CORNELL STUDIES IN CLASSICAL PHILOLOGY

EDITED BY

FREDERICK M. AHL * KEVIN C. CLINTON
JOHN E. COLEMAN * JUDITH R. GINSBURG
G. M. KIRKWOOD * GORDON R. MESSING
ALAN NUSSBAUM * PIETRO PUCCI
WINTHROP WETHERBEE

VOLUME XLV

Seneca's *Hercules Furens*

A Critical Text with Introduction and Commentary
by John G. Fitch

From Myth to Icon:
Reflections of Greek Ethical Doctrine in Literature and Art
by Helen F. North

Lucan: An Introduction
by Frederick M. Ahl

The Violence of Pity
in Euripides' *Medea*
by Pietro Pucci

Epicurus' Scientific Method
by Elizabeth Asmis

The Rhetoric of Imitation:
Genre and Poetic Memory in Virgil and Other Latin Poets
by Gian Biagio Conte, edited by Charles Segal

THE TOWNSEND LECTURES

Artifices of Eternity:
Horace's Fourth Book of Odes
by Michael C. J. Putnam

SENECA'S
Hercules Furens

A CRITICAL TEXT WITH
INTRODUCTION AND COMMENTARY

John G. Fitch

CORNELL UNIVERSITY PRESS
ITHACA AND LONDON

PA 6664 .H4 1987
Seneca, Lucius Annaeus, ca.
4 B.C.-65 A.D.
Seneca's Hercules furens

Copyright © 1987 by Cornell University

All rights reserved. Except for brief quotations in a review, this book, or parts thereof, must not be reproduced in any form without permission in writing from the publisher. For information, address Cornell University Press, 124 Roberts Place, Ithaca, New York 14850.

First published 1987 by Cornell University Press.

International Standard Book Number 0-8014-1876-3
Library of Congress Catalog Card Number 86-11582
Printed in the United States of America.
Librarians: Library of Congress cataloging information appears on the last page of the book.

The paper in this book is acid-free and meets the guidelines for permanence and durability of the Committee on Production Guidelines for Book Longevity of the Council on Library Resources.

TO MY PARENTS

CONTENTS

Preface	9
Abbreviations	11
INTRODUCTION	13
The Ambivalent Hero	15
The Senecan Drama	21
Conflicting views of Hercules	21
Hercules 'sane'	24
Hercules insane	28
The dominion of death	33
The final Act	35
Summary	38
Hercules Furens and Stoicism	40
Seneca's Sources	44
Date	50
Text and Apparatus Criticus	53
Sigla	63
HERCULES FURENS	65
COMMENTARY	115
Act I	115
Ode I	158
Act II	183
Ode II	252
Act III	274
Ode III	334

Contents

Act IV	350
Ode IV	390
Act V	412

APPENDIXES

1. Further Details of T (Par. Lat. 8031)	463
2. Addenda and Corrigenda to Giardina's Apparatus Criticus	465
3. The Colometry of the Anapestic Odes	467
4. Compound Adjectives and Adjectives in -*x*	469

BIBLIOGRAPHY   471

Addenda   478

INDEXES

1. Index of Latin Words	481
2. General Index	484

PREFACE

Recent decades have seen a resurgence of interest in Seneca's tragedies, inspired in the 1920s by T. S. Eliot's two essays on Seneca's translators and by Otto Regenbogen's study of suffering and death in the tragedies, and fostered in the 1960s by C. J. Herington's essay in *Arion*. There have also been more general cultural factors, among them a belated escape from the dictates of Romantic criticism, and a history of wars and superpower confrontations to which the Senecan themes of unreason, megalomania, and destructive self-assertion have an unmistakable relevance.

Only very recently, however, has this revival been supported by the appearance of fully annotated editions of individual plays: in English we now have C. D. N. Costa's *Medea* (1973), R. J. Tarrant's *Agamemnon* (1976) and *Thyestes* (1985), and Elaine Fantham's *Troades* (1982). Such editions are indispensable to progress in criticism for several reasons. First, the editor serves an ancillary function, by gathering pertinent information from widely scattered and often inaccessible sources, and so permitting the critic to make an informed assessment of a particular passage. Second, the editor-commentator, by virtue of close familiarity with the text, is particularly well placed to assess critical views. Third, intensive work on a single play may reasonably be expected to open up lines of enquiry about the whole corpus. Thus Tarrant's pioneering work shed new light on many areas: inter alia, diction, the pervasiveness of Ovidian influence, and above all dramatic technique. My own work on *Hercules Furens* has in turn suggested avenues of research into relative dating, diction, anapest colometry, and expressive use of meter.

My choice of *Hercules Furens* was determined in part by the challenges presented by the interpretation of the play, in part by its sheer literary power (notably in the choral odes), and in part by the significance of Hercules himself, the most important culture-hero of Greco-Roman civilization. *Hercules Furens* is the largest of the genuinely Senecan plays,

Preface

its size matching its hero, a fact that has contributed to the size of my commentary. To avoid even greater length I decided, albeit reluctantly, not to attempt full documentation of Seneca's literary influence (even on the pseudo-Senecan *Hercules Oetaeus*). Some notable examples of classical and postclassical influence are given, however, for their intrinsic interest and for the light they shed on the quality of Seneca's verse.

Portions of the Commentary were seen in an early draft by Frederick M. Ahl, C. J. Herington, and R. J. Tarrant. Of my colleagues at the University of Victoria, D. A. Campbell and P. L. Smith between them read the whole of the Commentary, while S. E. Scully read the Introduction. All of these scholars offered helpful comments and criticisms for which I am most grateful. I also thank Cornell University Press's anonymous referee for a detailed and expert critique of the whole work. Valuable advice on collation of manuscripts was given by M. D. Reeve, L. D. Reynolds, and A. P. MacGregor. Richard Tarrant was generous in his encouragement, lending microfilms and allowing me to see a typescript of his *Agamemnon* before publication. I cannot let this opportunity pass without expressing once again my admiration and gratitude to Fred Ahl, who first guided my Senecan studies; and to two other inspiring teachers of Classics, P. H. Vennis and the late J. L. Whiteley.

This book has been published with the help of a grant from the Canadian Federation for the Humanities, using funds provided by the Social Sciences and Humanities Research Council of Canada. I thank the editors of Cornell Studies in Classical Philology both for accepting my manuscript and for financial assistance in its publication. I am also grateful to S.S.H.R.C.C. and to the University of Victoria for financial support during study leaves in 1978–79, 1981–82, and 1984. The Canada Council provided funds to employ a research assistant, which was helpful at the preparatory stage: my thanks go to the Council and to P. J. Burnell for undertaking the useful though often tedious tasks involved. The Inter-Library Loans office of the University Library at Victoria has been diligent in pursuing many requests for out-of-the-way items. The burden of proofreading was lightened by the help of Pamela Hegedus and of my father, S. Gordon Fitch. A garland of praise, finally, to A. Nancy Nasser, who typed and retyped this magnum opus from my minuscule handwriting with unfailing accuracy and good humor.

JOHN G. FITCH

Victoria, British Columbia
October 1985

ABBREVIATIONS

ALL	*Archiv für lateinische Lexikographie und Grammatik.* Leipzig 1884–1909.
Axelson	Axelson, Bertil. *Unpoetische Wörter.* Lund 1945.
Bömer	Bömer, Franz. *P. Ovidius Naso: Metamorphosen. Kommentar.* Heidelberg 1960–.
D-S	Daremberg, C., and E. Saglio. *Dictionnaire des antiquités grecques et romaines d'après les textes et les monuments.* Paris 1877–1919.
EAA	*Enciclopedia dell' Arte Antica.* Rome 1958–.
Giardina	Giardina, Gian Carlo, ed. *L. Annaei Senecae Tragoediae.* 2 vols. Bologna 1966.
H-S	Hofmann, J. B. *Lateinische Syntax und Stylistik.* Rev. Anton Szantyr. Munich 1965.
Jocelyn	Jocelyn, H. D. *The Tragedies of Ennius.* Cambridge 1967.
K-S	Kühner, R., and C. Stegmann. *Ausführliche Grammatik der lateinischen Sprache: Satzlehre.* 5th ed. Hanover 1976.
Leo	Leo, Friedrich, ed. *L. Annaei Senecae Tragoediae.* 2 vols. Berlin 1878–79 (reprinted Berlin 1963).
L-S	Lewis, C. T., and C. Short. *A Latin Dictionary.* Oxford 1879.
LIMC	*Lexicon Iconographicum Mythologiae Classicae.* Zurich 1981–.
N-H	Nisbet, R. G. M., and Margaret Hubbard. *A Commentary on Horace: Odes Book I.* Oxford 1970. *A Commentary on Horace: Odes Book II.* Oxford 1978.
OCD	*The Oxford Classical Dictionary.* 2d ed. Oxford 1970.
OLD	*Oxford Latin Dictionary.* Oxford 1968–82.
Otto	Otto, A. *Die Sprichwörter und sprichwortlichen Redensarten der Römer.* Leipzig 1890 (reprinted Hildesheim 1962). "*Nachträge*" refers to R. Haussler, ed. *Nachträge zu A. Otto, Sprichwörter.* Hildesheim 1968.
Preller-Robert	Preller, L., and C. Robert. *Griechische Mythologie.* 4th ed. Berlin 1920–21 (reprinted Berlin 1966–67).
RE	Pauly A., G. Wissowa, and W. Kroll. *Real-Encyclopädie der klassischen Altertumswissenschaft.* Stuttgart 1950–.

Abbreviations

Roscher   Roscher, W. H. *Ausführliches Lexikon der griechischen und römischen Mythologie.* Leipzig 1884–1937 (reprinted Hildesheim 1965).
Sen. Trag.   Senecan tragedy excluding ps.-Sen. *Hercules Oetaeus* and *Octavia.*
Strzelecki   Strzelecki, L. *De Senecae Trimetro Iambico.* Krakow 1938.
Tarrant   Tarrant, R. J., ed. *Seneca: Agamemnon.* Cambridge 1976.
TrGF   Snell, B., R. Kannicht, and S. Radt, eds. *Tragicorum Graecorum Fragmenta.* Göttingen 1971–.
TLL   *Thesaurus Linguae Latinae.* Leipzig 1900–.
Wilamowitz   Wilamowitz-Moellendorf, U. von, ed. *Euripides: Herakles.* 2d ed. 3 vols. Berlin 1895 (reprinted Berlin 1959).

Other abbreviations are from the standard abbreviation lists in *OCD* and *L'Année Philologique*. Works listed in the Bibliography are generally cited in abbreviated form by the author's name and page: e.g. Ahl 25 = F. M. Ahl, *Lucan: An Introduction* (Ithaca 1976) p. 25. If several works by a single author appear in the Bibliography, my citations distinguish them by date, for example, Leo 1876 432. It should be noted that I use Sen. Trag. in reference to the genuine plays of the corpus only, that is, excluding *HO* and *Oct.*

INTRODUCTION

INTRODUCTION

The Ambivalent Hero

Hercules has appeared in many guises over the centuries, from aggressive bully to exemplar of virtue. This section of the Introduction will do no more than touch upon certain aspects of the Hercules tradition up to Seneca's time. It will not attempt to catalogue all authors who wrote about Hercules—which would in itself be a Herculean labor—nor to chronicle all the vicissitudes of his reputation.[1] Its purpose is simply to outline those earlier views and treatments of the hero which seem to me to have an important bearing on Seneca's play.

From the earliest times Hercules' heroism is ambivalent. On the one hand he is "the best of men,"[2] endowed with invincible strength and courage. On the other hand, any strength that goes so far beyond the human norm is potentially dangerous and unpredictable. His killing of wife and children shows how easily his strength may turn in the wrong direction. On that occasion he at least had the excuse of madness, but there was no such excuse for his murder of his music teacher Linus, who had simply angered him. The dangerous side of his personality is already evident in Homer, who mentions his attacks on the gods and his murder of his host Iphitus; for the former action he is described as σχέτλιος, ὀβριμοεργός, ὃς οὐκ ὄθετ' αἴσυλα ῥέζων, and for the latter as again σχέτλιος, and lacking in αἰδώς toward the gods (*Il.* 5.403, *Od.* 21.28). Yet this criticism is mild in comparison with the devastating condemnation implied in Sophocles' *Trachiniae*: here Hercules is portrayed as drunk at the court of Eurytus, vengeful and deceitful in his murder of Iphitus, lustful and brutal in destroying Oechalia to seize

---

1. For a valuable study of literary adaptations of Hercules from Homer to the twentieth century see G. Karl Galinsky, *The Herakles Theme* (Oxford 1972), to which I am heavily indebted in much of this section.
2. E.g. Soph. *Trach.* 811; cf. G. Murray, *Greek Studies* (Oxford 1946) 108.

Introduction

Iole; as a husband who neglects the admirable Deianira and insults her by taking a mistress openly, and finally as a tyrannical father in his commands to Hyllus.³ Such excesses might be appropriate to the folktale hero whose *arete* consists of getting his own way regardless of opposition, but they must appear savage and hubristic when set within the context of civilized reality.

It is not surprising, in view of Hercules' importance in religion and mythology, that there are many attempts to paint a more favorable picture, and in particular to justify that constant resort to violence which seems endemic in the labors. For example, the historian Timaeus insists that Hercules did his bloody deeds only under orders; when he was free to act on his own initiative, he established the Olympic Games, the epitome of civilized competition rather than barbaric conflict. Others portray Hercules' violence as justified by the barbaric nature of his opponents: Pisander calls him a "most just killer"; Aeschylus notes that Geryon's herdsmen were "unjust men"; Pindar describes the beasts slain by him as "knowing nothing of justice," and emphasizes the injustice of his human adversaries, the guest-cheating Augeas and the guest-cleaving Parians.⁴ As for the story of Hercules' hubristic attacks on the gods, Pindar with characteristic radicalism rejects it as palpably untrue (*Ol.* 9.30ff.). An even more radical reinterpretation and justification is seen in Prodicus' fable of Hercules at the crossroads: here Hercules undertakes the labors not under constraint but out of a free choice, deliberately prefering the hard road of Virtue to the easy path of Vice.⁵

Whether or not Hercules' labors can be justified, a rather different question continues to be asked, namely whether all this slaying of monsters represented an achievement of any real value. "What was so wonderful about his killing a marsh-hydra?" asks Euripides' Lycus (151f.), and Hercules himself comments that he would have been better employed in defending his family than in the labors (575f.). Lucretius scorns the labors as irrelevant; the genuine dangers to be faced are those of the mind, cares, fears and desires, and it was Epicurus, not Hercules, who showed men how to overcome such monsters (5.22–54). Seneca himself expresses doubts, though he does so more tactfully, and replaces Epicurus with the Stoic Cato as a foil to Hercules. Cato, he re-

---

3. In Homer a less unfavorable view of Hercules is taken at *Il.* 18.117–19 and *Od.* 11.601–26; and in Sophocles we find a much more favorable view of him once he is safely removed from contact with humans and translated to Olympus, viz. in *Phil.* On Hercules in *Trach.* see further R. P. Winnington-Ingram, *Sophocles: An Interpretation* (Cambridge 1980) 81–86, with references to more favorable views taken by some critics; also Galinsky 46–52 with n. 16.

4. Timaeus *FGrH* 566 F22; Pisander fr. 10 Kinkel; Aesch. fr. 74 N; Pind. *Nem.* 1.63 ἀϊδροδίκας, *Ol.* 10.34 ξεναπάτας, fr. 140a.56 ξενοδαΐκτα.

5. Xen. *Mem.* 2.1.21–43.

Introduction

marks, did not fight with wild beasts, which is a job for the hunter or peasant, but came into conflict with ambition and the lust for individual power.[6] Even those who are well-disposed toward Hercules sometimes define his heroism in terms not so much of his external achievements as of the qualities of spirit that made them possible. Just such an approach is found in Isocrates, who praises Hercules not for his labors but the excellences of his spirit, wisdom, desire for glory, justice, and philanthropy (5.109–14). The most memorable redefinition, however, is that given in Euripides' *Heracles*. By the end of that play Hercules' heroism, learned in facing the labors, has been brought to bear on a new and more difficult challenge, that of facing the tragic circumstances of human life. In such interpretations we see a tendency to place the focus less on physical conflicts than on spiritual ones. The process reaches its logical, if uninspiring, conclusion when Hercules' external foes are allegorized as dangers of the spirit: Cerberus represents earthly lusts and vices according to Servius, and Fulgentius takes Antaeus to mean lust, and Cacus to signify evil incarnate.[7]

But if the value of the labors was sometimes questioned, they were more frequently praised and justified as having a beneficent purpose, to make human life more secure. Hercules "made the straits kindly to seafarers," he "pacified the woods of Erymanthus,"[8] and in Euripides his task is defined by Amphitryon as nothing less than ἐξημερῶσαι γαῖαν, to civilize the earth (20, cf. 851f.). Thus he is a protector and savior from the evils of life. According to the possibly Hesiodic *Shield of Heracles*, Zeus fathered the hero "to be a defender against ruin (ἀτῆς ἀλκτῆρα) for gods and bread-eating men" (28f.), and in the certainly Hesiodic *Theogony* we are told that he "warded off the deadly plague (sc. the eagle) from Prometheus, and delivered him from his miseries" (527f.). In cult, one of the titles most frequently applied to him is ἀλεξίκακος, and he is invoked as a deliverer from troubles of all kinds, particularly disease.[9] In fact the notion of deliverance associated with the hero sometimes extends as far as deliverance from death. The idea of conquest over death is, of course, implicit in some details of the myth itself: like Orpheus, he descended to the land of death and returned; he also shot Pluto with an arrow, and wrestled with Thanatos for Alcestis' life.[10] It is hardly surprising, therefore, to find associa-

---

6. *Const. Sap.* 2.2. In similar vein, but in a nonphilosophical context, Tiberius compared Hercules' fights against beasts unfavorably with Augustus' struggles and achievements among men (Dio Cass. 56.36.4).
7. Serv. ad V. *Aen.* 6.395, Fulg. *Myth.* 2.3f., cf. also Dio Chrys. 5.22ff.
8. Pind. *Isthm.* 4.57, V. *Aen.* 6.802f.
9. *RE* Suppl. 3.1001.5ff., 1013.10ff.
10. Some of the other labors also appear to have connotations of defeating death;

Introduction

tions with some of the mystery-religions. According to one tradition he was initiated in the Eleusinia before his catabasis.[11] In the Pythagorean basilica at Rome, the representation of Hercules rescuing Hesione implies the liberation of the pure soul from the shackles of the body.[12] In Roman times, representations of Hercules are frequently found in funerary contexts, in which the hero is a prototype and guarantee of immortality. Sometimes he reclines at his ease after the toils of this life, as his human followers hope to do in their turn. Often the dead are actually represented with the attributes of Hercules, to suggest their identification with the hero.[13]

But this is an anonymous form of immortality, suitable for ordinary men. Hercules also becomes a model, in Hellenistic and Roman times, for the extraordinary individual who, by his personal merits and his services to his fellow men, becomes a god: the θεῖος ἀνήρ.[14] On the Greek side Alexander the κοσμοκράτωρ, with his far-flung conquests of the 'barbaric' world, was naturally likened to Hercules: Theocritus pictures him as deified, a companion in heaven of the divine Hercules, to whom in fact he traced back his lineage (17.13–33). In Rome, Ennius canonized the view that Romulus had become a god; he also attempted to bring Scipio Africanus into this company. In the first century B.C. there was considerable competition to inherit the mantle of Hercules between Pompey, Caesar, and Antony. It is Augustus, of course, whom we find most conspicuously cast in the Herculean role. Horace prophesies that Augustus will recline in heavenly bliss between Pollux and Hercules, having earned his place in heaven by qualities similar to theirs (*Carm.* 3.3.9ff.). Vergil's treatment of Hercules as an exemplar is somewhat more complex. Certainly Aeneas and Augustus are both seen as successors of Hercules, but the general parallel does not exclude the possibility of contrasts. In *Aeneid* 6 Aeneas' peaceful mission to the underworld is contrasted with Hercules' violence (see comm. on *HF* 762–827), and in *Aeneid* 8 Hercules' furious rage is emphasized as

---

cf. introductory note to Ode II (524–91). H. J. Rose 215f. suggests the possibility that in an early version of the catabasis myth, Hercules' purpose was indeed the conquest of death, and that the capture of Cerberus was substituted later when the original motive became unacceptable.

11. Apollod. 2.5.12 with Frazer ad loc., Diod. Sic. 4.14.3, 25.1; cf. Mylonas *Eleusis* 205ff., Boardman 1975 10 n. 35, and my comm. on 762–827.

12. J. Carcopino, *La basilique pythagoricienne de la porte majeure* (Paris 1927) 328–29.

13. The basic study is that of J. Bayet, "Hercule funéraire," *Mélanges de l'École Française de Rome* 39 (1921–22) 219–66, 40 (1923) 19–102; see also F. Cumont, *Recherches sur le symbolisme funéraire des Romains* (Paris 1942) 28 n. 3, 256 n. 5, 415–17.

14. See the valuable study of A. R. Anderson, "Heracles and His Successors," *HSCP* 39 (1928) 7–58.

he fights against Cacus (219f. *Alcidae furiis exarserat atro / felle dolor,* 228 *furens animis,* 230 *dentibus infrendens, fervidus ira*); although his anger has some justification, it must seem excessive to an audience which has learned from both Stoic and Epicurean teachers the supreme importance of controlling the emotions. There are hints, then, that Hercules is a somewhat archaic model, whom later heroes may not only emulate but also surpass. Nevertheless the parallels between him and Augustus are unmistakable and become explicit at *Aen.* 6.801–7. Among the later Julio-Claudian emperors there is relatively little evidence for association with Hercules, except in the case of Nero, but thereafter the association becomes popular, particularly with those emperors who laid some claim to military prowess.[15]

But opinions concerning Hercules' successors were by no means universally favorable. Particularly in the early Empire a more realistic view emerges, namely, that men like Alexander were not motivated primarily by a desire to make the world safe for civilization, but by an insatiable lust for power and conquest. With regard to Alexander, emphasis is also placed on the hubris of the conqueror who disregards the boundaries wisely set by Nature, and even dares embark on Ocean, traditionally the limit of human endeavor (Sen. Rhet. *Suas.* 1.5, 10 *Alexandrum rerum terminos supergressum,* 11). Such criticisms are found three times in Seneca's prose, at *Ben.* 1.13.1–3, 7.3.1, *Ep.* 94.63; although the chief target is Alexander, Seneca makes it clear that the criticisms apply also to such men as Marius, Pompey, and Caesar. The influence of such views is evident in Lucan's portrait of Caesar as a man obsessed with military conquest and characterized by megalomania and an assumption of invincibility.[16] Juvenal has a similar attitude to another great conqueror, Hannibal (10.133ff.). In such a climate of opinion it would not be surprising if the faults imputed to these men of action should be found also in their great exemplar, Hercules himself. That, I believe, is what has happened in Seneca's *Hercules Furens.*

Hercules is, in fact, explicitly associated with the hubristic violation of natural boundaries in Hor. *Carm.* 1.3, the second half of which is concerned with human audacity in exploring the various regions of the universe. Not content with the land, man has ventured onto the sea, while Daedalus violated the air and Hercules broke into the underworld (36 *perrupit Acheronta Herculeus labor*); finally, *caelum ipsum petimus stultitia* (38). This notion of the heavens as the last and most insane goal of human ambition may be seen also in an ironic epigram on Philip V of Macedon:

15. Cf. n. 49 and Roscher 1.2982ff.
16. Cf. Ahl chap. 6, "Caesar."

[*19*]

Introduction

χθὼν μὲν δὴ καὶ πόντος ὑπὸ σκήπτροισι Φιλίππου
δέδμηται, λοιπὰ δ' ἁ πρὸς Ὄλυμπον ὁδός.
(*Anth. Pal.* 9.518.3–4 [Alcaeus of Messene])[17]

and in a similar epigram on the ambitions of Rome by Alpheius of Mytilene (roughly contemporary with Seneca?):

ἤδη γὰρ καὶ πόντος ὑπέζευκται δορὶ Ῥώμης
καὶ χθών. οὐρανίη δ' οἶμος ἔτ' ἔστ' ἄβατος.
(*Anth. Pal.* 9.526.3–4)

Behind such poems lies a tradition hostile to the unfettered boldness of man's conquest of the world, a tradition which sees an attack on the heavens as its inevitable culmination; e.g. *Corp. Hermet.* fr. 23.45–46:

τολμηρὰς ἐκτενοῦσι χεῖρας καὶ μέχρι θαλάσσης, καὶ τὰς αὐτοφυεῖς ὕλας τέμνοντες μέχρι καὶ τῶν πέραν διαπορθμεύσουσιν ἀλλήλους . . . εἶτα οὐ καὶ μέχρις οὐρανοῦ περίεργον ὁπλισθήσονται τόλμαν οὗτοι;[18]

From the viewpoint of such a tradition, the deification of Hercules, Romulus, and Caesar can be seen not as a justified reward, but as a hubristic intrusion by human beings into the realm which should most of all be denied them, that of heaven itself. That is, in fact, precisely the interpretation found in a passage in which Ovid apostrophizes *hominum natura*:

quid tibi cum pelago? terra contenta fuisses!
  cur non et caelum, tertia regna, petis?
qua licet, adfectas caelum quoque: templa Quirinus,
  Liber et Alcides et modo Caesar habet.
(*Am.* 3.8.45–48)

Thus in Seneca's time, as in Homer's, two very different views of Hercules can be held: at one extreme he can be regarded as the greatest of men, a model to be emulated; at the other extreme he can be seen as an overreacher, the very exemplar of human hubris.

---

17. On the question of the tone of this epigram, which has sometimes been taken as sincerely intended flattery, see Gow and Page's commentary pp. 8–9. The suggestion of hubris seems to me too patent for the tone to be other than ironical.

18. Cf. Max. Tyr. 36.2b and Nemesius 40.533a Migne. Further on this tradition see Nisbet and Hubbard's introduction to Hor. *Carm.* 1.3, and A. S. Ferguson in W. Scott, *Hermetica* vol. 4 pp. 455ff.

Introduction

The Senecan Drama

Conflicting views of Hercules

The fact that Hercules' entry is delayed until almost halfway through the play means that our first impressions of him are shaped by the opinions of other characters.[19] Indeed, we are given a series of *conflicting* pictures, which compete for attention and credence; this forces us to choose between them, to make at least a preliminary judgment, which can then be tested against direct experience of his behavior in Acts III–V.

From the very outset, Juno leaves no doubt about Hercules' overwhelming might. He has overcome with ease all the challenges she could devise for him, and has covered himself with glory in the process. Yet according to Juno there is also a darker side to his invincible strength: she accuses him of violating the bounds of Nature in returning from the underworld (43ff.), and alleges that his next step will be to invade the heavens and unseat Jupiter (63–74). We recognize the pattern of escalating hubris familiar from the tradition mentioned earlier, and the possibility that these criticisms of Hercules may indeed be valid. But the charges are weakened by the obvious prejudice of the accuser. After all, Juno herself sent Hercules to the underworld, so it is hardly reasonable for her to complain about the results. And why is she suddenly so solicitous for the Jupiter from whom she is estranged and the heavens which she has abandoned? Her allegations appear to be a trumped-up excuse for continuing, or rather intensifying, her persecution of the hero.[20] Nevertheless these accusations remind us, at the opening of the play, of the ambivalence of Hercules' might, even if initially we reject Juno's specific charges.

It is less easy to ignore the doubts about Hercules raised by the members of the Chorus in the first ode: they do not share Juno's obvious

---

19. The view propounded in this Introduction, namely that the failings of Seneca's Hercules outweigh his virtues and that his madness arises from his own psyche, has been dominant in modern criticism of the play (though naturally there are differences of emphasis from one critic to another): it will be found in the studies by Frenzel, Marcosignori, Bishop, Henry and Walker, Tobin, Zintzen, Galinsky, Shelton, Wellmann-Bretzigheimer, and A. Rose. The chief dissenters are Edert, Dingel, Caviglia, Motto and Clark, Lawall, and Zwierlein (1984). My view of Act V and the question of Hercules' supposed transformation is less orthodox; I have attempted to combat the views of other critics in more detail in *Hermes* 107 (1979) 240–48, and I am pleased to find myself in agreement with Timpanaro 122–24 on this question.

20. Indeed, the audience can observe how the notion that Hercules will attack heaven forms in Juno's mind: see comm. on 63–74.

[21]

Introduction

prejudice, and their oblique approach to criticism tends to disarm objections. Nevertheless their criticism, whether implied or explicit, is extremely far-reaching. When they draw a contrast between the quiet life and the life of ambitious activity, there can be no doubt on which side Hercules is ranged. Their critique of the active life may be summarized as follows: first, it is dominated by the *affectus*, *spes*, and *metus* (161ff.); second, those obsessed by ambition rush toward death, in the sense of forgetting the ephemeral nature of human life and neglecting quiet enjoyment of each passing day (174ff.); third, the lofty positions attained by the ambitious are precarious: *alte virtus animosa cadit* (201). We can scarcely fail to perceive that Hercules is the outstanding exemplar of *virtus animosa*, and we know from Juno's predictions that he will suffer a great fall. Whether the other two criticisms also apply to Hercules remains to be seen. But coming so early in the play, and being introduced so persuasively, the Chorus' condemnation of the active, ambitious life is bound to have a great impact on the audience.

In contrast to these negative attitudes toward Hercules, a more favorable view begins to emerge in Acts II and III. It bears out Juno's comment that his *virtus* is honored throughout the world (39f.). His *virtus* has been established, of course, by his success in the labors and πάρεργα, frequently mentioned in Act II; Amphitryon catalogues many of them (215–48) in such a way as to confirm that his strength and courage are extraordinary, indeed superhuman. Amphitryon has every reason to be confident that his *virtus* will enable him to return from the underworld (312f., 319–24).[21] Moreover, the notion that Hercules' fame and significance are universal permeates the play. His conquests have created peace for the world, and consequently the whole world feels his absence (250f.). Peace for the world—indeed for the universe—is his prayer (925ff.), and world peace is what the Chorus believes he has established on his return (882f.).[22]

In keeping with Seneca's emphasis on Hercules' superhuman qualities are the frequent references to his imminent deification. Juno alleges, perhaps with malicious exaggeration, that he is already generally talked of as a god (39f.). The fact that he is a son of Jupiter is mentioned time and again during the play.[23] Further, Jupiter has prom-

---

21. The Chorus too is fairly confident of his eventual success (n.b. *poterit* 591), whereas in the corresponding stasimon in Eur. it assumes that he cannot return from Hades (426ff.).

22. Another significant contrast with the Euripidean play, where the corresponding ode is concerned only with the salvation of Thebes, not of the world (763–814).

23. Even Juno acknowledges, somewhat ruefully, Jupiter's paternity (24–26, 35–36). Amphitryon also has no doubts about the matter (see comm. on 1246–48). Only Lycus questions it, in his usual cynical fashion.

Introduction

ised his son divinity (23, 959). This prospect of deification is the subject of a lengthy argument between Amphitryon and Lycus (438ff.),[24] and Amphitryon clearly has the better of it. The presence of prayer elements in both Amphitryon's and Megara's first appeals to Hercules (see comm. on 277ff., 283ff.) suggests that they think of him already as at least semidivine; this tendency is seen again at the end of Act II, when Amphitryon breaks off his prayer to the gods and appeals instead to Hercules, with the implication that he is a more promising source of help (516–20). The signs that follow, indicating the approach of Hercules, are such as accompany the epiphany of a god or superhuman power (see comm. on 520–22).[25] All this contrasts most notably with Euripides' avoidance of any emphasis on the divine destiny of Hercules. Even when Theseus is laying down regulations for his cult in Athens, Euripides avoids drawing attention to the fact that it is to be the cult of a god.[26]

We receive a strong impression, then, of Hercules as a superhuman world-conqueror and one already close to deification—a picture reflecting Hellenistic-Roman concepts of the κοσμοκράτωρ and θεῖος ἀνήρ. It is vital for an understanding of Seneca's purpose, however, to realize that these favorable references to Hercules are regularly accompanied by reservations. The note of criticism heard in the prologue and first ode recurs as the play continues. Thus Amphitryon introduces his list of Hercules' labors not to glorify him, but rather to corroborate his complaints (207–13) that his son never enjoys any *quies*, nor his family any security. The immediately preceding ode had concluded that the ambitious man lacks *secura quies* and that the fortunes of his house are insecure (175, 199f.); Amphitryon's words seem designed to recall those criticisms and to show their applicability to Hercules and his *domus*. The Chorus in the second ode displays a similarly unfavorable attitude to the labors, seeing them as unpleasant and undesirable tasks, unfairly imposed by Fortune (524ff.); it doubts the wisdom of his having undertaken the underworld exploit (547f., cf. 186). Amphitryon notes further that Hercules' establishment of peace has been annulled in his absence, since injustice and terror have sprung up again like Hydra's heads (249ff.). The passage recalls Seneca's criticism of the βίος of another world-conqueror, Julius Caesar: *non ipse per*

---

24. Again, significantly, a feature that does not exist in the Euripidean version.
25. Kroll 409f. points out that Ode III recalls the scene in V. *Aen.* 8 in which the deified Hercules is honored by a hymn and sacrifice (see introduction to Ode III). Though in *HF* Hercules is the officiant at the sacrifice rather than its recipient (see comm. on 893f.), the recollection of the Vergilian scene must underline Hercules' closeness to divinity.
26. Wilamowitz on Eur. 1332.

Introduction

annos decem continuos patria caruit? [cf. *HF* 249 *orbe defenso caret*] . . . *nunc ecce trahit illum ad se Africa resurgentis belli minis plena, trahit Hispania, . . . trahit Aegyptus infida, totus denique orbis, qui ad occasionem concussi imperii intentus est. cui primum rei occurret? cui parti se opponet? aget illum per omnes terras victoria sua* (*Cons. Helv.* 9.7–8; cf. also the comments on Augustus' life at *Brev. Vit.* 4.5). The parallel is apt, for Caesar may be seen as one of Hercules' successors. It is also noteworthy that what is contrasted with the harried life of the world-conqueror, in that passage as in *HF*, is the quiet life.

Doubts of another sort are raised by Lycus' sustained attack on Hercules' character. When he questions Hercules' superhuman strength and bravery, Lycus is easily refuted. But it is a different matter when he dwells on his lack of manliness in the Omphale episode, or his brutal lust in his treatment of Iole and other women (465–71, 477–80). These criticisms remind us of an element of instability in Hercules' behavior which is familiar from the mythological tradition.

Hercules 'sane'

When Hercules appears, we scrutinize his words and actions to see if they bear out the various criticisms leveled against him. We quickly learn something significant: he is indeed a man incapable of relaxing; he is obsessed with facing challenges. Even before enquiring about his family's well-being, he is asking Juno what will be her next command; on learning of the situation in Thebes he bids his family "postpone" their embraces, in his eagerness to rush off again into combat; immediately on returning from killing Lycus, he prays that any further challenges should appear *quickly*. The suggestion that he should pray for well-deserved *otium* and *quies* is dismissed as unworthy of him (924ff.). Clearly the fact that he and his family lack *secura quies* is due to his own nature as much as to the tasks imposed on him.

This obsession with action leads to a manifest lack of concern for his family. There is a striking contrast here between Euripides' and Seneca's handling of Hercules' arrival in Thebes. In both plays the hero concerns himself immediately with necessary preparations for attacking Lycus. But in Euripides he also establishes beyond any doubt his love and concern for his family (622–36), which is just what Seneca's Hercules fails to do. We need not invoke Euripides here to illustrate Hercules' failure, for Seneca himself draws attention to it through his characterization of Amphitryon. Though Amphitryon acknowledges intellectually that Hercules is Jupiter's son, he nevertheless regards him emotionally as his *natus*,[27] and has a real yearning for him during his

27. Cf. lines 520, 621f., 647, 760, 918, 953, 1039, 1303.

Introduction

long absences, movingly expressed in 1252ff. *nullus ex te contigit / fructus laborum . . . semper absentis pater / fructum tui tactumque et aspectum peto*, cf. 621ff. This warmth of affection, which finds its expression in physical contact (see comm. on 1318^b–21^a), is all the more notable because of its rarity in Sen. Trag. But Hercules consistently fails to respond. His lack of love and concern cannot be dismissed as an inevitable and unimportant concomitant of his heroic mode of existence; Seneca brings it to our attention as a deficiency underlining what is lost in the life of *virtus animosa*.

Hercules' eagerness for action is often a desire specifically for *punitive* action, for elimination of evil, for which his characteristic method is an unthinking resort to violence.[28] To the examples just cited we may add his insistence in Act V, once he discovers the murders, on taking revenge personally and immediately, first against the unknown assailant, and then, when he learns the full truth, against himself. He wastes no time on mourning, but in a revealing phrase asks Amphitryon and Theseus to "postpone" their tears, just as earlier he requested a "postponement" of embraces; human tenderness comes a poor second to his obsession with punishment.[29] He brusquely rejects Amphitryon's argument that punishment may be more harmful than restorative; the appeal that he show *venia* to himself, in view of the mitigating circumstances of the murders, also falls on deaf ears.

It is significant that this eagerness for punishment is twice called *ira* (1167, 1277). This corresponds closely to Seneca's definition of anger, in his study of the subject, as *cupiditas poenae exigendae* (*Ira* 1.3.2). Both in Act III[30] and Act V, in fact, Hercules shows traits of the typical Senecan *iratus*. His haste is indicative of anger (*Ira* 1.5.3, 1.7.3); so is the way in which he spurs himself on to take action (1281ff., cf. *Ira* 2.3.5 *concitatio animi ad ultionem voluntate et iudicio pergentis*); so is his willingness to destroy the whole world, if need be, in satisfaction of his anger (1167ff., 1290ff., cf. *Ira* 2.35.5). Seneca in his prose works is much concerned with limiting the scope of retributive punishment, agreeing with Amphitryon's point that it can do more harm than good (see comm. on 1187). Seneca insists that punishment should *not* be in-

---

28. Even in other situations he tends to rely on brute force: Seneca reveals that reliance clearly in the encounter with Charon (see comm. on 762–827).
29. Cf. Seneca's question to a person similarly obsessed with punishment: "Tell me, unhappy man, will you ever find time to love?" (*age, infelix, ecquando amabis? Ira* 3.28.1).
30. Seneca's compressed version of the revenge on Lycus greatly reduces or removes those elements which tend to justify the attack on Lycus in Eur., viz. the hero's love for his family and our impression that he is their savior (especially Eur. 522, 532, 564, 574, 583), and the Chorus' belief that the act embodies divine justice (736, 757ff.). In Sen. the action is not a rescue but simply retribution, with no claim to divine sanction. See also introduction to Act III.

[25]

Introduction

flicted in haste or anger (e.g. *Ira* 1.6, 15–16, 18–19), and that it should be tempered by a generous display of *venia* or (as he prefers to say at a later stage) *clementia* (e.g. *Ira* 1.14.2, 2.10; *Clem.* 1.17, 2.4.1–4). All this confirms what is evident from the play, namely, that Hercules' behavior reveals not a justifiable rigor, but rather a destructive and unbalanced obsession.

Hercules is also marked by an intense preoccupation with himself, or rather with an image of himself as an invincible hero. This self-regard is so pervasive that it scarcely needs illustration, but there is a remarkable instance in Act V. On discovering the murder of his family he asks *quis tanta Thebis scelera moliri ausus est / Hercule reverso?* (1162f.)—as if his mere presence should have prevented it. A little later he addresses the murderer as *victor Alcidae* (1168), as if that were the most important aspect of the killings; and asks *cui praeda iacui?* (1186), though the word *praeda* would surely apply more accurately to those who have been murdered.

His boundless self-regard is linked, at least before the murders, with ambition. Why, after all, is there such urgency about completing the conquest of evil? Clearly because the next stage, as Jupiter promised, is to be his own deification (see comm. on 23 *promissa*). The ambition to gain the heavens is, in fact, one of the first ideas to emerge in his madness (955ff.). The supposed altruism of the labors, then, is actually mingled with a large element of vainglory and personal ambition—an unhealthy and unstable combination. Self-regard and ambition are reflected in the condescending tone he adopts toward the gods: he refers familiarly to many of them as his "brothers" (907f.), assumes that he can speak for Jupiter (922–24, 926f.), and even prays that Jupiter will desist from his unruly habit of hurling thunderbolts (932f.).

It might be argued that his extraordinary talents and destiny justify such an attitude, but the plain fact is that, although admittedly the mightiest of men, he is not yet a god, and should show more awareness of the distinction; failure to do so is hubristic. Further evidence of hubristic disregard of religious proprieties is given by his insistence on directing a sacrifice with bloodstained hands, despite Amphitryon's warning on the subject.[31] Equally unbalanced is his wish that he might pour out libations of Lycus' blood (920ff.). The clearest sign of hubris, however, is given soon after Hercules' first appearance, in his boastful

---

31. The detail has been taken from the same moment in Euripides' play, but tellingly remodeled: Euripides' hero was well aware of the need for purification (922ff.), and though he postponed it at the onset of madness, he did not even then deny its necessity (936ff.). For the importance of such purification cf. Hes. *Erga* 724–26. Neither Hector nor Aeneas forgets it even at moments of deep crisis (Hom. *Il.* 6.266–68, V. *Aen.* 2.717–20).

Introduction

descriptions of his conquest of the underworld. He could have ruled there if he had been so inclined (609f.), but instead *morte contempta redî* (612). Juno accused him earlier of despising the human lot (89f.); here he shows contempt for its most significant condition. Our knowledge of what is to come casts a deeply ironic light upon all Hercules' posturings and assumptions of invulnerability.

What of the prayer that Hercules addresses to Jupiter immediately before the madness comes upon him—a prayer for a new Golden Age free from evil both in the natural world and in human society (926ff.)? Initially it may seem a noble expression of Hercules' ideal. But notice the sheer impossibility of what he prays for—an end to sea storms, lightning, winter floods, poisonous herbs; these things belong to the very fabric of nature, and the wish to eliminate them reflects an unbalanced obsession with stamping out all possible sources of disorder.[32] In addition, the prayer is tainted by the atmosphere of hubris and ambition in which it is spoken.[33] Hercules' willingness to take on any *monstra* that might still threaten has an overreaching quality about it, an assumption, which we know to be false, that he is superior to any evil. This is underlined by the unconscious irony of the phrase *si quod parat / monstrum, meum sit* (938f.): the monstrous evil will indeed be his own, as the onset of madness immediately shows.

The impossibility of a Golden Age is relevant not only to our understanding of Hercules' failure in this play, but also to Rome herself. Vergil had expressed hopes for the establishment of a new Golden Age (*Ecl.* 4 passim, *Aen.* 6.791–94), and such hopes resurfaced on the accession of Nero (cf. Calp. *Ecl.* 1. 42ff., 4.6ff., *Einsied. Ecl.* 2.22ff., and Sen. himself at *Apocol.* 4, where, however, the context has a deflationary effect), though *HF* may have been written before that event. In each case these hopes were centered on a savior figure, as Hercules sees himself as the creator and guardian of the new age. Although it would be oversimple to see a direct answer to Vergil here, the passage certainly tends to suggest a more realistic appraisal of such hyperbolic hopes.

---

32. A similar point is made in Archibald MacLeish's verse play *Herakles:* "To want the world without suffering is madness!" Cf. Galinsky 244ff.

33. Joseph Campbell, speaking of the hero who acts as a representative of a divine father, notes that a deterioration may take place in his character, specifically in attributing all order to himself; he cites the Zoroastrian legend of the emperor Jimshad (*The Hero with a Thousand Faces* 2d. ed. [Princeton 1968] 347). Such an attitude is not far below the surface of Hercules' prayer. One may also note here the more general mythical pattern of the hero whose very invincibility leads him to become excessive. For example the Twins of Winnebago myth, after overcoming all monsters in heaven and earth, themselves become a threat to cosmic order: see Carl G. Jung, ed., *Man and His Symbols* (Garden City, N.Y. 1964) 113f. Such parallels illustrate Seneca's ability to sense what is inherent in the myth or appropriate to it.

Introduction

Hercules' *virtus*, then, is tainted by aggression, ambition, and megalomania. The questioning of *virtus* is in fact a notable theme of the play. The Chorus and Megara warn that *virtus* is endangered by its preeminence (201, 325f.), but in addition the very concept of *virtus* is threatened by distortion and misuse.[34] This point is established unmistakably in connection with Lycus, as if to prepare for its more subtle relevance to Hercules. Lycus glories in the fact that he owes nothing to noble ancestry and everything to *clara virtus* (337–40). For him, *virtus* is devoid of moral content and means simply strength or ability; it is a euphemism for self-assertion even by criminal means, as Amphitryon recognizes (251f. *prosperum ac felix scelus / virtus vocatur*). Indeed, Lycus may be seen as a Doppelgänger, if exaggerated and distorted, of the hero. He illustrates, before Hercules enters, how men of ambition are liable to disaster. Of course there are great differences between the petty tyrant and the mighty hero; Lycus is devoid of the altruism that Hercules at least professes. But the similarities are also evident: both men are ambitious and brutal, both rely on might more than right, and in both the claim to *virtus* is a cover for less desirable qualities.

Hercules insane

In the mad-scene Hercules' derangement is shown by a remarkable series of conflicting hallucinations. It will be useful to summarize them before attempting to analyze their content. As the madness comes upon him, he sees the sky darken, and the Nemean Lion, now translated into the heavens, threatening to attack stars. Next he decides that he will scale the heavens; and supposing that Jupiter denies him his promised place (though at one point the opposition seems to come from Juno) he prepares to lead the Titans in rebellion. Then it appears to him that the Giants are taking up arms against heaven, and shortly afterwards that the Furies are threatening him personally. Immediately after this, he mistakes his children for Lycus' and begins to kill them. This illusion is interrupted by another which shows him Megara as Juno, whom he attacks partly to settle his own scores, partly in the interest of Jupiter. But by the end of the scene he believes again that he has been attacking Lycus' family, and sarcastically refers to them as an *ex-voto* sacrifice to Juno. Moments later he collapses from exhaustion.

This series of hallucinations powerfully suggests the fluctuations of a

---

34. For distortions of *virtus* compare Medea's use of that term for her own intransigence (*Med.* 161) and Lucan's attribution to Julius Caesar of *nescia virtus / stare loco* (1.144f.); also Stat. *Silv.* 3.2.64 *temeraria virtus* (of the Giants attacking Olympus, significantly enough in a poem derived from Hor. *Carm.* 1.3), *Theb.* 9.6, 11.1 *virtutis iniquae*, Val. Fl. 2.647 *effera virtus*.

Introduction

distraught mind, and is very Senecan.³⁵ Particularly convincing is the *associative*, rather than logical, connection between some of the visions: thus the fact that he sees imminent conflict in the heavens (947ff.) leads to the idea of *scaling* the heavens, by force if necessary (955ff.); and the *intention* of leading the Titans in rebellion (967f.) turns into the *fear* of just such a rebellion by the Giants (976ff.).

The content of the first hallucinations may well have been influenced by medical observations of symptoms of disease and insanity (see comm. on 939–52). But it is the relevance of the visions to Hercules' individual psychology that is of primary importance in the play.³⁶ The various hallucinations result from anxieties and conflicts present, whether at a conscious or subconscious level, in his 'sane' mind. Thus every one of them involves violence, and in all but the first Hercules feels called upon to face a threat or take violent action; this obviously reflects his habitual obsession with conquest and revenge. As for the content of the individual hallucinations, the attacks on Lycus' family³⁷ and on Juno, and the planned attack on Eurystheus' Mycenae, clearly arise from his hatred of his enemies and persecutors.³⁸ Two of the other visions involve rebellions on the part of forces that Hercules had

---

35. In the Euripidean mad-scene there is a single consistent hallucination, namely that Hercules is attacking Mycenae (936ff.). Many instances come to mind of Seneca's ability to suggest poetically the shifts of a mind under intense pressure: one thinks of the shift from literal to symbolic in Cassandra's trance (*Ag.* 935–49); or of Phaedra's suicide-speech, in which death comes to signify both an escape from shameful love and a means of pursuing it; or on a larger scale of the minutely observed shifts in the life-and-death struggle between Andromache and Ulysses (*Tro.* 524ff.).

36. This is not to deny the poetic and thematic resonance of some details. Darkness as contrasted with daylight takes us back to the nightmare world of the prologue, where passions grow to monstrous size and the boundary between the upper world and the underworld is dissolved; Hercules sees into the underworld at 984ff. Darkness also suggests the underworld as a place of *death*, and that connotation is of course equally relevant here. Finally the picture of disorder in the heavens reestablishes the interplay between the individual and the universe, microcosm and macrocosm, which was seen in the prologue. Concerning the symbolism of the rebellion of Leo see comm. on 944–52.

37. Incidentally, by making the supposed victims Lycus' children, rather than Eurystheus' as in Euripides, Seneca has emphasized the continuity between Hercules' sane and insane behavior: the ruthlessness with which he attacks the children of 'Lycus' in madness is matched by the bloodthirstiness of his 'sane' attack on Lycus himself.

38. Similarly his imagined attack on Eurystheus in Eur. may be seen as the surfacing of a long-suppressed grudge against the tyrant; so J. C. Kamerbeek, "The Unity and Meaning of Euripides' *Heracles*," *Mnemosyne* 19 (1966) 14. But it is more doubtful whether the *origin* of the madness is psychological in Eur., as it is in Sen.: see fn. 40.

[29]

Introduction

already conquered or helped to conquer—the Nemean Lion and the Giants. These visions reflect the nightmare of the civilizer or pacifier, that the forces of chaos are never completely conquered, that they will regain strength and rebel—just as had in fact happened during Hercules' last absence from Thebes (251ff.).

Particularly significant is the hallucination in which Hercules envisages himself as attempting to enter the heavens (955ff.). In view of Jupiter's promise, the possibility of deification has long been present in his mind; as we have seen, it is not far below the surface in his last moments of 'sanity.' The element of madness here is that he sees his ascent as achieved by main force. Such an idea would not occur to him while he was sane. But at the same time we can see that it is actually "in character," because he normally thinks of new areas in terms only of conquest. The fear of opposition reflects his daily expectation of resistance in whatever task he undertakes. Yet his sudden anxiety that his *father* may deny him a place in heaven, and his instant determination to lead a rebellion, clearly reveal a latent aggression on the part of the ambitious son against the father who is perceived as hostile and repressive.[39] Not that Seneca means us to think of such an attitude toward Jupiter as part of Hercules' normal consciousness; but the hallucination suggests an understanding that in a personality such as Hercules', there would be sublimated aggression against the father.

In brief, then, Hercules' madness has a psychological origin. While sane, he is characterized by habitual aggression, ambition, and megalomania; in other words he is already close to insanity in his daily *modus vitae*. At this moment, when he has reached the highest pitch of megalomania, his mind topples over into madness. During the madness he has a series of hallucinations which embody—by a process familiar from dreams—the fears, conflicts, and ambitions that exist at different levels of consciousness in his mind. Seneca explores the *continuity* between the sane and insane mind.

This depiction of madness arising from uncontrolled *affectus* is close to the Stoic view, encountered repeatedly in Seneca's prose works, that all emotions are forms of mental derangement and therefore akin to madness. He applies the term *furor* to a wide range of dangerous emotions: to excessive mourning (*Cons. Pol.* 9.2) and greed (*Cons. Helv.* 10.6) as well as to passions which come closer to Hercules', namely obsession with conquest (*Ep.* 94.62), ambition (*Ep.* 104.9) and anger (*Clem.* 1.19.4, cf. *Ira* 1.1.2–4, 3.3.3). In other passages, rather than actually

---

39. The reference to Saturn in 965 strengthens this feeling by putting Hercules' rebellion into a series of such rebellions by younger generations: Saturn/Cronos against Uranus, and Jupiter against Saturn.

Introduction

identifying the passion with madness, he warns that *affectus* can *lead* to madness: fear can have this result (*QNat.* 6.29.2), as can attachment to possessions (*Ep.* 42.10) and, of course, anger (*Ira* 2.36.4–5, *Ep.* 18.15). Significantly Seneca mentions an example drawn from tragedy: Ajax's *ira* led to *furor*, and *furor* in turn to *insania* (*Ira* 2.36.5). But although Stoic psychology certainly explains why Seneca was prone to see Hercules' madness as an outgrowth of uncontrolled emotions, it would be a gross distortion to interpret his portrayal of Hercules, or the *HF* as a whole, as simply an illustration of his Stoic views conceived in a didactic spirit. This question will be discussed further in the section on Stoicism.

The interpretation of Hercules' madness as due to natural causes is not in itself new; what is original to Seneca, so far as we can tell, is the *psychological* causation of the madness.[40] The madness was widely explained as an attack of epilepsy, and indeed Ἡράκλειος νόσος, *Herculeus morbus*, became a term for that disease. The cause was sometimes given as an excess of black bile,[41] a standard medical explanation of madness in general. The paroemiographers, however, give a different cause for the epileptic seizure, namely exhaustion after the countless labors.[42] That explanation may well be reflected in the fact that Seneca's Hercules refuses to take rest between his tasks; in which case Seneca has transmuted the idea of physical exhaustion leading to epilepsy into that of psychological exhaustion leading to temporary insanity. Certainly he is aware that lack of rest makes a person vulnerable to the *affectus* (*Ira* 2.20.1, 3.9.1–5). However, that is not the only explanation implied in the play for the fact that Hercules goes mad just after the end of the labors: it is also clear that his ambition and megalomania

---

40. Attempts to show that the madness in Euripides' play has a psychological origin have met with little success. Wilamowitz in his edition (vol. 2, 127ff.) argued that the madness arises from the hero's megalomaniac attitudes; his *arete* is marked by violence and self-aggrandizement, which eventually lead to its destruction. But this ignores the humane side of his character, on which Euripides places great emphasis. The interpretation won little support, and was later disowned by Wilamowitz himself. Kamerbeek has proposed an alternative theory, namely that the madness in Euripides is "the violent reaction to the overstrain of a burdensome life" (p. 14). But evidence of such overstrain is difficult to find: the hero appears entirely capable of acting rationally and facing any challenges which he may encounter. In fact by bringing Iris and Lyssa onstage at the very moment when Heracles goes mad, Euripides underscores the external origin of the madness, and the discontinuity between the hero's behavior when sane and when insane.

41. Ps.-Arist. *Pr.* 30 953a; cf. Nicolaus of Damascus ap. *FGrH* 90 F13.

42. *Corpus Paroemiographorum Graecorum* 1 p. 91.26 (Zenobius). Macarius, quoted in the note ad loc., is even more emphatic: ἐπὶ τῶν μετὰ πολὺν κάματον ἐμπιπτόντων εἰς νόσον. ὁ γὰρ Ἡρακλῆς μετὰ μυρίους καμάτους τῇ ἱερᾷ ἐνέπεσεν. (These references from Soellner 312–14.) At *HO* 1396–98 one can surely see the ἐκ τῶν πόνων explanation being reused in a new context.

Introduction

have been increased by the supposed conquest of the underworld. It would be wrong to insist on a psychological explanation for the precise *timing* of the madness, for that is determined primarily by dramatic irony: it is just when Hercules believes himself to have mastered all evil, that evil masters his own mind.[43]

If Hercules' madness has its origin in his own psyche, how are we to understand Juno's part in it? The answer must be that here, as often in classical literature, we find two levels of motivation: one divine and the other human, or one mythological and the other psychological. In tragedy the form best suited to embody such double motivation is exactly that adopted in the *HF*, in which the divinity's appearance is confined to the prologue and therefore somewhat separated from the body of the play, where events unfold at the human level and from human motives.[44] The same pattern can be seen in Euripides' *Hippolytus* and *Troades*, and in Seneca's own *Thyestes*. The *Thyestes* with its infernal prologuists, the Fury and the ghost of Tantalus, gives a particularly close parallel, as Juno in the *HF* is also something of a hellish figure, a *Juno inferna*.

The question remains *why* Seneca decided to employ Juno in the prologue. On the one hand, he could not follow Euripides in introducing divine intervention at the time of the mad-scene, for that would have obscured his whole conception of the madness. On the other hand, to dispense with divine intervention altogether would have been a radical departure from mythical tradition, for the jealous Juno is a more integral part of Hercules' myth than, say, Venus is to that of Phaedra. Seneca therefore distanced the divine action as far as possible from the actual madness, and showed the planning stage, involving Juno herself, rather than her agents as in Euripides. These strategic considerations, so to speak, will have coincided with the powerful attraction of several literary models, particularly in Vergil and Ovid, for a monologue of Juno complaining about her rivals and enemies (see introduction to Act I). Seneca was as ready as any Roman to practice imitation and emulation of his predecessors.

The choice was a fortunate one, for the use of Juno in the prologue contributes greatly to the strength and cohesion of the play. Her forewarning of the denouement encourages the audience to examine Her-

---

43. For the irony that Hercules' challenge is immediately answered in an unexpected way, compare the similarly ironic timing in 613–17.

44. That is not to deny the obvious connection in *atmosphere* between the prologue and the mad-scene: both are filled with darkness and an oppressive, nightmarish atmosphere in which passions rule unchecked and even the constellations connote disorderly passion. But the connection is atmospheric and thematic, not causal. On the question of the Furies' appearance in the mad-scene see comm. on 982–84 ad fin.

cules' behavior for symptoms of approaching madness, which are indeed not difficult to find. But the portrayal of Juno is also relevant to that of Hercules in a more oblique (but no less effective) manner. Just as Lycus reflects certain Herculean characteristics, namely ambition and reliance on force, so Juno anticipates and parallels another destructive quality of the hero—his *ira*. Her chief motive is a desire to avenge herself—precisely that *cupiditas poenae exigendae* which for Seneca constitutes *ira* (*Ira* 1.3.2). Her feelings are in fact twice identified as *ira* (28, 75). Like Hercules, she deliberately spurs herself on to take action (75ff., cf. *Ira* 2.3.5). Her insistence on taking revenge personally is characteristic; her phrase *quid tanta mandas odia?* (77) closely parallels Seneca's statement about the angry person at *Ira* 3.3.3, *nec mandat ultionem suam*. Also characteristic is the fact that her anger finally approaches a state of frenzy, of loss of mental control, in a word of *furor* (109ff.). Furthermore, her anger, like Hercules', is not that of a sniveling slave, but of a great power in the universe.[45] They are figures at a similar level of existence. Because of their unique positions, they both see the macrocosm in personal terms, so to speak, as if it were a microcosm. Juno sees the heavens filled with her rivals, while Hercules sees them threatened by one of the monsters he himself has conquered. It is in such situations, in which personal passions can expand outward to affect the whole universe, that Seneca's poetry achieves its greatest resonance.

The dominion of death

A prominent theme in the *HF* is that of the underworld and its power. Its importance is particularly marked in Theseus' narrative and in the odes that precede and follow it (Odes II and III), but it is also felt throughout the play. What is emphasized is the vast population of the dead absorbed by this realm (e.g. 556f., 673f.). It is a mighty empire. But like most empires, it is eager for further increase. Death casts a rapacious eye on the living—on the whole company of the living, who are destined to swell the numbers of its subjects (870–74). In a powerful series of images Seneca sees the great crowds of the living, at Olympia or Rome, as no more than parallels and illustrations for the throngs of the dead (838ff.).

The underworld is seen largely as a world of evil, in two senses. On the one hand there is the negative evil constituted by the absence of all

---

45. One must not, of course, overlook the difference in the *quality* of their anger: Juno's is dark, female, frustrated; Hercules' brutal, male, unthinking, translated at once into action.

[33]

that accompanies life in the upper world—an absence of light, of color, of sound and movement (550ff., 698ff., 858ff.). But there is also the positive, active evil of the hellish forces harbored by the underworld. These include Dread, Resentment, Grief, Wars, and suchlike (690ff.) in addition to those Juno specifically summons, namely Crime, Error, Madness, and Impiety which laps its own blood. She also summons the Furies, and a power normally buried deep below Tartarus, the goddess Discord (92ff.).

This is the world that Hercules entered and supposedly conquered. It is noteworthy that he is repeatedly alleged not simply to have brought back Cerberus as commanded, but also to have achieved a wider conquest of death's power (e.g. 591, 610–12).[46] The Chorus praises him for having "pacified" the underworld (890). Elsewhere he is said to have opened a way from the underworld, with the implication that the dead now have access to the upper world (55–57), the latter idea becoming explicit in Megara's words (290–93; cf. 566–68). Sometimes, too, the impression is given that the journey resulted from his own initiative and decision, rather than the commands of Juno or Eurystheus (46ff., 186ff., 547ff.). The impression that Hercules has voluntarily achieved a conquest of death's power, benefiting all mankind, is a new element in the literary treatment of the twelfth labor. It is influenced by the religious conception mentioned earlier of Hercules as *mortis victor* and in some sense a deliverer from death.

But within the tragic context of this play, the idea of a conquest of death can only have hubristic overtones. Juno accuses him of the greatest arrogance (50–59), and Megara's language suggests unintentionally that hubris must be involved in the very idea of opening up the underworld (see comm. on 279ff. and 290); such passages recall the pattern of 'man's hubristic conquest of the universe' exemplified in Hor. *Carm.* 1.3. In addition to its hubris, the impossibility of the idea is underlined by the play's constant emphasis on the power of death. This pattern is particularly clear in Ode III, where rejoicing over Hercules' achievement is overshadowed by a meditation on the underworld and on human mortality (see introduction to the ode). Undeniably Hercules has overcome with ease the official rulers of the underworld, but we are constantly reminded that the underworld has other powers, less easily defeated. The Chorus' claim that Hercules has established control *Auroram inter et Hesperum* (882f.) is undercut for the audience by a reference only a few lines earlier to *death's* mastery over the living from east to west (871). Similarly, the Chorus' simple confidence that *nil ultra iacet inferos* (892) is countered by our knowledge of those powers lying

---

46. This point is developed in great and enlightening detail by Kroll 423ff.

in the lowest depths of Tartarus, precisely *ultra nocentum exilia* 93, *imo Ditis . . . regno* 95, namely, Crime, Impiety, Madness, and the like. Above all, the notion of a conquest of death is invalidated by our foreknowledge of Hercules' madness. He will and does become the agent, not the master, of the underworld: he does the work of its hellish forces and brings death to those around him. As Juno predicted (90f.), he has not fully escaped the *inferi*. It is appropriate that on recovering consciousness he finds himself still confronted by a *turba feralis* (1146), and that at the end of the play he longs to return to the underworld (1145f., 1338ff.).

Within the tragic purview of the play, then, the Herculean attempt to conquer death is doomed to failure, and indeed it has the opposite effect to that intended. In face of inevitable death the only sane mode of life, the Chorus suggests, is that of *secura quies*, which values each passing moment to the full (174ff.)—the polar opposite of *virtus animosa*. After being introduced in the first ode, the value of *quies* is consistently represented by Amphitryon. He points out early in the play that Hercules, beset by his constant labors, never has any free time or rest (212f.); after the punishment of Lycus he recommends that Hercules pray for *otium* and *quies* (924–26); and it is he who orders, as Hercules lies unconscious after murdering his family, that time be given to *quies* and the restorative power of sleep (1051f.). In this situation the two themes of rest and death are tellingly brought together in the fourth ode. Sleep is death's brother (1069), the experience of sleep is a daily *praeparatio mortis* (1075f.), and the power of sleep is as universal as that of death (see comm. on 1072 and 1074). Hercules has attempted to deny the importance of rest and death, but they will not be denied; if scorned, they will assert their power. As the Chorus sings the ode, Hercules lies mastered by sleep, and mastered in a different sense by death.

The final Act

Understanding of Act V has often been distorted by presuppositions about what *ought* to take place. Critics who remember the deeply impressive final episode of Euripides' play tend to assume that Seneca will likewise show Hercules learning in the end a new and deeper kind of heroism. Other critics insist that Seneca's tragic understanding of Hercules cannot differ completely from the more favorable view found in some of his philosophical writings; they therefore maintain, against all the evidence, that Hercules finally gains mastery over his powerful *affectus*. But if one allows the play to speak for itself, it is evident that the concluding Act has not shown any such redeeming transformation.

Introduction

On the contrary, it is the continuing harshness of Hercules' character, and the conflict and pain which result from it, that remain dominant throughout the Act. Such an ending is absolutely typical of Seneca's practice as a tragedian, as a glance at the endings of the other Senecan tragedies will show.

The continuity of Hercules' behavior with that which he displayed in the preceding Acts is very quickly evident. We have already seen that his angry insistence on revenge, first against the unknown assailant and then against himself, is entirely in keeping with his earlier behavior. Another trait still much in evidence in Act V is Hercules' narcissistic concern for himself and his self-image, which precludes the possibility of concern for others.[47] It is characteristic of him, as we have seen, that when he discovers the murders, he seems less perturbed by the untimely deaths of his family than by the damage to his own image as an invincible hero (1168–73, 1186). His inability to concern himself with others is crucial as his decision to commit suicide becomes more urgent. Amphitryon makes a powerfully expressed and moving appeal to him, stating the claims of *pietas*: he has never been able to rely on Hercules' support because of his continual absences, but now he needs his strength (1246ff.). But Hercules fails to respond to the appeal (1258ff.). Amphitryon's only recourse, therefore, is to renounce the argument in terms of his own needs (1302–5) and make his supreme appeal in terms of Hercules' reputation (1306f.), arguing that if Hercules commits suicide he will be damned as a parricide and this without the excuse of insanity (1308–13; see also comm. on 1300^b–1313). Hercules characteristically spends the whole of his final speech agonizing over his own destiny. He simply cannot bring his thoughts to bear on the question of caring for an aged father, and does not even show the concern over Amphitryon's eventual burial which we find in Euripides (1419ff.).

One can perceive minute signs of a thaw in Hercules' character. He thinks at the end, albeit only momentarily, of his father's plight (1317–19), and recognizes in Theseus (but only because he stands in need of

---

47. A detail of dramatic technique is relevant here. Although Act V contains sections of dramatically important dialogue, much of the Act is taken up by five lengthy speeches from Hercules (starting at 1138, 1202, 1221, 1278, and 1321). Long stretches of these speeches can be classified as monologue: in fact, of 157 lines spoken by H. in this Act, only 45 are properly in dialogue, in the sense of being clearly addressed to one of his interlocutors. In some cases it is not clear whether he is talking to himself or to an interlocutor: for example, the speech at 1278ff. seems to start as an oblique answer to Theseus, but by 1281 has definitely become self-address. This technique is appropriate to the situation and the character. H. is accustomed to proceed in terms of his own ideas and self-image, with no sensitivity to the feelings of others.

Introduction

its exercise) a quality he himself lacks, namely charitable love even for the guilty. But these signs are quite inadequate as evidence of a conversion in his outlook and values. Above all he fails to perceive that his excessive way of life led to the madness and the murders. He does admit responsibility for the deed, but only in an external sense—and his motive is to justify his insistence on punishment and to reject the plea of extenuating circumstances. The closest he comes to self-recognition is in the moving lines 1226–29:

> pectus o nimium ferum!
> quis vos per omnem, liberi, sparsos domum
> deflere digne poterit? hic durus malis
> lacrimare vultus nescit.

Here he perceives that his inability to weep is a failure, caused by the rigidity of his heroic persona; and the immediately subsequent proposal to destroy the weapons suggests a desire to destroy that persona, along with his life. But we cannot read into it a recognition that his heroic attitudes led directly to the deeds. It is also very short-lived, for he is soon immersed again in the Herculean persona, and calling for the weapons to use them punitively against himself (1242ff.). The usual inflexibility of that persona is strikingly illustrated in the way in which he reduces the issue to the familiar formula of the labors, monster-slayer versus monster:

> purgare terras propero; iamdudum mihi
> monstrum impium saevumque et immite ac ferum
> oberrat.
>
> (1279–81)

Of course the present situation, with its complex moral questions, is utterly different from the simple pattern of the labors, but Hercules' heroism can operate only in a single, rigid mode. Similarly the task of living on has to be categorized as another Herculean labor, done under a command, in order to become acceptable (1315f.).

This is not to underestimate the importance of Hercules' final decision for the dramatic economy of the play. Certainly Seneca has constructed the final Act so that tension gradually increases, reaching a climax in 1302–19. He liked such dramatic endings: compare Jocasta's suicide only moments before the end of *Oedipus*, or Medea's murder of the second son at a comparable point in *Medea*. Emotionally there is something right and satisfying about the outcome in which Amphitryon, the representative of love and sanity, gains the upper hand over Hercules' will to destruction. But this stops far short of a full resolution of the conflicts embodied in the play. On the one side, Amphitryon's

[37]

Introduction

victory is limited, for he will never enjoy that close relationship with his son for which he longs. On the other side, Hercules is conscious of defeat, not of a new beginning. He has taken the right decision, but in the wrong spirit—reluctantly, and under duress so extreme that it can only be called blackmail. Living on is another burdensome labor; death would be preferable. Like Theseus at the end of the *Phaedra* (1201ff.), he longs hopelessly for the underworld, the more poignantly because he has recently left it (1338ff.). In this way he fulfills to the letter Juno's plans: *me vicit: et se vincat, et cupiat mori / ab inferis reversus* (116–17). As Juno intended, he stands at the last with bloodstained hands (1323ff., cf. 122), longing for an obscure hiding-place rather than the position in heaven which he once coveted. There can be no sense of victory over the goddess or over the tragedy that has befallen him.

What of the last few lines of the play, in which Theseus offers Hercules sanctuary and purification in Athens? Does this not offer at least some possibility of recovery from the tragedy? Of course it does; and it is significant, in terms of the themes of the play, that the possibility is created by the power of tolerance and love (cf. 1336f.) as opposed to retributive punishment. But the very brevity of Theseus' speech marks it as essentially an epilogue: it solves the practical problem of Hercules' future, and even hints at the eventual deification which the myth requires, but it does not give a full resolution springing naturally from the development of the play.

The fact that the dominant notes of the last Act are anger, conflict, and suffering is consistent with the usual patterns of Senecan tragedy—in marked contrast to classical Greek tragedy, where there is often some sense of anguish being calmed, of ways being found to accept the disasters that have occurred. Seneca's *Troades* ends with the bitter contrast between the children's deaths and Hecuba's being denied death; his *Medea* with Medea's gloating murder of the children; *Phaedra* with Theseus' curse on his dead wife; *Oedipus* with Jocasta's suicide onstage and Oedipus' despairing exile; *Agamemnon* with Electra's defiance of her mother and Cassandra's prophecy of bloodshed yet to come; *Thyestes* with Atreus' taunting of his devastated brother. Seneca as tragedian maintains the tragic tone throughout his plays, and is not concerned to suggest possibilities of healing, reconciliation or new strength. So it should not be surprising that Hercules' decision to live on is not a source of new hope, and that his final speech is a long cry of pain.

Summary

The kernel of Seneca's play may be seen as the study of a passion-figure. In a characteristically Senecan pattern—one thinks of Medea,

Atreus, Phaedra, Pyrrhus, Clytemnestra—ungoverned emotional impulses lead to catastrophe. But Hercules is somewhat unusual within this group of passion-figures. First, he is not dominated by a single emotion, as Atreus by *ira*, nor by two conflicting emotions, as Phaedra by *amor* and *pudor*, but by a complex of interconnected impulses which may be summarized as aggression (including *ira*), ambition, and megalomania. Second, the evil that constitutes the tragedy, the killing of his family, is not consciously planned, but rather an accidental result of the disorder which these *affectus* create in his mind. Consequently, Act II of *HF* does not contain a Passion-Restraint scene of the normal type, that is, one in which the passion-figure, despite attempts at restraint by an interlocutor, makes evil plans which lead to the catastrophe later in the play.[48]

Hercules' significance goes beyond personal psychology. The play is also a study of a mythical hero and a culture-hero. Hercules is the paradigm of an influential cultural ideal: that of the exceptional man, the beneficent conquering hero and peace-bringer, exaggerated into the θεῖος ἀνήρ. Seneca explores this ideal from a tragic viewpoint; he draws on the ambivalence about Hercules' character evident in the myth itself, and on the dangers of such a cult of personality as evidenced by historical examples such as Alexander and Julius Caesar. Certainly he evokes the magnificence of this kind of heroism, as opposed to the small-mindedness of Lycus. He also shows that such a hero is likely in fact to be an unstable mixture of benevolence, self-seeking, compulsive activity, violence, and megalomania. Furthermore, the ideal of universal peace and order is endangered not only by the nature of the civilizer himself, but also by something endemic in human nature and in the nature of the universe: evil, violence, and death are stubbornly rooted and cannot be eradicated.

These conclusions might be seen in part as a warning to emperors (cf. comm. on 735–47). Indeed, as Augustus and other emperors were likened to Hercules, so Seneca's Hercules is in some ways an imperial figure, with his triumphs (58, 828) and his claim to have established peace from the orient to the occident. But such a didactic purpose should not be overstressed, and it is difficult to see a specific application to any of the emperors under whom the play might in theory have been written: the Herculean role would have little relevance to the teenaged Nero before 54; Tiberius, Gaius, and Claudius scarcely fell into the Herculean mold, and in any case Gaius was presumably beyond such subtle warnings.[49] And insofar as the play propounds an al-

---

48. See introduction to Act II.
49. There is no special significance in the fact that Gaius on occasion dressed as Hercules, as he also imitated most other members of the pantheon (Dio Cass.

Introduction

ternative to heroic activity, it is that of retirement and the quiet life, which could have little meaning for emperors. The play responds to myth,[50] as seen from a certain Hellenistic-Roman cultural perspective, and to the dictates of tragedy rather than to a particular political situation.

Another meaning inherent in the myth that Seneca explores from a tragic standpoint is that of liberation from death. As we have seen, the conquest of death is the theme of several of Hercules' labors, and as a natural development Hercules is sometimes seen as one who delivers mankind from death's power. Seneca's tragedy suggests that the hope of conquest over death or deliverance from it is empty. The only sane response, according to the Chorus in the first ode, is to accept the fact of death and live life in consciousness of its limited and ephemeral nature.

A study of a complex of *affectus*, an investigation of a mythical hero who represents a certain cultural ideal, even a critique of certain religious aspirations—this may seem a large amount of significance to claim for a single tragedy. But the meanings of a literary work arise in part from its very subject matter. The choice of Hercules as a subject brought with it a whole range of potential meaning, which Seneca was able to realize by virtue of his powerful imagination and his sensitivity to myth.

Hercules Furens *and Stoicism*

There are, not surprisingly, many similarities of thought and expression between Seneca's tragedies and his prose writings. These similarities can create a temptation for the critic to use the relatively clear-cut doctrines of the *philosophica* as a ready-made key to understanding the more elusive meaning of the tragedies. This approach entails the supposition that the dramas are somehow secondary to the prose works, and leads to a tendency to disregard those elements in the tragedies which do not agree with a Stoic interpretation. Such an approach has given rise to grossly distorted interpretations of the *HF*. On the one hand the play has been seen as "a hymn to the Stoic wise man"—

59.26.5ff.). Though Nero liked to act the part of mad Hercules, that was only one of his favorite dramatic roles (Suet. *Nero* 21, cf. fn. 70). His *identification* with Hercules apparently belongs to the period of the tour of Greece: on his return in A.D. 68 he was hailed as Nero Hercules (as well as Nero Apollo, Dio Cass. 62.20.5); he planned to emulate Hercules by killing a lion at the next Olympics (Suet. *Nero* 53); coins were issued at Rome with the inscription *Herculi Augusto* (Roscher 1.2982).

50. For Seneca's remarkable sensitivity to what is inherent in myth cf. fn. 33 and comm. on 1284ᵇ–94.

Introduction

though the view of Hercules as a prototypical wise man is treated by Seneca with some reserve even in his prose works. On the other hand, because of Seneca's interest in anger as evidenced in the *de Ira*, the *HF* has been seen as simply a study of *ira*—a view that oversimplifies the characterization of Hercules and ignores the more general themes summarized in the previous section.

The evident difference in general outlook and Weltanschauung between the tragedies and the prose works should warn against any simplistic correlation between the two. In the world of the dramas there is a general absence of overriding control or order. The gods, who might be expected to establish some moral order, appear ineffective or worse. The only Olympians who definitely intervene in human affairs are Juno in *HF*, Neptune in *Pha.*, and Apollo in *Ag.*; all of these interventions are either malignant in intention or evil in effect. On the other hand, when the gods might be expected to counter evil, assert right, or punish injustice, they are notably ineffectual (e.g. *Pha.* 671ff.). Jupiter in *HF* does not lift a finger to protect his son, and Amphitryon breaks off a prayer to him in disgust at its obvious pointlessness (516ff.). The Chorus of *Pha.* complains that while there is order in the outer reaches of the universe, it does not extend into human affairs (959–88). The strong impression of moral chaos cannot easily be reconciled with the Stoic conception of a universe governed by divine providence.

Certainly the picture of Hercules' *affectus* leading to madness corresponds in a general way to the Stoic association between passion and madness, as we have seen. But this observation must be qualified on several counts. First, the association of passion with madness is not a cabalistic doctrine that justifies separating Seneca's tragedies from the mainstream of Roman literature under the label Stoic: one need only mention the recurrent thematic importance of *furor* in the *Aeneid*.[51] Second, it is not simply a question of *ira*, or (more accurately) of a complex of *affectus*; rather these *affectus* are mingled with the virtues of beneficence and idealism. The ambivalence of this portrait owes more to contradictions inherent in the myth, and to historical examples of men who tried to emulate Hercules, than it does to Stoic categorization of the passions. Furthermore, the main contrast established within the play is not between passion and Stoic reason (*ratio* is never mentioned in the *HF*) but between *virtus animosa* and *secura quies*, the latter described in terms redolent of Horace and popular Epicureanism (see introduction to Ode I).[52] Thus the situation in *HF* is very different from

---

51. See especially B. Otis, *Virgil: A Study in Civilized Poetry* (Oxford 1964) index s.v. *furor*.

52. It is true that in Seneca's prose too the quiet life is sometimes favorably contrasted with the life of frenetic activity lived by Alexander, Julius Caesar, and their

Introduction

that in *Thyestes*, in some ways the most Stoic of the tragedies, where Atreus' abuse of kingship for unlimited self-assertion is set against the Stoic definition of kingship, enunciated in the second ode, as mastery of one's own soul.

Understanding of Act V in particular has been distorted by Stoic interpretation. Some critics believe that Hercules, having strayed far from the role of Stoic exemplar in the body of the play, returns to it at the end. But there is no basis for this belief; it is simply untrue to claim that from 1227ff. he is "increasingly controlled by *Ratio*," or that at the end of the play he is "resigned, decisive, steady," displaying "a consciously willed resolution to terminate upheaval."[53] Others have explained the importance of suicide as an issue in Act V by Seneca's own interest qua philosopher in that subject. There may be some truth in that assumption, but it should be remembered that Hercules' contemplation of suicide is already prominent in the Euripidean model. Nor can Seneca's treatment of the issue in the tragedy easily be assimilated to that of the *philosophica*. In the prose works Seneca frequently approves of suicide as an honorable means of escape from an intolerable life, but he also makes two important qualifications to his approval: first, one should not commit suicide if one's presence is important to family or friends (e.g. *Ep*. 104.3); second, by the doctrine of the *rationalis excessus*, suicide should not be undertaken in an emotional fashion—*etiam cum ratio suadet finire se, non temere nec cum procursu capiendus est impetus* (*Ep*. 24.24). By either of these criteria, Hercules' impulse to suicide stands condemned. He is motivated by exactly that *libido moriendi*, that *inconsulta animi inclinatio*, against which Seneca warns (*Ep*. 24.25). On the other hand, his decision *against* suicide is equally far removed from what Seneca would approve. As we have seen, it is not taken out of a generous concern for the needs of others,[54] but rather under emotional blackmail, and out of consideration

---

kind (*Cons. Helv.* 9.7–8, *Ep*. 94.69ff.). But Seneca regularly takes the Stoic view that leisure and retirement are justified only as an opportunity for intellectual and moral endeavor which will be of benefit to mankind (e.g. *Cons. Helv.* ibid., *Brev. Vit.* 14.1–2, 18.2, *de Otio* 3.4, 6.4–5). That Stoic justification is quite absent from the *HF*.

53. The first quotation comes from Zintzen 201, the second and third from Motto and Clark 112 and 103.

54. Contrast Seneca's personal decision against committing suicide, taken when a young man and recounted at *Ep*. 78.2:

saepe impetum cepi abrumpendae vitae; patris me indulgentissimi senectus retinuit. cogitavi enim non quam fortiter ego mori possem, sed quam ille fortiter desiderare non posset. itaque imperavi mihi, ut viverem.

There is a world of difference between Seneca's consideration of his father's ability to bear bereavement, and the way in which Hercules rejects, or more accurately ignores, this consideration as presented to him by Amphitryon himself.

for his own reputation. If this is meant to convey Seneca's Stoic teaching on suicide, even by means of a negative *exemplum*, Seneca has chosen a remarkably opaque means of instruction. The truth is that Hercules' behavior should be judged in the light of the play itself, rather than in the light of the prose works.

Why—to come to the essential question—can Seneca give so unfavorable a portrait of Hercules in the *HF*, while in prose he usually refers to him with admiration? Part of the answer must lie in the independence of literary genres in antiquity. As a Stoic philosopher Seneca inclines toward the orthodox, favorable view of Hercules; as a tragedian he has license to explore the tragic aspects of his heroism.[55] The importance of generic considerations is borne out by *Apocol.* (5–7, 9), which contains a burlesque portrait of Hercules appropriate to satire, but quite out of keeping with that of the *philosophica*.

This is not to reduce the significance of the *HF* to that of a literary exercise in a particular genre. Inasmuch as Hercules is representative of a certain heroic ideal, the writer's attitude toward him carries general implications concerning heroism and the conduct of life. Here too it might be argued that the differences are influenced by genre; in tragedy one takes a tragic view of life, in Stoic philosophy not. But poetry of any value at all is also truth-telling; the integration of themes in *HF* and their relevance to Roman concerns suggest that this work is something more than a literary trifle of no significance in comparison with the *philosophica*. Rather it appears that Seneca, like some other Roman writers, notably Vergil, could hold certain attitudes in tension without resolving them.

In any case, Seneca's opinion of Hercules in the prose works is not one of unqualified adulation. On the single occasion on which he mentions the notion of Hercules as an exemplar of the *sapiens*, he does not commit himself to that view, but attributes it to "Stoic teachers," *Stoici nostri*, and comments pointedly that Cato was a *certius exemplar* of a wise man; he also goes on to allude in sardonic style to Hercules' labors, contrasting them unfavorably with Cato's (*Const. Sap.* 2.1–2). Elsewhere his references to Hercules are more complimentary. But one cannot help but notice that the real point of three of them (*Ben.* 1.13.1–3, 7.3.1; *Ep.* 94.63)[56] is that Hercules' example has been disastrous as put into practice—admittedly misguidedly, and with the wrong motives—by men such as Alexander, Julius Caesar, and Pompey. Seneca's primary purpose in these passages is to criticize the obsession with conquest shown by such men. In the *HF*, then, instead of

---

55. Similarly Seneca acknowledges the Stoic view of Ulysses as a prototypical wise man at *Const. Sap.* 2.1–2, but portrays him as cunning and ruthless in *Troades*.
56. The others are *Ben.* 4.8.1, *Tranq.* 16.4.

Introduction

showing Hercules as an example on whom actual men of power might model themselves, Seneca reverses the process and models Hercules on the men of power themselves, attributing to him some of the failings which he attributes to Alexander and his kind in the prose works.

Seneca's Sources

The fact that the plot of Seneca's play derives ultimately from Euripides' *Heracles* is too evident to need demonstration. But the many differences between the two plays, and the long period of theatrical history that intervenes, make it necessary to ask whether Seneca took his dramatic material directly from Euripides, altering it to suit his own purposes, or whether he used non-Euripidean dramatic sources in part or in whole. I shall first examine the action of Seneca's play for signs of non-Euripidean influence; brevity is necessary to keep the discussion within bounds, and further details both of closeness to Euripides and of divergence from him will be found in the introductions to individual Acts, or in commentary on particular lines and passages.

Act I is modeled on several angry speeches of Juno in Vergil and Ovid. It would be entirely superfluous to postulate an intermediary between Vergil and Ovid on the one hand and Seneca on the other; nor are there any grounds for postulating a pre-Augustan dramatic source, whether Greek or Roman.[57]

Act II corresponds approximately to the prologue and first episode of Euripides, the chief difference lying in Lycus' offer of marriage to Megara. This scene is full of Senecan elements: the instability of unjust rule is a characteristically Senecan theme (341–45 comm.), and the theme of *novitas* has relevance to Seneca's own career (Tac. *Ann.* 14.53); equally Senecan are the arguments of 362ff. (see comm. on 362–67 and 365–67), the *adynata* of 373–78 and the exploitation of precedents in 386–96 and 398. It may be that the basic pattern of a marriage offer from a tyrant in such circumstances is borrowed from another plot, whether concerning Danae or Merope (see introduction to Act II), but that supposition is not obligatory. In any case, there is no need to assume with Friedrich 1934[58] that the borrowing, if such it

57. Hera does not appear as a dramatis persona in classical Greek tragedy, but there is a postclassical example in the alternative prologue of the *Rhesus*, preserved in the hypothesis (= *TrGF* adesp. 8L); one cannot therefore argue a priori against her appearance in a Hellenistic or Republican Hercules-play.

58. Friedrich worked on the assumption that any dramatically effective elements in Seneca which are not derived from Euripides must come from some lost tragedy;

Introduction

is, was made by an unknown tragedian writing on Hercules' madness; it could equally well have been made directly by Seneca, attracted by the opportunity to show the *instans tyrannus* being defied to his face.

At the end of this Act and the beginning of the next, we receive the impression that Hercules is emerging directly from the underworld (520–22, 592ff.). As has often been noticed, this contradicts Juno's statement that he has already returned and begun parading through Greece (58ff.), and Theseus' report that he emerged at Taenarum (813ff.). A concomitant inconsistency lies in the fact that at 600ff. Hercules has Cerberus with him, but the hound's presence is not mentioned again, and at 1105–7 he is back in the underworld. In these respects 520–23 and 592–615 represent a *Fremdkörper* within the Senecan play and might therefore be thought to derive from a non-Euripidean dramatic source. But it should be noted that the immediately preceding lines 501–20 are best explained as an extremely abbreviated and somewhat cavalier rehandling by Seneca himself of Euripides' lines 238–347 and 451–513. Sen. 501–8 corresponds to Eur. 238–51; Sen. then skips over Eur. 252–320 but picks up Amphitryon's request to die first (Eur. 321–22), recasting it so as to express stoical acceptance of death and to elicit a typically tyrannical rejoinder, and failing to notice that neither the request nor the reply makes sense as he presents them (see comm. on 509–10); finally in 516–19 he reuses Amphitryon's prayer at Eur. 498ff. It seems probable, then, that the direct emergence from the underworld is an equally opportunistic variation by Seneca on the Euripidean original, designed in part to end Act II on a note of high drama and in part to provide an occasion for Hercules' self-revealing musings on his underworld exploit (592ff.); Seneca either did not notice, or was not concerned by, the inconsistency with the rest of the play. He then returned to fidelity to Euripides in 618–25 (Eur. 516–19), failing to remember that for his Amphitryon Hercules' presence should come as a confirmation of the forewarnings in 520–22, not a complete surprise.

There remains the puzzle of the stage-direction at 515, where Lycus announces that he will go and pay a thank offering to Neptune (v. ad loc.). The explanation of the offering is not clear, since he has just met with failure rather than success; one deduces that the reason for gratitude must be his newly acquired kingship, but the earlier part of the Act definitely does not give the impression that he has just this moment won the throne (e.g. 343). Furthermore, Neptune's patronage

---

his hypothesis was rightly assailed by Haywood 1942. Friedrich rashly identified the hypothetical lost source first with the Republican drama represented for us by *inc. inc. trag.* 30f. R^2, and later with Accius' *Amphitruo*: see below p. 48.

[45]

Introduction

can only be explained by the tradition that he was Lycus' ancestor—a tradition Seneca suppressed earlier in portraying Lycus as an unknown upstart (see comm. on 269 *ignarum exulem*). This double inconsistency makes it virtually certain that the motive for Lycus' exit is drawn from another play. But that need not strengthen the hypothesis of an alien source for 520ff. If Seneca in 501ff. is adapting Euripides in piecemeal and cavalier fashion, as I suppose, then when faced by the need to explain the stay of execution and Lycus' departure he discards the Euripidean business of dressing for death[59] and substitutes a motive which he remembers from another play; then he returns to Euripides. But one must not underestimate the significance of the evidence of 515 that Seneca had another Hercules-drama on which he could draw.

In Act III the overshadowing of plot material (plans to kill Lycus) by an ecphrastic element (Theseus' narrative) may well reflect Hellenistic, and perhaps Augustan, practice in drama. But the model for the content of much of the ecphrasis is Vergil, with Amphitryon's questions at Eur. 610ff. providing a point of departure. There is no reason not to suppose, therefore, that Seneca shaped the Act himself in accordance with prevalent canons of dramatic form.

In Act IV, rather than having the mad-scene reported as in Euripides, Seneca brings it onstage as far as possible, though the murders themselves take place offstage (for details see introduction to Act IV). This is quite in keeping with Seneca's tendency to dramatize rather than narrate tragic violence, particularly late in the play (compare Medea's murders of her children, and the suicides of Jocasta and Phaedra). But although it is not beyond belief that Seneca himself could have managed the transposition of Euripides' narrative into dramatic action, it must be admitted that the clear awareness of stage realities, at least from 999ff., is not what one ordinarily associates with Seneca.

Here we must take into account the stage directions of 912–17, which are clearly designed to remove Theseus from the stage lest he be an inconvenient witness of the murders.[60] Seneca does not always trouble to give a specific reason for the absence of relatively minor characters, and it is particularly untypical of him to go about the business in such a fussy manner (so Friedrich 1934 306). This makes it likely that Seneca is following another dramatist, a probability strength-

---

59. In Euripides that provides a means whereby Lycus can be trapped; Seneca has no need for such a device and therefore discards it.

60. First recognized by H. Weil, *Rev. Arch.* 11 (1865) 26. Sacrifice is often used to motivate an exit in ancient tragedy: cf. 515 with comm. Hercules' words indicate that Theseus is to visit various locations, worshiping not just Zethus but his *antra*, not just Cadmus but his *lar*; similarly at Eur. *Ion* 422–24 instructions to Creusa to visit several altars motivate her exit and lengthy absence.

ened by the fact that Seneca's lines, though they must motivate an exit, are not written as if that purpose were uppermost in Seneca's mind: the exit is taken for granted, which suggests that Seneca has it at second hand. This hypothesis carries with it important implications, namely, that the unknown dramatist, like Seneca, had Theseus appear at an earlier point than he does in Euripides,[61] and very probably that he removed Theseus from the stage because the mad-scene was to be enacted there. This playwright is therefore a probable source for the dramatization of the madness in Act IV; perhaps also for the employment of Theseus as a narrator in Act III, though the length of the narrative, and particularly of the *descriptio inferorum*, is probably due to Seneca.

In Act V the person who dissuades Hercules from suicide is now Amphitryon, not Theseus as in Euripides; that is in keeping with Seneca's thematic contrast between the values of Amphitryon and Hercules, and there is no need to postulate another source. Although the dramatic climax, with Hercules' preparations for suicide thwarted by Amphitryon's collapse and counterthreat of suicide, is to some extent envisaged in terms of stage action (v. 1317f. and comm. on 1300^b–1313), the physical awkwardness, if not impossibility, of drawing a bow against oneself (1298–1300) suggests a certain remoteness from stage reality, which probably betokens the hand of Seneca rather than a predecessor.

In sum, internal evidence for Seneca's having used a non-Euripidean dramatic source is small but convincing: it consists of two stage directions, 515 and 915–17, the second of which implies a mad-scene enacted largely onstage and thus a precedent for Seneca. Can we identify the play or plays from which these elements might have come?

Greek dramas dealing with the events of Euripides' play were either few or obscure. We know of three Hellenistic dramas entitled *Heracles*, by Diogenes, Lycophron, and Timasitheus,[62] but nothing of their contents. No fragments known from literary sources or papyri appear to come from plays on this subject.[63] A scholiast on Hom. *Od.* 11.269 gives a version of the story which he ascribes to Asclepiades of Tragilos: "Lycus in obedience to Hera garlands Heracles' sons in order to sacrifice them. . . . But Heracles arrives and kills him and his sons. Becoming mad by Hera's agency he kills his own sons. He was about to

---

61. No doubt at the time of Hercules' first appearance: not a priori an unlikely supposition, since his belated arrival in Euripides smacks rather obviously of dramatic convenience.

62. Respectively, *TrGF* 88 F1c, 100 F1e, 214. Spintharos' *Heracles Perikaiomenos* (40 T1), whatever its nature, cannot have dealt with this plot in view of its title.

63. *TrGF* adesp. F126 and F653 both seem to come from plays dealing with Hercules' death.

Introduction

kill his brother Iphicles too, but Athena prevented him." (= *FGrH* 12 F27). This presumably came from Asclepiades' *Tragoidoumena*; if the scholiast's report is accurate, the play in question diverged in several details from Euripides, but none of the divergences is reflected in Seneca.[64]

Evidence of another drama may be provided by the krater in Paestan style painted by Assteas shortly after 350 B.C., which shows Hercules about to hurl a child onto a fire while Megara escapes through an open door.[65] The painting is generally thought to show theatrical influence, the nature of which is, however, difficult to evaluate. Insofar as it implies a play in which the madness was dramatized rather than narrated, and in which the palace door was important, it has affinities with Seneca's play; but insofar as it implies that the children were killed onstage, one at least by fire, it diverges from Seneca. In any case the element of burlesque, whether attributable to the painter or his dramatic inspiration, makes it impossible to take the vase as direct evidence of a tragic drama.

Other candidates have been proposed from Republican Roman tragedy. Mette (1964 132–34 and 174, 1966 478) and Friedrich (1967 108) have revived the old suggestion that Accius' *Amphitruo* dealt with the events surrounding Hercules' madness. It is true that fr. IV (86 R^2 *sed quaenam haec mulier est funesta veste, tonsu lugubri?*) could be spoken by Hercules on first catching sight of Megara. But fr. VI (88f. R^2 *tamen et staturae gracilitudo propemodum et luctus facit / ne dubitem*), which ought to belong to the same context, cannot be Hercules', unless one makes the awkward assumption that he has learned about the situation in Thebes before his return. The most serious obstacle, however, as Ribbeck noted,[66] lies in fr. I (82f. R^2 *cum patre parvos patrium hostifice / sanguine sanguen miscere suo*). This can only be fitted into the situation of Hercules' madness on the assumption that Hercules' sons fought against him and spilled his blood, which seems scarcely credible. Most of the other fragments can be fitted into the context of the madness, but their content is so general that they would also fit into a wide variety of other tragic plots. Finally we must note the difficulty of supposing that a play with a plot akin to Eur. *Heracles* or Sen. *HF* was entitled *Amphitruo*.

One other fragment of Republican tragedy may well belong to a Hercules play. Friedrich 1934 303ff. drew attention to *inc. inc. trag.* 30f. R^2 *nam sapiens virtuti honorem praemium, haud praedam petit. / sed quid*

---

64. It may be significant that Seneca's Hercules *thinks* he is killing Lycus' sons (987ff.), but this is not strong evidence.

65. A. D. Trendall, *Paestan Pottery* (Rome 1936) 31ff.; M. Bieber, *History of the Greek and Roman Theater*, 2d ed. (Princeton 1961) 130.

66. O. Ribbeck, *Die römische Tragödie* (Leipzig 1875) 559.

video? ferro saeptus possidet sedes sacras, and persuasively suggested that the speaker is Hercules, who after speaking line 30 catches sight of Amphitryon surrounded by Lycus' guards (cf. *HF* 616f.). That would put the passage shortly after Hercules' first entry, and line 30 would be spoken either at the end of an entrance-monologue akin to *HF* 592–615 in form (though not in content), or in dialogue with, say, Theseus. But further than that we cannot go.[67]

Attention has also been drawn to the painting of a tragic scene in the Casa del Centenario in Pompeii, which shows Hercules on the left, Amphitryon and Megara in the center, apparently with their hands tied, and Lycus reclining on the right.[68] The fact that Hercules appears unaware of Amphitryon and Megara, whereas they have seen him, suggests the moment of Hercules' arrival. The play illustrated can scarcely be Seneca's, in view of the tied hands and Lycus' posture. Bieber has argued that such paintings are likely to be representations of contemporary performances, rather than copies of earlier paintings, on the evidence of the costumes and stage conventions seen in them.[69] But again the evidence will not permit further conclusions.[70]

Tarrant (1978) has shown that Seneca's dramatic technique is in large part that of postclassical rather than fifth-century tragedy, marked by such characteristics as five-act structure, reduction of the role of the Chorus almost exclusively to delivering act-dividing odes, and use of entrance-monologues and asides. He has also argued persuasively that Seneca's familiarity with these techniques derives primarily from Augustan tragedy[71] rather than from Hellenistic or Republican Roman drama. (That would be in keeping with Seneca's deep indebtedness to Augustan writers whose work does survive, Horace, Vergil, and above all Ovid—an indebtedness illustrated repeatedly in my commentary.) But this does not warrant the assumption that the *HF*, or any other Senecan play, is based primarily on a specific Augus-

---

67. *Inc. inc. trag.* 249f. R² *quaenam te adigunt, hospes, / stagna capacis visere Averni?* is similar to *HF* 547–49, and may be addressed to Hercules (though there are alternative possibilities such as Theseus), but if so the present tense might suggest a different segment of the myth from that with which we are concerned.

68. Bieber (cf. fn. 65) 229. There is a similar scene in the Casa di Casca, but without Hercules.

69. Bieber 227. She takes the play in question to be Accius' *Amphitruo,* but we have seen reason to doubt whether that play contained such a situation.

70. One cannot tell whether the role of mad Hercules enacted by Nero (Suet. *Nero* 21) came from a tragedy, nor whether it predated Sen. *HF.* Certainly it was not the role created by Seneca, as it required Hercules to be bound with chains.

71. In addition there seems no reason to deny the probable influence of post-Augustan tragedians such as Pomponius Secundus.

Introduction

tan model.⁷² Although it is conceivable that the Augustan period produced one or more plays on the madness of Hercules, nothing compels us to assume that Seneca would have turned for inspiration exclusively to these, rather than to the great original of Euripides;⁷³ it seems at least equally possible a priori that he would have worked directly from Euripides' drama, remodeling it in accordance with the dramatic conventions familiar to him, and adding elements from diverse dramatic and nondramatic sources. But Tarrant's arguments do have the great merit of making it impossible to assume automatically that Seneca worked primarily from the *exemplaria Graeca*.

Our conclusions, then, must be largely agnostic. In the nature of things it is impossible to prove that Seneca used Euripides directly, because similarities of situation and even of wording⁷⁴ do not preclude the existence of an intermediary who was himself following Euripides closely. The stage-directions at 515 and 915–17, the early return of Theseus, and the dramatic handling of Act IV, probably come from a non-Euripidean Hercules drama or dramas, which we cannot identify further. But there is no compelling reason to attribute Seneca's other departures from Euripides to imitation of the same source or sources, for his notion of imitation, both in theory (*Ep.* 84.5–10) and in practice (see e.g. my introduction to Ode I), is to combine materials from the most diverse sources in order to create a new whole.

Date

A noteworthy piece of evidence is provided by Quintilian's reminiscence of a literary disagreement between Seneca and Pomponius Secundus: *memini iuvenis admodum inter Pomponium ac Senecam etiam praefationibus esse tractatum, an 'gradus eliminat' in tragoedia dici oportuisset* (*Inst.* 8.3.31). These *praefationes* appear to have been remarks delivered by the authors before recitations or performances of their tragedies. The phrase *iuvenis admodum* would suggest that Quintilian was some-

---

72. Tarrant's general thesis makes him too ready to assume (1978 261) that Accius' *Amphitruo* dealt with Hercules' madness, and that it inspired an Augustan drama which in turn inspired Seneca.

73. Tarrant believes that Seneca and his contemporaries did not have a wide or deep knowledge of fifth-century Greek tragedy (*Agamemnon* pp. 9f.); however that may be, he concedes that Seneca would have known such famous dramas as Euripides' *Heracles, Medea,* and *Troades* (1978 216).

74. Places where Seneca's wording comes particularly close to Euripides' are 268 *Cadmea proles,* 440 *partes meae sunt e.q.s.* (v. comm. on 439ff.), 509f., 519 *quid deos frustra precor?* (v. comm. on 516–20), 544, 548 *vias inremeabiles,* 761, 997f., 1025f., 1318f.; for details see my commentary ad locc., and see also index s.v. Euripides.

Introduction

where between seventeen and twenty-one years old at the time;⁷⁵ as he was born between A.D. 30 and 40,⁷⁶ and as Seneca did not return from exile until 49 and Pomponius was in Germany in 50 and 51, the probable period for the occasions Quintilian recalls is between 52 and 61. So at least one of Seneca's tragedies (we cannot know which) was presented publicly in this period. Probably the drama or dramas in question had been written since 49, or perhaps during the exile (41–49); the hypothesis that Seneca was reviving works written more than a decade earlier, that is, before the exile, is inherently much less plausible.⁷⁷

Attempts to date individual plays by supposed references in them to contemporary events have met with little success. But for *HF* we have more reliable evidence, consisting of echoes of the play in Seneca's *Apocolocyntosis*: this evidence establishes a *terminus ante quem* of late 54.⁷⁸ The echoes occur in two verse passages of *Apocol.*: the mock-tragic speech delivered by Hercules in section 7, and the *nenia* for the dead Claudius in section 12.⁷⁹

§ 7 poët. vv.1–3 exprome propere, sede qua genitus cluas,
                 hoc ne peremptus stipite ad terram accidas:
                 haec clava reges saepe mactavit feros.

Line 2 recalls *HF* 1296 *hoc en peremptus spiculo cecidit puer*. *Peremptus* is not in itself conclusive, because the participle occurs in this metrical position eleven times in Sen. Trag., but the overall similarity of the lines is unmistakable. Though there are parallels, e.g. in Ovid, for *stipes* = 'club', the frequency of this usage in *HF* is noteworthy (1029, 1119, 1230, 1232; only once elsewhere in Sen. Trag.). Hercules' suppression of tyrants (v.3) is given unusual emphasis in *HF*: see comm. on 271f.

ibid.v.8   Inachiam ad urbem nobile advexi pecus.

---

75. Tacitus uses the same phrase of himself at the age of nineteen, *Dial.* 1.2 (dramatic date A.D. 75).
76. See F. H. Colson's edition of book I (Cambridge 1924) ix–x and M. L. Clarke in *G&R* N.S. 14 (1967) 27f.
77. For a summary of other evidence which has been thought to date the tragedies either absolutely or relatively, with an acknowledgment of its inconclusive nature, see Fantham 9–14.
78. On the date of *Apocol.* see Griffin 129 fn. 3 with further references, and P. T. Eden's edition of *Apocol.* (Cambridge 1984) pp. 4–5.
79. In what follows I adduce only the evidence that seems to me to establish incontrovertibly the link between *HF* and *Apocol.* Several of the parallels were first noted by J. Mesk, *Philologus* 71 (1912) 361–75. A detailed examination of the relationship between the diction of the rhesis and *nenia* in *Apocol.* and that of Sen. Trag. in general is given by O. Weinreich, *Senecas Apocolocyntosis* (Berlin 1923) 75ff., 112ff.

Introduction

Advehere in the general sense of *adducere, adigere* with an animal object is paralleled by *TLL* 1.827.16ff. only from *HF* 604.

> ibid. vv.9–13
> vidi duobus imminens fluviis iugum,
> quod Phoebus ortu semper obverso videt,
> ubi Rhodanus ingens amne praerapido fluit,
> Ararque dubitans, quo suos cursus agat,
> tacitus quietis adluit ripas vadis.

These lines are full of reminiscences of the geography of the underworld as described in the first one hundred lines of Theseus' narrative (662ff.). Line 9 recalls the picture of *HF* 762 *ferale tardis imminet saxum vadis*. The contrast in vv.11–13 between a violent and a calm river is like that between the Acheron and the Styx at *HF* 711–16; note particularly that the word *fluvius*, used above in v.9, occurs in this passage of *HF* (713) but nowhere else in Sen. Trag., and only once in Seneca's prose. The *dubitatio* of the Arar about which direction to take (v.12) is inspired by that of the Maeander at *HF* 685 *instatque dubius litus an fontem petat*.[80] Finally, though the pleonasm of adjectives in line 13 could be paralleled many times from Sen. Trag. (see comm. on 536), the line is particularly similar to *HF* 680 *placido quieta labitur Lethe vado*.

> § 12 poët. v.2   resonet tristi clamore forum

Cf. *HF* 1108 *resonet maesto clamore chaos*. The specific similarity between these lines is evident, though the general idea of the world reechoing human grief is commonplace (see comm. on 1108–14).

> ibid. vv.8–12
> levibusque sequi
> Persida telis, certaque manu
> tendere nervum, qui praecipites
> vulnere parvo figeret hostes,
> pictaque Medi terga fugacis.

Cf. *HF* 1127–30 *telum Scythicis leve gorytis / missum certa librare manu, / tutosque fuga figere cervos / nondumque ferae terga iubatae*. Although individual phrases may be paralleled elsewhere, the overall similarity between the two passages is too great to be accidental.

Almost all critics have agreed that the nature of these parallels suggests the priority of *HF* over *Apocol.* rather than vice versa. The gratu-

---

80. Less similar is the *dubitatio* of sea waves caught between wind and tide, Ov. *Met.* 8.472, *Tr.* 1.2.26, Sen. *Ag.* 140 *incerta dubitat unda cui cedat malo*. Caes. *BGall.* 1.12.1 may have provided Sen.'s *information* about the Arar's current, but not his poetic coloring of it.

Introduction

itous introduction of the tragic speech in *Apocol.* 7 tends to confirm this: Seneca thinks of making Hercules temporarily tragic *because* he has experience of a tragic Hercules from writing *HF*. (Note that the other verse passages in *Apocol.*, with the exception of the *nenia*, are in dactylic hexameters.) The ease with which Seneca adapts phrases from *HF* suggests that the tragedy was fresh in his mind and had either been written, or at any rate presented in a *recitatio*, within a year or two of 54. It will be seen that such a date is not inconsistent with Quintilian's evidence for Seneca's activity in tragedy.

In the absence of further reliable evidence concerning the absolute dating of the tragedies, one looks for stylistic evidence that might establish at least the relative order of composition. Elsewhere[81] I have drawn attention to remarkable variations between individual plays in the incidence of sense-pauses falling within the iambic line rather than at the end of the line, and in the incidence of shortened final *o* (see 109 comm.). On the basis of this evidence I have divided the plays into three groups: an early group (group 1), represented by *Agamemnon, Oedipus*, and *Phaedra*; a middle group (2), made up of *HF, Medea*, and *Troades*; and a late group (3), consisting of *Thyestes* and *Phoenissae*. If this relative dating is correct, the plays of group 1, being prior to *HF*, must have been written before 54; in addition it would be rash, in my view, to place the other plays of group 2, viz. *Med.* and *Tro.*, much after 54.

Text and Apparatus Criticus

The text of Seneca's tragedies is preserved in two branches of manuscripts.[82] One of these is represented by the codex generally known as the Etruscus (E) and by a handful of its descendants. The other branch (A) has a larger number of witnesses and is the ancestor of the vulgate tradition, though contamination from E appears at an early stage in its transmission. The two branches differ inter alia in the order in which the plays are presented. E lacks *Octavia* and gives the other plays in the following order and with the following titles: *Hercules* (=*HF*), *Troades, Phoenissae, Medea, Phaedra, Oedipus, Agamemnon, Thyestes, Hercules* (=*HO*). In A the order and titles are: *Hercules Furens, Thyestes, Thebais* (=*Phoen.*), *Hippolytus, Oedipus, Troas, Medea, Agamemnon, Octavia, Hercules Oetaeus*.

---

81. Fitch 1981: discussion in Fantham 14 and Tarrant's edition of *Thyestes* 11–12.
82. For more detailed studies of the MS tradition see particularly Tarrant 23–87 and Zwierlein (1983) 7–181; also Philp, MacGregor (1971), and Richard H. Rouse, "The A Text of Seneca's Tragedies in the Thirteenth Century," *Revue d'Histoire des Textes* 1 (1971) 93–121.

[53]

Introduction

E   The Etruscus was written in the late eleventh century in central or northern Italy and reposes in the Laurentian Library in Florence (plut. lat. 37.13). In the fourteenth or fifteenth century, when a basically A text was dominant, the text of the Etruscus was found so unacceptable that many of its characteristic readings were erased in the first few folios, i.e. in the first four hundred lines or so of *HF*, and other readings, generally those of A, were inserted. Fortunately in the rest of the manuscript such alterations occur only occasionally. These alterations have generally left the original reading doubtful or completely illegible, and in such places it is necessary to turn to three descendants of E, namely

FMN   F, M, and N. All three were written in Italy: F (Paris, Bibliothèque Nationale Lat. 11855) belongs to the first quarter of the fourteenth century; M (Milan, Biblioteca Ambrosiana D 276 inf.) and N (Vaticanus Lat. 1769) are fourteenth-century, perhaps somewhat later than F. They

Σ   descend from a common parent Σ, which was copied from E before the corrections were made in that manuscript.[83] Usually, therefore, they supply the original reading of E. Occasionally matters are complicated by corruption through scribal error (particularly evident in M); in addition, these manuscripts exhibit, in varying degrees and at various places, a relatively light degree of contamination with A readings; they have also undergone a certain amount of correction of their original readings, usually in favor of the A reading. M has suffered damage to the upper parts of the first few folios, which has rendered small portions of its text difficult or impossible to read.

The great value of E lies in two facts: first, that it is a careful copy descended from carefully written ancestors; second, that it is largely free of deliberate alteration,[84] whereas A has undergone a process of quite extensive interpolation.[85] Gronovius was the first to recognize E's virtues,

---

83. The alternative view, which regards Σ as a gemellus of E, is improbable (Tarrant 63ff.). In *HF* the Σ manuscripts contain few correct or respectable readings which do not appear in E TP CS: 20 MN, 277 FMN, 497 M, 916 N, 1005 MN, 1021 (attribution) MN, 1032 M. These may readily be explained as conjectures (though 1032 is probably a fortunate error), whether originating in Σ or in FMN individually or in the manuscripts from which they drew their A readings. Elsewhere in the corpus, right readings peculiar to Σ are similarly explicable as conjectures (Zwierlein 1969 760).

84. Possible examples in *HF* are 188, 381 (arising from failure to understand *carior*), 683f., 759, 767, 980, 1284. The corrections at 683f., 759, and 1284 reflect a certain literal-mindedness about singulars and plurals; cf. *Med.* 430, where E alters the generalizing plural *potentes* to *potentem*.

85. Egregious examples in *HF* include the rewriting of 36f., 623, 671, and 1304, and the insertion of 162. The aim of the interpolator is often to simplify or normalize an expression (e.g. 212, 370, 916). Tampering with speaker attributions is another of his characteristic vices (see comm. on 1021).

Introduction

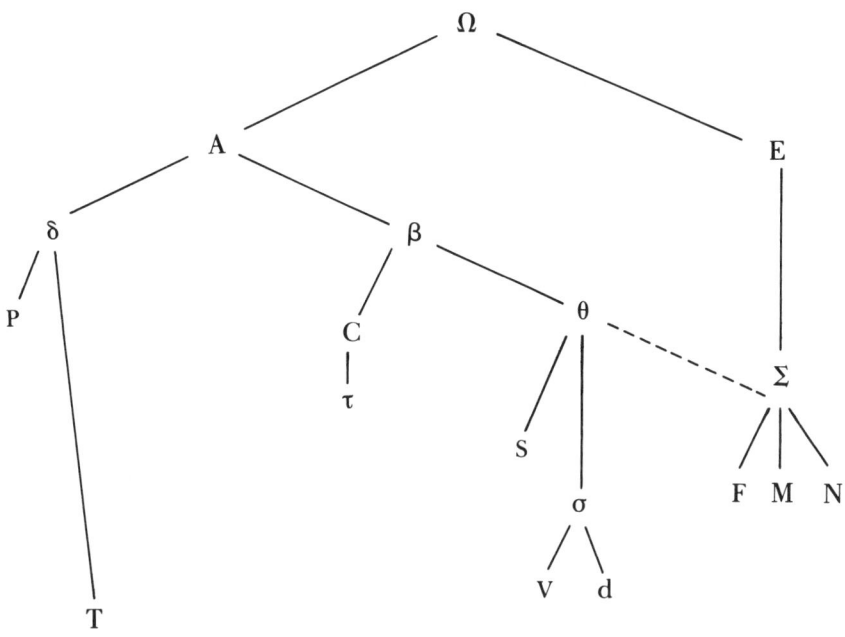

and he made much use of it in correcting the errors of the vulgate text. In Leo's influential edition of 1878–79 respect for E became exaggerated into a systematic preference for its readings, wherever they were not evidently corrupt, over those of A. The tendency of modern criticism, however, has been to perceive that E is by no means exempt from the ordinary processes of corruption through scribal error, and that A often preserves the truth where E is corrupt.[86] Therefore where E and A disagree, the choice between their readings must be made on the basis of the intrinsic quality of those readings. Only when the differences between E and A are so large as to suggest deliberate interpolation will suspicion fall ipso facto on A; and even here one must bear in mind the possibility of alternative explanations of the divergence, e.g. that a gloss has displaced the true reading in E (see comm. on 460).

In order to establish the text of A it is necessary to identify, among the large mass of A-branch manuscripts, those which are stemmatically closest to the hyparchetype. The generally accepted criterion for doing so was most fully developed by C. E. Stuart and concerns the lacunae that clearly stood in the hyparchetype, one of the most notable being *HF*

A

---

86. Gunnar Carlsson in particular reasserted the value of the A text and defended many A readings (1925, 1929, 1948).

Introduction

  124–161.[87] If a basically A-class manuscript fills these lacunae, it thereby convicts itself of contamination, whether direct or indirect, from the E branch. Stuart applied this test to more than three hundred manuscripts and uncovered three, PCS, which fill none of the primitive A-lacunae and whose stemmatic priority has generally been accepted by later critics. P and C are in fact the oldest complete A manuscripts to survive, both

P dating from the first half of the thirteenth century. P was written in northern France and is now in the Bibliothèque Nationale in Paris (Lat.
C 8260); C, probably written in England, is at Cambridge (Corpus Christi
S College 406).[88] S was written in Italy in the second half of the fourteenth century and passed in the sixteenth century to Spain (Escorial, Biblioteca Real T. III. 11). More recently, in the course of a new survey that has raised the number of known manuscripts to approximately four hundred, A. P. MacGregor has uncovered a fourth witness free from lacuna-

T filling, which he calls T (Paris, Bibliothèque Nationale Lat. 8031).[89] This was written in Franco-Flemish script between 1420 and 1430. Its value had not been noticed earlier, in part because of its relatively late date and in part because many of its original readings have been corrected to those of the vulgate tradition.[90] Its original readings can, however, usually be recovered in part or in whole, with the naked eye or under ultraviolet light.

  These four manuscripts represent two branches within the A tradition:
β C and S go back to a lost common ancestor β, which produced a numerous
δ progeny, while T and P belong to the family called δ, of which they are almost the only complete representatives. The presence of two members

87. C. E. Stuart, *The Tragedies of Seneca* (Diss. Cambridge 1907) 35 n. 1 persuasively argued that this lacuna and that at *Oed.* 430–71 were caused by loss of a folio in the hyparchetype. The *Oed.* lacuna suggests that the hyparchetype had forty-two lines per folio, twenty-one lines per page; the *HF* lacuna appears to be six lines shorter, but one must allow for the Chorus-heading (such headings occupy one line in TPCS) and for the possibility that A's arrangement of the anapests contained more monometers than E's, as it does in the second half of the ode (cf. *Med.* 787–842 and *Pha.* 959–88). The other primitive A-lacunae in *HF* are 19^b–21^a, 83–9, 543, 575–76, 1218.

88. In C several additions have been made in a hand very similar to, though not identical with, the first; this correcting hand may be studied to advantage in *HF* 1212–24 and in *Tro.* 261–70 and 602^b–07 (the *HF* passage added in the lower margin, the *Tro.* passages in the text in ras.). There are few reliable distinctions between the hands, the most consistent lying in the shape of the foot of *f* and *s*. I take the new hand to be that of the original scribe, perhaps after a lapse of some time.

89. Described and evaluated in *Philologus* 122 (1978) 88–110.

90. Paleographers may be able to distinguish at least two correcting hands in T. One of them, which imitates m.1, is responsible for the addition of 897 and of variants at 477, 518, 522, 604, 634, 659, 803, 846. Note the difference between the *al'* sign employed by this hand and that used at 49, 104, 107, 397, 697, 981, 1028, 1136, 1137, 1237, 1251.

Introduction

of each family enables us to distinguish the singular errors of β and δ from those of their surviving descendants. The discovery of T is particularly valuable as it unmasks, according to Zwierlein's calculations (1979 181 n. 1), the remarkable figure of more than fifteen hundred singular errors of P in the corpus as a whole. Zwierlein has also calculated that in the whole corpus β preserves the true reading (usually with E, except of course in *Oct.*) against δ on 276 occasions, while δ preserves the truth (again usually with E) against β in 267 places (1979 164). Though these figures are influenced to some extent by editorial choice between variants, it is clear that β and δ are of approximately equal value for the constitution of the text.

The purest of the remaining A manuscripts are V and d, which are gemelli and descendants of the subfamily marked in my stemma as θ. V (Vaticanus Lat. 2829) is a late-thirteenth or early-fourteenth-century manuscript of uncertain origin, while d (Naples, Biblioteca Nazionale IV.e.1) was written in Italy in the late fourteenth century. When C and S disagree it is sometimes helpful to cite a third witness to establish what stood in β, and on these occasions I have used V. In a handful of places where V is not available (e.g. in the V lacuna 674–82), or where its original reading is doubtful, I have turned instead to d.   V d

Other manuscripts are cited in the apparatus criticus only occasionally and when they contain a reading of special interest, usually a conjecture. The earliest and most prominent among them are KQ e H (whose present locations will be found in the list of sigla which follows). These are quite different in character from the manuscripts previously discussed, being conflations of E and A readings in which critical choice between the variant readings of these two branches has played a considerable part; their source of E readings lies within Σ, while their A text descends from θ. All were written in the fourteenth century, the last three in Italy, K either in northern France or perhaps in Italy; K and Q are gemelli. The siglum τ designates not a known manuscript but rather the text used by Nicholas Trevet, an English Dominican, for the commentary on the tragedies which he composed in the years 1314–16. The text can be recovered almost completely from the lemmata of the commentary:[91] basically it appears to be copied from C, but with some contamination from θ and E readings.   KQ e H   τ

My text is based on E TP CS throughout. In addition, where the reading of E^1 is doubtful or illegible I have regularly reported FMN.[92]

---

91. The commentary is published in V. Ussani, ed., *Nicolai Treveti Expositio Herculis Furentis* (Rome 1959).

92. I have also occasionally cited FMN for confirmation of an E reading that is certain but not easily seen or not previously recognized. These manuscripts are also

Introduction

I have collated all of these in microfilm;[93] in the case of E,T,P,C, and F I have also checked my collation from the manuscript itself. Fresh collation is always worthwhile, and it has proved possible to make numerous corrections to traditional reports of E P CS, ranging from minutiae to matters that affect the reading of the text (see comm. on 383). (My collations were independent of those undertaken by Zwierlein for his Oxford Classical Text, and each will therefore provide a useful check on the other.) In E use of ultraviolet light sometimes clarified the original reading. Collation of T presents considerable difficulties, because the countless erasures are neatly made and corrections entered in a hand that imitates that of the original scribe; during my first collation in 1979, and a reexamination in 1982, ultraviolet light frequently made it possible to recover the original reading, or at least to confirm that an erasure has occurred. Other manuscripts are reported only occasionally, as indicated earlier; for KQ e I rely almost entirely on the reports of Giardina, who collated these manuscripts himself; for Vd H, on my own collations from microfilm.

I have avoided burdening the apparatus criticus with material of no importance for the constitution of the text. (My own collation of P, for example, has added some thirty-five singular errors of that manuscript to the much larger number reported by Giardina, but there seems no point in constantly reminding the reader of the shortcomings of the P scribe.) Singular errors of the A manuscripts T, P, C, and S, and of θ, have therefore been eliminated, except when they consist of omissions of one or more lines of text. Variations in spelling have not been recorded (unless, of course, the reading is being reported for another reason), except where the deformation is such as to make the word ambiguous or unrecognizable. I have generally not reported cases in which the first scribe corrects his own error; and marginal variants and additions inserted by later hands have usually been excluded. (In all these categories, however, I have waived the principle of exclusion where the detail had some special importance or intrinsic interest.) Because Zwierlein also excludes material of this sort from the apparatus criticus of the Oxford Text, readers who require such information are referred to

---

cited when it is unclear whether a correction in E is by the first scribe or a later corrector; when they agree with E^{ac}, one will normally assume that E^{pc} is due to a later hand. Giardina did not collate FMN himself, and most reports of MN appear to rely on the apparatus criticus of Leo, who used only these two manuscripts to constitute Σ. Though Leo's reports are generally accurate, he sometimes uses Σ to designate the presumed reading of Σ rather than the actual agreement of MN (e.g. at 34, 63, 383).

93. The microfilm of S provided by the Escorial Library is less than perfectly clear, and I have therefore relied on Giardina's reports of that manuscript to a greater extent than with other manuscripts.

Giardina's edition, and for such readers I give a list of addenda and corrigenda to Giardina in Appendix 2. Furthermore, because no full collation of T has been published, and both Zwierlein's apparatus criticus and my own are selective, further details of T's readings in *HF* are given in Appendix 1. Again in the interests of lightening the apparatus, I have removed from it those conjectures which are methodologically unnecessary; most of them are, in any case, mentioned in the relevant text-discussions in the Commentary.

The apparatus is positively drawn, though occasionally a negative entry is used to record a variant of minor importance. I have also used a negative entry in places where E is corrected but Σ and A concur in what is clearly the right reading (e.g. at 101 and 689). In reporting agreement within each of the two A families I have written TP and CS rather than δ and β, out of a prejudice against hypothetical manuscripts with Greek sigla. On the other hand A is used to designate the unanimous agreement of TPCS; for example, at 13 the report *aureus E aureas A* is more convenient and more elegant, and better represents a division between two manuscript branches of equal status, than *aureus E aureas TP CS*. In the many places where T has been corrected by a later hand, I continue to write A if the original reading of T is legible and agrees with PCS; thus at 92 *conditam E T^{2pc} conditum A* the correct inference is that T^1 can be read (not guessed) as *conditum*, though this has been altered later to the E reading. When FMN are reported in the absence of E^1, their unanimous agreement is shown by Σ (despite the prejudice mentioned above) for simplicity, since text-reports in such places are usually rather complicated.

The various qualifications to sigla are explained in the list of sigla; they are adapted from those employed by R. D. Dawe, for example in his Teubner edition of Sophocles. I have not attempted to distinguish between the correcting hands that may appear in an individual manuscript; thus B^2 would designate any hand at work in the hypothetical codex B other than that of the original scribe. Where the original reading is only partially legible, as often in E and T, I have used a sublinear dash to indicate a letter about which I am not entirely confident (thus e̱), and a sublinear dash alone when the letter is quite uncertain (thus ̱).[94]

Florilegia and excerpt collections

Because of their epigrammatic character, Seneca's tragedies have often been used as a quarry by collectors of elegantly expressed *sententiae*.

---

94. Sublinear dots rather than dashes are sometimes used for this purpose, but such dots are often employed in manuscripts to expunge individual letters; I therefore use dashes to avoid giving the impression that I am reporting a correction of this sort in the manuscript.

Introduction

    Indeed, at certain periods the tragedies have been at least as widely known through such florilegia as in complete texts. For example, the tragedies are well represented in two collections of great popularity in the sixteenth
Poly. century, Mirabellius' *Polyanthea* (containing 26 excerpts from *HF*, rep-
Flor. resenting 53 lines of the play) and Mirandula's *Illustrium Poetarum Flores* (59 excerpts from *HF*, totaling 190 lines; the work was originally entitled *Viridarium Ill. Poet.*). B. J. Cohon has shown that in the sixteenth century *Polyanthea* went through at least 20 separate printings, and the *Flores* through at least 49; in the same century he counts 37 printings of editions of the complete tragedies.[95]

    I have sometimes referred to these florilegia (calling them respectively *Poly.* and *Flor.*), and to earlier excerpt collections, in my Commentary, to illustrate the popularity of certain lines and passages of the *HF*. Collections from the thirteenth century cited in this way include the
Gr. following: Exeter, Cathedral Library 3549 B (Gr.),[96] a manuscript that contains a complete text of the *Octavia* and a small number of excerpts from the other nine plays, with those from *HF* amounting to only eight
Vin. lines of that play's text; Vincent of Beauvais, *Speculum Historiale* (Vin.: excerpts from the tragedies at 9.113–14, with those from *HF* amounting to 12 lines), completed in 1244; anon., *Flores Paradysii* in Brussels,
Brux. Bibliothèque Royale 20030–32 (Brux.: tragedies on f.133^v and 176^r–177^v, with 61 lines of *HF*); and Cambridge, Gonville and Caius College
Gon. 225 (Gon.: 11 lines of *HF*).[97] From the fourteenth century we have Hiere-
Hier. mias de Montagnone, *Compendium moralium notabilium* (Hier., after 1295:
Leid. 19 lines of *HF*); Leiden, University Library 191 B (Leid.: tragedies on ff.155^r–159^v, with 82 lines of *HF*); and Paris, Bibliothèque Nationale
Par. Lat. 8049 (Par.: tragedies on ff.28^r–45^v, with 33 lines of *HF*).[98]

  95. Cohon 1960 240–50 (excerpts from *HF*), 137, 150, 403ff. (lists of printings).
  96. For the *Octavia*, where its text is complete, the manuscript is called G after an early owner, John Grandisson; that siglum was given by Herington 1958.
  97. Gon. originated in Bury St. Edmunds, and its excerpts were presumably taken from a manuscript of the tragedies which is known to have been at Bury in the second half of the thirteenth century (Tarrant 47f.; R. H. Rouse and A. C. de la Mare in *JWI* 40 [1977] 284). The fact that this manuscript is described in a fourteenth-century catalogue as containing nine plays, whereas Gon. has extracts from all ten, is no argument against the derivation (*pace* Zwierlein 1979 169), because in Gon. the excerpts from *Phoen.* run straight on into those from *Pha.*, with no *explicit* etc. such as marks the end of other plays. If *Phoen.* and *Pha.* were similarly merged in the full Bury manuscript, a cataloguer would naturally have counted them as one play, thus arriving at a total of nine. A parallel for the amalgamation of *Phoen.* (because of its brevity and lack of choral odes) with another play is provided by a Cambridge manuscript (Univ. Library Nn.II.35), in which *Oed.* follows directly after *Phoen.* with no indication of the start of a new play.
  98. The Senecan excerpts from several of these collections have been published: Leid. and Vin. by Leo, in *Commentationes in honorem F. Buecheleri—H. Useneri*, etc.

Introduction

Though of interest as documents of cultural history, the earlier excerpt collections have little importance for the constitution of the text. The amounts of material which they contain are too small to allow their stemmatic affiliations to be established with certainty. Brux. may be assigned with some measure of confidence, and Gr. and Vin. with less, to the δ family; because they are independent of T and P they could in theory be used to clarify the reading of δ at places where it is in doubt (much as V can be used in the β family), but in fact I have found no place in *HF* where any of them performs this service. Leid. had been thought to derive from an early A source independent of β and δ and free of several characteristic A errors. But now that the singular errors of δ can be distinguished from those of P, it has become clear that Leid. contains considerably more δ errors than it avoids; probably, therefore, its text derives basically from δ and its right readings result from contamination with an E source (Zwierlein 1979 167f.). Nevertheless the possibility still exists of its being used (in those places where its reading cannot derive from E) to clarify what was in δ, and I have cited it thrice in my apparatus criticus for that purpose. The other early collections, Gon., Hier., and Par., belong to the β family, and their testimony would be superfluous beside that of the complete and securely affiliated CSV. I have considered all the excerpt collections as possible *fontes coniecturarum*, but found only one occasion to cite any of them for this purpose.

(Bonn 1873) (Vin. pp. 39–40, Leid. pp. 43–60); Hier. and Par. by R. Peiper, *De Senecae Tragoediarum Vulgari Lectione Constituenda* (Breslau 1893) (Par. pp. 141–45, Hier. pp. 146–55, index pp. 171–79); Gr. by Herington 1958.

SIGLA

E	Laurentianus plut. 37.13
F	Parisinus Bibl. Nat. Lat. 11855
M	Ambrosianus D 276 inf.
N	Vaticanus Lat. 1769
Σ	consensus codicum FMN omnium
T	Parisinus Bibl. Nat. Lat. 8031
P	Parisinus Bibl. Nat. Lat. 8260
C	Cantabrigiensis Coll. Corp. Christi 406
S	Scorialis T. III.11
A	consensus codicum TPCS omnium, ut prima manu quisque scriptus est
V	Vaticanus Lat. 2829
d	Neapolitanus Bibl. Nat. IV.e.1
τ	codex quo Nicolaus Trevet usus est in exscribendo commentario
K	Cameracensis 555
Q	Casinensis 392P
e	Etonensis 110
H	Londiniensis Harleianus 2484
Brux	Bruxellensis 20030–32 (excerpta)
Leid	Leidensis Bibl. Univ. 191B (excerpta)
ς	codices recentiores (vel plures vel pauci)
B^1	ipse scriba codicis B
B^2	manus recentior quaelibet
B^{1pc}	lectio post correctionem a scriba ipso illatam
B^{2pc}	lectio post correctionem qualibet recentiore manu illatam
B^{ac}	lectio ante correctionem
B^{pc}	lectio post correctionem talem ut manus dinosci non possit

Sigla

mg.	in margine
var.	varia lectio
e̬	littera non omnino certa
‿	littera incerta

HERCULES FURENS

PERSONAE:

    Iuno
    Amphitryon
    Megara
    Filii Herculis (taciti)
    Lycus
    Hercules
    Theseus
    Chorus

Scaena Thebis

ACTUS PRIMUS

IUNO.

Soror Tonantis — hoc enim solum mihi
nomen relictum est — semper alienum Iovem
ac templa summi vidua deserui aetheris,
locumque caelo pulsa paelicibus dedi.
tellus colenda est; paelices caelum tenent.   5
hinc Arctos alta parte glacialis poli
sublime classes sidus Argolicas agit;
hinc, qua recenti vere laxatur dies,
Tyriae per undas vector Europae nitet;
illinc timendum ratibus ac ponto gregem   10
passim vagantes exserunt Atlantides.
ferro minax hinc terret Orion deos
suasque Perseus aureus stellas habet;
hinc clara gemini signa Tyndaridae micant
quibusque natis mobilis tellus stetit.   15
nec ipse tantum Bacchus aut Bacchi parens
adiere superos: ne qua pars probro vacet,
mundus puellae serta Cnosiacae gerit.
    Sed sero querimur; una me dira ac fera
Thebana tellus nuribus aspersa impiis   20
quotiens novercam fecit! — escendat licet
meumque victrix teneat Alcmene locum,

---

8 recenti *FM* re enti *E¹* tepenti *A E²ᵖᶜ Nᵖᶜ*(tep *in ras.*) ‖ 10 ac ponto *E A* a ponto *possis* ‖ 12 ferro _nax [minax *Σ*] hinc terret *E¹* fera coma hinc exterret *A E²ᵖᶜ* ‖ 13 aureus *E* aureas *A* ‖ 18–21, *quibus iam deerant* 19ᵇ–21ᵃ (*v. infra*), om. *P* (*homoeoteleuton vacet, licet*) ‖ 18 puelle serta gnosiace gerit *T CS* puellas fert anobis lac egerit *E* ‖ 19 sero *Leo* vetera sero *E A* vetera *ς* | 19ᵇ(una . . .)–21ᵃ(. . . fecit) *desunt A* (me dira ac fera *in textum inser. T² eraso* 21ᵇ, *et* 20–21 *add. mg. infr.*) ‖ 20 tellus nuribus aspersa *scripsi* tel. nur. sparsa *E* nur. sparsa tel. *KQ MN H T²mg.infr. ς* ‖ 21 escendat

Hercules Furens

    pariterque natus astra promissa occupet,
    in cuius ortus mundus impendit diem
    tardusque Eoo Phoebus effulsit mari   25
    retinere mersum iussus Oceano iubar,
    non sic abibunt odia: vivaces aget
    violentus iras animus, et saevus dolor
    aeterna bella pace sublata geret.
        — Quae bella? quidquid horridum tellus creat   30
    inimica, quidquid pontus aut aer tulit
    terribile dirum pestilens atrox ferum,
    fractum atque domitum est. superat et crescit malis
    iraque nostra fruitur; in laudes suas
    mea vertit odia; dum nimis saeva impero,   35
    patrem probavi, gloriae feci locum.
    qua Sol reducens quaque deponens diem
    binos propinqua tinguit Aethiopas face,
    indomita virtus colitur et toto deus
    narratur orbe. monstra iam desunt mihi,   40
    minorque labor est Herculi iussa exsequi
    quam mihi iubere; laetus imperia excipit.
    quae fera tyranni iura violento queant
    nocere iuveni? nempe pro telis gerit
    quae timuit et quae fudit: armatus venit   45
    leone et hydra.
            Nec satis terrae patent:
    effregit ecce limen inferni Iovis
    et opima victi regis ad superos refert.
    vidi ipsa, vidi nocte discussa inferum   50
    et Dite domito spolia iactantem patri
    fraterna. cur non vinctum et oppressum trahit
    ipsum catenis paria sortitum Iovi
    Ereboque capto potitur et retegit Styga?

N^{ac} exsc- E^1 ut vid. (x supr. e) extendat M ascendat CS E^{2pc} $F^{pc}N^{pc}$ ‖ 24 ortu E^{pc} T^{pc} (in utroque s post u era.) ς | impendit E A impedit vel impediit $N(^{pc}?)$ ς ‖ 34 fruitur A E^2(t in ras.) $N(^{pc}?)$ fruimur F,M^{1pc}(mur in ras.) ‖ 36 probavi FM probavit A E^2(t inser. m.2) N^2(avit in ras.) | glorie feci locum Σ inde qua lucem premit A E^2in ras. ‖ 37 qua sol reducens quaque reponens E (relucens pro reducens Σ, deponens pro reponens recte FM) aperitque thetis qua ferens titan A ‖ 38 aethyopes E^2(altera e in ras. ex a) ‖ 43 qu(a)e E T^{2pc} quo A | iura F^{ac}M iussa A E^2(ss in ras. unius lit.) F^{pc},N^2in ras. ‖ 49 post 54 collocavit Leo ‖ 52 vinctum E victum A | trahit: hit in ras. E^2(h ex r?) ‖ 54 potitur et E A potitur? en Baden | retegit E A relegit

Hercules Furens

parum est reverti, foedus umbrarum perît: 49
patefacta ab imis manibus retro via est 55
et sacra dirae Mortis in aperto iacent.
at ille, rupto carcere umbrarum ferox,
de me triumphat et superbifica manu
atrum per urbes ducit Argolicas canem.
viso labantem Cerbero vidi diem 60
pavidumque Solem; me quoque invasit tremor,
et terna monstri colla devicti intuens
timui imperasse.   Levia sed nimium queror:
caelo timendum est, regna ne summa occupet
qui vicit ima; sceptra praeripiet patri. 65
nec in astra lenta veniet ut Bacchus via:
iter ruina quaeret et vacuo volet
regnare mundo. robore experto tumet,
et posse caelum viribus vinci suis
didicit ferendo; subdidit mundo caput 70
nec flexit umeros molis immensae labor
meliusque collo sedit Herculeo polus.
immota cervix sidera et caelum tulit
et me prementem: quaerit ad superos viam.
   Perge, ira, perge et magna meditantem opprime, 75
congredere, manibus ipsa dilacera tuis;
quid tanta mandas odia? discedant ferae,
ipse imperando fessus Eurystheus vacet.
Titanas ausos rumpere imperium Iovis
emitte, Siculi verticis laxa specum, 80
tellus Gigante Doris excusso tremens
supposita monstri colla terrifici levet.
[sublimis alias Luna concipiat feras.]
sed vicit ista. quaeris Alcidae parem?
nemo est nisi ipse; bella iam secum gerat. 85
   Adsint ab imo Tartari fundo excitae

Bentley, Withof repetit *Bentley* ‖ 49 perît: perit *E* T^2*var.supr.*P^{pc} *CS* petit *T,P^{ac}* ‖ 56 dir(a)e *A*(e C^{pc} ex a) E^{pc} dur(a)e $E^{ac}\Sigma$ ‖ 62 et terna *FN* eterna *M* et tetra *A* E^{2pc}(the-) | devicti *A* E^{pc}(altera i *in ras.*) F^{pc} devicta F^{ac},*M?,N* ‖ 63 *post* levia *dist.* E^{ac} F^{ac} | nimium *A* E^{2pc} $F^{pc}N^{pc}$ minimum F^{ac},N^{ac}*ut vid. lectio incerta M* ‖ 65 praeripiet E^{pc}(*inter* e *et alteram* r *ras. 2 litt.*) ‖ 66 lenta *T CS* E^{2pc} lentus E^1 *P* | ut Bacch·ıs: ut bac *in ras.* E^2 ‖ 68 experto *E* expenso *A* ‖ 72 meliusque E^1 mediusque *A* E^{2pc} ‖ 76 dilacera *E*(iam *supr. add. m.*2) iam lacera *A* ‖ 81 gigantis E^1, *corr. m.*2 ‖ *post* 82: 123 *huc traicit A, omissis* 83–89 (*spat. unius vs. post* 123 *rel. P S, om. T C*)

Hercules Furens

Eumenides, ignem flammeae spargant comae,
viperea saevae verbera incutiant manus.
i nunc, superbe, caelitum sedes pete,
humana temne. iam Styga et manes feros   90
fugisse credis? hic tibi ostendam inferos.
revocabo in alta conditam caligine,
ultra nocentum exilia, discordem deam,
quam munit ingens montis oppositi specus;
educam et imo Ditis e regno extraham   95
quidquid relictum est: veniet invisum Scelus
suumque lambens sanguinem Impietas ferox
Errorque et in se semper armatus Furor —
hoc hoc ministro noster utatur dolor.
    Incipite, famulae Ditis, ardentem incitae   100
concutite pinum, et agmen horrendum anguibus
Megaera ducat atque luctifica manu
vastam rogo flagrante corripiat trabem.
hoc agite, poenas petite vitiatae Stygis.
concutite pectus, acrior mentem excoquat   105
quam qui caminis ignis Aetnaeis furit;
ut possit animum captus Alcides agi,
magno furore percitus, vobis prius
insaniendum est. — Iuno, cur nondum furis?
me me, sorores, mente deiectam mea   110
versate primam, facere si quicquam apparo
dignum noverca. vota mutentur mea:
natos reversus videat incolumes precor
manuque fortis redeat. inveni diem,
invisa quo nos Herculis virtus iuvet.   115
me vicit: et se vincat, et cupiat mori
ab inferis reversus. hic prosit mihi
Iove esse genitum. stabo et, ut certo exeant
emissa nervo tela, librabo manu,

‖ 83 *del.* Leo ‖ 90 *post* 91 E^1, *ord. corr. m.2* ‖ 90 feros Σ ferox A E^2(x *in ras.*) ‖ 92 conditam E T^{2pc} conditum A ‖ 94 *locus nondum satis enarratus: v. comm.* | quam A E^{2pc} qua E^1 ‖ 96 *post* veniet *dist.* E^1 $F^{ac}N^{ac}$ | veniet. invisum E^1 veniet et invisum T veniet et in invisum P vel veniet utinam et invisum CS veniet vel invisum E^{2pc} ‖ 100 incite A citae E(in *supr. add. m.2*) ‖ 101 anguibus: *in ras.* E^2 ‖ 102 luctifica E T^{2pc} CS ludifica T^1P ‖ 104 viciatae E violate A ‖ 107 animum A animo E ‖ 108 vobis E P CS nobis T d KQ ς ‖ 109 furis E furit A ‖ 110 deiectam A E^{pc} delecta E^{ac} delectat FM derectam N^2(r *et* m *in ras.*) ‖ 111 versate: *altera* e *in ras. 2 litt.* E^2 ‖ 112 vota Σ iam odia A E^2*in ras.* ‖ 116 vicit FN vic__ M pariter A E^2*in ras.* ‖ 118 certo A E^{pc} M,N^{pc} certa E^{ac} F,N^{ac} ‖ 119 manu E manum

regam furentis arma, pugnanti Herculi 120
tandem favebo. scelere perfecto licet
admittat illas genitor in caelum manus.
   Movenda iam sunt bella; clarescit dies
ortuque Titan lucidus croceo subit.

CHORUS.

   Iam rara micant 125
sidera prono languida mundo; 125bis
nox victa vagos contrahit ignes
luce renata;
cogit nitidum Phosphoros agmen;
signum celsi glaciale poli
septem stellis Arcados Ursa 130
lucem verso temone vocat.
iam caeruleis evectus equis
Titan summa prospicit Oeta;
iam Cadmeis inclita Bacchis
aspersa die dumeta rubent, 135
Phoebique fugit reditura soror.
   Labor exoritur durus et omnes
agitat curas aperitque domos.
pastor gelida cana pruina
grege dimisso pabula carpit; 140
ludit prato liber aperto
nondum rupta fronte iuvencus;
vacuae reparant ubera matres;
errat cursu levis incerto
molli petulans haedus in herba. 145
pendet summo stridula ramo
pinnasque novo tradere soli
gestit querulos inter nidos
Thracia paelex,
turbaque circa confusa sonat 150
murmure mixto testata diem.
carbasa ventis 152
credit dubius navita vitae, 152bis

A ‖ 123 *v. post* 82 ‖ 124–161 *desunt A* ‖ 125–61 *et* 163–203 *dimetri (praeter* 151ᵇ *tes. diem* monometrum*)* E 162–203 *dimetri (praeter* 194bisᵇ *tol. et art. et* 197ᵇ *tut. teg.* monometros*) A: v. Append. 3* ‖ 128 phosforos *E*²ᵖᶜ fofforos *cod. Burney* 250 bosforos *E¹* ‖ 130 del. Leo | Ursa *scripsi* ursae *E* ‖ 131 vocat ς vocant *E* ‖ 132 equis *E* aquis ς ‖ 133 summa *E* summum *e* | oeta *E* oetā (-am *an* -an?) *e* oetan *vel* -en ς ‖ 161ᵇ

Hercules Furens

laxos aura complente sinus.
hic exesis pendens scopulis
aut deceptos instruit hamos 155
aut suspensus
spectat pressa praemia dextra;
sentit tremulum linea piscem.
    Haec, innocuae quibus est vitae
tranquilla quies 160ᵃ
et laeta suo parvoque domus. 160ᵇ–1ᵃ
spes immanes urbibus errant 161ᵇ–3ᵃ
trepidique metus. 163ᵇ
ille superbos aditus regum
durasque fores expers somni 165
colit; hic nullo fine beatas
componit opes,
gazis inhians 167ᵇ
et congesto pauper in auro;
illum populi favor attonitum
fluctuque magis mobile vulgus 170
aura tumidum tollit inani;
hic clamosi rabiosa fori
iurgia vendens 173
improbus iras et verba locat. 173bis
    Novit paucos secura quies,
qui velocis memores aevi 175
tempora numquam reditura tenent.
dum fata sinunt, vivite laeti.
properat cursu vita citato,
volucrique die
rota praecipitis vertitur anni; 180
durae peragunt pensa sorores
nec sua retro fila revolvunt.
at gens hominum fertur rapidis
obvia fatis incerta sui;
Stygias ultro quaerimus undas. 185

[turbine magno spes sollicitae] 162

immanes *Schmidt*   in magnis *Gronovius*   iam magnis *E* ‖ 162 *deest E, habet A; del. Gronovius* ‖ 164 regum *E T²*(um *in ras.*) *CS*   regno *P* ‖ 166 hic *Ascensius*   ac *E A* ǀ beatas *E T²ᵖᶜ CSV*   beatus *T¹P Cvar.supr.Vvar.mg.* ‖ 171 tollit *E TP CᵖᶜVvar.mg.*   volvit *CᵃᶜSV* ‖ 180 vertitur *E A*   volvitur *Brux Q ς* ‖ 181 dur(a)e *E TᵃᶜP CV*   dura *Tᵖᶜ Cvar.supr.S* ‖ 183 gens: genus *P*(g'ns *ut* 1075)*Leid* ǀ fertur *A E²in ras. Fᵖᶜ*(fer *in*

nimium, Alcide, pectore forti
properas maestos visere manes.
certo veniunt tempore Parcae.
nulli iusso cessare licet,
nulli scriptum proferre diem; 190
recipit populos urna citatos.
 Alium multis gloria terris
tradat et omnes
Fama per urbes garrula laudet, 194
caeloque parem tollat et astris; 194bis
alius curru sublimis eat:
me mea tellus
lare secreto tutoque tegat.
venit ad pigros cana senectus,
humilique loco sed certa sedet
sordida parvae fortuna domus; 200
alte virtus animosa cadit.
 — Sed maesta venit crine soluto
Megara parvum comitata gregem,
tardusque senio graditur Alcidae parens.

ACTUS SECUNDUS

AMPHITRYON. MEGARA.

AM. O magne Olympi rector et mundi arbiter, 205
iam statue tandem gravibus aerumnis modum
finemque cladi. nulla lux umquam mihi
secura fulsit; finis alterius mali
gradus est futuri. protinus reduci novus
paratur hostis; antequam laetam domum 210
contingat, aliud iussus ad bellum meat;

---

ras.)*N*^{pc} flatur *M,N*^{ac} ‖ 184 sui *T,P*^{pc} *CS E*^{pc} suis *E*^{ac} *Σ* suus *ut vid. P*^{ac} ‖ 188 tempore *Σ* ordine *A E*²*in ras.* ‖ 190 proferre *E T*^{pc}*P C,V*^{2pc} preferre *T*^{ac} *S,V*¹ ‖ 193 (trad. et o. fa. per ur.) *post* 194 (gar. laud. cael. par.) *E*¹, *ord. corr. m.2* ‖ 204 *uno versu E duobus versibus A* (t.s.g./a.p.) ‖ *ante* 205 *inscribitur*: AMPHITRYON. MAEGERA. LYCUS *E* Megera. amphitrion. licus *A* (amphy-, lu- *P*) (*v. ante* 332) ‖ *inter* 208^a *et* 208^b *sententiam excidisse ci. Leo* ‖ 209 reduci novus: i, no, us *add. in ras. E*^{pc} ‖ 210 paratur *E T*^{2pc} *CS* paratus *T*¹*P* ‖ 211 meat *E* exeat *A* ‖ 212 vacat *E P*

Hercules Furens

    nec ulla requies, tempus aut ullum vacat,
    nisi dum iubetur. sequitur a primo statim
    infesta Iuno; numquid immunis fuit
    infantis aetas? monstra superavit prius   215
    quam nosse posset. gemina cristati caput
    angues ferebant ora, quos contra obvius
    reptabat infans igneos serpentium
    oculos remisso lumine ac placido intuens;
    artos serenis vultibus nodos tulit,   220
    et tumida tenera guttura elidens manu
    prolusit hydrae. Maenali pernix fera,
    multo decorum praeferens auro caput,
    deprensa cursu; maximus Nemeae timor
    pressus lacertis gemuit Herculeis leo.   225
    quid stabula memorem dira Bistonii gregis
    suisque regem pabulum armentis datum,
    solitumque densis hispidum Erymanthi iugis
    Arcadia quatere nemora Maenalium suem,
    taurumque centum non levem populis metum?   230
    inter remotos gentis Hesperiae greges
    pastor triformis litoris Tartesii
    peremptus, acta et praeda ab occasu ultimo;
    notum Cithaeron pavit Oceano pecus.
    penetrare iussus solis aestivi plagas   235
    et adusta medius regna quae torret dies
    utrimque montes solvit ac rupto obice
    latam ruenti fecit Oceano viam.
    post haec adortus nemoris opulenti domos
    aurifera vigilis spolia serpentis tulit.   240
    quid? saeva Lernae monstra, numerosum malum,
    non igne demum vicit et docuit mori,
    solitasque pinnis condere obductis diem
    petît ab ipsis nubibus Stymphalidas?

---

datur *T CS* ‖ 213 a primo: aprimo E^{ac} Σ a prima *P CS*   apprime T^2(*prima* p *inser.*, e *in ras. add. m.*2) *H*(*explicat* valde) ς   aprime E^{pc} ‖ 216 posset *A* E^{pc} F^{pc}(e *in ras.*)*M* possit E^{ac} *N* ‖ 218 reptabat *E*   reptavit $T^{2pc}P$ *CS*   raptavit T^1 | serpentium E^{ac} *FN TP*   serpentum E^{pc} *M CS* ‖ 219 oculos *in fine vs.* 218 *habent CS* | lumine Σ pectore *A*   vultu E^2*in ras.* ‖ 224 cursu *E*   cursu est *A, fort. recte* ‖ 225 pr. lac. gemuit *E*   gemuit lac. pr. $T^{2pc}P$ *CS*   genuit l.p. T^1 ‖ 228 iugis: *in ras.* E^2 (*prima* i *ex* h?) ‖ 233 acta et praeda *Jac. Gronovius*   acta est pr. *E A*   acta pr. *Peiper* ‖ 236 quae: qua E^1, *corr. m.*2 ‖ 237 solvit *E* T^{2pc} *Cmg.SV*   solum *P* C^{ac} sol⁻ T^1 solvet C^{pc} | ac rupto *Gronovius*   abrupto *E A* ‖ 238 latam *E*   etiam (ec-) *A* ‖ 239 adortus: ad ortus *TP S* ‖ 244 petît: petit *E*   petiit *S*   peciit *TP C* ‖ 248 stabuli T^{2pc}(u *ex* i)*P* Σ(-ulli *M*) E^{2pc}

non vicit illum caelibis semper tori 245
regina gentis vidua Thermodontiae;
nec ad omne clarum facinus audaces manus
stabuli fugavit turpis Augei labor.
   Quid ista prosunt? orbe defenso caret.
sensere terrae pacis auctorem suae 250
abesse. rursus prosperum ac felix scelus
virtus vocatur; sontibus parent boni,
ius est in armis, opprimit leges timor.
ante ora vidi nostra truculenta manu
natos paterni cadere regni vindices, 255
ipsumque, Cadmi nobilis stirpem ultimam,
occidere; vidi regium capiti decus
cum capite raptum. — quis satis Thebas fleat?
ferax deorum terra, quem dominum tremis?
e cuius arvis eque fecundo sinu 260
stricto iuventus orta cum ferro stetit,
cuiusque muros natus Amphion Iove
struxit canoro saxa modulatu trahens,
in cuius urbem non semel divum parens
caelo relicto venit, haec quae caelites 265
recepit et quae fecit et (fas sit loqui)
fortasse faciet, sordido premitur iugo.
Cadmea proles atque Ophionium genus,
quo reccidistis? tremitis ignarum exulem,
suis carentem finibus, nostris gravem. 270
qui scelera terra quique persequitur mari
ac saeva iusta sceptra confregit manu
nunc servit absens fertque quae fieri vetat,
tenetque Thebas exul Herculeas Lycus.
   — Sed non tenebit. aderit et poenas petet 275
subitusque ad astra emerget; inveniet viam
aut faciet. adsis sospes et remees precor
tandemque venias victor ad victam domum.

stabuli *an* stabili *ambiguum* CS   stab_lis *E¹*   stabulis *Q* | augei *A*   angaei *Eᵖᶜ*(n *in ras.*) ‖ 251 abesse. rursus *Wilamowitz*   abesse terris. *E A*   abesse tristes. *Peiper* ‖ 257 capiti *E¹*   capitis *A E²ᵖᶜ* ‖ 258 quis *A*   qui *E* | thebas *E P*   thebis *T CS* ‖ 259 tremis *ς*   tremit *A E²*(it *in ras.*) *N²*(i *in ras.*)   tremet *FM* ‖ 262 natus: us *in ras. Eᵖᶜ* ‖ 268 Ophionium genus *Bentley, Leo* (*iam* Echionium genus *Nic. Heinsius*)   ophionius cinis *E*(ophyon-) *P*(ophon-) *CS*   ophionius civis *T* ‖ 269 quo reccidistis *N²*(re *in ras. maioris spatii; prima* c *ex* x?)   q. rectid- *Tᵃᶜ*   q. recid- *TᵖᶜP CS E²ᵖᶜ*   quo_ _xcidistis *E¹*   quorsum excidistis *FM* | ignarum *E A*   ignavum τ *T²ᵖᶜ* ‖ 271 mare *E¹, postea corr.* ‖ 272 confregit *T CS*   confringit *E P* ‖ 273 fieri *E A*   ferri *ς* ‖ 274 herculeas *E*   herculeus *TP*   herculis *CS* ‖ 277 assis sospes *FM,N*(*¹ᵖᶜ*?) *Ke*   adsiso

Hercules Furens

MEG. Emerge, coniunx, atque dispulsas manu
abrumpe tenebras. nulla si retro via 280
iterque clausum est, orbe diducto redi,
et quidquid atra nocte possessum latet
emitte tecum. dirutis qualis iugis
praeceps citato flumini quaerens iter
quondam stetisti, scissa cum vasto impetu 285
patuere Tempe — pectore impulsus tuo
huc mons et illuc cessit, et rupto aggere
nova cucurrit Thessalus torrens via —
talis, parentes liberos patriam petens,
erumpe rerum terminos tecum efferens, 290
et quidquid avida tot per annorum gradus
abscondit aetas redde, et oblitos sui
lucisque pavidos ante te populos age.
indigna te sunt spolia, si tantum refers
quantum imperatum est.
       Magna sed nimium loquor 295
ignara nostrae sortis. unde illum mihi
quo te tuamque dexteram amplectar diem
reditusque lentos nec mei memores querar?
tibi, o deorum ductor, indomiti ferent
centena tauri colla; tibi, frugum potens, 300
secreta reddam sacra: tibi muta fide
longas Eleusin tacita iactabit faces.
tum restitutas fratribus rebor meis
animas, et ipsum regna moderantem sua
florere patrem. si qua te maior tenet 305
clausum potestas, sequimur; aut omnes tuo
defende reditu sospes aut omnes trahe.
— trahes, nec ullus eriget fractos deus.

AM. O socia nostri sanguinis, casta fide
servans torum natosque magnanimi Herculis, 310
meliora mente concipe atque animum excita.

---

sospes *E*(adsis o *postea dist.*) assis hospes *A* | precor *E* tuis *A* ‖ ante 279 *nota Megarae deest A* ‖ 279 emerge *E T* emergere *P CS* | dispulsas *E* depulsas *A* ‖ 280 retro *E* vento *P* vē_ *T¹* vetito *T²ᵖᶜ CS* ‖ 281 diducto *E T,Pᵖᶜ C¹ᵖᶜSV* de- *Pᵃᶜ Cᵃᶜ* ‖ 284 flumini *T CS* -is *P* fulmini *E* ‖ 285 stetisti scissa *E T CV* fetistis cissas *Pᵃᶜ*(*altera s postea era.*) fecisti scissa *S* ‖ 287 cessit *Leo* cecidit *E A* ‖ 295 imperatum *E¹ A* impertitum *E²* | loquor: locu *E¹, corr. m.2* ‖ 301 muta *E* multa *A* ‖ 302 eleusin tacita *A*(n *postea era. T*) eleus intacita *Eᵃᶜ*(in *postea era.*) | iactabit *E* iactabo *A* ‖

Hercules Furens

    aderit profecto, qualis ex omni solet
    labore, maior.

MEG.   Quod nimis miseri volunt,
    hoc facile credunt.

AM.   Immo quod metuunt nimis
    numquam moveri posse nec tolli putant;   315
    prona est timoris semper in peius fides.

MEG. Demersus ac defossus et toto insuper
    oppressus orbe quam viam ad superos habet?

AM.   Quam tunc habebat cum per arentem plagam
    et fluctuantes more turbati maris   320
    abît harenas bisque discedens fretum
    et bis recurrens, cumque deserta rate
    deprensus haesit Syrtium brevibus vadis
    et puppe fixa maria superavit pedes.

MEG. Iniqua raro maximis virtutibus   325
    Fortuna parcit. nemo se tuto diu
    periculis offerre tam crebris potest;
    quem saepe transit casus, aliquando invenit.
    — Sed ecce saevus ac minas vultu gerens
    et qualis animo est talis incessu venit   330
    aliena dextra sceptra concutiens Lycus.

      LYCUS. MEGARA. AMPHITRYON.

LYC. Urbis regens opulenta Thebanae loca
    et omne quidquid uberis cingit soli
    obliqua Phocis, quidquid Ismenos rigat,
    quidquid Cithaeron vertice excelso videt,   335

---

313 quod: quid *E¹*, *corr. m.2* ‖ 315 moveri *E* amoveri *A* ‖ 316 *Amphitryoni continuat E, Megarae dat A* | timoris *E^{ac} Σ* timori *A E^{pc}* ‖ 318 viam: vim *E¹*, *corr. m.2* ‖ 321 abît: abiit *A E^{2pc}* adit *E¹* adiit *Σ* ‖ 322 deserta *E A* defecta *Damsté* ‖ 324 superavit *A E²*(*avit in ras.*) *F^{pc}*(*peravit in ras.*) super habuit *N* semper h. . . (*lectio post* h *incerta*) *M* ‖ 326 tuto: *prior* t *ex* p, o *in ras. E²* ‖ 330 animo *E T CV* in animo *P S* | incessu *T CV* in cessu *E P S* ‖ *ante* 332 *scaenae tit. inserui* (*v. ante* 205) ‖ 332–36 *Lyco dat E, Megarae continuat A* ‖ 332 urbis *TP E^{2pc}* urbi *CS* urbe *E¹* ‖ 333 uberis cingit soli *Karsten* uberi c. solo *A* ubere c. solo *E* uberi iungit solo *vel*

[77]

Hercules Furens

      [et bina findens Isthmos exilis freta]
      non vetera patriae iura possideo domus
      ignavus heres; nobiles non sunt mihi
      avi nec altis inclitum titulis genus,
      sed clara virtus. qui genus iactat suum,   340
      aliena laudat. rapta sed trepida manu
      sceptra obtinentur; omnis in ferro est salus;
      quod civibus tenere te invitis scias,
      strictus tuetur ensis. alieno in loco
      haud stabile regnum est; una sed nostras potest   345
      fundare vires iuncta regali face
      thalamisque Megara; ducet e genere inclito
      novitas colorem nostra. non equidem reor
      fore ut recuset ac meos spernat toros;
      quod si impotenti pertinax animo abnuet,   350
      stat tollere omnem penitus Herculeam domum.
      invidia factum ac sermo popularis premet?
      ars prima regni est posse in invidia pati.
      — Temptemus igitur, fors dedit nobis locum:
      namque ipsa, tristi vestis obtentu caput   355
      velata, iuxta praesides adstat deos,
      laterique adhaeret verus Alcidae sator.

MEG.   Quidnam iste, nostri generis exitium ac lues,
      novi parat? quid temptat?

LYC.   O clarum trahens
      a stirpe nomen regia, facilis mea   360
      parumper aure verba patienti excipe.
      si alterna semper odia mortales gerant,
      nec coeptus umquam cedat ex animis furor,
      sed arma felix teneat infelix paret,
      nihil relinquent bella; tum vastis ager   365
      squalebit arvis, subdita tectis face
      altus sepultas obruet gentes cinis.
      pacem reduci velle victori expedit,
      victo necesse est. — particeps regno veni;

---

uberis iungit soli *Nic. Heinsius* ‖ 335 *post* 336 *E¹*, *ord. corr. m.2* ‖ 336 *del. Leo (Peiper deleverat* 335–36) ‖ 343 tenere te Σ   tenetur *A E²*(tur *in ras.*) ‖ 345 haut: aut *E¹*, *corr. m.2* (haud) ‖ 347 thalamisque *A*   thalamis *E* | et genere *E A*, *corr.* ς ‖ 352 factum *E¹*   fastum *A E²ᵖᶜ* ‖ 353 in invidia *Richter*   invidiam *E*   ad invidiam *A*(ad *postea era. T*)   et invidiam *Grotius* ‖ 354 fors *E P SV*   sors *T C* | locum nobis *E*(*ord. postea corr.*) ‖ 356 om. *E.* ‖ 362 alterna *Zwierlein*   aeterna *E A* | gerant *E*   agent *A* ‖ 368 reduci

	sociemur animis. pignus hoc fidei cape:	370
	continge dextram. quid truci vultu siles?	
MEG.	Egone ut parentis sanguine aspersam manum	
	fratrumque gemina caede contingam? prius	
	exstinguet ortus, referet occasus diem,	
	pax ante fida nivibus et flammis erit	375
	et Scylla Siculum iunget Ausonio latus,	
	priusque multo vicibus alternis fugax	
	Euripus unda stabit Euboica piger.	
	patrem abstulisti, regna, germanos, larem,	
	patriam — quid ultra est? una res superest mihi	380
	fratre ac parente carior, regno ac lare:	
	odium tui, quod esse cum populo mihi	
	commune doleo — pars quota ex isto mea est!	
	dominare tumidus, spiritus altos gere;	
	sequitur superbos ultor a tergo deus.	385
	Thebana novi regna: quid matres loquar	
	passas et ausas scelera? quid geminum nefas	
	mixtumque nomen coniugis nati patris?	
	quid bina fratrum castra? quid totidem rogos?	
	riget superba Tantalis luctu parens	390
	maestusque Phrygio manat in Sipylo lapis.	
	quin ipse torvum subrigens crista caput	
	Illyrica Cadmus regna permensus fuga	
	longas reliquit corporis tracti notas.	
	haec te manent exempla. dominare ut libet,	395
	dum solita regni fata te nostri vocent.	
LYC.	Agedum efferatas rabida voces amove,	
	et disce regum imperia ab Alcide pati.	
	ego rapta quamvis sceptra victrici geram	
	dextra, regamque cuncta sine legum metu	400
	quas arma vincunt, pauca pro causa loquar	
	nostra. cruento cecidit in bello pater?	
	cecidere fratres? arma non servant modum;	

A E^{2pc}(i *in ras. 3 litt.*)   reducere Σ ‖ 370 sotiemur animis E^1(r *era., s in ras. inser. m.2*) sociemus animos A ‖ 377 vicibus: vic *in ras.* E^2 ‖ 380 patriam E A patrem (*et patria abstulisti regna in* 379) *Peiper*   patrium *ed. Patavina (1748)* ‖ 381 carior A E^{2pc} N^{2pc} careo F,M *ut vid.*   car__ E^1 car_o N^1 ‖ 383 ex isto TP (existo E^{2pc} F^{pc})   ex ista CS (exista N^{2pc})   exicio E^1 exitio M exiti_ N^1 ‖ 385 victor E A, *corr.* ς ‖ 397 efferatas T CS FN effratas P effrenatas E^{2pc}(ren *in ras.*)   effreistas M^{pc} ‖ 400 regamque E geramque A ‖ 403 modum E T^{2pc} domum P CS d__um T^1 ‖ 408

Hercules Furens

    nec temperari facile nec reprimi potest
    stricti ensis ira; bella delectat cruor.   405
    sed ille regno pro suo, nos improba
    cupidine acti? quaeritur belli exitus,
    non causa. — sed nunc pereat omnis memoria;
    cum victor arma posuit, et victum decet
    deponere odia. non ut inflexo genu   410
    regnantem adores petimus; hoc ipsum placet,
    animo ruinas quod capis magno tuas.
    es rege coniunx digna; sociemus toros.

MEG. Gelidus per artus vadit exsangues tremor.
    quod facinus aures pepulit? haud equidem horrui,   415
    cum pace rupta bellicus muros fragor
    circumsonaret; pertuli intrepide omnia.
    thalamos tremesco; capta nunc videor mihi.
    gravent catenae corpus et longa fame
    mors protrahatur lenta: non vincet fidem   420
    vis ulla nostram. moriar, Alcide, tua.

LYC. Animosne mersus inferis coniunx facit?

MEG. Inferna tetigit, posset ut supera assequi.

LYC. Telluris illum pondus immensae premit.

MEG. Nullo premetur onere, qui caelum tulit.   425

LYC. Cogere.

MEG.   Cogi qui potest nescit mori.

LYC. Effare thalamis quod novis potius parem
    regale munus.

MEG.   Aut tuam mortem aut meam.

LYC. Moriere demens.

MEG.   Coniugi occurram meo.

pereat E T^{2pc} pergat P CS perg__ T^1 ‖ 423 supera E^1 T^1P superna CS E^{2pc} T^{2pc} ‖ 425 premetur A Σ E^{pc} premer_tur E^{ac} ‖ 427 thalamis quod novis potius E A pot.

LYC.	Sceptroque nostro potior est famulus tibi?	430
MEG.	Quot iste "famulus" tradidit reges neci!	
LYC.	Cur ergo regi servit et patitur iugum?	
MEG.	Imperia dura tolle: quid virtus erit?	
LYC.	Obici feris monstrisque virtutem putas?	
MEG.	Virtutis est domare quae cuncti pavent.	435
LYC.	Tenebrae loquentem magna Tartareae premunt.	
MEG.	Non est ad astra mollis e terris via.	
LYC.	Quo patre genitus caelitum sperat domos?	
AM.	Miseranda coniunx Herculis magni, sile;	
	partes meae sunt reddere Alcidae patrem	440
	genusque verum. post tot ingentis viri	
	memoranda facta postque pacatum manu	
	quodcumque Titan ortus et labens videt,	
	post monstra tot perdomita, post Phlegram impio	
	sparsam cruore postque defensos deos	445
	nondum liquet de patre? mentimur Iovem?	
	Iunonis odio crede.	
LYC.	Quid violas Iovem?	
	mortale caelo non potest iungi genus.	
AM.	Communis ista pluribus causa est deis.	
LYC.	Famuline fuerant ante quam fierent dei?	450
AM.	Pastor Pheraeos Delius pavit greges.	
LYC.	Sed non per omnes exul erravit plagas.	

quod nov. thal. *Wilamowitz* ‖ 430 sceptroque: quoque *ex* que *E*² | potior (-ius *P*) est famulus *A*   famulus est potior *E, fort. recte* ‖ 431 quot: t *ex* d *E*^pc *C*^pc ‖ 438 sperat *E* penetrat *A* ‖ 440 meae *E*   mee hee (*sic*) *TP S*   mee he *C* ‖ 449 pluribus causa est *E T*²pc*P*¹pc *SV*   pluribus est causa *T*¹   pluribus est *P*ac   est causa *C*(plur. ca. est

Hercules Furens

AM. Quem profuga terra mater errante edidit?

LYC. Num monstra saevas Phoebus aut timuit feras?

AM. Primus sagittas imbuit Phoebi draco. 455

LYC. Quam gravia parvus tulerit ignoras mala?

AM. E matris utero fulmine eiectus puer
mox fulminanti proximus patri stetit.
quid? qui gubernat astra, qui nubes quatit
non latuit infans rupis exesae specu? 460
sollicita tanti pretia natales habent,
semperque magno constitit nasci deum.

LYC. Quemcumque miserum videris, hominem scias.

AM. Quemcumque fortem videris, miserum neges.

LYC. Fortem vocemus cuius ex umeris leo, 465
donum puellae factus, et clava excidit
fulsitque pictum veste Sidonia latus?
fortem vocemus cuius horrentes comae
maduere nardo, laude qui notas manus
ad non virilem tympani movit sonum, 470
mitra ferocem barbara frontem premens?

AM. Non erubescit Bacchus effusos tener
sparsisse crines nec manu molli levem
vibrare thyrsum, cum parum forti gradu
auro decorum syrma barbarico trahit; 475
post multa virtus opera laxari solet.

LYC. Hoc Euryti fatetur eversi domus
pecorumque ritu virginum oppressi greges.
hoc nulla Iuno, nullus Eurystheus iubet:
ipsius haec sunt opera.

Cmg.) ‖ 453 terra mater *E*   mater mater *P CS*   terre mater *K T²*(terre *in ras.*) |
errante edidit *E*   errantem dedit *A* ‖ 454 num *E*   non *T²in ras. CS*   nunc *P* | sevas
A   saeva *E* ‖ 456 Amphitryoni continuant *E A, corr. Gruter* | parvus *E A*   partus
Housman ‖ 460 exese *A*(ex ese *P*)   ideae *E* ‖ 461 tanti pretia (prec-) *A*   precia tanti
E ‖ 462 constitit *E T CS*   conscit *P*   consistit *Leid* ‖ 466 factus *E A*   pactus *Nic.
Heinsius* ‖ 474 vibrare *E A*   -asse ς ‖ 475 barbarico *E*   barbaricum *A* ‖ *ante* 477 Lyci

AM.   Non nosti omnia: 480
   ipsius opus est caestibus fractus suis
   Eryx et Eryci iunctus Antaeus Libys,
   et qui hospitali caede manantes foci
   bibere iustum sanguinem Busiridis;
   ipsius opus est vulneri et ferro invius   485
   mortem coactus integer Cycnus pati,
   nec unus una Geryon victus manu.
   eris inter istos — qui tamen nullo stupro
   laesere thalamos.

LYC.   Quod Iovi hoc regi licet:
   Iovi dedisti coniugem, regi dabis;   490
   et te magistro non novum hoc discet nurus,
   etiam viro probante meliorem sequi.
   sin copulari pertinax taedis negat,
   vel ex coacta nobilem partum feram.

MEG. Umbrae Creontis et penates Labdaci   495
   et nuptiales impii Oedipodae faces,
   nunc solita nostro fata coniugio date.
   nunc nunc, cruentae regis Aegypti nurus,
   adeste multo sanguine infectae manus.
   dest una numero Danais; explebo nefas.   500

LYC. Coniugia quoniam pervicax nostra abnuis
   regemque terres, sceptra quid possint scies.
   complectere aras: nullus eripiet deus
   te mihi, nec orbe si remolito queat
   ad supera victor numina Alcides vehi.   505
   — congerite silvas; templa supplicibus suis
   iniecta flagrent, coniugem et totum gregem
   consumat unus igne subiecto rogus.

AM.   Hoc munus a te genitor Alcidae peto,
   rogare quod me deceat, ut primus cadam.   510

---

notam habent A F,M² E², ante 479 E¹ M¹(et ante 478)N ‖ 478 oppressi *E A*   pressi
Bentley ‖ 483 hospitali cede manantes *A*   hospitalem caedem minantes *E* ‖ 485 vulneri
E T²ᵖᶜP C   vultum *T¹ S,V¹*   inultum *V²ᵖᶜ* | invius *Nic. Heinsius*   obvius *E A* ‖ 486
integer cycnus *E*   ante geriones *A* ‖ 490 dabis *E A*   dabit *Leo* ‖ 497 nostro τ *Q M*
T²ᵖᶜ   vestro *E T¹ut vid.,P CS* ‖ 499 multo *E A*   iuncto *Gronovius* ‖ 500 ex plebo
P   ex phebo *T¹, corr. m.2* ‖ 504 remolito *A*   demol- *E* ‖ 505 numina *E A*   lumina

Hercules Furens

LYC. Qui morte cunctos luere supplicium iubet
nescit tyrannus esse. diversa irroga:
miserum veta perire, felicem iube.
ego, dum cremandis trabibus accrescit rogus,
sacro regentem maria votivo colam. 515

AM. Pro numinum vis summa, pro caelestium
rector parensque, cuius excussis tremunt
humana telis, impiam regis feri
compesce dextram! — quid deos frustra precor?
ubicumque es, audi, nate. — Cur subito labant 520
agitata motu templa? cur mugit solum?
infernus imo sonuit e fundo fragor.
audimur! est est sonitus Herculei gradus.

CHORUS.

O Fortuna viris invida fortibus,
quam non aequa bonis praemia dividis. 525
Eurystheus facili regnet in otio;
Alcmena genitus bella per omnia
monstris exagitet caeliferam manum:
serpentis resecet colla feracia,
deceptis referat mala sororibus, 530
cum somno dederit pervigiles genas
pomis divitibus praepositus draco.
  Intravit Scythiae multivagas domos
et gentes patriis sedibus hospitas,
calcavitque freti terga rigentia 535
et mutis tacitum litoribus mare.
illic dura carent aequora fluctibus,
et, qua plena rates carbasa tenderant,
intonsis teritur semita Sarmatis.
stat pontus, vicibus mobilis annuis, 540

Nic. Heinsius ‖ 508 rogus *cod. Vat. Reg. 1500(in ras.)* Avantius locus *E A* ‖ 512 irroga *A* in loca *E* ‖ 513 veta *E T²ᵖᶜ(t ex r ut vid.)P* vita *CS* ‖ 515 colam *E* rogem *A* ‖ 516 pro... pro *E* proh... proh *T* proth... proth *P* pro... oro *CS* | numinum *E T²ᵖᶜ CS* nimium *P* ‖ 521 agitata *E T C¹ᵖᶜSV* agita *P Cᵃᶜ* ‖ 522 sonuit e *Eᵖᶜ Σ T²(e in ras. 3 litt.) CS* sonu ite *Eᵃᶜ* sonuit est *P* ‖ 523 est est *E TP* ē(= est *vel* en) est *CS* en est *ςς* ‖ 526–32 *verba Fortunae esse putat Bothe et sic dist.:* "Eurystheus ... draco." ‖ 529 ferocia *E A, corr. ς* ‖ 536 multis *E A, corr. Kς* ‖ 538 tenderant *T CV* tenderent *E* tendantur *P* tendeant *S* ‖ 539 semita *E CS* -tas *Tᵃᶜ(sed corr. m.1)P*

navem nunc facilis, nunc equitem pati.
illic quae viduis gentibus imperat,
aurato religans ilia balteo,
detraxit spolium nobile corpori
et peltam et nivei vincula pectoris, 545
victorem posito suspiciens genu.
   Qua spe praecipites actus ad inferos,
audax ire vias irremeabiles,
vidisti Siculae regna Proserpinae?
illic nulla noto nulla favonio 550
consurgunt tumidis fluctibus aequora;
non illic geminum Tyndaridae genus
succurrunt timidis sidera navibus;
stat nigro pelagus gurgite languidum,
et, cum Mors avidis pallida dentibus 555
gentes innumeras manibus intulit,
uno tot populi remige transeunt.
   Evincas utinam iura ferae Stygis
Parcarumque colos non revocabiles!
hic qui rex populis pluribus imperat, 560
bello cum peteres Nestoream Pylon,
tecum conseruit pestiferas manus
telum tergemina cuspide praeferens;
effugit tenui vulnere saucius
et mortis dominus pertimuit mori. 565
fatum rumpe manu: tristibus inferis
prospectus pateat lucis, et invius
limes det faciles ad superos vias.
   Immites potuit flectere cantibus
umbrarum dominos et prece supplici 570
Orpheus, Eurydicen dum repetit suam.
quae silvas et aves saxaque traxerat
ars, quae praebuerat fluminibus moras,
ad cuius sonitum constiterant ferae,
mulcet non solitis vocibus inferos 575
et surdis resonat clarius in locis.
deflent Eumenides Threiciam nurum,
deflent et lacrimis difficiles dei;
et qui fronte nimis crimina tetrica

‖ 543 *deest A (spat. unius vs. rel. S, sine spat. TP C)* ‖ 546 suscipiens *E A, corr.* ς ‖ 548 inremeabiles (irr-) *A* inremediabiles *E* ‖ 559 non revocabiles *E A* irrevocabiles *τ* ‖ 561 bello *E TP S^{pc}* bella *C,S^{ac}* | peteres *T^{2pc}ς* peteret *E T^{1}P C^{2pc}S* -erit *C^1* ‖ 566 tristibus *E* tristis et *A* ‖ 571 repetit *E* recipit *A* ‖ 575–76 *desunt A* ‖ 577 *post* 580

[85]

quaerunt ac veteres excutiunt reos 580
flentes Eurydicen iuridici sedent.
tandem mortis ait "Vincimur" arbiter,
"evade ad superos, lege tamen data:
tu post terga tui perge viri comes,
tu non ante tuam respice coniugem, 585
quam cum clara deos obtulerit dies
Spartanique aderit ianua Taenari."
odit verus amor nec patitur moras:
munus dum properat cernere, perdidit.
   Quae vinci potuit regia carmine, 590
haec vinci poterit regia viribus.

ACTUS TERTIUS

HERCULES. AMPHITRYON. MEGARA tacita. THESEUS.

HER.   O lucis almae rector et caeli decus,
qui alterna curru spatia flammifero ambiens
illustre latis exseris terris caput,
da, Phoebe, veniam, si quid illicitum tui 595
videre vultus; iussus in lucem extuli
arcana mundi. tuque, caelestum arbiter
parensque, visus fulmine opposito tege;
et tu, secundo maria qui sceptro regis,
imas pete undas. quisquis ex alto aspicit 600
terrena, facie pollui metuens nova,
aciem reflectat oraque in caelum erigat
portenta fugiens. hoc nefas cernant duo,
qui advexit et quae iussit. — in poenas meas
atque in labores non satis terrae patent 605
Iunonis odio. vidi inaccessa omnibus,
ignota Phoebo quaeque deterior polus
obscura diro spatia concessit Iovi;

A | Eumenides Threiciam nurum *Schmidt* euridicē (-cidē S) treicie nurus A eurydicem threiciae nurus E Eurydicen Tartareae nurus *Withof* ‖ 583 evade *E T²ᵖᶜ* et vade *A* ‖ 586 quam cum clara deos *E A* quam clarus radios *Zwierlein* ‖ 590 carmine *E* cantibus *A* ‖ *ante 592 scaenae tit. inserui (v. ante 618)* ‖ 592 decus *E TP* deus *CS* ‖ 594 latis *E* letis *A* ‖ 597 archana *E* secreta *A* | celestum *Tᵖᶜ CV* celestium *E*(cael-) *Tᵃᶜ P S* ‖ 598 tege *E T CV* rege *P S* ‖ 601 pollui metuens *E T* pollui timens *P* metuens pollui *CS* ‖ 604 iussit *E* vexit *A* ‖ 606 inaccessa *E* in acc- *CV* inactessa

Hercules Furens

	et, si placerent tertiae sortis loca,	
	regnare potui. noctis aeternae chaos	610
	et nocte quiddam gravius et tristes deos	
	et fata vici; morte contempta redî.	
	quid restat aliud? vidi et ostendi inferos.	
	da si quid ultra est, iam diu pateris manus	
	cessare nostras, Iuno; quae vinci iubes?	615
	— Sed templa quare miles infestus tenet	
	limenque sacrum terror armorum obsidet?	
AM.	Utrumne visus vota decipiunt meos,	
	an ille domitor orbis et Graium decus	
	tristi silentem nubilo liquit domum?	620
	estne ille natus? membra laetitia stupent.	
	o nate, certa at sera Thebarum salus,	
	teneone in auras editum an vana fruor	
	deceptus umbra? tune es? agnosco toros	
	umerosque et alto nobilem trunco manum.	625
HER.	Unde iste, genitor, squalor et lugubribus	
	amicta coniunx? unde tam foedo obsiti	
	paedore nati? quae domum clades gravat?	
AM.	Socer est peremptus, regna possedit Lycus,	
	natos parentem coniugem leto petit.	630
HER.	Ingrata tellus, nemo ad Herculeae domus	
	auxilia venit? vidit hoc tantum nefas	
	defensus orbis? — cur diem questu tero?	
	mactetur hostia, hanc ferat virtus notam	
	fiatque summus hostis Alcidae Lycus.	635
	ad hauriendum sanguinem inimicum feror;	
	Theseu, resiste, ne qua vis subita ingruat.	
	me bella poscunt; differ amplexus, parens,	
	coniunxque differ. nuntiet Diti Lycus	
	me iam redîsse.	

T in accensa *P* inacensa *S* ‖ 607 queque *A* quaque *E* ‖ 612 vici *E A* vidi *Leo* | redî: redi *E* redii *A* ‖ 614 iam diu *E* tam diu *P CS* tandiu *T* ‖ 615 quae *E* quid *A* ‖ *ante* 618 *inscribitur*: AMPHYTRION. HERCVLES. MEGERA. THESEVS *E* Amphitrion. hercules. theseus *A* (*v. ante* 592) ‖ 622 at *Gruter* et *E A* ‖ 623 teneone in auras editum an vana fruor *E* verumne cerno corpus an fallor videns *TP* ver. c. c. an fallor vel tua videns *CS* ‖ 629 regna *E TP* regnaque *CS* ‖ 632 vidit *E P C*^{ac} vide *T*^{1} videt *T*^{2pc} *C*^{pc}*SV* ‖ 634 hostia *Leo* hostis *E A* ‖ 634^{b}–36 *Herculi continuat*

Hercules Furens

THE.   Flebilem ex oculis fuga,   640
    regina, vultum, tuque nato sospite
    lacrimas cadentes reprime; si novi Herculem,
    Lycus Creonti debitas poenas dabit.
    lentum est "dabit": dat. hoc quoque est lentum: dedit.

AM.   Votum secundet qui potest nostrum deus   645
    rebusque lassis adsit. — o magni comes
    magnanime nati, pande virtutum ordinem,
    quam longa maestos ducat ad manes via,
    ut vincla tulerit dura Tartareus canis.

THE.   Memorare cogis acta securae quoque   650
    horrenda menti. vix adhuc certa est fides
    vitalis aurae; torpet acies luminum,
    hebetesque visus vix diem insuetum ferunt.

AM.   Pervince, Theseu, quidquid alto in pectore
    remanet pavoris, neve te fructu optimo   655
    frauda laborum: quae fuit durum pati,
    meminisse dulce est. fare casus horridos.

THE.   Fas omne mundi teque dominantem precor
    regno capaci teque quam tota irrita
    quaesivit Aetna mater, ut iure abdita   660
    et operta terris liceat impune eloqui.
       Spartana tellus nobile attollit iugum,
    densis ubi aequor Taenarus silvis premit.
    hic ora solvit Ditis invisi domus
    hiatque rupes alta et immenso specu   665
    ingens vorago faucibus vastis patet
    latumque pandit omnibus populis iter.
    non caeca tenebris incipit primo via;
    tenuis relictae lucis a tergo nitor
    fulgorque dubius solis affecti cadit   670

E, *Theseo dat* A ‖ 641 vultum *E A* luctum *Nic. Heinsius* ‖ 644 est lentum *E TP* lentum *CS* ‖ 646 lassis *E A* lapsis *ς* ‖ 654 pervince *A* pervincet *E* | alto in *E* alto *A* ‖ 659–60 tota . . . ethna *E TP C^{ac}*(rota . . . e. *C^{pc}*)*S* amotam . . . Enna *Heimsoeth* (*iam* raptam . . . Enna *Bentley*) toto . . . orbe *Schmidt* nocte . . . Aetna *possis* ‖ 660 iure *codd. Par. Lat. 8030, 8035* iura *E A* ‖ 661 eloqui *A* loqui *E* ‖ 664 invisi *E* invicti *TP C* inviti *S* ‖ 665 hiatque *A E^{2pc}*(at *in ras. 3 litt.*) *F^{2pc}M^{2pc}N* hitque *F^{1}* iatque (*vel* i atque) *M^{1}* | immenso *E T^{2pc}*(e *in ras.*, ĩm *et* n *corr.*) *CS* universo *P* ‖ 667 pandit: nd *in ras. E^{pc}* ‖ 670 affecti *Bentley* afflicti *E A* ‖ 671 nocte sic mixta *E* tale non

et ludit aciem; nocte sic mixta solet
praebere lumen primus aut serus dies.
hinc ampla vacuis spatia laxantur locis,
in quae omne mersum pergat humanum genus.
nec ire labor est; ipsa deducit via. 675
ut saepe puppes aestus invitas rapit,
sic pronus aer urget atque avidum chaos,
gradumque retro flectere haud umquam sinunt
umbrae tenaces.
            Intus immensi sinus
placido quieta labitur Lethe vado 680
demitque curas; neve remeandi amplius
pateat facultas, flexibus multis gravem
involvit amnem, qualis incerta vagus
Maeander unda ludit et cedit sibi
instatque dubius litus an fontem petat. 685
palus inertis foeda Cocyti iacet;
hic vultur, illic luctifer bubo gemit
omenque triste resonat infaustae strigis.
horrent opaca fronde nigrantes comae,
taxum imminentem qua tenet segnis Sopor 690
Famesque maesta tabido rictu iacet
Pudorque serus conscios vultus tegit.
Metus Pavorque, Funus et frendens Dolor
aterque Luctus sequitur et Morbus tremens
et cincta ferro Bella; in extremo abdita 695
iners Senectus adiuvat baculo gradum.

AM.   Estne aliqua tellus Cereris aut Bacchi ferax?

THE.   Non prata viridi laeta facie germinant,
nec adulta leni fluctuat Zephyro seges;
non ulla ramos silva pomiferos habet; 700

---

dubie A ‖ 674 in qu(a)e E T^{2pc} CS   inque T^{1}P | mersum TP C   versum E   mensum S
| pergat *Peiper* (*iam pergit cod. Par. Lat. 8034^{2pc}*)   pereat E A ‖ 678 umquam
E T Cd   numquam P S ‖ 679 immensi sinus E   immenso (inm-) sinu A ‖ 680
lethe E^{2pc}(*altera e in ras. 2 litt.*) Σ   lethes A ‖ 683–4 incerta . . . unda A
incertis . . . undis E^{1pc}(*incertis ex -tus*) Σ ‖ 684 meander E T^{2pc} leander A | ludit
E T^{2pc}(ludum T^{1})P CS   errat ludit E ‖ 687 illic E TP V   *om. in textu, add. mg.* C   hic
S | luctifer E T^{2pc} CV   lucifer T^{1}P S ‖ 688 omenque E T CV   omneque P S(*ut vid.*)
‖ 689 horrent: t *in ras. 2 litt* E^{2} ‖ 690 taxum imminentem qua *Leo*   taxo imminente
quam E T CS   raxo iminente quam P ‖ 691 famesque m(a)esta E A   Fames quoque
istic *Withof* | iacet *Withof*   iacens E A ‖ 693 metus A   metusque E ‖ 697 cerereris

Hercules Furens

sterilis profundi vastitas squalet soli
et foeda tellus torpet aeterno situ —
rerumque maestus finis et mundi ultima.
immotus aer haeret et pigro sedet
nox atra mundo; cuncta marcore horrida,   705
ipsaque morte peior est mortis locus.

AM.   Quid ille opaca qui regit sceptro loca,
qua sede positus temperat populos leves?

THE.   Est in recessu Tartari obscuro locus,
quem gravibus umbris spissa caligo alligat.   710
a fonte discors manat hinc uno latex,
alter quieto similis (hunc iurant dei),
tacente sacram devehens fluvio Styga;
at hic tumultu rapitur ingenti ferox
et saxa fluctu volvit Acheron invius   715
renavigari. cingitur duplici vado
adversa Ditis regia, atque ingens domus
umbrante luco tegitur. hic vasto specu
pendent tyranni limina, hoc umbris iter,
haec porta regni. campus hanc circa iacet,   720
in quo superbo digerit vultu sedens
animas recentes. dira maiestas deo,
frons torva, fratrum quae tamen specimen gerat
gentisque tantae; vultus est illi Iovis,
sed fulminantis. magna pars regni trucis   725
est ipse dominus, cuius aspectus timet
quidquid timetur.

AM.   Verane est fama inferis
iam sera reddi iura et oblitos sui
sceleris nocentes debitas poenas dare?
quis iste veri rector atque aequi arbiter?   730

THE.   Non unus alta sede quaesitor sedens
iudicia trepidis sera sortitur reis:
aditur illo Cnosius Minos foro,

E^1, *corr. m.2* | ferax *E* tenax *A* ‖ 705 marcore *Richter* maerore *E A* ‖ 709 recessu *E* secessu *A* ‖ 717 adversa *E T* aversa *P CS* ‖ 722 deo *A* dei *E* | *in fine vs., non post recentes, interpunxit Leo (legens* dei) ‖ 723 fratrum qu(a)e *E T²ᵖᶜ CS* fratrumque *P* fratrum q⁻ *T¹* | specimen *E A* speciem *ς* ‖ 728 iam *Ageno* tam *E A* | reddi *A* reddit *E* ‖ 730 veri rector *E A* veri exactor *Bentley* ‖ 733 aditur *E* auditur *A* ‖

>   Rhadamanthus illo, Thetidis hoc audit socer.
>   quod quisque fecit, patitur; auctorem scelus   735
>   repetit, suoque premitur exemplo nocens.
>   vidi cruentos carcere includi duces
>   et impotentis terga plebeia manu
>   scindi tyranni. quisquis est placide potens
>   dominusque vitae servat innocuas manus   740
>   et incruentum mitis imperium regit
>   animaeque parcit, longa permensus diu
>   vivacis aevi spatia vel caelum petit
>   vel laeta felix nemoris Elysii loca,
>   iudex futurus. sanguine humano abstine   745
>   quicumque regnas; scelera taxantur modo
>   maiore vestra.

AM.   Certus inclusos tenet
> locus nocentes? utque fert fama, impios
> supplicia vinclis saeva perpetuis domant?

THE.   Rapitur volucri tortus Ixion rota;   750
> cervice saxum grande Sisyphia sedet;
> in amne medio faucibus siccis senex
> sectatur undas; alluit mentum latex,
> fidemque cum iam saepe decepto dedit,
> perit unda in ore, poma destituunt famem.   755
> praebet volucri Tityos aeternas dapes,
> urnasque frustra Danaides plenas gerunt;
> errant furentes impiae Cadmeides,
> terretque mensas avida Phineas avis.

AM.   Nunc ede nati nobilem pugnam mei.   760
> patrui volentis munus an spolium refert?

THE.   Ferale tardis imminet saxum vadis,
> stupente ubi unda segne torpescit fretum.
> hunc servat amnem cultu et aspectu horridus

---

734 hoc A   hos E ‖ 739 tyranni E T²ᵖᶜ CS   tyrannum T¹P ‖ 741 regit FM A Eᵖᶜ regis Eᵃᶜ   regist (sic) N ‖ 742 anim(a)eque E P CS   animoque τ T²(o in ras.) ς ‖ 743 vivacis Bentley   felicis E A ‖ 747 vestra E A   nostra N e Leid T²ᵖᶜ ‖ 751 sisyphea E A(sysi- T sysy- P sisi- CS) ‖ 753 alluit Eᵃᶜ F¹N T¹   aluit M P   abluit Eᵖᶜ F²ᵖᶜ T²ᵖᶜ CS ‖ 757 gerunt E   ferunt A ‖ 759 terretque m. avida phineas (phy-) avis A terrentque m. avidae fineas aves E ‖ 763 stupente ubi unda A   stupent ubi undae E ‖

Hercules Furens

    pavidosque manes squalidus gestat senex.   765
    impexa pendet barba, deformem sinum
    nodus coercet, concavae lucent genae;
    regit ipse longo portitor conto ratem.
    hic onere vacuam litori puppem applicans
    repetebat umbras; poscit Alcides viam;   770
    cedente turba dirus exclamat Charon:
    "Quo pergis audax? siste properantem gradum."
    non passus ullas natus Alcmena moras
    ipso coactum navitam conto domat
    scanditque puppem. cumba populorum capax   775
    succubuit uni; sedit et gravior ratis
    utrimque Lethen latere titubanti bibit.
    tum victa trepidant monstra, Centauri truces
    [Lapithaeque multo in bella succensi mero;]

              *   *   *

    Stygiae paludis ultimos quaerens sinus   780
    fecunda mergit capita Lernaeus labor.
      Post haec avari Ditis apparet domus.
    hic saevus umbras territat Stygius canis,
    qui trina vasto capita concutiens sono
    regnum tuetur. sordidum tabo caput   785
    lambunt colubrae, viperis horrent iubae
    longusque torta sibilat cauda draco.
    par ira formae: sensit ut motus pedum,
    attollit hirtas angue vibrato comas
    missumque captat aure subrecta sonum,   790
    sentire et umbras solitus. ut propior stetit
    Iove natus, antro sedit incertus canis
    et uterque timuit. — ecce latratu gravi
    loca muta terret; sibilat totos minax
    serpens per armos. vocis horrendae fragor   795

---

765 gestat *E A* vectat *Des. Heraldus* ‖ 766 impexa *E T²ᵖᶜ CS* impensa *T¹P* ‖ 767 lucent *T CS* luent *P* squalent *E* ‖ 768 longo por. conto *E* conto por. longo *TP C* cinto p. l. *Sᵃᶜ*(*male corr., o non supra i sed supra o inserta*) ‖ 769 vacuam *E* vacuus *A* ‖ 770 umbras *E* undas *A* ‖ 770ᵇ–71ᵃ *post* viam *dist. TP necnon Bentley, post* turba *S vulgo* ‖ 776 succubuit *E TP SV* succumbit *C* ‖ 777 titubanti *E* titubato *A* ‖ 778 tum *E* tunc *A* ‖ victa *E* vasta *A* ‖ 779 *delevi* (*de versu delendo cogitaverat Ageno*) *et lacunam post* 778 *statui* ‖ in bella *E* bella *A* ‖ 782 avari ditis *A F,M*(t *in ras.?*) avariditis *Eᵖᶜ*(idit *in ras.*) avari diris *N* ‖ 784 trina *E P CS* terna *T²ᵖᶜ* ς trin. *T¹* ‖ 785 caput *fort. corruptum* ‖ 787 torta *E A* tota *Cvar.mg.* ‖ 788 par *A* per *E* ‖ 790 subrecta *E* subiecta *A* ‖ 791 propior *E T²ᵖᶜ CS* prior *T¹*(ut

per ora missus terna felices quoque
exterret umbras. solvit a laeva feros
tunc ipse rictus et Cleonaeum caput
opponit ac se tegmine ingenti tegit;
victrice magnum dextera robur gerens 800
huc nunc et illuc verbere assiduo rotat,
ingeminat ictus. domitus infregit minas
et cuncta lassus capita summisit canis
antroque toto cessit. extimuit. sedens
uterque solio dominus et duci iubet; 805
me quoque petenti munus Alcidae dedit.
    Tum gravia monstri colla permulcens manu
adamante texto vincit. oblitus sui
custos opaci pervigil regni canis
componit aures timidus et patiens trahi, 810
erumque fassus, ore summisso obsequens,
utrumque cauda pulsat anguifera latus.
postquam est ad oras Taenari ventum, et nitor
percussit oculos lucis ignotae novos,
resumit animos victus et vastas furens 815
quassat catenas; paene victorem abstulit
pronumque retro vexit et movit gradu.
tunc et meas respexit Alcides manus;
geminis uterque viribus tractum canem
ira furentem et bella temptantem irrita 820
intulimus orbi. vidit ut clarum diem
et pura nitidi spatia conspexit poli,
[oborta nox est, lumina in terram dedit,]
compressit oculos et diem invisum expulit
aciemque retro flexit atque omni petît 825
cervice terram; tum sub Herculeas caput
abscondit umbras.
                — Densa sed laeto venit
clamore turba frontibus laurum gerens,
magnique meritas Herculis laudes canit.

---

vid.)P ‖ 797 feros ς   ferox *E A* ‖ 799 tegit *E*   clepit *TP C^{pc}*(d *exp.*, cl *supr.*)*S* ‖ 801 assiduo: sid *in ras. E²* ‖ 807 tum *E T*   tunc *P CS* ‖ 814 ignotae novos *Ageno* (*v. comm.*)   ignot(a)e bono *E A*   ignote bonos τ *T^{2pc}* ς   ignoto bono *vel* ignotum bonum *Gronovius*   ignotae novus *Bücheler* ‖ 815 victus *E*   vinctus *A* ‖ 821 diem *E*   ethera *A* ‖ 822 nitidi *E T^{2pc} CS*   mundi *T¹P* ‖ 823 *del. Bothe* | oborta nox est *E A*   aborta vox est *Weber* ‖ 824 compressit *A*   comspexit *E* ‖ 826 tum *E T^{2pc}*   cum *A* ‖ 826–27 herculeas ... umbras *E*   herculea ... umbra *A* ‖ 834 es *E* ·est *A* ‖

Hercules Furens

CHORUS.

Natus Eurystheus properante partu 830
iusserat mundi penetrare fundum.
derat hoc solum numero laborum,
tertiae regem spoliare sortis.
ausus es caecos aditus inire,
ducit ad manes via qua remotos 835
tristis et nigra metuenda silva,
sed frequens magna comitante turba.
 Quantus incedit populus per urbes
ad novi ludos avidus theatri;
quantus Eleum ruit ad Tonantem, 840
quinta cum sacrum revocavit aestas;
quanta, cum longae redit hora nocti
crescere, et somnos cupiens quietos
Libra Phoebeos tenet aequa currus,
turba secretam Cererem frequentat 845
et citi tectis properant relictis
Attici noctem celebrare mystae:
tanta per campos agitur silentes
turba. pars tarda graditur senecta,
tristis et longa satiata vita; 850
pars adhuc currit melioris aevi:
virgines nondum thalamis iugatae
et comis nondum positis ephebi
matris et nomen modo doctus infans.
his datum solis, minus ut timerent, 855
igne praelato relevare noctem;
ceteri vadunt per opaca tristes.
qualis est vobis animus remota
luce cum maestus sibi quisque sensit
obrutum tota caput esse terra? 860
stat chaos densum tenebraeque turpes
et color noctis malus ac silentis
otium mundi vacuaeque nubes.
 Sera nos illo referat senectus!
nemo ad id sero venit, unde numquam, 865
cum semel venit, potuit reverti;

836 nigra met. silva *E* silva met. nigra *A* ‖ 840 quantus ς qualis *E A* | ruit *E P* currit *T²in ras. CS* coit *T iterum correctus, cod. Vat. Reg. 1500²* ‖ 841 revocavit *E T CS* renovavit *P* ‖ 842 nocti *E* noctis *A* ‖ 844 phebeos *A* thebeos *E* ‖ 849 graditur *E* gradiens *A* ‖ 855 his *E CS* hiis *TP* ‖ 858 vobis *E T¹P SV* nobis *T²pc*

quid iuvat durum properare fatum?
omnis haec magnis vaga turba terris
ibit ad manes facietque inerti
vela Cocyto. tibi crescit omne, 870
et quod occasus videt et quod ortus
(parce venturis); tibi, Mors, paramur.
sis licet segnis, properamus ipsi;
prima quae vitam dedit hora, carpit.

   Thebis laeta dies adest. 875
aras tangite supplices,
pingues caedite victimas;
permixtae maribus nurus
sollemnes agitent choros;
cessent deposito iugo 880
arvi fertilis incolae.
pax est Herculea manu
Auroram inter et Hesperum,
et qua sol medium tenens
umbras corporibus negat; 885
quodcumque alluitur solum
longo Tethyos ambitu,
Alcidae domuit labor.
transvectus vada Tartari
pacatis redit inferis. 890
iam nullus superest timor;
nil ultra iacet inferos.

— Stantes sacrificus comas
dilecta tege populo.

ACTUS QUARTUS

HERCULES. THESEUS tacitus. AMPHITRYON.
   MEGARA. CHORUS.

HER. Ultrice dextra fusus adverso Lycus 895
  terram cecidit ore; tum quisquis comes

C || 872ᵇ *post* 870ᵃ, 872ᵃ *ante* 870ᵇ *transpos.* Schmidt || 870 vela: a *in ras.* E², et a *era. ante* cocyto | crescit A crescet E || 874 *uno verso* E T, *duobus versibus* P CS (p.q.v./d.h.c.) | carpit E carpsit T²ᵖᶜ(psit *in ras.*)P CS || 876–93 *coniuncti bini, sed initiis versuum distinctis* E || 876 aras E A aram *Terentianus Maurus (qui vv. 875–77 affert de metris 2673 sq.*) || 878 maribus A matribus E || 894 tege E T rege P CS || *ante* 895 *inscribitur:* HERCVLES. AMPHYTRION. MEGERA. CHORVS

Hercules Furens

    fuerat tyranni iacuit et poenae comes.
    nunc sacra patri victor et superis feram,
    caesisque meritas victimis aras colam.
     Te te laborum socia et adiutrix precor,   900
    belligera Pallas, cuius in laeva ciet
    aegis feroces ore saxifico minas;
    adsit Lycurgi domitor et Rubri Maris,
    tectam virenti cuspidem thyrso gerens,
    geminumque numen Phoebus et Phoebi soror   905
    (soror sagittis aptior, Phoebus lyrae),
    fraterque quisquis incolit caelum meus
    non ex noverca frater.
          Huc appellite
    greges opimos; quidquid Indi arvis secant
    Arabesque odoris quidquid arboribus legunt   910
    conferte in aras, pinguis exundet vapor.
    populea nostras arbor exornet comas,
    te ramus oleae fronde gentili tegat,
    Theseu; Tonantem nostra adorabit manus,
    tu conditores urbis et silvestria   915
    trucis antra Zethi, nobilis Dircen aquae
    laremque regis advenae Tyrium coles.
    — date tura flammis.

AM.   Nate, manantes prius
    manus cruenta caede et hostili expia.

HER.   Utinam cruorem capitis invisi deis   920
    libare possem! gratior nullus liquor
    tinxisset aras; victima haud ulla amplior
    potest magisque opima mactari Iovi,
    quam rex iniquus.

E Hercules. theseus. amphitrion. megera *A* ‖ 895 ultrice *T²ᵖᶜP²ᵖᶜ CS* altrice *T¹P¹* victrice *E* | adverso *E* adversam *T¹ᵖᶜP CS* -sus *Tᵃᶜ* ‖ 896 tum *A* tunc *E* ‖ 897 deest *T¹P (homoeoteleuton), inser. T²mg.infr.* ‖ 899 aras colam: sacra scolam *E¹, corr. m.2* ‖ 904 virenti *A* virente *E* ‖ 909 Indi arvis secant *Schmidt* indorum seges *E A* Indorum genus *Withof* Indo fert seges *Koetschau de lacuna post 909 cogitavit Leo* ‖ 911 conferte *E T²ᵖᶜ CS* conferre *T¹P* ‖ 913 te ramus *E T²ᵖᶜ S* teramus *T¹P C* ‖ 915–7 *Herculi continuat E, Theseo dat A* ‖ 915 tu *E* dii *A* | conditores *A* conditor es *E¹(corr. m.2)* ‖ 916 zethi *E* theti *T CS* tethi *P* | nobilis *E T¹P S* nobiles *T²ᵖᶜ C* | dircen aque *N* dircenaque *E* dirces (dy-) aquas *A* ‖ 917 coles *E* colis *A* ‖ 920 cruorem *A* cruore *E* ‖ 922 haud *TLeid* haut *C,S²ᵖᶜ* aut *E P S¹d* ‖ 924

AM.   Finiat genitor tuos
opta labores, detur aliquando otium   925
quiesque fessis.

HER.   Ipse concipiam preces
Iove meque dignas. stet suo caelum loco
tellusque et aequor; astra inoffensos agant
aeterna cursus, alta pax gentes alat;
ferrum omne teneat ruris innocui labor   930
ensesque lateant. nulla tempestas fretum
violenta turbet, nullus irato Iove
exsiliat ignis, nullus hiberna nive
nutritus agros amnis eversos trahat.
venena cessent, nulla nocituro gravis   935
suco tumescat herba. non saevi ac truces
regnent tyranni. si quod etiamnum est scelus
latura tellus, properet, et si quod parat
monstrum, meum sit.
                 — Sed quid hoc? medium diem
cinxere tenebrae. Phoebus obscuro meat   940
sine nube vultu. quis diem retro fugat
agitque in ortus? unde nox atrum caput
ignota profert? unde tot stellae polum
implent diurnae? primus en noster labor
caeli refulget parte non minima Leo   945
iraque totus fervet et morsus parat.
iam rapiet aliquod sidus: ingenti minax
stat ore et ignes efflat et rutilat, iubam
cervice iactans; quidquid autumnus gravis
hiemsque gelido frigida spatio refert   950
uno impetu transiliet, et verni petet
frangetque Tauri colla.

AM.   Quod subitum hoc malum est?
quo, nate, vultus huc et huc acres refers
acieque falsum turbida caelum vides?

tuos *Cvar.* ϛ   tuus *E A* ‖ 928 aequor *Nic. Heinsius*   (a)ether *E A* ‖ 934 amnis *E CS*   annis *TP* ‖ 937 etiamnum est: etiam num est *E CV*   eciam nunc est *T²in ras.*(eciam est nunc *T iterum correctus*)   etiam ñ est *P* (ñ = num *vel* non)   etiam non est *S* ‖ 947 rapiet *TP C^{pc}SV*   rapiat *E C^{ac}* ‖ 948 rutilat *E^{ac} A*   rutilam *E^{1pc}*   rutila *Lipsius* | iactans *E A*   iactat *cod. Vat. Lat. 7611 (in comm. Treveti) necnon Lipsius* ‖ 951 verni *E P SV*   verum *C^{ac}*   iterum *T²in ras.*(it ex v) *C^{pc}* ‖ 953 et huc *E T¹P*   et

Hercules Furens

HER. Perdomita tellus, tumida cesserunt freta, 955
inferna nostros regna sensere impetus;
immune caelum est, dignus Alcide labor.
in alta mundi spatia sublimis ferar,
petatur aether; astra promittit pater.
— quid, si negaret? non capit terra Herculem 960
tandemque superis reddit. en ultro vocat
omnis deorum coetus et laxat fores,
una vetante. recipis et reseras polum?
an contumacis ianuam mundi traho?
dubitatur etiam? vincla Saturno exuam, 965
contraque patris impii regnum impotens
avum resolvam. bella Titanes parent,
me duce furentes; saxa cum silvis feram
rapiamque dextra plena Centauris iuga.
iam monte gemino limitem ad superos agam; 970
videat sub Ossa Pelion Chiron suum,
in caelum Olympus tertio positus gradu
perveniet aut mittetur.

AM.   Infandos procul
averte sensus; pectoris sani parum,
magni tamen, compesce dementem impetum. 975

HER. Quid hoc? Gigantes arma pestiferi movent.
profugit umbras Tityos, ac lacerum gerens
et inane pectus quam prope a caelo stetit!
labat Cithaeron, alta Pallene tremit
marcentque Tempe. rapuit hic Pindi iuga, 980
hic rapuit Oeten, saevit horrendum Mimas.
flammifera Erinys verbere excusso sonat
rogisque adustas propius ac propius sudes
in ora tendit; saeva Tisiphone, caput
serpentibus vallata, post raptum canem 985
portam vacantem clausit opposita face.
— sed ecce proles regis inimici latet,
Lyci nefandum semen. inviso patri

---

illuc *CS*   illuc T^{2pc} ‖ 957 dignus *T CS* E^{2pc} dignum E^1 *P* | alcide *A*   alcidae *E* ‖ 959 promittit *E T CS*   promisit *P* ‖ 963 recipis et *A*   recipi. sed *E* ‖ 967 parent *E T CS*   parant *P* ‖ 971 sub ossa *E* T^{pc} *C*   sub osse T^{ac} *SV*   suborse *P* ‖ 973 mittetur *E* T^{2pc} mutetur *E* ‖ 973^b–74^a averte sensus *in eodem versu ac* infandos procul *A* (sensus averte *C, ord. postea corr.*) ‖ 976 pestiferi *E P*   pestifera *T CS* ‖ 979 pallene *A*   pellene *E* ‖ 980 marcentque *A*   macetumque *E* ‖ 981 Mimas *Avantius*   minans *E A* ‖

| | haec dextra iam vos reddet. excutiat leves
nervus sagittas. tela sic mitti decet
Herculea. | 990 |

| AM. | Quo se caecus impegit furor?
vastum coactis flexit arcum cornibus
pharetramque solvit, stridet emissa impetu
harundo — medio spiculum collo fugit
vulnere relicto. | |

| HER. | Ceteram prolem eruam
omnesque latebras. quid moror? maius mihi
bellum Mycenis restat, ut Cyclopia
eversa manibus saxa nostris concidant.
huc eat et illuc valva deiecto obice
rumpatque postes; columen impulsum labet.
perlucet omnis regia; hic video abditum
natum scelesti patris. | 995

1000 |

| AM. | En blandas manus
ad genua tendens voce miseranda rogat.
— scelus nefandum, triste et aspectu horridum!
dextra precantem rapuit et circa furens
bis ter rotatum misit; ast illi caput
sonuit, cerebro tecta disperso madent.
at misera, parvum protegens natum sinu,
Megara furenti similis e latebris fugit. | 1005 |

| HER. | Licet Tonantis profuga condaris sinu,
petet undecumque temet haec dextra et feret. | 1010 |

| AM. | Quo misera pergis? quam fugam aut latebram petis?
nullus salutis Hercule infesto est locus.
amplectere ipsum potius et blanda prece
lenire tempta. | |

989 leves *A*   levis *E* ‖ 991 impegit *E*   invergit *A* ‖ 993 stridet *E*   stridit *A* ‖ 994 medio *A*   medium *E* ‖ 995 eruam *E TP*   eruat *CS* ‖ 996 omnisque *E*   omnes *A* ‖ 997 cyclopea *E A* ‖ 999 et *A om. E* | valva *Baden*   aula *E A*   clava (*et rotet pro* eat) *Withof* | deiecto *E*   disiecto *T CS*   obiecto *P* ‖ 1000 columen *A* (-mem *P*)   culmen *E* ‖ 1001 perlucet *E*   procumbat *A* ‖ 1005 dextra precantem *MN Q H*   dextra precante *E*   dextram precantem *A*   dextram precantis *τ* ‖ 1006 ast *E TP*   at *CS* ‖ 1009–10 *om. P.* (*homoeoteleuton*) ‖ 1009 e *E T^{pc} C*   est *T^{ac}*   ē (= est *vel* en) *SV* ‖ 1010–11 *Herculi dat E, Amphitryoni continuat A (omisso* 1010 *P*) ‖ 1012 latebram

Hercules Furens

MEG.   Parce iam, coniunx, precor,   1015
agnosce Megaram. natus hic vultus tuos
habitusque reddit; cernis, ut tendat manus?

HER.   Teneo novercam. sequere, da poenas mihi
iugoque pressum libera turpi Iovem —
sed ante matrem parvulum hoc monstrum occidat.   1020

AM.   Quo tendis amens? sanguinem fundes tuum?
— pavefactus infans igneo vultu patris
perit ante vulnus, spiritum eripuit timor.
in coniugem nunc clava libratur gravis:
perfregit ossa, corpori trunco caput   1025
abest nec usquam est. — cernere hoc audes, nimis
vivax senectus? si piget luctus, habes
mortem paratam. — pectori en tela indue,
vel stipitem istum caede monstrorum illitum
converte; falsum ac nomini turpem tuo   1030
remove parentem, ne tuae laudi obstrepat.

CHO.   Quo te ipse, senior, obvium morti ingeris?
quo pergis amens? profuge et obtectus late
unumque manibus aufer Herculeis scelus.

HER.   Bene habet, pudendi regis excisa est domus.   1035
tibi hunc dicatum, maximi coniunx Iovis,
gregem cecidi; vota persolvi libens
te digna, et Argos victimas alias dabit.

AM.   Nondum litasti, nate; consumma sacrum.
stat ecce ad aras hostia, exspectat manum   1040
cervice prona; praebeo, occurro, insequor:
macta. — quid hoc est? errat acies luminum

E latebras $T^{2pc}P$ CS lateas ut vid. T^1 ‖ 1017 tendat A tendam E ‖ 1020 occidat E auferam A ‖ 1021–31 *Amphitryoni tribuunt* MN, *Herculi dat* E; 1021 Megarae, 1022–31 *Amphitryoni dat* A ‖ 1021 fundes E T^1P fundens T^{2pc} CS ‖ 1023 eripuit E rapuit A | timor E puer P CS pavor T^2(avor *in ras.*) ς ‖ 1024 coniugem A coniuge E ‖ 1028^b–31^a(. . . converte): *utrum his verbis Amphitryon Herculem compellat (ut ego puto) an secum etiamnum loquatur non constat* ‖ 1028 pectori en *scripsi* pectus in E A | indue E CS move TP ‖ 1029 monstrorum E A nostrorum *cod. Vat. Lat. 2827 (m.1) necnon* Schmidt ‖ 1032–34 *Choro tribuit* M, *Theseo dant* E A ‖ 1032 senior E genitor A ‖ 1033 late A latet E ‖ 1038 dabit E T^{2pc}(t *in ras.*) dabis P CS ‖ 1041 prebeo A praebe E ‖ 1043 meror A maemor E marcor Wilamowitz

[*100*]

Hercules Furens

visusque maeror hebetat, an video Herculis
manus trementes? vultus in somnum cadit
et fessa cervix capite summisso labat;   1045
flexo genu iam totus ad terram ruit,
ut caesa silvis ornus aut portum mari
datura moles. vivis, an leto dedit
idem tuos qui misit ad mortem furor?
sopor est: reciprocos spiritus motus agit.   1050
detur quieti tempus, ut somno gravi
vis victa morbi pectus oppressum levet.
removete, famuli, tela, ne repetat furens.

CHORUS.

Lugeat aether   1054
magnusque parens aetheris alti   1054bis
tellusque ferax
et vaga ponti mobilis unda,
tuque ante omnes   1057
qui per terras tractusque maris   1057bis
fundis radios
noctemque fugas ore decoro,
fervide Titan;   1060
obitus pariter   1060bis
tecum Alcides vidit et ortus
novitque tuas utrasque domos.
   Solvite tantis animum, o superi,
solvite monstris;   1064
rectam in melius flectite mentem.   1064bis
tuque, o domitor Somne malorum,
requies animi,
pars humanae melior vitae,
volucre o matris genus astriferae,
frater durae languide Mortis,
veris miscens falsa, futuri   1070
certus et idem pessimus auctor,

‖ 1047 portum mari *E* portus manet *A* (net era., ri *in ras. inser.* T^2) ‖ 1050 motus *A* in ortus *E* ‖ 1051 gravi *E* gravis *A* ‖ 1054–1137 *dimetri praeter* 1111^b (se. aer) *monom. et* 1135^b–36 (gen.o.p.n.p.i.t.l.) *trim. A dim. praeter* 1114^b (tr.r.s.) *monom. et* 1136^b–37 (tr.l.i.i.v.r.) *trim. E: v. Append. 3* ‖ 1054 (a)ether *E* T^{2pc} *CS* et h__ T^1 et hoc *P* ‖ 1063–64 *verba sic disposuit Leo* solvite tantis animum monstris solvite superi *A* sol. t. a. m. sol. o sup. *E* ‖ 1068 volucre *o Leo* volucer *E P CV* volucre *T* -er *an* -re *ambiguum S* | astriferae *scripsi* astre(a)e *E A* ‖ 1070 futuri T^{2pc}

Hercules Furens

    pax o rerum, portus vitae,
    lucis requies noctisque comes,
    qui par regi famuloque venis,
    pavidum leti genus humanum   1075
    cogis longam discere noctem:
    placidus fessum lenisque fove,
    preme devinctum torpore gravi;
    sopor indomitos alliget artus,
    nec torva prius pectora linquat,   1080
    quam mens repetat pristina cursum.
        En fusus humi
    saeva feroci corde volutat   1082bis
    somnia — nondum est
    tanti pestis superata mali —
    clavaeque gravi   1085
    lassum solitus mandare caput   1085bis
    quaerit vacua pondera dextra,
    motu iactans bracchia vano.
    nec adhuc omnes expulit aestus,
    sed ut ingenti vexata noto
    servat longos unda tumultus   1090
    et iam vento cessante tumet.
    pelle insanos fluctus animi;
    redeat pietas virtusque viro.
    vel sit potius
    mens vesano concita motu;   1095
    error caecus qua coepit eat.
    solus te iam praestare potest
    furor insontem;   1098
    proxima puris sors est manibus   1098bis
    nescire nefas.
        Nunc Herculeis
    percussa sonent pectora palmis;   1101
    mundum solitos ferre lacertos   1101bis
    verbera pulsent ultrice manu.
    gemitus vastos audiat aether,

CS futuris *E T¹P* ‖ 1072 pax o rerum *Traina* pater o rerum *E A* pax errorum *Wilamowitz* ‖ 1074 famuloque *E T²ᵖᶜ CS* famulosque *T¹P* ‖ 1076 noctem *I. Douza fil.* mortem *E A* ‖ 1077 *ante* 1075 *A* ‖ 1077 fove *E A* foves *ς* ‖ 1078 devinctum *CS* devictum *E TP* | torpore *TP Cᵖᶜ S* corpore *E Cᵃᶜ* ‖ 1080 torva *E T²ᵖᶜP* tortua *T¹* tot tua *CS* ‖ 1082 en fusus (enfus-) *A* infusus *E* ‖ 1082bis volutat *A* volvat *E* ‖ 1085bis lassum *E T²ᵖᶜ CS* lassim *T¹P* | caput *E CS* capᵗ(= caput *vel* capit) *T* capit *P* ‖ 1102 ultrice *Nic. Heinsius, Bentley* victrice *E A* ‖ 1104 regina *A* regia

Hercules Furens

audiat atri regina poli
vastisque ferox 1105
qui colla gerit vincta catenis
imo latitans Cerberus antro.
resonet maesto clamore chaos
latique patens unda profundi
et (qui melius 1110
tua tela tamen senserat) aer.
pectora tantis obsessa malis
non sunt ictu ferienda levi;
uno planctu tria regna sonent.
   Et tu, collo decus ac telum
suspensa diu, fortis harundo,
pharetraeque graves, 1117
date saeva fero verbera tergo; 1117bis
caedant umeros robora fortes
stipesque potens
duris oneret pectora nodis; 1120
plangant tantos arma dolores.
   Non vos patriae laudis comites
ulti saevos vulnere reges,
non Argiva membra palaestra
flectere docti 1125
fortes caestu fortesque manu — 1125bis
iam tamen ausi
telum Scythicis leve gorytis
missum certa librare manu,
tutosque fuga figere cervos
nondumque ferae terga iubatae. 1130
ite ad Stygios, umbrae, portus
ite, innocuae,
quas in primo limine vitae
scelus oppressit patriusque furor.
ite, infaustum genus, o pueri, 1135
noti per iter triste laboris.
   — ite, iratos visite reges.

E ‖ 1105 vastisque *A* vastusque *E* ‖ 1109 unda *E T CS* ora *P* ‖ 1110–11 *del. Schmidt* ‖ 1110 melius *A* medius *E* ‖ 1111 aer *E TP* ether *CS* ‖ 1117 graves *E* leves *A* ‖ 1117bis saeva *E* sera *A* ‖ 1120 oneret (hon-) *E A* laceret *Cornelissen, Leo* ‖ 1123 ulti sevos *KQ* viliscevos *E* ulti sevo *A* ‖ 1124 non argiva *E T²ᵖᶜ CS* nargiva *T¹P* ‖ 1125 docti *E* forti *A* ‖ 1127 scithycis leve corytis *E* scythici leve goryti *vel sim. T²ᵖᶜP CS* (stithici l. coriti *T²ᵖᶜ* sitici l. goryti *P* scyctici l. choriti *C* sitici l. gorriti *S*) sythi_ et leve gory__ *T¹* ‖ 1129 tutosque *E A* fretosque *Bentley* ‖ 1135–36 *post*

[103]

Hercules Furens

ACTUS QUINTUS

HERCULES. AMPHITRYON. THESEUS.

HER.   Quis hic locus, quae regio, quae mundi plaga?
ubi sum? sub ortu solis, an sub cardine
glacialis Ursae? numquid Hesperii maris   1140
extrema tellus hunc dat Oceano modum?
quas trahimus auras? quod solum fesso subest?
certe redîmus: unde prostrata domo
video cruenta corpora? an nondum exuit
simulacra mens inferna? post reditus quoque   1145
oberrat oculis turba feralis meis?
pudet fateri: paveo; nescioquod mihi,
nescioquod animus grande praesagit malum.
ubi es, parens? ubi illa natorum grege
animosa coniunx? cur latus laevum vacat   1150
spolio leonis? quonam abît tegimen meum
idemque somno mollis Herculeo torus?
ubi tela? ubi arcus? arma quis vivo mihi
detrahere potuit? spolia quis tanta abstulit
ipsumque quis non Herculis somnum horruit?   1155
libet meum videre victorem, libet —
exsurge, virtus. quem novum caelo pater
genuit relicto? cuius in fetu stetit
nox longior quam nostra?

                        — Quod cerno nefas?
nati cruenta caede confecti iacent,   1160
perempta coniunx. quis Lycus regnum obtinet,
quis tanta Thebis scelera moliri ausus est
Hercule reverso? quisquis Ismeni loca,
Actaea quisquis arva, qui gemino mari
pulsata Pelopis regna Dardanii colis,   1165
succurre, saevae cladis auctorem indica.
ruat ira in omnes: hostis est quisquis mihi
non monstrat hostem. victor Alcidae, lates?

1121 *traiecit Leo* ‖ 1136 per iter *E*   pariter *A* ‖ 1140 glacialis *A*   glatiali *E* ‖ 1143 domo *E A*   ad domum *Schmidt* ‖ 1144 exuit *E T*^{2pc} *CS*   ex_uit *T*^{1} exivit *P* ‖ 1146 oberrat *A*   oborrat *E* | oculis . . . meis *E*   oculos . . . meos *A* ‖ 1149 es *E*   est *A* ‖ 1150 cur *A*   cur en *E* | vacat *E*^{pc} *CS*   vocat *E*^{ac} vagat *TP* ‖ 1151 abît: abit *E*   abiit *TP C*^{pc}*S*   ad huc *C*^{ac} ‖ 1155 quis *A*   qui *E* | somnum *E C,S*^{pc} somnium (sompn-) *TP S*^{ac} ‖ 1157 virtus *E*   victor *A* ‖ 1158 in foetu *E*   incestu *T*^{2pc},*P*(in ce-) *CS*   incessu *T*^{1} ‖ 1162 *del. Leo* ‖ 1166 saevae: seve *T CS*   saeve *E*   sive *P* ‖ 1167

>   procede, seu tu vindicas currus truces
>   Thracis cruenti sive Geryonae pecus   1170
>   Libyaeve dominos; nulla pugnandi mora est.
>   en nudus adsto; vel meis armis licet
>   petas inermem.
>   Cur meos Theseus fugit
>   paterque vultus? ora cur condunt sua?
>   differte fletus. quis meos dederit neci   1175
>   omnes simul, profare — quid, genitor, siles?
>   at tu ede, Theseu — sed tua, Theseu, fide.
>   uterque tacitus ora pudibunda obtegit
>   furtimque lacrimas fundit. in tantis malis
>   quid est pudendum? numquid Argivae impotens   1180
>   dominator urbis, numquid infestum Lyci
>   pereuntis agmen clade nos tanta obruit?
>   per te meorum facinorum laudem precor,
>   genitor, tuique nominis semper mihi
>   numen secundum, fare: quis fudit domum?   1185
>   cui praeda iacui?

AM.   Tacita sic abeant mala.

HER.   Ut inultus ego sim?

AM.   Saepe vindicta obfuit.

HER.   Quisquamne segnis tanta toleravit mala?

AM.   Maiora quisquis timuit.

HER.   His etiam, pater,
        quicquam timeri maius aut gravius potest?   1190

AM.   Cladis tuae pars ista quam nosti quota est!

HER.   Miserere, genitor, supplices tendo manus.
        quid hoc? manus refugit — hic errat scelus.

ruat ira *TP C^{pc}V*   ruit ira *C^{ac}*   ritat ira *S*?(it an u *dubium*)   ruatur *E* ‖ 1169 currus *E T^{2pc} CV*   curru *T¹P*   curris *S* ‖ 1170 sive gerione *P CS*   -ionis τ *T^{2pc}*(is *in ras.*)   sivergeryone *E* ‖ 1171 lybiaeve *E*   libieve *CS*   libiene *TP* ‖ 1175 differte fletus *T C*   differre fletus *P S*   defer tellus *E* ‖ 1177 at tu ede *T CS*   at tue de *P*   aut tuae de *E* ‖ 1180 impotens *E*   potens *A* ‖ 1181 lyci *E T²in ras.*   mihi *A* ‖ 1185 fudit domum *E TP*   domum fudit *CS* ‖ 1188 toleravit *A*   tolerabit *E* ‖ 1191 tu(a)e

Hercules Furens

        unde hic cruor? quid illa puerili madens
        harundo leto? tincta Lernaea est nece.   1195
        iam tela video nostra. non quaero manum.
        quis potuit arcum flectere aut quae dextera
        sinuare nervum vix recedentem mihi?
        ad vos revertor, genitor: hoc nostrum est scelus?
        tacuere — nostrum est.

AM.   Luctus est istic tuus,   1200
        crimen novercae; casus hic culpa caret.

HER.   Nunc parte ab omni, genitor, iratus tona;
        oblite nostri, vindica sera manu
        saltem nepotes. stelliger mundus sonet
        flammasque et hic et ille iaculetur polus.   1205
        rupes ligatum Caspiae corpus trahant
        atque ales avida; cur Promethei vacant
        scopuli? vacat cur vertice immenso feras
        volucresque pascens Caucasi abruptum latus
        nudumque silvis? illa quae Pontum Scythen   1210
        Symplegas artat hinc et hinc vinctas manus
        distendat alto, cumque revocata vice
        in se coibunt saxaque in caelum expriment
        actis utrimque rupibus medium mare,
        ego inquieta montium iaceam mora.   1215
        quin structum acervans nemore congesto aggerem
        cruore corpus impio sparsum cremo?
        sic, sic agendum est; inferis reddam Herculem.

AM.   Nondum tumultu pectus attonito carens
        mutavit iras, quodque habet proprium furor,   1220
        in se ipse saevit.

HER.   Dira Furiarum loca
        et inferorum carcer et sonti plaga

E T^{2pc} me $T^{1}P$ ne CS ‖ 1195 Lernaea est *Leo* lernae E lernea A ‖ 1197 dextra P C ‖ 1198 sinuare E T^{2}(inu *in ras.*) $C^{pc}SV$ sumare *ut vid.* P sinuate C^{ac} | nervum A nervos E ‖ 1206 ligatum E T^{2}(tu *in ras.*) CS ligavi P ‖ 1207 ales: aves P^{ac} C^{ac}, *utrumque corr. m.1* ‖ 1208 vacat cur *Leo* vagetur E paretur T^{2pc} CS parent $T^{1}P$ ‖ 1209 abruptum E T^{2}(tum *in ras.*)P abrutum CS abrupunt T^{1} ‖ 1210 nudumque: nondumque T^{1}(*corr. m.2*) C | silvis: illius T^{1}(*corr. m.2*)P ‖ 1212–24 *om. in textu, add. mg.* C (*omisso* 1218) ‖ 1213 coibunt E Cd cohibunt T^{2pc} S(h *postea exp.?*) cohibent $T^{1}P$ ‖ 1215 inquieta TP S in quieta E C ‖ 1216 structum E T^{2pc} CS struetur $T^{1}P$ | congesto E T^{2pc} S agesto $T^{1}P$ coniesto C ‖ 1218 *om.* A ‖ 1219 attonito E attonitum A | carens E caret A ‖ 1220 mutavit E T^{2pc} CS mutant $T^{1}P$

decreta turbae! si quod exilium latet
ulterius Erebo, Cerbero ignotum et mihi,
hoc me abde, Tellus; Tartari ad finem ultimum   1225
mansurus ibo.
              Pectus o nimium ferum!
quis vos per omnem, liberi, sparsos domum
deflere digne poterit? hic durus malis
lacrimare vultus nescit. huc arcum date,
date huc sagittas, stipitem huc vastum date.   1230
tibi tela frangam nostra; tibi nostros, puer,
rumpemus arcus; at tuis stipes gravis
ardebit umbris; ipsa Lernaeis frequens
pharetra telis in tuos ibit rogos —
dent arma poenas. vos quoque infaustas meis   1235
cremabo telis, o novercales manus.

AM.   Quis nomen usquam sceleris errori addidit?

HER. Saepe error ingens sceleris obtinuit locum.

AM.   Nunc Hercule opus est: perfer hanc molem mali.

HER. Non sic furore cessit exstinctus pudor,   1240
populos ut omnes impio aspectu fugem.
arma, arma, Theseu, flagito propere mihi
subtracta reddi. sana si mens est mihi,
referte manibus tela; si remanet furor,
pater, recede: mortis inveniam viam.   1245

AM.   Per sancta generis sacra, per ius nominis
utrumque nostri, sive me altorem vocas
seu tu parentem, perque venerandos piis
canos, senectae parce desertae, precor,
annisque fessis; unicum lapsae domus   1250
firmamen, unum lumen afflicto malis

‖ 1223 si *E* et si *A* ‖ 1225 hoc *E* huc *A* ‖ 1227 vos *E T²ᵖᶜ C* nos *T¹P SV* ‖ 1228 deflere *E CS* desse *TP* ‖ 1229 arcum *Bentley, Withof* ensem *E A* ‖ 1230 om. *E* (*homoeoteleuton*) ‖ 1232 tuis *E T CV* tuus *P S* ‖ 1235 vos *E T²in ras. CS* nos *P* | infaustas *E TP* infausta *C*(in fau-)*S* ‖ 1237, 1239 Amphitryoni tribuit *E*, Theseo dat *A* ‖ 1237 usquam *E* umquam *TP* numquam *CS* ‖ 1238 sepe error *A* semper furor *E* ‖ 1240 furore cessit *A* furor recessit *E* ‖ 1244 referte *E T²*(efer *in ras.*) reverte *P CS* ‖ 1247 altorem ς auctorem *E A* ‖ 1250 laps(a)e *E P CS* lasse *T KQe* quassae *Nic. Heinsius* ‖ 1251 lumen afflicto *A* lu. afflictis *E* columen afflicto *Dan.*

[*107*]

Hercules Furens

   temet reserva. nullus ex te contigit
   fructus laborum; semper aut dubium mare
   aut monstra timui; quisquis in toto furit
   rex saevus orbe, manibus aut aris nocens,   1255
   a me timetur; semper absentis pater
   fructum tui tactumque et aspectum peto.

HER. Cur animam in ista luce detineam amplius
   morerque nihil est; cuncta iam amisi bona,
   mentem arma famam coniugem natos manus,   1260
   etiam furorem. nemo polluto queat
   animo mederi; morte sanandum est scelus.

AM. Perimes parentem.

HER.   Facere ne possim, occidam.

AM. Genitore coram?

HER.   Cernere hunc docui nefas.

AM. Memoranda potius omnibus facta intuens   1265
   unius a te criminis veniam pete.

HER. Veniam dabit sibi ipse, qui nulli dedit?
   laudanda feci iussus; hoc unum meum est.
   succurre, genitor, sive te pietas movet
   seu triste fatum sive violatum decus   1270
   virtutis. effer arma; vincatur mea
   Fortuna dextra.

THE.   Sunt quidem patriae preces
   satis efficaces, sed tamen nostro quoque
   movere fletu. surge et adversa impetu
   perfringe solito. nunc tuum nulli imparem   1275
   animum malo resume, nunc magna tibi
   virtute agendum est; Herculem irasci veta.

Heinsius col. afflictae *Nic. Heinsius* ‖ 1252 contigit *E T CV* contingit *P S(sed altera n exp.?)* ‖ 1263^a, 1264^a, 1265–66 *Amphitryoni tribuit E, Theseo dat A* ‖ 1266 pete *E T^{1}P* peto *T^{2pc} CS* ‖ 1269 sive *E T^{2pc} CS* si non *T^{1}P* ‖ 1270 fatum *A* factum *E* | violatum *E* violate *T^{1pc}(e corr.)P^{pc}(e in ras.) CS* ‖ 1272 fortuna *T^2(in ras. praeter* f) *CS* forma *P* fortu *E^1(na add. supr. m.*2) | quidem *E P C^{pc}S* quidam *T^{2pc} C^{ac}*

Hercules Furens

HER. Si vivo, feci scelera; si morior, tuli.
purgare terras propero; iamdudum mihi
monstrum impium saevumque et immite ac ferum   1280
oberrat. agedum, dextra, conare aggredi
ingens opus, labore bis seno amplius.
ignave, cessas, fortis in pueros modo
pavidasque matres? — arma nisi dantur mihi,
aut omne Pindi Thracis excidam nemus   1285
Bacchique lucos et Cithaeronis iuga
mecum cremabo, aut tota cum domibus suis
dominisque tecta, cum deis templa omnibus
Thebana supra corpus excipiam meum
atque urbe versa condar, et, si fortibus   1290
leve pondus umeris moenia immissa incident
septemque opertus non satis portis premar,
onus omne media parte quod mundi sedet
dirimitque superos, in meum vertam caput.

AM. Reddo arma.

HER.   Vox est digna genitore Herculis.   1295
hoc en peremptus spiculo cecidit puer.

AM. Hoc Iuno telum manibus immisit tuis.

HER. Hoc nunc ego utar.

AM.   Ecce quam miserum metu
cor palpitat pectusque sollicitum ferit.

HER. Aptata harundo est.

AM.   Ecce iam facies scelus   1300
volens sciensque.

quaedam T^{ac} ‖ 1280 et T C^1sup.S om. E P | immite T CS immitte E P(inm-) ‖ 1281 agedum: age dum E T agendum P CS ‖ 1283 ignave E A ignava *Iac. Gronovius, fort. recte* ‖ 1284 pavidasque matres A pavidamque matrem E | dantur E dentur A ‖ 1285 excidam E T SV excindam P C ‖ 1287 aut τ ς *deest E A* | domibus E A laribus *Peiper* ‖ 1288 tecta E A regna *Damsté* ‖ 1290 versa A eversa E *metro nolente* ‖ 1291 m(o)enia E TP media CS | incident E CS incidunt T^1P incidant T^{2pc} ‖ 1293 quod mundi E quo mundus A ‖ 1295–1300 *ut exhibui personis dividit* E 1295^a(r.a.) *Herculi continuat* A, *cetera tribuit ita:* 1295^b(vox e.q.s.)–97 *Amphitryoni*, 1298^a *Herculi*, 1298^b–1300 *Amphitryoni* ‖ 1295 reddo E redde A |

[*109*]

Hercules Furens

HER.   Pande, quid fieri iubes?

AM.   Nihil rogamus; noster in tuto est dolor:
nātum potes servare tu solus mihi,
eripere nec tu. maximum evasi metum;
miserum haud potes me facere, felicem potes.   1305
sic statue, quidquid statuis, ut causam tuam
famamque in arto stare et ancipiti scias:
aut vivis aut occidis. hanc animam levem
fessamque senio nec minus fessam malis
in ore primo teneo. tam tarde patri   1310
vitam dat aliquis? non feram ulterius moram,
letale ferrum pectori impresso induam;
hic, hic iacebit Herculis sani scelus.

HER.   Iam parce, genitor, parce, iam revoca manum.
succumbe, virtus, perfer imperium patris.   1315
eat ad labores hic quoque Herculeos labor:
vivamus. artus alleva afflictos solo,
Theseu, parentis. dextra contactus pios
scelerata refugit.

AM.   Hanc manum amplector libens,
hac nisus ibo, pectori hanc aegro admovens   1320
pellam dolores.

HER.   Quem locum profugus petam?
ubi me recondam, quave tellure obruar?
quis Tanais aut quis Nilus aut quis Persica
violentus unda Tigris aut Rhenus ferox
Tagusve Hibera turbidus gaza fluens   1325
abluere dextram poterit? Arctoum licet

---

digna genitore A   dignatore E ‖ 1297 immisit E   emisit A ‖ 1299 pectusque
Gronovius corpusque E A ‖ 1301ᵇ *Herculi dat cod. Neapol. Oratorianus CF.4.5 necnon
Rutgers, Amphitryoni continuant* E A ‖ 1304 eripere nec tu E   theseu. ipse necdum
A *(sine punct. TP)* ‖ 1305 potes me T CS   potes E   me potes me P ‖ 1309 fessam
malis E   quassam ma. A ‖ 1312 letale E A   senile *Withof (qui* pectus *retinet)* |
ferrum pectori impresso *scripsi (iam* ferrum pectori impressum *ς)*   ferro pectus
impresso E   ferro pectus impressum A *(fero p. i. P)*   ferro vulnus impresso *Peiper*
‖ 1315 perfer E T²ᵖᶜ   profer P CS   pr_fer T¹ ‖ 1316 herculeos A   herculeus E ‖
1319 hanc E   hanc ego A ‖ 1320 pectori A   pectore E | egro E P*(sic:* eg̊) ego T CS
‖ 1322 obruar E   obruam A ‖ 1324 renus A   thenus E ‖ 1325 tagusve P CS

Hercules Furens

        Maeotis in me gelida transfundat mare
        et tota Tethys per meas currat manus,
        haerebit altum facinus. in quas impius
        terras recedes? ortum an occasum petes?   1330
        ubique notus perdidi exilio locum.
        me refugit orbis, astra transversos agunt
        obliqua cursus, ipse Titan Cerberum
        meliore vultu vidit. o fidum caput,
        Theseu, latebram quaere longinquam, abditam;   1335
        quoniamque semper sceleris alieni arbiter
        amas nocentes, gratiam meritis refer
        vicemque nostris: redde me infernis, precor,
        umbris reductum, meque subiectum tuis
        restitue vinclis; ille me abscondet locus —   1340
        sed et ille novit.

THE.   Nostra te tellus manet.
        illic solutam caede Gradivus manum
        restituit armis; illa te, Alcide, vocat,
        facere innocentes terra quae superos solet.

---

thagusne *T* padusve *E* | hibera (hy-) turbidus *A* hiberatur bibus *E* ‖ 1330 recedes *A* recidis *E* ‖ 1332–33 *om. P* (*homoeoarcton* me, meliore) ‖ 1336 quoniamque *E* cum ia̱̱ *T¹* cum iamque *P* quique *CS* quicunque *T²ᵖᶜ* ‖ 1340 restitue *E A* substitue *Bentley, Leo* ‖ 1342 illic *E* illuc *A* | cede *A* crede *E* | gradivus *E T²ᵖᶜ CS* gradimus *T¹ ut vid. P*

[*111*]

COMMENTARY

COMMENTARY

Title. The addition of *Furens*, found in TPS (C omits the title), distinguishes the play from the *Oetaeus*, and may therefore not be Senecan. In E both this play and *HO* are called simply *Hercules*.

Act I (1–124)

As in three other plays of Seneca (*Tro., Med., Ag.*) the prologue consists of a monologue; in keeping with general Senecan practice it is preliminary in character, and somewhat separate from the main action of the plot. In both respects Seneca's usage shows Euripidean influence, whether direct or indirect.[1]

There are important differences from Euripidean technique, however, which may be summarized by describing Juno's speech as a true soliloquy rather than a monologue addressed to the audience. In place of a formal self-introduction, for example, Juno's identity is revealed 'accidentally' in her opening complaints about her status. Background information emerges incidentally, rather than in expository narrative, and it is limited to the point that interests her, namely Hercules' return from the underworld; there is no word of the situation in Thebes until Act II. In keeping with the convention that Juno is thinking aloud, she decides on her plan of campaign against Hercules during the course of the speech (rather than having prepared it in advance, as Aphrodite has done in Eur. *Hipp.*). Indeed, the audience observes the process of thought by which she arrives at it. Her vow to wage *aeterna bella* against Hercules first raises the question *quae bella?* (30), which leads to the reflection that all previous efforts have been counterproductive; the latest example of this, Hercules' victory over the powers of the under-

---

1. On Senecan prologues v. Frenzel, Pratt 1939, Runchina 19–70, Anliker 11–48, Tarrant 157f.

world, leads in turn to the suspicion that he will now be tempted to attack Jupiter himself (see comm. on 63–74). This thought increases the urgency of finding a means of checking him, and by a process of elimination Juno realizes that there is no match for Hercules—except himself.[2] This rather roundabout train of ideas is suggestive of everyday thought processes rather than of formal speech. It is also consistent with the general technique of the prologue that Juno, after deciding on her plan, does not give an explicit outline of it (here again one may contrast Eur. *Hipp.*); it is clear in her own mind, but is revealed to the audience only incidentally, through allusive hints (96–98, 113–21).[3]

These hints create a certain amount of foreboding about the catastrophe, all the more effective in view of their veiled nature. Seneca's chief purpose in the prologue was not to arouse anticipation of specific events, but rather to create a portrait of violent, uncontrolled emotion, and the atmosphere of horror and suspense that naturally accompanies it. Clearly, Seneca liked monologues of this type, using them not only in prologues but elsewhere in his dramas, particularly at the beginning of Act II (cf. *HF* 279ff., *Med.* 116ff., 397ff., 893ff., *Pha.* 85ff., *Ag.* 108ff., *Thy.* 176ff.). Such monologues no doubt reveal the influence of Euripides, as in the famous speech in his *Medea* (1021ff.). More recent models were provided by the monologues of Vergil's Dido (*Aen.* 4.534ff.) and of Ovid's many impassioned heroines in the *Metamorphoses* (Medea in 7, Scylla and Althaea in 8, Deianira, Byblis, and Iphis in 9, Myrrha in 10). The contemporary practice of rhetorical exercises on emotional themes probably also influenced the popularity and style of such monologues.[4]

The suitability of Juno for this type of monologue was suggested not only by her close involvement with the episode of Hercules' madness, but also by the fact that Juno's complaints about her rivals or enemies were a familiar literary *locus*: compare V. *Aen.* 1.37ff., 7.293ff., Ov. *Met.* 2.508ff., 3.259ff., 4.420ff.,[5] all of which are monologues except

---

2. The traditional division of the speech into two halves, the first (ending at 74) concerned with complaints, the second with plans for action, quite obscures the organic development of thought in the prologue, and ignores the fact that at line 30 Juno is already looking for a means of attack. The division appears in Trevet's commentary (p. 6 of Ussani's edition), cf. Paratore 16.

3. On the technique, v. Leo's often-quoted sentence on Senecan prologues generally (1908 91): "zwar werden die ὑποκείμενα mitgeteilt, aber durchaus in Affect, so daß sie entweder nur in Andeutungen (Herc. f., Med.) oder in pathetischer Schilderungen (*Oed. Tro. Agam.*) herauskommen, Vorgeschichte und Gegenwärtiges, auch das Kommende in dunkler Einkleidung."

4. Leo 1908 90 and Bonner chaps. 3 and 8. Juno's complaints were a declamation theme in Augustine's boyhood (*Conf.* 1.17.27) and no doubt much earlier.

5. In Greek there are complaints about rivals at Callim. *Del.* 240ff., and Hera's lack of success in dealing with her enemies is frequently the burden of her speeches in the *Iliad*, e.g. 4.25ff., 5.716ff., 8.462ff.

Commentary: Act I

the example in *Met.* 2. All these speeches had some degree of influence on this prologue. Seneca's primary model in the opening lines was the passage in *Met.* 2, where Juno has similarly abandoned heaven for earth because she feels her place has been usurped—by a *paelex* (Callisto), who has been transformed into a constellation along with her bastard son by Jupiter; the stargazing of 6–18 was suggested by *Met.* 2.514ff.: *mentior, obscurum nisi nox cum fecerit orbem, / nuper honoratas summo mea vulnera caelo / videritis stellas.* The gist of 21ff.—"granted I cannot prevent what Jupiter intends for my enemies, yet I can make things unpleasant for them"—is close to V. *Aen.* 7.313–22. A complaint about her lack of power or the ineffectiveness of her efforts is a standard element of the Juno-speeches, but Seneca's lines 33ff. are probably an adaptation of *Met.* 2.519–22 in particular, because they share the paradoxical point that Juno's persecution has actually increased her enemy's fame. Finally, Juno's appeal to the Furies for help in revenge has precedents at *Aen.* 7.324ff. and *Met.* 4.451ff. (For further details of influence from the Vergilian and Ovidian passages see comm. on 1f., 4f., 6–7, 28^b–29, 96–98.) It would be mistaken to suggest that the Senecan speech is a mere patchwork of borrowed materials, however; on the contrary, the motifs mentioned are well integrated and arise naturally in the context.

Juno's jealousy and vindictiveness are so unbalanced that one is forced to ask whether this is really the queen of the gods, Juno Caelestis herself. *Tantaene animis caelestibus irae?* asks Vergil in a similar situation. In fact, as she appeals to the Furies to madden her, she herself becomes something of an infernal power, a Juno Inferna.[6] The fact that she appears at night strengthens this impression. It is noteworthy that Seneca's other supernatural prologue figures, in *Ag.* and *Thy.*, are indeed from the underworld; further, these extravagant and erring spirits vanish at dawn, just as Juno does (cf. Tarrant on *Ag.* 56). This infernal aspect of Juno is obviously consistent with the emphasis throughout this play on the power of the underworld.

Time. The play begins toward the end of night, and the arrival of dawn is noted at the end of the prologue (123ff.). A similar pattern occurs in several ancient tragedies: Soph. *Ant.* (lines 16, 100ff.); Eur. *El.* (54ff., 102), *Ion* (82ff.), *IA* (4ff., 156ff.), *Phaethon* (63ff., cf. Diggle ad loc.); and Sen. *Ag.* (56), *Thy.* (120f.). Other tragedies also begin during the night or at dawn, e.g. Aesch. *Ag.*, Soph. *El.*, Eur. *Hec.*, Sen. *Pha.* (39ff.), *Oed.* (1ff.) and ps.-Sen. *Oct.* (1ff.).

1f. Juno's opening words establish her angry mood, and at the same time serve neatly to identify her. Seneca here combines echoes of Ver-

---

6. See Kroll 434, 404.

Commentary: Act I

gil and Ovid. The idea of Juno being only the *soror* of Jupiter is influenced by Ov. *Met.* 3.265f. *si sum regina Iovisque / et soror et coniunx— certe soror* (which itself plays on the familiar formula *soror et coniunx*, cf. e.g. V. *Aen.* 1.46f.; for other variations of the formula v. Tarrant on *Ag.* 348). The *solum nomen* remaining, that of *coniunx* being lost, comes from Vergil's Dido: *hospes, hoc solum nomen quoniam de coniuge restat* (*Aen.* 4.323).

2 alienum. "Belonging to another"—a sense often found in the context of love- and marriage-relationships (v. *OLD* s.v. 1b); and perhaps also "hostile" (*OLD* s.v. 7), as he often is toward Juno in the *Iliad*, for example.

3 templa summi ... aetheris. *Templa*, modified by *caeli*, is used poetically for "regions" of the sky, e.g. Enn. *Ann.* 48 Skutsch, Lucr. 1.1014 *nec mare nec tellus neque caeli lucida templa*. This is probably the primary meaning here (*aether* being used as a synonym for *caelum* as often in poetry, v. *TLL* 1.1149.66ff.), but the sense of "abodes" of the gods is no doubt also present; cf. Enn. *trag.* 163 R², Lucr. 5.1188 *in caeloque deum sedes et templa locarunt*.

vidua. The adjective means "single, without a mate," whatever the reason for that state (e.g. Seneca uses it of Amazons 246, 542); Miller's translation "widowed" creates more paradox than Seneca intended. In poetry the word first becomes popular in Ovid (eighteen uses) and in Sen. Trag. (sixteen uses).

4f. The lines contain one definite and one possible reminiscence of the Ovidian Juno's speech in *Met.* 2: *paelices caelum tenent* recalls *pro me tenet altera caelum* (2.513); and *pulsa* may echo *pulsa Iunone* (2.525).

paelicibus, paelices. Another word that becomes popular with Ovid (forty-four uses), though generally uncommon in earlier poets. For its use for Juno's rivals, see Plaut. *Merc.* 689f. and Prop. 3.22.35; in Ovid it becomes almost the standard term in such contexts (three times in the Callisto passage in *Met.* 2). In Sen. *paelex* completely replaces *adultera*.

5. Seneca likes to round off a movement of thought with an epigrammatic line such as this; cf. e.g. *HF* 706 *ipsaque morte peior est mortis locus*, and, in the opening lines of other plays, *Oed.* 5, *Ag.* 4 *fugio Thyestes inferos, superos fugo* (cf. Tarrant 160, Wilkinson 198f.). The epigrammatic effect here is heightened by the contrast *tellus/caelum* (cf. *inferos/*

Commentary: Act I

superos in *Ag.* 4), by paronomasia of *paelex* from 4 (cf. *morte/mortis* in 706), and by the chiastic alliterative pattern *te-c-l / l-c-te*.

6–18. Juno points to the evidence in the sky of Jupiter's infidelities. The list takes as its starting point the Bear (= Callisto), and then mentions the Bull, the Pleiades, Orion, Perseus, Gemini (= Castor and Pollux), Apollo and Diana (= sun and moon), and the Garland of Ariadne. Catalogues, particularly of proper names, are a familiar feature of Sen.'s style (Canter 74–76); examples at the beginnings of plays are *Tro.* 8–13, *Med.* 1–12, *Pha.* 1–30, *Ag.* 15–21, ps.-Sen. *HO* 16–27. The present list helps to establish from the outset the expansive, indeed cosmic purview that characterizes this play.

Five distichs, marked off by *hinc–hinc–illinc–hinc–hinc*, compose the main part of the list. As *illinc* (10) does not point in a new direction (the Pleiades being in the vicinity of Taurus), the function of these adverbs is to indicate the rhetorical structure as much as the positions of the constellations. The climax and conclusion of the catalogue is marked by a single tristich 16–18.

The phrasing of the list suggests that Juno can actually see all these heavenly bodies in the night sky as she speaks.[7] (Hence Bacchus and Semele, as they were not transformed into constellations, are mentioned only in a kind of *praeteritio*.) Yet the reference to Apollo in 15 violates this principle, as he must be represented in the heavens by the sun.[8] Here it seems that Sen. has allowed the attraction of a neat rhetorical structure in the list of Jupiter's illegitimate children (two heroic sons in 12–13, two pairs of twins in 14–15) to blind him to the dramatic difficulty. Like *illinc* in 10, *hinc* in 14, though purportedly designating a particular region of the sky, in fact serves to articulate the structural pattern.

Apart from the characteristic allusiveness with which Sen. refers to some of the constellations (e.g. *puella Cnosiaca* for Ariadne), the whole passage is allusive in that Juno does not explain the particular infidelity of Jupiter that each constellation represents (she comes closest to doing so with *vector Europae* in 9). To understand these allusions would have

---

7. For observations of the constellations in plays that begin in darkness, cf. Aesch. *Ag.* 4ff., Eur. *IA* 6ff.

8. Opelt 111 has attempted to solve the difficulty by suggesting that Apollo is represented by the constellation Lyra rather than by the sun, but this is improbable. First, Lyra could at best represent only an attribute of Apollo, not Apollo himself; in 16–18 Seneca clearly distinguishes between the deification of Ariadne and the catasterism of her attribute, viz. the garland. Second, the lyre of the constellation is in any case more often associated with Mercury (Arat. *Phaen.* 270f., 597, 674) and Orpheus (Manil. 1.325, 5.326) than with Apollo (v. *RE* 13.2.2495ff.).

[119]

Commentary: Act I

required mental agility on the part of the original audience, but not great erudition. Virtually all the references could be understood with a knowledge of Ovid's *Fasti* and *Metamorphoses*, for example; the only exception is the deification of Semele, which appears in mythological handbooks, e.g. Diodorus (see comm. on 16).

6–7. The Bear (Ursa Major) is the catasterized form of Callisto, a nymph loved by Jupiter; cf. particularly Ov. *Met.* 2.409ff., *Fasti* 2.155ff. It may be that Sen. made the Bear his starting point because Juno's complaints about it in *Met.* 2 were in his mind, or because as the most northerly constellation it is a natural beginning for starlists (e.g. Aratus).

alta parte ... sublime. Ennius describes Ursa Major as *sublimum agens / ... noctis iter* (*trag.* 190f. J = 179 R²). Ovid describes the Bears as positioned *summo ... caelo* (*Met.* 2.515, cf. Manil. 1.276). Compare *HF* 129 *signum celsi glaciale poli*, with comm.

glacialis poli. This phrase for the northern pole comes from Ov. *Met.* 2.173. For the association *Arctos–glacialis–polus* cf. *HF* 129, 1140 *glacialis Ursae*, *Pha.* 288; ps.-Sen. *HO* 89, 336; *TLL* 6.2000.27ff.

7 classes Argolicas agit. At least since Aratus (*Phaen.* 37–39) it was a commonplace that the Greeks found north by the Great Bear, but the Phoenicians by the Lesser Bear; cf. Ov. *Tr.* 4.3.1–2 *magna minorque ferae, quarum regis altera Graias, / altera Sidonias ... rates*, Sen. *Med.* 696f., Pease on Cic. *Nat. D.* 2.105 and 106.

Agere naves can be used of an admiral or helmsman guiding ships (Livy 9.38.2, Apul. *Flor.* p. 102 Oud.); for the metaphor of constellations "guiding" ships cf. Tib. 1.9.10 *ducunt instabiles sidera certa naves*, Ovid cited above, and the compressed phrase at Val. Fl. 5.46 *agentes noctibus Arctos*.

8f. Taurus is mentioned as the catasterized form of the bull that ferried Europa to Crete, cf. Ov. *Fasti* 5.605ff., *RE* 5.56.53ff.

hinc, qua ... dies. That is, in a more southerly part of the sky than the *glacialis polus* of the Bears. The widespread association of Taurus with spring in antiquity (cf. 951f. *verni ... Tauri*) was established in Babylonian times, when the sun was in Taurus at the vernal equinox. Vergil still speaks of Taurus as opening the year, *Georg.* 1.217f. *candidus auratis aperit cum cornibus annum / Taurus*, though in his time the

[120]

sun did not enter Taurus until late April.⁹ For Seneca the association has become purely notional (v. comm. on 10 *timendum . . . ponto*): he obscures its properly zodiacal nature by speaking of Taurus as a visible constellation, though it would scarcely be so at the time of the sun's entry into it;¹⁰ and he seems to think of the association as one of place rather than time.

I am inclined to prefer *recenti*, the reading of Σ and probably therefore of E before correction, to the *tepenti* of A. Because *tepens* or *tepidus* is a standard adjective for spring (Ov. *AA* 3.185, *Fasti* 1.664, 5.602; ps.-Ov. *Cons. Liv.* 102; ps.-Sen. *HO* 1576; cf. Cat. 46.1, Ov. *Met.* 1.107), the reading *tepenti* appears to be an example of the normalization frequently found in A (so Zwierlein 1969 254f.). In view of the vagueness of Seneca's astronomy here, there is perhaps no objection to taking *recenti vere* to mean "in early spring," for which one can compare V. *Georg.* 1.43 *vere novo* and the equally specific phrase *medio vere* in Sen. *Med.* 589 and *Oed.* 601. Alternatively, *recenti* may be a decorative adjective, "fresh," for which cf. Ov. *Met.* 2.27 *ver novum*.

laxatur dies. The primary reference is to the lengthening of the period of daylight. (Cf. *OLD* s.v. *laxo* 1a, "to make larger, widen, extend": the verb in this sense is very rarely used of time, but cf. *Med.* 420 *laxare tempus immitis fugae*.) Verbs of "opening, releasing" are used of the relaxing effect of warmth on the climate, earth, and so on, e.g. V. *Georg.* 4.51f. *ubi pulsam hiemem sol aureus egit / sub terras caelumque aestiva luce reclusit*, Hor. *Carm.* 1.4.1. *solvitur acris hiems* (with N-H ad loc.), Ov. *Her.* 2.123 *sive die laxatur humus*, Stat. *Silv.* 4.4.12f. *iam terras volucremque polum fuga veris aquosi / laxat*, and that must be an additional connotation of *laxatur* here; the range of meaning of *dies* includes not only "daylight" but also "sky, weather" (Germ. fr. 4.46, Phaedr. 4.17.5, Sen. *Thy.* 263), which suits this connotation of *laxatur*.

9 per undas vector. When a prepositional phrase with adverbial force modifies a noun, the noun is usually abstract, e.g. *profectio ex Sicilia, ante oculos trucidatio civium*. Personal nouns are normally modified only by prepositional phrases with adjectival force, e.g. *homo de plebe*. But the present phrase is not unnatural in view of the strong verbal content of

---

9. Cf. R. J. Getty, *TAPA* 79 (1948) 24ff.
10. Cf. E. L. Brown, *Numeri Vergiliani* (Brussels 1963) 24f. It might be objected that Taurus would be more clearly visible at an earlier period of spring, i.e. February (Varro dates the beginning of spring to February 7, *RR* 1.28) or March. But as a *visible* constellation Taurus would more naturally be associated, then as now, with winter.

Commentary: Act I

vector; for a parallel cf. Val. Fl. 6.113 *superas Hecates comitatus in auras*. The active sense of *vector* seen here (= *qui vehit*) appears three times in Sen. Trag. and three times in *HO*; it is rare before Sen., but as often there is an Ovidian precedent, at *Fasti* 1.433 *Sileni vector asellus*.

nitet. The verb may allude to the traditional brightness of the Bull, snow-white (Ov. *Met.* 2.852, *Anth. Lat.* 14.3ff.), with gilded horns (V. *Georg.* 1.217f.). Germ. *Arat.* 174f. speaks of *ignea Taurus / cornua fronte gerens et lucidus ore minaci*. Aldebaran (α Tauri), a very bright star, is usually pictured as one of the Bull's eyes, and El Nath (β Tauri) as the tip of a horn.

10–11. The Pleiades, daughters of Atlas (hence *Atlantides*), are included because three of their number—Maia, Electra, and Taygete—lay with Jupiter and bore him sons, respectively Mercury, Dardanus, and Lacedaemon. Another three of them could also be called *paelices*, two having lain with Poseidon and one with Mars (Ov. *Fasti* 4.172ff.).

timendum ... ponto. The morning *setting* of the Pleiades in November was associated with the onset of winter storms, cf. Hes. *Erga* 618ff.; Arat. *Phaen.* 1065f., 1085; Val. Fl. 2.357ff. Hence, more loosely, the constellation itself is spoken of as heralding storms, cf. Ov. *AA* 1.409 *tunc tristis hiems, tunc Pliades instant*, Stat. *Silv.* 1.3.95; at Val. Fl. 2.405, 4.269 *Plias* is virtually a synonym for "storm at sea."

ac ponto. Karsten's conjecture *ex ponto* (45) is untenable because *exserere* is one of the verbs with which *ex* is not repeated (*TLL* 5.2.1854.69ff.): on the other hand, the small alteration to *a ponto* would be supported by Luc. 5.598 *primus ab oceano caput exseris Atlanteo*, and is worth considering, as *ac ponto* is somewhat otiose in sense. Similar phrases with *exserere* include Ov. *Met.* 2.271f. *Neptunus aquis cum torvo bracchia vultu / exserere ausus erat*, 13.838 *nitidum caput exsere ponto*, *Fasti* 1.458 *patriis exserit ora vadis*; Sen. *Ag.* 484 *ora Corus Oceano exserens*, 554 *Neptunus imis exserens undis caput*.

There are grounds for caution, however. Senecan parallels for *exserere* of heavenly bodies (*HF* 594, *Pha.* 747) show that an indication of place whence is not de rigueur. The suggestion that the sea fears storms is paradoxical, but paradox is part of the lifeblood of Senecan tragedy. Also characteristically Senecan is the exploitation of the idea of sentient nature: for examples with *timere* cf. *Thy.* 119 *timentque veterem nobiles Argi sitim*, 594f. *hic ubi ingenti modo sub procella / Cyclades pontum timuere motae*. There is a touch of zeugma about the pairing of ships and sea, but that too is not un-Senecan (e.g. *Pha.* 1101f., 1178).

gregem ... exserunt. A slightly recherché expression. *Exserere* is not uncommon of heavenly bodies (*TLL* 5.2.1856.52ff.), but the object is usually *caput, vultus* et sim. (v. preceding comm.) or a word indicating light (e.g. Luc. 10.212 *ignes*, Avien. *Arat.* 1397 *lumina*).

11 passim vagantes. Such phrases are sometimes used by the poets with reference to the apparent movements of stars in general, rather than specifically to the planets: cf. 126f., *Thy.* 834 *vaga ... sidera*, *Pha.* 962 *cursus vagos ... astrorum*, ps.-Sen. *Oct.* 1, Lucr. 2.1031 *palantia sidera passim* with Bailey ad loc., V. *Aen.* 9.21. It is unclear whether the application of such a description to the Pleiades has any special significance.

Atlantides. The long Greek name rounds off the couplet, cf. 244 *Stymphalidas*, 246 *Thermodontiae*, with comm. on 244–46.

12. The inclusion of Orion in Juno's list is puzzling. It may be that he is mentioned as a quasi-illegitimate child of Jupiter: since he is followed in the catalogue by Perseus and other illegitimates, this is perhaps the most likely explanation. He was not born of a *paelex* but from the οὖρον of Jupiter and others (Ov. *Fasti* 5.531ff.: see Bömer on 5.493, 535). Seneca may also have in mind the tradition that at the moment of catasterism Orion was amorously pursuing the Pleiades and continued the pursuit in the heavens (cf. Athen. 11.490f., Schol. Apollon. 3.225, Schol. A ad Hom. *Il.* 18.486, Schol. Pind. *Nem.* 2.17): thus like the Garland of Ariadne (17–18) he is a further source of *probrum* in the heavens, by memorializing the passions of Jupiter's offspring. In fact, since the Pleiades have just been mentioned, it may have been their close association with Orion that first suggested his inclusion to Sen.[11] Juno adds further color to his inclusion with her complaint that he *terret deos*. Orion's aggressive stance was normally thought to be directed toward the Pleiades (in addition to Athen. et al. cited above, cf. Hes. *Erga* 618f. Πληιάδες σθένος ὄβριμον Ὠρίωνος / φεύγουσαι and Quint. Smyrn. 5.368): Juno indicates that it makes the gods themselves nervous (no doubt a further reason why she finds the heavens uninhabitable).

The drawn sword alluded to in *ferro minax hinc terret* (the reading of Σ, and so almost certainly of E[ac]) is a detail found in several Latin poets, cf. Cic. *Arat.* 369 *et dextra retinens non cassi luminis ensem*, Ov. *Met.* 8.207 *strictumque Orionis ensem*, and (influenced by the present passage) Stat. *Silv.* 1.1.45f. *magnus quanto mucrone minatur / noctibus hibernis et*

---

11. Alternatively Seneca may have thought of Orion because of his proximity to other constellations mentioned in the list, Gemini and Taurus, particularly if he consulted a globe or planisphere; cf. Opelt 113f.

Commentary: Act I

sidera terret Orion. The A reading *fera coma hinc exterret* refers to the brilliance of Orion's stars (Manil. 5.723 *mersit et ardentes Orion aureus ignes*). But the sword is clearly the more effective threat in the present context; in addition, A's version creates an awkward rhythm, and *coma* is not used of stars other than comets before Avienus (though *crinis* is so used at Germ. *Arat.* 624 *exilit Oceano tum toto crine Bootes*, cf. Pliny *NH* 2.92).[12]

13 aureus. Compare such phrases as *aureus sol, aurea sidera* in the poets; the adjective is used of specific constellations at Ov. *Fasti* 5.316 (Corona), Manil. 5.538 (Andromeda), 5.723 (Orion). There may also be an allusion to Perseus' unusual conception, cf. *aurigena* Ov. *Met.* 5.250, and *aureus* of the shower of gold Ov. *Met.* 6.113, ps.-Sen. *Oct.* 207.

14. The adjective *gemini* alludes to the name of the constellation into which Castor and Pollux were translated. It is often said that both heroes are sons of Jupiter by Leda (*Hymn. Hom.* 33.1ff., Theoc. 22.1, Ap. Rhod. 1.149ff.), as their title Dioscuri would imply, though another version (e.g. Pind. *Nem.* 10.80ff.) calls Castor the son of Leda's mortal husband Tyndareus, and at Hom. *Od.* 11.298ff. they are both sons of Tyndareus.

The Twins seem to attract appositional phrases, cf. 552 *geminum Tyndaridae genus*, Hor. *Carm.* 4.8.31 *clarum Tyndaridae sidus*, 1.3.2 *fratres Helenae, lucida sidera*; Germ. *Arat.* 541f. *sed caelo, semper nautis laetissima signa, / Ledaeos statuit iuvenis pater ipse deorum*; Ov. *Met.* 8.372 *at gemini, nondum caelestia sidera, fratres*. Seneca's interweaving of two noun-adjective phrases here (*abAB*) is typical of his style (cf. line 7 above, and v. 216-48 comm. ad fin.); contrast the common *enclosure* of an appositional phrase (*abBA* vel sim.) as in several of the phrases just cited, cf. V. *Ecl.* 2.3 *inter densos, umbrosa cacumina, fagos*, Ov. *AA* 1.125 *raptae, genialis praeda, puellae*.

clara. This adjective is applied to Gemini by Cicero (*Arat.* 331) and Horace (*Carm.* 4.8.31) before Seneca: the stars Castor and Pollux (re-

---

12. Since the Σ reading is satisfactory, there is no need for N. Heinsius' conjecture (209ff.) *ferro comanti hinc terret*, which is also open to the objection that *comans* is not used of heavenly bodies except comets before Avienus. W. H. Owen, *CJ* 64 (1969) 225f. ingeniously attempts to remove the problem of Orion by writing *fera coma illinc eminens terret deos*, the subject now being Perseus in 13. He understands *fera coma* here to refer to the Gorgon's head, held in Perseus' hand as part of this constellation (Manil. 1.359f., *RE* 19.1.993.25ff.). But the allusion seems very obscure, and it is a further objection that if both 12 and 13 are devoted to Perseus in this way, the content of 13 becomes a heavy anticlimax.

[124]

Commentary: Act I

spectively α and β Geminorum) are in fact among the twenty-five or so brightest stars in the sky.

15. The line alludes to the story that on the birth of Apollo and Diana the island of Delos, previously floating in the Aegean at the mercy of the winds, became fixed. Allusions to this story are frequent in the poets, v. 453 below; V. *Aen.* 3.75ff. with R. D. Williams ad loc.; Ov. *Met.* 6.188ff., 333f., 15.336f.; Prop. cited below; Sen. *Ag.* 384ff. with Tarrant ad loc. On the difficulties caused by the reference to Apollo here, see 6–18 comm.

mobilis . . . stetit. The contrast is borrowed from Prop. 4.6.27f. *cum Phoebus linquens stantem se vindice Delon / (non tulit iratos mobilis una Notos)*. In the Senecan version the verb takes on a slightly different sense, that is, "stopped and remained fixed," cf. Ov. *Met.* 5.132 *in obliquo missum stetit inguine ferrum*, Sen. *Tro.* 428.

16 Bacchi parens. For Semele among the gods cf. Pind. *Ol.* 2.25f. ζώει μὲν ἐν Ὀλυμπίοις ἀποθανοῖσα βρόμῳ / κεραυνοῦ τανυέθειρα Σεμέλα, Philostr. *Imag.* 1.14, Nonn. 8.408ff.; some versions say that after her death Bacchus rescued her from the underworld, and made her immortal under the name Thyone (Diod. Sic. 4.25.4, Apollod. 3.5.3).

nec . . . aut . . . adiere. *Nec* joins the clause as a whole with what precedes, and *aut* alone has the function of linking *Bacchus* with *Bacchi parens*, cf. ps.-V. *Aetna* 197f. *nec tamen est dubium penitus quid torqueat Aetnam, / aut quis mirandus tantae faber imperet arti*, TLL 2.1567.84ff. As *aut* is not exclusive here, the two singular subjects have a cumulative effect and may be followed by a plural verb (cf. H-S 434).

17 ne . . . vacet. For this ironically suggested motive cf. V. *Aen.* 8.205f. *ne quid inausum / aut intractatum scelerisve dolive fuisset*, Ov. *Met.* 1.151 *neve foret terris securior arduus aether*, Sen. *Phoen.* 271 *ne parum sceleris foret*, Tarrant on Sen. *Ag.* 184f. The verb *vacare* often figures in rhetorical points in Sen., e.g. *Pha.* 174, *Phoen.* 121f. *dira ne sedes vacet, / monstrum repone maius*, *HF* 1207f.

18. The line refers to Ariadne's *corona*, set in the heavens by Bacchus as a memorial of his love for her. The catasterism of the crown is a popular theme in Hellenistic-Roman literature, e.g. Arat. *Phaen.* 71ff., Ap. Rhod. 3.1002ff., Ov. *Fasti* 3.513ff., *Met.* 8.177ff., cf. *RE* 2.805.46ff. Ovid in the passages cited describes the *corona* as originally a golden

Commentary: Act I

crown inlaid with gems (cf. Pherecydes *FGrH* 3 F148 στέφανον . . . χρυσοῦν). Other writers, however, agree with Sen. in describing it as a garland of flowers (*serta*): cf. Bacchyl. 16.113ff. ἀμεμφέα πλόκον . . . ῥόδοις ἐρεμνόν (for the identity of this garland with Ariadne's cf. Preller-Robert 1.682 fn. 2), Athen. 15.684f., Prop. 3.20.18 *sidereae torta corona deae*. On the Farnese globe, the constellation is represented as a laurel garland with a ribbon.

puellae . . . Cnosiacae. *Puella* conveys not only "girl" but also "mistress" here, cf. its use in 466 of Omphale; the word is common in lyric and elegy, but unusual in epic and in Sen. Trag., cf. Axelson 58. Though Ariadne is usually described as Bacchus' wife from Hesiod on (*Theog.* 947f.), Juno refuses to recognize her as more than a mistress. Ariadne is often identified allusively, perhaps because of the metrical difficulties presented by her name: e.g. *Cnosia* Prop. 1.3.2, [Tib.] 3.6.39; *Cnosias* Ov. *AA* 1.556; *Cnosis* ibid. 1.527, 3.158; *Cressa Am.* 1.7.16; *Minois* Cat. 64.247, *Aetna* 22. For the spelling of *Cnosiacus* with initial *c* rather than *g*, cf. Housman *CQ* 22 (1928) 6–7 = 1972 1142–43.

19ff. Juno's first reference to Hercules, in 19^b–21^a, is an allusive one, and her most pressing concern (H.'s imminent deification along with Alcmene, as she supposes) is mentioned in a subordinate clause rather than in expository statement. All this is in keeping with the "thinking aloud" character of the monologue; to Juno the deification is a familiar if unwelcome prospect, and she is more concerned here with her own reaction to it.

Line 19 is preserved in the hypermetrical form *sed vetera sero querimur; una me dira ac fera* (so E: A omits everything from *una* in 19^b to *fecit* in 21^a).[13] Suspicion has naturally centered on *vetera sero*; omission of either word will restore meter. I prefer to write *sed sero querimur* (for *serŏ* cf. *Thy.* 964) as Leo did in 1876, though not in his edition. This phrase will imply not "I should have complained earlier" (as though earlier complaints would have done any good) but rather "given the situation, complaints are pointless"; cf. Sen. *Ben.* 1.1.1 *sequitur enim, ut male collocata* (sc. *beneficia*) *male debeantur; de quibus non redditis <u>sero querimur</u>; ista enim perierunt, cum darentur*, *Brev. Vit.* 6.2. The gist of Juno's thinking in 19–29 will then be as follows: "But there is no point in complaints; all this is a fait accompli, and the deification of Alcmene

---

13. There is no justification for regarding the clause from *una* to *fecit* as an E interpolation, despite the fact that its deletion would remove the metrical problems in both 19 and 20. Such an interpolation would be quite uncharacteristic of E, whereas omissions are not infrequent in A.

and Hercules will soon be another. Nevertheless (that is, although these things are settled, and complaints useless) I shall not abandon my resentment and opposition." To some extent one may compare Medea's prologue speech, 26f. *querelas verbaque in cassum sero? / non ibo in hostes?* though that is a more direct contrast between complaints and action. On this interpretation the rhetorical function of the clause from *una* to *fecit* will be to illustrate the uselessness of complaints, by pointing out that a single city has been able to flout Juno so often.

If we read *sed vetera querimur* with many editors, that will imply a contrast between old indignities and new; compare the contrast in Hecuba's prologue speech between *vetus malum* and *luctus recentes* (*Tro.* 42f.). The new indignity is not of course H.'s birth, as one might at first suppose from 19^b-21^a—surely a *vetus malum* by now—but his imminent deification along with Alcmene. The sentence from 19^b to 21^a will now illustrate the word *vetera*. But the thought does not proceed so smoothly with this reading, for the case of H. is awkwardly divided between old indignities (his birth) and new (his deification).[14]

The phrase *dira ac fera* alludes to the Theban tradition of horrendous deeds, involving inter alios Oedipus and his sons, the Danaids, and the fates of Dirce and Pentheus (cf. comm. on 20 *nuribus impiis*, and Stat. *Theb.* 1.4 *gentis . . . primordia dirae*, sc. *Thebanae*).

querimur . . . me. Rapid changes are sometimes found between plural and singular in first-person verbs, pronouns, and adjectives referring to one person, e.g. *nostra—mea* 34–35, *inveni—nos—me* 114–16; cf. H-S 20, Bömer on Ov. *Met.* 1.772. (Euripides allows even more blatant juxtapositions, e.g. *Her.* 858 μαρτυρόμεσθα δρῶσα; further examples collected by A. Katsouris in *RhM* 120 [1977] 228f.)[15]

---

14. More radically, Richter 1894 17f. postulated a lacuna after *querimur*, to be filled *exempli gratia* thus: *sed vetera sero querimur.* <*haec etiam nova / inulta patimur?*> *una me dira ac fera* e.q.s. This would solve the metrical difficulty in line 19, but in my view there is no room for any supplement between the clause ending *querimur* and that beginning *una*, because the latter amplifies and illustrates the former, whatever reading is adopted there. The difficulties of Richter's supplement are evident: it makes Hercules' birth an illustration of *haec nova*, but it is surely ancient history.

15. In Sen. the most common form of first-person plural for singular is the use of *noster* for *meus*: *HF* has twenty-six such usages as against thirty of *meus* itself and only six of *noster* with a plural sense. In the pronoun the usage is much less common: five examples of *nos = ego* as against fifty-four of *ego* and one of *nos* as a genuine plural. It is also relatively uncommon in first-person verbs: eight certain examples (19, 354, 411, 1142, 1143, 1232, 1302, 1317) and two doubtful instances (446, 523, where Amphitryon may be speaking of the family rather than himself, cf. 306).

Commentary: Act I

20. The line as transmitted in E, *Thebana tellus nuribus sparsa impiis*, is unmetrical.[16] The rearrangement found in KQ, etc., *Thebana nuribus sparsa tellus impiis*, creates an awkward word order, in which the referent of *dira ac fera*, that is, *tellus*, is postponed until after a further adjective *and* a participial phrase. This order is partially paralleled at 997f. *ut Cyclopia / eversa manibus saxa nostris concidant*, but the clumsiness of the present instance is evident. Furthermore, it violates the modified Porson's law observed in Senecan trimeters, according to which a final cretic word beginning with a vowel is normally preceded either by elision (as in 62 *devicti intuens*) or a monosyllable (as in 406 *nos improba*); Strzelecki finds only twelve exceptions in the genuine tragedies, of which two are excused by proper names (p. 18 fn. 2, 19 fn. 1). Again, when Sen. permits a succession of word breaks after the first elements of feet 2, 3, 4, and 5 (sometimes also foot 1), there are usually word breaks at other points, or a sense-pause at mid-line (as e.g. 641, 1333), to interrupt the monotonous rhythm. The only contrary examples I have noticed in *HF* are 698, 715, and again 998.

I suggest *Thebana tellus nuribus aspersa impiis*, which creates the familiar metrical pattern of word break with elision in the fifth foot. *Aspersa* will mean the same as *sparsa*, that Jupiter's women are scattered throughout Thebes, cf. Mela 1.91 *is [sinus] parvis urbibus aspersa est*, Ov. *Pont.* 1.4.1 *iam mihi deterior canis aspergitur aetas*, Pliny *NH* 37.155 *[gemma] quae . . . aureis guttis aspersa sit*. It may also carry some of its familiar moral sense, "sullied": an instance where this moral sense is present together with a physical sense (though not that seen here) is *Tro.* 255f. *quid caede dira nobiles clari ducis / aspergis umbras?* Corruption of *aspersa* to *sparsa* would not be difficult, particularly if it was written *asparsa* as sometimes happens in MSS (for the spelling *aspargo*, etc., v. *TLL* 2.818.40ff.). See Addenda for Axelson's conjecture.

nuribus . . . impiis. Juno is thinking particularly of the Theban *paelices* of Jupiter, who include (besides Alcmene) Bacchus' mother Semele, and Antiope, mother of Amphion and Zethus. They are called *impiae* as representing an insult to Juno's godhead. The adjective, however, indicates that she also has other groups of women in mind: the daughters of Cadmus, who killed Pentheus (*impiae Cadmeides* 758), and

---

16. Bücheler's rearrangement *Thebana tellus sparsa nuribus impiis*, accepted by most modern editors, is inadmissible as Seneca avoids an iambic fifth foot in trimeters; this rule is broken only five times in the genuine tragedies, and then only to accommodate a final quadrisyllabic word (*Tro.* 195, 1080, *Med.* 512, 709, *Thy.* 115; cf. ps.-Sen. *HO* 804). Baehrens' suggestion *Thebana tellus nuribus a! sparsa impiis* has rightly won little acceptance: v. *TAPA* 111 (1981) 66. Bücheler's conjecture was published in Leo's app. crit.; Baehrens' in his *Miscellanea Critica* (1878) 34 n. 1.

[*128*]

Commentary: Act I

the Danaids, who killed their husbands (*cruentae regis Aegypti nurus* 498). Seneca uses *nurūs* here for "young women" without distinction as to whether they are married (as Alcmene) or not (as Semele): Ovid had already used the word in this general sense, cf. *Met.* 3.529 *matresque nurusque*, Bömer on *Met.* 2.366.

21 quotiens novercam fecit. Vergil and Ovid both pointedly refer to Juno as Hercules' *noverca* (*Aen.* 8.288; *Met.* 9.15, 135, 181; *Her.* 9.8); this appealed to Sen. (cf. 112, 908, 1018, 1201, 1236), who extends the term to apply also to Juno vis-à-vis Jupiter's other illegitimate children; v. *Oed.* 418, 487 (Bacchus), *Ag.* 809 with Tarrant's note.

The conventional image of the stepmother is already present in Hesiod (*Erga* 825); for Roman examples see Otto s.v. *noverca*. Quintilian complains about *saeviores tragicis novercas* (*Inst.* 2.10.4).

21f. The suggestion that Alcmene will be elevated to the gods is not inspired by any known mythological account (though she was the object of a minor cult, cf. *RE* 1.1574.62ff.), but is simply a supposition by Juno based on Jupiter's treatment of the other *paelices* mentioned earlier. The most common mythological version speaks of Alcmene as translated after death to the Elysian Fields as the wife of Rhadamanthus (*RE* ibid. 51ff.).

escendat[17] or *ascendat*? In defense of *ascendat*, Carlsson (1925 37) points out that *ascendere* is a *vox propria* for ascent to heaven (cf. *TLL* 2.756.5ff.), and that Sen. uses the verb absolutely in this sense at *Ep.* 73.15, *Apocol.* 1.3. *Escendere* cannot be excluded from contexts of ascent to heaven, however, and is so used absolutely by Sen. at *Prov.* 5.11 (of Phaethon about to scale the heavens) *ille generosus adulescens "placet" inquit "via: escendo."* (Cf. ibid. 10 *vide quam alte escendere debeat virtus.*) As the rarer *escendere* is more likely to have been displaced by *ascendere* than vice versa, and it can carry the required meaning, *escendat* is the preferable reading.

23 astra. The word is used as a virtual synonym for *caelum* as at 195, *Pha.* 1008 and often; with reference to deification, cf. Prop. 3.18.74 *Caesar ab humana venit in astra via*. Seneca may also allude to specific stars associated with Hercules; the constellation known to the Greeks as Engonasin was sometimes identified in antiquity as Hercules, the name

---

17. The initial *e* of E¹ is clearly visible under ultraviolet light. The faint but clear *x* above it, also E¹, has not previously been reported. This reading explains M's *extendat*.

[*129*]

Commentary: Act I

by which it is known today (cf. Eratosth. *Catast.* 4, Schol. Arat. 74, Cook *Zeus* 3.1.483–92).

promissa. Compare Hercules' words at 959: *astra promittit pater*. At the time of H.'s birth, Zeus persuaded Hera to agree that he would receive the gift of immortality once he had performed the labors; this version is found in Diodorus (2.9.5). According to Pindar, Tiresias prophesied to Alcmene that immortality would follow the labors (*Nem.* 1.69ff., followed by Theoc. 24.79ff.). The same prophecy was made to H. himself by the Pythia, when she ordered him to serve Eurystheus (Diod. 4.10.7, Apollod. 2.4.12).

24–26. The lengthening of the night on which H. was conceived is a familiar theme, alluded to again at 1159 *nox longior quam nostra*. Versions vary between a night of twice and three times the normal length. Seneca's phrase *mundus impendit diem* is constructed primarily for point, and should not be pressed too closely for a precise meaning. It is probably to be understood of a double night, the version Sen. follows elsewhere (*Ag.* 815, *Brev. Vit.* 16.5; for this interpretation cf. also the phrasing of Hyg. *Fab.* 29 *[Iuppiter] tam libens cum ea concubuit ut unum diem usurparet, duas noctes congeminaret*, also ps.-Sen. *HO* 1697f. *nocte commissa dies / quievit unus*, 1865f. *lux una periit noctesque duas / contulit Eos*), but it would clearly not be inappropriate of a triple night.[18]

ortus. The accusative is clearly preferable on stylistic grounds to the ablative. The word has a general sense, best rendered here "creation, origin." When it is accusative the plural is normal in poetry (see Mass, *ALL* 12.487, 494; Landgraff, *ALL* 14.73); in Sen. Trag. the word is found in the singular only in the ablative, or when coupled with *occasus*, which is regularly singular in Sen. Trag.

25 Eoo. *Ĕous* occurs only here in Sen. Trag.: *Ēous* five times. Cf. Servius ad *Aen.* 2.417 *notandum sane, quod, cum "Eous" "e" naturaliter longum habeat, metri necessitate correptum est propter sequentem vocalem. rarum autem est*, etc. (cf. also ad *Aen.* 11.4). The two forms correspond to ἑῷος and ἠῷος.

26. The detail that the Sun actually received orders to delay his rising is relatively rare, but cf. Sen. *Ag.* 816ff., Lucian *Dial. D.* 10 passim (Helios does not approve of the orders), Schol. Townl. in Hom. *Il.* 14.324.

---

18. For other versions supporting a double night cf. Prop. 2.22.25f., Ov. *Am.* 1.13.45, *Tr.* 2.402; Stat. *Silv.* 4.6.17, *Theb.* 10.77f. (with R. D. Williams ad loc.); ps.-Sen. *HO* 147; for a triple night see citations in *RE* Suppl. 3.1016.25ff.

27 sic abibunt. *Sic abire* means "pass off just like that," viz. without further action being taken (cf. 1186 *tacita sic abeant mala*); the phrase has a colloquial sound. Elsewhere the subject of the verb is a pronoun, Ter. *An.* 175; Cic. *Att.* 14.1 *non posse istaec sic abire, Fin.* 5.3.7; Cat. 14.16 *non non hoc tibi, salse, sic abibit.* The phrase οὕτως ἄπει is used somewhat similarly (= *impune abibis*) at Eur. *Alc.* 680, but with a personal subject. For *sic* and οὕτως in this sense cf. N-H on Hor. *Carm.* 2.11.14.

27–29 vivaces aget e.q.s. Passions such as *dolor, furor, ira* are frequently personified in Senecan tragedy (e.g. *HF* 99, *Tro.* 282f., *Phoen.* 299ff., *Med.* 540ff., 671, *Pha.* 268, 366, 824, *Thy.* 552ff.). Speakers often objectify their passions, speaking of them as independent agencies, cf. *HF* 75ff. with comm., *Med.* 406f. *numquam meus cessabit in poenas furor / crescetque semper,* 951ff., *Pha.* 99ff., 178f., 184, *Thy.* 496, 942ff. The combination of intense emotion with an objective style of self-analysis is characteristic of Senecan drama; cf. Tarrant on *Ag.* 132ff.

28 iras. Normally plural in the accusative in Sen. Trag., as in Vergil, whereas Ovid uses the singular accusative much more than the plural.

28ᵇ–29. There are three similarities here to the speech of the angry Juno at the beginning of V. *Aen.* 1: for the metaphor of her warfare with her enemies cf. *una cum gente tot annos / bella gero* (47f.); for *aeterna* cf. *Iuno aeternum servans sub pectore vulnus* (36: on *aeternus* in contexts of hatred and revenge see 362 comm.); for *saevus dolor* cf. the introductory passage *necdum etiam causae irarum saevique dolores / exciderant animo* (25f.).

30–32 quidquid . . . . Seneca uses indefinite clauses with very similar phrasing elsewhere, again in allusion to sinister resources, cf. *Med.* 681f., 691 *et vile telum est, ima quod tellus creat,* 714 *quodcumque tellus vere nidifico creat, Oed.* 591f., and compare *HO* 14f., 28f. More generally v. N-H on Hor. *Carm.* 2.13.9 *quidquid usquam concipitur nefas.*

tellus . . . pontus . . . aer. Hercules is traditionally described as master of land and sea: Pind. *Nem.* 1.62f. ὅσους μὲν ἐν χέρσῳ κτανών, / ὅσους δὲ πόντῳ θῆρας ἀϊδροδίκας, Eur. *Her.* 851f., Ov. *Her.* 9.15 *se tibi pax terrae, tibi se tuta aequora debent,* Sen. *Med.* 640. Most of the monsters defeated by H. were in fact terrestrial, Antaeus and the Giants being literally children of Earth. Sea monsters H. encountered include the one sent by Neptune against Troy to punish Laomedon, and those subdued on H.'s voyage to the far west.[19] *Aer* alludes to the Stymphalian Birds,

---

19. For the latter cf. Pind. *Nem.* 3.23 δάμασε δὲ θῆρας ἐν πελάγεσιν; they are perhaps to be identified with Triton, with whom Hercules is often shown fighting in works of art, cf. *RE* 7A. 257ff.

Commentary: Act I

cf. 1111f. Seneca's enumeration of the three regions is perhaps suggested particularly by Ov. *Met.* 8.830 *quod pontus, quod terra, quod educat aer*, cf. *Pont.* 1.10.9. Such enumerations of earth, sea, and sky naturally carry the suggestion of "everywhere," for example Lucr. 5.592, V. *Aen.* 1.280, 6.724, Sen. *Thy.* 833f.; thus these lines introduce the theme of the universal scope of H.'s conquests, which constantly recurs throughout the play.

32. A spectacular line consisting purely of adjectives in asyndeton, for which cf. *Pha.* 939 *longinqua clausa abstrusa diversa invia*, *Phoen.* 223. For similar asyndetic lists of adjectives or nouns cf. e.g. Hom. *Od.* 15.406 εὔβοτος εὔμηλος οἰνοπληθὴς πολύπυρος, Eur. fr. 866 N ἥδε μοι τροφὸς / μήτηρ ἀδελφὴ δμωῖς ἄγκυρα στέγη, Men. fr. 213.4f. Κ ἄρχων στρατηγὸς ἡγεμὼν δήμου πάλιν / σύμβουλος, Ter. *Ad.* 866, Hor. *Ars P.* 121. The device is popular in Republican tragedy, cf. Pacuv. 53, 301, 336 R^2, Acc. 348, 415, 468, 550, 595 R^2. For a collection of asyndeta in Senecan drama see Canter 169ff.

Seneca employs two unusual adjectives in constructing the line: *terribilis* does not recur in the tragedies, *pestilens* only once. The non-dactylic word *pestilens* is in fact rare in poetry generally, but *terribilis* is common enough outside Sen.

atrox. In view of Sen.'s avoidance of iambic fifth feet (cf. comm. on 20), the quantity of the first syllable must be long, as at *Tro.* 289, *Thy.* 745. In earlier writers it is short where its quantity can be discerned, cf. *TLL* s.v.

33ff. The subject of *superat* and so on is Hercules, although he has not yet been named except as son of Alcmene in 23. For the significant omission cf. 275, 312, 807f., 831; H. is so prominent in the mind of Juno, as of other characters, that he does not need to be named. *Superat* perhaps conveys both "survives" and "is victorious, has the upper hand" (L-S s.v. I B 3 and I B 1, respectively). The point that Juno's persecutions are counterproductive comes from Ovid, who uses it in connection with both H. (*Her.* 9.11f. *illa premendo / sustulit*) and Callisto (*Met.* 2.519 *quae prosum sola nocendo*). For the phrasing of *superat et crescit malis* cf. *Med.* 910 *crevit ingenium malis*, *Pha.* 101 *alitur et crescit malum*.

36f. The E and A traditions diverge completely between the caesura of 36 and the end of 37: see app. crit. (In the second half of 36 the original text of E itself has been erased, but may be recovered from Σ.) Almost all editors since Commelinus have rightly preferred the E read-

Commentary: Act I

ing in general, but there is doubt about *rēponens* in 37. This scansion is sometimes defended by analogy with the occasional lengthening of the initial syllable of *recido* and *reduco* in the poets; however, this usage seems to be limited to these verbs, to *religio, reliquus, reliquiae,* and to the perfects *rettuli reppuli repperi.* It is best therefore to correct to *deponens* with M and some recc. Line 37 recalls Vergil's *cum sol referetque diem condetque relatum* (*Georg.* 1.458): for *reducere diem* cf. ibid. 1.249, Sen. *Ep* 93.9. A's version is an amalgam of *Oed.* 121f., *Pha.* 571 (with Tethys written *thetis* as often in A manuscripts) and *HO* 488.

37f. The tradition of two tribes of Aethiopians, at the sun's rising and setting, goes back to Hom. *Od.* 1.23f., cf. *RE* 1.1095ff., F. Snowden, *Blacks in Antiquity* (Cambridge, Mass. 1970) 102ff. Dark-skinned races were thought to have their faces burned by the closeness of the sun, as is indicated by the derivation of αἰθίοψ from αἴθω, ὤψ; cf. Serv. on V. *Aen.* 4.481 *dicta Aethiopia a colore populorum, quos solis vicinitas torret,* Snowden 258 n. 6, N-H on Hor. *Carm.* 1.22.21f. *nimium propinqui / Solis.* For the torch of the Sun (an appropriate image in this context) cf. Jocelyn on Enn. *trag.* 243 *candentem in caelo sublimat facem,* Lucr. 5.401f.

"From the Sun's rising to his setting" is a natural synonym for "everywhere" (e.g. 871, *Tro.* 382f., Cic. *Nat. D.* 2.66.164, Ov. *Met.* 5.445, Sen. *Ep.* 92.32). Similar phrases are often used in this play in connection with Hercules, indicating the extent of his journeys and fame, cf. 442f. *postque pacatum manu / quodcumque Titan ortus et labens videt,* 882f. *pax est Herculea manu / Auroram inter et Hesperum,* 1060ff., 1139ff., 1330, Owen 305f. See comm. on 30–32 *tellus . . . pontus . . . aer.*

39 indomita virtus colitur. The phrase may suggest that Hercules is not only spoken of as a god (*narratur* below) but worshipped as one. *Colitur* could connote worship, although it need mean no more than "is honored." *Virtus* is par excellence the quality that justifies and is associated with deification, cf. V. *Aen.* 9.641f.; ps.-Sen. *HO* 1942f., 1971; Sil. 3.594f.; *CIL* 7.45 *Virtuti et n(umini) Aug(usti) . . . reddidit C. Severius Emeritus.* The adjective *indomitus* (used again of H. at 1079) recalls *invictus,* a cult title of H. in Rome (Bömer on Ov. *Met.* 3.56, *Fasti* 1.562) as of other gods (*TLL* 7.2.187.11ff.). According to Diodorus, H. began to accept divine honors, which he had previously refused, at the end of the tenth labor (4.24); the Ara Maxima was thought to have been consecrated to him during his lifetime (cf. Gransden on V. *Aen.* 8.269–72).

41f. Seneca here reworks—with a nice touch of humor in *labor*—the pointed contrast made by Ovid's Hercules at *Met.* 9.198f. *defessa iubendo*

[*133*]

Commentary: Act I

est / *saeua Iouis coniunx, ego sum indefessus agendo*. Ovid uses the weary Juno again at *AA* 2.217 *fatigata praebendo monstra nouerca*. Ovid's picture of Juno herself ordering each of the labors (again at *Met.* 9.15 *iussa nouercae*) is a new one;[20] Sen.'s borrowing of it leads to some ambiguity about whether she or Eurystheus was H.'s taskmaster (contrast 41f. with 43).

43f. The rhetorical question is equivalent to a negative statement: "No matter what cruel rights the tyrant had over Hercules, they could not harm him." *Iura* is no doubt the original reading of the E-branch manuscripts, though unaltered only in M. The A reading *iussa* involves a repetition of this word from 41 with no clear rhetorical purpose; repetition of this kind is not uncommon in many classical writers (cf. 706ff. *locus . . . loca . . . locus*, V. *Aen.* 8.378ff. *labores . . . laborem* with Austin on 2.505, Ov. *Met.* 3.55ff. *corpora . . . corporis . . . corpora*), but it would be particularly awkward here, as the *iussa* would be ascribed both to Juno and to Eurystheus.

45 timuit. Juno is not suggesting cowardice on Hercules' part, but a natural reaction to fearful sights, cf. 454 with comm., 793, 1147, *HO* 291f. *Herculis . . . timentis* (i.e. when facing monsters) and see comm. on 502 *terres*. Attempts to defend H.'s character by removing *timuit* (*domuit* Lipsius, *triuit* Herrmann) are therefore unnecessary.

46 leone et hydra. That is, the pelt of the Nemean Lion (cf. 465, ps.-Ov. *Hal.* 71 *caeso decorantur terga leone*) and the Hydra's poison. The synecdoche perhaps hints that the qualities of these monsters are still alive (cf. comm. on 939–52).

nec satis terrae patent. Hercules echoes the phrase with unconscious irony 605f. *non satis terrae patent* / *Iunonis odio*. Seneca quotes the Ovidian phrase *qua terra patet* (*Met.* 1.241) at *QNat.* 4A *praef.* 19: for *satis patere*, cf. *Tranq.* 9.1, *Ben.* 6.31.3. The transition here is similar to that at ps.-V. *Aetna* 85 *nec tu, terra, satis: speculantur numina diuum*, cf. also Ov. *Met.* 1.151.

47–57. Juno's allusive account of the catabasis suggests that Hercules broke open a way into (or out of) the underworld (*effregit, rupto*), thus allowing the entry of daylight (50, 56) and permitting the shades to re-

---

20. Elsewhere she is occasionally said to have been responsible for the fact that Hercules undertook the labors, but only in a vague and general sense (Eur. *Her.* 20f., V. *Aen.* 8.291ff.). She is also sometimes alleged to have played a part in one or two specific labors, e.g. Hes. *Theog.* 314f., cf. *RE* Suppl. 3.1098.67ff.

[*134*]

Commentary: Act I

turn to the upper world (49, 55). These details are not reflected in Theseus' narrative of the catabasis, but one may compare the language at 279ff., 290ff., 566ff., 613 *ostendi inferos*, *Tro.* 723f., *Med.* 638, and Horace's phrase *perrupit Acheronta Herculeus labor* (*Carm.* 1.3.36). The idea of the underworld being opened to view by some cataclysm is seen in Hom. *Il.* 20.61ff., imitated in Vergil's splendid simile *Aen.* 8.243ff.: v. also Ov. *Met.* 2.260f., 5.356ff., *Fasti* 4.449f. At what stage this idea became associated with H.'s catabasis is unclear, but an association with H., albeit an oblique one, is present in the Vergilian passage. That the rending of the earth allows the ascent of spirits is a familiar motif from Roman necromancy, cf. Tib. 1.2.45f., Ov. *Met.* 7.205f., *Rem. Am.* 252f., Sen. *Oed.* 572f., Luc. 6.728f. Permitting the return of the dead is of course in keeping with H.'s religious role as savior from death, as discussed in the Introduction. But Juno's language, like that of Horace, presents H. as a violator of natural boundaries.

47 limen. Cf. *perfracto limine Ditis* of the same event, *Tro.* 723. The door of the underworld is a familiar image, cf. Hes. *Theog.* 773, Lucr. 6.762, V. *Aen.* 6.127 *patet atri ianua Ditis*, Ov. *Met.* 1.662 *praeclusaque ianua Leti*, 4.450, 453, v. N-H on Hor. *Carm.* 1.24.17. To souls newly entering the underworld, the door is ever-open, but closed to any return. Hercules' violence contrasts with Aeneas' peaceful emergence through one of the *Somni portae*, V. *Aen.* 6.893ff.

inferni Iovis. Such periphrases for Hades-Dis appear in both Greek and Latin, cf. Hom. *Il.* 9.457 Ζεὺς καταχθόνιος, Hes. *Erga* 465 Διὶ χθονίῳ, Aesch. *Ag.* 1386f. al., V. *Aen.* 4.638 *Iovi Stygio*, Ov. *Fasti* 5.448, and descriptions of Proserpina as *Iuno inferna* (V. *Aen.* 6.138) and *I. Averna* (Ov. *Met.* 14.114); see further Tarrant on *Ag.* 1. Elsewhere Sen. writes *diro Iovi*, *HF* 608. Juno emphasizes the parallel between Dis and Jove, as in 53, in order to stress Hercules' hubris.

48 opima. Strictly speaking, the term *spolia opima* refers to the Roman custom whereby a victorious general stripped arms from an enemy ruler he had personally killed, v. Livy 1.10. It is used in a heroic Greek context, and in a much more general sense, by Accius *trag.* 145f. R^2 *sed ita Achilli armis inclutis vesci studet / ut cuncta opima levia iam prae illis putet*. In Seneca the word retains the connotation that Hercules has defeated a hostile *rex* and carried off his chief means of defense, that is, Cerberus. For the substantival use of *opima* in verse, in addition to the Accian example, there is an Ovidian precedent, fr. 3 Owen *Larte ferox caeso Cossus opima tulit*.

[135]

Commentary: Act I

ad superos. From the viewpoint of the underworld, *superi* indicates this world and its inhabitants, cf. 318, 568, 583; from the viewpoint of the earth, the word has its more usual meaning of heaven and its occupants, e.g. 17, 74, 423, 898.

50 vidi ipsa vidi. Immediate repetition of *vidi* conveys emotional emphasis, as at *Tro.* 170 *vidi ipse vidi*, *Ag.* 656, *HO* 207. (See 254–57 comm.) The change of verse-accent between the two words creates a variation within the repetition, as at 75 *perge ira perge*; cf. V. *Aen.* 2.306 *sternit agros, sternit sata laeta*, 8.71 *Nymphae, Laurentes Nymphae*, N. Herescu *Poésie latine* (Paris 1960) 197ff.

51f. patri / fraterna. Seneca creates several effective juxtapositions with words indicating relationship, cf. *Tro.* 1074 *paterna puero bella monstrabat senex*, *Ag.* 35f. *avo parentem (pro nefas!), patri virum, / natis nepotes miscui*, Canter 152f. This juxtaposition is neatly pointed by the line end, as at 251f. *felix scelus / virtus vocatur*. The effect is increased by the unusual sense-pause. Comparable examples of a strong sense-pause before the caesura underlining a contrast are 277f. *inveniet viam / aut faciet*, 408f. *quaeritur belli exitus, / non causa*.

52–54. Juno's sarcastic suggestions extrapolate from what Hercules has already done. He has conquered Dis: why not drag him off in fetters and take possession of his kingdom? He has broken a gap through the barrier between the lower and upper worlds: why not completely unroof the underworld? (For this general sense of *Styx* cf. 104, *Tro.* 520, *Oed.* 396.) Lines 49 (rightly placed by Leo after 54, see ad loc.) and 55f. then justify the latter suggestion by elaborating on the point (made only briefly before, *effregit . . . limen* 47, *nocte discussa* 50) that he has already broken his way through the *claustra profundi*.

Some may believe that *retegit Styga* does not convey clearly the idea of a complete unroofing, as opposed to what H. has done so far; but the context of sarcastic exaggeration surely helps to clarify the meaning. For *retegere* with this sense cf. *QNat.* 6.32.4 *securus aspiciet ruptis compagibus dehiscens solum, illa licet inferorum regna retegantur*, which refers to a cataclysmic rending of the earth.

If emendation is thought necessary, the most attractive suggestion is Baden's *potitur? en retegit Styga*.[21] Combining this with Leo's later transposition of 49, one might punctuate as follows:

---

21. Made in 1798, according to Pierrot (cf. comm. on 49 *perît*); abandoned in Baden's edition of 1821, but adopted by Herrmann and Viansino.

Commentary: Act I

> Ereboque capto potitur? en retegit Styga;
> parum est reverti, foedus umbrarum perît:
> patefacta ab imis manibus retro via est e.q.s.[22]

Attempts to alter *retegit* alone have met with little success;[23] and the verb in this context is a reminiscence of Ov. *Met.* 5.356f. *rex pavet ipse silentum / ne pateat latoque solum retegatur hiatu*, which speaks for its authenticity.[24]

52f. vinctum et oppressum trahit . . . catenis. That is, as he treated Cerberus, cf. 807–21, Ov. *Met.* 7.412f. *nexis adamante catenis / Cerberon abstraxit. Vinctum* is clearly the superior reading: *victus* has just been used of Dis in line 48.

53 ipsum . . . paria sortitum Iovi. The phrase hints that it is a short step from overcoming Jove's equal to attacking Jove himself, cf. 64f. On the casting of lots for the three realms of the sky, sea, and underworld, the *locus classicus* is Hom. *Il.* 15.187ff., where Poseidon in a similar phrase describes himself as ἰσόμορον καὶ ὁμῇ πεπρωμένον αἴσῃ with Zeus. For *sortitus* in this context cf. [Tib.] 3.5.22, Ov. *Met.* 8.596, also *sors* at *HF* 609.

49. Leo's relocation of this line after 54 is justified. The line is out of place between 48 and 50f., as the chief subject of those lines is Hercules' *spolia*: but it forms an excellent introduction to lines 55–57, which

---

22. Alternatively one might consider *Ereboque capto potitur? en retegit Styga — / parum est reverti. foedus umbrarum perît: / patefacta* e.q.s. But this produces an awkward and broken sequence of thought: *parum est* plus infinitive is more naturally linked with a following clause than a preceding one, as e.g. Ov. *Met.* 6.3 *laudare parum est, laudemur et ipsae*, *Her.* 3.25, *Pont.* 3.1.35, ps.-Sen. *Oct.* 825.

23. Bentley and Withof both conjecture *relegit Styga*. Withof 32f. wants this to indicate a recrossing of the Styx on H.'s way *out* of the underworld again, i.e. with Dis as his *spolia*: but this is a very feeble *variatio* on 52f., and indeed it is difficult to see how it could be understood in this way. More naturally, Kroll 433 n. 1 takes the phrase to denote a reentry *into* the underworld, to take possession of that realm; it could mean either "recross the Styx" or "retrace his way through the underworld." But this is still an anticlimax after the magnificent hubris involved in Juno's other suggestions (i.e. 52–54ᵃ), and the same is true of Bentley's colorless alternative *repetit Styga*.

24. Tarrant, *MH* 36 (1979) 242f. deletes 54 *in toto* on the grounds that Hercules has already done what is suggested in it. But *potitur* does imply a complete take-over as opposed to a momentary victory, *pace* Tarrant; to argue that Juno's first suggestion (52–53) would already have brought H. *out* of the underworld is to insist on logic and precision in the midst of sarcastic rhetoric.

Commentary: Act I

are concerned with the opening of the underworld. A possible explanation of the MSS mistake is initial omission of the line in the archetype, because of the similarity of its opening letters to those of 55, followed by erroneous reinsertion.

parum est. This phrase with an infinitive (only here in Sen. Trag.) occurs some eight times in Ovid but is absent from poetry before him, so far as I know, though common in prose. The Ovidian examples occur only in speeches or where the poet is speaking *in propria persona*; examples in Lucan and Statius occur only in speeches.

foedus umbrarum. This is one of the *bene dissaepti foedera mundi* (*Med.* 335, cf. Costa ad loc.); specifically the natural covenant by which the underworld and its inhabitants are separated from contact with the world above. Such phrases in the poets (e.g. V. *Georg.* 1.60, Manil. 2.301) are influenced by Lucretius' frequent use of *foedera* (*foedus*) *naturae*, e.g. 1.586, 2.302. In similar contexts of a breach of the underworld, Manilius uses the phrase *naturae foedere rupto* (2.48), and Statius has an indignant Pluto exclaim *pereant discrimina mundi!* (*Theb.* 8.37).

perît. The tense of the verb is almost certainly perfect, though taken as present by Pierrot (editor of *HF* in the *editio Lemairiana* of 1829).

55 patefacta . . . retro via est. Compare, of the same event, *Tro.* 724 *caecum retro patefecit iter*, *Med.* 638 *post feri Ditis patefacta regna*, and in a similar context Stat. *Theb.* 2.13f. *Tellus / miratur patuisse retro*.

ab imis manibus. The phrase *imi manes* is Vergilian, used four times in *Aen.* (cf. Pease on 4.387); Ovid borrows it once (*Fasti* 2.52) and Sen. thrice (cf. *Tro.* 146, *Med.* 968).

56. Probably not a reference to the presence of Cerberus, although 596f. *in lucem extuli / arcana mundi* does refer to the hound. In view of the content of 54^b–55 and 57, Juno appears more concerned in this immediate context with violation of the *claustra profundi* and its consequences; she then returns to the topic of Cerberus in 59ff. The present line will therefore indicate that it is now possible to see into the underworld, a point frequently met in comparable passages, cf. Hom. *Il.* 20.64f. (Aidoneus feared lest) οἰκία . . . θνητοῖσι καὶ ἀθανάτοισι φανείη / σμερδαλέ' εὐρώεντα, V. *Aen.* 8.243ff. *non secus ac si qua penitus vi terra dehiscens / infernas reseret sedes et regna recludat / pallida, dis invisa, superque immane barathrum / cernatur*, Ov. *Met.* 5.357, Sen. *HF* 613 *ostendi*

Commentary: Act I

inferos. The term "sacred things" refers primarily to the places of the underworld, but need not exclude its activities.

dirae. So A: *durae* E^(ac)Σ. Though either adjective can be paralleled as a description of death (for *dirae* cf. Tib. 1.10.4, Sen. *Tro.* 783, *TLL* 5.1. 1273.51ff., and comm. on 608; for *durae* V. *Aen.* 10.791, Sen. *HF* 867, 1069), the *dreadfulness* of death is clearly more apposite to the present context, and virtually all editors have rightly preferred *dirae*. The corruption is of course an easy one, cf. Prop. 3.23.20, Hor. *Carm.* 2.12.2, Sen. *Pha.* 1164, ps.-Sen. *HO* 1732.

57 rupto carcere umbrarum ferox. "Arrogant at having broken . . ."; the adjective is closely connected in sense with the ablative absolute, as at Hor. *Carm.* 1.37.29 *deliberata morte ferocior*, Luc. 4.533f. *stabat devota iuventus / damnata iam luce ferox*. On the metaphor *carcer* = underworld see 1222 comm.

58f. The suggestion of a triumph is clearly a Roman touch (though hardly an obtrusive one), which Seneca repeats elsewhere in a Greek context, cf. *Tro.* 150ff., *Phoen.* 577f., *Ag.* 804; see comm. on 195, 827–29, and Walter 81–89. Cerberus is being publicly paraded, as eminent captives were in a Roman triumph. *Superbificus* is found only here: on such compounds see Appendix 4.

59. This detail is not paralleled in our scanty literary sources for the raising of Cerberus (comm. 762–827), unless there is a trace of Hercules' having exhibited the hound in Diodorus' phrase τὸν δὲ κύνα . . . ἀπήγαγε καὶ φανερὸν κατέστησεν ἀνθρώποις (4.26.1). Euripides' H. leaves him at Hermione until he has an opportunity to convey him to Argos (614f., 1386f.).

The "silver" type of line, with the pattern *abCBA* or some variant of it, "frames" the line between a noun and an adjective in agreement; such lines often provide an effective end to a period in Sen. Trag., as here: see comm. on 216–48 ad fin.; also Eden on V. *Aen.* 8.32.

atrum. Black is a natural color for the underworld's creatures, e.g. Tityus' vultures, *atras aves* (*Thy.* 10); for Cerberus' blackness cf. Hor. *Carm.* 2.13.34f., Tib. 1.3.71, Sen. *Ag.* 14. *Ater* is much more common than *niger* in Sen. Trag. (32:10).

60f. A very Senecan touch: *Thy.* 120f. and *Ag.* 53ff. also speak of the sun recoiling at the presence of beings from the underworld (cf. *HF*

Commentary: Act I

595ff.). The idea that the sun and elements can be affected by sights on earth is traditional, e.g. Soph. *OT* 1425ff., Eur. *Her.* 1231ff.; but Sen. exploits it as part of his general tendency to seek cosmic reactions to evil and disaster (see 1054–62 comm.). Thus after the murders Hercules speaks of the stars and sun recoiling from his presence (1332ff.); similarly Medea and Hippolytus *pray* that the sun will turn back in reaction to great crimes (*Med.* 28ff., *Pha.* 677ff.).

61 invasit tremor. Cf. *Oed.* 659 *artus gelidus invasit tremor. Invasit* and other perfect forms of the verb are frequently used in prose and verse with subjects such as *terror, furor, libido*, cf. *OLD* s.v. 4. *Tremor* is a favorite line ending in Senecan descriptions of emotion (see 414 and comm.).

62 terna monstri colla. Here and elsewhere Sen. gives Cerberus three heads in accordance with the usual tradition, though some writers credit him with as many as a hundred; cf. Frazer on Apollod. 2.5.12. The phrase is influenced by Ov. *Met.* 10.22 *terna Medusaei vincirem guttura monstri*. Though distributives are frequently used by the poets for metrical convenience, *terna*[25] in this context (cf. 784, 796, *Thy.* 675f.) perhaps has some excuse as the three necks belong to one dog: cf. *capita bina* on one liver *Oed.* 360.

intuens. Metrical considerations result in this verb being associated primarily with drama: there are ten uses in republican comedy and two in tragedy, twelve in Sen. Trag. and six in ps.-Sen, but no other poet up to Statius uses it more than once.

63 levia sed nimium queror. Compare the transition at 19 *sed vetera querimur*. Such transitions illustrate two Senecan tendencies: first, *Steigerung*, that is, movement to what is still more important, impressive, terrible; and second, classification and subdivision of material (Liebermann 64ff.). For both points compare *Ag.* 528 *ecce alia clades*, 557 *nos alia maior naufragos pestis vocat*. For the present phrase cf. also Ov. *Met.* 2.214 = *AA* 2.631 *parva loquor*, Sen. *HF* 295 *magna sed nimium loquor*, *Med.* 48 *levia memoravi nimis*.

The last two phrases cited and the present phrase are somewhat ambiguous, as the adverb might wrongly be taken with the verb, as is done here by Miller. Postponement and hyperbaton are occasionally found with adverbs of quantity such as *nimium, nimis, parum*, cf. 186, 313f.

---

25. *Terna* is clearly right against A's *tetra* = *taetra*; corruption of *terna* to *tetra* occurs again at *Pha.* 943, in P.

quod nimis miseri volunt / hoc facile credunt (again ambiguous: see comm. ad loc.), 579, 974 *pectoris sani parum*, Med. 326 *avidus nimium navita*, 1011 *nimium est dolori numerus angustus meo*, and the references given by Nisbet on Cic. *Pis.* 17. On postponement of *sed* and other connectives see Eden on V. *Aen.* 8.91, Norden *Aeneis VI* Anhang III B 3.

63-74. In these lines we see the development of Juno's suspicion that Hercules will attack the heavens, already latent in the comparison of Dis with Jupiter (51, 53); note again the "thinking aloud" character of the speech. What begins as a fear (*timendum est*) is no sooner voiced than it turns into an expectation (*praeripiet, veniet, quaeret, volet*); its likelihood is then backed up by arguments (68-74) which turn it into a certainty in the present (*quaerit*). Cf. Anliker 46. Juno seems determined to believe the worst of her stepson, and to find any excuse to intensify her persecution of him.

65 sceptra. A symbol of royalty among gods as well as men, carried not only by Jupiter but also by the rulers of the other two realms (599, 707). The scepter of Zeus-Jupiter is often shown in visual representations; in literature cf. e.g. Eur. fr. 912.7 N σκῆπτρον τὸ Δίος μεταχειρίζων, Ov. *Met.* 1.178, 596 with Bömer's note.

66. Accounts of Bacchus' ascent to heaven are uncircumstantial and found only in connection with his raising of Ariadne or the catasterism of the Corona (cf. comm. on 16, 18). Probably the point is that his divinity was gradually and thoroughly established on earth before his elevation. Bacchus is frequently mentioned in connection with Hercules, more often as a parallel than as a contrast (cf. comm. on 472-76). *In astra venire* is an Ovidian phrase for ascent to heaven, *Fasti* 2.478, 3.186, 3.808.

67f. vacuo volet regnare mundo. Such a gibe is naturally used of one who wishes to rule without opposition, cf. Soph. *Ant.* 739 καλῶς ἐρήμης γ' ἂν σὺ γῆς ἄρχοις μόνος, *OT* 630: Juno is perhaps suggesting in addition that Hercules will want to expel the other inhabitants of heaven, so that there may be no other god besides himself. *Mundo* = *caelo* as in 70.

68 experto. Preferable in sense to the A reading *expenso*, as *expertus* can mean "proven, tried, and tested," cf. Livy 3.44.3 *viro ... expertae virtutis*, 24.28.6 *quinquaginta annis feliciter expertam amicitiam*, Quint. *Inst.* 2.6.7 *expertas vires*. *Expenso* on the other hand would mean "having been judged, weighed," without so clear an implication about a positive re-

Commentary: Act I

sult; *TLL* 5.2.1639.62 gives only one late example of *expendere* in the sense of *probare*, Symm. *Ep.* 1.98 *amicitia usu credita et expensa documentis*.

69f. "Learning" is often the basis of a Senecan point (cf. 398 comm.); compare particularly *Tro.* 263f. *magna momento obrui / vincendo didici.* Ovid also makes a pointed connection between Hercules' bearing of the heavens and his ascent to them (in this case without violence): *quod te laturum est, caelum prius ipse tulisti* (*Her.* 9.17).

70–74. The story of how Hercules briefly assumed Atlas' burden is alluded to again at 425, 528, 1101, *Pha.* 327. Qua philosopher, Seneca is naturally skeptical, as in his comparison of Cato with H.: *nec* (sc. Cato) *in ea tempora incidit quibus credi posset caelum umeris unius inniti* (*Const.* 2.2). Note the *variatio* of *caput, umeros, collo, cervix*.

71f. Perhaps an echo of V. *Aen.* 2.708 (Aeneas to Anchises) *ipse subibo umeris nec me labor iste gravabit*, itself a phrase with overtones of Herculean endurance.

72 melius. That is, better than on the shoulders of Atlas, who sometimes had difficulty in supporting his burden (Ov. *Met.* 2.296f., *Fasti* 2.489f., Stat. *Theb.* 1.98f.). This reading of E (A has *medius*) makes 72 a pointed *variatio* on 71, entirely Senecan in character. Imitations by Claudian and Sidonius Apollinaris show that their texts had *melius*, and that they thought it an effective point: Claud. *Rapt. Pros.* 2 *praef.* 47 *firmior Herculea mundus cervice pependit, Cons. Stil.* 1.143ff. *sic Hercule quondam / sustentante polum melius librata pependit / machina*, Sid. *Carm.* 7.582ff. *pondera suscepit caeli simul atque novercae* [cf. *HF* 73f.] */ . . . cum / tutior Herculeo sedisset machina collo.*

In support of the A reading *medius*, which has since been accepted by Giardina and by Zwierlein (1979 170), Carlsson (1948 39) cited Eur. *Her.* 403ff. οὐρανοῦ θ' ὑπὸ μέσσαν / ἐλαύνει χέρας ἕδραν, / Ἄτλαντος δόμον ἐλθών, / ἀστρωπούς τε κατέσχεν οἴ-/ κους εὐανορίᾳ θεῶν. But Euripides clearly did not intend οὐρανοῦ μέσσαν ἕδραν to mean the same as μέσος οὐρανός, *medius polus*, which could not rest on the neck of anyone standing on earth. Furthermore if *medius* is read, line 72 disrupts the sequence of thought, since it describes only the fact of the burden, as 70[b], not H.'s endurance of it, as 71 and 73; it is then desirable to transpose 72 before 71 with Zwierlein.[26] But why prefer a flat line that needs transposition over a pointed line that fits its context and is supported by late classical imitations?

26. Peiper also moved 72 before 71, but this must have been for a different reason, as he read *melius*. The sequence *nec . . . -que* is unobjectionable in a series of clauses, cf. *Tro.* 2f., *Phoen.* 605ff.

73. Compare Hercules' words at Ov. *Met.* 9.198 *hac caelum cervice tuli.*

immota cervix. The phrase *praebenti immotam cervicem*, describing Cicero about to be beheaded, occurs in a fragment of Livy quoted by Seneca's father, *Suas.* 6.17.

74 prementem. The weight of a god is itself formidable (e.g. Hom. *Il.* 5.838f., Ov. *Fasti* 3.330, *Met.* 9.273), but Juno means that she also pressed down deliberately to increase the burden.

75ff. The objectification of the *affectus* in Sen. Trag. sometimes goes as far as an address by a speaker to his or her passion, as if it were an independent entity; cf. *Med.* 916 *quo te igitur, ira, mittis?* 953 *ira, qua ducis, sequor*, Canter 144. Such addresses often occur as here in contexts of *Selbstantreibung*, when the speaker urges on his *affectus* or *animus* to take some action; e.g. *Med.* 914, *Ag.* 192, *Thy.* 192.

76–82. D. Heinsius, followed by Ageno, finds it inconsistent that *quid tanta mandas odia?* should be followed so soon by *Titanas emitte*, etc., "quod rursum mandantis est." Both critics consequently propose emendations. But lines 76–77 mean only that Juno will take personal charge of the persecution of Hercules, rather than entrusting it to Eurystheus (so Pierrot): this need not exclude the use of allies. On the other hand there is a real inconsistency between the idea of summoning the Titans and the phrase *congredere, manibus ipsa dilacera tuis*. Yet this is natural in a character who is thinking aloud about various possibilities; her plan shifts from personally *making* an attack to personally *directing* an attack.

76. Two resolutions in the first two feet are sufficiently unusual to be noteworthy (one example in every thirty-five iambic lines in *HF*), and here as at 100 *incipite famulae Ditis* they express the urgency and vehemence of the speaker. The effect is increased by *dilacera*; in *HF* lines containing three resolutions occur only once every seventy-five lines (cf. 229 comm.).

dilacera. The *iam* of A's reading *iam lacera* has some point—"attack him now in person, not by proxy as before"—but in fact the contrast is pointed in terms of personal involvement (*ipsa, tuis* vs. *mandas*) rather than time.[27] In view of endemic imitation of *HF* in *HO*, and as *dilacerare* is found nowhere else in the corpus, *HO* 826 *artus ipse dilacerat suos* gives support to the E reading.

27. Similarly at 112 the A interpolation *iam odia mutentur* for *vota mutentur* is a misguided attempt to "improve" a contrast with *iam* (see ad loc.).

Commentary: Act I

77. Compare Seneca's description of a man inflamed by anger (*Ira* 3.3.3): *nec mandat ultionem suam, sed ipse eius exactor animo simul ac manu saevit.*

78 imperando fessus. Another echo of Ovid's *defessa iubendo est / saeva Iovis coniunx* (cf. 41f. comm.).

79–85. One means by which Sen. heightens horror is to have his characters contemplate blood-chilling possibilities, only to reject them in favor of something still more fearful. Cf. *Med.* 37–50 and *Thy.* 257–60, where the ultimate inspiration of using one's enemy against himself (259) is similar to that seen here (84f.).

79. Originally the Titanomachy seems to have involved a successful attempt by Jupiter to depose the ruling Titans; cf. West on Hes. *Theog.* 632. Hesiod's own account at *Theog.* 629ff., however, could be taken to indicate a revolt of the Titans against Jupiter, though probably not so intended; later Titanomachy and Gigantomachy became thoroughly conflated, and for Hyginus (*Fab.* 150) as for Sen. the former represents an attempt to depose Jupiter; cf. also Hor. *Carm.* 3.4.42–64, where Titans and Giants are to some extent merged, along with the Aloidae and Typhoeus, in a single vast battle against the Olympians.

ausos rumpere imperium Iovis. *Audere* can sometimes mean "to attempt daringly," without implying success in the attempt, e.g. V. *Aen.* 10.811 *quo moriture ruis maioraque viribus audes?* If that is the case here, the rest of the phrase will mean "to smash Jove's power." Alternatively the whole phrase may mean "having dared to violate Jove's sway," which they would have done as soon as they rebelled against him.

80 emitte. Probably from Tartarus, their traditional place of imprisonment from Hesiod on (*Theog.* 717ff.). For *emittere* of release from the underworld cf. 283, *Oed.* 394, *Ag.* 2, *Thy.* 672, *TLL* 5.2.502.44ff. The author of *HO* in remodeling these lines speaks rather of releasing the Titans from Etna (1308f. *emitte Siculo vertice ardentes, pater, / Titanas in me*), but that does not seem to be Sen.'s meaning here.

80–82. Who is this prisoner of Etna? In referring to him as an unnamed *Gigas*, Sen. is probably following Ovid, cf. *Pont.* 2.10.23f. *Aetnaea . . . flamma / suppositus monti quam vomit ore Gigas*, *Met.* 14.1, *Ibis* 597f. Elsewhere Ovid identifies the prisoner as Typhoeus (*Fasti* 1.571, 4.491), whom he calls a Giant (*Met.* 5.346); actually Typhoeus was no such thing, but conflation of Jupiter's foes is common in Augustan and

Commentary: Act I

later poetry. There is no need, therefore, to suppose from *Gigante* that Sen. has in mind Enceladus, a true Giant, though Enceladus does displace Typhoeus as prisoner of Etna in a minor tradition seen at V. *Aen.* 3.578 (see Williams ad loc., Apollod. 1.6.2, Langen on Val. Fl. 2.24). At *Med.* 410 Sen. calls the prisoner, still unnamed, a Titan—a further example of conflation.

Siculi verticis laxa specum. There are often said to be caverns in Etna from which come its volcanic fires (e.g. *Pha.* 102f. *Aetnaeo vapor / exundat antro*, Luc. 6.294, 10.448), and a *specus* is also a natural place of imprisonment, cf. 94. It is not clear whether *Siculi verticis* indicates that the *specus* is near the summit, in which case one might compare Luc. 1.545 *ora ferox Siculae laxavit Mulciber Aetnae* and 5.99f. *Siculus . . . apex*, or whether *vertex* here is approximately equivalent to *mons*, as at 1208, *Phoen.* 22, Ov. *Am.* 2.11.2.

81 tellus . . . Doris. The predominantly Doric character of Sicily was established by its earliest Greek colonies, including Syracuse, Megara Hyblaea, and Gela, which in turn founded important colonies of their own. The phrase is, however, rather surprising as an allusion to Sicily, despite the fact that the context makes its meaning clear: contrast Pind. *Nem.* 3.3 ἵκεο Δωρίδα νᾶσον Αἴγιναν, Soph. *OC* 695 τᾷ μεγάλᾳ Δωρίδι νάσῳ Πέλοπος, Sid. *Carm.* 2.475 *Dorica tellus* (= Greece). The explanation may lie in an association of Sicily with the pastoral tradition, in which Dorian dialect and identity are important. Cf. particularly line 1 of anon. *Lament for Bion*, where Δώριον ὕδωρ virtually = "Sicilian water," and lines 12, 18, 96, 122.

excusso. "When he shakes himself": for *excutere* meaning much the same as *quassare* cf. *Ag.* 5 *pavor membra excutit*, *Thy.* 669, *Med.* 112, and for the middle use with a reflexive sense cf. *excutior somno* V. *Aen.* 2.302, Ov. *Met.* 9.695. The discomfort of the prisoner is frequently emphasized, e.g. Pind. *Pyth.* 1.28 στρωμνὰ δὲ χαράσσοισ' ἅπαν νῶτον ποτικεκλιμένον κεντεῖ, Claud. *Rapt. Pros.* 2.159 *pressaque Gigas cervice laborat*; for the idea that Sicily trembles when he shifts position cf. V. *Aen.* 3.581f. *et fessum quotiens mutet latus, intremere omnem / murmure Trinacriam*, Ov. *Met.* 5.354ff. The usage of *excusso* is a bold one, but there seem to be no good grounds for conjecture.

83. This line flatly contradicts *discedant ferae* (77) and was rightly excised by Leo (cf. 1876 444), followed by Richter and by Garrod 213f. It might be argued that the *ferae* of 77 are specifically those employed by Eurystheus, and that Juno intends to send fresh beasts into combat, but

[145]

Commentary: Act I

this is to defend the indefensible. In 79–82 Juno is clearly proposing allies who will be more dreadful than mere *ferae*, and 83 comes as a complete anticlimax: "Well, it must be Nemean Lions again after all!" (Garrod).[28]

The Nemean Lion is sometimes said to have come from the moon (perhaps first in Herodorus *FGrH* 31 F4), which is later described as the origin of the Cretan Bull (*Laus Herculis* 120) and even of all gigantic creatures (Lact. Plac. on Stat. *Theb.* 2.58; these and further references in Garrod).

84f. Some of the force of these lines is captured by Jean Rotrou in the prologue of *Les Sosies* (1636):

> D'autres armes manquant à ma fureur extrême,
> Je n'opposerai plus que lui-même à lui-même;
> Lui-même il se vaincra; s'il naît pour vaincre tout,
> De ce dernier ouvrage il viendra bien à bout.

(The whole of Rotrou's prologue, spoken by Junon, is a close adaptation of the Senecan speech.) Another echo is Massinger, *Duke of Milan* 4.3: "Her goodness doth disdain comparison, / And, but herself, admits no parallel." But both imitations lack Sen.'s telling conciseness.

vicit. Hercules' help was indispensable to the gods in defeating the Giants, most of whom were dispatched by his arrows: Pind. *Nem.* 1.67f., Eur. *Her.* 178–80, 1193f., Apollod. 1.6.1–2, Hor. *Carm.* 2.12.6f. *domitosque Herculea manu / telluris iuvenes.*

85 bella. Frequently used of H.'s labors and struggles, cf. 211, 527, 638, 997.

86ff. The immediate inspiration for Juno's summoning of the Furies comes from the similar passages in V. *Aen.* 7.312ff. and Ov. *Met.* 4.447ff. The primary function of the Furies here is to cause madness, in contrast with their role in early Greek thought as avengers or punishers (for the contrast cf. Jocelyn 218f.); they can even be asked to madden Juno herself (108ff.) as well as H. Their function as punishers is not completely forgotten here (cf. 104 *poenas petite*), but it is clearly mentioned as an afterthought, in an attempt at self-justification by Juno.

Seneca generally writes within the conventions of stage drama, whether or not he expected stage performance, and it is therefore

---

28. The inept interpolator imitated the phrase *terra concipiat feras* HO 34, 1327.

worth asking whether the Furies summoned by Juno appear "onstage." Probably they do; compare the Fury of the prologue of *Thy.*, and those of Aesch. *Eum*. It is true that visions of the Furies elsewhere in Sen. Trag. do not imply stage appearance (*HF* 982ff., *Med*. 958ff., *Ag*. 759ff.); but Juno's relationship to the Furies is different, and in 100ff. she is clearly addressing them directly and in person, as she does in the Vergilian and Ovidian source passages. It seems likely that they appear before the beginning of 89; this gives special point to *i nunc* e.q.s. Then, after threatening further action, which does not have to be realized in the prologue, Juno turns back to the Furies at 100. Alternatively, they may come onto the stage immediately before 100 (so Frenzel 38), but that is less effective.

86 ab imo Tartari fundo. Influenced by V. *Aen*. 6.577ff. *tum Tartarus ipse / bis patet in praeceps . . . / hic genus antiquum Terrae, Titania pubes, / fulmine deiecti, fundo volvuntur in imo.* Thus Sen. seems to locate the Furies in the place that is traditionally the prison of the Titans (cf. Hes. *Theog.* 717ff.). Usually the Furies are said to live in the underworld but with no specific location, cf. *RE* Suppl. 8.127.33ff. Ovid sets them in front of the *sedes scelerata*, *Met*. 4.456; Vergil puts Tisiphone there, *Aen*. 6.555f., but places the *Eumenidum thalami* at the very entrance to the underworld, ibid. 280.

87f. Fire, snakes, and whips are traditional attributes of the Furies, cf. *RE* Suppl. 8.125f. More usually they have the snakes in their hair and blazing brands in their hands, e.g. *Med*. 14f. Sometimes, however, the snakes are held in their hands, as at Eur. *El*. 1345, V. *Aen*. 6.572; here Seneca envisages the snakes used as whips, as at *Ag*. 760 *anguinea* (N. Heinsius: *sanguinea* codd.) *iactant verbera*, *Med*. 961f. *ingens anguis excusso sonat / tortus flagello*. The flaming hair is an unusual detail, but fire is closely associated with the Furies, and is said to come from their clothes (Eur. *IT* 288), their eyes (*Hymn. Orph.* 70.6) and their mouths (Aesch. *Eum*. 137ff.).

89 i nunc. *I* or *i nunc* followed by imperative may be used to give ironic encouragement to take an action that the speaker regards as foolish, dangerous, etc. Compare Juvenal's comment on Hannibal, *i demens et saevas curre per Alpes, / ut pueris placeas et declamatio fias* (10.166f.). A particularly close parallel in Sen. Trag. is *Med*. 1007f. *i nunc, superbe, virginum thalamos pete, / relinque matres*; other examples include *Tro*. 191ff., *Med*. 197, 650f., *Oed*. 880f. The construction is primarily poetic, occurring in several genres including epic, but is also found in Livy and in Seneca's prose; lists of passages in E. B. Lease, *AJP* 19 (1898) 59–69.

89f. The notion of despising earthly things and honoring heaven is of course a common one, though not usually spoken ironically: cf. e.g. Cic. *Rep.* 6.20 *haec caelestia . . . spectato, illa humana contemnito, Off.* 1.67 *humana contemnentes.* As the rare *temnere* appears only here in Sen. Trag. (and not at all in Ovid or Lucan), its use was perhaps suggested to Sen. by one or both of the following *loci*: Lucr. 5.1238 *si se temnunt mortalia saecla*, V. *Aen.* 1.542 *si genus humanum et mortalia temnitis arma.*

caelitum. *Caeles* is primarily a poetic word, largely restricted to the elevated style, but for metrical reasons little used in dactylic poetry (except in Ovid), where it is replaced by *caelicola* or *caelestis*. It is therefore most common in tragedy: six uses in Republican tragedy (including one in Cicero's translations), seventeen in Sen. Trag.

90 feros. It is not easy to choose between this reading of Σ (and presumably of E¹) and *ferox* (A): *ferox* could have been corrupted to *feros* (as at *Thy.* 96 in C), particularly under the influence of *inferos* in 91, but the opposite corruption of *feros* to *ferox* is familiar in the MSS (*HF* 797 EA, *Oed.* 90 CS, 761 E, *Thy.* 582 E). *Ferox*, if correct, would presumably be nominative with *credis*, i.e. "do you arrogantly believe?"; for *ferox* of the arrogance born of victory cf. 57 *rupto carcere umbrarum ferox*, Livy 3.61.13 *feroces ab re bene gesta*. I am inclined to think that after *superbe* in 89 another adjective describing Hercules' attitude is excessive; on the other hand, *feros* appropriately notes the fearfulness of the underworld powers which, as Juno implies, are far from completely defeated.

91 fugisse credis? Omission of the subject-accusative of an infinitive is not uncommon in poetry or in prose, cf. 117f. *hic prosit mihi / Iove esse genitum* (sc. *Herculem*), H-S 362.

92–94. The *discordem deam* of 93 is none other than Discordia, the Roman equivalent of Greek Eris: for the transparent periphrasis cf. *dea dira* = Dira V. *Aen.* 7.324, 12.914, *dea venustissima* = Venus Plaut. *Poen.* 1177, *dea magna* = Magna Mater Cat. 63.91, Ov. *Fasti* 4.194; for her association with the other "abstracts" of the netherworld (96ff.) cf. Hes. *Theog.* 224ff., V. *Aen.* 6.273ff., Hyg. *Fab. praef.* 1, Stat. *Theb.* 2.287f., 5.73f., 7.47ff., Val. Fl. 2.204ff., Claud. *In Ruf.* 1.29ff. Discordia would normally cause conflict with others rather than mental disharmony within an individual. Vergil virtually identifies her with the Furies at *Aen.* 6.280f., however, where Fury-like she has *vipereum crinem* (cf. 8.701f.), and Sen. completes the identification at *Thy.* 251 where the figure called *discors Erinys*, and distinguished from Megaera and the rest of the Furies, can only be Discord; so she can share the Furies' maddening function.

Commentary: Act I

92f. Seneca creates a sense of mystery and foreboding by postponement of the object. The effect is increased by the heaviness of *conditam caligine* (note also the initial alliteration of this phrase and of *discordem deam*); final words of four or more syllables are quite rare in Sen., as opposed to other iambic writers (cf. comm. on 244, 246). The *caligo* involved is of course that of the underworld, as at 710 and (e.g.) *inc. inc. trag.* 75 R² *crassa caligo inferum*.

93 ultra nocentum exilia. That is, in the same area as the Furies, *imo Tartari fundo* (86). The *nocentes* are Ixion, Tantalus, and the other famous sinners, as at 748 and elsewhere in Sen. Trag. The archaic ending *-um* is frequently employed by the poets in place of *-ium* for metrical convenience, particularly with participles used as substantives (e.g. *Tro.* 1009 *dolentum, Med.* 740 *silentum*), but also with adjectives so used (e.g. *HF* 597 *caelestum*).

Exilia is a striking metaphor, which may have been suggested by Hor. *Carm.* 2.3.27f. *nos in aeternum / exilium impositura cumbae*. Seneca's use is more specific, of places where the guilty are segregated from other inhabitants of the underworld, cf. 1223f. *si quod exilium latet / ulterius Erebo*, and probably *Thy.* 1019 (*exilia* Gronovius, *exitia* codd.).

94. Not a clear picture. The word *oppositi* suggests that what keeps Discordia prisoner is the whole bulk of the mountain that stands between her and the rest of the underworld. But if she is imprisoned *within* the mountain in a *specus*, what keeps her prisoner is the fact that the mountain surrounds her on all sides, and that is difficult to reconcile with *oppositi*.

As Discordia seems to be imprisoned in a similar manner to the prisoner of Etna (cf. 80 *Siculi verticis laxa specum* e.q.s.), one solution would be to alter *oppositi* to *impositi*, the *specus* being now not a cave in the mountainside but a hollow space deep within: cf. V. *Aen.* 1.60ff. *sed pater omnipotens speluncis abdidit atris* (sc. *ventos*) / . . . *molemque et montis insuper altos / imposuit*. I am more inclined to focus suspicion on *ingens . . . specus*, because in such a context it would be more natural to mention the vastness of the barrier than the spaciousness of the prison. One might then write *quam munit ingens montis oppositi latus* with Bentley, but conjecture of this kind can only be *exempli gratia*. It is also noteworthy, though not necessarily a ground for suspicion, that *munire* = "imprison, hedge in" is very rare, the earliest parallel cited by the dictionaries being Ulp. *Dig.* 9.2.27.9 *ignem extinguere vel ita munire, ne evagetur*.

95. The line is "framed" between two verbs, and the effect is heightened by the fact that the verbs have similar prefixes (further empha-

[149]

Commentary: Act I

sized by *e* within the line) and endings. For such framing in Vergil, cf. Norden *Aeneis VI* Anhang III A 2; the closest parallel there is *Aen.* 6.850 *describent radio et surgentia sidera dicent*. *Educam* and *extraham* must both govern *quidquid relictum est*, pace Miller who translates "I will bring her forth" (sc. Discord).

96 quidquid relictum est. That is, after the release of the Furies and Discord. This is the interpretation suggested by the context; strictly it would require a future-perfect, but Latin is not always precise about indications of futurity, cf. 1306 *statue quidquid statuis* (i.e. *quidquid statues*) and comm. on 306 and 1284 *arma nisi dantur*. The phrase seems unlikely to mean "whatever was left behind by Hercules" (so Miller et al.), because he did not penetrate to these depths of the underworld.

96–98. Such groups of personifications are found in poetry from Hesiod on (cf. 690–96 with comm.) but usually they simply reside in the underworld; the idea of their emerging with the Furies to aid Juno's revenge is suggested by Ov. *Met.* 4.484f. and 502f. Seneca has chosen personifications that are highly relevant to Juno's plan. Impietas is not paralleled as a personification, except at ps.-Sen. *Oct.* 432, until a much later period, though Pietas is frequently personified. Furor first becomes an underworld figure in Sen. Trag. (v. *Oed.* 590); Vergil has her imprisoned behind the *Belli portae* in Rome (*Aen.* 1.294ff.). Scelus and Error come from the Ovidian passage.

veniet. A garbled report of a variant *veniat* had got into the text of β, the common ancestor of CS. *Veniet* is clearly the transmitted reading of A as of E, and preferable to *veniat* after the future tenses of 91–95.

97 suumque lambens sanguinem. For this nightmarish image cf. Pliny's description of Domitian, who lurked in his palace and *propinquorum sanguinem lamberet* (*Pan.* 48.3).

98. Furor perhaps replaces the Insania of Ovid's list, but with very different connotations (contrast *trepidoque Insania vultu*): it represents a raging, aggressive type of madness. For the self-destructive tendency of *furor* cf. 1220f. *quodque habet proprium furor, / in se ipse saevit*, with comm.

99. Similarly Oedipus expresses perverse satisfaction after summoning Pestis, Dolor, and the like: *ducibus his uti libet!* (*Oed.* 1061).

hoc hoc. Seneca likes immediate anaphora of a monosyllable for emphasis, particularly in the first foot. The various forms of *hic* provide seven examples in Sen. Trag.: other words so used are *iam* (six), *me* (two), *nunc* (three), *sic* (three), *te* (four). On emphatic gemination in Latin see Wölfflin, *Ausgew. Schriften* 288ff.

100–106. The literal fire of the Furies' torches becomes the metaphorical fire of *furor*. Compare *Aen.* 7, where Vergil first has Allecto hurl her torch into Turnus' breast, and then introduces a simile comparing his madness to water seething over a blazing fire (456f., 462ff.). The use of fire imagery in connection with madness is traditional: cf. Aesch. *Ag.* 1256, Soph. *El.* 887f., and Sen. *Ag.* 723, and in *Aen.* 7, in addition to the simile mentioned above, note the language used of Amata's growing madness 354ff. *ac dum prima lues . . . / . . . ossibus implicat ignem / necdum animus toto percepit pectore flammam.* (Cf. comm. on 1022, and for the Furies' torches as maddening instruments v. 982–84 and comm.)

In this play fire imagery recurs particularly in the mad-scene. At the beginning of the madness Hercules has a hallucination of the fiery constellation Leo (944ff.), and later of a Fury thrusting a brand into his face (982ff.); note also the description of his expression as *igneus* (1022). Elsewhere fire is frequently associated with evil and/or destruction: thus the serpents sent against the infant H. have fiery eyes (218) and lightning is mentioned among the destructive forces of nature (932f.); Lycus intends to burn H.'s family on a pyre (506–8), and after the murders H. frequently threatens to burn himself and his weapons (1216f. with comm., 1233–36, 1284–87). Though such fire imagery is in many cases very traditional, it occurs with sufficient frequency in this play to acquire some thematic force, though it is less fully developed here than e.g. in *Medea* (v. Pratt 1963, esp. 205ff.).

100–105. For the dramatic impact of a series of plural imperatives cf. Pacuv. *trag.* 350–52 R² *Agite ite, evolvite rapite, coma / tractate per aspera saxa et humum, / scindite vestem ocius!* and 263–67 R², also Sen. *Phoen.* 340–45. In the present passage the sequence of *-ite* endings, apart from its alliterative quality, continues the metrical effect established in *incipite famulae* (cf. 76 comm.).

100 famulae Ditis. Such a description could scarcely be used of the Erinyes of the early Greek writers, who punish the transgressions of gods as well as of men (Hes. *Theog.* 220; see West ad loc. and on 217). But given the concept of punishments in the underworld, which the Furies carry out (V. *Aen.* 6.571f., Sen. *Thy.* 78), they can be described as functionaries of that realm. The beginning of this line echoes a regular form of address to palace servants in Sen. Trag., cf. *Pha.* 387 *removete,*

Commentary: Act I

famulae, purpura, HF 1053, *Med.* 188, *Ag.* 997 *abripite, famuli, monstrum*, and the description of the Furies was no doubt suggested to Sen. by such phrases.

incitae. So A: E has *citae. Incitae*, the less common word, is more likely to have been displaced (particularly if it was written *īcitae*), and the alliteration it creates with *incipite* is perhaps also in its favor. The word also carries stronger connotations than *citus* of excitement or violent movement, appropriate here, cf. Lucr. 1.271 *venti vis verberat incita pontum*, Sen. *Ag.* 720ff. *quid me furoris incitam stimulis novi / . . . rapitis?*

101 concutite. The action is necessary to keep a pine-torch alight, cf. Ov. *Am.* 1.2.11f. *vidi ego iactatas mota face crescere flammas, / et vidi nullo concutiente mori*, Pliny *Epist.* 4.9.11; but here the movement is also threatening, cf. 331 *sceptra concutiens, Tro.* 683 *arma concussit manu*, and for the Furies' threatening use of their torches 983f., *Med.* 960ff.

agmen. The use of this word for the Furies is suggested by Vergil, *Aen.* 4.474 *Eumenidum agmina*, 6.572 *agmina sororum*; in Seneca cf. *Med.* 960, *Thy.* 78, and similar uses of *turba Med.* 958, *cohors Thy.* 250. Such terms suggest a larger number than the traditional three; otherwise Megaera here and Tisiphone in *Aen.* 6 would be leading an *agmen* of two. The number three becomes canonical with Euripides, but larger and less definite numbers are sometimes found, notably in the Chorus of Aesch. *Eum.* (cf. *RE* Suppl. 8.122).

102 Megaera. In the Latin poets a single Fury is often given special mention. Probably for metrical reasons, Tisiphone is popular in dactylic poetry, but Sen.'s favorite is Megaera, singled out again at *Med.* 963, *Thy.* 252.

luctifica. The most popular of the *-ficus* adjectives in Sen. Trag. (cf. Appendix 4), probably suggested here by Vergil's *luctificam Allecto, Aen.* 7.324.

103. Megaera carries a *trabs* at *Med.* 962 also. The word naturally indicates something larger than a regular torch, and that seems to be the case here as the *trabs* is stolen from a pyre, cf. *HF* 514 (though at *Phoen.* 547 it is simply a synonym for *fax*). Hence the adjective *vastam* is appropriate here (cf. e.g. *HF* 815, 992), and there is no need to consider conjectures such as *ustam* (N. Heinsius, Bentley).

For brands stolen from funeral ceremonies or pyres cf. Prop. 4.3.13f., Ov. *Met.* 6.430 (of the Eumenides), Sen. *HF* 983 (again of the Furies), *Med.* 798f., *Oed.* 550f., 874f.

Commentary: Act I

104 hoc agite. The phrase calls for concentrated action or attention, as often in comedy, but perhaps also has sinister overtones, for which see *Med.* 562 with Costa's note. *Hoc age* was a ritual phrase spoken at Roman sacrifices (Plut. *Numa* 14.2), and it is sometimes used or alluded to in connection with murder (cf., in addition to the passage in *Med.*, Sen. *Clem.* 1.12.2, Suet. *Cal.* 58, *Galba* 20). Thus there is a suggestion of Hercules as a sacrificial victim. For sacrificial imagery in the play cf. 634, 922ff., 1036ff.

vitiatae. E's reading suggests "desecrated" (cf. *profanatum chaos* in a similar context at Stat. *Theb.* 8.52), or even "defiled" by Hercules' living presence, as the upper world would be by an underworld creature (cf. *HF* 601, *Thy.* 103ff.). A's *violatae* is typical of the tendency of that tradition to normalize unusual expressions. The absence of *vitiare* elsewhere in Sen. Trag., and its rarity in poetry generally, might cast suspicion on the E reading, if it were not that Ovid uses the verb more than twenty times.

105. There are two echoes here of Juno's appeal to Allecto in *Aeneid* 7: *concutite pectus* comes from 338 *fecundum concute pectus*, and *excoquat* from 345 *femineae ardentem curaeque iraeque coquebant*. *Excoquere* constitutes a strong metaphor here, both because of intensive *ex-* and because the verb (unlike *coquere*) is rarely used metaphorically (but cf. Sen. *Ben.* 4.13.11 where *luxuria* is said to be a fever which *cor ipsum excoquat*). The metaphor *acrior mentem excoquat [ignis]* follows naturally on the torches of the Furies: indeed it would be difficult to say where "literal" fire ends and metaphor begins.

Whose *pectus* and *mens* is meant? The translators generally suppose Hercules' (so Heywood, "Strike through his breast, let fyercer flame within his bosome boyle"); but in Vergil the *pectus* is Allecto's own, and Wagenvoort 173f. follows Ageno in supposing that Juno likewise means the Furies' breast here. The Vergilian precedent is not conclusive for the interpretation of the phrase, for at *Thy.* 85f. *concute insano ferum / pectus tumultu* the *pectus* is probably not Tantalus' own but someone else's. In the present passage lines 107–9[a] have an important bearing on the question: their rhetorical structure suggests that they are not introducing a new idea, but rather confirming and explaining the preceding lines; thus *concutite pectus* e.q.s. indicates that the Furies must first madden themselves.[29]

29. Vergil's *fecundum concute pectus* means "sift your fertile imagination," i.e. for ways of doing harm (cf. the preceding words *tibi . . . mille nocendi artes*). Seneca's phrasing makes it unlikely that his *concutite pectus* could have that meaning (*pace* Wagenvoort); it probably means "arouse yourselves," for which cf. Juv. 10.327f. *et se / concussere ambae*, i.e. to take revenge.

[*153*]

106. Etna's fires often provide a simile or comparison, particularly for love, cf. *Pha.* 102f., Cat. 68.53, Ov. *Met.* 13.867ff., *Rem. Am.* 491, ps.-Sen. *HO* 285f., but also for fury, cf. *Med.* 409f., and for fever, cf. Hor. *Epod.* 17.30ff.

caminis. A metaphor for Etna's fiery recesses, rather than a mythological allusion to the smithies of the Cyclopes. In connection with Etna both *caminus* and *fornax* are used in this metaphorical way, cf. Lucr. 6.681, V. *Georg.* 1.472, *Aen.* 3.580, Ov. *Met.* 15.340, ps.-V. *Aetna* 1, 556, 606; both words are also used in reference to the Cyclopes' activities, but then the mythological meaning is made clear, e.g. with *Cyclopum* at Ov. *Fasti* 4.473, cf. V. *Aen.* 6.630, 8.418ff., ps.-V. *Aetna* 37, Sen. *Pha.* 191.

107 animum captus. A variation on the usual idiom *mente captus*, for which see L-S s.v. *capio* I B 1 e (B), *TLL* 3.340.31ff. Of the variant readings, *animum* is more likely to have been displaced by *animo* than vice versa. For variation on the usual ablative in this phrase cf. Tac. *Hist.* 3.73 *captus animi*; for the accusative construction e.g. Plato *Symp.* 218a τὴν καρδίαν ἢ ψυχὴν πληγείς, and in Seneca *Oed.* 442 *membra remissae, Med.* 800 *mota caput.*

108f. vobis prius insaniendum est. So EPCS, but *nobis* appears in T, Trevet, and many recc., and has occasionally been adopted by modern editors. The run of the lines from 107 favors the paradosis; the sentence beginning *ut possit* seems insufficiently pointed to introduce a new thought ("I too must become mad": see comm. on 105), whereas the sudden self-address in the second half of 109 appropriately heralds a new idea. For such abrupt and lifelike shifts of thought or feeling in self-address cf. 307f., 519, *Tro.* 606f.

109 Iuno. The *o* is short again at 615, 1297. The practice of shortening final *o* is extended considerably by Ovid, and taken still further by Sen. The latter often shortens the *o* not only in iambic and spondaic words, but also in trisyllables of various metrical shapes (except cretics), e.g. *compello* (*Oed.* 1043), *regio* (*HF* 1138 al.), *cremabo* (*HF* 1236), and in longer words, e.g. *accipio* (*Thy.* 542), *Agamemno* (*Ag.* 514). He even applies the license occasionally to gerunds, e.g. *vincendo* (*Tro.* 204), though there was no precedent for shortening a second-declension dative or ablative ending. See Austin on V. *Aen.* 2.735, R. Hartenberger *De O Finali apud Poetas Latinos*, diss. Bonn 1911. Since the practice of shortening final *o* increases rapidly during the first century, the notably higher frequency of this usage in *Thy.* and *Phoen.* than elsewhere in

Commentary: Act I

Sen. Trag. probably indicates a relatively late date for those two plays. See Fitch 1981 303–5.

furis. So E: A *furit*. Either reading could conceivably be intrusive. For an intrusive third person, with a vocative taken as a nominative, cf. 1149 *ubi es, parens* E (*recte*), *ubi est parens* A; for the opposite error cf. 1038 *Argos victimas alias dabit* E (*recte*), *Argos, victimas alias dabis* A. From a rhetorical point of view, however, the self-address introduces the new idea much more vigorously and effectively than would a third-person reference (cf. 108f. comm.). The scribe of A may have been influenced by *furit* in 106.

110 mente deiectam mea. "Driven out of my mind": an unusual expression, but one may compare such phrases as Varro *L.* 6.44 *a mente sua discedit*, Suet. *Aug.* 48 *mente lapsis*.

112 dignum noverca. Senecan *irati* sometimes embrace an identity with criminal overtones, and use it as a guide or criterion for their crimes; cf. *Thy.* 176ff. (tyrant), 271 (Thyestes, Atreus), *Ag.* 116–24, *Med.* 43, 910. On Juno as *noverca* cf. 21 comm.

vota mutentur mea. This reading of Σ (and so presumably of E¹) makes good sense, with *vota* matching *precor* in 113: previously Juno's hopes and prayers were that Hercules would fail to return safely, but now they are for the opposite. A's reading *iam odia mutentur mea* is unclear: it might perhaps be "let my hatred be changed to solicitude" (said sarcastically) or "let my hatred become covert rather than overt," but in either case the phrase is awkward here, as Juno has just declared her intention of furthering her hatred. Perhaps the A interpolator is attempting to strengthen the jussive with *iam*, as at 76 he writes *iam lacera* for *dilacera*; his substitution of *odia* in conjunction with *mutare* was inspired by *Pha.* 575 [*Amor*] *odia mutat*.[30]

113–22. Though Juno's general decision to use Hercules against himself was made earlier (85), the details of her plan are kept back until this point, as a climax and finale for the whole prologue.

---

30. Zwierlein has argued (1976 200ff.) that both *vota* here and *precor* in 113 are inappropriate, because Juno is now intending to take an active, directing role, rather than simply "praying" for success. (He accepts A's *iam odia*, and writes *pater* for *precor*.) But the argument is misconceived: Juno's intended "action," viz. to madden Hercules and make him kill his children, can happen only when he has returned home, and she must therefore hope for a safe return. Zwierlein also objects to prayers in the mouth of a goddess, but of course the usage is metaphorical: she is not addressing *preces* to the Furies here (though she does so at *Met.* 4.472), for their function is to madden H., not to ensure his homecoming.

[155]

Commentary: Act I

114f. inveni . . . iuvet. Compare the similar phrase used by another supernatural prologuist, the Fury of *Thy.*: *inveni dapes, / quas ipse fugeres* (66f.).

diem. That is, the one now dawning, cf. 123ff.

116 me vicit: et se vincat. For the effective parallelism compare 490 *Iovi dedisti coniugem, regi dabis*. Seneca likes to use paronomasia of verb forms, cf. 60 *viso . . . vidi*, 266f. *fecit . . . faciet*, 274f. *tenet . . . tenebit*, 590f. *potuit . . . poterit*, 776f. *timet . . . timetur*, Canter 162. *Et* here means "also," and some punctuation is needed after *vicit* (Müller 4f.), though this has oddly been overlooked by several modern editors. Failure to understand how the line should be pointed perhaps accounts for the rewriting in A.

116f. et cupiat . . . reversus. Juno does not intend H. to die, but to have a hopeless longing for death—a much more sadistically effective punishment (cf. 511–13 with comm.). The poignancy of his longing will be all the greater because he has just left the world of death (*ab inferis reversus*). On the latter point v. H.'s own last words 1338–41.

117f. hic . . . esse genitum. Compare Ov. *Met.* 11.319f. *et forti genitore et progenitore nitenti / esse satam prodest?* (with a similar omission of the subject-pronoun; cf. 91 comm.).

hic. "Herein, in this regard" (L-S s.v. I B, cf. *Tro.* 553 with Wertis' defense of the MSS reading, *Thy.* 473) rather than "at this juncture" (L-S II).

118 stabo. In readiness for action, cf. 458 with comm.

119 manu. The choice between this reading and the alternative *manum* is not an easy one. I prefer *manu*, particularly in view of the similar phrase at 1127f. *telum . . . / missum certa librare manu*; cf. also *Med.* 534 *tela librentur manu*, *Phoen.* 437 *librata dextrā tela*. In favor of *manum* one could cite *Ag.* 900 *impiam librat manum*, V. *Aen.* 5.479 *libravit caestus*. It is true that these phrases do not indicate someone else's hand, as would be the case here, but it does not seem difficult to suppose such an extension of sense. Compare *HO* 313 *aderit noverca quae manus nostras regat*.

121f. That is, "*Then*—if he still wishes to—Jupiter may admit Hercules to heaven." For such ironic granting of permission with *licet* cf. Ov.

Met. 3.192f. (Diana to Actaeon) *nunc tibi me posito visam velamine narres, / si poteris narrare, licet.* This is preferable to taking *licet*, with Kingery, as a concessive conjunction, "though Jupiter may later admit H. . . ."

122 illas . . . manus. That is, polluted by the blood of his family. Hercules' powerful hands are frequently mentioned during the play. Their tragic connotations, established by the present phrase in conjunction with *manuque fortis redeat* above, are particularly important at three points. The first is after H.'s return from the underworld, when he jeeringly asks Juno to find more work for his *manus* (614). The second comes after the killing of Lycus, when there is something ominous about the blood on H.'s hands and his refusal to wash them (918–24 comm.). Finally, in Act V the fresh blood on his hands reveals H.'s guilt to him (1192ff.); he then becomes obsessed with the need to punish them and the impossibility of cleansing them. Although Eur.'s play naturally contains many references to H.'s hands, the dramatic use of them to foreshadow the tragedy, and to reveal H.'s guilt, is new in Sen.

123f. Dawn urges the end of preparatory discussion and the beginning of action; cf. particularly Eur. *IA* 156ff. ἴθι· λευκαίνει / τόδε φῶς ἤδη λάμπουσ' ἠὼς ἢ πῦρ τε τεθρίππων τῶν Ἀελίου· / σύλλαβε μόχθων.

bella. The question *Quae bella?* (30) has been answered, and the answer is leading to action.

clarescit dies. The only use of *clarescere* in Sen. Trag., and the first surviving use in Latin with reference to *visual* clarity. *Dies* may mean either "daylight" or "sky" (cf. comm. on 8 *laxatur dies* ad fin.).

124ff. Poetic periphrases for dawn and other times or seasons are frequently found from Homer on. Seneca elsewhere has an ironic comment on Julius Montanus, who specialized in sunrises and sunsets (*Ep.* 132.11), and there are amusing parodies of the *topos* at *Apocol.* 2.

124 Titan. From the earliest Greek literature on, the sun is called Hyperion (Hom. *Il.* 8.480) or Hyperion's child (Hes. *Theog.* 374), Hyperion being a Titan (ibid. 134). The poetic use of *Titan* for "sun" is first popularized by Ovid, but remains a poor third in that writer to *Phoebus* and *Sol* (cf. Pease on V. *Aen.* 4.119, J. Fontenrose in *AJP* 61 [1940] 429ff.). In Seneca however it is almost as widely used as *Phoebus*, and much more so than *Sol* (*Phoebus* twenty times, *Titan* seventeen, *Sol* eight).

[157]

Commentary: Ode I

croceo. The adjective is applied by Vergil and Ovid to the robe, couch, hair, etc. of Aurora, in the tradition of Homer's κροκόπεπλος Ἠώς. Seneca is the first to apply it to the color of dawn itself.

Ode I (125–204)

In subject matter the first half of the ode is heavily indebted to the dawn description that opens the parodos of Euripides *Phaethon*.[31] It is instructive to see how Seneca reshapes this source material.[32] I give the relevant lines (63–90) in full:

ἤδη μὲν ἀρτιφανὴς
 Ἀὼς ἱ[ππεύει] κατὰ γᾶν,
ὑπὲρ δ' ἐμᾶς κεφαλᾶς
 Πλειά[δων πέφευγε χορός],
μέλπει δὲ δένδρεσι λεπτ-
 ὰν ἀηδὼν ἁρμονίαν
ὀρθρευομένα γόοις
  Ἴτυν Ἴτυν πολύθρηνον.

σύριγγας δ' οὐριβάται
 κινοῦσιν ποιμνᾶν ἐλάται,
ἔγρονται δ' εἰς βοτάναν
 ξανθᾶν πώλων συζυγίαι·
ἤδη δ' εἰς ἔργα κυνα-
 γοὶ στείχουσιν θηροφόνοι,
παγαῖς τ' ἐπ' Ὠκεανοῦ
 μελιβόας κύκνος ἀχεῖ.

ἄκατοι δ' ἀνάγονται ὑπ' εἰρεσίαις
 ἀνέμων τ' εὐαέσσιν ῥοθίοις,
ἀνὰ δ' ἱστία ν[αῦται] ἀειράμενοι
 ἰαχοῦσιν ["Επου] πότνι' αὔρ[α]
[ἡμῖν ὑπ'] ἀκύμονι πομπᾷ
 σιγώντων ἀνέμων
[ποτὶ τέκνα] τε καὶ φιλίας ἀλόχους·
 σινδὼν δὲ πρότονον ἐπὶ μέσον πελάζει.

---

31. The parodos of the *Phaethon* was already an anthology piece by the third century B.C. (J. Diggle, ed., Euripides *Phaethon* [Cambridge 1970] 34). Strabo and Plutarch quote lines from outside the parodos, however, and Diggle believes that Ovid knew the full play (p. 200). So Seneca could have known a full text of the play.

32. The most detailed study of Seneca's use of sources in the odes of *HF* is that of Kapnukajas; compilations of material include those of Spika for Horace, Haar Romeny for Vergil, and Charlier for Ovid. For Ode I, I have also profited from A. Rose 1978 chap. 2, "The Dawn Songs of Euripides and Seneca."

Commentary: Ode I

> τὰ μὲν οὖν ἑτέροισι μέριμνα πέλει,
> κόσμον δ' ὑμεναίων δεσποσύνων
> ἐμὲ καὶ τὸ δίκαιον ἄγει καὶ ἔρως
> ὑμνεῖν.[33]

In broad outline Seneca follows Euripides in moving from the heavens to the land and finally to the sea. In more detail the order of topics in the two poets may be summarized thus (but see p. 478 on 146–51):

Euripides	Seneca
dawn	stars
stars	sun, mountains
nightingale	toil
shepherds	shepherd
grazing animals	grazing animals
hunters	nightingale
swan	other birds
sailors	sailor
	fisherman

The following are the more notable changes introduced by Seneca.

1. He expands the opening four lines of Euripides to twelve, in keeping with the general emphasis in this play on the heavens and their phenomena. The expansion is influenced by Ov. *Met.* 2.114–18, from the Phaethon episode (clearly Seneca associated Ovid's version with Euripides' play):

> diffugiunt stellae, quarum agmina cogit
> Lucifer et caeli statione novissimus exit.
> quem petere ut terras mundumque rubescere vidit
> cornuaque extremae velut evanescere lunae,
> iungere equos Titan velocibus imperat Horis.

See comm. on 126–28 and 136. The mountains of 113ff., not in Ovid, are introduced for their associations (see ad loc.).

2. The note of *hardship* in 137f. is foreign to the Arcadian atmosphere of Euripides' lines,[34] and Seneca maintains it in what follows: the shepherd must collect fodder, the sailor faces dangers, the fisherman's task is neither easy nor comfortable. In Roman poetry such a note is associated particu-

---

33. The text is that of Diggle, reproduced by kind permission of the editor. Square brackets indicate conjectural supplements.

34. Eur. uses μέριμνα of the tasks of the countryside (87): that may have suggested Sen.'s *curas*, but in Eur. the word carries no connotation of hardship, for the line means simply "these things are the concern of others" (Diggle).

larly with Vergil's *Georgics*, and indeed the phrase with which Seneca introduces it, *labor durus*, occurs there twice (2.412, 4.114).

3. Euripides' passing reference to colts is expanded into a list of animals at pasture and their activities; these are described with sympathy, particularly for young creatures. This note may be found in several Roman poets (e.g. comm. on 144f.), but again it is associated especially with the *Georgics*.

4. The nightingale is postponed from its earlier position in Euripides and subjoined to Seneca's list of animals. In keeping with that list, Seneca gives a sympathetic picture of the bird's activities, rather than a conventional reference to its supposedly mournful song. Euripides' singing swans were in place by the streams of Ocean (see Diggle on 77), but would not be so in the environs of Thebes: Seneca replaces them by a general *turba* of birds, a fitting conclusion to his catalogue of creatures.

5. Seneca discards the sailors' prayer: he wants to portray typical activities, whereas the prayer gives a degree of characterization to Euripides' sailors. To fill out the final section he adds the shore fisherman.

The vivid pictures in 139–58 contrast with the vagueness of most of Seneca's descriptions. This may be attributed in part to Euripidean influence, but the most striking details—the shepherd gathering fodder by hand, the bird warming its wings, the whole fisherman description—have no counterpart in Eur. *Phaethon*. In details of language the dominant influence, as so often in Seneca, is Ovidian (see comm. on 131, 136, 143, 146–49, 151, 152–54, 157). For further instances of verbal influence from the *Georgics* see comm. on 139f. and 146.

The second half of the ode begins by contrasting the simple lives of the countryside with the busy activities of the city.[35] These lines recall two famous passages, Horace's first ode and the end of *Georgics* 2 (particularly 503ff.). Both have two types in common with Seneca's list, the φιλοχρήματος and the φιλότιμος, and Vergil possibly shares a third type (v. 164 *regum* comm.); Seneca's description of the φιλότιμος is certainly influenced verbally by the Horatian ode, and probably also by Vergil (v. comm. on 169–71). But the influence of these passages should not be overestimated. The *locus* concerning the variety of human activities was highly traditional, and the φιλοχρήματος and φιλότιμος were among the most traditional types (see N-H on Hor. *Carm.* 1.1); it is relevant that in this *locus* other ways of life are often contrasted unfavorably with the βίος θεωρητικός, though what Seneca has in mind at 174ff. is contentment, εὐθυμία, rather than philosophical contemplation, θεωρία). Seneca's description of the miser contains many reminiscences of Horace, but not of the first ode. Finally, the

---

35. A familiar contrast, usually weighted in favor of rustic simplicity: cf. e.g. Cic. *S.Rosc.* 75, Lucr. 2.22–36, Hor. *Epod.* 2, *Carm.* 3.29.9ff., Sen. *Pha.* 483ff., Quint. 2.4.24.

pattern *ille—hic—illum—hic* that introduces Seneca's types may echo the *hunc—illum* of Hor. *Carm.* 1.1.7—9, but some such pattern of pronouns was inevitable given the nature of the topic.

The themes of the remainder of the ode—'live in the present, for life passes swiftly' and 'eminence is dangerous'—are associated with Horace: for the first cf. e.g. *Carm.* 1.11.7f., 2.11, *Epod.* 2, for the second *Carm.* 2.10.9ff., 3.16.18ff. Both themes are commonplace, however (v. N-H on *Carm.* 1.11 passim and 2.10.9). There is no evidence of influence from specific passages in Horace, and indeed lines 199f. contradict the Horatian Golden Mean (see ad loc.). This section is best described as using conventional themes with Horatian-Epicurean overtones. The language too is largely conventional (but see 189—91 comm.). Seneca's originality here lies in his application of these themes to the understanding of the play.

The ode is integrated, to a degree that is unusual in Senecan tragedy, into its dramatic context. Thus at its opening there is a strong awareness of dramatic time which agrees with the indications at the end of the prologue. The end of the ode provides a transition into the following scene (202—4), a technique that is unusual outside the plays of group 1 (see ad loc.). There is also some degree of verbal integration both with the preceding prologue (cf. 6 *Arctos alta parte glacialis poli* with 129 *signum celsi glaciale poli*[36]) and with the following Act (comm. on 207—13).

The ode proceeds through a remarkable series of shifts in thought and feeling. First it engages the audience emotionally through the lyrical images of light and peace in 125—61[37]; the effect is like that of waking from a nightmare. Now an element of moral judgment is introduced with the contrast between alternative ways of life. The topic seems to grow naturally out of the first half of the ode, and the audience is hardly likely to object to the choice implied, given the terms in which the contrast is presented. Next the discussion of ways of life is lifted onto a philosophical plane: life is so brief that we should live each moment to the fullest (174ff.). Again the transition is skillfully done,

36. Note that at 129 the Bear is introduced by Sen. independently of Ov. *Met.* 2.114—18. Other verbal similarities between ode and prologue (e.g. *micare* 14, 125, *vagantes* 11 cf. *vagos* 126) may be seen as due to the similarity of subject, but nevertheless increase the links between the two. It should be noted, however, that these links are somewhat ironic in nature. For Juno the starry heavens are evidence of Jupiter's infidelities, but in the ode they are described for their own sake and seem to connote the regular processes of nature. This technique of ironic recall is used to greater effect in the opening odes of *Med.* and *Thy.*

37. Even here, however, references to tragic passion are not completely excluded: note the allusions in 134 and 149.

with this section seeming at first no more than a recapitulation of 159ff. (*tranquilla quies* 160—*secura quies* 175, *laeta* 160—*laeti* 178), and the ideas are thoroughly familiar from Horace and elsewhere. Only at the end of this section does the audience realize, surely with a considerable shock, that these generalities are extremely pertinent to the judgment of the play. Hercules' descent to the underworld is seen as a metaphor for the human tendency to rush deathward in pursuit of ambitious aims, rather than savoring each passing moment. The ode quickly moves away again into generalities, but by now their purport is clear: the audience cannot but identify the *alius* of 192ff. at least in part with H. himself, and understand that he is a notable exemplar of the *animosa virtus* that leads to a fall (201). Thus the ode has brought the audience, through a series of modulations of traditional topics, toward condemnation of Hercules' βίος and expectation of his tragedy.

The Roman contrast between country and city contains certain anachronistic details: the *salutatio* of 164–66, the lawyer's activity in the forum in 172–74, the triumphal *currus* of 195. In general, though Seneca occasionally introduces deliberate Grecisms (v. comm. on 853), he does not go out of his way to avoid anachronism (on the subject v. Walter). Here the anachronisms may be seen as related to the strategy of moving through familiar material to an unfamiliar conclusion. But the anachronisms work both ways: if they assist a Roman audience in perceiving what is objectionable in Hercules' way of life, they also hint that Herculean ambition and disregard of the evanescent quality of life are ills to be found in contemporary Rome; *de nobis fabula narratur*.

Is the lyrical description of dawn in the countryside used simply to lead into the contrast with urban activities, and so ultimately to permit the condemnation of ambition? I suggest a deeper thematic integration. The first half of the ode presents humanity within the much larger setting of nature. Here the sympathetic description of animals and birds is important: human beings do not dominate, but take their place among other sentient creatures in the natural setting, subject to the powers of nature, whether the fickle winds or the daily return of the light (152f., 137f.). This is in the most literal sense life according to nature,[38] in complete contrast to the solipsistic world of the city where human passions attain such importance that Seneca speaks of them as haunting the streets (163). The second half of the ode also advocates life in accordance with nature, in a sense that is more philosophical but

---

38. Needless to say, life according to nature in this sense does not guarantee a Nirvana-like peace; Sen. has perhaps short-circuited his argument in attributing *tranquilla quies* to those who are subject to *labor durus, curae*, and danger. But the underlying coherence of thought is clear: such men enjoy the peace of a quiet conscience.

Commentary: Ode I

not fundamentally at variance with the first sense. Human life can only be lived well by those who realize that it is subject to nature, to the turning year, in a word to time. The theme of the ode may be seen in part as nature and the life according to nature, as opposed to lives which attempt to deny the ephemeral quality of human existence.

The ode is not only integrated into the drama in a technical sense, but also indispensable for our understanding of the play. It establishes a standard of normality in the conduct of human life, and indicates that by that standard Hercules is condemned. It was essential for Seneca to formulate these judgments early in the play, so that the developing action could be viewed in these terms. And only the Chorus could give an objective view of this kind, as the other *dramatis personae* all have a prejudiced view of Hercules.

The meter is anapestic monometers and dimeters. On the question of colometry see Appendix 3.

125ff. iam. For the repetition of *iam* (132, 134) cf. ἤδη at *Phaethon* 63, 75. Initial anaphora of *iam* or ἤδη in asyndeton is sometimes used to enumerate various aspects (concurrent rather than successive) of a certain time or season: cf. *Ag.* 456ff. (dusk), Julius Montanus ap. Sen. *Ep.* 122.13, Stat. *Theb.* 1.336ff. (night), Cat. 46.1ff., Hor. *Carm.* 4.12.1ff., *Anth. Pal.* 10.5.1ff. (spring), Hor. *Carm.* 3.29.17ff. (midsummer), *Anth. Lat.* 465 Riese (autumn).

125–27. These lines refer to both reasons for the stars' disappearance, that is their setting (*prono . . . mundo*) and their being outshone by the sun. The latter is of course frequent in dawn descriptions, but the stars' setting (or movement toward setting) usually indicates a somewhat earlier time of night: the small hours at V. *Aen.* 2.9 *suadentque cadentia sidera somnos*; the approach of dawn rather than its arrival at Hom. *Il.* 10.252f. ἀλλ' ἴομεν· μάλα γὰρ νὺξ ἄνεται, ἐγγύθι δ' ἠώς, / ἄστρα δὲ δὴ προβέβηκε, παροίχωκεν δὲ πλέων νύξ.

rara micant sidera. *Micare* is not unusual of stars, but *rara micant* perhaps echoes Vergil's evocative reference to campfires in an unguarded enemy camp: *lumina rara micant, somno vinoque sepulti / procubuere* (*Aen.* 9.189f.).

prono . . . mundo. Either ablative of place, "in the heavens as they turn downward," or ablative absolute, for which cf. Luc. 4.28f. *prono . . . Olympo / in noctem.* For the phrase cf. also V. *Aen.* 8.280 *devexo . . . Olympo.*

[*163*]

126–28. Military metaphors are common in dawn descriptions (see comm. on 136 *fugit*, and for *nox victa* cf. *Tro.* 171 *vicerat noctem dies*), but this lively extended metaphor is suggested specifically by the Ovidian passage quoted in the introduction to Ode I. *Contrahit ignes* interprets the fact that stars now appear only in the western sky to mean that night has rallied her forces there; for *contrahere* of concentrating scattered troops cf. Cic. *Att.* 8.1.2 *ut Luceriam omnes copiae contrahantur*, Caes. *BGall.* 7.43.5, Curt. 8.4.9 *contrahere dispersos* (sc. *milites*). *Agmen cogere* is the standard term for bringing up the rear and thus keeping the column in close formation. The latter phrase comes from the Ovidian passage (cf. also *Met.* 11.97f. *et iam stellarum sublime coegerat agmen / Lucifer*), but *contrahit* is Seneca's contribution.

126 vagos. A standard description of stars in Sen. (see comm. on 11 *passim vagantes*), but the adjective here also contributes to the military metaphor (cf. Livy 3.5.10 where a band of defeated Aequi are described as *vagi dissipato agmine fugientes*).

128 Phosphoros. As a variation on Ovid's *Lucifer* (*Met.* 2.115, 11.98), the standard Latin form, Sen. introduces the much rarer *Phosphoros*, for which only one precedent survives in Latin verse (Germ. fr. 4.73).

129–31. "In classical Roman poetry . . . the position of the Bear seems regularly to fix the time of night and that of the Pleiades the season of the year" (Jocelyn 329). Thus Sen. substitutes the Bear for the Pleiades of *Phaethon* 65f. Diggle. Vergil makes the same substitution in adapting a passage of the *Odyssey*, and Ennius in adapting Euripides (*Aen.* 3.512ff.–*Od.* 5.270ff., Enn. *trag.* 188ff. Jocelyn–Eur. *IA* 6ff.; Jocelyn 329–30).

129. The northern pole is traditionally described as "high," cf. Arat. *Phaen.* 25f. ἀλλ' ὁ μὲν [sc. πόλος] οὐκ ἐπίοπτος, ὁ δ' ἀντίος ἐκ βορέαο / ὑψόθεν ὠκεανοῖο (Germ. *Arat.* 22f. *pars mersa sub undas / Oceani, pars celsa sub horrifero Aquilone*), V. *Georg.* 1.342f. The northerly Bears are naturally associated with cold, as in the phrase *gelidas Arctos* V. *Aen.* 6.16, Ov. *Met.* 4.625. See comm. on 6 *glacialis poli*.

130f. E's text *Arcados Ursae . . . vocant* can only be construed with *Ursae* as nominative plural, but this is open to objections on linguistic, astronomical, and mythological grounds. First, the singular *signum* in 129 would not naturally refer to two constellations. Second, the phrase *septem stellis* clearly alludes to the term *septentriones*, as at Acc. *trag.* 566

R² *sub axe posita ad stellas septem*, Sen. *Tro.* 439. *Septentriones* may be used of either the Great or the Lesser Bear, but it would be an obvious error in astronomy to describe the Bears jointly as having seven stars. Third, there is no mythological justification for the phrase "the Bears of Arcas." Arcas is closely associated with the Great Bear; according to the version familiar from Ovid (*Fasti* 2.153ff., cf. *Met.* 2.409ff.), he was transformed into the Bear-Ward, Arctophylax, when his mother became Ursa Major. But this gives no connection with Ursa Minor, and indeed the versions that link the catasterism of the two Bears are incompatible with the Callisto myth[39] (cf. Arat. *Phaen.* 30ff., Roscher 869–72).

It therefore seems necessary to correct to *Ursa . . . vocat*. As Arcas in the heavens can be called *Custos Ursae* (Ov. *Fasti* 2.153), so the Great Bear can reasonably be described as *Arcados Ursa*.[40] Leo deletes 130 *in toto*, presumably regarding it as interpolated (as does Zwierlein 1976 182f.), but this leaves the colon insipid.

131 verso temone. From the earliest times the Bear is also known as the Wain, cf. Hom. *Od.* 5.273 Ἄρκτον θ', ἣν καὶ Ἄμαξαν ἐπίκλησιν καλέουσιν. In Latin the term is *Plaustrum* (e.g. Ov. *Met.* 10.447, cited below); sometimes, by metonymy, *Temo* (e.g. Stat. *Theb.* 1.371), though *temo* more often indicates part of the constellation, as in the citations below. Finally, the term *septentriones* seems to picture the constellation as ploughing oxen, cf. Varro *Ling.* 7.74. Conflation between some or all of these conceptions becomes traditional in Roman poetry, as the following passages illustrate: Cic. *Nat. D.* 2.109 (from Aratus) *Arctophylax, vulgo qui dicitur esse Bootes, / quod quasi temone adiunctam prae se quatit Arctum,* Ov. *Met* 10.446f. cited below, Luc. 4.523, ps.-Sen. *HO* 1523 *quique sub plaustro patiuntur Ursae,* Stat. *Theb.* 1.692f.

The turning of the Wain usually indicates an advanced hour of the night, rather than dawn, cf. Ov. *Met.* 10.446f. *tempus erat, quo cuncta silent, interque Triones / flexerat obliquo plaustrum temone Bootes,* Sen. *Tro.* 438f. *partes fere nox alma transierat duas / clarumque septem verterant stellae iugum,* Anacreont. 33.1ff. West μεσονυκτίοις ποτ' ὥραις / στρέφετ' ἦμος

---

39. The only exception known to me is the obscure version in Schol. Arat. 27 (p. 343 Maass), according to which Ursa Minor is not a bear at all, but the hunting dog of Callisto.

40. The conjecture *Arcades Ursae* (found in Q and some recc.) fails because there are no grounds for describing Ursa Minor as "Arcadian." Furthermore the conjecture does not satisfy the first two objections raised above to E's text. (I assume that at *Oed.* 477 *sidus Arcadium* refers only to Ursa Major, and is not synonymous with the following phrase *geminumque Plaustrum*.)

Ἄρκτος ἤδη / κατὰ χεῖρα τὴν Βοώτου. Seneca introduces the constellation in an unusual context for two reasons; his adaptation of the *Phaethon* passage, and the link with the prologue (v. introduction to Ode I).

lucem ... vocat. For the metaphor in this context cf. Tib. 1.9.62 *dum rota Luciferi provocet orta diem*, Ov. *Met.* 4.629f. *dum Lucifer ignes / evocat Aurorae*, *Pont.* 1.4.58 [*Memnonis mater*] *quam primum roseo provocet ore diem!*

132 caeruleis ... equis. The horses of the Sun are too familiar an image to need illustration, but one notes particularly line 118 of the passage in *Met.* 2, *iungere equos Titan velocibus imperat horis*. They are sometimes given an appropriate color, being *nivei* at Ov. *Am.* 2.1.24, *purpurei* at *Fasti* 2.74 (cf. Tib. 1.3.94, ps.-Ov. *Cons. Liv.* 282). Here *caeruleus* carries its associations with the sky, for which cf. Enn. *Ann.* 48 Skutsch *caeli caerula templa*, Ov. *Fasti* 3.449 *caeruleum ... caelum*, *TLL* 3.104.18ff. The closest parallel to the present phrase is perhaps ps.-V. *Ciris* 37f. *candida lunae / sidera, caeruleis orbem pulsantia bigis*, where *candida* suggests that *caeruleis* connotes brightness rather than darkness. Cerulean horses of a darker hue appear at Ov. *Her.* 7.50 and *Fasti* 4.446, belonging to Triton and Pluto, respectively. The variant *caeruleis ... aquis*, found in recc., may be regarded as a trivialization, introducing the more usual associations of *caeruleus* with the sea, and perhaps borrowed from *Ag.* 69 *caeruleis immunis aquis*.

evectus. Something of a *vox propria* for rising on high, cf. V. *Aen.* 6.130 *evexit ad aethera virtus*, Ov. *Met.* 2.73 (the Sun speaking to Phaethon) *rapido contrarius evehor orbi* (with Bömer ad loc.), 2.587f. *mox alta per auras / evehor*; of the Sun, Mela 3.57 *sol se altius evehens*.

133 summa ... Oeta. Oeta is mentioned because of two relevant associations: with Hercules, who will die in the pyre on its summit; and with dawn. (Silius has both associations at 6.452f. *vixdum clara dies summa lustrabat in Oeta / Herculei monumenta rogi*.) For the link with dawn cf. ps.-V. *Ciris* 349f. *postera lux ... /... gelida venientem ignem quatiebat ab Oeta*, ps.-Sen. *HO* 861f.: no doubt it arose from the association of the mountain with Eous-Hesperus, for which cf. Cat. 62.7, V. *Ecl.* 8.30, ps.-V. *Culex* 203, *Ciris* 351f., Stat. *Silv.* 5.4.8. Here it is notional rather than literally accurate, as Oeta lies northwest of Thebes and more than 60 miles away.

The Etruscus gives the phrase in the ablative, but the Etonensis and many recc. offer an accusative, *summum . . . Oetam* or *Oetan /-en*.[41] Silius 6.452f. and *HO* 861f. *haec haec renatum prima quae poscit diem / Oeta* seem to support an accusative, but *Ciris* 349f. provides a parallel for the ablative.[42] I am inclined to accept the reading of the Etruscus, and assume that the original ablative was altered to an accusative to provide an object for the verb *prospicit*.

134f. A striking and indeed surrealistic couplet: the reddish light of dawn transfigures the slopes of Cithaeron once more into the bloody scene of Pentheus' *sparagmos*. Though *Cadmeis inclita Bacchis* may be interpreted to mean "the famed site of the biennial festival of Theban Bacchants" (cf. V. *Aen.* 4.302f., Stat. *Theb.* 4.371 *te, bacchate Cithaeron*), it seems impossible to exclude a reference, particularly in *Cadmeis*, to the deeds of Agave and her sisters. An allusion to Pentheus' death in 134 is not in itself unusual in a poetic reference to Cithaeron, e.g. *Phoen.* 17ff., 256f., *Oed.* 930ff., Stat. *Theb.* 1.328f. But 135 creates a *visual* reminiscence of it, by the words *aspersa* and *rubent*. *Aspergere* is very rarely used of light; *TLL* cites only one other passage before Augustine, Sil. 15.223 *qua Titan ortu terras aspergit Eoo*.[43] On the other hand, all other uses of *aspergere* in Sen. Trag. (with the exception of 20 above) are in connection with blood, cf. *HF* 372, *Phoen.* 268, *Tro.* 256, 1107, *Thy.* 95. The image of blood is confirmed by *rubent*. *Rubere, rubescere* are of course commonly used of dawn light (cf. especially *mundumque rubescere* in the Ovidian source passage, *Met.* 2.116), but they are also frequently used of things stained by blood, e.g. Ov. *Met.* 12.71, Sen. *Pha.* 552; particularly striking parallels are Claud. *In Ruf.* 2.418f. *sic mons Aonius rubuit, cum Penthea ferrent / Maenades*, ps.-Sen. *HO* 861ff. (Hercules on Oeta) *abrupta cautes scindat et partem mei / ferat omne saxum, pendeant lacerae manus / totumque rubeat asperi montis latus*.

41. The surprising masculine adjective *summum* can be paralleled from a handful of the places in the poets where some MSS report a masculine adjective agreeing with Oeta or Ossa. They are Prop. 2.1.19f., Ov. *Met.* 1.155 (v. Lee and Bömer ad loc.), 9.165, 204, Claud. *Carm. Min.* 53 [Gigantomachia] 66. Perhaps in these cases the masculine noun *mons* exerts some influence, even though it does not actually appear in the text.

42. If we consider mountains other than Oeta, there are parallels both for peaks *receiving* the first sunlight (supporting an accusative here), e.g. Eur. *Tro.* 1066ff., *Ion* 86ff., V. *Aen.* 12.112f., Ov. *Met.* 7.804 *sole fere radiis feriente cacumina primis*, Sen. *Tro.* 170f., Sil. 9.33f., and for the sun *shining from* a peak (supporting an ablative), e.g. Ap. Rhod. 3.1223f., Lucr. 5.663ff., V. *Aen.* 2.801, Ov. *Met.* 7.702f., Luc. 10.434f. *Lucifer a Casia prospexit rupe, diemque / misit*.

43. *Spargere* is the word used by poets in connection with light, e.g. Lucr. 2.44, V. *Aen.* 4.584 with Pease ad loc., 9.459, 12.113, Sen. *Med.* 74.

Commentary: Ode I

136. Seemingly somewhat misplaced, as 134–35 have turned our attention from heaven to earth. Perhaps the explanation lies in the order of topics in the Ovidian source: *HF* 125–31 elaborates *Met.* 2.114–15, 134–35 expands 2.116 *mundum rubescere*, and the present line on the moon is suggested by 2.117. The sun is mentioned earlier in Seneca than Ovid, however.

fugit. The metaphor of flight, which here takes up the military language of 126–28, is frequently found in dawn descriptions, e.g. Eur. *Ion* 84 ἄστρα δὲ φεύγει πυρὶ τῷδ' αἰθέρος, Ov. *Met.* 2.114 *diffugiunt stellae* (with Bömer ad loc.), cf. *TLL* 6.1.1493.14ff. (*fugio*), 1501.15ff. (*fugo*).

reditura. In this context the word perhaps conveys a hint of human mortality: contrast the *tempora numquam / reditura* of human life (176f.), and note *redire* in contexts of mortality at Cat. 5.4–6 *soles occidere et redire possunt; / nobis cum semel occidit brevis lux, / nox est perpetua una dormienda*, Prop. 2.15.24 *nox tibi longa venit, nec reditura dies*.

137f. Dawn is naturally associated with the beginning of the day's tasks, cf. Hes. *Erga* 579ff., *Hymn. Hom.* 4.98, Callim. fr. 760 Pf. 63–69, V. *Aen.* 11.182f. *Aurora interea miseris mortalibus almam / extulerat lucem, referens opera atque labores*, Ov. *Met.* 4.664f. and *Fasti* 4.165ff. *nox ubi transierit, caelumque rubescere primo / coeperit . . . / . . . et ad solitum rusticus ibit opus*, Am. 1.6.65f., 1.13.13ff., Manil. 1.243f. The note of *hardship*, however, conveyed by *durus* and *curas*, may reasonably be called Roman and specifically Vergilian: see introduction to Ode I.

exoritur. *Labor* arises like the sun (cf. *Oed.* 1f. *Titan . . . exoritur*), and together with it: an excellent metaphor in this couplet which makes the transition from the heavens to earthly matters.

omnes agitat curas. The verb means "sets in motion" (with an effective touch of personification in *curas*). It is well chosen, as *curae* and other perturbations could also be said *agitare* humans in the sense of "disturb," cf. Plaut. *Cist.* 688ᵃ *ita nunc . . . metus me agitat*, Hor. *Epist.* 1.18.98 *num te semper inops agitet vexetque cupido*. N. Heinsius' conjecture *omnes agitat curis* produces a much more ordinary expression (he concludes the sentence with *operitque domos*).

139f. Suggested by *Phaethon* 71f., but Sen.'s herdsman works much harder than his piping counterparts in Euripides. He gathers leaves

[168]

Commentary: Ode I

from trees and plants to supplement the animals' grazing: cf. Soph. fr. 502 P (again at dawn), Theoc. 11.73f., Babr. 45.7, Longus 1.21, Cato *R.R.* 30 *bubus frondem ulneam, populneam, querneam, ficulneam usque dum habebis dato: ovibus frondem viridem usque dum habebis praebeto*, Hor. *Epist.* 1.14.28; Vergil even speaks of plucking grain, in addition to leaves and sedge, for the purpose of strengthening calves (*Georg.* 3.175f.).

The lines may be influenced by V. *Georg.* 3.325ff. *Luciferi primo cum sidere frigida rura / carpamus, dum mane novum, dum gramina canent / et ros in tenera pecori gratissimus herba*. But *pabula carpere* is an Ovidian phrase, used four times by that poet of grazing animals (so also *Dirae* 92); and the collocation *cana pruina*, though here the words do not agree, recalls passages where they do, Hor. *Carm.* 1.4.4 *nec prata canis albicant pruinis*, V. *Georg.* 2.376 *frigora nec tantum cana concreta pruina*, Ov. *Her.* 5.16 *defensa est humili cana pruina casa*. Vergil's *carpamus* is generally taken to denote eager motion ("let us take to the fields"), though the sense of pasturing cannot be far distant. Servius overemphasized the latter by interpreting *carpamus* as *carpere cogamus animalia*, and similarly *TLL* 3.492.56f. unconvincingly glosses Sen.'s *carpit* here with *carpere iubet*; in view of the parallels cited earlier, Sen. must mean that the shepherd himself plucks fodder, cf. also Ov. *Met.* 13.943f. *manuque / pabula decerpsi*.

141–46. The word-pattern of 141 is echoed almost exactly in 144 and 146, which begin parallel cola (but not in 143, which is something of a pendant to 141–42); the resulting series of initial verbs *ludit, errat, pendet*, has an enumerative effect, for which cf. 756–59 with the series *praebet, errant, terret*. Two lines particularly similar to 141 which may have influenced its wording are Hor. *Carm.* 3.18.9 *ludit herboso pecus omne campo* and Ov. *Fasti* 1.156 *ludit et in pratis luxuriatque pecus*.

142 nondum rupta fronte. That is, by horns. For the description cf. Ov. *Am.* 3.13.15 *vituli nondum metuenda fronte* and *Hal.* 2f. *vitulus . . . / qui nondum gerit in tenera iam cornua fronte*, Sen. *Tro.* 538, Stat. *Theb.* 6.267.

143 vacuae. I take this to mean that their udders are empty, rather than that they are left at peace by their young ("at leisure" Kingery, Miller), but perhaps both senses are present. There is a less striking example of a transferred adjective in such a context at Ov. *Met.* 15.472 *ubera dent saturae manibus pressenda capellae*. Seneca loves to exploit *plenus* and *vacuus*: some of the more spectacular passages are *Pha.* 1268, *Oed.* 1012, *Ag.* 26, 858, *Thy.* 12.

reparant ubera. An extension of the verb's meaning from such phrases as *reparare membra* (Ov. *Met.* 4.216); I know of no parallel for *reparare* in the sense of "refill."

144f. This picture of the kid's wobbling steps in the soft grass is particularly reminiscent of Lucr. 1.259ff. *hinc nova proles / artubus infirmis teneras lasciva per herbas / ludit*, cf. 3.7 *tremulis . . . artubus haedi.* (145 also recalls V. *Georg.* 4.10f. *neque oves haedique petulci / floribus insultent.*)

144. The unusual rhythm seems expressive of the kid's unsteadiness. There is only one other dimeter with double spondee followed by anapest-spondee in this ode (175 *qui velocis memores aevi*), and it lacks the word-break after the second syllable of the anapest, which contributes to the effect here.

146–49. Seneca takes the nightingale from *Phaethon* 67ff.,[44] but follows Roman tradition concerning her mythical identity; *paelex* alludes to Philomela, debauched by her sister's husband, as at Ov. *Met.* 6.537 *paelex ego facta sororis*, *Tr.* 2.389f. According to the usual Greek tradition, it was Procne who became a nightingale, and Philomela a swallow; most Roman writers, however, reversed the roles, cf. V. *Georg.* 4.15, 511, ps.-V. *Aetna* 587ff., Ov. *Fasti* 2.853ff., Petron. 131, Mart. 11.18.19, *Anth. Lat.* 13, Serv. ad V. *Ecl.* 6.78.[45]

146 pendet summo . . . ramo. The verb indicates "to be perched" here, as at 155, ps.-Sen. *Oct.* 921f. (also of a nightingale) *tenui / ramo pendens*, Ov. *Pont.* 1.8.51 *pendentis . . . rupe capellos.* For mention of the singing nightingale's perch on a branch cf., in addition to *Oct.*, V. *Georg.* 4.514f. *ramoque sedens miserabile carmen / integrat*, Sen. *Ag.* 671 *ramo cantat*, *Anth. Lat.* 808.39. The bird's liking for woodland habitat is often noted, cf. Tarrant on *Ag.* 670–73 *verno . . . ramo . . . tectis.*[46]

---

44. For evidence of the nightingale singing at dawn see Diggle 101–2; the bird will in fact sing at any time of day or night, cf. Arist. *HA* 9.632b ἡμέρας καὶ νύκτας, Witherby et al. *Handbook of British Birds* 2.188. Seneca also makes the bird sing after the young are hatched, cf. V. *Georg.* 4.512. According to modern observations in Italy, the bird sings well into July and may sometimes be heard in August (*Ibis* series 12.3A [1927] 266, 269, cf. Arist. loc. cit).

45. Seneca follows the Roman version again at *Ag.* 670–77 (*pace* Tarrant ad loc.). The swallow is clearly identified with Procne at 675 *furta mariti garrula narrat*; for Philomela mourning Itys (672) cf. ps.-V. *Culex* 250f., Ov. *Am.* 2.6.7, Mart. 10.51.4.

46. The nightingale "sings chiefly from low cover or amongst foliage of lower branches of trees [the usual tradition in classical poetry, e.g. Hom. *Od.* 19.520, Soph. *OC* 673, Cat. 65.13], but sometimes fully exposed" (Witherby et al. 2.188).

Commentary: Ode I

stridula. An odd adjective for what was considered, in ancient as in modern times, the most musical of birds, but it is similarly called ὀξύφωνος at Soph. *Trach.* 963, Babr. 12.3.19, which Jebb explains as referring to the clear and supposedly mournful nature of the song.

147. For the wording cf. V. *Georg.* 1.398f. *tepidum ad solem pennas in litore pandunt / . . . alcyones.*[47] The unusual use of *tradere*, in conjunction with the phrase *novo . . . soli*, suggests that there may also be verbal influence here (as Heyne thought) from ibid. 2.332f. *inque novos soles audent se gramina tuto / credere.* For *sol novus* in reference to dawn cf. ibid. 1.288 *aut cum sole novo terras inrorat Eous.*

148 querulos . . . nidos. Cf. Ov. *Med. Fac.* 77 *querulo volucrum . . . nido* (where however the noun means "nest" rather than "nestlings"); also V. *Aen.* 12.475 *nidisque loquacibus*, Julius Montanus ap. Sen. *Ep.* 122.12 *argutis . . . nidis. Querulus, queror, querela*, etc. are frequently used of the sounds of birds and other creatures (V. *Georg.* 1.378 *ranae cecinere querelam*, Ov. *Met.* 4.413 of bats). Sometimes the birds' complaints are said to be directed at a mythological cause, as at Ov. *Am.* 2.6.7ff., *Tr.* 5.1.60, Stat. *Theb.* 12.478ff. (cf. Eur. *Phaethon* 69f.), but elsewhere, as here, the metaphor is more general, cf. Hor. *Epod.* 2.26 *queruntur in silvis aves*, Sen. *Pha.* 508.

inter. In poetry *inter* sometimes stands between two words which it governs (whether adjective-noun or two nouns), as if its meaning were reflected in its very position: see J. Marouzeau *L'Ordre des mots* (Paris 1922–49) 3.58, Eden on V. *Aen.* 8.32. In Sen. the order adjective–*inter*–noun is associated with anapests and lyric meters, cf. *Med.* 621, 649, 667, *Oed.* 148, 436, *Ag.* 678. On postposition of prepositions generally see Marouzeau 3.44ff., R. D. Williams on Stat. *Theb.* 10.97.

149 Thracia. Philomela and Procne were Athenian in origin, but as their tragedy occurred in Thrace, the poets often use such adjectives to allude to it; v. Tarrant on *Ag.* 673 *Bistonis*.

Here the bird is thought of as seeking the sun's first rays, cf. Lactant. *Phoenix* 39ff. *summo considit in arboris altae / vertice . . . / exspectat radios et iubar exoriens*. But Sen. is wrong in placing the nest on the treetop, v. Bannerman *Birds of the British Isles* 3.302.
47. The nightingale sometimes flutters its wings during song (Bannerman 3.299) or display (Witherby et al. 4.3), but the notion that the wings are spread to the sun probably derives from seabird behavior such as that described by Vergil.

Commentary: Ode I

150–51. The close of Robert Bridges' *Nightingales* is very similar: "while the innumerable choir of day / Welcome the dawn." (The short closing line parallels the traditional colometry *confusa sonat murmure mixto / testata diem.*)

151 murmure. Rarely used of birds in earlier poetry, but Ovid provides a precedent at *AA* 2.465f. *columbae / quarum blanditias verbaque murmur habet.*

152–54. Much abbreviated from Eur., but the detail of the wind filling out the sail occurs in both passages. Seneca's wording of it, however, is Ovidian, cf. *Am.* 2.11.38 *impleat . . . aura sinus.*

152f. carbasa ventis credit. For the phrase cf. *Ag.* 443 *credita est vento ratis*, Quint. 12 *praef.* 2 (a nautical metaphor) *multos . . . iisdem se ventis credere ausos habemus.* Ovid has comparable phrases, e.g. *Fasti* 6.715 *Zephyro data carbasa*, *Her.* 7.171 *praebebis carbasa ventis*, but the use of *credere* in particular suggests the danger involved in trusting the winds, cf. V. *Aen.* 5.850 *Aenean credam . . . fallacibus auris?*

152bis dubius . . . vitae. In Eur. the weather is fair and the sailors seem more confident. Seneca's phrase reflects the traditional theme of the dangers of seafaring, often found in descriptions of the trader's life: cf. Solon 13.46 φειδωλὴν ψυχῆς οὐδεμίαν θέμενος, Hor. *Carm.* 1.1.14 *pavidus nauta*, 1.14.14, Juv. 14.265ff., K. F. Smith on Tibullus 1.3.37ff. *Dubius vitae* occurs at Ov. *Tr.* 3.3.25.

153 laxos . . . sinus. In reference to sails, the phrase is paralleled at Germ. *Arat.* 408f. *[auster] turbavit lintea puppis / incubuitque sinu laxo*: but it more usually refers to the loose folds of a garment, as at Sen. *Oed.* 423, *Ag.* 889, *Ep.* 53.12.6.

154–58. Descriptions of fishing from shore are found in classical literature from Homer on; particularly relevant to the present passage are Hom. *Il.* 16.406ff., *Od.* 12.251ff., Theoc. 21.41ff., Opp. *Hal.* 3.460ff. The fisherman regularly stations himself on a rock or headland: cf. Hom. *Il.* 16.406 πέτρῃ ἔπι προβλῆτι, Opp. *Hal.* 3.460, Ov. *Met.* 3.592 *scopulis . . . in isdem*, Petron. 3 *in scopulo*. For illustrations of the awkward positions involved (n.b. *pendens*), see W. Radcliffe, *Fishing from the Earliest Times* (London 1921) 11, 131.

154 hic. Unusually contrasted with the noun *nauta* rather than with another *hic* or *ille*; cf. *TLL* 6.2735.84ff.

Commentary: Ode I

155 deceptos. Housman's explanation of *deceptos* as = *celatos*, "concealed by the bait" (*CR* 14 [1900] 259 = 1972 521f.) seems likely, though the only parallel is the difficult phrase at Livy 22.4.4 *ab tergo ac super caput deceptae insidiae*. The alternative is to understand *deceptos piscibus hamos*, "his cheated hooks" (Miller): this could be illustrated by the clever trick attributed to the mullet, *at mugil cauda pendentem everberat escam, / excussamque legit* (ps.-Ov. *Hal.* 38f.).

157 spectat . . . praemia. The phrase is borrowed from Ov. *Met.* 6.518 *spectat sua praemia raptor*, of an eagle gloating over a captured hare. Seneca has altered the meaning of the phrase, as his fisherman has not yet made his catch but is watching the fish in the water in order to judge the right moment to strike: cf. Theoc. 21.42f., Opp. *Hal.* 4.229f. ἁλιεὺς δέ μιν αἶψα δοκεύσας / χαλκείαις ξυνέπειρεν ἀνακρούων γενύεσσιν, Mart. 10.30.18 *spectatus alte lineam trahit piscis*, Sil. 7.500ff.

pressa . . . dextra. *Pressa* means "*rigida, firmata*" (Gronovius), that is, to prevent any movement that might alarm the fish. For the importance of a firm hand for the fisherman, see Philip's epigram on the retirement of Peison, who is described as ἔντρομος ἤδη / δεξιτερήν *Anth. Pal.* 6.5.7f.

158. A vivid phrase. *Tremulus* is expressively used of the fish itself; more conventionally of the rod or line, cf. Ov. *AA* 2.77 *tremula dum captat harundine pisces* (the same phrase *Met.* 8.217), Mart. 1.55.10, 3.58.27 *tremulave captum linea trahit piscem*, 4.30.9. The single line, grammatically isolated, makes an effective close to this section of the ode: cf. the similar effect at 185, 191, 201.

159 haec. (Sc. *agunt ii, quibus est*. . . .) For the ellipse cf. V. *Georg.* 4.528 *haec Proteus* (sc. *dixit*), *Aen.* 8.18 *talia per Latium* ("*gerebantur*" *subaudis*, Serv.), Ov. *Met.* 15.807 *talibus hanc genitor* (sc. *allocutus est*). The present example, however, is unusually harsh. *Haec* perhaps reflects τὰ μὲν in the similar summary and transition at *Phaethon* 87f.

161^{b}f. Line 162 has long been recognized as an interpolation in the A tradition, designed to give the ode a comprehensible opening in the absence of lines 125–61. This leaves the question of E's text in 161^b *spes iam magnis*. *Iam*, having meant "at dawn on this date in the Heroic Age" at 125, 132, 134, can scarcely mean "in these degenerate Roman times" here; although the activities listed in 164–74 are clearly Roman in character, it would take more than a *iam* to turn a covert anachronism into an overt one. (The case of *nunc iam* at *Med.* 364 is quite different,

[*173*]

as there the preceding part of the ode has clearly established a temporal succession [329ff., 336ff.]). Nor can *iam* continue to mean "at dawn," as there is no awareness of dramatic time in the following list of activities, despite *expers somni* 165. Among conjectures, Gronovius' *spes in magnis* seems rather flat. Schmidt's *spes immanes* (1860 62f.) is more attractive: an unusual expression, but cf. Ov. *Met.* 5.678 *studiumque immane loquendi*, Stat. *Theb.* 12.167f. *immanis eundi / impetus*. (For *in* or *im-* corrupted to *iam* cf. *TLL* 7.80.78ff.).

163 urbibus errant. For evils wandering around, as if in search of victims, cf. Hes. *Erga* 100 ἄλλα δὲ μυρία λυγρὰ κατ' ἀνθρώπους ἀλάληται (with West ad loc.), Aesch. *PV* 275f., Gratt. 345 *errantis per tot divertia morbos*, Sen. *Tranq.* 11.7. *Urbibus* makes the picture more definite, suggesting muggers roaming through dark city streets.

164–72 ille–hic–illum–hic. Occasionally one finds strict alternation, as here and *Med.* 720ff. *illas–has–illa–has–illos–has*; more often not, cf. *HF* 6ff. *hinc–hinc–hinc–illinc–hinc*, *TLL* 6.2735.15ff., 2736.4ff., Bömer on Ov. *Met.* 3.48.

164–66. The early-morning *salutatio* is often described in satirical fashion, e.g. Hor. *Epod.* 2.7f.; V. *Georg.* 2.461ff.; Sen. *Tranq.* 12.6, *Brev. Vit.* 14.3, *Ep.* 4.10, 68.10; Juv. 1.95ff., 3.126ff., 5.19ff. In the first two passages mentioned it is treated, as here, as a characteristic of city life as opposed to country life. The present context shows clearly that Seneca has in mind here not simply a dutiful *cliens* but an ambitious social climber: cf. the list of such a person's activities in *Ep.* 68.10, *pulsare superbas potentiorum fores, digerere in litteram senes orbos, plurimum in foro posse*; also *Brev. Vit.* 2.1 *sunt quos ingratus superiorum cultus voluntaria servitute consumat*.

164 superbos aditus. Such phrases are almost formulaic in references to the levée, cf. Hor. *Epod.* 2.7f. *superba civium / potentiorum limina*, V. *Georg.* 2.461 *foribus domus alta superbis*, Sen. *Ep.* 4.10 *superbis adsidere liminibus*, 68.10 cited above.

regum. "Patrons, great men," as often in Plautus and Horace. The word may well have the same sense (as Conington and others think) at V. *Georg.* 2.504 *penetrant aulas et limina regum*, in which case the social climber is a third type which Sen.'s list shares with Vergil's (cf. introduction to Ode I).

165 duras fores. The phrase was perhaps suggested to Sen. by the similar situation of the sleepless *exclusus amator*: cf. Ov. *Am.* 2.1.22

mollierunt duras lenia verba fores, Tib. 1.1.56 *sedeo duras ianitor ante fores*, TLL 5.2309.11f.

expers somni. Elsewhere Sen. describes the *salutatores* as *illis miseris suum somnum rumpentibus ut alienum expectent* (*Ep.* 14.4). Cf. Juv. 3.127ff., 5.19ff., Mart. 10.70.5. For the phrase cf. Lucr. 6.1181 *lumina . . . expertia somno*.

166–68. This picture of the φιλοχρήματος is rich in reminiscences of Horace. *Gazis*, and the ironic use of *beatas*, come from *Carm.* 1.29.1f. *Icci beatis nunc Arabum invides / gazis*; *inhians* from *Sat* 1.1.70f. *congestis undique saccis / indormis inhians*, which also suggested *congesto* (though the word is not uncommonly used of wealth, cf. Cic. *Rep.* 6.2, Ov. *Her.* 16.224, Tib. 1.1.1, Sen. *Ep.* 92.31); and the paradox of 168 recalls *Sat.* 2.3.142 *pauper Opimius argenti positi intus et auri* and *Carm.* 3.16.28 *magnas inter opes inops*.

169–71. Again the description owes much to Horace, cf. *Carm.* 1.1.7f. *hunc si mobilium turba Quiritium / certat tergeminis tollere honoribus* (however, the phrase *mobile vulgus* occurs in Ovid, cf. *Tr.* 1.9.13 *mobile sic sequitur Fortunae lumina vulgus*).

169 attonitum. Used by Vergil of the φιλότιμος in a very similar context, *Georg.* 2.509f. *hic stupet attonitus rostris, hunc plausus hiantem / . . . corripuit*. The adjective is common in Sen. Trag. (fifteen uses), and need not necessarily be ascribed to Vergilian influence here.

170. The comparison of the common people to the sea for changeability is traditional, cf. Dem. 19.136, Cic. *Muren.* 35–36, Livy 28.27.11 *multitudo omnis sicut natura maris per se immobilis est, at venti et aurae cient: ita aut tranquillum aut procellae in vobis sunt* (cf. Polyb. 11.29.9ff.).

171 aura tumidum. The most frequent nonmetaphorical use of *tumidus* in Sen. Trag. is for the swelling of the sea. Both words are often used metaphorically (*aura* frequently of popular favor, e.g. Hor. *Carm.* 3.2.20, Sen. *Pha.* 488 *aura populi*), and it is unlikely that they convey any precise image here.

172f. clamosi rabiosa fori iurgia. *Clamosi* refers to the shouts of σοφῶς and the like which greeted rhetorical hits, cf. Pliny *Ep.* 2.14.5ff. The phrase is modeled on Ov. *Tr.* 3.12.17f. *ludis / cedunt verbosi garrula bella fori* (cf. 4.10.18 *fortia verbosi natus ad arma fori*). Similar adjectives are applied to the forum at V. *Georg.* 2.502 *insanum . . . forum* (cf. Prop. 4.1.134 *insano verba tonare foro*), Ov. *AA* 1.80 *arguto . . . foro*.

Commentary: Ode I

173 vendens. For complaints of the venality of lawyers cf. Cic. *Parad.* 46 passim, Sen. *Apocol.* 12 poët. v. 28 *o causidici, venale genus*, Tac. *Ann.* 11.5 *nec quicquam publicae mercis tam venale fuit quam advocatorum perfidia.*

173bis iras et verba locat. *Manus (suas) locare* is a similar phrase that Seneca likes, cf. *Ben.* 6.17.1, *Ep.* 37.2, 44.3. Cf. also Ovid's phrase *reos empta ... defendere lingua*, *Am.* 1.10.39.

174 secura quies. The phrase clearly carries Epicurean overtones. It is used by Lucretius (3.211 and 939) of death, by Vergil (*Georg.* 2.467) of the farmer's life, by Ovid (*Fasti* 6.734) of sleep, and in *AA* 1.639 for the Epicurean view of the gods' existence.

175–78. The language is simple and conventional; cf. particularly the philosophy expounded by the town mouse, Hor. *Sat.* 2.6.96f. *dum licet, in rebus iucundis vive beatus: / vive memor, quam sis aevi brevis.* A *dum* clause is standard in such contexts (v. N-H on Hor. *Carm.* 2.11.16), and *fata sinunt* is a common tag, e.g. Tib. 1.1.69f. *interea, dum fata sinunt, iungamus amores*, Prop. 2.15.23, V. *Aen.* 4.651 *dum fata deusque sinebat*, 11.701, Ov. *Met.* 13.624, *Tr.* 5.3.5.

176 tempora. The plural perhaps has the connotation of "moments" or "days," whereas *aevum* means the life span seen as a single unit.

177 vivite laeti. The address is less to a specific dramatic audience than to the *gens humana* at large, cf. *Oed.* 980 *fatis agimur: cedite fatis*, *Tro.* 407 *quaeris quo iaceas post obitum loco?*

179 volucrique die. "With the fleeting passage of time." *Volucris dies* is a Horatian phrase, used at *Carm.* 3.28.6, 4.13.16. In the second of these passages it is particularly clear that *dies* stands for passing time; for this meaning cf. *OLD* s.v. 10.

180. The cycle of the year is a familiar image, cf. Eur. *Or.* 1645, *Phoen.* 477 ἐνιαυτοῦ κύκλον; Livy 9.18.4 *circumegit se annus*; V. *Georg.* 2.401, *Aen.* 3.284 *magnum sol circumvolvitur annum*; Stat. *Theb.* 2.400f. *astriferum iam velox circulus orbem / torsit*.

181f. The use of *sorores* for the Fates, and of *fila* for the threads of human life they spin, are both common in poetry, e.g. Hor. *Carm.* 2.3.15f., Ov. *Her.* 12.3 *quae dispensant mortalia fila sorores*. For 182 cf. e.g. Prop. 4.7.51 *Fatorum nulli revolubile carmen*, and line 559 below *Parcarumque colos non revocabiles*.

Commentary: Ode I

183–85. Compare 867 *quid iuvat durum properare fatum?* The most natural interpretation of these lines is that people literally shorten their lives by constant activity and dangerous enterprises, cf. 198 *venit ad pigros cana senectus*. Compare the familiar point that men in general have shortened their life span by their own misplaced ambition and ingenuity, whether through the invention of seafaring (Prop. 3.7.31f., Sen. *QNat*. 5.18.8 *itaque eamus in pelagus et vocemus in nos fata cessantia*, Luc. 3.193ff.) or of weapons (Tib. 1.10.3f.), or through the Promethean theft of fire (Hor. *Carm*. 1.3.29ff.). But in view of the gist of 174–82, the lines might also be taken metaphorically, as meaning that people cheat themselves of the full measure of their days by thinking of the future and allowing the present to slip through their grasp; they "wish their lives away." Cf. Epicurus fr. 204 σὺ δὲ τῆς αὔριον οὐκ ὢν κύριος ἀναβάλλῃ τὸν καιρόν. ὁ δὲ πάντων βίος μελλησμῷ παραπόλλυται καὶ διὰ τοῦτο ἕκαστος ἡμῶν ἀσχολούμενος ἀποθνῄσκει, Sen. *Brev. Vit*. 7.6–8 (esp. *praecipitat quisque vitam suam et futuri desiderio laborat, praesentium taedio*), 9.1, *Ep*. 98.6. Perhaps it would be a mistake to exclude either of these interpretations.

183f. fertur . . . obvia. For *fertur* M and N^{ac} have *flatur*, which may therefore have been the original reading of E; however, the reading is almost certainly corrupt, though accepted by Leo and Giardina out of excessive respect for E. Timpanaro 134f. thinks *flatur* could mean "is blown along," and considers the image to be that of a feather swept off by the Fates, drawn from Eur. *Her*. 509f. καὶ μ' ἀφείλεθ' ἡ τύχη / ὥσπερ πτερὸν πρὸς αἰθέρ' ἡμέρα μία. But such a use of *flare* is unparalleled and highly improbable. In any case a suggestion of passive helplessness would be most inappropriate, for the Chorus' point in 183–87 is that human beings deliberately and willfully seek out death; the most important word in 183–84 is *obvia*. For *obvius* in a context of hastening one's death (though not in the precise sense indicated here) cf. Lucr. 3.1041 (Democritus) *sponte sua leto caput obvius obtulit ipse*, Cic. *Tusc*. 5.56 *praestat . . . morti iam ipsi adventanti paullum procedere ob viam*. There is a comparable manuscript confusion of *affert/afflat* at Hor. *Sat*. 2.6.109.

184 incerta sui. (The E reading *suis* is clearly an assimilation to the case of *fatis*.) The phrase may have a causal sense: it is because people are unsure of themselves, that is of their nature and their true good, that they rush through their lives; cf. *Ep*. 32.4 *vis scire, quid sit quod faciat homines avidos futuri? nemo sibi contigit* (i.e. "no one has found himself, his true nature"). Alternatively, the phrase may simply indicate the spiritual condition in which the majority live. It recurs in a similar context at *Ep*. 23.2 *sollicitus est et incertus sui, quem spes aliqua proritat*. The present context makes it unlikely that the phrase means "uncertain of their survival from day to day," as might be suggested by the uses of *certus sui* at *Ag.* 61, *Ep.* 91.16. (Cf. 292f. comm. for similar phrases.)

185. A neat conclusion and transition, as it applies both to humanity in general in the sense indicated above on 183–85, and also in a very specific way to Hercules' descent to the underworld. The thought also appears, in a less appropriate context, at *Pha.* 477f. *sic* (sc. by celibacy) *atram Styga / iam petimus ultro*.

Stygias . . . undas. A common poetic formula for the underworld, e.g. V. *Aen.* 3.215, 7.773; Ov. *Met.* 3.272; *Tr.* 1.2.65; Sen. *Med.* 805.

186f. Apostrophe is very frequently used in Seneca's choral odes, and contributes to their vigor. Here it is as though the Chorus suddenly thinks of H. as a striking example of its theme. The odes of this play alone provide other instances of apostrophe at 178, 524ff., 549, 558ff., 834, 858, 870ff., 1057ff., 1063ff., 1065ff., 1092, 1115ff., 1135ff.

186 nimium . . . forti. For the hyperbaton see 63 comm.

187 maestos . . . manes. Seneca uses the phrase again at 648 *quam longa maestos ducat ad manes via* (also 566 *tristibus inferis*). Compare Vergil's use of *maestus* for the dead at *Aen.* 6.333, 340, 434, 445, and 10.820f. *tum vita per auras / concessit maesta ad manis*.

188–91. The paratactic style makes it difficult to follow the train of thought, and there are two possible ways of reading the implications of these lines: either "You are acting hubristically in subverting the proper arrangements made by the Fates," or "You are wasting the short span of life granted to you: death comes soon enough, and once it arrives there is no postponing it."

In the first interpretation there seems little point in repeating the idea "no one may postpone his death" (189f.) as H. is doing just the opposite, i.e. forestalling it. *Proferre* must therefore be altered to *praeferre* (a simple enough correction, found already in T^{ac}, S, and V^1), and the sense of 189f. now becomes "just as no one may postpone his death, so no one is allowed to forestall it," with the implication that H. is doing what is forbidden. With this interpretation, the A reading *ordine* in 188 is definitely preferable to the *tempore* of Σ: H. is not just forestalling the time of his own death, but disrupting the orderly process established by the Fates. In line 191 great emphasis will fall on *citatos*: the crowds of the dead come *when summoned*, not before or after.

In the second interpretation, *tempore* is the preferable reading in 188, as we are simply concerned with the moment of an individual's death. *Citatos* in 191 now means "hurried to their doom" (Miller). (The participle usually implies haste in Sen. Trag.) This interpretation of the passage fits better with the argument of the preceding lines, 174–87, and I therefore prefer it, though it must be admitted that 188 does not easily yield the necessary implication "Death comes soon enough." Given this interpretation of the passage, it seems necessary to punctuate as I have done in 187f., rather than with a colon or semicolon after *manes* and a full-stop after *Parcae* as in modern editions.

189–91. The language here has the atmosphere of public life and the courts, though there is no term that could be identified as purely technical. *Cessare* may be used in legal contexts of failure to act or to appear in court, cf. *OLD* s.v. 3b, particularly Callim. *Dig.* 49.14.2.4 *quotiens . . . delator adesse iussus cessat.* For *scriptum diem* cf. Cic. *Verr.* 1.141 *locare incipit non proscripta neque edicta die,* Phaedr. 4.11.8 *cum adscriptus venerit poenae dies. Proferre diem* is a technical phrase in business and legal contexts, cf. *TLL* 5.1.1051.22ff. *Citare* is regularly used of a summons by the magistrates for trial or some similar event, cf. *TLL* 3.1200.38ff.

189 iusso. Probably dative of the participle with *nulli*, rather than ablative of *iussum* with *cessare*. There are, however, instances of the latter construction, particularly Livy 42.6.8 *se nullo usquam cessaturum officio.*

191. The *urna* is most naturally interpreted as the cinerary urn. There may be some conflation with the urn used by the judges of the dead (cf. V. *Aen.* 6.432 *quaesitor Minos urnam movet* and comm. on 732 *iudicia . . . sortitur*), which would "receive" the names of those to be judged. The urn of fate, which determines the order of death (Hor. *Carm.* 2.3.26, 3.1.16), seems less relevant, because here the peoples have already been summoned.

populos. The plural of this noun is frequently used in this play to emphasize the number of the dead, cf. 293, 557, 560, 667, 708, 775.

192ff. In conclusion the Chorus returns to the *locus* concerning the variety of human pursuits, with which it began the second half of the ode. Here the *locus* takes the form of a brief priamel (N-H on Hor. *Carm.* 1.1, pp. 2f.), in which the list of others' pursuits prefaces a statement of personal preference.

Commentary: Ode I

193f. The frequency with which *Fama* is personified is illustrated by the passages collected by Pease on V. *Aen.* 4.173. Naturally enough she is thought of as spreading through cities in particular, as is illustrated by Pease's collection, e.g. V. *Aen.* 4.173 *Libyae magnas it Fama per urbes,* Stat. *Theb.* 6.1f. *Danaas perlabitur urbes / Fama.*

194[bis] **caeloque parem tollat et astris.** At one level, perfectly conventional language, as is shown by the dictionaries s.vv. *caelum, astrum;* cf. such phrases as *in caelum ferre, ad astra tollere.* But as often in Sen. Trag. (cf. comm. on 1138–41 and 1206ff.), the conventional phrases have a particular relevance to the present context: we think of Hercules, whose destined assumption into heaven has been mentioned in the prologue (23, 74, 89, 122), and who is the very type of *animosa virtus* (201).

195 alius curru sublimis eat. That is, in a triumph (again a Roman touch, cf. 58f. comm.). For the phrase cf. Livy 28.9.15 *iret alter consul sublimis curru,* Juv. 10.36f. *praetorem curribus altis / extantem et medii sublimem pulvere circi;* also ps.-Sen. *HO* 1682f. *quis sic triumphans laetus in curru stetit / victor?*

196–201. The security of an unambitious life is frequently contrasted in Sen. Trag. with the dangers of high estate, cf. *Pha.* 1124–40, *Oed.* 882–913, *Ag.* 57–107, *Thy.* 391–403, 447–70; ps.-Sen. *HO* 644–57, 675–99, *Oct.* 377–84, 895–98. In some of these passages it is the Horatian Golden Mean (*media sors*) that is praised, as at *Oed.* 890f., *Ag.* 102ff., but in other passages, as here, Sen. has in mind the polar opposite of high station, a life of the utmost simplicity. *Sordida* (200) in particular contradicts the Golden Mean, cf. Hor. *Carm.* 2.10.5ff. *auream quisquis mediocritatem / diligit tutus caret obsoleti / sordibus tecti, caret invidenda / sobrius aula;* contrast also *Anth. Lat.* 5.11 *otia contingant pigrae non sordida vitae.* (For a similar contradiction of the Horatian Golden Mean, cf. *Ag.* 105 with Tarrant's note.) Here the adjective is "descriptive rather than disparaging" (Howell on Mart. 1.49.28 *infante cinctum sordido*); in addition to Martial's phrase cf. Aesch. *Ag.* 772ff. Δίκα δὲ λάμπει μὲν ἐν δυσκάπνοις δώμασιν, V. *Ecl.* 2.28 *sordida rura.*

For the characteristic elements of the simple life, compare, in addition to the passages cited above, *Med.* 331ff. (the life of primitive man) *sua quisque piger litora tangens / patrioque senex factus in arvo, / parvo dives, nisi quas tulerat / natale solum, non norat opes.* For praise of the simple, quiet life cf. some of the epigrams attributed to Seneca, *Anth. Lat.* 407, 440, 444.

Commentary: Ode I

196 me. The singular of the first person is occasionally used by the Chorus in Seneca, but by no means as commonly as in Greek tragedy. Instances in Sen. are *Tro.* 115 *sum, Med.* 90 *precor, Pha.* 356 *canam, Oed.* 882ff. *mihi, meo, temperem, me, Ag.* 332 *velim*, 656 *vidi vidi*, 694 *putem, Thy.* 393ff. *me, perfruar, moriar.* In the present passage the emphatically contrastive *me* is clearly suggested by the priamel pattern, cf. Hor. *Carm.* 1.1.29, 1.7.10, Tib. 1.1.5. *Oed.* 882ff. and *Thy.* 393ff., the other passages where the singular pronoun occurs, have a similar theme of personal preference for the simple life.

198 cana senectus. A familiar phrase, cf. Cat. 108.1, Tib. 1.8.42 (*senecta*), Ov. *Her.* 14.109.

201. On the thematic importance of *virtus* see the Introduction. For *virtus animosa* cf. Sen. *Ep.* 71.18 *virtutem enim intellego animosam et excelsam.*

202–4. Cf. Eur. *Her.* 442–48, spoken by the Chorus as the family emerges from the palace after dressing in preparation for death: ἀλλ' ἐσορῶ γὰρ τούσδε φθιμένων / ἔνδυτ' ἔχοντας, τοὺς τοῦ μεγάλου / δήποτε παῖδας τὸ πρὶν Ἡρακλέους, / ἄλοχον τε φίλην ὑποσειραίους / ποσὶν ἕλκουσαν τέκνα, καὶ γεραιὸν / πατέρ' Ἡρακλέους. In the Senecan plays that I regard as early (see Introduction, discussion of date), it is not uncommon for the Chorus to refer at the end of an ode to action onstage (usually, as here, an entrance), and so to lead in to the next Act: cf. *Pha.* 358f., 824ff., 989f., 1154f., *Oed.* 911ff., *Ag.* 408ff., 693f. The technique almost disappears in the later plays (the only other example is *HF* 893f.); therefore this instance is probably due to the Euripidean precedent. The Senecan transitional passages are usually in iambic trimeters, though the two passages in *Oed.* continue the meter of the ode. This passage is unique in containing a transition from the odic meter to iambic trimeter.[48]

The purpose of the family's entrance is not stated, but immediately becomes clear from 205ff.: to make prayers for Hercules' return. Am-

---

48. There seems no good reason to doubt the tradition, as Seneca's willingness to experiment with meter is proved by the polymetric odes of *Oed.* and *Ag.* and by the witchcraft scene of *Med.* 740ff. He had, of course, plentiful precedents in Greek tragedy for the use of isolated iambic trimeters in conjunction with other meters in choral passages. The chief dissenter from the paradosis has been Peiper, who normalized the passage by rewriting 204 as an anapestic dimeter plus monometer, *graditurque comes tardus senio / pater Alcidae* (1863 34) or *graditurque gravi tardus senio / pater Alcidae* (1867).

[*181*]

Commentary: Ode I

phitryon should probably be imagined, therefore, as advancing to the stage altar, or perhaps to a statue or shrine associated with it (comm. on 356, 506). The situation differs somewhat from Eur., where the family have sought sanctuary at the altar σωτῆρος Διός (48) before the play begins: in Sen. there is no indication of their seeking refuge until the entrance of Lycus (cf. 356, 503). The altar assumes dramatic importance again later in the play, when the Chorus and H. refer to it as a place for thanksgiving sacrifices (876, 899, 911; cf. 1040 with comm.). On the various functions of stage altars in classical drama, see Tarrant on *Ag.* 392a f.

202 crine soluto. In mourning for her father and brother, cf. 355f. *tristi vestis obtentu caput / velata* (with comm.), 626f. *lugubribus amicta*. These details of Megara's mourning garb are absent from Eur., where the family are first described as χρεῖοι . . . σίτων ποτῶν ἐσθῆτος (51f.), and later put on shrouds in readiness for death (329, 442f.). For *crinem solvere* in mourning contexts cf. V. *Aen.* 3.65, Tib. 1.1.67f., Sen. *Tro.* 84, 99f.

203 Megara. Here and at 1009 the final *a* is long, as in Greek.[49] The scansion is presumably to make the name tractable in verse: *Electra* and *Phaedra* have short final *a* in Sen. See Lachmann on Lucr. 6.971.

parvum comitata gregem. The participle must be active (*pace* Pierrot and others). The regular construction with *comitatus* passive is an ablative, though *per* plus accusative is found once, v. *TLL* 3.1815.11ff. *Gregem* means her sons, cf. 1149 *natorum grege*; *parvum* refers to the age of the group rather than its numbers.

204 tardusque senio graditur. Compare Eur. *Her.* 1040f. πρέσβυς ὑστέρῳ ποδὶ / πικρὰν διώκων ἤλυσιν πάρεσθ' ὅδε, where, however, Amphitryon's slowness is perhaps indicative of grief as much as age. A character's walk is often described in Sen. Trag., generally at his or her entrance, and usually indicates attitude or age: see 330 (and comm. on 329–31), 474 with comm., *Pha.* 583 *sed Phaedra praeceps graditur, impatiens morae*, *Thy.* 421, and for old age *Pha.* 431 *quid huc seniles fessa moliris gradus*, *Oed.* 289. *Senium* is found three times in early tragedy, three times in Plautus, seven times in Sen. Trag., but it is rare in nondramatic verse until after Sen.

---

49. But the name has a Latin accusative at 1016 *agnosce Megaram*. For variation of Greek and Latin forms cf. *Tro.* 555 *Andromacham*, 700 *Andromachen*; *Ag.* 648 *Hecabe*, 706 *Hecuba*.

Act II (205–523)

The first part of Act II, up to Lycus' entrance, is modeled in some respects on the prologue of Euripides' *Heracles*. Both scenes open with a long speech by Amphitryon, which refers to the present situation in Thebes. This is followed in both cases by a speech by Megara, who expresses despair about the possibility of Hercules' returning to rescue them; and this in turn by a dialogue, in which Megara's pessimism is contrasted with Amphitryon's optimism. The idea of recasting the first two speeches as consecutive *appeals*, by Amphitryon to Jupiter and by Megara to Hercules, was probably inspired by a later passage in Eur. *Her.* 490–500, where similar appeals are made consecutively though in the opposite order.

Amphitryon's first speech, being a prayer, is within the dramatic framework in Seneca, whereas in Euripides it is an expository prologue speech, outside the action of the play. Accordingly, such background information as is imparted in Seneca about the situation in Thebes and its history—a relatively small amount in comparison with the Euripidean speech—emerges through Amphitryon's complaints rather than in formal narrative. He refers to the situation allusively, as is natural in the dramatic context: Creon is not mentioned by name, and Hercules and Lycus not until the end of the speech. The technique here is similar to that of Juno's speech (see introduction to Act I).

Another difference from Euripides lies in the quality of Megara's pessimism. The Euripidean Megara has a resigned and clear-eyed acceptance that all hope is lost. In Seneca the near-hysteria of her first appeal to Hercules gives way to an underlying despair. In fact, from Megara's monologue up to the entrance of Lycus, the scene is molded in a pattern familiar in Sen. Trag. (and normally found in Act II, as here), in which one character expresses passionate emotion while the other attempts to exercise a restraining influence.[50] The present scene does, however, differ from the other Passion-Restraint scenes in one important respect, namely, that in the latter the passion is the chief cause of the tragedy (e.g. Phaedra's love for Hippolytus, Atreus' desire for revenge).

The development of this Act is particularly similar to the third Act of

---

50. Herington 1966 453f. notes that the Passion-Restraint pattern is typical of Act II of the Senecan dramas, and cites those instances where the passion leads to the catastrophe, viz. *Tro.* 203ff., *Med.* 150ff., *Pha.* 129ff. (actually Act I, but after Hippolytus' monody), *Ag.* 108ff., *Thy.* 176ff. The person attempting restraint is a servant in *Med.*, *Pha.*, *Ag.*, and *Thy.*, but a named character in *Tro.* as in *HF*. On Passion-Restraint scenes outside Act II see introduction to Act V (where Amphitryon is again the restraining influence).

Commentary: Act II

Tro. There too a modified Passion-Restraint scene (Andromache-Old Man) is followed by a confrontation with a tyrant (Andromache-Ulysses). And both Megara and Andromache undergo a drastic, but natural and understandable, change of attitude: they give way to weakness and despair when among friends, but show strength of character in facing the tyrant. In *HF* note especially the contrast between Megara's pessimism over Hercules' return at 308ff. and the confidence she expresses at 423ff.

In the Lycus scene, which begins at 332ff., two elements may be distinguished. One is Lycus' attempt to persuade Megara to marry him, the other is his questioning of Hercules' greatness. The latter element has antecedents in the Euripidean debate between Lycus and Amphitryon (140ff.). There as here Lycus denies H.'s divine paternity, refuses to believe that he will return from the underworld, and questions the amount of heroism involved in fighting wild beasts. But the argument in Euripides is primarily concerned with the rights and wrongs of using a bow, as H. does, in preference to a spear—a question that would have had little interest for an audience in the first century A.D. In Seneca the focus is rather on the question of H.'s divine paternity and his prospect of eventual deification—the latter is an issue of considerable importance in Act I also.

Lycus' wooing of Megara, on the other hand, has no precedent in *Heracles.* Whether Seneca invented it himself or borrowed it from a post-Euripidean dramatist, one cannot know.[51] Whatever its origin, however, it was particularly attractive to Seneca because it enabled him to show a tyrant being defied to his face. Similar scenes, again with the defiance being offered by a woman, appear in *Tro.* (Andromache-Ulysses) and *Ag.* (Electra-Aegisthus). One should beware of seeing too definite a didactic purpose in such scenes. Although it is true that Seneca in his prose works talks of the strength philosophy offers in resisting tyranny (e.g. *Tranq.* 14.3, *Ep.* 28.8), it would be a distortion to see Megara in this scene as a Stoic heroine.[52] She is in fact a highly emotional woman, and her defiance of Lycus is based on a passionate hatred of him (see particularly 380ff.).

---

51. The only authorities apart from Sen. who suggest that Lycus' intentions toward Megara were other than murderous are Serv. ad V. *Aen.* 8.299 (Hercules) *Lycum regem, qui . . . Megaram uxorem eius temptaverat, reversus peremit,* Tzetzes ad Lycophr. 38 ὁ Ἡρακλῆς εἰς Θήβας παραγενόμενος κατὰ Λύκου βασιλεύοντος τῆς πόλεως καὶ βιαζομένου τὴν γυναῖκα αὐτοῦ Μεγάραν, τοῦτον κατατοξεύσας κ.τ.λ. Krischan in *RE* 15.151.29ff. believes that these both derive from Sen. One cannot prove or disprove the point, but in Tzetzes neither βιαζομένου nor κατατοξεύσας is the most obvious way of describing what happens in Sen.

52. As is done e.g. by Zintzen 173–75.

Wilamowitz pointed out a similar motif of wooing in two lost plays of Euripides, the *Dictys* and *Cresphontes* (2.161 n.75). In the former, the tyrant Polydectes paid suit to Danae, who had an aged supporter (Dictys, cf. Amphitryon) and an absent champion (Perseus, cf. Hercules) who returned and slew the suitor. If the detail in Apollod. 2.4.3, that Danae and Dictys had to take refuge from Polydectes at an altar, goes back to Euripides,[53] that would be an additional similarity. In the Cresphontes story, the usurper Polyphontes married his murdered brother's wife Merope, no doubt to legitimize his rule; but these events had taken place long before the dramatic date of the play, which cannot therefore have contained a scene similar to the present one. Such a scene may have existed in Ennius' *Cresphontes* (though there is no direct evidence for it), if Jocelyn (pp. 271–74) is right that the subject of that play was Polyphontes' usurpation.[54] If any of these plays influenced Seneca— or his model—it seems most likely to have been Eur. *Dictys*.

The end of the Act (501ff.) briefly borrows certain elements from the second half of episode 1 and the beginning of episode 2 in Euripides (see Introduction and comm. on 506–8, 509f., 516–20). Seneca eliminates the Euripidean business of dressing for death, because he does not wish to use it as a means whereby Hercules can kill Lycus (see introduction to Act III).

Words with prosaic or colloquial connotations appear with more than usual frequency around Lycus' entry and first interchange with Megara, as if the dialogue becomes more vigorous there. The technical term *novitas* is startling in poetry (see on 348). *Aliquando* (328) is an uncommon word in iambic and hexameter poetry (v. *TLL* 1.1599.28ff., adding Ov. fr. 19.18; contrast 5 uses in Seneca's tragedies with 213 in his prose). Most poets completely avoid *obtinere* (342), presumably as a prosaic word (Axelson 69); Seneca is an exception in using it 6 times. The periphrasis *fore ut / futurum esse ut* (349) is also generally avoided by poets: it occurs only here in Sen. Trag., only once in Ovid (*Her.* 16.279f., a couplet suspected by Palmer), 4 times in Lucretius.

Other words are more closely associated with the forceful language of drama than with nondramatic poetry: they include *quisnam* and

---

53. As is supposed by T. B. L. Webster, *The Tragedies of Euripides* (London 1967) 62.

54. Interestingly enough, Voltaire's *Mérope* was influenced by the *HF*: compare Lycus' scheme with that of Polyphonte in 1.4.291–94:

> J'ai besoin d'un hymen utile à ma grandeur,
> Qui détourne de moi le nom d'usurpateur,
> Qui fixe enfin les voeux de ce peuple infidèle,
> Qui m'apporte pour dot l'amour qu'on a pour elle.

quinam (cf. *quidnam* 358), used eight times in early tragedy, frequently in comedy, eleven times in Sen. Trag., and *agedum* (397), with twenty-two uses in Plautus and Terence and five in Sen. Trag. Axelson 76f. points out that Seneca is exceptional among poets of elevated style in making considerable use (thirty-four times) of *nemo* (326), but one should note that it occurs with comparable frequency in the fragments of earlier tragedy (six instances in the index of Ribbeck's *TRF*). The use of *egone ut* (372) and variants to introduce questions expressing indignation, incredulity, etc. is familiar in comedy, cf. Enn. *trag.* 227 R² and six uses in Sen. Trag. *Parumper* (361) is more frequent in drama, both comedy and tragedy, than in other poetry (except Enn. *Ann.*); in drama, furthermore, it is associated almost exclusively with requests and appeals, which is not the case in other genres. For other instances of diction associated with drama (though the association differs from instance to instance, and each case must be weighed individually) see comm. on 62 *intuens*, 204, 206, 618f., 864 *illo*, 1050 *reciprocos*, 1140, 1151 *quonam*, 1200, 1225, 1242 *propere*, and p. 469.

205–308. E gives 205–78 to Amphitryon and 279–308 to Megara, whereas the A manuscripts assign the whole of 205–308 to Megara. The following arguments seem conclusively in favor of E's arrangement (for important discussion see Friedrich 1933 52–55).

In 279ff., which certainly belong to Megara, there is a new and somewhat unbalanced emphasis on *vis Herculea*. This change of tone suggests a change of speaker: and the vocative *coniunx* in 279 is appropriate to such a change.

As indicated in the introduction to Act II, 205–308 is modeled in part on two pairs of speeches by Amphitryon and Megara in Eur. *Heracles*. As Sen. combines the Euripidean Amphitryon's prologue speech with the same character's prayer to Zeus, it seems that he intends the result (i.e. 205ff.) to be spoken by Amphitryon.

Some elements in 205–78 suit Amphitryon better than Megara. The complaint about lack of security and *requies* (206–13) is repeated in Amphitryon's speeches at 925f. and 1252–57. Furthermore, "aliter de fratribus et de patre Megarae loquitur Amphitryon 255–257, aliter Megara ipsa 303–305" (Viansino on 277): in particular, *natos* 255 seems too objective for Megara.[55]

Stylistically the tricolon at 277f., with strong alliteration in the second line, appears to signal the close of a speech.

---

55. Herrmann believed that *paterni* in 255 must mean "*my* father's," thus proving the speaker to be Megara; this view has gained a certain currency, but is of course completely indefensible.

The prayer elements in 277f. mean that Amphitryon's speech ends with a prayer, as it began (Zwierlein 1966 120).

205. From the earliest times, gods may be invoked by description rather than by name, cf. Hom. *Il.* 3.278f. γαῖα, καὶ οἳ ὑπένερθε / καμόντας ἀνθρώπους τίνυσθον, Ar. *Thesm.* 315ff. Ζεῦ μεγαλώνυμε, / χρυσολύρα τε Δῆλον ὃς ἔχεις ἱεράν. In Sen., instances are plentiful, e.g. *HF* 299f., 516ff., 597ff., 904f., *Med.* 2ff., 62ff.; the more elaborate examples, at least, owe something to his liking for allusiveness. (On single lines devoted to the name and/or titles of the addressee v. 592 comm.) *Olympi rector* is an Ovidian phrase (*Met.* 2.60 with Bömer, 9.499, cf. Sen. *Pha.* 960), though a highly traditional concept. *Arbiter* here means "lord, controller" (not "judge," Miller), as at 597f. *caelestum arbiter / parensque.*

206 aerumnis. This word is generally more common in drama, both tragic and comic, than in other poetic genres; for details v. Tarrant on *Ag.* 305, *TLL* s.v.

207–13. Amphitryon's two complaints, about his son's constant absence and his own consequent anxiety, are repeated at 1252–57; see there for possible antecedents. There are deliberate verbal and thematic links here with the preceding ode: absence of *securitas* and *requies* (cf. *secura quies* 175) is precisely what might be expected, given Hercules' commitment to *animosa virtus*. Further, the phrasing of *nulla lux . . . fulsit* recalls the dawn theme of the ode.

Critics have suspected this passage, on the grounds that there is an abrupt change of topic in 209 from the troubles of Amphitryon to those of Hercules, and in particular that *reduci* in 209 must be understood to refer to H. with no help from a proper noun. Leo postulated a lacuna between *fulsit* and *finis* in 208, and supplied *exempli gratia* (from 1252f.) *nullus e nati datur / labore fructus.* But Hoffa 467 rightly defends the passage. The omission of H.'s name may be paralleled from 33, 275, 831. The supposedly abrupt change of topic is mitigated by the fact that the *aerumnae* and *clades* of 206f., though primarily Amphitryon's, are inseparable from the toils of Hercules: indeed the sentence *finis alterius mali / gradus est futuri* may be taken ἀπὸ κοινοῦ of Amphitryon and Hercules, and so eases the transition. Schulze 33 n. 63 well compares 924ff. *finiat genitor tuos / opta labores, detur aliquando otium / quiesque fessis,* where *fessis* similarly refers both to H. and to his family. Wilamowitz's conjecture *umquam Herculi* for *umquam mihi* in 207 is therefore not needed.

[187]

Commentary: Act II

212 vacat. *Datur*, the reading of T CS, appears to be a characteristic A interpolation (possibly borrowed from 1051 *detur quieti tempus*), designed to simplify the construction by making *requies* and *tempus* subjects of the same verb. The fact that P has *vacat* with E suggests that the reading of the archetype survived, at least as a variant, in δ.

213 nisi dum iubetur. A *nisi* at the beginning of the line is particularly effective in making rhetorical points, cf. *Med.* 486f. *nil exul tuli / nisi fratris artus*, *Thy.* 195f. *scelera non ulcisceris / nisi vincis*, 240f. *certi nihil / nisi frater hostis*, *Phoen.* 34, *Pha.* 628.

sequitur. Perhaps a historic present, but more probably a present of the type used with *dudum, olim*, etc., indicating that the action still continues (H-S 305).

215 infantis aetas. That is, *infantia*, a noun rarely used in poetry in the sense of "infancy." Cf. Sen. *Ep.* 121.16 *alia est aetas infantis, pueri, adulescentis, senis*.

216–48. The labors of Hercules constitute one of the most familiar commonplaces of classical literature. Among treatments in Latin poetry up to Seneca's time one may cite Cic. *Tusc.* 2.8–9, Lucr. 5.24–36, V. *Aen.* 8.288–300, Ov. *Her.* 9.85–100, *Met.* 9.182–98 (cf. H. H. Huxley in *Proc. Leeds Philos. and Lit. Soc.* 7 [1952] 20ff.). Other extended treatments of the topic in Sen. Trag. are *HF* 529ff. (highly selective) and *Ag.* 829ff.

As an illustration of the laboriousness of H.'s life, the present list may be compared particularly with Eur. *Her.* 1266–80, which also begins *in cunis* with the strangling of the serpents. The commonplace nature of Sen.'s list is indicated by the fact that although it begins as a complaint, it immediately turns into praise of H.'s achievements; however, this laudatory tone is not inappropriate in the mouth of Amphitryon, who regularly expresses pride in his son's achievements.

Seneca here includes eleven of the canonical twelve labors (see lists in Apollod. 2.5.1–12, Diod. Sic. 4.11–26; cf. H. J. Rose 205–29), omitting the yet unfinished quest for Cerberus. He inserts the opening of the Straits of Gibraltar, usually treated as a *parergon*, presumably in order to restore the standard number of twelve (see comm. on 235–38). The list is prefaced by the strangling of the snakes, which has an obvious relevance to Amphitryon's argument.

Two stylistic principles are evident in Sen.'s handling of the material. One is variation on straightforward narrative statement: 216–25 statement, 226–30 *praeteritio*, 231–40 statement, 241–44 rhetorical question, 245-48 statement by negation (neatly taking up the *non* of the rhetorical question). The other principle is parallelism of structure within this variation of approach. Thus the first two labors are introduced by similar labeling phrases *Maenali pernix fera* and *maximus Nemeae timor*; in the *praeteritio* we have the parallelism of the line openings *suisque, solitumque, taurumque*; then come two blocks of four lines (231-35, 236-39), whose closing lines have a similar pattern; finally there is a series of distichs each devoted to a single labor.

Chronological and geographical considerations have much less importance. Seneca virtually ignores the usual order of the labors, though he knows, for example, that the Nemean Lion is normally called the first labor (*primus . . . labor* 944). He also ignores the distinction sometimes made between Peloponnesian and extra-Peloponnesian tasks. The only geographical consideration evident is the grouping together of the three labors that belong to the far west, 231-40; and the only chronological indication occurs in the same section, *post haec* 239.

The passage is remarkable inter alia for a stylistic reason: of its thirty-two lines, ten contain two epithet-noun pairs arranged in interwoven order, e.g. 220 *artos serenis vultibus nodos tulit*. This pattern, first introduced into Latin poetry by the Neoteroi (v. Wilkinson 215) is common in Sen.'s verse: on average it occurs once every ten lines in *HF* (once every seven lines in Cat. 64, and once every nine lines in Ov. *Am.* 1.1-10). Even this figure does not allow for the many instances in which the interlocking pattern runs over the line end, e.g. 27f. *vivaces aget / violentus iras animus*. Like several of the poets, Seneca likes to use lines composed of the double epithet-noun pattern plus a verb. The balance of such lines makes them particularly effective for rounding off a colon or paragraph, e.g. 124, 274, 367, 1034. In cases where the verb falls in the middle of the line, Sen. prefers the "silver" pattern (*abCBA, aBCbA*, etc.; seventeen examples in *HF*) to the "golden" (*abCAB, aBCAb*, etc.; six examples), no doubt because the former "frames" the line between the adjective and its noun (v. 59 comm.).

216-22. One of the more circumstantial accounts of the strangling of the snakes extant in poetry; cf. particularly Pind. *Nem.* 1.33ff., fr. 52 u Snell (= *POxy.* 2442 fr. 32 col. 1), Theoc. 24, Plaut. *Amph.* 1107ff. The snakes are regularly two in number. For Sen.'s wording in 216f. and 221 cf. V. *Aen.* 8.288f. *ut prima novercae / monstra manu geminosque premens eliserit angues*, but the parallel may be due to the similar context rather than to a specific reminiscence.

Seneca presents the scene in 216-19 as a balanced tableau, in which the combatants advance gradually toward each other, meeting each other's gaze. (Contrast the crawling of Sen.'s infant with Plaut. *Amph.*

Commentary: Act II

115 *citus e cunis exilit, facit recta in anguis impetum.*) In view of this effect, E's imperfect tense *reptabat* in 218 is preferable to A's *reptavit*, as providing an exact balance to the imperfect *ferebant* in 217; the perfect *tulit* (220) is then the decisive action which interrupts the steady movement represented by the imperfects.

216 cristati caput. Similarly, at Plaut. *Amph.* 1108 they are *iubati*. Crests or manes are a traditional feature of supernatural serpents, cf. 392 below; Eur. *Phoen.* 820; Livy 41.21.13, 43.13.4; V. *Aen.* 2.206; Ov. *Met.* 3.32.

217 ferebant ora. Compare V. *Aen.* 3.490 *sic oculos, sic ille manus, sic ora ferebat*, 8.229 *huc ora ferebat et illuc*. Here the phrase has a greater sense of forward movement, on analogy with *se ferre, pedem ferre*, etc.: the *ora* are mentioned as threatening and horrific.

218f. igneos oculos. Eur. 1266 calls the snakes γοργωπούς; according to Theocritus ἀπ' ὀφθαλμῶν δὲ κακὸν πῦρ / ἐρχομένοις λάμπεσκε (24.18f.). For the fiery eyes of serpents cf. Gow on the latter passage, citing inter alia V. *Georg.* 3.433 *flammantia lumina*, *Aen.* 2.210 *ardentisque oculos suffecti sanguine et igni*: add Ov. *Met.* 3.33 *igne micant oculi*.

219 lumine. This is clearly the right reading: Sen. contrasts the glare of the serpents with the calm gaze of H. The A reading *pectore* is another instance of interpolation in that tradition from elsewhere in the corpus, in this case from *Phoen.* 187 *remisso pectore ac placido feras*.

220. In other accounts too the serpents coil around the child's limbs (Theoc. 24.30, Ov. *Her.* 9.85f.), as is frequently shown in artistic representations of the scene. *Tulit* = "endured": this sense is suggested by *serenis vultibus*, and the verb would be weak in a physical sense ("raised," Miller).

221. The alliterative pattern was perhaps suggested by Ov. *Met.* 3.73 *plenis tumuerunt guttura venis*: Sen.'s alliteration is more intense (cf. also *tulit* in 220), and effective in combination with the double initial resolution (comm. on 76).

tenera. Compare Theoc. 24.54 χείρεσσιν . . . ἀπαλαῖσιν, Ov. *Her.* 9.21f. *tene ferunt geminos pressisse tenaciter angues, / cum tener in cunis iam Iove dignus eras?*

222 prolusit hydrae. Pindar makes a similar but less pointed comment concerning this exploit, *Nem.* 1.43 πειρᾶτο δὲ πρῶτον μάχας. The serpents were good practice for the killing of the Hydra because of the snakelike nature of the latter, cf. 529 *serpentis*, *Ag.* 835 *draconem*.

Proludere is one of Sen.'s favorite metaphors, cf. *Tro.* 182f. (Achilles) *proludens tuis / iam, Troia, fatis, Pha.* 1061, *Med.* 970f. *prolusit dolor / per ista noster, Ira* 2.2.5, *Ep.* 102.23, *QNat.* 3.28.3.

Maenali pernix fera. The hind is usually associated with Mt Ceryneia, but cf. *Anth. Plan.* 91.6 Μαιναλίην ἔλαφον. It is likely that Sen. uses the genitive here as he uses the adjective at 229 to mean simply "Arcadian" (for the usage v. Bömer on Ov. *Fasti* 5.89); cf. *Ag.* 831 *cerva Parrhasis*.

223. The golden horns are frequently shown in artistic representations of the hind, e.g. Brommer ill. 13b, 15a and b, 17, and mentioned in early Greek sources (Pind. *Ol.* 3.29, Eur. *Her.* 375) and in the mythographers (Apollod. 2.5.3, Diod. Sic. 4.13.1, Hyg. *Fab.* 30). The literal-minded were already perturbed in antiquity by the anomaly of a horned hind, cf. Preller-Robert 2.448 n.3.

224 deprensa cursu. Seneca, like other Latin poets, sometimes omits auxiliary *est* with a deponent or passive participle, cf. 233 *peremptus*, 855, 955, *Tro.* 424, *Med.* 369, 729f., *Oed.* 348, 550, 571, 977, *Thy.* 677. (See Leo I 184ff., an important discussion of the usage.) It is not always easy to decide for or against omission in places where, as here, E omits but A does not (cf. *Pha.* 227, *Oed.* 398, *Thy.* 576, *HO* 26, 940); is it a case of erroneous omission by E, as at *HO* 1215, 1763, or interpolation by A as at *Pha.* 964, *HO* 1338? I prefer E's version, but not with great confidence.

cursu. It is generally agreed that the pursuit was a long one; versions of the capture differ, but Diodorus reports one tradition that H. exhausted the creature συνεχεῖ διωγμῷ (4.13.1).

224f. The lion is regularly said to have been squeezed to death; Hercules had first attempted to use his bow and other weapons, but found that the lion's skin was impervious to them. Similar wording at Cic. *Tusc.* 2.8.20 *o lacertorum tori, / vestrone pressu quondam Nemeaeus leo / frendens efflavit . . . halitum*, Sen. *Ag.* 830 *pressus lacerto fulmineus leo*, cf. Eur. *Her.* 154 βραχίονος . . . ἀγχόναισιν.

226f. On the man-eating horses of Diomedes see particularly Eur. *Her.* 380ff., *Alc.* 483ff.; Apollod. 2.5.8; Diod. Sic. 4.15.3; Sen. *Ag.* 841ff. The detail that H. fed Diomedes to his own beasts is rare, and first found in Diodorus; it may be influenced by the similar fate of

Commentary: Act II

Glaucus of Potniae, who also kept anthropophagous horses which eventually devoured him, cf. V. *Georg.* 3.267f. with Probus ad loc., Preller-Robert 2.175f., 461.

stabula . . . dira. The horses' gruesome stalls are a standard feature of the story, cf. Eur. *Her.* 382 φονίαισι φάτναις, *Alc.* 496, Diod. Sic. 4.15.3, Ov. *Met.* 9.195 *plenaque corporibus laceris praesepia vidi*, Sen. *Ag.* 844f. *stabulis . . . saevis* (note also the conjunction of *dirus stabulis*).

227 pabulum. Borrowed from Ovid, who uses it of Diomedes' victims *Pont.* 1.2.120 *quique suis homines pabula fecit equis*; the point is sharpened by the application of the word to Diomedes himself, and appealed to Boethius, *Consol.* 4.7.20f. *victor immitem posuisse fertur / pabulum saevis dominum quadrigis*, and to Racine, *Phèdre* 3.5.970 "À ses monstres lui-même a servi de pâture."

armentis. That is, horses, as probably at *Tro.* 818 (v. Fantham ad loc.); there are precedents in Vergil (*Georg.* 3.129, *Aen.* 3.540, 11.494), who applies the word also to deer and even seals.

228f. The woods of Erymanthus are mentioned in connection with the boar at Ov. *Her.* 9.87 *cupressifero Erymantho*, V. *Aen.* 6.802f. *Erymanthi . . . nemora*, cf. Ap. Rhod. 1.126f. κάπριον, ὅς ῥ' ἐνὶ βήσσης / φέρβετο Λαμπείης, Ἐρυμάνθιον ἂμ μέγα τῖφος.

densis hispidum. There is some interplay between the juxtaposed adjectives, both of which could be glossed with *horridus* (*densus* is used of heavily coated swine Col. 1 *praef.* 26 *glabrae sues densaeque*). The absolute use of *densus* = "heavily wooded" is unusual, but cf. [Tib.] 3.9.7 *densos colles*, Sen. *Pha.* 506 *nemoris alti densa . . . loca*, *Thy.* 412f. *silvestres fugas / saltusque densos*. (The alternative meaning, "close-set," is not impossible, cf. Stat. *Theb.* 7.266 *densamque iugis Eteonon iniquis*, but unlikely in the context.) For *hispidum* cf. Lucr. 5.25 *horrens Arcadius sus*: *hispidus* is used of nonmythological boars at Phaedr. 5.10.4, Sen. *Ag.* 892. The bristles are a feature of some artistic representations of the exploit, e.g. Brommer ill. 13a.

229. The splendid run of resolutions suggests the trembling of the woods. Other examples of multiple resolutions with expressive effect include *Tro.* 1178 *repetite celeri maria, captivae, gradu* (impatient command), *Med.* 170 (vehement argument), *Oed.* 60f. *mater hunc amens gerit, / properatque ut alium repetat in eundem rogum* (distraught haste), *Ag.* 787f. *famuli, attollite, / refovete gelido latice* (urgency); cf. also 76 comm. Lines with three or four resolutions are notably more common in Sen. Trag. than in Greek tragedy (Strzelecki 90, cf. Hoche 14ff.).

Maenalium. Maenalus lies at some distance from Erymanthus, but the adjective here means "Arcadian," as often in poetry. *Tegeaeus* is used in exactly the same way at Ov. *Her.* 9.87f. *ut Tegeaeus aper cupressifero Erymantho / incubet.*

230 centum . . . populis. This allusive use of the phrase is inspired immediately by Ov. *Met.* 7.481 *rector populorum . . . centum* (viz. Minos), echoed also at *Pha.* 105 *ille lato maria qui regno premit / populisque reddit iura centenis.* In Homer, Crete is ἑκατόμπολις at *Il.* 2.649 but has ἐννήκοντα πόληες at *Od.* 19.174; in Latin poetry the rounder and metrically more convenient number becomes standard, cf. Bömer on Ov. *Met.* 7.481.

231 gentis. Virtually equivalent to "land," as e.g. Manil. 4.602f. *laeva freti caedunt Hispanas aequora gentes, / teque in vicinis haerentem, Gallia, terris.*

232 pastor triformis. For the allusive reference to Geryon cf. Eur. *Her.* 423f. τὸν τρισώματον . . . βοτῆρ' Ἐρυθείας, Ov. *Met.* 9.184f. *pastoris Hiberi / forma triplex,* ps.-V. *Eleg. Maec.* 1.84, Sen. *Apocol.* 7 poët. 6f. *tergemini . . . regis.* At *Ag.* 837ff. Sen. apparently thinks of him as three-headed (n.b. *pectore ex uno*; cf. Hes. *Theog.* 287 τρικέφαλος), whereas he is more usually three-bodied (Aesch. *Ag.* 870, Lucr. 5.28, V. *Aen.* 6.289; the regular type in art, cf. M. Robertson in *CQ* N.S. 19 [1969] 207ff.).

litoris Tartesii. Another Ovidian phrase, from *Met.* 14.416 *sparserat occiduus Tartessia litora Phoebus.*[56] Seneca's phrase, like Ovid's, probably refers generally to the west coast of Spain, whereas Stesichorus is more precise in locating Geryon's birth σχεδὸν ἀντιπέρας κλεινᾶς Ἐρυθείας Ταρτησσοῦ ποταμοῦ παρὰ παγάς (ap. Strabo 3.2.11, cf. Roscher 1.1633–36).

233 peremptus, acta et praeda. The transmitted text, *peremptus, acta est praeda,* seems excessively awkward; contrast the more natural pattern of V. *Ecl.* 8.2f. *quos est mirata iuvenca / certantis, quorum stupefactae carmine lynces,* where the auxiliary is inserted in the first verb and then

---

56. *Tartessia* here is the conjecture of Farnaby, widely accepted by editors. As in the present passage, the MSS deform the unfamiliar name, writing *cartesia*, etc.

Commentary: Act II

omitted from the second. Gronovius' replacement of *est* by *et* is a simple and convincing solution.[57]

234. An elegant variation on the contrast indicated at *Ag.* 839 *duxitque ad ortus Hesperium pecus*. Hercules would have to pass through Boeotia en route to deliver the cattle to Eurystheus, whether he entered Greece from Thrace (Apollod. 2.5.10) or Epirus (Diod. Sic. 4.25.1; on his route see Preller-Robert 2.473ff.). The pastures of Cithaeron are well known in tragedy, cf. Soph. *OT* 1026ff., 1134ff.; Eur. *Bacch.* 677f.; Sen. *Oed.* 808ff., 845f.

pavit. Verbs of eating and more particularly of drinking, which frequently indicate geographical location (cf. Hor. *Carm.* 4.15.21 *qui profundum Danubium bibunt*, Costa on Sen. *Med.* 372–74), may also be used to indicate dislocation, foreignness, etc., cf. V. *Ecl.* 1.63 *aut Ararim Parthus bibet aut Germania Tigrim*, Ov. *Her.* 12.10 *turbaque Phasiacam Graia bibistis aquam*, Sen. *Med.* 372ff.

235–38. Hercules is usually said to have visited Libya and Gibraltar en route for Geryon, but Sen. seems to raise the visit to the status of an independent labor. This is suggested by the use of *iussus* in 235, because the *athloi* were commanded whereas the *parerga* and *praxeis* were not; by the fact that he detaches the visit from the Geryon exploit, and gives it equal space with that exploit; and by his choice of the version that H. actually opened up the Straits of Gibraltar, a sufficiently laborious task. Seneca's motive is probably to maintain the canonical number of twelve with this substitute for the yet uncompleted capture of Cerberus: at *Ag.* 829ff. he likewise balances insertion of the capture of Troy by exclusion of the Stables of Augeas. (Similarly Eur. 359ff., while making several substitutions, keeps the total at twelve.) This particular task, out of H.'s many *parerga*, may well have come to Sen.'s mind for thematic reasons, in view of the emphasis later on H.'s need to force his way out of the underworld; cf. particularly *viam facere* in 276f., and the similar opening of the Vale of Tempe mentioned at 283ff.

235 solis aestivi plagas. The regions around the Tropic of Cancer, also called the summer tropic (Manil. 1.571 *aestivum medio nomen sibi sumit ab aestu*); that is, North Africa. For *sol aestivus* in connection with the tropic cf. Cic. *Arat.* 263ff. *Cancer, / in quo consistens convertit curriculum Sol / aestivus*. It might be thought that the phrase means simply "regions of the ever-summerlike sun," cf. V. *Aen.* 7.226 *plaga solis iniqui*

---

57. Another possibility would be simply to omit *est*, with Peiper. Less convincing is the conjecture of Withof 150f. *peremptus; actā et praedā ab occasu ultimo, notum* e.q.s.

Commentary: Act II

(where *plaga* = "zone"), but *aestivus* could not carry this meaning without further elaboration as at Sen. *QNat.* 3.6.2 *paucosque inveniri in interiore Africa fontes, quia fervida natura caeli sit et paene semper aestiva.*

236. The areas scorched by the midday sun are those lying below it, that is, in the South; cf. 883f. *Auroram inter et Hesperum, / et qua sol medium tenens / umbras corporibus negat* (with comm.), Luc. 1.15f. *unde venit Titan, et nox ubi sidera condit, / quaque dies medius flagrantibus aestuat horis, / et qua bruma rigens* e.q.s. *Medius dies* may of itself sometimes indicate "the South" (cf. V. *Georg.* 3.302f. *stabula . . . ad medium conversa diem*), though its derivative *meridies* is more common in this sense.

237f. Pindar speaks only of the setting up of the Pillars of Hercules, *Nem.* 3.21, cf. Apollod. 2.5.10. The version according to which H. broke through a land barrier that joined Africa to Europe, and thus created the straits between the Mediterranean and Ocean, is not attested until comparatively late, cf. Diod. Sic. 4.18.5, Pliny *NH* 3.4, Mela 1.27. The *montes* are Calpe on the northern side and Abyla on the southern; these rocks became identified with the Pillars, cf. Frazer on Apollod. 2.5.10.

ac rupto obice. The MSS have *abrupto obice*, which causes an awkward asyndeton whether taken with what precedes or what follows. Gronovius' conjecture eliminates this problem and is supported by the structure of the closely parallel lines 287f. *huc mons et illuc cessit et rupto aggere / nova cucurrit Thessalus torrens via.* For the phrase *rupto obice* cf. in a similar context V. *Georg.* 2.479f. *qua vi maria alta tumescant / obicibus ruptis, rursusque in se ipsa residant.*

238 ruenti. That is, rushing into the newly created space. There is no need for N. Heinsius' conjecture *irruenti*; the simple verb is used rather than the compound as frequently in poetry, cf. 409f. comm.

239 post haec. The canonical order of H.'s labors places the Apples of the Hesperides among the last of them: the order in Apollod. 2.5 and Hyg. *Fab.* 30 is (10) Geryon (11) Hesperides (12) Cerberus; in Diod. Sic. 4.17ff. and the Tabula Albana (*FGrH* 40) it is (10) Geryon (11) Cerberus (12) Hesperides.[58]

---

58. The phrase may suggest that H. visited the Garden of the Hesperides as part of the same journey during which he opened the Straits of Gibraltar. This would be an unconventional version; the usual account speaks of the visit to the Hesperides as involving a separate journey through Africa, during which he killed Busiris and Antaeus (Apollod. 2.5.11). Confusion about the two journeys would not be surprising: Diodorus recounts the killing of Antaeus and Busiris under both labors ten and twelve.

[195]

Commentary: Act II

opulenti. That is, gold-bearing, cf. *Phoen.* 604 *trahens opulenta Pactolus vada, HF* 532 *pomis divitibus* with comm.

domos. The meaning is illuminated by *Med.* 766ff. *nemoris antiqui domus / amisit umbras, vocis imperio meae / die reducto* (cf. Costa ad loc.). In both places *domus* = "sheltering enclosure." *TLL* 5.1972.12ff. gives no further instances apart from the doubtful case of *Oed.* 228. It would be too specific to limit the meaning to the homes of birds and animals (e.g. Lucr. 1.18 *frondiferasque domos avium*) or of the Hesperides themselves, though these senses are not excluded from the more general meaning of *domos*. There may be influence from Eur. 394ff. ὑμνῳδούς τε κόρας / ἤλυθεν ἑσπέριον ἐς αὐ-/λάν, where, however, the αὐλά is specifically the Hesperides'.

240. Seneca's other references to this labor also emphasize H.'s victory over the snake that guarded the apples, cf. 530–32 with comm. Cicero too uses *aurifer* in a poetic reference to the Golden Apples, fr. 33 Baehrens (*Tusc.* 2.9.22) 43 *draconem auriferam optutu adservantem arborem*: on such compounds see Appendix 4.

vigilis. Guardian snakes are properly watchful (see Tarrant on *Ag.* 856). The insomnia of this particular serpent is mentioned as early as Panyassis (ap. Hyg. *Poet. Astr.* 2.6), cf. Preller-Robert 2.492 n. 1, Pease on V. *Aen.* 4.484.

241f. For this reference to the slaying of the Hydra cf. Eur. 419ff. τάν τε μυριόκρανον / πολύφονον κύνα Λέρνας / ὕδραν ἐξεπύρωσεν. The similarity between the two passages is natural in the context, and there is no need to assume direct imitation by Sen. Hercules' initial strategy was to cut off the Hydra's heads, but he found that the creature thrived on decapitation; Iolaus therefore seared the roots of each head as it was cut off, to prevent its regrowth, cf. Apollod. 2.5.2, Diod. Sic. 4.11.6, Serv. on V. *Aen.* 6.287. The use of fire is first mentioned in Eur.; Hesiod speaks simply of H. and Iolaus destroying the Hydra νηλέϊ χαλκῷ (*Theog.* 316).

docuit mori. A modest point for a labor that sometimes inspires elaborate paradoxes, cf. Ov. *Her.* 9.95f. *quaeque redundabat fecundo vulnere serpens / fertilis et damnis dives ab ipsa suis*, Sen. *Ag.* 836 *vetuitque collo pereunte nasci*.

243f. The pattern of the couplet is similar to that of 228f., beginning with *solitus* and ending with the name of the creature involved.

Commentary: Act II

pinnis condere obductis diem. The point is used again by Sen. at *Phoen.* 422f. *atra nube subtexens diem / Stymphalis*. It does not appear in other accounts of the Stymphalian Birds, but is somewhat proverbial; cf. the anecdote about Persian arrows hiding the sun (Hdt. 7.226, Cic. *Tusc.* 1.42.101). *Pinnis* probably means "wings," by a common metonymy, here and at *Phoen.* 423, but with special reference to the feathers the birds were able to discharge like arrows, cf. Ap. Rhod. 2.1088, Hyg. *Fab.* 30, Serv. ad V. *Aen.* 8.300. At *Med.* 783 the word perhaps means "feathers."

244. The version implied here is that made explicit at *Ag.* 849 and *Med.* 784 (cf. *HF* 1110f. with comm.), namely that H. shot the birds down with his arrows, cf. Hyg. *Fab.* 30, Paus. 8.22.4. Other authorities speak of his having simply frightened the birds off with a rattle or castanets, cf. Peisander ap. Paus. loc. cit., Diod. Sic. 4.13.2; according to Apollod. 2.5.6 he first flushed the birds in this way and then shot them. Artistic representations usually show the birds being shot with bow and arrows or a sling.

petit. A offers *petiit* here, and similar uncontracted perfects before a vowel at 321 *abiit*, *Tro.* 806 *rediit* (E has the contracted forms in each case). If correct, these forms would be anapests, not tribrachs (cf. Strzelecki 68f.), using the archaic long quality of the final vowel; on such forms v. R. D. Williams on Stat. *Theb.* 10.25. Lachmann, an enthusiast for perfects in *-iit*, believed A to be right, arguing (on Lucr. 3.1042) that Seneca, Phaedrus, and Silius avoid contracted perfects before a vowel. But since other poets use contracted perfects either before a vowel exclusively or indifferently before a vowel or consonant (Munro on Lucr. 3.1042), there seems little to commend Lachmann's view. I believe that A is simply inserting an unambiguous perfect, as e.g. at 612, 1151. On the other hand, *adiit*, attested by both E and A, may be right at *Pha.* 221, and though this form occurs before a consonant, it may suggest a liking for this metrical pattern in the first foot.

ab ipsis nubibus. For the hyperbole cf. *Ag.* 850f. *nube percussa Stymphalis alto / decidit caelo*. The *HO* as usual takes exaggeration one stage further, 1237 *astris ab ipsis depulit Stymphalidas*.

244, 246 Stymphalidas, Thermodontiae. Final long words are quite common in the *senarii* of Republican drama and in Greek tragic trimeters, but Sen. is sparing in his use of them (Hahlbrock 181ff., Soubiran passim). He has 69 uses of final four-syllable words, 14 of five-syllables

Commentary: Act II

and 3 of six-syllables.[59] As many as one-third of the quadrisyllables are proper names or adjectives derived from them, almost all naturally of Greek provenance; by contrast in Republican tragedy there is only one Greek proper name among 106 long final words. Seneca clearly reflects the increased admittance of Greek names in Neoteric and later poetry. Here he uses the Greek names to round off their respective couplets, cf. 11 *Atlantides*, 484 *Busiridis*.

245f. A relatively unadorned reference to H.'s encounter with Hippolyte, such as suits the style of this catalogue; contrast the vivid, detailed picture in lyric at 522–26.

caelibis ... tori. The phrase also appears at *Ag.* 185 *caelebs torus*; cf. Cat. 68.6 *in lecto caelibe*, repeated at Ov. *Her.* 13.107.

246. Compare the similar verse at *Med.* 215 [*cohors*] *inclusa ripis vidua Thermodontiis*. Seneca often uses *viduus* in reference to the Amazons, cf. also *HF* 542, *Tro.* 13.

Thermodontiis. The River Thermodon is traditionally associated with the Amazons since Aesch. *PV* 724f. αἱ Θεμίσκυράν ποτε / κατοικιοῦσιν ἀμφὶ Θερμώδονθ', cf. *RE* 5A.2396.66ff., Sen. *Med.* cited above, *Oed.* 481 *Thermodontiacae catervae*. On other locations v. Roscher 1.272ff., and comm. on *HF* 533–46.

248 Augei. I take this as an adjective (with *OLD*), as the line seems designed to create the interweaving of two noun-adjective pairs in which Sen. delights; for other examples of such a line rounding off the description of a labor cf. 225, 227, 230, 238, 240, 246. (The adjective is attested only here: the form *Augei* appears three times elsewhere, Hyg. *Fab.* 30, *Anth. Lat.* 627.7, 641.7, in each case as the genitive of a noun.) But Gronovius may be right in his suspicion that Sen. wrote *Elei*, which has been displaced by a gloss. He compares Ov. *Met.* 5.576 *fluminis Elei veteres narravit amores*, where several MSS replace *Elei* with *Alphei*.

249ff. Seneca notes similar difficulties—enforced absences, and the resurgence of disorder when his back is turned—in the life of another world-conqueror, Julius Caesar: *Cons. Helv.* 9.7f., quoted pp. 23f.

In Eur., Amphitryon attributes Lycus' success to the state of *stasis*

---

59. To Soubiran's list p. 467 n. 1, I add four uses of quadrisyllables of metrical shape ˉ˘˘ˉ: three of *memoria* (*HF* 408, *Med.* 268, *Oed.* 847), one of *facinorum* (*Med.* 266).

Commentary: Act II

among the citizens, 34, 272f., 588ff. This characteristically Greek element is absent from Sen., who implies that the reason is simply the absence of Hercules; this is in keeping with the greater emphasis here on the importance of H. (cf. Zintzen 166).

250 sensere terrae. The idea of a universal sympathy and reaction to certain events is characteristic of Senecan tragedy; for *sentire* in such contexts cf. *Oed.* 159 *omnia nostrum sensere malum, Ag.* 824f. *sensit ortus, sensit occasus / Herculem nasci.* The notion is particularly apt in this play because of the universality of H.'s exploits, cf. 1054ff., 1331ff. For the pointed phrase cf. also Sen. Rhet. *Suas.* 1.2 (to Alexander about to set sail on the Ocean) *resiste, orbis te tuus revocat.*

pacis auctorem. A phrase with a strongly Roman color: Cicero and Livy both use it several times; Ovid applies it to Augustus (*Pont.* 1.1.32).

251. Withof, ever alert for absurdity (except in some of his own conjectures), was the first to reject the MSS reading *abesse terris.* The paradosis might be defended as an example of *traductio*, the repetition of a word in a somewhat different sense, with *terrae* in the previous line meaning "the inhabited lands" and here "the upper world"; for repetitions of this kind cf. *Thy.* 470 *immane regnum est posse sine regno pati*, 994 *noxque se in noctem abdidit, Tranq.* 5.3 *qui tuto insultaverat agmini tyrannorum* (sc. Socrates), *eius libertatem libertas non tulit, Ep.* 90.35 [*philosophia*] *cuius hoc pretium est non posse pretio capi.* What these examples in fact demonstrate, however, is the feebleness of the present instance; and this, taken together with the likelihood of dittography, makes it impossible to accept the transmitted text. The conjecture by Wilamowitz, which I have printed, is the best that has been made, but it is not entirely convincing, for the overturning of moral values indicated in *prosperum . . . vocatur* might be thought of as a characteristically "modern" development, exemplified by Lycus (cf. 340).

251 prosperum−253. For this picture of a morally upside-down state of affairs, in which the wicked flourish like a green bay tree, cf. *Pha.* 978−88, *Tranq.* 15.1 (n.b. the phrase *scelerum felicium turba*). For crime made honorable by success, cf. *Pha.* 598 *honesta quaedam scelera successus facit.*

The passage was popular in the Renaissance, appearing in two *florilegia*, the *Flores* (see Introduction) and the *Senecae Flores sive Sententiae* of 1547 (cf. Cohon 158), and in Sir William Cornwallis, *Discourses upon Seneca the Tragedian* (1601). The sententia *prosperum . . . vocatur* is trans-

Commentary: Act II

lated by Marston as "Mischiefe that prospers men do vertue call" (*The Malcontent* 5.3), and reused with vigor by Ben Jonson in *Catiline* 3.540f.: "Let 'hem call it mischiefe; / When it is past, and prosper'd, 'twill be vertue."

253. Variations on the proverbial idea that ὅπου βία πάρεστιν, οὐδὲν ἰσχύει νόμος (ps.-Men. *Gnomai* 409 Meineke); cf. 401 [*leges*] *quas arma vincunt*, Otto s.v. *lex* (3). *Ius est in armis* is a particularly pointed version, "might is right," cf. *Pha.* 544 *pro iure vires esse*, Sil. 2.504 *iurisque locum sibi vindicat ensis*, 11.183f. The form of expression is possibly paralleled at Hes. *Erga* 192f. δίκη δ' ἐν χερσὶ καὶ αἰδώς / ἐσσεῖται (text conjectural; see West ad loc.).

254, 257 vidi ... vidi. Apart from immediate anaphora as at 50 *vidi ipsa vidi* (v. comm.), one also finds repeated εἶδον or *vidi* used to enumerate horrors that the speaker has witnessed, as at Eur. *Tro.* 479, 482; Enn. *trag.* 83, 86, 91 R²; V. *Aen.* 2.499, 501; Ov. *Her.* 3.45, 47, 49; Sen. *Tro.* 36, 44, *Phoen.* 543, 545.

255f. For these sons of Creon cf. Eur. 539 (Megara) τεθνᾶσ' ἀδελφοὶ καὶ πατὴρ οὑμὸς γέρων, 541 Λύκος σφ' ὁ καινὸς γῆς ἄναξ διώλεσεν. In Sen. they are said to have been two in number (373), and there are several references to their deaths (cf. 303, 379, 403). Eur. *Her.* and Sen. *HF* appear to be the only places where these sons are mentioned.

There is so little connection in myth between (a) Creon qua friend of Amphitryon and father of Megara and her brothers, and (b) Creon qua brother of Jocasta and father of Megareus, Haemon, and Menoeceus, that they have been regarded as two distinct individuals (so Rose in *OCD*² s.v. Creon); the only link known to me between the myths is late, Hyg. *Fab.* 72.3. But Eur. identifies them in calling Creon (a) son of Menoeceus and a descendant of the Sown Men (*Her.* 4–8), things which are true of Creon (b).

Seneca's reference to Creon as *Cadmi nobilis stirpem ultimam* (256) is perhaps a variation on Eur. *Phoen.* 942ff. (Tiresias to Creon) σὺ δ' ἐνθάδ' ἡμῖν λοιπὸς εἶ σπαρτῶν γένους / ἀκέραιος, ἔκ τε μητρὸς ἀρσένων τ' ἄπο, / οἱ σοί τε παῖδες. Creon was a Cadmeid as well as a descendant of the Spartoi, because his ancestor Echion married Cadmus' daughter Agave. The claim that he was the *last* Cadmeid is justified rhetorically if not genealogically: Oedipus' descendants (Cadmeids through Jocasta) may be ignored in view of the separation of the myths noted above, and Hercules' children, though strictly Cadmeids through their mother, are more likely to be considered Heraclids.

[*200*]

Commentary: Act II

paterni. The use of an adjective in place of the genitive of a noun is found in both poetry and prose, cf. Austin on V. *Aen.* 2.543, Bömer on Ov. *Met.* 1.779. *Paternus* and *patrius* are particularly frequent in this usage: in *HF* cf. 337, 380, 534, 1122, 1134, 1272. On juxtapositions of words indicating relationships, see 51f. comm.

vindices. Clearly "as defenders, while defending." The odd idea of some commentators that the word indicates "prospective avengers" or "liberators" here may be dismissed.

257 regium capiti decus. Something of a set phrase in Sen. Trag. for "the crown," cf. *Ag.* 8f. *hinc auspicari regium capiti decus / mos est Pelasgis* (with Tarrant ad loc.), *Thy.* 701f. *regium capiti decus / bis terque lapsum est.* Ovid uses *regale decus* in the same sense, *Met.* 9.690. The unusual dative *capiti* is probably to be attributed to the influence of V. *Aen.* 10.134f. *qualis gemma micat, fulvum quae dividit aurum, / aut collo decus aut capiti* (echoed also at *HF* 1115 *collo decus*); cf. also *Aen.* 1.429 *scaenis decora alta futuris,* ps.-V. *Culex* 137 *magnum Argoae navi decus.* In Sen.'s phrase, however, the dative is virtually equivalent to a genitive. (Hence A's *capitis* here, clearly a trivialization.)

258 cum capite. For the pointed use of *cum* v. comm. on 1287f. *cum dominis, cum deis.*

quis satis ... fleat? For this type of question cf. 1227f. *quis vos ... / deflere digne poterit?* with comm.

259 ferax deorum. In addition to Bacchus one could mention Ino, daughter of Cadmus, and her son Melicertes, both transformed into sea divinities, cf. *Oed.* 444ff. But the plural may simply generalize from the single instance of Bacchus, cf. comm. on 1284 *pavidasque matres.*

262f. According to Hom. *Od.* 11.262f., Amphion and Zethus built the walls of Thebes together, cf. Eur. *Antiope* (Page, *Greek Literary Papyri* 68), Ap. Rhod. 1.735ff., Paus. 9.5.6, Hyg. *Fab.* 9. In Roman poetry, however, Amphion alone tends to be given credit (cf. 915–17 comm.): Hor. *Carm.* 3.11.2, *Ars P.* 394f.; Prop. 1.9.10; Ov. *Met.* 6.178, 15.427, *AA* 3.323f.; Sen. *Oed.* 611f., *Phoen.* 566ff.; Stat. *Theb.* 4.357ff.

263 modulatu. An expressive resolution. The noun is rare, first attested here and not again until Fronto; it is no doubt inspired by the use of *modulor* in poetry. Expressive metrical effects with the verb in-

Commentary: Act II

clude Manil. 2.767f. *fata / Pieridum numeris etiam modulata*, Sen. *Ag.* 672 *Ityn in varios modulata sonos* (a rare purely anapestic dimeter).

264f. Compare Juno's complaints about her rivals in Thebes at 20f.

265f. quae caelites recepit. Apart from Jupiter's illicit visits one thinks particularly of the wedding of Cadmus and Harmonia, to which the Olympians came as guests: Apollod. 3.42, Pind. *Pyth.* 3.89ff., Eur. *Phoen.* 822f., Diod. Sic. 5.49. But *caelites* could be a generalizing plural based solely on the instance of Jupiter (259 comm.).

266 (fas sit loqui). The phrasing is borrowed from V. *Aen.* 6.266 *sit mihi fas audita loqui*, in a passage Sen. imitates again at 658f. For this familiar type of apotropaic phrase cf. also Lutatius Catulus fr. 2.3f., Cic. *Tusc.* 5.13.18 *cum ipse deo, si hoc fas est dictu, comparari potest*, Ov. *Pont.* 4.8.55.

268–70. Primarily a sad reflection on the present state of affairs in Thebes, rather than an imputation of cowardice. Contrast two otherwise similar passages: Eur. *Her.* 217ff., where Amphitryon uses λόγους ὀνειδιστῆρας in accusing Thebes of ingratitude for failing to protect H.'s family; and Pentheus' speech in Ov. *Met.* 3.531ff., criticizing the present generation of Thebans as unworthy of their traditions. In the present passage, although *tremitis* e.q.s. might suggest cowardice, the main point, as in 259 *quem dominum tremis*, is simply the contrast between Thebes' great destiny and her present degradation; the burden of the phrases is that of 267 *sordido premitur iugo*. In what follows in 271–74 the implication is that the only person who could conceivably deal with Lycus would be H. (cf. 249ff. comm.).

268. For the apostrophe cf. Eur. 217 (Amphitryon) ὦ γαῖα Κάδμου and 252 ὦ γῆς λοχεύμαθ᾽, οὓς Ἄρης σπείρει ποτὲ. Phrases with *proles* and an adjective indicating an ancestor are common, but usually designate an individual; for a people cf. particularly Ov. *Met* 3.531f. *quis furor, anguigenae, proles Mavortia, vestras / attonuit mentes?* (the beginning of the speech of Pentheus mentioned above).

Ophionium genus. N. Heinsius was the first to correct the transmitted *cinis* to *genus*, comparing Ov. *Fasti* 1.591 where the MSS differ between *cinerosa* and *generosa*. *Ophionius* appears again at *Oed.* 484f. *Cithaeron sanguine undavit / Ophioniaque caede* (a reference to Pentheus' death), but the Ophion in question is utterly obscure (Roscher s.v. 4); the dictionaries assume that he is a double of Echion, the father of

[202]

Pentheus (ἔχις = ὄφις), but without supporting evidence. In *Oed.*, Jac. Gronovius emended him away, writing *Amphionius* (*āphionius* could easily be corrupted to *oph-*), but here he is protected by meter from that fate, and Heinsius' conjecture *Echionium* is unpersuasive paleographically. One is inclined to respect the testimony of the MSS at these two places.

269 quo reccidistis? For *recidere* in the sense of "sink, be degraded" with *quo* cf. Livy 30.42.18 *ex quantis opibus quo reccidissent Carthaginiensium res*; with other adverbs such as *eo*, *illuc*, cf. Cic. *Verr.* 2.5.63.163; Livy 4.2.8, 25.31.4; Quint. 2.10.3; Juv. 12.53f.[60]

ignarum exulem. Euripides invented this Lycus for the purposes of his *Heracles* (Wilamowitz I 112), coloring the invention by making him the son of an earlier Lycus who had ruled Thebes, as the husband of Dirce, before the coming of Amphion and Zethus (26f.). The younger Lycus, however, is not Theban-born but has come to the city from Euboea (32, cf. 257). Seneca simplifies the situation by making his Lycus come from humble and obscure origins (cf. 337ff. on his *novitas*), and blackens his character by the detail that he has been banished from his homeland.

Ignarus passive = *ignotus* is rare, but used before Sen. by Sallust, Vergil, and Ovid. *Ignotus* is frequently used in reference to lowly origins. Lycus as portrayed by Sen. could scarcely be described as *ignavum* (τΤ^{2pc}), even by Amphitryon; contrast *truculentus* above in 254.

271f. For Hercules as *defensor iustitiae* and chastiser of tyrants cf. particularly Diod. Sic. 4.17.5 τοὺς παρανομοῦντας ἀνθρώπους ἢ δυνάστας ὑπερηφάνους ἀποκτείνας τὰς πόλεις ἐποίησεν εὐδαίμονας κ.τ.λ. In this play his hatred of tyrants is expressed at 922ff., 936f., and his punishment of them is alluded to at 431 and 1123f.; for the theme of the punishment of unjust kings cf. 737ff., which describes their fate in the underworld. Tyrants put down by H. include Busiris, Antaeus, Eryx, and Diomedes.

---

60. The second word of the phrase in E^{ac} was almost certainly *excidistis* (as in FM), the original *x* being plainly visible though corrected. Presumably the error in E or its exemplar was caused by the unfamiliar form *reccidistis*, leading to wrong word division and attempted correction. The first word may have been left as *quor*, but the traces after the *o* are illegible; FM write *quorsum*. Strangely, some recent editors have accepted *quorsum excidistis* into the text, though Leo I 112 n. 12 had shown it to be untenable: *quorsum* is not used by poets after Horace, and *excidere* could not have the required meaning.

Commentary: Act II

272 confregit. Carlsson, who boldly preferred this reading of CS despite the agreement of EP in *confringit* (1925 18f.), is now vindicated by the fact that T has *confregit*; this shows that P has accommodated the tense to that of *persequitur*, and it seems probable that E did the same. For tense-variation such as *persequitur/confregit*, Carlsson compares 30f. *quidquid horridum tellus creat / inimica, quidquid pontus aut aer tulit*, *Tro.* 675f. *terret, dedit, sensit*, *Thy.* 103f. *sentit, horruit*.

273 fieri. The earlier editors generally preferred the reading of recc. *ferri*, Pierrot arguing that the paronomasia *fert–ferri* was characteristic of Sen.'s style. Corruption of *ferri* to *fieri* would not be surprising, cf. e.g. Cic. *Cael.* 61, but the paradosis sounds genuinely Senecan, cf. 1301 *fieri iubes*, *Ag.* 306 *fieri sinam* (both at line end), *Tro.* 334 *hoc vetat fieri pudor*.

274f. tenet ... sed non tenebit. On paronomasia of verbs see comm. 116. Senecan characters often take up something they have just said (epanalepsis), as if the word itself suggested a new train of thought or the need for self-correction: cf. 30f., 307f., 643f.

275 aderit. Sc. Hercules, a natural omission as he is at the center of Amphitryon's thoughts (cf. 312, and 33ff. with comm.).

276 ad astra. That is, *ad caelum* (23 comm.), but in the special sense of "to *sight* of the heavens," i.e. to the land of the living, for which cf. *Pha.* 1213 *patuit ad caelum via*, of Theseus' return from the underworld, and *Ag.* 859. Perhaps Sen. wants the audience to hear a second meaning also, "to take his place among the stars" (23 comm.).

276f. inveniet viam / aut faciet. For the pattern of this contrast, followed by an unusual sense-pause in the second foot, cf. comm. on 51f. ad fin.

277f. Amphitryon's speech closes effectively with an emotional apostrophe to Hercules. The appeal is phrased as a prayer, in keeping with the frequent impression in this play of the superhuman status of H.; there are also prayer elements in the following monologue of Megara. For *adesse* in prayers cf. 903 *adsit Lycurgi domitor*, V. *Aen.* 8.78 *adsis o tantum et propius tua numina firmes*, Ov. *Met.* 3.613, Bömer on Ov. *Fasti* 1.65. For *tandemque venias* cf. Hor. *Carm.* 1.2.30ff. *tandem venias precamur / ... augur Apollo*; for *venire* in prayers v. N-H on that passage, Cat. 61.8f. *flammeum cape laetus, huc / huc veni*, Tib. 1.7.53 *sic venias hodierne* (following *huc ades* in 49).

Commentary: Act II

The wording of this passage is similar to *Ag.* 395–96a *telluris altum remeat Argolicae decus / tandem ad penates victor Agamemnon suos.*

precor. A frequent line ending, occurring eight times elsewhere in *HF*. Here it is the reading of E, preferred by editors since Gronovius to A's *tuis*; however, Zwierlein (1976 202 and n. 80) defends *tuis*, arguing that *precor* is more likely to be intrusive in this context. But *precor* in conjunction with *tandem venias* is supported by the Horatian passage cited above, whereas *tuis* creates an awkward tautology with *ad victam domum*.

278 venias victor ad victam domum. Strong alliteration marking the end of the speech, as at *Pha.* 482 *civium coetus cole.* The play on *victor-victus* is at home in the pointed style of the tragedies, cf. 368f., 409, *Tro.* 257, 914, and in Sen.'s prose, e.g. *Const. Sap.* 6.6. It is also Ovidian (cf. Bömer on *Met.* 3.95, *Fasti* 3.101), but less frequent in Vergil (only *Aen.* 2.368, 10.757).

279ff. The first half of Megara's speech is marked by an ominous violence of language; there is hubris in the phrases *orbe diducto redi* and *erumpe, rerum terminos tecum efferens,* and in the idea of releasing the dead, 291ff. But at 295 *magna sed nimium loquor* she makes an effort to control herself, speaking more gently of what H.'s return would mean to her. The despair that breaks through at 308 is clearly the underlying cause of her earlier outburst. Among the Passion-Restraint scenes (v. introduction to Act II) Megara's monologue may be compared particularly with that of Medea (*Med.* 116ff.), which has a similar shift of feeling (at 137): there, too, violent unrestrained emotion gives way to gentler language expressing an underlying feeling of love, albeit frustrated and sore-tried.

Megara takes up the direct appeal to H. with which Amphitryon ended his speech, seconding it on the basis of her personal relationship to him (*coniunx*). The opening word *emerge* was certainly suggested by *emerget* at the end of Amphitryon's speech (276: the verb occurs only once elsewhere in Sen. Trag.), and may well be intended as a deliberate echo of the word on Megara's part.

Note the series of imperatives emphatically placed at the beginnings of lines, *emerge, abrumpe, emitte*; cf. the series at 100ff. *incipite, concutite, hoc agite, concutite.*

280 retro via. Clearly influenced by 55 *patefacta ab imis manibus retro via est*; the words do not appear together again in Sen. Trag.

[205]

Commentary: Act II

283ff. qualis . . . talis. The passage is redolent of prayer style in its use of the formula "as you did before, so give help now" (Norden *Agnostos Theos* 152; for *qualis* in such a context cf. Tib. 2.5.7ff., Sen. *Med.* 16f.). Here the formula carries the further implication δύνασαι γάρ.

283–88. Other authors who credit Hercules with opening the Vale of Tempe are Diodorus (4.18.6) and Lucan (6.347ff., 8.1). Herodotus' rationalistic view that the mountains had been separated by an earthquake (7.129) is followed by Sen. himself qua natural scientist, *QNat.* 6.25.2. Diodorus mentions this feat as a parallel to the opening of the Straits of Gibraltar; in *HF* it is noteworthy that the two exploits are mentioned within fifty lines of each other, and that the language of 287f. is remarkably similar to that of 237.

284 praeceps . . . iter. Presumably this phrase indicates that the river falls steeply in its passage through Tempe. In fact it does not, but cf. Ov. *Met.* 1.569f. *Tempe, per quae Peneus ab imo / effusus Pindo spumosis volvitur undis / deiectuque gravi* e.q.s.

quaerens. "Obtaining, winning," rather than "seeking"; cf. Ter. *Eun.* 260f. *ille . . . videt mi esse tantum honorem, / tam facile victum quaerere*, Prop. 3.2.25 *ingenio quaesitum nomen*, Sen. *Ag.* 927 *Aegisthus arces venere quaesitas tenet.* Contrast *Tro.* 187, where the same line-end (*quaerens iter*) is used, again of a blocked river, but where *quaerens* = "seeking."

285 stetisti. That is, in heroic stance, either in preparation for the task (cf. 118 *stabo*) or in triumph at having accomplished it (cf. *Tro.* 22 *stat avidus irae victor*, 188).

287 cessit. *Cecidit* codd.: the conjecture is that of Leo, comparing *QNat.* 6.25.2 *aiunt aliquando Ossan Olympo cohaesisse, deinde terrarum motu recessisse et fissam unius magnitudinem montis in duas partes*, Luc. 6.347f. *postquam discessit Olympo / Herculea gravis Ossa manu.* The mountain range was divided, not leveled as would be indicated by *cecidit* (cf. Lucr. 6.546 *quippe cadunt toti montes*).

289 parentes liberos patriam petens. For lists of nouns in asyndeton, v. 32 commentary. These lists frequently contain words denoting relatives, home, country, cf. 379f. *patrem abstulisti regna germanos larem / patriam*, 388 *mixtumque nomen coniugis nati patris*, 630 *natos parentem coniugem leto petit*, 1260, *Med.* 982, *Phoen.* 663, ps.-Sen. *Oct.* 645.

Commentary: Act II

290 rerum terminos. The boundaries between the natural divisions of the universe, specifically between the upper world and the underworld. Compare *Med.* 369 *terminus omnis motus*, a phrase that indicates that the *bene dissaepti foedera mundi* (ibid. 335) have now been annulled; also Sen. Rhet. *Suas.* 1.10 *Alexandrum rerum terminos supergressum.* The idea of disrupting such boundaries is of course hubristic; for the association of this theme with H., see Introduction. I take it that the *termini* here are conceptual, as at *Med.* 369: H. will "carry them away with him" by virtue of breaking through to the upper world as Megara suggests.

291f. avida . . . aetas. Greed is a traditional attribute of death, cf. Callim. *Epigr.* 2.6f. ὁ πάντων / ἁρπακτὴς Ἀίδης, Tib. 1.3.4, Gratt. 347 *avidissimus Orcus*, Sen. *HF* 555 *Mors avidis . . . dentibus* with comm., 782, *Ag.* 752; here it is transferred to time as an agent of death, cf. *Tro.* 400 *tempus nos avidum devorat.*

tot per annorum gradus. An unusual phrase. *Gradus* is more conventionally applied to the "stages" of human life, e.g. *Pha.* 451f. *propria descripsit deus / officia et aevum per suos duxit gradus*, Tac. *Dial.* 28 *per singulos aetatis gradus.*

292f. oblitos sui lucisque pavidos . . . populos. A memorable description of the insubstantial dead, though its elements are thoroughly traditional. Their forgetfulness of self is due to their having drunk from Lethe, cf. 681 (Lethe) *demitque curas* with comm. For their fear of the light cf. V. *Aen.* 8.246 *trepident immisso lumine manes*, Ov. *Met.* 5.358 *immissusque dies trepidantes terreat umbras.* Even more substantial inhabitants of the underworld react with fear to daylight, cf. Ov. *Met.* 2.261 [*lumen*] *infernum terret cum coniuge regem*, Sen. *Ag.* 862 (Cerberus) *lucis ignotae metuens colorem.* On the *populi* of the dead cf. 191 comm. For the line-ending *oblitos sui* cf. 728f. *oblitos sui / sceleris* (also of the dead), 808 *oblitus sui*, *Med.* 560 *oblitus mei.*

295ff. The sudden shift in emotion is typical of Sen.'s characters, women in particular. Apart from *Med.* 137 (see comm. 279ff.), cf. particularly *Tro.* 474ff.; here Andromache lays aside the extravagant hopes in which she has been indulging, realizing the precariousness of her present position. Note the similarity of language, *sed mei fati memor / tam magna timeo vota.*

The phrase *magna sed nimium loquor* is similar to 63 *levia sed nimium queror*, also in a transition (see comm.).

Commentary: Act II

296–305. This *anticipated* welcome not unnaturally contains several elements that might be expected in an *actual* welcome, listed by Cairns, *Generic Composition* 21–23 in his analysis of the *prosphonetikon*: demonstrations of affection by the welcomer (297, Cairns no. 4), indications of the welcomer's sufferings during the other's absence (298, Cairns no. 10), payment of vows made by the welcomer for the other's return (299–302, Cairns no. 15–16), benefits conferred by the other's arrival (303–5, Cairns no. 11).

296f. unde illum mihi . . . diem. "How shall that day come for me?" For the construction with an accusative cf. Hor. *Sat.* 2.5.101f. *ergo nunc Dama sodalis / nusquam est? unde mihi tam fortem tamque fidelem?*, 2.7.117, Sen. *Ben.* 3.36.2, Luc. 7.28, Stat. *Silv.* 1.2.188f.

297. The greeting involves both an embrace and a clasping of hands, cf. V. *Aen.* 6.697f. *da iungere dextram, / da, genitor, teque amplexu ne subtrahe nostro.* For *dexteram amplecti* cf. ibid. 8.124 *excepitque manu dextramque amplexus inhaesit.*

298. As Megara envisages this moment of intimacy, her language is colored by the *sermo amatorius*: clearly there is influence here from Ovid, whose heroines especially in *Her.* speak the language of elegiac love poetry. For *lentus* in such contexts cf. Prop. 1.15.4 *tu tamen in nostro lenta timore venis*, Ov. *Her.* 2.23 *at tu lentus abes*, 19.70, R. Pichon, *De Sermone Amatorio* (Paris 1902) 186. For *memor* cf. Prop. 1.11.5 *nostri cura subit memores a! ducere noctes?*, Ov. *Her.* 1 (Penelope to Ulixes) 44 *at bene cautus eras et memor ante mei*, Pichon 198. *Queror, querela* are of course extremely common in such poetry, e.g. Ov. *Her.* 2.1f. *tua te Rhodopeia Phyllis / ultra promissum tempus abesse queror*, 26 *vela queror reditu, verba carere fide*, cf. Pichon 248f. For such language in Sen. Trag. cf. particularly the complaints of Andromache *Tro.* 802ff. (with Fantham ad loc.).

299–301. Anaphora of *tu* is at home in hymn- and prayer-style, cf. Norden *Agnostos Theos* 149ff., N-H on Hor. *Carm.* 1.10.9. But line 300 is somewhat unusual, because asyndetic anaphora usually refers to a single divinity, whereas a new addressee is normally introduced by *tuque* vel sim., as at 597, 599, 658f., 1057, 1065. For a similar distributive anaphora, but not addressed to divinities, cf. 1231ff. *tibi tela frangam nostra; tibi nostros, puer, / rumpemus arcus* e.q.s.

deorum ductor. *TLL* cites only this passage for *ductor* used of a god. The word has the sense here of *rector* or *dominus*: cf. *HO* 560 [*Plutonem*] *turbae ducem maioris et dominum Stygis. Ductor* is a Vergilian word in verse (twenty-four uses), avoided by Ovid (only a variant at *Met.* 12. 524).

299f. indomiti . . . colla. A hecatomb is described in similar language at *Pha.* 500 *centena nivei colla summittunt boves*; for *colla ferre* of a *victima* cf. *Med.* 59f. *colla Tonantibus / taurus celsa ferat*. Hecatombs are frequently described in Latin poetry as involving literally a hundred cattle, cf. Cat. 64.389 *centum procumbere tauros*, Hor. *Epod.* 17.39, Ov. *Tr.* 2.75f. But as early as Homer ἑκατόμβη is used of any large sacrifice. Cf. Bömer on Ov. *Met.* 8.152.

indomiti. That is, unbroken to the yoke, a detail frequently found in sacrifices (e.g. Hom. *Il.* 10.292f.; V. *Georg.* 4.540, *Aen.* 6.38; Ov. *Fasti* 1.83, 4.335f.; Sen. *Oed.* 300, *Med.* 61f.).

300–302. Why does Megara pray to Ceres in particular? According to some sources, Hercules had requested initiation in the Eleusinian Mysteries in preparation for his descent to the underworld (Apollod. 2.5.12, Diod. Sic. 4.25.1; see 762–827 comm.). Ceres might therefore be thought to have a special interest in his safe return.

Megara apparently vows a special celebration of the Mysteries if H. should return. In historical times the Mysteries were celebrated only at a set time, in the month of Boedromion every year (cf. 842ff.), but it is not unreasonable to picture matters as less regulated in the heroic age: the Lesser Mysteries are said to have been established specially to accommodate H.'s request for initiation. Seneca associates torch waving with thanksgiving for a return again at *Ag.* 362f. (see Tarrant's note).

300 frugum potens. Compare Ov. *Am.* 3.10.35 *diva potens frugum silvis cessabat in altis*. The poets like to use phrases with *potens* plus genitive in reference to the gods, often allusively: e.g. Hor. *Carm.* 1.3.1 *diva potens Cypri*, *Carm. Saec.* 1 *Phoebe silvarumque potens Diana*, V. *Aen.* 1.80 *nimborumque facis tempestatumque potentem*, Ov. *Met.* 9.315 *diva potens uteri*, Sen. *Oed.* 868 *tenebrarum potens*.

301. The phrase *muta fide* refers, like *secreta sacra*, to secrecy about the Eleusinian rites. For the phrase of keeping a secret cf. *Oed.* 799 *praestare tacitam regibus soleo fidem*, *Thy.* 317f. *tacita tam rudibus fides / non est in annis*; compare also Hor. *Carm.* 3.2.25f. *est et fideli tuta silentio / merces*, V. *Aen.* 3.112 *hinc fida silentia sacris*, both with reference to Mysteries (of Ceres and Cybele, respectively). I take it that *tacita* in 302 also refers to silence about, rather than during, the rites (as at *Pha.* 107 cited below);

Commentary: Act II

what we know of the Eleusinian Mysteries does not suggest that they were conducted in silence.

302. Compare similar language in reference to the Mysteries at *Pha.* 106f. *Atthidum mixtam choris / iactare tacitis conscias sacris faces.* Torches were important in the rites: according to Lactantius' account, *facibus accensis per noctem Proserpina inquiritur, et ea inventa ritus omnis gratulatione ac taedarum iactatione finitur* (*Div. Inst.* epit. 18 (23); cf. also Nilsson, *GGR* 1^3 656). The length of the torches may be seen on monuments associated with the Mysteries, e.g. Mylonas *Eleusis* ill. 81, 83–85, 88.

303–5. The hyperbole is characteristic of impassioned characters in Sen., cf. Atreus (*Thy.* 1098f.) *liberos nasci mihi / nunc credo, castis nunc fidem reddi toris*, and Medea (*Med.* 982ff.) *iam iam recepi sceptra germanum patrem* e.q.s. In the present passage there is the suggestion that Hercules will actually replace Megara's lost relatives: cf. Andromache's words to Hector at *Il.* 6.429f. Ἕκτορ, ἀτὰρ σύ μοί ἐσσι πατὴρ καὶ πότνια μήτηρ / ἠδὲ κασίγνητος, σὺ δέ μοι θαλερὸς παρακοίτης, and those of Briseis to Achilles at Ov. *Her.* 3.51f. *tot tamen amissis te compensavimus unum; / tu dominus, tu vir, tu mihi frater eras.*

305f. maior . . . potestas. Both *maior quam tua* and *maior quam ut erumpere possis.*

306 sequimur. The present tense suggests immediate willingness (cf. H-S 307f.). The present tense with a future sense is particularly common in comedy with verbs of motion, e.g. Plaut. *Stich.* 623 *deos salutabo modo, poste ad te continuo transeo*, and *sequor* is not infrequently so used (C. E. Bennett, *Syntax of Early Latin* [Boston 1910–14] 1.18ff.). For the sense of *sequor* here, viz. "follow to death," cf. Ov. *Met.* 1.361f. *namque ego (crede mihi), si te quoque pontus haberet, / te sequerer, coniunx.*

308. Megara's underlying despair is activated by the last words she has spoken, and overwhelms her show of bravery. For a word or phrase triggering a new train of thought cf. 29f. *bella . . .—Quae bella?* and v. comm. on 274f.

fractos. Many readers must have thought of *tractos* before it was proposed by Hoffa 469. The conjecture is rhetorically attractive, taking up *trahe-trahes*, but unacceptable on grounds of sense. It introduces a reference to a hope of salvation at a later stage, when some god will "raise" the family again to the upper world, but there is no preparation or justification for such an idea. As it stands, the line satisfactorily summarizes the immediate prospects as Megara sees them: "it will be the case that you will drag us down, it will not be the case that any god will restore our fortunes." Thus Megara implicitly rejects as useless her appeals to Jupiter and Ceres.

309 O. A more emotional form of address than a vocative alone (N-H on Hor. *Carm.* 1.9.8), as is clear at 622 and 1334. In some other passages *o* appears to create a more formal or elevated address than a plain vocative, as in Lycus' opening words to Megara 359ff. and in addresses to the gods, e.g. 205, 299, 592.

socia nostri sanguinis. An echo of *Titanum suboles, socia nostri sanguinis*, the first line of Cicero's translation of a speech from Aeschylus' lost Προμηθεὺς λυόμενος (*Tusc.* 2.10.23ff.).

309f. casta fide servans torum. For such phrases of marital fidelity cf. *toros . . . tutari* and *casta . . . fide* at *Ag.* 110f.; for *servare torum* cf. V. *Aen.* 8.412f. *castum ut servare cubile / coniugis . . . possit*, Prop. 2.32.55 *lectum servare pudicum*, Ov. *Pont.* 2.2.69 *coniunx sua pulvinaria servat*, with such precedents as λέκτρα σῴζειν at Eur. *IA* 1203, *Her.* 1372.

310 magnanimi. The word has an epic ring, cf. Vergil's *magnanimi heroes* (*Aen.* 6.649); it is reminiscent of Homer's frequently used μεγάθυμος. See Skutsch, *ALL* 12.208ff. = *Kl. Schr.* 207ff., and Norden on *Aen.* 6.307. In using the word here, Amphitryon no doubt hints that Megara should be worthy of her husband's *magnanimitas*.

313f. quod nimis . . . credunt. "How easily / Doe wretched men beleeve, what they would have!" (Ben Jonson, *Sejanus* 4.491f.). For the credulity of the wretched, cf. Menander fr. 322.1 Κ εὔπιστον ἀτυχῶν ἐστιν ἄνθρωπος φύσει; however, people in general proverbially believe what they want to believe, cf. Dem. *Olynth.* 3.19 ὃ γὰρ βούλεται, τοῦθ' ἕκαστος καὶ οἴεται, Caes. *BGall.* 3.18.2 *fere libenter homines quod volunt, credunt*, Otto s.v. *credere* 1 and the *Nachträge*, pp. 42, 54, 71, 266.

nimis. Modifies *volunt. Nimis* et sim. may be used in hyperbaton even when an intervening adjective seems likely to cause at least momentary confusion, cf. Ov. *AA* 1.354 *neve parum tacitis conscia fida iocis*, where *parum* modifies *conscia*, and (less confusing) Sen. *Med.* 293 *parumne miserae temporis lacrimis negas?* See comm. on 63.

315 moveri. The simple verb (transmitted by E) is more elegant than the compound *amoveri* (A), cf. comm. on 409f.

Commentary: Act II

316. "The belief of fear (i.e. of the fearful) always inclines to the worse." The phrasing of the *sententia* is influenced by Ov. *AA* 3.674 *prona venit cupidis in sua vota fides* (in itself another variation of *homines quod volunt, credunt*; see comm. on 313f. above). For the thought cf. Luc. 1.484ff. *sic quisque pavendo / dat vires famae, nulloque auctore malorum / quae finxere timent*, Stat. *Theb.* 3.5f. E's genitive *timoris* is preferable to A's dative *timori*, which would sound at first as though it were dependent on *prona*.

317f. Seneca likes such tricola of verbs expressing "burial," cf. *Ben.* 7.10.2 *terra . . . ista* (sc. *metalla*) *defodit et mersit et ut noxiosis rebus . . . toto pondere incubuit*, *QNat.* 5.15.3 *quae tanta necessitas hominem ad sidera erectum incurvavit et defodit et in fundum telluris intimae mersit?*

318 ad superos. That is, to the world of the living; but perhaps Sen. wants the audience to catch a second possible meaning, "to join the gods above" (v. comm. 148 *ad superos*). Compare the potential ambiguity of *ad astra* 276.

319–24. These lines attest an otherwise unknown adventure in which a vessel in which Hercules was traveling ran aground in the Syrtes and the hero made his way to safety on foot. (The Syrtes threatened ships by a combination of shallows and an unusually high tide, which might leave them stranded as it ebbed, cf. Ap. Rhod. 4.1235ff., Hor. *Carm.* 2.6.3f., N-H on Hor. *Carm.* 1.22.5.) I take it that the reference is to a single episode, despite *cum . . . cumque*. H. in his quest for Geryon's cattle made use either of the goblet of the sun or of a bronze urn (cf. Apollod. 2.5.10, Athen. 11.469d–470d, Serv. ad *Aen.* 7.662, 8.300); on the present occasion he may have been traveling in one of these, or in some more prosaic vessel. One is reminded of the episode in Ap. Rhod. 4.1232–1484, in which the *Argo* similarly became stuck in the Syrtes, and the Argonauts, struggling inland, found themselves hard on H.'s heels: they learned that he had visited and plundered the grove of the Hesperides only the previous day, and when they searched for him, the keen-eyed Lynceus thought he glimpsed him far off. As the Argonauts literally follow in H.'s footsteps in this adventure, is the grounding of the *Argo* modeled on an original grounding of H.'s ship?

Seneca's language creates an almost surrealistic impression of land and sea confounded. The land imitates the sea, with its sand dunes like waves; the sea repeatedly invades the land and departs; H. walks through the sea as if on land (*pedes*). Lucan makes the point by statement rather than suggestion, 9.303ff. *Syrtes . . . natura . . . in dubio pelagi terraeque reliquit* e.q.s.

320. For the shifting sands of the desert in this area cf. Hdt. 3.26, 4.173; Sall. *Jug.* 79; Luc. 9.455ff.

321 abît. That is, from the useless ship. Twentieth-century editors have followed Leo I 18f. in preferring *adiit*, the reading of Σ. (It looks as though E^ac had *adit*.) Leo thought that H. first made his way to the sea and then traveled through it on foot; but this seems highly unlikely if his ship had stuck fast in the shallows. Furthermore, to take *bisque discedens fretum / et bis recurrens* as governed by *adiit*, with Leo, gives most awkward Latin, whereas there is no difficulty if the phrase is governed by *per*. For the contracted form *abît* here see comm. on 244 *petît*.

322 deserta rate. *Defecta rate*, proposed by Damsté 431, appears to make better sense of the passage: Hercules' ship failed him, and he was stuck. (For this sense of *defectus* cf. Ov. *Met.* 9.154 *quae vires defecto reddat amori*, 13.477 *illa super terram defecto poplite labens*.) But as we know so little of the episode, it seems wisest to make no change: H. may, for example, have become caught (*deprensus haesit*) in the notorious quicksands of the Syrtes after abandoning ship.

323 Syrtium brevibus vadis. Vergilian phrasing, cf. *Aen.* 1.111f. *in brevia et syrtis urget . . . / inliditque vadis*, 5.221 *brevibusque vadis*, echoed again at Sen. *Ag.* 572 *brevia . . . vada*.

325f. For the idea that danger awaits those who aspire to *virtus animosa* cf. 201; for the idea that fortune shows no favor to such men cf. 525 *O Fortuna viris invida fortibus*.

328. "Whom chance hath often missed, chance hits at length" (Thomas Hughes, *The Misfortunes of Arthur* [1587]). For the wording cf. Publ. Syr. 515 Friedrich *quemcumque quaerit calamitas, facile invenit*, and for the thought Sen. *QNat.* 6.1.3 *circumit fatum et, si quid diu praeterit, repetit*. The single-line *sententia* is used to summarize and round off the passage, v. 5 comm.

329 sed ecce. Examples of *sed ecce, sed en*, and similar phrases drawing attention to the entrance of a new character are collected by Liebermann 50 n. 137.

329–31. Facial expression is frequently noted as revealing emotions or character, cf. 371, *Tro.* 933 *subdolo vultu*, 1152, *Pha.* 363 *proditur vultu furor*, 433, *Thy.* 898f., *Ag.* 128 with Tarrant ad loc.; for characterization by gait see 204 comm. Entrance-announcements sometimes con-

Commentary: Act II

vey character by both expression and walk, as here, cf. *Tro.* 522f. *adest Ulixes, et quidem dubio gradu / vultuque: nectit pectore astus callidos,* 999f., *Med.* 380, 394, *Pha.* 431ff. Even Lycus' handling of his scepter suggests his aggression, for he brandishes it (*concutiens*) as a weapon, cf. Livy 22.1.12 *Mavors telum suum concutit,* Ov. *Met.* 12.79, Sen. *Ira* 2.35.6 *sanguineum quatiens dextra Bellona flagellum, Tro.* 683.

Descriptions of physical manifestations of states of mind are found in the literary tradition in both tragedy and epic (e.g. Eur. *Med.* 27–30, V. *Aen.* 2.774). Their frequency and fullness in Sen. Trag., however, may be influenced by a Stoic tradition of interest in such revelations of *ethos,* cf. Sen. *Ep.* 52.12, 95.65, E. C. Evans in *TAPA* 81 (1950) 169–84.

332–57. One of two entrance-monologues in *HF,* the other being that of Hercules at 592ff. (which opens as a prayer). Such monologues are a familiar feature of late Euripidean tragedy (with some precedents in Aeschylus) and of New Comedy (D. Bain, *Actors and Audience* [Oxford 1972] 61ff., 68ff., 135ff.), as well as of Sen. Trag.: on the technique in Sen. and its antecedents see Tarrant 1978 231–41. Conventionally the entering character at first fails to notice (or to take account of) the characters already onstage; only after expressing what is on his mind does he become aware of their presence. In that the speaker gives a full account of his attitude and intentions, the present speech is similar to Eur. *Bacch.* 215ff. (Pentheus) and *Tro.* 860ff. (Menelaus).

332–35. Lycus proudly enumerates the areas he rules. He might simply have said "the whole of Boeotia," but the list of its regions gives a vivid impression of his kingdom's size and resources; cf. Aesch. *Suppl.* 254–59 and fr. 158 N, Eur. *Alc.* 588ff. with Dale ad loc., Sen. *Med.* 211ff. The passage may also be compared with the tragic fragment quoted by Sen. at *Ep.* 80.7, which presumably comes from a *Thyestes* or *Atreus: en impero Argis, regna mihi liquit Pelops, / qua ponto ab Helles atque ab Ionio mari / urgetur Isthmos.*

333f. The paradosis *et omne quidquid uberi (ubere* E) *cingit solo / obliqua Phocis* is open to two objections. First, Phocis is not fertile but mountainous, as Sen. indicates by *obliqua* (Ovid's *terra ferax, Met.* 1.313, is purely conventional); to talk of Phocis encircling Boeotia *uberi solo,* as though Boeotia were less fertile, would be ridiculous. Second, Phocis was not historically subject to Thebes (except for a short period after Leuctra). The conjecture of Karsten 47 *quidquid uberis cingit soli*[61]

---

61. Later proposed also by Müller 7, and usually attributed to him. N. Heinsius 216 had already suggested a partitive genitive in his conjecture *quidquid uberis iungit soli.*

solves the problem: Lycus is now indicating that he rules not only the immediate area of Thebes (332) but also northwest Boeotia, bordered by the mountains of Phocis. For the phrase in description of Boeotia cf. *Phoen.* 129f. *Boeotios / colonus agros uberis tondes soli.*

334 obliqua. "Sloping," that is, mountainous but not precipitous: for the word in this sense cf. Livy 38.22.1 *cum quoad viam colles obliqui dederunt escendissent, postquam ad invia ventum est, flexere iter* (where *obliqui* contrasts with *invia*), Val. Fl. 1.484; and for this characterization of the area cf. Sen. *Oed.* 281 *clementer acto colle Parnasos biceps.*

quidquid Ismenos rigat. The Ismenus rises a little to the south of Thebes and flows north into the Theban plain, its course being roughly parallel to that of the Dirce (cf. Eur. *Phoen.* 824ff.). The river is frequently mentioned in connection with Thebes, cf. Bömer on Ov. *Met.* 2.244. For the use of a river name to designate a region see Tarrant on *Ag.* 318ff., adding to his references from Sen. Trag. *Tro.* 8ff., *HF* 1163, and omitting *HF* 1323ff., *Med.* 707ff.

336. Peiper in the 1867 Teubner deleted 335 (which seems unjustified) and 336, Leo only 336. Geographically the line is not intolerable, as the Megarid, the northern half of the Isthmus, does march with part of southern Boeotia. For the expression cf. Ov. *Met.* 6.491f. *quaeque urbes aliae bimari clauduntur ab Isthmo, / exteriusque sitae bimari spectantur ab Isthmo*, where the first line refers to the Peloponnese, the second to central Greece. But 336 adds little to the definition of Boeotia's southern border in 335; as the only place reference in 333–36 without a separate verb, it has the air of being tacked on; and the fact that E has 336 before 335 could support the hypothesis of an early interpolation (possibly inspired by the Ovidian lines just quoted?).

337–41. Lycus plumes himself on having gained his position by his own efforts rather than by inheritance. The contrast between those who make their way by individual worth and those who rest on the laurels of their ancestors is not unknown in Greek literature: cf. Men. fr. 533 K = 612 S. Seneca, however, expresses the contrast here in very Roman terms; e.g. the *tituli* in 339 suggest the honorific titles of ancestors a noble family at Rome would prize, cf. Prop. 4.11.32 *et domus est titulis utraque fulta suis*, Luc. 8.73 *femina tantorum titulis insignis avorum*. The language of the passage reflects the conflict at Rome between *novi homines* (n.b. *novitas* 348) and *nobiles* (cf. 338f.)—a conflict still felt in Seneca's day, cf. Tac. *Ann.* 14.53 (Sen. speaking to Nero) *inter nobiles et longa decora praeferentes, novitas mea enituit. Virtus* as opposed to *genus*

Commentary: Act II

(339f.) was exactly what the new men emphasized, e.g. Sall. *Jug.* 85.31f., Cic. *Verr.* 5.180 (Cato) *se virtute non genere populo Romano commendari putaret*, cf. T. P. Wiseman, *New Men in the Roman Senate* (London 1971) 109f. Similarly *ignavus heres* 338 is the sort of phrase a new man might throw at a *nobilis*, cf. Sall. *Jug.* 85.14 *contemnunt novitatem meam, ego illorum ignaviam.*

For examples of the topic of nobility and personal worth in tragedy cf. Eur. fr. 336 N, Acc. *trag.* 272 R² *non genus virum ornat, generis vir fortis loco.* Seneca uses the theme in a philosophical context at *Ep.* 44.5 *non facit nobilem atrium plenum fumosis imaginibus. nemo in nostram gloriam vixit, nec quod ante nos fuit, nostrum est.* (For philosophical and rhetorical developments of the theme v. G. Highet, *Juvenal the Satirist* [Oxford 1960] 272.) The whole of Juvenal's eighth satire is an extended treatment of the question *stemmata quid faciunt?*

340 sed clara virtus. The play increasingly casts doubt on the value of *virtus*; Lycus is using the term merely as a euphemism for ruthless self-assertion (v. Introduction).

340f. qui genus . . . laudat. Cf. Ov. *Met.* 13.140f. *nam genus et proavos et quae non fecimus ipsi, / vix ea nostra voco*, Plut. *Mor.* 5d εὐγένεια καλὸν μέν, ἀλλὰ προγόνων ἀγαθόν, Apul. *de Deo Socratis* 23.175 *igitur omnia similiter aliena numeres licebit. "Generosus est": parentes laudas.* The Greek proverb τίς πατέρ' αἰνήσει εἰ μὴ κακοδαίμονα τέκνα (*Corp. Paroem. Gr.* 1 p. 314) was directed against people who relied on their ancestors' merits rather than their own.

genus iactat. For the phrase cf. Hor. *Carm.* 1.14.13 *iactas et genus et nomen inutile*, Ov. *Her.* 16.51 *genus et proavos et regia nomina iactas*.

341–45. Having expressed his pride at winning power with his own hands, Lycus acknowledges that there are inherent difficulties in a position so won. The points he makes are reminiscent of views frequently expressed in Sen.'s work about the nature of supreme power, e.g. those who rule by fear must live in fear, *Oed.* 705f.; hated rule, or rule based on force, is unstable, *Tro.* 258, *Phoen.* 660, *Clem.* 1.11.4, 1.25.3ff. Lycus is unusual in appreciating these points and seeking a solution; tyrants are more typically portrayed as riding roughshod over their people's hate (cf. *Phoen.* 654ff., *Thy.* 205ff., *Oed.* 703f.), as indeed Lycus is prepared to do if his solution fails (352f.).

Shakespeare echoes the wording, though not the sense, of 341f. *rapta sed trepida manu / sceptra obtinentur* in *King John* 3.3(4).135f.

A sceptre snatch'd with an unruly hand
Must be as boisterously maintain'd as gain'd.⁶²

342 sceptra obtinentur. A variation on the more usual *sceptra tenere* (e.g. V. *Aen.* 1.57, Ov. *Met.* 3.265), perhaps by analogy with *obtinere regnum, imperium, dominationem* et sim.

345 haud stabile regnum est. Seneca could have written *instabile regnum est* as at *Thy.* 217, but avoids it for euphonic reasons after *in loco*. Also he likes to use *haud*, which is associated particularly with the diction of high poetry (Axelson 91f.).

347f. ducet . . . colorem. *Colorem ducere* is used once each by Vergil and Ovid, of grapes taking on color. Seneca has four uses of it, the others being *QNat.* 1.5.6, *Ep.* 71.31, 108.5 (the last metaphorical). Cf. also Curt. 10.3.14 (again metaphorical).

348 novitas. The only use of the word in Sen. Trag., and its first use in poetry, so far as I know, in the technical sense of "lack of ancestry" (cf. above on 337ff.). The noun in all senses is rare in poetry, except in Lucretius and Ovid.

349 toros. Virtually = "marriage" (cf. *thalamus*), though not entirely without sexual connotations; the usage appears to be Ovidian, e.g. *Met.* 7.91, *Fasti* 3.484, *Pont.* 3.3.50.

351. Euripides' Lycus has decided from the outset and unconditionally to destroy H.'s family, his motive being to prevent H.'s sons growing up as avengers (38ff.). Seneca does not specify a motive, and for him perhaps the decision primarily reveals the ruthlessness of the tyrant. For similar phrases for the collapse or destruction of a *domus* see Tarrant on *Ag.* 912.

---

62. Cf. Baldwin II 556f. Pierrot cites an erroneous interpretation of the Senecan lines: "Qui genus iactat suum, aliena laudat; at qui sceptrum rapuit, ei laborandum et vigilandum est, ut vi partum vi retineat"; *trepida manu* is taken to mean *periculose*, and *sed* is regarded as adversative to 340f. *qui genus . . . laudat* rather than to the whole of 337–341ᵃ. If it could be shown that Shakespeare knew this misinterpretation, we would have the explanation of the couplet cited above, and a clue as to the source of Shakespeare's knowledge of Sen. Unfortunately Pierrot does not attribute it, and I have not been able to trace it. Could it in fact be a product of the Shakespearean lines rather than their source?

Commentary: Act II

352f. The question and answer are reminiscent of the many stichomythic debates in Sen. Trag., particularly between passion-figures and those who seek to restrain them. These often contain a similar sententious reply, taking up a word used by the interlocutor (cf. *invidia-invidiam*), e.g. *Oed.* 685f. Creo *parumne me tam longa defendit fides? /* Oedipus *aditum nocendi perfido praestat fides.* See comm. 422ff. For an objection by an interlocutor with similar content cf. *Thy.* 204f. Satelles *fama te populi nihil / adversa terret?*

premet. Probably "attack, harass" rather than "restrain, prevent" (Miller, *OLD* s.v. 20). The first is rhetorically more satisfactory: Lycus brings up a conceivable objection, simply in order to dismiss it. For the usage cf. Cic. *de Orat.* 1.228 *cum et invidia et odio populi tum Galba premeretur*, *Cat.* 2.4 *invidia oppressus*, Quint. *Inst.* 6.1.4 *invidia premere maluerit*.

353. The *sententia* is characteristic of a tyrant, cf. *Phoen.* 654 (Eteocles) *regnare non vult, esse qui invisus timet*, *Oed.* 703f. (Oedipus) *odia qui nimium timet / regnare nescit*.

After *ars prima regni est* E has the unmetrical *posse invidiam pati*, and A the meaningless *posse ad invidiam pati*. The best conjectures are *posse in invidia pati* (Richter in the 1867 Teubner) and *posse et invidiam pati* (Grotius, apud Gronovium). I prefer the first. The phrase *in invidia esse* is common enough, e.g. Sall. *Jug.* 25.5, Livy 29.33.17, Ov. *Met.* 6.403; and the use of *pati*, in the sense "to endure living," with a prepositional phrase is supported by the similar line *Thy.* 470 *immane regnum est posse sine regno pati*, and by *QNat.* 3 *praef.* 6 (Hannibal) *sine patria pati poterat, sine hoste non poterat* (cf. also V. *Ecl.* 10.52f. *certum est in silvis inter spelaea ferarum / posse pati*, Luc. 5.313, 9.262, ps.-Sen. *HO* 1523).[63]

354. Lycus catches sight of the characters who are already onstage. Conventionally there would be some expression of surprise at this point, but Lycus—who is not without a certain self-possession, cf. 410–12—takes the situation in his stride.

---

63. Peiper's *posse cum invidia pati* (in the 1902 Teubner) is less attractive because *cum invidia* is normally used when an action causes, or is accompanied by, *invidia*: cf. Cic. *Har. Resp.* 17 *vir in rebus magnis cum invidia versatus*, Quinct. 85, *Sest.* 49, Livy 42.22.4 *ingenti cum invidia in senatum venit*. Of conjectures which discard *posse*, the best is *noscere invidiam pati* (Kiessling, *teste* Garrod 214), though I know of no parallel for *noscere* (as opposed to *nosse*) with infinitive. The line with *noscere* may be compared with *Tro.* 256f. *noscere hoc primum decet, / quid facere victor debeat, victus pati.* It seems wiser to retain *posse*, because of Seneca's liking for *pati posse* (some twenty-seven times in his work), and because *posse* suits Lycus' self-confidence better than does *noscere*.

Commentary: Act II

igitur. It is indicative of the paratactic style of the tragedies that they contain only 7 uses of words for "therefore" (4 of *ergo*, 3 of *igitur*); contrast Seneca's prose works, with 745 uses of *ergo*, 10 of *igitur*, 579 of *itaque*. (*Itaque* is avoided by poets: *TLL* 5.2.760f.)

fors dedit nobis locum. For the formula in a similar situation cf. *Pha.* 425f., where Phaedra's nurse catches sight of Hippolytus approaching: *dedit / tempus locumque casus.*

355f. tristi . . . velata. Megara is in mourning garb, cf. 202 *crine soluto*, 626f. *lugubribus amicta*. To cover the head is a standard gesture of grief or extreme distress, e.g. Soph. *Ajax* 245, Eur. *IA* 1550, Plato *Phaedo* 117c, Livy 4.12.11. Mourning veils are feminine attire, cf. Hom. *Il.* 24.93f., *Hymn. Hom.* 2.42, 182; at Rome the *ricinium* was worn at funerals by women, cf. Cic. *Leg.* 2.23, Varro ap. Non. Marc. 14 p. 542 M.

356 iuxta praesides . . . deos. The phrase indicates that Sen. envisages statues onstage, probably associated with the stage altar (comm. on 202–4 ad fin.). Such statues are frequently found in Greek drama as the object of appeals and prayers: relevant passages are collected by P. D. Arnott, *Greek Scenic Conventions* (Oxford 1962) 65ff. Eur. *Hipp.*, for example, requires statues of Artemis and Aphrodite; similarly in Sen. *Pha.* we must imagine a statue of Diana, to which prayers are offered by Hippolytus and later by the nurse (54ff., 406ff.). The statues envisaged here must certainly include one of Jupiter. Probably *praesides* indicates that Megara looks to these gods for protection, and it may derive from Eur. *Her.* 48 where Megara and her family are suppliants at the βωμὸν . . . σωτῆρος Διός; if *praesides deos* meant "the gods who protect the land," one would expect an explanatory genitive as at *Pha.* 109 *praesidem terrae deam.*

357 laterique adhaeret. Lycus speaks with contempt of Amphitryon as clinging to a woman's skirts; similarly at Val. Max. 3.5.3 Clodius Pulcher is described as *adhaerens Fulvianae stolae*, cf. Mart. 5.61.1f. *crispulus iste quis est, uxori semper adhaeret / qui, Mariane, tuae?* Seneca uses *lateri adhaerere* only here; before him Livy likes it, using it three times; Ovid has it once in this sense.

verus Alcidae sator. That is, Amphitryon as opposed to Jupiter; Lycus, as at Eur. 148f., refuses to believe in H.'s divine paternity (cf. 438ff.).

All known uses of *sator* before the present passage are of Jupiter as *hominum sator atque deorum* (V. *Aen.* 1.254, 11.725, cf. Pacuv. *trag.* 295

Commentary: Act II

R², Cic. *Tusc.* 2.9.21, Phaedr. 3.17.10). The transference of the word here to Amphitryon almost requires ironic quotation marks.

358 nostri generis exitium ac lues. Compare *Tro.* 892f. *pestis exitium lues / utriusque populi* (of Helen). There are other parallels for *exitium* of a single individual, though it is not as common in this sense as *pestis*: *inc. inc. trag.* 16 R² *eum esse exitium Troiae, pestem Pergamo* (of Paris), Hor. *Carm.* 1.15.21f., ps.-V. *Ciris* 292, Ov. *Met.* 13.500. But there is only one precedent for *lues* so used, at Cic. *Har. Resp.* 12.24, and even that may refer to Clodius' action rather than his person. *Lues* in all senses is uncommon before Sen., who has more uses of it (thirteen, of which twelve are in trag.) than all previous writers together.

359–71. This short speech of persuasion falls into three clearly demarcated parts: opening address (359–61), argument (362–69ᵃ), concluding appeal (369ᵇ–71). The opening lines contain a *captatio benevolentiae* both in their reference to Megara's illustrious descent and in their unctuously polite request for attention.

359f. The address with *o* and vocative participle is very formal, suiting Lycus' ultra-politeness, cf. Cat. 36.11 *nunc o caeruleo creata ponto*, Hor. *Carm.* 2.7.1f. *o saepe mecum tempus in ultimum / deducte*, with N-H ad loc.; and the reference to Megara's illustrious descent is deferential, cf. *Pha.* 129 (Nurse to Phaedra), *Ag.* 125 (Nurse to Clytemnestra), *Phoen.* 129 (probably Messenger to Oedipus, v. Zwierlein 1978 145ff.).

Nomen may be meant literally: as one of Creon's sons was called Megareus (Aesch. *Sept.* 474, Soph. *Ant.* 1303), Sen. may think of it as a family name. Alternatively *nomen* may mean "distinguished position," as at Livy 22.22.13 *parentibus quorum maximum nomen in civitatibus est suis*, Cic. *Clu.* 154 *domi splendor, apud exteras nationes nomen et gratia*.

360f. The phrase *aure . . . patienti* echoes Hor. *Epist.* 1.1.40 *patientem commodet aurem*. For *aure excipere* cf. Sen. *Tro.* 617 *missasque voces aure sollicita excipit*. *Facilis* is frequently used in such phrases of paying attention, e.g. Hor. *Sat.* 1.1.22f., Prop. 2.21.15 *a! nimium faciles aurem praebere puellae*, Publ. Syr. N 36 *non semper aurem facilem habet Felicitas*, Sen. *Pha.* 414.

362–67. For a similar argument that the unrelenting pursuit of hatred would lead to total devastation, cf. Sen. Rhet. *Contr.* 1.1.6 *redite in gratiam: . . . perierat totus orbis, nisi iram finiret misericordia*.

362 alterna . . . odia. "Mutual hatred, hatred answering hatred," cf. Manil. 2.63 *alterno consensu*, Stat. *Theb.* 4.400 *alterna . . . moriuntur in ira*,

Commentary: Act II

9.671 *alternos . . . furores. Alterna* here is the conjecture of Zwierlein (1976 202) for codd. *aeterna*. Admittedly such pleonasm as *aeterna semper* is not unthinkable in Sen.'s style, cf. 742f. *longa permensus diu / felicis aevi spatia*, and comm. on 536; nevertheless the present example seems particularly awkward, and the correction simple and convincing (for confusion of *alternus* and *aeternus* cf. *TLL* 1.1754.40f. and ps.-Sen. *HO* 1637). Zwierlein points out that *alternus* is often used in contexts of strife and conflict, particularly by Sen., cf. *Phoen.* 435f. *iamque in alternam necem / illinc et hinc miscere cupientes manus*, *Ag.* 44 *sanguine alterno* (again at *Ep.* 95.31), 77 *scelus alternum*, *Thy.* 25f. *alterna vice / stringatur ensis*, 133ff., 340.[64]

gerant. So E. There are two objections to A's reading: the error over mood (*agent* for *agant*), which may have been made by an interpolator; and the fact that it renders the clause ambiguous, as *odia* might be either the object (cf. 27f. *vivaces aget / violentus iras animus*) or the subject (cf. *Phoen.* 299 *illos ira praecipites agit*, *Pha.* 541f. *quaeque succensas agit / libido mentes*). I suspect that the reading is an interpolation intended to enliven the line by making *odia* the subject. For *odia gerere* cf. *Thy.* 328f., *TLL* 9.2.465.2ff.

365-67. This picture of the desolation which would be caused if an attitude were persisted in may be compared with *Pha.* 471ff. (without sexual union) *orbis iacebit squalido turpis situ, / vacuum sine ullis piscibus stabit mare, / alesque caelo derit et silvis fera, / solis et aer pervius ventis erit.* In both cases the argument is intentionally specious, but the picture presented is a powerful one, the last line of the *Pha.* passage being one of the finest in Sen. Pictures of cataclysmic destruction caused by human passions are characteristic of his imagination, e.g. 1293f., *Med.* 414, 424f. *invadam deos / et cuncta quatiam*, *Thy.* 828ff.

relinquent, squalebit, obruet. The future indicatives, following present subjunctives in the protasis, perhaps state the consequence more vividly. For other examples cf. Hor. *Carm.* 3.3.7f. *si fractus illabatur orbis, / impavidum ferient ruinae*, V. *Aen.* 12.203ff., Ov. *Tr.* 2.333, Sen. *Ep.* 94.17 *si quis furioso praecepta det, erit ipso quem monebit insanior*. Blase

---

64. In defense of *aeterna* one might cite 28f. *saevus dolor / aeterna bella pace sublata geret*, but there, as in the Vergilian source, the word is particularly appropriate to the divinity. There is a superficial similarity between the contrast *aeterna/mortales* in the paradosis and the argument at *Ira* 3.42.2 that the brevity of human life forbids human feuds: *nec ulla res magis proderit quam cogitatio mortalitatis. sibi quisque atque alteri dicat: "quid iuvat tamquam in aeternum genitos iras indicere et brevissimam aetatem dissipare?"* In fact, however, it is clear that this philosophical argument is not one which Lycus is using.

Commentary: Act II

(*ALL* 9.25) shows that the construction is not rare: in the elegiac poets there are fifty examples of the *si sit, erit* construction as against seventy-three of *si sit, sit*; in Seneca's prose, twenty of the first as against nine of the second (cf. also Handford, *The Latin Subjunctive* [London 1947] 133).

365f. tum vastis ager squalebit arvis. *Vastis* = "waste, desolate," as e.g. at Cic. *Agr.* 2.26.70, Livy 28.11.10 *agrum vastum et desertum habere.* For the wording cf. 702 *sterilis profundi vastitas squalet soli* (of the underworld). *Squalere* of fields is probably influenced by V. *Georg.* 1.507 *squalent abductis arva colonis,* cf. Manil. 1.877 *squalidaque elusi deplorant arva coloni.*

367. The "silver" pattern *abCBA* is finely used as the climax and conclusion of the picture, cf. 216–48 comm. ad fin. For *altus cinis* cf. V. *Aen.* 11.211, Ov. *Fasti* 1.526 *hic toto est altior orbe cinis* (sc. *Troiae*), Sen. *Med.* 147. The line is curiously prophetic of the eruption of Vesuvius, cf. Pliny *Ep.* 6.20.18 *occursabant trepidantibus adhuc oculis mutata omnia altoque cinere tamquam nive obducta.*

368f. There is a somewhat similar sententia at Tac. *Hist.* 3.70 *pacem et concordiam victis utilia, victoribus tantum pulchra esse.* For the play on *victori-victo* v. 278 comm.

369ff. Lycus introduces his proposal in the most delicate manner: *particeps regno veni* need offer no more than a share of royal authority, and *sociemur animis* only hints at marriage (v. comm. 370). Thus Megara at this point responds only to the idea that she might touch his hand in reconciliation. At 414ff., after Lycus has proposed marriage in unmistakable terms, Megara reacts to it as a newly introduced idea.

particeps regno veni. *Particeps* normally governs a genitive. Post-Augustan writers like to vary such constructions, cf. Suet. *Cal.* 56 *in quadam coniuratione quasi participes nominati,* Tac. *Ann.* 15.50 *Natalis particeps ad omne secretum Pisoni erat,* and comm. on 107 above.[65] Here the choice of the dative is influenced somewhat by *venire*: for verbs of motion constructed with a dative cf. Enn. *Ann.* 391 Skutsch *undique conveniunt . . . tela tribuno,* V. *Aen.* 5.451 *it clamor caelo,* Löfstedt *Syntactica* I² 180ff.

[65]. Curt. 6.6.36 *sceleris in regem suum particeps Besso* and 6.7.6 *seque eius consilii fortibus viris et illustribus esse participem* are not parallels to the present passage, because in them the dative indicates not the thing shared but the person with whom it is shared.

Commentary: Act II

370 sociemur animis. By no means an obvious phrase for marriage. When *sociare* is used of marriage, which is not often, the meaning is usually conveyed by a more specific word; so V. *Aen.* 4.16 *vinclo . . . sociare iugali*, Ov. *Ibis* 15 *sociatam foedere lecti*, *Met.* 10.635 *sociare cubilia*, the latter the model for *sociemus toros* below at 413 (cf. also the Ovidian *socia tori* = *uxor*, e.g. *Pont.* 2.8.29). A's *sociemus animos* is clearly a simplification of the more elegant phrase preserved by E.

370f. pignus . . . dextram. Faith, friendship, etc. are regularly pledged by joining hands, cf. Livy 25.16.13 *contingere dextram et ita pignus fidei secum ferre*, V. *Aen.* 3.610f. *ipse pater dextram Anchises . . . / dat iuveni, atque animum praesenti pignore firmat*.

371 truci vultu. See 329–31 comm. for such indications of feelings.

373. The strong sense-pause at the end of the fifth foot is unusual in Sen. Trag.; 644 is the only other line in *HF* where more than a comma is required in this position.

373–78. A list of *adynata* is often used in classical, and particularly Latin, poetry to illustrate the impossibility of some event; cf. E. Dutoit, *La thème de l'adynaton dans la poésie antique* (Paris 1936), Canter 60ff. This figure, with its picture of the natural order reversed, is particularly congenial to Sen.'s imagination and style, though not overused by him, cf. *Med.* 401ff., *Pha.* 568ff., *Oed.* 504ff., *Thy.* 476ff., *Phoen.* 85ff.

373f. The impossibility of the sun's course being altered is a favorite topic in *adynata*, cf. Dutoit 167f. For this particular point, that the sun will never rise in the west and set in the east, cf. Soph. *Phil.* 1330f. ἕως ἂν αὐτὸς ἥλιος / ταύτῃ μὲν αἴρῃ, τῇδε δ' αὖ δύνῃ πάλιν, Sen. *Pha.* 570f. *ante ab extremo sinu / Hesperia Tethys lucidum attollet diem*, ps.-Sen. *HO* 335f., Sil. 7.477. The use of *ortus* and *occasus*, as they mean primarily "rising" and "setting," underlines the impossibility.

375. Fire and water are traditional opposites, and to substitute snow for water intensifies the opposition. For the proverbial irreconcilability of fire and water cf. Dio Cass. 55.13 θᾶσσον . . . πῦρ ὕδατι μιχθήσεσθαι, Otto s.v. *aqua* (1); in *adynata* cf. Ov. *Ibis* 31 *desinet esse prius contrarius ignibus umor*, Tr. 1.8.4, Sen. *Pha.* 568 *ignibus iunges aquas* e.q.s., *Thy.* 480.

376. For the phrasing cf. V. *Aen.* 3.417f. *venit medio vi pontus et undis / Hesperium Siculo latus abscidit*. One cannot be certain whether *Scylla* re-

Commentary: Act II

fers to the rock on the Straits of Messina, or to the mythological monster of the same name, but in the context the former seems more likely.

377f. The shifting currents of the narrow strait between Chalcis and the mainland of Greece are frequently mentioned in classical literature from Aeschylus on (*Ag.* 189f.), and indeed the Euripus becomes proverbial for changeability; passages are collected by Pease on Cic. *Nat.D.* 3.24, to which add Claud. 3.91 *Euripi refluis incertius undis*. In Sen. cf. *Tro.* 837f. *an premens litus maris inquieti / semper Euripo properante Chalcis*. For a similar *adynaton* cf. *Thy.* 477f. *Siculi rapax / consistet aestus unda*.

vicibus alternis fugax. "Alternately ebbing" (sc. and flowing), cf. V. *Aen.* 11.627f. *[pontus] nunc rapidus retro . . . fugit* (opp. *nunc ruit ad terram* 625), Sen. *Tro.* 384 *[Oceanus] quidquid bis veniens et fugiens lavat*. *Fugax* also indicates that the ebb is fast, cf. *TLL* 6.1.1474.61ff.; the currents are so strong as to make the passage of the straits difficult (cf. Mela 2.108), and sometimes reach a speed of over 6 knots.

378 piger. Similarly used of turbulent water magically calmed *Med.* 763f. *et Hister, in tot ora divisus, truces / compressit undas, omnibus ripis piger*; of a calm sea, *Ag.* 161, Luc. 5.435.

380 patriam. The list concludes with a hyperbole: Lycus has deprived her, not literally of her country, but of all that she valued in it. Cf. 1259f. *cuncta iam amisi bona: / mentem arma famam coniugem natos manus*, where Hercules has not literally lost his hands, but their meaning and worth.[66] The unusual sense-pause at the end of the first foot points up the hyperbole; for a pause here used to rhetorical effect cf. *Med.* 19f. *mihi peius aliquid, quod precer sponso, malum est* (Hoffa: *malum* codd.): */ vivat*.

380–83. An extreme example of the reification of emotions characteristic of Sen. Trag. Megara speaks of her hatred as something existing independently of her (she must "share" it with the people), and as objectively as her father, home, etc. Cf. *Med.* 238f. *virgini placeat pudor / paterque placeat*, 488 *tibi patria cessit, tibi pater, frater, pudor*; see also comm. on 75 and Liebermann 120 (with n. 142), 129f.

---

66. The conjecture *larem / patrium*, adopted by Leo and some later editors, gives a flat and unsatisfactory ending to the list; if conjecture be thought necessary, Peiper's *patria abstulisti regna germanos larem / patrem* is somewhat better.

una res superest mihi. For a similar rhetorical point based on "survival amid total loss" cf. *Med.* 164ff. Nutrix *abiere Colchi, coniugis nulla est fides / nihilque superest opibus e tantis tibi. /* Medea *Medea superest.*

381. Echoing the list in 379. Such mannered repetitions have an Ovidian ring: for repetition in a comparison cf. *Met.* 2.722f. *quanto splendidior quam cetera sidera fulget / Lucifer, et quanto quam Lucifer aurea Phoebe*; for a series of nouns repeated, *Met.* 1.15ff. *utque erat et tellus illic et pontus et aer, / sic erat instabilis tellus, innabilis unda, / lucis egens aer.*

carior. Seneca is well aware that passions such as grief and anger may become obsessive and a source of perverse pleasure. On grief cf. *Cons. Marc.* 1.7 *fit infelicis animi prava voluptas dolor, Cons. Pol.* 4.1, *Ep.* 99.25ff. For hatred the best illustration is Atreus, who delights in planning and executing his revenge, *Thy.* 279, 716, 889, 903–6, 911f., cf. *Med.* 991f., 1016f.

382f. A somewhat comparable selfishness about hatred is seen in Atreus' insistence on inflicting his revenge with his own hand, *Thy.* 691ff.: cf. *Ira* 3.3.3 *nec mandat ultionem suam* (sc. *iratus*), *sed ipse eius exactor animo simul ac manu saevit.* For the notion that the intensity of an emotion is diminished if it is shared with others cf. *Cons. Pol.* 12.2 [*dolor*] *quia dispensatur inter plures, exigua debet apud te parte subsidere, Tro.* 1011f.

383 pars quota ex isto.[67] That is, "How small a part of it." This is the regular sense of *pars quota* in Sen.'s work, both prose and verse, and its usual meaning in Ovid (the only exception among ten uses of the phrase being *Met.* 7.522, where it means "how large a part," *pace* Bömer ad loc.). *Pars* followed by *ex* rather than a genitive is unusual, but cf. Cic. *Caec. Div.* 57 *ex illa pecunia magnam partem ad se verrit,* Tib. 2.6.54 *moverit e votis pars quotacumque deos,* Ov. *Pont.* 3.6.30 *ex illis mergi pars quota digna fuit?*; for *ex* used partitively cf. *TLL* 5.2.1116.10ff., H-S 265.

385. Note the imitative word order, with *deus* coming literally *a tergo*; similarly Tib. 1.8.72 *nescius ultorem post caput esse deum.* An *ultor deus* who punishes pride is referred to also at Ov. *Met.* 14.750, *Laus Pis.* 251. It would be overprecise to refer these phrases to the Erinys or Neme-

---

67. Editors have traditionally reported the original reading of E as *ex illo* (an error originating with Gronovius), and followed Bothe and Baden in accepting that reading into the text. But inspection of the MS leaves no doubt that E^{ac} has *exicio*; hence M *exitio*. I take it that the error in E^{ac} arose originally through misreading T as I in majuscule script. For other majuscule errors in E cf. Tarrant 58.

sis: indeed at Ov. *Met.* 14.693 the *ultores dei* are mentioned separately from Nemesis. Rather *deus* is used vaguely as in Greek ὁ θεός. For the phrase in other contexts cf. Prop. 3.20.22 *non habet ultores nox vigilanda deos*, Tac. *Hist.* 4.57.2 with Heubner ad loc. EA here have *victor* for *ultor*: confusion of *ult-/vict-* is frequent in manuscripts, cf. 895, 1103, *Ag.* 220, ps.-Sen. *Oct.* 263.

386–96. For the thought that a ruler of Thebes cannot hope to escape disaster in view of so many precedents, cf. *Phoen.* 648ff. *sceptra Thebano fuit / impune nulli gerere* e.q.s., Stat. *Theb.* 11.701ff. (Oedipus to Creon) *habeas Thebana regasque / moenia, quo Cadmus, quo Laius omine rexit / quoque ego; sic thalamos, sic pignora fida capessas.* For the disastrous traditions of Thebes cf. more generally *Oed.* 626f., 711ff., *Phoen.* 276ff.

The use of *exempla* is a standard technique of argument, cf. *Ag.* 208–18, K. Alewell, *Über das rhetorische* ΠΑΡΑΔΕΙΓΜΑ (Leipzig 1913), Bonner 62, N-H on Hor. *Carm.* 1.12.37. More generally one may see "precedent" as the basis of many arguments and rhetorical points in Sen. Frequently it is the basis also for action, as at 500 where Megara sees herself as potentially completing the Danaids' murders of their husbands. Naturally it can provide a specious excuse for evil action, as at *Tro.* 249 (Pyrrhus) *solita iam et facta expeto.* (*Solere* appears often in points based on precedent, cf. *solita fata* here and at 497, also 1101f. with comm., 1344.) The precedent may be one's own actions (*Med.* 52f. *paria narrentur tua / repudia thalamis*) or those of others (*Thy.* 242f. *Tantalum et Pelopem aspice: / ad haec manus exempla poscuntur meae.*).

386–89. The allusiveness of these references is not untypical of Seneca, but particularly appropriate to the *praeteritio*; contrast the fuller detail of 390–94.

386f. matres ... passas et ausas scelera. Both participles apply to Jocasta, in view of her incest and suicide, and Ino, who, before Athamas attacked her and her sons, had plotted against the life of Phrixus. *Ausas* could also suggest Niobe in view of her hubris (but not *passas*, as her punishment could hardly be called *scelus*) and Agave.

387 geminum nefas. A suggestive phrase: primarily it refers to Oedipus' double crime of parricide and incest, but also perhaps alludes to the "doubling" of relationships created by Oedipus' incest, cf. Soph. *Ant.* 53 μήτηρ καὶ γυνή, διπλοῦν ἔπος, *OT* 1249f., 1257 διπλῆν ἄρουραν οὗ τε καὶ τέκνων and note also Ov. *Met.* 6.537f. (Philomela to Tereus) *paelex ego facta sororis, / tu geminus coniunx.*

Commentary: Act II

389 bina. Distributives rather than cardinals are regularly used with nouns which are *pluralia tantum*, cf. H-S 212.

totidem rogos. The phrase may mean no more than "their two deaths," but it probably contains an allusion to the tradition that when Eteocles and Polynices were placed on the pyre, the flames divided in token of their discord during life; cf. *Anth. Pal.* 7.399, Luc. 1.552, Stat. *Theb.* 12.429ff. (The story is also told of the fire or smoke of sacrifice to the brothers, Ov. *Tr.* 5.5.33ff., *Ibis* 35f., ps.-V. *Aetna* 576, Hyg. *Fab.* 68, Paus. 9.18.3).

390f. Niobe belonged to the royal house of Thebes through her marriage with Amphion. For the traditions concerning her bereavement see Bömer on Ov. *Met.* 6.146ff., and in greater detail Lesky in *RE* 17.644ff.; her transformation to stone on Sipylus is mentioned as early as Hom. *Il.* 24.614–17 (v. Lesky 645). Seneca's treatment of the subject here is similar in several respects to that at *Ag.* 392ff. (address to Diana) *tu Tantalidos funera matris / victrix numeras: / stat nunc Sipyli vertice summo / flebile saxum / et adhuc lacrimas marmora fundunt / antiqua novas*: in particular compare *maestus lapis* with *flebile saxum*. Both passages are influenced by Ov. *Met.* 6.311f. *ibi fixa cacumine montis / liquitur et lacrimas etiam nunc marmora manant* and *Her.* 20.105f. *quaeque superba parens saxo per corpus oborto / nunc quoque Mygdonia flebilis adstat humo*.

riget ... luctu. Suggested by a phrase earlier in the *Met.* 6 account, *orba resedit / exanimis inter natos natasque virumque / deriguitque malis* (301f.). This version that Niobe turned to stone from grief (cf. *Pont.* 1.2.30, Hyg. *Fab.* 9) differs from that at Apollod. 3.5.6, according to which Zeus turned her into stone out of pity, in answer to her prayer.

superba Tantalis ... parens. *Superba parens* comes from Ov. *Her.* 20.105 cited above; Seneca calls her *superba Tantalis* again at *Med.* 954, *Oed.* 613f.

391. Tears continue to flow from the rock into which Niobe was transformed—a regular detail of the myth: in addition to the Ovidian passages cited above, cf. Soph. *Ant.* 829f., *El.* 149, Callim. *Ap.* 22ff., Prop. 2.20.7f., 3.10.8.

Phrygio ... Sipylo. The mountain is actually in Lydia, but Ovid associates the Niobe story with Phrygia (*Met.* 6.146, 166, 177, *Her.* 20.106, cf. Callim. *Ap.* 23); Strabo 12.8.2 remarks, with reference to Sipylus

[227]

Commentary: Act II

and Tantalus' family, that the boundaries of Phrygia are somewhat fluid.

manat. From Ov. *Met.* 6.312 *lacrimas . . . marmora manant* (see comm. 390f.). The verb is used intransitively of things flowing with tears, etc., but normally with an accompanying ablative, e.g. Cat. 101.9 *fraterno multum manantia fletu*; this is the first instance cited by *TLL* of the verb used absolutely in this sense.

392–94. The climax and conclusion of the list, involving the very founder of the dynasty. For *quin ipse* so used cf. V. *Georg.* 4.481f. *quin ipsae stupuere domus atque intima Leti / Tartara*. On Cadmus' metamorphosis see particularly Eur. *Bacch.* 1330ff., Apollod. 3.5.4 (with Frazer ad loc.), Ov. *Met.* 4.563ff. Seneca's wording in 393f. is influenced by lines 567f. of Ovid's version, *longisque erroribus actus / contigit Illyricos profuga cum coniuge fines*; *fuga*, then, means only that Cadmus was *profugus* from Thebes. Both Ovid and Apollodorus locate the metamorphosis itself in Illyria; Sen.'s *regna* could allude to the detail found in Apollodorus, that Cadmus ruled there. For *crista* cf. Ovid's *cristati . . . draconis* (599) of the transformed Cadmus; supernatural snakes are regularly crested, v. 216 comm.

395 manent. *Manere* transitive is used particularly of an individual's destiny, cf. Cic. *Phil.* 13.45 *me aliud fatum manet*, Tib. 1.8.77 *te poena manet, TLL* 8.291.37ff.

dominare ut libet. The second half of the speech began *dominare tumidus, spiritus altos gere* (384); the present phrase echoes that line and so helps to conclude the speech neatly. For the ironic granting of permission used as a rhetorical flourish to end a speech cf. 121f. with comm.

396. For the phrasing cf. 497 *nunc solita nostro fata coniugio date* and *Phoen.* 276f. *optime regni mei / fatum ipse novi*, both alluding to the fateful traditions of the Theban royal family.

397 voces amove. Cf. *Tro.* 570 *cassa consilia amove*, *Med.* 202 *tuam causam amoves*, both at line end. The use of *amovere* with abstract nouns belongs to everyday language, cf. Plaut. *Asin.* 254 *quin tu abs te socordiam omnem reice et segnitiem amove*, *Ps.* 1282, Hor. *Sat.* 1.1.27 *amoto quaeramus seria ludo*, Livy 4.41.9 *ab se . . . enixe amovens culpam*. Seneca has a liking for such noun-verb phrases where in prose a verb alone might be used,

[228]

cf. *Phoen.* 459f. *cui . . . / verba admovebo?* (i.e. *quem adloquar?*), *Med.* 801 *voces dedi, Pha.* 587 *dimove vocis moras.*

398. "Learning," from one's own previous experience or from others', often forms the basis of a Senecan point, cf. 69f., 491, *Tro.* 242, 264, 730, *Pha.* 1200, *Ag.* 932, *Phoen.* 330f. Conversely an action may be called "practice" for some later undertaking, v. 222 with comm. These usages may be seen as part of a general exploitation of precedent in Sen. Trag., v. 386–96 comm.

399f. victrici . . . dextra. Metrically a remarkably adaptable phrase, cf. 800 *victrice . . . dextera,* 895 *victrice dextra,* Ov. *Fasti* 1.335 *dextra victrice.* See also 800 comm.

400f. The rule of force proverbially overrides that of law, cf. comm. on 253.

401f. pauca pro causa loquar nostra. Similarly, Aeneas prefaces his self-defence to Dido with a somewhat legalistic phrase, *pro re pauca loquar,* V. *Aen.* 4.337. For *pro causa dicere* et sim. cf. *TLL* 3.698.10ff.

403–5. The suggestion that weapons draw men on to use them is found already in Hom. *Od.* 16.294, 19.12 αὐτὸς γὰρ ἐφέλκεται ἄνδρα σίδηρος, cf. Sen. *Tro.* 284f. *gladiusque felix, cuius infecti semel / vecors libido est,* Tac. *Hist.* 1.80 *visa inter temulentos arma cupidinem sui movere.* Note the reference to *ira*; at *Ira* 1.7 Seneca rejects the view that anger is helpful in war, arguing that once admitted, it cannot be restrained.

The sword is personified in several writers, e.g. V. *Aen.* 10.394, 12.731f. *at perfidus ensis / frangitur in medioque ardentem deserit ictu,* Ov. *Met.* 3.534f.; 5.77, 108; 14.574, 801f. The extent of personification in this passage is remarkable (*arma* in 401 and 403, *ensis ira, bella, cruor*), and characteristic of a tendency in Sen. Trag. to speak of things (and passions, cf. 27–29 comm.) as independent agencies (cf. Liebermann 111f.).

406f. An example of πρόληψις, *occupatio* (Quint. 4.1.49f.): Lycus anticipates an objection, and responds to it. The ellipse of the verb (*pugnavit, pugnavimus* vel sim.) is appropriate, as though Lycus need not complete the thought because Megara has already formulated it in her own mind. (Ellipse of verbs is common in Cicero's letters, where it similarly implies a tacit understanding: H-S 423f.)

Commentary: Act II

sed. *At (enim)* would be a more usual introduction to an anticipated objection, but *sed* is often used in this way by Sen., v. H-S 488.

407–10. A good example of the importance of nouns in articulating style and meaning in Seneca (v. comm. on 397 *voces amove*). Thus *pereat omnis memoria* for "let us completely forget the past"; cf. *Med.* 555f. *melioris tibi / memoria nostri sedeat,* where *memoria* expresses the central concept and the verb is merely auxiliary. Similarly here with *deponere odia* for "be reconciled," cf. *Pha.* 238 *tibi ponet odium, Thy.* 921 *sollicitas ponite curas.* See Liebermann 113, and passim for incidental comments on noun-style in Sen. Trag. Smereka 1996 similarly characterizes the style of the tragedies as *dictio nominis,* which he contrasts with the *dictio verbi* of the prose works; he finds that in the tragedies the proportion of nouns to verbs is two to three times as high as in a sample of the *Epistles.*

408 pereat omnis memoria. An extremely rare metrical pattern in Sen. Trag.: a resolved fifth-foot arsis is permitted only with two final quadrisyllabic words, *memoria* and *facinorum* (v. fn. to 244, 246 comm.; *arietis Med.* 471 is probably a cretic). *Memoria* is also allowed to create unusual metrical patterns elsewhere in the line (Strzelecki 33, 55, 67, 45, 58). It is clear that Sen. allows metrical anomalies in the case of certain word groups, including useful quadrisyllables; v. 1183 *facinorum* comm.

409f. In sense the simple verb *posuit* is here interchangeable with the compound *deponere*; compare some of the phrases cited in 407–10 comm., where *ponere* = *deponere*, and Ov. *Met.* 3.1f. *iamque deus posita fallacis imagine tauri / se confessus erat.* The use of a simple verb in the sense of a compound may often be seen as a poeticism, v. H-S 298f., Bömer on Ov. *Fasti* 5.480 and *Met.* 3.52.

410f. ut inflexo genu regnantem adores. That is, that you should do obeisance, as to an eastern monarch, cf. Sen. Rhet. *Suas.* 1.2 *quae tam ferae gentes fuerunt quae non Alexandrum posito genu adoraverunt?* and Sen. *Thy.* 599f. *ille qui donat diadema fronti, / quem genu nixae tremuere gentes* e.q.s.

413 sociemus toros. See comm. on 370 *sociemur animis.*

414. Such descriptions of psychosomatic reactions occur quite frequently in Sen. Trag. (Canter 76f.), and tend to be formulaic in phrasing: for the present line cf. particularly *Oed.* 659 *et ossa et artus gelidus* *invasit tremor*, and for final *tremor HF* 61 *invasit tremor, Pha.* 1034 *os quassat tremor, Ag.* 711. Descriptions of this kind have a long literary pedigree, appearing particularly in epic, e.g. Hom. *Il.* 10.93ff., and less elaborately in Greek tragedy, e.g. Eur. *Hec.* 438, *Andr.* 1077f. In Roman epic they are notably formulaic: thus *Aen.* 2.120f. *gelidusque per ima cucurrit / ossa tremor* recurs verbatim at 12.447f. (cf. also 6.54f.); likewise the line-ending *tremor occupat artus* occurs at *Aen.* 7.446, 11.424, Ov. *Met.* 3.40 (cf. 1.548, 5.632). *Gelidus* (or *frigidus*) is common in such contexts, cf. Bömer on Ov. *Met.* 2.200 *gelida formidine*. Seneca's language is heavily influenced by this tradition. This is also one of the poetic *loci* taken up by the declaimers, cf. Bonner 60, ps.-Quint. *Decl. Mai.* 9.7 *obstipui, totumque corpus percurrit frigidus pavor*.

415 quod facinus aures pepulit? For the indignant question cf. Plaut. *Aul.* 796 *ei mihi, quod ego facinus ex te audio?*, 822 *quod ego facinus audio ex te? Facinus* is freely used by Plautus and Terence, but avoided in classical poetry until Ovid (36 uses) and Sen. Trag. (39).

416f. muros . . . circumsonaret. Suggested by V. *Aen.* 8.474 *hinc Rutulus premit et murum circumsonat armis*. *Circumsonare* occurs only there in Vergil, only here in Sen. Trag., four times in Ovid. Such heavy words are rare in Sen. Trag., the only other instances in *HF* of words of five or more syllables being at 58, 109, 246, 268, 716: contrast nineteen instances in the first 500 lines alone of the *Aeneid*.

417 intrepide. In verse the adjective *intrepidus* appears first in Ovid, and the adverb first in Sen. Trag. (here only).

418 capta nunc videor mihi. A somewhat perfunctory use of a point that appears more convincingly and appropriately at *Tro.* 988f. *nunc victa, nunc captiva, nunc cunctis mihi / obsessa videor cladibus* (Hecuba, assigned as a slave to Ulysses).

419–21. Megara anticipates the threats which despots, on the stage as off it, make against those who defy them: cf. Aesch. *Ag.* 1621ff., Soph. *OT* 1152ff., *El.* 379ff., Plaut. *Asin.* 145, Pacuv. *trag.* 158f. R[2], Sen. *Tro.* 573ff., *Pha.* 882ff., *Oed.* 518, 707, 852, 862, *Ag.* 988ff.

422ff. A characteristic feature of Senecan stichomythia is its use of link words: thus in the first five lines here *inferis-inferna, premit-premetur, cogere-cogi*. This technique is found in Greek tragedy, but Sen. makes greater use of it, in keeping with his general tendency to intellectualism and verbal dexterity, cf. Hancock 35–39, Seidensticker 25

[231]

ff., 38ff. T. S. Eliot, in his essay "Seneca in Elizabethan Translation," commenting on this passage as example of the technique, notes the "crossing of rhythms" involving the link words: *ínferis-inférna, cogére-cógi, regés-régi, vírtús-vírtutem-virtútis* (cf. *Med.* 160), *Phoébus-Phoebí*, cf. also 352f. above *invídia-invidiám*.

426–29. Antilabe occurs in all of Sen.'s plays but *Phoen.*, which has little stichomythia. He occasionally exploits it for virtuoso display (*Ag.* 792–99, *Med.* 168–73), but more normally restricts it to one or two lines at a time: often he uses it, as here, in conjunction with speeches of one and one-half lines, giving a freer and more varied dialogue than that of pure stichomythia, cf. 1186–91, 1295–1301.

426 cogi qui potest nescit mori. The Stoic teaching that death (suicide) is the ultimate guarantee of freedom from compulsion or servitude is presented frequently and passionately in Seneca's prose works, cf. *Prov.* 6. 7, *Ira* 3.15.3f., *Cons. Marc.* 20.3, *Ep.* 12.10 *qui mori didicit, servire dedidicit; supra omnem potentiam est, certe extra omnem. quid ad illum carcer et custodia et claustra? liberum ostium habet.* Among the tragedies, this idea is a constant theme of *Tro.*: for its use in defying a tyrant's threats cf. 573f. Ulixes *coacta dices sponte quod fari abnuis.* / Andromacha *tuta est, perire quae potest debet cupit* e.q.s. Of course it would be wrong to infer that Megara and Amphitryon are Stoic characters.

nescire mori. Readiness to face death is a lesson that must be learned, cf. *Tranq.* 11.4 *male vivet quisquis nesciet bene mori, Brev. Vit.* 7.3 *tota vita discendum est mori, Vit. Beat.* 19.2, *Ep.* 12.10 cited above, 26.9 *egregia res est mortem condiscere, HF* 1075f., *Ag.* 611 (*nescire mori* again).

427f. Lycus tries a different approach, working on the principle *munera (crede mihi) capiunt hominesque deosque* (Ov. *AA* 3.653). Cf. *Tro.* 589ff., where Ulysses, finding Andromache impervious to threats, tries more subtle means.

There is probably no need to see a reference to the Roman custom of *donatio ante nuptias*, whereby the man presented his fiancée with a gift some time before the marriage (see references in J. P. V. D. Balsdon, *Roman Women* [London 1962] 312 n. 20). Lycus' proposed gift seems to be a special case, as e.g. Polynices' gift to his bride of Harmonia's necklace (Stat. *Theb.* 2.265).

Alteration of the word order to *effare potius, quod novis thalamis parem* e.q.s. by Wilamowitz was accepted by Leo and Richter, but Hoffa 469 gave the correct interpretation of the paradosis: *potius* goes primarily with *parem* and means "instead of forcing you." The hyperbaton *thala-*

Commentary: Act II

mis quod novis (which would be removed by the conjecture) also speaks in favor of the transmitted word order.

429. The terseness of the death threat is characteristic of stage tyrants, cf. Eur. *Med.* 352ff., Cic. *Rab. Post.* 29 *regum autem sunt . . . illae minae: "si te secundo lumine hic offendero, moriere"* (cf. Jocelyn 349), Sen. *Ag.* 971 *morieris hodie,* 1012. See further Tarrant on *Ag.* 971. In *Ag.*, as here, the threats are defied in a way that combines stoical endurance with rhetorical point.

430. It is difficult to find adequate grounds on which to choose between A's word order *sceptroque nostro potior est famulus tibi?* and that of E, *sceptroque nostro famulus est potior tibi?* Seneca could have chosen to point the contrast between *sceptro nostro* and *famulus* either by juxtaposition (cf. e.g. 448 *mortale caelo*) or by separation (e.g. 450 *famuline fuerant antequam fuerant dei?*). I prefer A's version, in part because *famulus* is then taken up more immediately by *iste famulus* in 431.

sceptroque. There is no reason to reject this reading, though most editors have followed recc. in altering to *sceptrone*, the sole objectors being Gruter and Baden. Questions expressing skepticism, expostulation, etc. not infrequently begin with *et* or *-que* (cf. *TLL* 5.2.890.68ff.). For an example in Sen. Trag. with similar tone and in a similar context cf. *Ag.* 961 *et esse demens te parem nobis putas?* and for an instance of *-que Thy.* 320 *ipsosque per quos fallere alium cogitas / falles?* (so E: A already normalizes to *ipsosne*).

431 tradidit . . . neci. *Neci* or *leto dare* (*tradere, dedere*) are among the more common periphrases for "to kill" in Vergil, Ovid, and Sen. Trag.: see comm. on 1048f.

433, 435, 437. Sententiae, like link words, are much more common in Sen.'s dialogue than in that of Greek tragedy (instances are collected by Canter 85–99). The importance Sen. placed on such sententiae in dramatic poetry is shown by *Ep.* 8.8f. *quam multi poetae dicunt quae philosophis aut dicta sunt aut dicenda! non attingam tragicos nec togatas nostras . . . quantum dissertissimorum versuum inter mimos iacet!* e.q.s. It is characteristic of Sen.'s style that his sententiae (like those of Publilius) are linguistically self-contained, their relationship to the preceding argument implied rather than expressed: contrast e.g. Soph. *Ant.* 519 ὅμως ὅ γ' Ἅιδης τοὺς νόμους ἴσους ποθεῖ, *El.* 398 καλόν γε μέντοι μὴ 'ξ ἀβουλίας πεσεῖν, v. Seidensticker 180ff.

Commentary: Act II

433. The thought is amplified at *Prov.* 2.4 *marcet sine adversario virtus; tunc apparet quanta sit quantumque polleat, cum quid possit patientia ostendit.* Epictetus similarly makes the point that the challenge of the labors was necessary for the exercise of Hercules' virtues (1.6.32–36).

434f. Lycus implies that fighting wild beasts is not a sufficiently noble task to allow of the display of *virtus.* Cf. *Const. Sap.* 2.2, where Cato is compared with H., to the disadvantage of the latter: *Cato non cum feris manus contulit, quas consectari venatoris agrestisque est.* He may also suggest that there is no great risk involved in facing such creatures, a point made more definitely by Euripides' Lycus (151–61).

In Megara's reply, the phrase *quae cuncti pavent* presumably points to the courage required for such actions (rather than to their philanthropic effect of freeing mankind from fear); that is the meaning also at *Prov.* 4.1 *calamitates terroresque mortalium sub iugum mittere proprium magni viri est.*

obici. The passive reinforces the sneering tone of Lycus' question, suggesting that H. has no more choice about facing wild beasts than a prisoner in the circus, cf. Sall. *Jug.* 14.15 *pars bestiis obiecti sunt,* Sen. *Ira* 3.23.1 *qui leoni obiectus est, Ep.* 7.4 *mane leonibus et ursis homines . . . obiciuntur,* Suet. *Cal.* 27.4 *equitem R. obiectum feris.*

Contrast the scansion ŏ*bici* with the noun ō*bice* at 237, 999. The first syllable is regularly long in the noun, the earliest exception occurring in Silius; but in the present stem of the verb, though long in hexameters until Lucan, it is short at Plaut. *Asin.* 814 and again in Sen. at *Med.* 237, 496 (indifferent *Med.* 497). Cf. *TLL* s.vv.

436. Implying a λόγος/ἔργον contrast: Hercules' inability to escape shows the emptiness of his boasts.

437. The path of *virtus* is proverbially hard, cf. Cornelius Severus fr. 2 Baehrens *ardua virtuti longoque per aspera nisu / eluctanda via est,* Ov. *Pont.* 2.2.113 *tendit in ardua virtus,* Sen. *Prov.* 5.9–11, Otto s.v. *arduus.*

438 caelitum sperat domos. Cf. V. *Georg.* 4.325 *quid me caelum sperare iubebas?*

439ff. Amphitryon feels it appropriate that he, as H.'s human father, should argue the question of paternity: *miseranda coniunx* perhaps suggests also that he feels Megara has borne enough of Lycus' attack. Dramatically his intervention gives some variation in this lengthy debate. The division of the argument in connection with the question of H.'s father probably derives from Eur. 170ff. τὸ τοῦ Διὸς μὲν Ζεὺς ἀμυνέτω μέρει / παιδός· τὸ δ' εἰς ἔμ', Ἡράκλεις, ἐμοὶ μέλει / λόγοισι τὴν τοῦδ' ἀμαθίαν ὑπὲρ σέθεν / δεῖξαι (though there Amphitryon leaves the question of paternity to Zeus).

441–45. The series of prepositional phrases produces a fine rhetorical effect, cf. *Med.* 478ff. *per spes tuorum liberum et certum Larem, / per victa monstra, per manus pro te quibus / numquam peperci, perque praeteritos metus, / per caelum et undas, coniugi testes mei, / miserere.*

443. A variation on the more usual *occasus et ortus*, for which see comm. on 24 *ortus*. Such phrases occur several times in this play indicating the extent of H.'s travels and fame, cf. 37f. comm. ad fin.

444f. Hercules played an important part in defeating the rebellious Giants (v. 84 comm.). In Eur. too this episode is mentioned by Amphitryon shortly after his division of the argument (177ff.). For the phrasing cf. ps.-V. *Culex* 28 *Phlegra giganteo sparsa est quo sanguine tellus*. Similar wording at *HF* 1217 *cruore corpus impio sparsum; sparsus cruore* recurs as a line-opening *Med.* 709, *Ag.* 448.

448 mortale ... genus. *Mortale genus* appears in the sense of "the human race" (cf. τὸ θνητὸν γένος) only in poetry, whereas *humanum genus*, used below at 674, 1075, is found *passim per totam Latinitatem* (*TLL* 6.1892.82).

449. Clear examples are Bacchus, Castor and Pollux (v. 14 comm.), Aristaeus (son of Apollo and Cyrene), and Plutus (son of Ceres and Iasius).

451. That is, "even a fully-fledged god endured servitude." The response discards the categories set up in the previous three lines, in order to give a more striking instance. (Apollo was not the son of a mortal mother, 448f., nor was his servitude to Admetus a precondition of his divinity, 450.)

The animals Apollo tended are generally cattle (e.g. *Anth. Pal.* 9.241, Tib. 2.3.113; so Sen. at *Pha.* 296ff.), but Homer speaks of him rearing horses (*Il.* 2.766f.), and Callimachus adds goats and sheep (*Ap.* 48–54).

453. Latona's long wanderings before she gave birth on Delos are generally attributed to Juno's jealous persecution; for details of her journeys see *Hymn. Hom.* 3.30–46, *RE* Suppl. 5.569f., and for Delos as a wandering island at this time see the references given on 15 above. A parallel between the wanderings of the goddess and the island is made explicitly

Commentary: Act II

by Ovid, *Met.* 6.190 (address of Delos to Latona) "*hospita tu terris erras, ego*" *dixit "in undis."*

454. The E reading *num monstra saeva Phoebus* e.q.s. appears to be an accommodation of the adjective to the adjacent noun. For *aut* postponed by two words cf. Ov. *Pont.* 3.3.94, ps.-Sen. *Oct.* 422, Val. Fl. 8.167f. Seneca may be echoing the similar hyperbaton at Ov. *Her.* 9.34 *monstraque terribiles persequiturque feras.*

timuit. Not an imputation of cowardice; if it were, Amphitryon would certainly respond to it. Rather Lycus suggests that to undergo such dangers is unworthy of a prospective god (cf. 434), and that is the point to which Amphitryon replies. *Timuit* here as at 45 (see comm.) emphasizes the fearsome nature of the monsters, rather than H.'s feelings in facing them.

455. For the tradition that the killing of Python was Apollo's first major deed cf. Eur. *IT* 1249ff. ἔτι μιν ἔτι βρεφός, ἔτι φίλας / ἐπὶ ματέρος ἀγκάλαισι θρῴσκων / ἔκανες, ὦ Φοῖβε, Callim. *Ap.* 97ff., Ap. Rhod. 2.704ff., Ov. *Met.* 1.441ff., Luc. 5.80f., Hyg. *Fab.* 140, Serv. ad *Aen.* 3.73. According to some of these accounts, Juno had sent Python to pursue the pregnant Latona, so Apollo took revenge soon after his birth by slaying the creature.

456. A reference to the snakes that he had to strangle in his cradle. Housman argued that in this episode Hercules suffered a fright but not *gravia mala*; accordingly he conjectured *partus* (genitive) for *parvus* (*CQ* 17[1923]164 = 1972 1075), the allusion now being to "the prolonged labour of Alcmena and her son's retarded birth" (cf. Ov. *Met.* 9.281–323). But although *gravia mala* certainly does not describe H.'s experience as retold by Amphitryon in 216ff., exaggeration and misrepresentation are part and parcel of such debates, not least in Sen. Trag. Furthermore, of the two *exempla* adduced in Amphitryon's reply, only Bacchus would fit *partūs mala*, whereas *parvus* is sufficiently general to suit both the embryonic Dionysus and the infant Jupiter. Finally, it would be unskillful argument to raise this point when a counterexample, that of Apollo's difficult birth, has just been mentioned (453; according to *Hymn. Hom.* 3.71f. Latona was in labor for nine days and nights). *Parvus* in this context probably derives from Ov. *AA* 1.187f. *parvus erat, manibusque duos Tirynthius angues / pressit.*

457f. Jupiter's appearance in full panoply to Semele, and the consequent premature birth of Bacchus, *proles fulminis improbi* (*Med.* 84), are too familiar to need illustration. But the part Bacchus played in defeating the Giants, to which 458 alludes, is a less frequently mentioned element of his myth: cf. Eur. *Ion* 216ff., *Cycl.* 5ff.; Apollod. 1.6.2; Diod. Sic. 3.70.6; Hor. *Carm.* 2.19.21ff. N-H on the last passage note that the artistic tradition (for which they give references) is a fuller source than literature for Bacchus' role in the Gigantomachy.

The skillful ordering of the couplet is evident, with paronomasia *fulmine–fulminanti* and chiasmus *matris–fulmine–fulminanti–patri*. But there is also an unpatterned contrast between *ex . . . utero . . . eiectus* and *proximus . . . stetit*, which saves the couplet from excessive schematism.

457 eiectus. A *vox propria* for miscarriage, cf. Val. Max. 4.6.4 *partum . . . subita animi consternatione . . . eicere coacta est*, Pliny *NH* 11.210 [suis] *volva eiecto partu melior quam edito*, and the absolute use Ulp. *Dig.* 9.2.27.22 *si mulier pugno . . . a te percussa eiecerit*.

458 stetit. That is, in battle-readiness, as at 118, 261, 948, *Pha.* 1063.

459f. There is a somewhat similar contrast at Ov. *Am.* 3.10.21f. *illic, sideream mundi qui temperat arcem, / exiguus tenero lac bibit ore puer.*

459. Jupiter traditionally hurls thunder and lightning from the clouds, which are shaken and rent (V. *Aen.* 3.199 *ingeminant abruptis nubibus ignes*, Ov. *Met.* 15.70 *Iuppiter an venti discussa nube tonaret*; *nubem quatere* at V. *Aen.* 7.143 has a different sense, "brandish"). But *gubernat astra* is best paralleled by *Pha.* 959ff. *o magna parens Natura deum, / tuque igniferi rector Olympi, / qui sparsa cito sidera mundo / cursusque vagos rapis astrorum* e.q.s.; this is the Stoic identification, found also in Sen.'s prose, of Jupiter with Nature and Providence, the powers that guide the universe and the stars in their courses.

460. Cf. *Phoen.* 359 *latebo rupis exesae cavo*, *Tro.* 831 *montis exesi . . . antro*. Here A has *exesae*, E *Idaeae*. One cannot exclude the possibility that A interpolated *exesae* from one of the passages just cited, but it seems more likely that *Idaeae* is a clarifying interpolation, or else an intrusive gloss; in favor of *exesae* is the fact that it continues the allusive character of 457f. Classical authors frequently locate Jupiter's cave on Mt Ida, e.g. Arat. *Phaen.* 33f., Diod. Sic. 5.60, Ov. *Met.* 4.289 *Idaeis . . . sub antris* (but not so Hesiod, the earliest source, cf. West on *Theog.* 484).

461f. Metaphors drawn from finance and trade appear with unusual frequency throughout Sen.'s work, one of the most remarkable instances in the tragedies being *Oed.* 942 *solvendo non es. Constare* in the sense of "to cost" is used metaphorically four times in the tragedies (and some twenty-two times in the prose works); contrast one instance in Ovid's verse (*Her.* 7.47) and none in Vergil.

sollicita . . . pretia. Not "a price consisting of anxiety," which the Latin could scarcely mean, but "a price that causes anxiety" (for this sense of *sollicitus* cf. e.g. Hor. *Serm.* 2.6.79 *sollicitas . . . opes*, Sen. *Pha.* 518f. *sollicito . . . auro*); e.g. in Hercules' case the actual *pretium* would be persecution by Juno.

463f. These were among the most popular of sententiae from *HF* in later centuries: one or both of them appear in all the *florilegia* listed in the Introduction except Brux., *Polyanthea*, and the eccentric Gonville collection.

In the stichomythia of Greek tragedy, as of Sen. Trag., a speaker sometimes echoes not merely a word from the previous speech (422ff. comm.) but a phrase or even the whole structure of the speech; one of the most striking examples is Soph. *OT* 547–52, v. Hancock 33–35. The device is not particularly common in Sen. Trag., but cf. *Thy.* 1111f. Thyestes *his* (sc. *deis*) *puniendum vota te tradunt mea.* / Atreus *te puniendum liberis trado tuis, Tro.* 325ff., 343-344-347. One may also discern here Seneca's liking for pairs of parallel verses, which he draws from Ovid rather than from Greek tragedy, cf. 590f. *quae vinci potuit regia carmine,* / *haec vinci poterit regia viribus* with comm.

463. There is a somewhat similar thought at Acc. *trag.* 614ff. R² *quem ego ubi aspexi, virum memorabilem* / *intui viderer, ni vestitus taeter, vastitudo,* / *maestitudo praedicarent hominem esse*, though there *homo* means "an ordinary man," here "a human being."

464. Reminiscent of the Stoic position, frequently stated in Sen.'s prose works, that the Good Man is necessarily happy, e.g. *Ep.* 92.15 *potest virtus efficere, ne miser aliquis sit*, 16 *non est miser vir bonus, quamvis omnibus prematur incommodis, Vit. Beat.* 16.1–3. In his philosophical works Sen. would not describe *fortitudo* as itself guaranteeing happiness, though it is one of the qualities of the Good Man, cf. *Vit. Beat.* 3.3 *beata est ergo vita conveniens naturae suae, quae non aliter contingere potest, quam si primum sana mens est . . . deinde fortis ac vehemens, tunc pulcherrime patiens* e.q.s., *Ep.* 45.9. The philosophical doctrine is here adapted to fit the particular instance.

465–76. Accounts in Roman poetry of Hercules' *affaire* with Omphale regularly speak of the hero having worn women's clothes; this

Commentary: Act II

was a popular subject in Hellenistic-Roman painting, as evidenced by Pompeii (cf. also Lucian *Hist. Conscr.* 10, Plut. *Mor.* 785e). (According to the standard earlier version H. was literally the slave of Omphale, but Roman poetry presents the situation as a *servitium amoris*, cf. *RE* 18.389f.) The poets add that Hercules plied the maidservant's task of working wool while so dressed: Prop. 4.9.45ff. (cf. 3.11.17ff.), Ov. *Her.* 9.57–118, *AA* 2.217f., ps.-V. *Eleg. Maec.* 1.69ff., Sen. *Pha.* 317–24, ps.-Sen. *HO* 371ff. The present passage is the first to mention perfume (echoed at *HO* 376). However, all the details are familiar in allegations of Eastern effeminacy: e.g. V. *Aen.* 4.216f. (*mitra*, unguents), 9.614ff. (gaudy clothes, dancing, *mitra*, *tympanum*).

Lycus is not alone in making disparaging remarks about H.'s transvestitism, cf. notably Deianira in Ov. *Her.* 9. On the other hand Amphitryon's defence *post multa virtus opera laxari solet* is the attitude taken also in *Eleg. Maec.*, where the episode is used to justify Maecenas' luxurious tendencies. (Bacchus' effeminate traits are there used as a parallel, 57ff., as here; cf. Stat. *Ach.* 1.260ff.)

465f. At *Eleg. Maec.* 79 H. simply discards the lion-skin and club, at Ov. *Her.* 9.111ff., *Fasti* 2.325 (cf. Lucian *Hist. Conscr.* 10) Omphale dons them. That H. actually presented the skin to her is a new detail. For the metonymy *leo* for "lion-skin" v. 46 with comm.

466 donum puellae factus. For the somewhat flat *factus* of the paradosis, N. Heinsius conjectured *pactus*, which would presumably hint at *pro nocte pactus*, cf. Ov. *Am.* 1.10.47 *parcite, formosae, pretium pro nocte pacisci*, *Rem. Am.* 505 *pacta nocte*. Such a meaning would not be out of keeping with the elegiac-erotic associations of *puellae* (for which cf. comm. on 18 *puellae . . . Cnosiacae*), but I do not have sufficient confidence in the conjecture to adopt it.

467. Hercules wears a *Sidonia palla* in Prop. 4.9.47, *tunicas Gaetulo murice tinctas* at Ov. *Fasti* 2.319, a *tenuem Tyrio / stamine pallam* at Sen. *Pha.* 328f., and at Ov. *Her.* 9.101 he is *Sidonio insignitus amictu*. *Sidonius* is used here in its general sense of "Phoenician," and doubtless implies purple, cf. Sen. *Thy.* 345 *vestis Tyriae color*, Pease on V. *Aen.* 4.137.

Pictum may mean "brightly decorated," i.e. brightly dressed; or it may denote "embroidered" (cf. Pease loc. cit.), with the adjective transferred from the garment to its wearer as at V. *Aen.* 9.582 *[Arcentis filius] pictus acu chlamyden*. The word is frequently used in contexts of brightly colored dress, cf. V. *Aen.* 4.137 (Dido) *Sidoniam picto chlamyden circumdata limbo*, Ov. *Met.* 3.556 *purpuraque et pictis intextum vestibus aurum*.

469f. That is, he busied his hands with spinning, to the accompaniment of the tympanum. This interpretation of the general phrase *ma-*

Commentary: Act II

nus movere, "to occupy one's hands" (e.g. Plaut. *Pers.* 772, Varro *RR* 2 *praef.* 3, Sen. *QNat.* 6.18.9), is assured by the fact that almost all the verse passages listed on 465–76 mention H.'s hands in describing how he spun the wool. (For spinning to musical accompaniment cf. Hom. *Od.* 10.221f., Cat. 64.321, Sen. *Apocol.* 4.1.15ff.) Otherwise one might take *manus movit* to mean he danced (cf. Ov. *Rem. Am.* 334 *fac saltet, nescit si qua movere manus*, Hor. *Sat.* 1.9.24f. *quis membra movere / mollius* (sc. *possit*)?, Sen. *Tranq.* 17.4 *Scipio . . . corpus movebat ad numeros*, Stat. *Silv.* 3.5.66 *molli diducit bracchia motu*), but the other accounts do not mention dancing. The Latin could not mean that he *played* the tambourine, as Miller supposes, despite the fact that he does so at Stat. *Theb.* 10.649.

469–71. Seneca here builds on contrasts made in Ov. *Her.* 9: the glorious hands unworthily employed in spinning at 75f. *non fugis, Alcide, victricem mille laborum / rasilibus calathis imposuisse manum*, and the warlike head inappropriately wrapped in a *mitra* at 63 *ausus es hirsutos mitra redimire capillos*. The *mitra* was associated with the East, and particularly Lydia, Omphale's kingdom, cf. Pind. *Nem.* 8.15, Prop. 3.17.30 *Lydia mitra*; and it is primarily a woman's garment, cf. Ar. *Thesm.* 941f., Serv. ad *Aen.* 4.216 *quibus effeminatio crimini dabatur, etiam mitra eis adscribebatur*. (I doubt that 470f. need refer specifically to participation in Bacchic rites, though both *tympana* and *mitrae* were used in these, cf. Eur. *Bacch.* 833 with Dodds' note.)

471–75. There are strong similarities of phrasing between these lines and the ode to Bacchus in *Oed.* For 471–73 cf. *Oed.* 414ff. *[decet] te caput Tyria cohibere mitra / hederave mollem / bacifera religare frontem, / spargere effusos sine lege crines*, for 473ᵇ–474ᵃ cf. *Oed.* 440f. *thyrsumque levem / vibrante manu*, and for the *syrma* of 475 cf. *Oed.* 423 (the word occurs only in these two places in Sen. Trag.).

472–76. Bacchus' general effeminacy is traditional, particularly since the fifth century B.C., cf. Eur. *Bacch.* 453ff. with Dodds ad loc., Ov. *Met.* 3.555f., 607 *virginea puerum . . . forma*.

472f. effusos . . . sparsisse crines. Bacchus' long hair is characteristically tossed freely, cf. *Hymn. Hom.* 7.4 καλαὶ δὲ περισσείοντο ἔθειραι, Eur. *Bacch.* 150 πλόκαμον εἰς αἰθέρα ῥίπτων, 240f.; the same is true of his followers, cf. V. *Aen.* 7.394, Ov. *Met.* 3.725f. (with Bömer ad loc.), Livy 39.13.12 *matronas Baccharum habitu crinibus sparsis . . . decurrere ad Tiberim*. This is clearly the meaning of *sparsisse* here (cf. *crinibus sparsis* in Livy, also Ov. *AA* 1.541 *ecce Mimallonides sparsis in terga capillis* and Sen. *Pha.* 393), not "to sprinkle with perfume" (Kingery, Miller), which would require an ablative.

Commentary: Act II

473f. sparsisse, vibrare. Such variation in the tense of the infinitive is found in Latin first at V. *Georg.* 3.435f. *ne mihi tum mollis sub divo carpere somnos / neu dorso nemoris libeat iacuisse per herbas*, and frequently in Tibullus, e.g. 1.1.29ff., 45f., 73f. Apart from considerations of style, meter may also play a part here, because *sparsisse* gives a metrical equivalent to *vibrare* (on perfect infinitives used for metrical purposes cf. Brink on Hor. *Ars P.* 98 *tetigisse*, Austin on V. *Aen.* 6.79). It might also be argued that *sparsisse* is not exactly equivalent to *spargere* but connotes *sparsos crines habere*.

levem vibrare thyrsum. A characteristic gesture of the god, e.g. Eur. *Bacch.* 240 κτυποῦντα θύρσον, Ov. *Met.* 3.667 *pampineis agitat velatam frondibus hastam*, as again of his followers, cf. Eur. *Bacch.* 187f., Sen. *Oed.* 440f. *thyrsumque levem / vibrante manu* (of Agave). For *levem* cf. Ov. *Met.* 6.593 *umero levis incubat hasta* (of Procne dressed as a Bacchante); the thyrsus, being made of a hollow fennel-stalk (cf. Dodds on Eur. *Bacch.* 113), would be light in comparison with a regular spear (*gravis* at Hor. *Carm.* 2.19.8 refers to its supernatural force).

474 parum forti gradu. For *gradus, incessus* as reflecting moral character cf. *Ep.* 114.3 *non vides, si animus elanguit, trahi membra et pigre moveri pedes? si ille effeminatus est, in ipso incessu adparere mollitiam?*, 52.12, and comm. on 204 and 329–31 above. Elsewhere Sen. complains of the flowing walk that was fashionable in his own day, *Tranq.* 17.4 *ut nunc mos est etiam incessu ipso ultra muliebrem mollitiam fluentibus*, *QNat.* 7.31.2.

475. Bacchus wears a trailing garment adopted also by his followers, cf. Eur. *Bacch.* 833 πέπλοι ποδήρεις, Prop. 3.17.32, Sen. *Oed.* 422f. *inde tam molles placuere cultus, / et sinus laxi fluidumque syrma*; for its gold embroidery cf. Ov. *Met.* 3.556 *purpuraque et pictis intextum vestibus aurum*, Stat. *Ach.* 1.262f. In Greek, σύρμα is the technical term for the flowing costume worn by tragic actors. Seneca, the first Roman writer to use the word so far as we know, gives it a broader sense (perhaps thinking the garment appropriate to the patron of tragedy), but later Latin writers use it exclusively of the tragic robe. *Trahit* perhaps alludes to the origin of the Greek word in σύρω. For the verb used of luxurious garments v. N-H on Hor. *Carm.* 2.18.8 *trahunt . . . purpuras*.

auro . . . barbarico. Cf. V. *Aen.* 2.504 *barbarico postes auro spoliisque superbi*; in both passages *barbaricus* means simply "eastern" (see Austin on the Vergilian line), whereas Lycus' *barbara* (471) has more pejorative connotations. The E reading *barbarico* (A *barbaricum*) is guaranteed both by the Vergilian parallel and by Sen.'s liking for such interwoven patterns of noun-adjective pairs, cf. 216–48 comm. ad fin.

[241]

Commentary: Act II

476. Compare the examples of great men's relaxations given in *Tranq.* 17.4, e.g. *Cato vino laxabat animum curis publicis fatigatum*, and the discussion ibid. 4ff. of the need for occasional recreation; also *Ira* 2.20.3 *lusus quoque proderunt; modica enim voluptas laxat animos et temperat.*

477f. Lycus ironically refers to instances of Hercules' lust, suggesting that the hero carries his relaxation of *virtus* much too far. The reference in 477 to the Iole episode, like Eur.'s reference to the sack of Oechalia at *Her.* 427f. (see Bond ad loc.), has been criticized by some commentators as mythologically anachronistic, as it occurred at the end of the hero's life, his death being caused by Deianira's jealousy of Iole (e.g. Soph. *Trach.* passim, Diod. Sic. 4.38.1, Apollod. 2.7.7, Ov. *Met.* 9.136ff.). But the capture of Iole is after all a reasonably self-contained event, and one doubts whether ancient audiences, deprived of the commentators' help, would have noticed the anachronism. It would be a different matter if Lycus had referred to Deianira herself.

eversi. "Overthrown, ruined"; here the sense of the line indicates that the participle is transferred from *domus* (cf. *Ag.* 733 *evertet domum*, 912 *eversa domus est funditus*), though the verb may be used with people as its object, e.g. Cic. *Verr.* 3.47 *aratores proximus [annus] . . . funditus everterat.* Seneca does not specify what happened to Eurytus himself: some sources say that he was killed by H. along with his sons (Soph. *Trach.* 281f., Scythinus of Teos *FGrH* 13 F1, Apollod. 2.7.7, ps.-Sen. *HO* 207ff., Hyg. *Fab.* 35), others that he fled to Euboea (Pherecydes *FGrH* 3 F82a, Herodorus *FGrH* 31 F37).

478. This has been taken as a reference to the fifty daughters of Thespius, all enjoyed by Hercules (a feat sometimes called the thirteenth labor). Passing references to the episode at Ov. *Her.* 9.51, ps.-Sen. *HO* 369f. suggest that it was well known; other sources include Herodorus *FGrH* 31 F20, Ephorus *FGrH* 70 F8, Diod. Sic. 4.29, Apollod. 2.4.10, 2.7.8, Paus. 9.27.6f., Stat. *Silv.* 3.1.42f., Hyg. *Fab.* 162, cf. Roscher 5.770ff. But *oppressi* is not equivalent to *compressi*, but must mean "harried" (Miller), though obviously with reference to sexual molestation. Now the sources (except perhaps Statius) agree that H. did not take the Thespiades by violence, but at the request of their father *prolis creandae causa*. It may be that Lycus is misrepresenting H.'s behavior in this episode for rhetorical effect, but I think it more likely that the reference is to *all* girls debauched by H., many of them (including Iole) less willingly than the Thespiades: for lists of them v. Apollod. 2.7.7, *RE* Suppl. 3.1091–93. (Those who do not find either of these explanations convincing may wish to adopt Bentley's conjecture *pressi*.)

Commentary: Act II

The phrase *pecorum ritu* suggests promiscuous sexual activity even though the meaning of *oppressi* is not explicitly sexual: cf. Herod. 4.180 κτηνηδὸν μισγόμενοι, Hor. *Sat.* 1.3.109f., Livy 3.47.7 *placet pecudum ferarumque ritu promiscue in concubitus ruere*, Pease on V. *Aen.* 4.551 *more ferae*. *Grex* of people is normally a weak metaphor, but here considerably strengthened by *pecorum ritu*.

479 iubet. The tense indicates that the point is more important for its relevance to the present discussion ("You cannot call these things Juno's commands") than as a historical fact, cf. 959 *promittit* comm.

480–88. Amphitryon mentions tasks voluntarily undertaken by Hercules which have benefited the human race by quelling lawless violence. The opponents he names, except Geryon, were *saevi reges* (1255, cf. 272), so that their mention is relevant to the case of Lycus and to the wider theme of the punishment of tyrants (cf. 737ff.). Most of them showed their cruelty particularly in their treatment of strangers. Busiris used to sacrifice them at an altar of Zeus; Antaeus challenged them to wrestling matches which he invariably won, and then used their skulls as building material for a temple to Neptune. As he mentions Eryx in this company, Sen. presumably has in mind the tradition that he similarly challenged strangers to a contest, though this tradition is less well attested (cf. Lycophr. *Alex.* 866 with Tzetz. ad loc. and ad 958, Hyg. *Fab.* 31, Serv. ad *Aen.* 1.570, and comm. below on 483f.). Cycnus too was a killer of strangers by some accounts (Eur. *Her.* 391f., schol. Pind. *Ol.* 10.19b); other sources agree at least that he threatened law and order ([Hes]. *Aspis* 479f., Paus. 1.27.6, schol. Pind. *Ol.* 2.147c).

Geryon (487) might seem out of place for two reasons: first because H. encountered him as a direct result of orders from Eurystheus; and second because Geryon was not generally known for lawlessness. Nevertheless, he is represented in Hesiod as a fearful monster (*Theog.* 287ff., n.b. 295), and it is clear from Lucr. 5.28 that the *vis Geryonai* was one of the pests from which H. was said to have freed mankind. On the first point, one could argue that Eurystheus' orders said only "fetch the cattle of Geryon," so that Geryon's death was in a sense *ipsius opus*. In fact the material of Sen.'s lists is not always entirely apposite, as line 15 shows (v. 6–18 comm.).

The rhetorical effects of the speech are noteworthy: *ipsius opus est* in 481 echoing Lycus' *ipsius haec sunt opera* in order to refute it (v. 463f. comm.), and anaphora of the phrase in the same metrical position in 485 (cf. *fortem* 464—*fortem vocemus cuius* 465, 468); contrast between the short, sharp *eris inter istos* in 488 and the lengthy list that precedes it.

[243]

481 caestibus . . . suis. That is, probably, "with the weapons of his own choice." For this use of *suus* cf. such phrases as Sall. *Jug.* 61.1 *suo loco pugnam dare*, Livy 42.43.3 *suo maxime tempore et alieno hostibus incipere bellum*, 22.39.21 *neque occasioni tuae desis, neque suam occasionem hosti des*. Alternatively *suus* might be taken more literally, suggesting that Eryx kept a pair of gloves for his opponents to use; but Vergil indicates that H. wore his own lethal gloves in this contest, *Aen.* 5.410. At any rate Seneca and Vergil agree that it was a boxing match, whereas Paus. 4.36.4 calls it a wrestling bout (cf. Hyg. *Fab.* 31, Tzetz. ad Lycophr. *Alex.* 866, 958).

482 Eryx et Eryci iunctus. *Iungere* here has the sense of *addere* (sc. *occidendo*), cf. V. *Aen.* 11.673 *his addit Amastrum*, Ov. *Met.* 12.380 *additur his Dorylas*. The idea of "addition" is frequently expressed by paronomasia of the noun, cf. *Oed.* 62 *luctu in ipso luctus exoritur novus*, 131f., *Ag.* 342f. *montes montibus altis / super impositi*; cf. also the pattern *ille et cum illo alius*, TLL 4.1377.28ff.

483f. H. allowed himself to be led to the altar, but at the last minute he broke his bonds and killed the king and his attendants there; cf. Hdt. 2.45, Pherecydes *FGrH* 3 F17, Hyg. *Fab.* 31, and particularly Ov. *Ibis* 399f. *frater ut Antaei quo sanguine debuit aras / tinxit, et exemplis occidit ipse suis*. (Preller-Robert 2.2.518 describes vase paintings of the scene.)

iustum. That is, *iure fusum*, cf. *Pha.* 708f. *iustior numquam focis / datus tuis est sanguis, arquitenens dea*.

485f. The phrase *mortem integer pati* must mean roughly "to die without being wounded." Seneca has confused two heroes of the same name: Cycnus son of Mars, killed by Hercules, and Cycnus son of Neptune, killed by Achilles at Troy. The latter was invulnerable (Arist. *Rhet.* 2.22.1396b), and the only way Achilles could dispatch him was by strangulation (Ov. *Met.* 12.72–145). Seneca has not completely conflated the two heroes; at *Tro.* 183f. he knows that the Neptunian Cycnus died at Achilles' hands (cf. *Ag.* 215), but he has transferred this Cycnus' invulnerability, and consequent unusual manner of death, to the Martian Cycnus. (This was all the easier to do because the tradition of the Neptunian Cycnus' invulnerability was not unanimous: Apollod. *epit.* 3.31 says Achilles smashed his head with a rock. Seneca has in mind some such tradition at *Tro.* 184, where *perculit* suggests a wound rather than strangulation.) In view of this it seems necessary to correct codd. *obvius* to *invius* with N. Heinsius (*teste* Baden) and most later editors. (A's mistaken reading *ante Geryonem* for *integer Cycnus* in 486 re-

Commentary: Act II

veals both faulty word-division and influence from *Geryon* in the following line.)

487. Number is often the basis of a point in Ovid and Seneca (500 comm.). For play on *unus* and larger numbers cf. e.g. Ov. *Met.* 1.721 *centumque oculos nox occupat una,* 3.473 *nunc duo concordes anima moriemur in una* (v. Bömer on 3.544), and of Geryon *Her.* 9.92 *quamvis in tribus unus erat*; Sen. *HF* 19f. *una me . . . tellus . . . quotiens novercam fecit,* 500, 507f., 557, 1114, *Tro.* 489, *Med.* 354, *Pha.* 665, *Oed.* 282, *Ag.* 646, 838, etc.

488 stupro. This noun occurs twelve times in Sen. Trag., more often than in any other poet, though Plautus comes close with eleven uses. Compare the relatively high frequency of *paelex* in Sen. (4f. comm.). The only other poets to use *stuprum* at all often are Ovid (5) and Propertius (3).

489–92. For the rhetorical exploitation of precedent v. 386–96 comm. and for the idea in 491 of "learning" from precedent v. comm. on 398.

The sense of 490 is "You gave a wife (i.e. an already married woman) to Jove, and you shall give one to a king." Leo altered *dabis* to *dabit* (sc. *Hercules*), arguing (II 375) that this was necessitated by the phrase *etiam viro probante* in 492, which he must therefore have taken to mean "when (or "if") the husband actually gives his approval." But the pointing of the line, and particularly the polyptoton, seems to demand the same subject in both clauses (cf. Ov. *Her.* 4.144 *oscula aperta dabas, oscula aperta dabis*). With *dabis* in 490, line 492 must mean "to follow the better man—and actually find her husband approving!" The idea that Hercules could approve appears to be one of Lycus' more farfetched notions, but of course he does not actually believe that the hero will return from the underworld. The phrase is introduced primarily in order to score off Amphitryon.

negat. For *negare* = *recusare*, "refuse to," cf. V. *Georg.* 3.207f., Ov. *Pont.* 3.6.20 *nec . . . Leucothoe ferre negavit opem*, Sen. *Tro.* 903f., *OLD* s.v. 4.

494 ex coacta partum feram. *Ferre* is not common in the sense of "have children" (of the father), but cf. ps.-Sen. *HO* 1604, Suet. *Aug.* 4.1 *superstitibus liberis . . . Octavia minore item Augusto, quos ex Atia tulerat*, id. *Otho* 1.3 *ex Albia Terentia splendida femina duos filios tulit*.

[245]

Commentary: Act II

495–500. By a type of ring composition Megara is made to assert her final defiance of Lycus in very similar terms to those which she first used, referring here to the fateful precedents of Theban royal marriages, as there to those of the Theban throne (386ff.: note particularly *solita fata* in 396 and 497). But here she determines to realize these precedents by her own action.

495 penates Labdaci. The doom-ridden royal family of Thebes is frequently called the Labdacid house, cf. Soph. *Ant.* 594f. τὰ Λαβδακιδᾶν οἴκων ὁρῶμαι / πήματα, 861, *OT* 489, 496, 1226, *OC* 221, Eur. *Phoen.* 800 Λαβδακίδαις πολυμόχθοις, Sen. *Oed.* 710ff. *non hinc Labdacidas petunt / fata, sed veteres deum / irae secuntur.*

496. The torches themselves seem somewhat ominous in this context. Torches frequently carry connotations of madness and destruction (e.g. 100ff., 983f.), and in particular marriage torches are often associated with funeral brands and the torches held by the Furies, cf. Prop. 4.3.13f. *quae mihi deductae fax omen praetulit, illa / traxit ab everso lumina nigra rogo*, Ov. *Her.* 2.120, 6.41f., 11.101ff., 20.172 *et face pro thalami fax mihi mortis adest*, Sen. Rhet. *Contr.* 6.6.

Oedipodae. Forms from a nominative Οἰδιπόδης are found in Greek from Homer on (*Il.* 23.679 Οἰδιπόδαο). In Latin forms from *Oedipodes, -ae* appear first in Sen.; he uses them always in the same metrical position as here, where forms from *Oedipus, -i* would give an undesired iambic fifth foot.

498f. Medea similarly summons the Danaids to her aid, *Med.* 748f. *vos quoque, . . . / Danaides, coite: vestras hic dies quaerit manus.* (For the phrasing *nunc nunc . . . adeste* cf. *Med.* 13 *nunc nunc adeste, sceleris ultrices deae.*)

Line 498 is influenced by Ov. *Ibis* 178 *exulis Aegypti, turba cruenta, nurus* (cf. *Pont.* 3.1.121 *nurus Aegypti*). Seneca's *cruentae* need not be tautologous with *sanguine infectae manus*, as Gronovius thought, as it often means "bloodthirsty" rather than "bloodstained."

499 multo sanguine. *Multo* alludes to the massacre of Aegyptus' sons (in reference to mass slaughter cf. *multa . . . caede* at V. *Aen.* 1.471 and Sen. *Tro.* 446), and it also has some significance for the Danaids' present appearance: Megara wants them to look as fearful as possible. There seems little justification for Gronovius' conjecture *iuncto* (sc. "*et per genus et per nuptias*").

500. Number is often the basis of a Senecan point: v. 487 comm. and for the conceit of "making up a total" cf. 832f. *derat hoc solum numero*

[246]

Commentary: Act II

laborum, / tertiae regem spoliare sortis, *Ag.* 811f. Megara's reference to the Danaids is probably derived from Eur. *Phoen.* 1675 (spoken by Antigone when being forced into marriage with Haemon) νὺξ ἆρ' ἐκείνη Δαναΐδων μ' ἕξει μίαν. The phrasing is also influenced by V. *Aen.* 6.545 *explebo numerum* (sc. *manium*) *reddarque tenebris*, a passage that also influences Sen. *Pha.* 1153 *constat inferno numerus tyranno*.

501ff. Lycus now abandons his hope of having children by Megara, and reverts to his alternative plan (cf. 350f.) of wiping out Hercules' whole family.

502 terres. "Threaten," as at Cic. *S. Rosc.* 117 *terret etiam nos ac minatur, Phil.* 13.14, Sen. *Thy.* 96f., 705f. *immotus Atreus constat atque ultro deos / terret minantes, Pha.* 727f. The emphasis in these usages is on the tendency rather than the actual effect, as is the case in 45 *timuit* (v. comm.).

sceptra quid possint scies. This may well be suggested by the corresponding speech in Eur. 244ff. πυροῦτε σώματα / πάντων, ἵν' εἰδῶσ' οὕνεκ' οὐχ ὁ κατθανὼν / κρατεῖ χθονὸς τῆσδ', ἀλλ' ἐγὼ τὰ νῦν τάδε. But the intention of "teaching a lesson" is a common element in the threats of rulers, e.g. Aesch. *Ag.* 1619ff., Soph. *OT* 403 παθὼν ἔγνως ἂν οἷά περ φρονεῖς, and (particularly close) *Oed.* 519 *quid arma possint regis irati scies*.

503 complectere aras. The phrase implies that Megara has grasped the altar, claiming its protection, in response to the threat of 502. For the stage altar see comm. on 202–4. The expression is Ovidian: *Met.* 9.772 *aram complexa*, 5.103 *amplexo . . . altaria, Pont.* 1.2.149 *amplectitur aras* (though cf. also Plaut. *Rud.* 695 *aram amplexantes*). *Tangere* or *tenere* are more usual verbs in this context, v. Pease on V. *Aen.* 4.219. *Ara* is always plural in Sen. Trag.

504 orbe . . . remolito. Modeled on Ov. *Met.* 5.354 (Typhoeus) *saepe remoliri luctatur pondera terrae*, which is the first appearance of the verb in Latin, and the only instance of it before Sen.[68] The hyperbole of *orbe* here emphasizes the difficulty of the task. The unusual and heavy metrical pattern of *remolito* also conveys a sense of strenuous effort; for a very similar effect cf. 1198 *sinuare nervum vix recedentem mihi*. (There are only six other examples in *HF* of a single word covering the whole of the fourth and fifth foot.)

---

68. Sen. uses *remoliri* again at *QNat.* 6.13.4, and Ovid's phrase is also echoed in *Tro.* 682 *molire terras*, in a similar context to the present one.

Commentary: Act II

In classical Latin only a limited number of deponent past participles (notably *pactus, potitus*) are used passively in the ablative absolute, but this usage becomes more widespread from Livy on (H-S 139).

505 ad supera numina. A variation on *ad caelum* in the sense of "to the upper world, to the world of the living" (*Pha.* 1213, *Ag.* 859); cf. 586 *cum clara deos obtulerit dies*, where *deos* = *caelum* in this sense, and for other variations cf. *Pha.* 848 *aether*, *HF* 276 *astra* with comm.[69] Perhaps Sen. has deliberately created some ambiguity between this unusual transferred meaning of the phrase and its literal meaning. His purpose would be to gain irony by having Lycus suggest, unconsciously, the possibility of Hercules' deification.

506–8. Lycus' intention of burning the suppliants derives from Eur. 240ff. Building a fire around the altar was thought less sacrilegious than slaughtering the suppliants there or dragging them away: for other examples in drama cf. Eur. *Andr.* 257f., Ar. *Thesm.* 726ff., Men. *Perinth.* 1ff. (with Gomme and Sandbach ad loc.), Plaut. *Most.* 1114, *Rud.* 768. But in view of *templa . . . flagrent* it is clear that the original motive of avoiding sacrilege has been lost sight of here.

506 congerite silvas. Other instances of *silva* of the material of a pyre are Ov. *Met.* 9.235 *congeriem silvae* (cf. *congerite* here), *Consol. Liv.* 255 [*flamma*] *tandem ubi complexa est silvas alimentaque sumpsit*.

templa. This temple or shrine is mentioned again at 521 and 616f. (n.b. singular *limen sacrum* 617). The present lines suggest it is close to the altar, probably just behind it. One cannot be certain to what extent Sen. envisages the scene in terms of actual stage conventions, but in Greek drama a temple is often spoken of as the immediate background to the action, e.g. Aesch. *Eum.* 35ff., 242, Eur. *Ion* 184ff.

506f. supplicibus suis iniecta flagrent. A similar Senecan point concerns temples falling on their own gods, cf. *Ag.* 653 *templa deos super usta suos*, *Const. Sap.* 6.2 *inter fragorem templorum super deos cadentium*, ps.-Sen. *HO* 173 *templa suis collapsa deis*, and 1288 with comm.

---

69. If *deos* is displaced by conjecture at 586 (see ad loc.), however, it will be necessary to consider N. Heinsius' *lumina* for *numina* here; for MSS confusion of these words cf. V. *Aen.* 3.600, Sen. *Pha.* 790, Luc. 7.199. *Lumina* could be either a poetic plural (cf. Lucr. 1.5 *lumina solis*) or a genuine plural, "heavenly lights" (cf. V. *Georg.* 1.5f. *vos o clarissima mundi / lumina*, Sen. *Thy.* 795).

Commentary: Act II

508 igne subiecto. The phrase contributes little in terms of meaning, but adds weight to the concluding clause; cf. 29 *pace sublata* in the same metrical position.

509f. Derived from the similar request of Amphitryon at Eur. 321f. μίαν δὲ νῷν δὸς χάριν, ἄναξ, ἱκνούμεθα· / κτεῖνόν με καὶ τήνδ' ἀθλίαν παίδων πάρος. The motive for the requests is characteristically more heroic in Sen. In Eur. Amphitryon explains that he wants to avoid seeing his grandchildren dying (323ff.); in Sen. he feels that the request becomes him as H.'s father, presumably because it would enable him to show the ready courage in face of danger and death which characterizes his son.

Dramatically the request seems to make no sense in Sen., as there can be no question of a set order of death if all are to die by burning. The explanation is that Sen., in abbreviating the corresponding scene in Eur., has omitted the development which makes the request meaningful: after Lycus' announcement that he intends to burn them, Megara persuades Amphitryon that they should leave the altar, to die with more dignity at Lycus' own hands. In Sen. it is just conceivable that we are to envisage some stage business that would explain the request: Amphitryon could simply leave the altar before or during this speech. But it seems likely that Sen. borrowed the request in order to elicit the typically tyrannical sententiae of 511–13 from Lycus. Those lines are equally inappropriate dramatically, as Lycus has every intention of killing Amphitryon in the near future. This is Sen. at his most neglectful.

genitor Alcidae. The phrase implies what can be expected of such a person, cf. 1295 *vox est digna genitore Herculis*. For similar meaningful references by speakers to their identity cf. V. *Aen.* 11.688f. *nomen tamen haud leve patrum / manibus hoc referes, telo cecidisse Camillae* (with Austin on 1.48, Norden on 6.510f.), Hor. *Carm.* 1.7.27 *Teucro duce et auspice Teucro* (with N-H ad loc.), Sen. *Ag.* 4 *fugio Thyestes inferos, superos fugo*, and comm. on *HF* 631, 635.

511–13. The hallmark of the tyrant, cf. *Thy.* 247f. (Atreus) *perimat tyrannus lenis; in regno meo / mors impetratur*, *Ag.* 995 *rudis est tyrannus morte qui poenam exigit*. The point that living may be a fate worse than death is a familiar one, e.g. Eur. *Hipp.* 1047, *Tro.* 637, Plaut. *Rud.* 675f., Sall. *Cat.* 51.20, Hor. *Ars P.* 467 *invitum qui servat idem facit occidenti*, Sen. Rhet. *Contr.* 8.4 *non magis crudeles sunt qui volentes vivere occidunt quam qui volentes mori non sinunt*, Publ. Syr. 502 *plus est quam poena sinere miserum vivere*, Sen. *Phoen.* 98ff., Tac. *Ann.* 12.29. In Sen.'s own lifetime some of the emperors showed that they had learned the lesson

[249]

Commentary: Act II

well, cf. Suet. *Tib.* 61 *mori volentibus vis adhibita vivendi. nam mortem* . . . *leve supplicium putabat,* Sen. *QNat.* 4A *praef.* 17.

515. Seneca shares with Euripides the need to remove Lycus from the stage so that H. can return without his knowledge. In Eur. he is given no reason for leaving, other than to wait while H.'s family array themselves for death; in Sen. he is given some specific business to attend to while the pyre is being built. Sacrifice is a frequent motive for an exit both in Greek tragedy (e.g. Aesch. *Ag.* 1056ff., Soph. *OC* 503, Eur. *Ion* 663ff.) and in Sen. Trag. (cf. *HF* 915ff., *Med.* 299, *Oed.* 399ff., *Ag.* 583f., 806f., *Thy.* 545). But it is unclear what debt Lycus is paying with this sacrifice (n.b. *votivo*).

Furthermore, why is sacrifice offered to Neptune? The reason must be the traditional relationship between that god and bearers of the name Lycus. The sources differ about the precise relationship: Apollod. 3.10.1 calls the original Lycus (viz. Lycus père in Eur.'s version, v. 269 comm.) a grandson of Neptune, but late Roman sources call him a son (Hyg. *Fab.* 76, 157, *Astr.* 2.21, *Myth. Vat.* 1.234, schol. Germ. p. 76 Breysig); by a further confusion, Hyginus also calls the present Lycus a son of Neptune (*Fab.* 31, 32). This relationship is inconsistent with Sen.'s picture of Lycus as a man of obscure origins and his silence about the previous Lycus. These difficulties suggest that Sen. has borrowed the motive for departure from a play which kept the Euripidean link between this Lycus and the earlier Lycus: see Introduction.

516–20. The prayer to Jupiter broken off in despair derives from Eur. 498ff. (Amphitryon) ἐγὼ δὲ σ', ὦ Ζεῦ, χεῖρ' ἐς οὐρανὸν δικὼν / αὐδῶ. τέκνοισιν εἴ τι τοισίδ' ὠφελεῖν / μέλλεις, ἀμύνειν, ὡς τάχ' οὐδὲν ἀρκέσεις. / καίτοι κέκλησαι πολλάκις· μάτην πονῶ. These lines come at a similar dramatic point, i.e. just before H.'s return is first noticed. (For the thought cf. also 339ff. ὦ Ζεῦ, μάτην ἄρ' ὁμόγαμόν σ' ἐκτησάμην κ.τ.λ.) The appeal to H. in 520 perhaps comes from the immediately preceding speech in Eur., in which Megara makes a last appeal to her husband (490ff.), but the somewhat impious-sounding substitution of H. for the gods as a potential source of help is new in Sen.

516. For the rhetorical effect of the repeated *pro* cf. *Pha.* 903 *pro sancta pietas, pro gubernator poli.*

numinum vis summa. For *vis* of the gods' power cf. Cic. *Nat. D.* 3.36.88 *vim omnem deorum et potestatem,* V. *Aen.* 1.4 *vi superum,* 7.432 *caelestum vis magna,* 12.199 *vimque deum infernam.* For the word in connection with *numen* cf. Cic. *post red.* 25 *qui apud me deorum immortalium* *vim et numen tenetis*, Ov. *Ibis* 433 *teque aliquis posito temptet vim numinis opto*.

caelestium. For metrical reasons the form *caelestum* is regular in dactylic verse (except Pers. 2.61), but iambic verse gives more freedom: thus Sen. has *-ium* here but *-um* at 597, and Accius similarly has *-ium* at *trag.* 101 R^2, *-um* at 209 (v. 93 comm. and Neue-Wagener *Formenlehre* 2.65). Nevertheless, genitive plurals in *-ium* remain very rare in Sen. Trag., except for the trisyllabic noun forms *civium gentium hostium montium*: the only other instance known to me is *HF* 218 *serpentium*, also at line end.

517 rector parensque. The "father and ruler" formula for Jupiter is expressed in Ennius (*Ann.* 203, 591 Skutsch) and Vergil by *pater* and *rex*. Ovid uses *pater* and *rector* (*Met.* 2.848, 9.245, 15.860: cf. 205 comm.), followed by Sen. *Ag.* 400 (see Tarrant); Germ. *Arat.* 4 has *rector satorque*; further Senecan variations are *HF* 597f. *arbiter / parensque*, *Ep.* 107.11 *parens . . . dominator*.

517f. cuius . . . telis. One standard means of listing a god's attributes at the beginning of a prayer is by a relative clause, cf. 593f., 659f., 901f., 1057ff., 1074, Norden *Agnostos Theos* 168ff. Here the clause hints that Amphitryon would like to see Jupiter's power put to use.

518 humana. "The earth," with special reference to its human inhabitants; cf. Cic. *Rep.* 6.20 *haec caelestia spectato, illa humana contemnito*, Luc. 4.689 [*Curio*] *quo superos humanaque polluit anno*.

520–22. Such phenomena regularly accompany an epiphany from the underworld, notably in Sen.: the earth trembles and gives a rumbling sound. Cf. V. *Aen.* 4.490f. (with Pease ad loc.), 6.256f. *sub pedibus mugire solum et iuga coepta moveri / silvarum*, Ov. *Met.* 7.206, 14.406ff., Sen. *Tro.* 171ff., *Med.* 785f., *Oed.* 569ff., and of the influence of hellish evil *Thy.* 104, 262ff., 696ff. The sound is regularly described with *mugit solum* vel sim. For the phrasing of 521f. cf. particularly *Thy.* 262 *imo mugit e fundo solum*.

Thus the phenomena suggest the imminent epiphany of a *numen*, a suggestion quite in keeping with the implication of 519f. The wording of 520f. strengthens this suggestion, as the shaking of a *temple* would normally be caused by the advent of a god, cf. Callim. *Ap.* 1f. οἷον ὁ τὠπόλλωνος ἐσείσατο δάφνινος ὄρπηξ, / οἷα δ' ὅλον τὸ μέλαθρον, V. *Aen.* 3.90f. *tremere omnia visa repente, / liminaque laurusque dei*.

The phenomena indicate that Hercules is about to emerge from the

Commentary: Ode II

underworld in or close to Thebes. This is consistent with the impression given in 592ff. that H. has just emerged into the light of day, but inconsistent with indications elsewhere in the play (58ff., 813ff.). As elsewhere, Sen. is ignoring consistency in favor of immediate dramatic impact. His intention in presenting H.'s return as imminent at 520ff. but then postponing it until after the choral ode is to finish the Act on a note of suspense and anticipation; the ode is no doubt to be thought of as covering the time needed for H. to complete his ascent (Wagenvoort 177). The way Sen. ends the Act may be compared to a dramatic technique found in New Comedy.[70] "The pattern of introducing a new development toward the end of an act is a recurrent one in Menander, and, naturally enough, the development is often brought by the arrival of a character new to the play, or at least new to the preceding sequence." So E. G. Turner, *Ménandre* (Entretiens Hardt 16) 11, with examples, to which may be added *Misoum.* 270ff. Sandbach, where Kleinias enters to play an important part in the next Act. In Sen. Trag. cf. *Tro.* 999ff., where Pyrrhus enters to claim Polyxena. For foreshadowing of an appearance one could compare Men. *Peric.* 261ff., where the slave is going to look for Moschion.

523 audimur. Similarly at *Oed.* 571 Tiresias concludes *audior* after comparable phenomena have occurred.

Ode II (524–91)

The first part of Ode II is concerned with the subject of Hercules' labors; in this it resembles the corresponding stasimon in Euripides (348ff.), and two close verbal parallels make direct or indirect Euripidean influence highly probable (see comm. on 544 and 548). But Seneca's treatment of the topic is very different: this is no garland of praise (cf. Eur. 355), but an illustration of the laboriousness of Hercules' life; and as Amphitryon has already catalogued the labors (222ff.), Seneca is free to select a few of them to illustrate the point, rather than give a complete list as Euripides does.

Of the four labors mentioned, two—the quests for the Amazon's girdle and for Cerberus—are developed at some length, largely by description of the landscapes (or seascapes) in which they are set. Critics have not noted how careful a parallel is drawn between the two. In both cases the physical setting is pictured as a wasteland, indeed a *Gegenwelt*. Seneca dwells on the waters of both regions: those of Scythia

---

70. Dramatic techniques common to Seneca and New Comedy may well have been used also in post-Euripidean tragedy, cf. Tarrant 1978 218.

lack waves and their sounds, those of the underworld lack waves and the winds which create them (n.b. the parallel *illic* of 537, 550); after these negative descriptions there are parallel positive statements, *stat pontus* 540, *stat . . . pelagus* 554. (Note also the close parallel between 542 *illic quae viduis gentibus imperat* and 560 *hic qui rex populis pluribus imperat.*)

This parallel has a deep appropriateness to the nature of the Hercules myth, as several of his adventures involve journeys to the ends of the earth which seem in origin to be of a type with—perhaps even variants of—his journey to the land of the dead.[71] But the meaning of such episodes in Seneca is quite different from their folktale significance of conquering death or winning the keys of immortality. In the first ode, H.'s descent to the underworld was seen as symbolic of the tendency to hasten through life, to rush toward death, in pursuit of ambition (185 *Stygias ultro quaerimus undas*). Ode II goes further, by suggesting (though this is to reduce the matter from poetic implication to prosaic statement) that the experience of H.'s various toils, and so of the men who toil like him, is that of death-in-life. In Ode I, lives of *tranquilla quies* were set in a context of living nature, of sunrises, animal life, winds, and sounds (125–61); here, the life of *virtus animosa* is set in a context of barren landscapes, silence, stillness, and death.[72]

The rest of the ode also depends largely on development of parallels and precedents to Hercules' situation: as previously he conquered Dis, so now he can escape his realm (560ff.); as Orpheus returned from the underworld, so Hercules can return (569ff.). But although the Chorus is optimistic, its words have ominous overtones. Its emphasis on the violence H. will have to use, and the consequent disruption of the *foedus umbrarum* (566–68, 591), carries unintended overtones of hubris as clearly as Megara's first speech (279–95). And although the return of Orpheus is meant by the Chorus to have a positive significance, the audience cannot fail to attach greater significance than the Chorus does to its tragic outcome (588f.), familiar from Vergil's and Ovid's accounts. Orpheus did not in any real sense overcome the realm of death. He appeared to have rescued Eurydice, but shortly thereafter destroyed her in error; the parallel with what will happen to H. and his family is too close to be missed.

The parallelism that dominates the whole structure is also found at

---

71. Preller-Robert 2.430f., H. J. Rose 214ff., Kirk 190–93.

72. Although Seneca's description of the frozen Euxine owes several details to Ovid (v. 535–41 comm.), the link between the Scythia-ecphrasis and the theme of death suggests a debt to book 3 of Vergil's *Georgics*: see Otis, *Virgil* 177f. Seneca's immobile seas, and their association with death both physical and spiritual, irresistably remind one of the becalmed ocean of Samuel Coleridge's *Rime of the Ancient Mariner*.

Commentary: Ode II

the level of clauses and individual lines. Thus the power of Orpheus' song on earth is illustrated in three parallel relative clauses (572–74), and its power in the underworld by three parallel main clauses (577–81); note also the parallelism of the final couplet (590f.). Often the parallelism takes the form of "theme and variation," in which a second line varies or amplifies the idea of a preceding line: instances include 533f., 535f., 540f., 547f., 558f., 564f., 575f., 586f. (cf. also 566ᵇ–68). The pattern of theme and variation is not uncommon in Roman poetry from Vergil on,[73] though rarely found in such concentration as here. It is entirely appropriate to the serious atmosphere and deliberate onward movement of the ode; one may compare passages from the Psalms, where of course the pattern is pervasive, e.g. 18.14ff.

Echoes and parallels also appear to a remarkable degree in the verbal texture of the ode. In some cases the parallel is pointed by anaphora, 541 *navem nunc . . . nunc equitem*, 550 *nulla noto nulla favonio*, 577ff. *deflent . . . deflent . . . flentes sedent*, 584f. *tu . . . perge, tu . . . respice*. Elsewhere it is a matter of wordplay: apart from examples where the words are related in meaning (565 *mortis . . . mori*, 567f. *invius . . . vias*), there are some striking examples where they are not, 539 *semita Sarmatis*, 581 *Eurydicen iuridici*, 586 *deos . . . dies*.[74] From such wordplay it is a short step to alliteration, examples of which are plentiful and sometimes elaborate. The following list of instances from the first few sentences of the ode is highly selective:

    524 O Fortuna viris invida fortibus
    532 pomis divitibus praepositus draco
    533 intravit Scythiae multivagas domos
    535 calcavitque freti terga rigentia
    543 aurato religans ilia balteo
    545 et peltam et nivei vincula pectoris

And although such forceful alliteration is particularly noticeable early in the ode, it by no means disappears thereafter, cf. e.g. 550, 552, 554, 572, 578, 585. All this suggests either that the ode has received an unusual amount of verbal polishing, or that Seneca struck an unusually

---

73. E.g. V. *Georg.* 1.208f. *Libra die somnique pares ubi fecerit horas / et medium luci atque umbris iam dividit orbem*; see J. Henry, *Aeneidea* index s.v. "Theme and Variation," and note on *Aen.* 1.546ff., also Eden on *Aen.* 8.171.

74. Naturally such wordplay on unrelated words is by no means exclusively Senecan, cf. e.g. Enn. *trag.* 212 R² *era errans*, 41 *mulier melior mulierum* (with Jocelyn p. 211 foot), Pacuv. *trag.* 246 *minuam manuum*, V. *Georg.* 2.328 *avia . . . avibus*, *Aen.* 2.271 *teris otia terris*, 6.204 *auri . . . aura* with Norden ad loc., Ov. *Met.* 2.101 *dubita, dabitur*, 126 *pārere pārentis* with Bömer ad loc. In *HF* cf. 153 *navita vitae*, 1184f. *nominis . . . numen*, 1263 *perimes parentem*.

Commentary: Ode II

rich vein of *melopoiea* (to use the word in Pound's sense) when composing it.

It is noteworthy that the Chorus is ignorant of the developments at the end of the preceding Act, that is, the indications of Hercules' imminent arrival and, apparently, the imminent danger to his family from Lycus (contrast 430ff. of the corresponding ode in Eur.). Similarly in the ode at *Med.* 579ff. the Chorus shows no knowledge of the specific plans for revenge just formed by Medea. One might conclude that the Chorus has been absent from the stage before each of these odes. Yet there is no other indication that it leaves the stage, and indeed the bridge-passage at *HF* 202–4, in which the Chorus observes what is happening onstage, argues against an exit at that point or soon thereafter. It is true that in fifth-century Greek tragedy the Chorus is assumed to be present from the parodos onward, and to be aware of what occurs onstage, so that choral ignorance can occur only if it has been temporarily absent, as at Soph. *Ajax* 815–65.[75] In the odes of Senecan tragedy, however, choral knowledge or ignorance seems to depend not on its presence or absence during the previous scene, but rather on the playwright's *fiat*.[76] Thus the Chorus is apparently absent from the confrontation between Hippolytus and Phaedra (*Pha.* 601),[77] but in the following ode it knows that Hippolytus' flight was innocent, a fact it cannot have learned from Phaedra or the nurse. Conversely, the Chorus of *Thy.* is told the reason for the sun's turning back (776ff.), and yet is ignorant of the explanation in the following ode (e.g. 802, 827). It appears, therefore, that some choral odes are subject to the same tendency toward independence as is found in some iambic scenes.[78]

Though the Chorus of classical Greek tragedy intervenes in the dialogue under a wide range of circumstances, such interventions in Senecan tragedy are limited almost exclusively to two types: bridge-passages immediately following odes, which lead into the next scene; and cases in which no other interlocutor is available (see, respectively, comm. on 202–4 and 1032–34 ad fin.). Obviously these remnants of

---

75. Tarrant 1978 223 with nn. 49 and 54.
76. This might be thought an argument against staging, particularly in an ode like the present one, where the Chorus must 'ignore' the tableau of the suppliants. But some degree of cutting-off of the Chorus from stage reality is already visible in late Euripides (Tarrant 1978 n. 48), and, if Tarrant is right, will have become more pronounced in Agathon and in later Greek dramatists who certainly wrote for the stage.
77. I say "apparently" because 404f. would seem to indicate its presence. In fact the question of presence or absence is entirely conventional.
78. On this see Tarrant 1978 228ff.

[255]

Commentary: Ode II

classical technique have been preserved because of their usefulness to the dramatist, and are purely conventional; they do not imply continuous awareness or presence on the Chorus' part. Hence it should not cause surprise that the Chorus of *Med.* does not react to Medea's plans to murder the children, despite having reacted to the messenger only moments earlier (879ff.); or that the Chorus of *Pha.*, though appalled by Phaedra's schemes against Hippolytus (824ff.), does not reveal them to Theseus. In sum, the Chorus in Senecan tragedy cannot be assumed to have a continuous existence outside the odes. It springs to life intermittently at the dramatist's convenience, and may also be regarded as absent when that is convenient; elsewhere it is not so much "present" or "absent" as simply in abeyance. Correspondingly the amount of knowledge the Chorus displays in the odes depends not on its previous presence onstage but on the dramatist's decision.

Despite its independence of the immediate stage situation, the present ode is designed for this place in this play, and cannot be called an *embolimon*. The Chorus' concern with Hercules' return, and its confidence that he *will* return successfully, is clearly appropriate to a point shortly before he does in fact emerge; contrast Ode I, in which his return is not even considered.

The meter is lesser Asclepiad.

524–32. Reproachful addresses to Fortune are found in Latin from Republican drama on, cf. Enn. *trag.* 307 R^2 *eheu mea Fortuna ut omnia in me conglomeras mala*, Ter. *Hec.* 406. Such complaints usually concern Fortune's caprice or blindness, e.g. Pacuv. *trag.* 366 R^2 *Fortunam insanam esse et caecam et brutam perhibent philosophi*, Hor. *Sat.* 2.8.61f., Otto s.v. *fortuna* (1). But Seneca suggests that Fortune deliberately favors the unworthy and envies energy and industry, cf. *Ep.* 118.4, *Cons. Pol.* 3.3 *o dura Fata et nullis aequa virtutibus*, *Pha.* 979f. *Fortuna . . . peiora fovens*, *HF* 325f.;[79] compare Pliny's phrase *indignorum fautrix* (*NH* 2.22) and Stat. *Theb.* 10.384f. *invida Fata piis et Fors ingentibus ausis / rara comes*, also earlier Kaibel *Epigr. Gr.* 489.4 ἡ φθονερὰ τοῖς ἀγαθοῖσι Τύχη. Such *invidia* is different from φθόνος θεῶν, which is aimed at eminence rather than *virtus*: that concept is rather more evident in the address to Fortune at *Ag.* 57ff. (cf. Tarrant ad loc.).

Seneca's *Fortuna invida fortibus*, though in complete contrast to the

---

[79]. At *Prov.* 1.6 Sen. takes a more Stoic view: he notes that good men toil while the bad live in ease, but regards this as the work not of an amoral Fortune but a provident god, who tests and toughens the good through hardships. But the imagined complaint at 5.9 is similar to *HF* 524f.: *quare tamen deus tam iniquus in distributione fati fuit, ut bonis viris paupertatem et vulnera et acerba funera ascriberet?*

proverbial idea that *fortes Fortuna adiuvat* (cf. Otto s.v. *fortuna* (9)), nevertheless echoes its play on the syllable *fort-*; for the wording of 524 cf. particularly Enn. *Ann.* 233 Skutsch *fortibus est Fortuna viris data*.

525. *Aequa* probably agrees with *praemia*, in view of Sen.'s liking for noun-adjective pairs. *Dividis* = "assign, apportion," νέμεις, cf. Acc. *trag.* 533f. R², Livy 28.9.17 *militibus M. Livius quinquagenos senos asses divisit*, Hor. *Carm.* 1.36.6 *nulli plura tamen dividit oscula / quam dulci Lamiae*.

526–32. There is a somewhat similar contrast in Ov. *Met.* 9: Hercules for all his *virtus* is dying an agonizing death, *at valet Eurystheus: et sunt qui credere possint / esse deos!* (203f.). Several editors have followed Bothe in presenting these lines in inverted commas, as the actual words of Fortune. This might be paralleled particularly by *Prov.* 2.6 *patrium deus habet adversus bonos viros animum et illos fortiter amat, et "operibus," inquit, "doloribus, damnis exagitentur, ut verum colligant robur."* But the present passage has no specific indication of direct speech; I am therefore inclined to take the subjunctives as representing an inference, drawn from events, about Fortuna's wishes, rather than words actually put into her mouth: "Eurystheus (it seems) is to rule at his ease, while Hercules must labor constantly." The subjunctives have been taken as indignant questions ("Is Eurystheus to reign?" etc.), but the subordinate clause in 531f. would create too anticlimactic an end to such a series of questions.

527. For *bella* of the conflicts faced by H. in his labors cf. 85 comm.

528 exagitet. The verb emphasizes the laboriousness of Hercules' life, suggesting that he cannot allow himself peace or rest. It recurs in a similar context in the passage cited in 526–32 comm., where again it implies harassment and difficulty (contra *TLL* 5.2.1152.82ff.).

caeliferam. The adjective makes a point, viz. that such a hand is unworthily employed on mere monsters (comm. on 434f.). For similarly pointed contrasts cf. 1101f. *mundum solitos ferre lacertos / verbera pulsent*, *Pha.* 327ff. *umerisque quibus / sederat alti regia caeli / tenuem Tyrio stamine pallam*. The last passage is certainly influenced by Ov. *Her.* 9.55f. [*Meandros*] *vidit in Herculeo suspensa monilia collo / illo, cui caelum sarcina parva fuit*, and the same is probably true of the *HF* passages. *Caelifer* is a standard adjective of Atlas (V. *Aen.* 6.796, Ov. *Fasti* 5.83, Germ. *Arat.* 264, Sil. 15.142, Stat. *Silv.* 1.1.60, *Theb.* 5.430), here appropriately transferred to the hero who acted as his substitute.

529. Both *resecet* and *feracia* suggest the difficult and wearisome nature of this conflict (cf. *exagitet*): cutting only stimulated the growth of the Hydra's heads, until at last H. realized that he must cauterize them (v. 242 comm.). *Feracia* is the certain Renaissance correction for EA *ferocia*: Sen. likes to use exactly this point in reference to the Hydra, cf. 781 *fecunda capita*, *Ag.* 835 *morte fecundum domuit draconem*. The inspiration for these adjectives is Ov. *Her.* 9.96f. *quaeque redundabat fecundo vulnere serpens / fertilis* (cf. also Germ. *Arat.* 543f. *fecundam meteret cum comminus Hydram / Alcides*), rather than Eur. *Her.* 1274f. τήν τ' ἀμφίκρανον καὶ παλιμβλαστῆ κύνα / ὕδραν φονεύσας, where the point is less similar.

530–32. There are two well-known literary versions of how Hercules obtained the Golden Apples of the Hesperides: according to one, he persuaded Atlas to fetch the apples, meanwhile relieving him of the burden of the heavens (Pherecydes ap. schol. Ap. Rhod. 4.1396): the other says that he plucked them himself, after killing the fearsome serpent that guarded them (Panyassis fr. 10K, Eur. *Her.* 396ff.). The allusions in the present lines do not agree with either of these standard versions. They may, however, be related more closely to a version attested in artistic representations of the exploit, particularly in the South Italian and Roman traditions,[80] which show the Hesperides offering the serpent a bowl (which must contain either food or a drug), and plucking the apples for Hercules. These representations agree with Sen. in giving the Hesperides a significant role, but one cannot be certain whether Sen. has the same concept of that role, nor how they were "deceived." Seneca may mean that Hercules tricked them into picking the apples for him; alternatively the trick may have consisted of Hercules' drugging the serpent himself, without being detected by the Hesperides, as Preller-Robert suggest (2.493 n. 2: one type does in fact show Hercules stroking the serpent and offering it a cup).[81] Other references to the exploit in Sen. Trag. (*Ag.* 852ff., *Phoen.* 316f.) agree that the serpent was not killed; but in the *Ag.* passage it seems to have been not drugged but simply distracted during the theft.[82]

---

80. Cf. E. Gerhard, *Gesammelte Akademische Abhandlungen* 1, pp. 52 (5), 54 (415), 58 (2), 62–68 (1–7, 9, 10), taff. XIX–XXI; Brommer 1953 p. 52 ab. 10, taff. 29, 30; Preller-Robert 2.493f.

81. Gerhard p. 54 (7).

82. Vergil's Dido speaks of a *sacerdos, / Hesperidum templi custos, epulasque draconi / quae dabat et sacros servabat in arbore ramos, / spargens umida mella soporiferumque papaver* (*Aen.* 4.483–86). Unfortunately the last line is as difficult to interpret as the Senecan passage. It might be thought to allude to a tradition that the serpent was drugged so that the apples could be stolen, but such an allusion would be inconsistent with *servabat*.

531. For this serpent as normally watchful, cf. comm. on 240 *vigilis*. The lulling of another usually sleepless guardian, that of the Golden Fleece, is described in similar language at *Med.* 472f. *somnoque iussum lumina ignoto dare / insomne monstrum.*

532 divitibus. "Precious," as golden: cf. V. *Aen.* 6.195f. *ubi pinguem dives opacat / ramus humum*, Manil. 5.16 *Hesperidumque vigil custos et divitis auri*, Luc. 9.659, and comm. on *HF* 239 *opulenti*.

533–46. Hercules is usually said to have undertaken this expedition against the Amazons with several other heroes, but this passage gives the impression that he went alone. This is in keeping with the emphasis in this ode on the difficulty of the labors, and with the general emphasis in the play on H.'s unique and superhuman capabilities.

The Amazons are sometimes located on the north coast of the Euxine, around the Maeotis, cf. Eur. *Her.* 409, Prop. 3.11.14, Sen. *Pha.* 399ff.; similarly at *Tro.* 12f. Sen. makes them neighbors of the Scythians. Elsewhere, however, writers, including Sen. himself at 246 (comm.) place them on the southern coast, around the River Thermodon: Hdt. 4.110 says that they moved from the Thermodon to the Maeotis. The present description would suit the Maeotis area better than the south coast, but it may be doubted whether Sen. distinguishes clearly between these locations. For similar poetic vagueness about the Amazons' location cf. V. *Aen.* 11.659f. *quales Threiciae cum flumina Thermodontis / pulsant . . . Amazones*, Prop. 4.4.71f. *qualis celerem prope Thermodonta / Strymonis.*

533f. The phrase *multivagas domos* is influenced by Hor. *Carm.* 3.24.9f. *Scythae, / quorum plaustra vagas rite trahunt domos* (in the same meter). For *intrare* = "come among" cf. V. *Aen.* 6.59 *intravi . . . penitusque repostas / Massylum gentes*, Ov. *Her.* 18.175 *intravit Colchos Pagasaeus Iason*. But the usage is rare and poetic, and the use of *intrare domos* in this transferred sense seems particularly bold. *Multivagus* is first attested in Sen.: on such compounds v. Appendix 4.

535–41. Of several passages in poetry describing the frozen Euxine, including V. *Georg.* 3.360–62 and a number in Ov. *Tr.* and *Pont.*, the fullest is *Tr.* 3.10.27–50, which seems to have most inspired Seneca's lines. Thus Ovid's *durum calcavimus aequor* (39) suggests Sen.'s *calcavit* and *dura . . . aequora*. Furthermore, the contrasts made by Sen. in 538f. and 541 derive from 31f. *quaque rates ierant, pedibus nunc itur, et undas / frigore concretas ungula pulsat equi, / perque novos pontes subter labentibus undis / ducunt Sarmatici barbara plaustra boves*: n.b. Sen.'s opening words

Commentary: Ode II

et qua . . . rates, and his reference to the Sarmatians. Such contrasts do occur elsewhere, V. *Georg.* 3.362 [*unda*] *puppibus illa prius, patulis nunc hospita plaustris*, Ov. *Pont.* 4.10.32ff. *hic freta vel pediti pervia reddit hiems, / ut, qua remus iter pulsis modo fecerat undis, / siccus contempta nave viator eat.*

535 terga. This metaphor for the sea's surface appears as early as Homer, in the formula ἐπ' εὐρέα νῶτα θαλάσσης. It is used specifically of the frozen surface of a body of water in the Vergilian passage, *undaque iam tergo ferratos sustinet orbes* (361), and at Ov. *Pont.* 1.2.80 [*gentes*] *dura meant celeri terga per amnis equo.*

536. An imaginative touch which does not appear in the Vergilian or the Ovidian passages; it increases the similarity of this *Gegenwelt* to the underworld, cf. 576 *surdis . . . in locis*, 848 *per campos . . . silentes.*

mutis tacitum. The proximity of adjectives of similar meaning is characteristic of Sen.'s style. Examples in *HF* include 284 *praeceps citato*, 301f. *muta . . . tacita*, 397 *efferatas rabida*, 680 *placido quieta labitur Lethe vado*, 683f. *incerta vagus / Maeander unda ludit*, 689 *opaca . . . nigrantes*, 762f. *tardis . . . vadis, / stupente ubi unda segne torpescit fretum*, 744 *laeta felix*, 822 *pura nitidi*, 950 *gelido frigida*, 1056 *vaga ponti mobilis unda*, 1082 *saeva feroci*, 1109 *latique patens unda profundi* (instances from other plays in Canter 173). Such pairing of adjectives seems to be favored particularly in descriptions of waters: in addition to the instances in *HF*, cf. Hor. *Carm.* 1.31.7f. *quae Liris quieta / mordet aqua taciturnus amnis*, Tib. 1.7.13f. *Cydne . . . tacitis qui leniter undis / caeruleus placidis per vada serpis aquis*, Sen. *Apocol.* 7 v. 13 [*Arar*] *tacitus quietis adluit ripas vadis*, Avien. *Or. Mar.* 121 *sic segnis humor aequoris pigri stupet*. For pleonasm in descriptions of silence cf. Lucr. 4.583 *taciturna silentia*, V. *Aen.* 2.255 *tacitae per amica silentia lunae*, Ov. *Met.* 4.433 [*via*] *ducit ad infernas per muta silentia sedes* (*muta silentia* again 7.184, 1053).

538 tenderant. For the pluperfect cf. *ierant* and *fecerat* in the Ovidian passages cited on 535–41. This seems the most certain instance, among those cited by Neue-Wagener *Formenlehre* 3.350, of the perfect stem of *tendere* without reduplication.[83] For *tendere* of spreading sails to the wind, cf. *Med.* 320f. *lina sinu tendere toto.*

---

83. Bücheler in *RhM* 37 (1882) 527 n. 3 accepted E's *tenderent*, which he took as a potential subjunctive, "where ships might have sailed." But this seems awkward and very improbable: the potential use of the imperfect subjunctive in the third person is largely limited to questions such as *quis posset dubitare* and expressions of opinion such as *quod minime quis crederet* (K-S 1.179).

Commentary: Ode II

539 intonsis. A standard indication of uncouthness, cf. Livy 21.32.7 *homines intonsi et inculti*, Ov. *Pont.* 4.2.2 *ab intonsis . . . Getis*.

540 stat pontus. For initial *stat* emphasizing lack of motion cf. 554 *stat nigro pelagus gurgite languidum*, 861 *stat chaos densum*, Sen. Rhet. *Suas.* 1.1 *stat immotum mare*. More generally, cf. the use of the verb at the beginning of a *descriptio loci*, e.g. V. *Aen.* 8.233 *stabat acuta silex* e.q.s. *Stat* is a favorite line-opening in Sen.'s lyrics, cf. *Oed.* 131, *Ag.* 394, *Thy.* 152, 391.

mobilis. There is some interplay between two senses: "moving" (as opposed to "standing frozen") and "changing its nature."

541. The epigrammatic line sums up and rounds off the passage, as in 5 (comm.). The paradoxical contrast derives from the passages cited on 535–41, but in form the line may be influenced also by Hor. *Carm.* 4.8.8 *sollers nunc hominem ponere, nunc deum* (in the same meter).

542–46. The scene is strikingly visualized, but not particularly close to known artistic representations.[84] Nor is it close to literary accounts of the winning of the girdle, though these vary greatly (*RE* Suppl. 3.1055.45ff.): sometimes H. is said to have stripped the girdle from the queen by force (Apollod. 2.5.9, Quint. Smyrn. 6.240ff.; Sen. follows this at *Ag.* 847ff.); according to Ap. Rhod. 2.966ff. Hippolyte herself was not defeated, but gave up the girdle as ransom for her sister Melanippe, captured by Hercules (cf. Diod. Sic. 4.16.4). Seneca's description here has a faintly erotic atmosphere; this element in the encounter was emphasized by Diogenes the Cynic, according to Dio Chrys. 8.32.

542 viduis. Compare 246 *regina gentis vidua Thermodontiae* with comm.

543 aurato . . . balteo. The same noun is used of this girdle at Ov. *Met.* 9.189, *Her.* 20.119, where it is described as *caelatus balteus auro*; for the gold cf. Eur. *Her.* 414 χρυσεόστολον φάρος.

544 spolium nobile. A slightly inappropriate phrase in this context (*detraxit spolium* would be more appropriately said of Hercules, cf. the more natural use of *spolium* at *Ag.* 849), and probably borrowed from

---

84. Admittedly, Greek vase paintings often show the Amazon falling on one knee (n.b. *posito . . . genu*), but no importance is given to the girdle (*LIMC* s.v. Amazones 1–89). Those few Italiot vases that do show her handing over the girdle represent the scene as peaceful, with the queen standing (ibid. 777–82). Several sarcophagi show H. stripping the girdle from the prostrate queen (ibid. 122–38).

Commentary: Ode II

Eur. 416f. τὰ κλεινὰ δ' Ἑλλὰς ἔλαβε βαρβάρου κόρας λάφυρα. There "famous" has a special point, viz. that the girdle was preserved at Mycenae.

545 nivei vincula pectoris. Suggested by Vergil's description of Penthesilea at Troy as *aurea subnectens exsertae cingula mammae* (*Aen.* 1.492): Seneca clearly thinks of this as an element of Amazon battle-dress, now removed together with the *pelta*. Amazons were traditionally believed to bare one breast when fighting, as the Vergilian passage shows, cf. Arrian 7.13.2 and *LIMC* s.v. Amazones passim.[85] *Nivei* is redolent of the *sermo amatorius*, where it is used of various parts of the body, v. Pichon 213 (cf. 298 comm.): Tibullus uses *niveum pectus* at 1.4.12.

547–49. Apostrophe is frequently found in Seneca's odes, cf. 186f. with comm. This question is similar to that of *inc. inc. trag.* 249f. R^2 *quaenam te adigunt, hospes, / stagna capacis visere Averni?* which was perhaps also addressed to Hercules (cf. Introduction fn. 67).

547 praecipites. I know of no parallel for this adjective used of that which lies at the bottom of a steep slope, as opposed to that which constitutes the slope or drop; but the extension in sense is not unnatural.

548 audax ire. Compare line 3 of the passage from Albinovanus Pedo cited by Sen. Rhet. in *Suas.* 1.15, *per non concessas audaces ire tenebras*. The construction is not particularly unusual (cf. 541 with comm., Hor. *Carm.* 1.3.25 *audax omnia perpeti*), but the somewhat similar subject matter, and Sen.'s familiarity with the passage (v. 703 comm.), make it probable that it influenced him here.

vias inremeabiles. The phrase probably comes from Eur. 431ff. τὰν δ' ἀνόστιμον . . . βίου κέλευθον; the Latin version of the adjective is certainly borrowed from V. *Aen.* 6.425 *ripam inremeabilis undae* (cf. 5.591 *inremeabilis error* of the Labyrinth), for *inremeabilis* does not appear elsewhere before Sen., and only here in him. On such adjectives in connection with death v. Gow on Theoc. 12.19.

549. Both *vidisti* and the verse-end *regna Proserpinae* come from Hor. *Carm.* 2.13.21f. *quam paene furvae regna Proserpinae / et iudicantem vidimus*

---

85. Kapnukajas takes the *vincula* as identical with the *balteus* (in support he might have cited *Ag.* 847ff. and Claud. 11.37f., where Hippolyte at sight of Honorius *seminudo pectore cingulum / forti negatum solveret Herculi*), but *et . . . et* makes this impossible: the queen here wears the *balteus* around her hips, the *vincula* around her breast.

Aeacum. Seneca adopts Horace's unusual short scansion of the first syllable of *Proserpina*. Elsewhere in the poets, including Horace himself, the *o* is long (Sen. uses the name only here). For *regna Proserpinae* of the underworld see N-H ad loc., and for *videre* of an unpleasant experience see their notes on *Carm.* 1.2.13, 1.3.19, and compare the passages cited above on 50 and 254, 257.

550–54. For the stillness of the waters of the underworld cf. 762f. *tardis . . . vadis, / stupente ubi unda segne torpescit fretum.* Part of Sen.'s purpose in emphasizing it here is to parallel the frozen immobility of the Euxine. There is no precedent for such emphasis on the absence of wind and movement on the underworld's rivers, though some earlier poets call them "sluggish," v. comm. 554. (At V. *Aen.* 6.296f., in contrast, the waters over which Charon ferries the dead are turbulent.) But one may compare Pedo's description of the North Sea (v. 548 comm.), which is also presented as a *Gegenwelt*: *alium flabris intactum . . . orbem* (v. 19: *flabris* Haupt, *libris* vel *liberis* codd.), cf. 5 *pigris . . . undis,* 9 *rapido desertam flamine classem.* For the technique of description by negative clauses followed by positive statement cf. 698–703 with comm.

550 Noto . . . Favonio. The south wind is associated with storms, cf. 1090, Hom. *Il.* 16.765, V. *Aen.* 6.355f., Hor. *Carm.* 1.3.14 *rabiem Noti,* Ov. *Am.* 2.6.44 *procelloso . . . Noto*; on the other hand the westerlies are more usually associated with spring and calmer seas, e.g. 699, *Anth. Pal.* 10.1.1f., Cat. 46.2f. *iam caeli furor aequinoctialis / iucundis Zephyri silescit auris.* But the native Latin term *Favonius* appears much less frequently in verse than *Zephyrus,* partly for metrical reasons, partly because of a liking for Grecisms: the comparative figures are Vergil 0:18, Ovid 1:22, Sen. Trag. 1:10. Perhaps therefore *Favonius* has less definite associations than *Zephyrus.*

552 geminum Tyndaridae genus. For appositional phrases of the Twins cf. *HF* 14 with comm. Senecan examples of this pattern of apposition, in which a noun is enclosed within an adjective-noun phrase, include *Tro.* 63 *turba captivae mea, Med.* 980, *Pha.* 1105, *Ag.* 800 *fida famuli turba* (v. Tarrant ad loc.).

553. Castor and Pollux were regarded as patrons and protectors of sailors. In particular they were associated with "St. Elmo's fire," an electrical phenomenon that appears on the masts and rigging of ships during storms, regarded as evidence of protection by the Dioscuri. (Compare the references collected by N-H on Hor. *Carm.* 1.3.2, 1.12.27.) *Sidera* alludes to this phenomenon, which is commonly described as starlike, cf. Xenophanes A 39 Diels-Kranz τοὺς ἐπὶ τῶν πλοίων φαινομένους οἷον ἀστέρας, οὕς καὶ Διοσκούρους καλοῦσί τινες, Hor. *Carm.* 1.3.2 *sic fratres Helenae, lucida sidera,* [*navem regant*], 1.12.27ff. *quorum simul alba nautis / stella refulsit, / . . . concidunt venti* e.q.s., 4.8.31f. *clarum Tyndaridae sidus ab infimis / quassas eripiunt aequoribus rates,* Sen. *QNat.* 1.1.13 *in magna tempestate apparere quasi stellae solent velo insidentes,* Stat. *Silv.* 3.2.8ff. *proferte benigna / sidera et antemnae gemino considite cornu, / Oebalii fratres.* The phrase *succurrunt . . . sidera* therefore means "give help as stars, in starlike form"; the Dioscuri do not simply send the fire as an encouragement to sailors, but are actually manifest in it, as is the case in most of the passages cited. In view of these parallels, and of the tendency to use apposition in phrases describing the Dioscuri, I retain the paradosis rather than adopting Housman's conjecture *sidere* (ad Manil. 2.556, p.126 of ed. maior; also made by A. Ker, *CQ* N.S. 12 [1962] 49[86]).

The general similarity of the line to 551 is varied by the grammatical chiasmus *fluctibus aequora / sidera navibus.*

timidis . . . navibus. That is, *nautis*: for the metonymy cf. 10 *timendum ratibus ac ponto gregem,* and for the transferred adjective 676 *puppes . . . invitas.* At Ov. *Fasti* 1.4 *timidae dirige navis iter* the phrase is a metaphor.

554. The combination of "black" and "sluggish" in description of underworld waters comes from Hor. *Carm.* 2.14.17f. *ater flumine languido / Cocytos* (note interwoven word order and ablative of description. N-H ad loc. cite Pindar frag. 130.2 βληχροὶ δνοφερᾶς νυκτὸς ποταμοί.) Cf. also *Thy.* 665f. *fons stat sub umbra tristis et nigra piger / haeret palude,* of a spring compared with Styx. For blackness, add V. *Aen.* 6.132 *Cocytusque sinu labens circumvenit atro.* The word *gurges* here as often lacks any connotation of turbulence. For. *stat* cf. 540 with comm., and the passage from *Thy.* cited above.

pelagus. The water the shades must cross (cf. 557) is usually described as a river or marsh; Sen.'s *pelagus* increases the parallelism with the Euxine, cf. particularly 540 *stat pontus.* (The word was perhaps suggested by Vergil's phrase *languentis . . . pelagi, Aen.* 10.289.) The description is not entirely without precedent, as Acheron is a λίμνη as well as a river (Soph. *El.* 138, fr. 523 P, Plato *Phaedo* 113a), and it is sometimes said to be Acheron that the dead must cross (e.g. Alcaeus 38A.8

---

86. Ker objected to the two appositions *geminum . . . numen* and *sidera,* but they have quite different functions: the first refers to a permanent state, the second to a particular form which the Gemini take on special occasions.

L-P, Aesch. *Sept.* 856, Ar. *Ran.* 137ff., Theoc. 17.46ff., [Plato] *Ax.* 371b). Cf. also Vergil's phrase *Stygios . . . lacus* of the waters the dead must cross (*Aen.* 6.134), and Sen.'s use of *fretum* at 763 below.

languidum. For "sluggish" as a description of underworld waters cf., in addition to the passages cited in the penultimate note, V. *Georg.* 4.479 *tardaque palus inamabilis unda / alligat,* Prop. 4.11.15 *vada lenta paludes,* Sen. *HF* 682f., 686.

555 Mors . . . pallida. Cf. Hor. *Carm.* 1.4.13 *pallida Mors,* also V. *Georg.* 1.277 *pallidus Orcus,* Sen. *Oed.* 584 *pallentes deos* (contrast 164 *Mors atra*). *Pallidus, pallens* are also used of those faced with death, of the dead, and of the underworld, cf. Pease on V. *Aen.* 4.26.

avidis. . . dentibus. Cf. *Oed.* 164f. *Mors atra avidos oris hiatus / pandit,* and the more metaphorical phrase Lucr. 1.852 *Leti sub dentibus ipsis.* Death is traditionally greedy, v. 291 comm. The grotesque detail is more reminiscent of the death-demons of Etruscan art (e.g. P. J. Riis, *Introduction to Etruscan Art* [New York 1954] ill. 69) than of Thanatos as represented in Greek art.

556f. gentes innumeras . . . tot populi. A borrowing from V. *Aen.* 6.706 *hunc circum innumerae gentes populique volabant,* which itself echoes Homer's ἔθνεα . . . μυρία νεκρῶν (*Od.* 11.632). The plural *populi* is used thematically with reference to death in this play, emphasizing the great numbers involved: v. 191 comm.

557 uno tot. For such play on numbers cf. 487 comm.

559 non revocabiles. Perhaps suggested, in a context of mortality, by ps.-Ov. *Cons. Liv.* 427f. *non est revocabilis istis* (sc. *lacrimis*), / *quem semel umbrifera navita lintre tulit*; or, if that is post-Senecan, by Prop. 4.7.51 *Fatorum . . . nulli revolubile carmen.* (The only certainly pre-Senecan use of *revocabilis* is Ov. *Met.* 6.264 *revocabile telum / non fuit.*)

560–65. There are two somewhat separate traditions concerning Hercules' attack on Pylos. One concentrates on his human adversaries, and reports that he killed all the sons of Neleus except Nestor (Hom. *Il.* 11.690ff., Apollod. 1.9.9, Ov. *Met* 12.549ff., Paus. 2.18.7, Hyg. *Fab.* 10). The other tradition is more interested in the gods he fought: Apollod. 2.7.3 and Paus. 6.25.2 report that Hades, fighting on the Pylian side, was wounded by him; Hom. *Il.* 5.392ff. mentions both Hades and Hera, but it is not clear whether the latter was wounded at

Pylos (cf. Preller-Robert 2.537 n. 2); Pind. *Ol.* 9.30ff. says that Hercules fought Poseidon who was defending Pylos, and that Apollo and Hades were also on the Pylian side; ps.-Hes. *Aspis* 359ff. mentions only Ares. Seneca's reference to a *tenue vulnus* is somewhat at variance with Homer's account, cf. 399f. κῆρ ἀχέων, ὀδύνῃσι πεπαρμένος· αὐτὰρ ὀϊστός / ὤμῳ ἔνι στιβαρῷ ἠλήλατο, κῆδε δὲ θυμόν. The point of the allusion is that having defeated Pluto once, H. can do so again; but it is characteristic of Sen.'s paratactic style that there is no *ut quondam* vel sim., no explicit indication of the relationship.

560 hic qui. This line-opening occurs again in choral odes at *Pha.* 1143 and *Thy.* 844, 848, 852. Here *hic* must be an adverb (cf. *illic* in the corresponding line 542), referring back to *Stygis* and modifying *imperat*.

populis pluribus. See 556f. comm.

562 pestiferas manus. Compare Ov. *Met.* 4.496 *pestiferaque manu*, of Tisiphone. The adjective appears first in V. *Aen.* 7.570, of an entrance to the underworld. Ovid with seven instances and Sen. with four are the only poets who make much use of the word.

563 telum tergemina cuspide. Cf. Ov. *Met.* 1.330 *tricuspide telo*, 12.594f. *faxo, triplici quid cuspide possim, / sentiat*, both of Neptune's trident. So Sen. envisages Pluto as wielding a trident:[87] but why? Admittedly the use of the trident is sometimes extended from Neptune to other divinities, e.g. Triton (cf. Accius *trag.* 400 R², Roscher 5.1179 [b]), but these are normally sea gods.[88] Harder 451 supposed a confusion between the trident and the *bidens* of Pluto, but the authenticity of the two-pronged fork as an attribute of Pluto is in doubt (cf. Cook *Zeus* 2.798ff.). Another possibility is that Pluto traditionally wielded a staff in this battle (cf. Pind. *Ol.* 9.32ff. οὐδ' Ἀΐδας ἀκινήταν ἔχε ῥάβδον), and that Sen. or a predecessor substituted the trident as a more formidable weapon. (There could have been a visual source of confusion, as

---

87. Attempts to explain the *telum tergemina cuspide* as some other weapon fail to take into account the antecedents of the phrase. H. Blümner, *Hermes* 54 (1919) 328f., interpreted it as a triangular-headed spear such as Hades holds on a vase from Orvieto (illustrated in Roscher 1.1807f.). C. Robert, *Hermes* 53 (1918) 446, transposed lines 562 and 563, thus referring *praeferens* to Hercules, and regarded the *telum* as an ὀϊστὸς τριγλώχις such as that with which the hero wounded Hera (*Il.* 5.392ff.). This suggestion is open to further objections: neither Robert nor *TLL* provides a parallel for *cuspis* of an arrowhead, and *telum ... praeferens* would be a pretentious phrase for an arrow.

88. Aeolus is given a trident at Quint. Smyrn. 14.481, however.

tridents and sceptres are often represented with similar lotus-shaped heads, v. Cook *Zeus* 2.786ff.) For the trident as a battle-weapon cf. e.g. Eur. *Ion* 281ff. and the illustrations in Roscher 3.2.2861ff., not to mention its use in gladiatorial combats.

There is a similar line in the same meter at *Pha.* 755 *tigres pampinea cuspide territans.*

565. The paradox is entirely in Sen.'s manner, but one thinks also of the ironical comment in Homer on Hades' speedy recovery: οὐ μὲν γάρ τι καταθνητός γε τέτυκτο (*Il.* 5.402).

pertimuit. The verb occurs only here in Sen. Trag. and ps.-Sen.; it is very rare in poetry generally before Sen., except in comedy and in Ovid.

566 fatum rumpe manu. Reminiscent of V. *Aen.* 6.882 *si qua fata aspera rumpas*, which may be seen as a compressed version of such phrases as Livy 1.42.2 *rupit fati necessitatem,* Lucr. 2.254 *fati foedera rumpat*. But Sen.'s addition of *manu* gives the phrase a more physical sense, as if it were a condensed version of *fati claustra rumpere* (cf. *Oed.* 160 *rupere Erebi claustra, HF* 57 *rupto carcere umbrarum*): in this respect it is similar to Hor. *Carm.* 1.24.17 *fata recludere* (cf. N-H ad loc.). In addition the unqualified use of *fatum* suggests that Hercules could completely cancel the power of death, not only for himself but for others: the latter idea is expanded in what follows in 566-68.

tristibus inferis. *Tristis* is often used of the underworld and its inhabitants, e.g. V. *Aen.* 4.243 *Tartara tristia,* 5.734 *tristes umbrae* (cf. the similar use of *maestus*, 187 comm.). It also often has the connotation of "gloomy," i.e. lacking in light, cf. *Aen.* 6.534 *tristes sine sole domos,* Ov. *Met.* 2.761ff., Sen. *HF* 620, *Oed.* 545f. That connotation is clearly present here: by letting in the light, H. would relieve the gloom of the netherworld.

The A reading *tristis et inferis* refers to the fear the dead feel for the light (cf. 292f. comm.), but such a reference would be inappropriate here, where H. is presented as a potential savior of the dead, offering them light and the possibility of return (contrast 291ff., where he is envisaged as driving them out willy-nilly). Furthermore, the repeated *et* . . . *et* in 566f. would be awkward.

567f. invius . . . vias. This consequence of Hercules' breaking out of the underworld, i.e. the release of the dead, is envisaged also at 55 and

Commentary: Ode II

291ff., and belongs to the concept of H. as *victor mortis* which underlies several passages of the play (see Introduction).

For the paradox and wordplay of *invius limes det . . . vias* cf. V. *Aen.* 3.383 [*Italiam*] *longa procul longis via dividit invia terris*, Ov. *Met.* 14.113 *invia virtuti nulla est via.*

568 faciles. Return will be as easy as descent has always been: the adjective in this context is suggested by V. *Aen.* 6.126ff. *facilis descensus Averno: / . . . sed revocare gradum superasque evadere ad auras, / hoc opus, hic labor est.* That passage is echoed again at 675, 678f.

569–89. This account of Orpheus' catabasis is inspired by the narratives of Vergil (*Georg.* 4.467–503) and Ovid (*Met.* 10.11–63), and their influence may be seen in many details of the passage. A particularly Senecan touch is the speech of Pluto, which breaks up the third-person narrative (though its content is thoroughly traditional): compare the frequent use of apostrophe in the odes for variation and lively effect (186f. comm).

As Ovid himself owed much to Vergil's lines, it is sometimes impossible to say which of them suggested a particular detail or phrase in Sen. Thus in the opening lines *umbrarum dominos* (i.e. Pluto and Proserpina, cf. 805 comm.) comes from Ovid (15f. *inamoenaque regna tenentem / umbrarum dominum*) and *immites* from Vergil (492 *immitis . . . tyranni*), but the phrase *Eurydicen . . . suam* is used both by Vergil and Ovid (lines 490 and 66, respectively). See comm. 583–87, 587, 589.

In typically paratactic style, this narrative begins with no explanation of its relevance, like that of the wounding of Pluto: *potuit* in an emphatic position in 569 implies *tu quoque potes*, but Sen. does not make the parallel explicit until the end of the ode.

Boethius' lyric on Orpheus' descent to the underworld (*Cons. Phil.* 3.12^{bis}), based on the present passage and on *HO* 1031–99, makes an interesting comparison with the present lines. He follows Sen. in giving Pluto a speech, and the influence of *HF* is most evident in that passage (ll.40–51):

```
40  Tandem "vincimur" arbiter           fas sit lumina flectere."
    umbrarum miserans ait,              Quis legem dat amantibus?
    "donamus comitem viro               maior lex amor est sibi.
    emptam carmine coniugem.            heu, noctis prope terminos
    sed lex dona coerceat,          50  Orpheus Eurydicen suam
45  ne, dum Tartara liquerit,           vidit, perdidit, occidit.
```

Commentary: Ode II

571 repetit. So E. The A reading *recipit* might be defended as conative (cf. in a *dum* clause Plaut. *Capt.* 234 [*homines*] *quod sibi volunt, dum id impetrant, boni sunt*), but it seems more likely to have been written in error for *repetit*, as at *HO* 1751 *repetit* MN *recte* (*repedit* E), *recipit* A.

572–74. Lists of the creatures and natural objects charmed by Orpheus' music are found as early as Simonides 567: cf. Hor. *Carm.* 1.12.7ff. *vocalem temere insecutae / Orphea silvae / arte materna rapidas morantem / fluminum lapsus celerisque ventos,* and the passages cited by N-H ad loc., particularly Hor. *Carm.* 3.11.13f. *tu potes tigris comitesque silvas / ducere et rivos celeris morari,* Ov. *Met.* 11.1f. *carmine dum tali silvas animosque ferarum / Threicius vates et saxa sequentia ducit,* Sen. *Med.* 626ff. *cuius ad chordas . . . / restitit torrens, siluere venti, / cum suo cantu volucris relicto / adfuit tota comitante silva.*

saxaque traxerat. For the alliterative phrase cf. *Oed.* 612 *qui saxa dulci traxit Amphion sono.*

573. The use of the word *ars* in connection with the delaying of rivers perhaps comes from Hor. *Carm.* 1.12.9f., quoted on 572–74, but the similarity is not remarkable. For Orpheus' ability to halt rivers cf. also Ap. Rhod. 1.26f. πέτρας / θέλξαι ἀοιδάων ἐνοπῇ ποταμῶν τε ῥέεθρα, N-H on Hor. *Carm.* 1.12.9.

praebuerat fluminibus moras. Another example of Senecan "noun-style," the central idea being conveyed by *moras* whereas Horace in the passages quoted on 572–74 uses verbs *morantem, morari*; v. comm. on 407–10. For *mora* used periphrastically cf. e.g. 1171 *nulla pugnandi mora est* for "I am ready to fight"; more elaborate examples include *Phoen.* 246 *uterique nondum solveram clausi moras* for "I had not yet been born," and *Tro.* 939 *abrumpere ense lucis invisae moras* of suicide. On Sen.'s liking for *mora* v. Leo I 154f.

576 surdis . . . in locis. The combination of the vague *loca* with an adjective creates an evocative phrase for the underworld, cf. 673 *vacuis . . . locis,* 707 *opaca . . . loca,* 794 *loca muta,* 1221, Enn. *trag.* 71f. R^2 (cf. Jocelyn 255f.) *nubila tenebris loca,* V. *Aen.* 6.462 *loca senta situ,* Ov. *Met.* 4.436, 10.29, 14.125. The underworld is "unhearing" because its denizens cannot normally be moved; perhaps also because there are usually no sounds to be heard (cf. comm. on 620 *silentem domum,* and for *surdus* in such a sense cf. Stat. *Silv.* 5.3.16f. *post Orpheu raptum / . . . iam surda ferarum / agmina*).

[269]

577 deflent Eumenides Threiciam nurum. This is the convincing conjecture of Schmidt (1865 16f.) for codd. *deflent Eurydicen Threiciae nurus* (vel sim.; v. app. crit.). In the transmitted text it is hard to believe that *Threiciae nurus* without qualification could mean what it would have to mean, i.e. "the shades of Thracian women."[89] More important, it would be no great testimony to the power of Orpheus' music that his wife's fate should be mourned by her own compatriots. One might add that in the context of the Orpheus story, Thracian women are better known for having finally torn the singer to pieces. The general idea of the paradosis may be paralleled from an epigram of Antipater of Sidon on the death of Aretemias, a young mother from Dorian Cnidos (*Anth. Pal.* 7.464): ἦ πού σε χθονίας, Ἀρετημιάς, ἐξ ἀκάτοιο / Κωκυτοῦ θεμέναν ἴχνος ἐπ' ἀϊόνι, / . . . ᾤκτειραν θαλεραὶ Δωρίδες εἰν Ἀΐδᾳ / πευθόμεναι τέο κῆρα. The parallel is admittedly a striking one, but it does not dispel the objections indicated above; in connection with the first objection, note that Sen. has no equivalent to Antipater's εἰν Ἀΐδᾳ.

Strongly in favor of Schmidt's conjecture, on the other hand, is the parallel with Ovid's account, *Met.* 10.45f. *tum primum lacrimis victarum carmine fama est / Eumenidum maduisse genas*; cf. also V. *Georg.* 4.481f. *stupuere . . . / Tartara caeruleosque implexae crinibus angues / Eumenides,* Stat. *Theb.* 8.58f. *blanda inter carmina turpes / Eumenidum lacrimas.* Schmidt's correction has the additional advantage of avoiding an unskillful triple repetition of *Eurydicen.* As to the source of the error, *Eurydicen* could easily have been substituted inadvertently for *Eumenides,* from 571 or 581 or from a marginal gloss on *Threiciam nurum*: the latter phrase would then tend to be altered to nominative plural to provide a subject for *deflent.* Attempts to alter *Threiciae* alone have met with little success: the best of them, Withof's *Tartareae nurus,* is unexceptionable, but again it does not provide a remarkable instance of Orpheus' powers.

578–81. Variations on the theme of 577. There is a precedent for Pluto's tears at Manil. 5.328 (Orpheus) *silvis addidit aures / et Diti lacrimas,* but none for those of the judges of the dead; other poets illustrate the power of Orpheus' music by its effect on the famous sinners such as Ixion, cf. Hor. *Carm.* 3.11.21ff., Ov. *Met.* 10.41ff., ps.-Sen. *HO* 1068ff.

---

89. Giardina and Viansino follow Richter in citing 149 *Thracia paelex, HO* 953 *Threicia coniunx,* and apparently regarding this as a defense of the paradosis. But what relevance Procne and Philomela could have here is obscure. They became birds, not shades; nor are they obvious types of imperviousness to sorrow, in that at least one of them mourns for Itys.

Commentary: Ode II

578. The line refers primarily to Pluto and Proserpina, the objects of Orpheus' address in Ov. *Met.* 10.15f., 46f.: but it perhaps also carries a more general connotation, cf. 611 *tristes deos* and the common phrase *di inferi*; also the generality of *corda* in V. *Georg.* 4.469f. *manesque adiit regemque tremendum / nesciaque humanis precibus mansuescere corda*.

lacrimis difficiles. "Unyielding to tears." The phrase refers to the implacability of such gods, but in the context it must also carry the sense that they themselves are not easily moved to tears. For the second sense cf. Hor. *Carm.* 2.14.6f. *illacrimabilem / Plutona*. The first sense is the more natural with *difficilis*, cf. Ov. *Pont.* 2.2.20 *difficilem precibus*, *Fasti* 1.146 *difficilem mihi*; for the traditional inexorability of the gods of the underworld cf. Hom. *Il.* 9.158 'Ἀΐδης τοι ἀμείλιχος ἠδ' ἀδάμαστος, V. *Georg.* 4.470 cited above, Hor. *Carm.* 2.3.24 *nil miserantis Orci*.

579–81. On Minos, Rhadamanthus, and Aeacus, the judges of the dead, v. 731–34 with comm.

579 fronte nimis... tetrica. Compare the description of Pluto sitting in judgment at 722ff. *dira maiestas deo, / frons torva* e.q.s. *Nimis* has the sense of "very, extremely," with no connotation of excess, which would have little point here: cf. Cic. *Leg.* 1.27 *oculi nimis arguti*, Ov. *Pont.* 1.5.60 *nimis intenti... laboris*.

580 veteres... reos. That is, *reos veteris criminis*, an unusual but not unnatural usage. For the thought, cf. V. *Aen.* 6.739f. *ergo exercentur poenis veterumque malorum / supplicia expendunt*.

581 iuridici. Something of a neologism, as this is the first extant use of the word in a general sense (here "judges"), though there are Tiberian and Neronian examples from inscriptions of its use as a magistrate's title, cf. *TLL* s.v., *RE* 10.1154. Seneca uses it here to echo the sound of *Eurydicen*.

583–87. The Vergilian and Ovidian passages lie close behind these lines, cf. *Georg.* 4.485ff. *iamque pedem referens casus evaserat omnes, / redditaque Eurydice superas veniebat ad auras / pone sequens: namque hanc dederat Proserpina legem* and *Met.* 10.50ff. *hanc simul et legem Rhodopeius accipit Orpheus, / ne flectat retro sua lumina, donec Avernas / exierit valles*. The words *evade* and *lege... data* come from Vergil (though Ovid too uses *lex*); the condition that Eurydice must follow behind comes from Vergil (though implicit in Ovid); the condition that Orpheus must not look back comes from Ovid (though implicit in Vergil). Seneca's statement of *both* conditions is typical of the "theme and variation" style of this ode.

584f. For distributive anaphora of *tu* in asyndeton cf. *tibi* . . . *tibi* in 299f. and 1231.

585 non. Sometimes used in place of *ne* when a particular part of the wish or command is emphasized. So here the prohibition is not against looking back ever, but against doing so prematurely; cf. Livy 9.34.15 *non die, non hora citius quam necesse est magistratu abieris*, i.e. "do not leave office a moment sooner than necessary," and Sen. *HF* 936f. with comm. *Non* frequently replaces *ne* with no such distinction, however, particularly in the poets: v. K-S 191f.

586. Objections have been raised to the use of *deos* by metonymy for "the upper world," but it is precisely paralleled by *numina* in 505, and further supported by the similar examples of metonymy cited in the comm. there. No doubt Sen. chose this phrasing in part for the sake of the wordplay *deos* . . . *dies*, in view of the frequency of such effects in this ode (cf. introductory note). The naturalness of the metonymy is illustrated by the fact that Hercules addresses the gods as soon as he regains the upper world (592ff.). The only difficulty of the line lies in the pleonasm *ante* . . . *quam cum*, for which there appears to be no parallel earlier than *Carm. adv. Marc.* (fourth cent.?) 5.189 *ante diem quam cum pateretur*; examples of a rather different type of pleonasm associated with *ante/prius quam* palliate the difficulty, but do not remove it (V. *Aen.* 4.24–27 *prius* . . . *ante* . . . *quam*, Prop. 2.25.25 *prius* . . . *quam* . . . *ante*, Sen. *Ag.* 898f. *prius* . . . *antequam*, where *prius* is defended by Zwierlein 1978 156).

If conjecture is thought necessary, much the best solution is Zwierlein's *quam clarus radios obtulerit dies* (1978 144);[90] use of an abbreviation *clar' radios* might well have led to haplography of *r* and incorrect word division, with *dios* then being "corrected" to *deos* and *cum* being added to fill out the line. The conjunction of *dies* and *radios* in this context is supported by Ov. *Met.* 7.411f., where Cerberus is described, as he enters the upper world, as *restantem contraque diem radiosque micantes / obliquantem oculos*, a passage in Sen.'s mind when he wrote *HF* (comm. on 808 and 813–27). I am inclined, like Zwierlein, to tolerate the grammatical anomaly of *ante* . . . *quam cum* and to retain the paradosis.

---

90. Bentley had conjectured *quam cum sol radios obtulerit suos* or *q. c. iam radios o. dies*, neither of which removes the real difficulty, viz. the offending *cum*.

Commentary: Ode II

clara ... dies. When the gender can be determined, *dies* is always masculine in Sen. Trag. outside the nominative singular, and usually in that case also; the few instances of nominative singular feminine (cf. *HF* 875 *laeta dies*, and four examples of *nulla dies* in other plays) reflect the metrical convenience of a final short syllable on the accompanying adjective, rather than any distinction of meaning in *dies* itself. The same is true of Vergil's usage (v. Austin on *Aen.* 4.169).[91]

587. It appears that Taenarum was first associated with Hercules' descent to fetch Cerberus, and was later regarded as a standard place of entrance to or exit from the underworld; v. 662-67 comm. Both Vergil and Ovid mention Taenarum as the place of Orpheus' descent, and both have the metaphor of the door: *Georg.* 4.467f. *Taenarias etiam fauces, alta ostia Ditis, / ... ingressus*, *Met.* 10.13 *Taenaria est ausus descendere porta.*

588 nec patitur moras. Seneca has several examples of *pati moras*, particularly in the negative, cf. 773, *Pha.* 583, *Oed.* 99, *Ag.* 131, *Thy.* 158, 769, also *HF* 1311 *non feram ulterius moram.* Such phrases appear to be Ovidian, cf. *pati* at *Met.* 4.350 and *Fasti* 2.722, *ferre* at *Met.* 10.497 and 11.307.

589. Orpheus' eagerness to see Eurydice probably comes from Ovid, *Met.* 10. 56f. *avidusque videndi / flexit amans oculos*, though it is implicit in Vergil.

590f. The parallelism of these lines makes an appropriate close to an ode full of parallelism. Other examples may be found in the tragedies, e.g. in an ode *Thy.* 613f. *quem dies vidit veniens superbum, / hunc dies vidit fugiens iacentem*, in an episode *Tro.* 510ff. *fata si miseros iuvant / habes salutem; fata si vitam negant, / habes sepulcrum*; similar parallelism appears in the prose, e.g. *Ep.* 10.5 *sic vive cum hominibus tamquam deus videat; sic loquere cum deo, tamquam homines audiant* (cf. A. Gercke, *Seneca-Studien* [Leipzig 1896] 155ff.). In verse the mannerism is Hellenistic in origin, e.g. Theoc. 11.22f. φοιτῆς δ' αὖθ' οὕτως ὅκκα γλυκὺς ὕπνος ἔχῃ με, / οἴχῃ δ' εὐθὺς ἰοῖσ' ὅκκα γλυκὺς ὕπνος ἀνῇ με (though in Greek tragedy one speaker sometimes echoes another for rhetorical effect, cf. 463f. with comm.). Seneca's immediate model, however, is Ovid, e.g. *Met.* 1.325f. *et superesse virum de tot modo milibus unum / et superesse videt de tot*

---

91. Zwierlein's suggestion that *dies* = "daylight" is regularly masculine in Sen. Trag. is wrongheaded, and in any case disproved by *Oed.* 689.

[273]

Commentary: Act III

modo milibus unam (v. Bömer ad loc. and on 3.98), 481f. *saepe pater dixit, "generum mihi, filia, debes"; / saepe pater dixit, "debes mihi, nata, nepotes."*

carmine. So E: A has *cantibus*, which seems the more likely of the two to be intrusive, in view of *viribus* in the following line and *cantibus* in 569. Boethius has *carmine* in his imitation of this passage, 42f. *donamus comitem viro / emptam carmine coniugem.*

Act III (592–829)

Act III falls into two unequal parts: a short scene in which Hercules appears, is greeted by his family, learns of the situation in Thebes, and prepares to kill Lycus; and a lengthy description by Theseus of the underworld and Hercules' catabasis. The first corresponds, in the most general sense and in summary fashion, to the bulk of the third episode in Euripides (514–636). There is no need to assume that Seneca is using Euripides directly, but a comparison of the two playwrights' handling of events is nevertheless instructive for their conception of the hero, particularly as concerns his relationship with his family: see Introduction.

The methods by which Hercules deals with Lycus are also instructive. In Seneca he relies simply on his superhuman strength, and there is no doubt about the outcome. But in Euripides he has no such overwhelming superiority: Lycus and his followers represent a real danger, and H. has to use caution and concealment in order to ensure victory. As a result we have the scene in which Amphitryon tricks Lycus into entering the house (701–33); here the focus is on Lycus' hubris, which provides a strong feeling of justification for his killing. In Seneca, while the justification of his death cannot be doubted, the focus is rather on H.'s overwhelming strength, and on the relish which he takes in the task, reflected in language which verges on the brutal (634, 636, 639f., cf. 920–24).

It is noteworthy that Hercules' interlocutor in Seneca is Amphitryon (618ff., 629), whereas the roughly corresponding speeches in Euripides are Megara's (516ff., 539ff.).[92] This is in keeping with the increased

---

92. Zwierlein 1966 48 attempts to explain Megara's silence in Act III by the three-speaker rule (Hor. *Ars P.* 192 *nec quarta loqui persona laboret*): "Seneca sacrifices dramatic reality (*Wahrheit*) in order to introduce Theseus as third speaker with his description of the underworld." But elsewhere Sen. circumvents the three-speaker rule, when he wishes to introduce another speaking character, by eliminating a previous speaker (usually by removing him from the stage); there is a good example in

Commentary: Act III

importance of Amphitryon in Seneca, and with the thematic contrast between his humanity and Hercules' inhuman obsession with action; we have on the one side Amphitryon's loving greeting, and on the other side Hercules' failure to respond except with "postpone your embraces."

The rest of the Act is occupied by Theseus' lengthy narrative (see comm. on 662–827). Sen. Trag. contains several narratives or scenes developed largely as independent set-pieces which have little or no importance for the advancement of the plot. The examples that involve narrative only are, apart from the present instance, the necromancy of *Oedipus* (530–658) and the storm-description of *Agamemnon* (421–578). The other two examples are not purely narrative: the sacrifice and extispicy of *Oedipus* (299–383) occurs onstage, but is fully described by Manto; the conjuration scene of *Medea* includes both narrative and action. There is little or no precedent for these elements in the *exemplaria Graeca*. In Eur. *Her.*, for example, questions and answers about the catabasis and the fetching of Cerberus are limited to 10 lines (610–19), whereas in Seneca they occupy almost 200. Conversely these scenes in Seneca displace, or at least overshadow, scenes of more traditional dramaturgy: in Eur. *Her.* the entrapment of Lycus, in Eur. *Med.* the meeting of Medea with Aegeus and her second meeting with Jason (663–758, 866ff.), in Soph. *OT* the quarrel of Oedipus with Tiresias (316–462) and with Creon (513ff.). Though such set-pieces are characteristic of Senecan drama, it is unwise to assume that the technique originated with Seneca. The tendency to develop ecphrastic elements at the expense of traditional plot development is found in Hellenistic literature, and may well have been seen in Greek tragedy of that period.

Undeniably such scenes have a considerable degree of independence from the body of the play, and offer an opportunity for display of rhetorical-poetic technique and in particular for δείνωσις, that is, treatment of the gruesome or horrific. It would be a mistake to underestimate their relevance to the rest of the play, though naturally this differs both in degree and in type from play to play. In *Medea*, for instance, the conjuration scene illuminates the identity of "Colchian witch" to which Medea reverts when her identity as "wife of Jason" is

---

the last Act of *Ag.*, during the course of which five characters speak. He could therefore have begun the present Act, if he had so wished, with Megara, Amphitryon, and Hercules as speakers, and then introduced Theseus as a speaker after H.'s exit at 640. So the use of Amphitryon in place of Megara was a matter of choice, not necessity. This is confirmed by Act IV, where Megara is in fact the third speaker but says not a word before her final appeals, whereas Amphitryon has much to say.

denied her. It is also the culmination of various indications earlier in the play that her powers are cosmic (v. Fitch 1974 133–48). In *HF* Theseus' narrative has important connections with the rest of the play in terms of both theme and characterization. The characterization is that of Hercules: in the underworld, as in the world above, he relies on his own strength to a degree which makes him appear brutal and hubristic (see comm. 762–827). The theme is that of death, the world of death and its ability to absorb the countless throngs of the dead. Both in Theseus' long narrative and in a lengthy section of the following ode (834ff.) our attention and imagination are focused on that world and its power. H.'s claim of triumph over it therefore seems somewhat hollow, and that impression is confirmed in the events of Act IV.

592–617. This speech begins as a prayer, but is skillfully altered around 603f. into a soliloquy, which reveals Hercules' present frame of mind. Only at the end of the speech does the hero notice the presence of others onstage. Thus the second half of the speech is in effect an entrance-monologue (v. comm. 332–57), but it is given dramatic color by the preceding prayer.[93] Comparison with the corresponding speech in Euripides' play (523ff.) reveals the difference in dramatic technique between the two writers, as there is no element of soliloquy in Eur.: H. notices the stage situation after only two lines of joyful address to his home.

592–95. Hercules' emphasis on the light of the sun not only expresses his own relief at returning from the underworld, but also forms a powerful contrast to the Chorus' preoccupation with the gloom of other worlds (cf. the dark/light contrast between Act I and Ode I).

A god may be invoked by name, or by reference to his or her attributes, as in 597f. and 599 (cf. 205 comm.), or by a combination of the two methods, as here; for this third type of invocation cf. 900–2, 1057–60.

592. For the rhythm and wording cf. the opening prayer of Act II, *o magne Olympi rector et mundi arbiter*. To begin an invocation or address with a single line devoted to the name and titles of the addressee is a natural pattern from Homer on, e.g. *Il.* 8.31 ὦ πάτερ ἡμέτερε Κρονίδη, ὕπατε κρειόντων, 9.308 διογενὲς Λαερτιάδη, πολυμήχαν' Ὀδυσσεῦ, V.

---

93. In a similar way Amphitryon's long monologue at the beginning of Act II is given some dramatic plausibility by opening as a prayer.

Commentary: Act III

Aen. 12.142 *nympha, decus fluviorum, animo gratissima nostro*, 5.45 *Dardanidae magni, genus alto a sanguine divum*.

caeli decus. The phrase occurs at V. *Aen.* 9.18 of Iris and at Hor. *Carm. Saec.* 2 of Diana, but in view of the frequency with which *decus* is used of people and gods (*TLL* 5.1.243.6ff., cf. N-H on Hor. *Carm.* 1.32.13) there is no need to assume influence from one of those passages. Elsewhere Sen. uses *mundi decus* of Bacchus, *Oed.* 405.

593 alterna . . . spatia. That is, the two hemispheres. The conception of these was by no means fixed in antiquity, least of all in poetry, but for the notion that the sun shines on another half of the world when it drops below the horizon cf. V. *Georg.* 1.250f. *nosque ubi primus equis Oriens adflavit anhelis, / illic sera rubens accendit lumina Vesper*, Manil. 1.242f. *hanc ubi ad occasus nostros sol aspicit actus, / illic orta dies sopitas excitat urbes*, Luc. 8.159ff.

curru . . . flammifero. Cf. the Sun's *ignifera . . . iuga, Med.* 34. The immediate source of these descriptions is the Phaethon episode in book 2 of the *Metamorphoses*, cf. 59 *ignifero . . . in axe*, 154 *hinnitibus . . . flammiferis* of the horses. *Flammifer* occurs only once (in Enn. *trag.*, cf. 982-84 comm.) before Ovid takes it up, using it five times: Sen. Trag. then has three uses.

594. The "golden" pattern of the line gives a sense of breadth that matches its content. *Illustre . . . caput* comes from Ov. *Met.* 2.50 *concutiens illustre caput*, also of the Sun. In Sen. it may allude to the Sun's crown of rays, for which cf. ibid. 40f. *genitor circum caput omne micantes / deposuit radios* with Bömer ad loc. But it may refer more generally to the Sun's characteristic brightness: Ovid's phrase at *Met.* 2.50 is of a moment when the Sun has removed his crown. For *exseris . . . caput* cf. comm. on 10 *ac ponto* and *gregem exserunt*.

latis. The A reading *laetis* would have a proleptic sense, i.e. the earth is gladdened by the sun.[94] The closest parallel known to me is Ov. *Fasti* 6.253f. (of an apparition of Vesta) *caelestia numina sensi, / laetaque purpurea luce refulsit humus*. More generally cf. Theogn. 8f. (at the birth of Apollo) πᾶσα μὲν ἐπλήσθη Δῆλος ἀπειρεσίη / ὀδμῆς ἀμβροσίης, ἐγέλασσε δὲ Γαῖα πελώρη. (*HO* 1529 *pallidus maestas speculare terras* may

---

94. *Laetus* can be applied to fields, etc., in the sense of "in good heart, fertile," cf. 698 *prata . . laeta*, but that meaning would not be appropriate to *terris*.

parallel the proleptic use of the adjective, but there it seems possible that the earth is already sad.) *Latis* seems the more likely reading given the context, cf. Ov. *Met.* 9.795 *postera lux radiis latum patefecerat orbem*, 2.307 [*Iuppiter*] *solet nubes latis inducere terris*.

595–604. For reluctance to let the Sun see evil sights cf. Soph. *OT* 1425ff., Eur. *Her.* 1231. Juno in her version of Hercules' return has already spoken of Cerberus striking fear into the Sun, cf. 60f. with comm. Other gods of the upper world are also vulnerable to pollution, particularly through contact with death, cf. Soph. *Ant.* 1016–22, Eur. *Hipp.* 1437f. (Artemis) ἐμοὶ γὰρ οὐ θέμις φθιτοὺς ὁρᾶν, / οὐδ' ὄμμα χραίνειν θανασίμοισιν ἐκπνοαῖς with Barrett ad loc., *Alc.* 22.

In this passage Hercules speaks of Cerberus as present with him, but hereafter we hear no more of the hound until 1106f., where he is back in the underworld. In production it would be easy to solve the stage problem, by having Cerberus exit with H. at 640 and not return. But the long silence about the hound's movements, and the lack of explanation in the later reference, suggests that in fact after this speech Sen. quite forgot about the creature, until he saw the opportunity of making a rhetorical point with him at 1106f. In Eur. Cerberus does not appear onstage, and the dramatist carefully has H. explain that he has left him in a grove of Demeter (614f.).

596 vultus. "Eyes, gaze," cf. comm. 640f.

597 arcana. So E; *secreta* A. In such a case, where there seems to have been a deliberate change in one of the traditions, A is the more probable culprit. *Arcana* also receives support from Luc. 5.198 *arcanaque mundi*, 6.514 *arcanaque Ditis operti*, which may well be echoes of the present phrase.

597f. caelestum arbiter parensque. For "father and lord" as a description of Jupiter cf. 516f. *caelestium / rector parensque* with comm. *Arbiter* is a verbal variation on the more usual *rex/rector*, but without discernible difference in meaning.

599 secundo . . . sceptro. A reference to the casting of lots for the three divisions of the universe (cf. 53 comm.). The assumption that Neptune drew the second lot and Pluto the third (cf. [Tib.] 3.5.22) appears several times in Ovid: of Neptune *Met.* 4.532f., 8.595f. *o proxima mundi / regna vagae . . . sortite tridentifer undae*; of Pluto *Met.* 5.368 *cui triplicis cessit fortuna novissima regni*, 14.111, *Fasti* 4.584. (Elsewhere such

Commentary: Act III

phrases refer only to the triple division, with no indication of order: thus Hom. *Il.* 15.195 τριτάτη μοίρα, Ov. *Am.* 3.8.50 *tertia regna*, both of heaven.) In Sen. cf. *Med.* 598 *regna secunda*, *Pha.* 904 *et qui secundum fluctibus regnum moves* (a similar line to the present one), and *tertia sors* at *HF* 609, 833.

600–603. Just as it was customary, after listing a god's names, to add a precautionary phrase in case any had been forgotten (cf. Cat. 34.21f. with Fordyce ad loc.), so it was usual to add a catch-all phrase to a list of gods in order to avoid omitting any relevant deity: cf. Cic. *Rab. Perd.* 5, Livy 1.32.10 *audi Iuppiter et tu Iane Quirine, dique omnes caelestes vosque, terrestres, vosque, inferni, audite*, V. *Georg.* 1.21ff. with Serv. ad loc., *post specialem transit ad generalem invocationem, ne quod numen praetereat*, Sen. *HF* 900–8.

facie. Of a fearful form, as e.g. V. *Aen.* 7.447f. *tot Erinys sibilat hydris / tantaque se facies aperit*, 8.194, 298 *nec te ullae facies, non terruit ipse Typhoeus*, Sen. *Pha.* 1046f. *ultima in monstrum coit / facies*.

601 pollui metuens. The infinitive in place of *ne* plus subjunctive is unusual but not unparalleled, cf. *TLL* 8.903.65ff.

603 nefas. That is, Cerberus. The word is very unusual of an object, whether animate or inanimate, but cf. V. *Aen.* 2.585 (of Helen), Corn. Sev. ap. Sen. Rhet. *Suas.* 6.26 (of Cethegus and Catiline, if Gronovius' generally accepted conjecture *nefas extinctum et* is right for codd. *nefas est tunc*).

604ff. Hercules' reference in 604 to Juno's commands triggers his subsequent reflections that he is capable of dealing with any challenge which Juno imposes. For similar thought processes in monologue cf. introduction to Act I.

604 poenas. "Sufferings, hardships" (not "punishment," for Juno is persecuting H., not punishing him). Seneca several times uses the word in this sense, e.g. *Tro.* 300 *patri, quem coli poena iubes* (i.e. by Polyxena's death), *Pha.* 399, *Ep.* 5.5 *frugalitatem exigit philosophia, non poenam*.

605 non satis terrae patent. With unconscious irony Hercules refers to Juno's difficulty in finding new challenges for him in the same phrase which she used to illustrate his overreaching, cf. 46 *nec satis terrae patent* with comm.

[279]

606f. The double elision of *vidi inaccessa omnibus* and the heaviness of the adjective combine to suggest the effort involved in this task. *Inaccessus* is rare (only here in Sen. Trag.). The point that the sun does not penetrate to the underworld is standard (e.g. Eur. *Her.* 607f. ἐξ ἀνηλίων μυχῶν / Ἄιδου), but for *ignota Phoebo* cf. particularly Ov. *Met.* 2.45f. (Phoebus to Phaethon) *promissis testis adesto / dis iuranda palus, oculis incognita nostris.* Sen. likes to use periphrases with *polus* for the underworld, cf. 1104f. *atri / regina poli*, *Pha.* 836 *umbrantem polum*, *Ag.* 756 *nigrantis poli* (*HO* 773 *peiorem polum* imitates *deterior polus* here, cf. also 938 *nigrantis poli*); it is evident that in these passages *polus* means "world" rather than "pole" or "sky."

608 diro . . . Iovi. For such periphrases for Dis cf. 47 *inferni Iovis* with comm. *Dirus* is used of Dis again at 722 *dira maiestas deo*; Sen. often uses it of the underworld, etc., thus 56 *Mortis*, 771 *Charon*, 1221 *Furiarum loca* (with comm.), cf. *TLL* 5.1.1270.31ff. The adjective is popular with the post-Ovidians (ibid. 1268.61f.).

609 tertiae sortis. See comm. 599 *secundo . . . sceptro.*

610 noctis aeternae chaos. Seneca likes to use *chaos* of the underworld; usually it seems to be evocative rather than having a specific meaning, though at 861 it means an oppressive, formless mass, and at *Thy.* 1009 *inane Chaos* it refers to the yawning chasm of the underworld (v. West on Hes. *Theog.* 116). *Noctis aeternae* is a Senecan formula used always in this position in the line and always in reference to the underworld, cf. *Med.* 9 (with *chaos* again), 484, *Pha.* 835, *Oed.* 393 (also *Pha.* 221 *silentem nocte perpetua domum*). Earlier the phrase is used of death, etc., Cat. 5.6 *nox est perpetua una dormienda*, V. *Aen.* 10.746 *in aeternam clauduntur lumina noctem*, 12.310, Ov. *Her.* 10.112.

611 nocte quiddam gravius. Such Senecan phrases work by suggestion rather than statement, cf. 30 *quidquid horridum tellus creat* with comm., *Thy.* 269f. *haud quid sit scio, / sed grande quiddam est.* I take the present phrase to refer to a darkness more impenetrable and oppressive than that of night. In *Ag.* a night of preternatural blackness (472ff.) is called *dirae Stygis / inferna nox* 493f.; cf. also Ap. Rhod. 4.1697f. οὐρανόθεν δὲ μέλαν χάος, ἠέ τις ἄλλη / ὠρώρει σκοτίη μυχάτων ἀνιοῦσα βερέθρων, Luc. 5.627 *non caeli nox illa fuit*. Alternatively the phrase might be taken to refer to some other grim aspect of the underworld, but it would then seem so vague as to lose its effect.

tristes deos. As applied to the gods of the underworld, *tristis* connotes grimness, rather than sadness and gloom as at 566: cf. Varro ap. Macrobius 1.16.18 *deorum tristium atque inferum*, V. *Aen.* 2.337 *tristis Erinys* (= Ov. *Her.* 6.45), 6.315 *navita tristis* (i.e. Charon), [Tib.] 3.3.35 *tristesque Sorores*.

612 et fata vici. For *fata vincere* cf. V. *Aen.* 11.160, Ov. *Met.* 2.617 with Bömer ad loc., Sen. *Cons. Marc.* 6.6.2, and the similar phrase *fata (fatum) rumpere*, 566 comm. Leo here conjectured *vidi* for *vici*, presumably in order to create a rhetorical series with *vidi* in 606 and 613 (cf. 254, 257 comm.). But the sense requires *vici*, as both 610 *regnare potui* and 612 *morte contempta redi* emphasize H.'s superiority to the underworld and its powers. Cf. also 615 *quae vinci iubes?* (In contrast, *vidi* in 606 is concerned with the prior achievement of simply reaching the underworld, and in 613 *vidi* is used for rhetorical balance with *ostendi*.)

morte contempta redi. Hercules has scorned both the power of death, by returning victoriously, and its estate, by rejecting its throne (609f.).

613 ostendi inferos. By smashing his way out, and so making the underworld visible from above; cf. 56 *sacra dirae Mortis in aperto iacent*, and comm. on 47–57. (For the line-end cf. 91 *hic tibi ostendam inferos*.)

613–15. The dramatic irony of these lines is evident. "There can only be one answer to the question *quid restat aliud?*" (Pratt 1939 20); and H.'s confidence that he will be victorious in any struggle imposed by Juno is, we know, ill-founded. There is also a more local irony in the dramatic timing in 615f.: no sooner has H. demanded a challenge than he finds himself facing one. Compare the similar development at 937ff.

614 ultra. H. probably means just "further," but there is a touch of irony here as the word could also mean "greater"; the experience to come will be more terrible than any so far undergone.

615 quae. Preferable on stylistic grounds to A's *quid*, since *quid* has occurred in 613 and 614.

616 miles. For the collective singular cf. Livy 22.37.7 *milite atque equite . . . nisi Romano Latinique nominis non uti populum Romanum*, V. *Aen.* 2.20 *uterumque armato milite complent* with Austin ad loc., K-S 1.67ff.

Commentary: Act III

616f. templa, limenque sacrum. On this shrine v. comm. on 506 *templa*.

617 terror armorum obsidet. For *terror* with a subjective genitive as the subject of a verb cf. Cic. *Tusc.* 2.20 (from Soph. *Trach.*) *nec mihi Iunonis terror implacabilis / nec tantum invexit tristis Eurystheus mali*, Sen. *Ag.* 547 *non me fugavit bellici terror dei*.

618–25. It is a little odd that Amphitryon speaks as if he had had no advance warning of Hercules' approach, despite 520–23. The probable explanation is that Sen. has not fully integrated the present lines, where he follows Eur. closely, with the earlier lines where he diverges from him. See Introduction p. 45, and for another problem caused by selective imitation of Eur. v. comm. 509f.

618–24. Amphitryon's doubts about whether H. is real derive from Megara's similar doubts at the corresponding moment in Eur.: ὅδ' ἐστὶν ὃν γῆς νέρθεν εἰσηκούομεν, / εἰ μή γ' ὄνειρον ἐν φάει τι λεύσσομεν. / τί φημί; ποῖ' ὄνειρα κηραίνουσ' ὁρῶ; (516ff.). For the idea in Sen. (618) that longing can cause hallucinations, cf. V. *Ecl.* 8.108 *credimus? an qui amant ipsi sibi somnia fingunt?* (and more generally *HF* 313f.); Sen. dramatizes an instance of such wish-fulfillment at *Tro.* 683ff.

618f. utrumne ... an. Seneca is unusual among the poets in using *utrum(ne) ... an* in direct questions (seven instances). Other poets who do so are Plautus (thirteen uses), Terence (two) and Martial (five); elsewhere in poetry it occurs only once each in Lucretius (1.971ff.) and Horace (*Epod.* 1.7) (cf. Axelson 90, *TLL* s.v. *an*; my figures are based on the concordances and differ slightly from *TLL*'s). The comparatively high frequency of this construction in the dramatists suggest that it is appropriate to the liveliness of dialogue. The more usual constructions in alternative direct questions in poetry are *-ne ... an* (as in 623) or *an* alone in the second part of the question (the latter much the most common in Ovid and Sen. Trag., though not in other poets).

619. Similar to the "heraldic" type of line, e.g. 592 *o lucis almae rector et mundi decus* (see comm.). *Graium decus* is particularly reminiscent of μέγα κῦδος Ἀχαιῶν in such lines in Homer. (Similarly *Fin.* 5.18.49 *o decus Argolicum* is Cicero's translation of that phrase at *Od.* 12.184.) *Graium* is genitive plural (*pace* Oldfather: this short form occurs six times in Vergil), as is *Argolicum* in Cicero's phrase; a genitive is the usual construction with *decus* of people and gods, cf. *TLL* 5.1.243.6ff.

Commentary: Act III

domitor orbis. The phrase has a Roman ring: Manilius 1.793 uses it of Pompey (cf. Sen. Rhet. *Contr.* 7.2.6), Val. Max. 6.7.1 of the elder Africanus.

620 silentem ... domum. Compare *Pha.* 221 *adît silentem nocte perpetua domum*. The shades of the dead are usually silent, or able only to squeak and gibber (v. Costa on *Med.* 740). Seneca makes much of the underworld's silence in *HF*, cf. 576 *surdis ... in locis*, 713 *tacente ... fluvio* (of the Styx), 794 *loca muta*, 848 *campos ... silentes*, 862f. *silentis ... mundi*.

nubilo. Of the underworld cf. the tragic fragment *nubila tenebris loca* (576 comm.), Ov. *Met.* 4.432, *Fasti* 3.322 *nubila ... Styx*.

domum. *Domus* singular or plural is often used of the underworld, cf. V. *Georg.* 4.481, *Aen.* 5.731, 6.269 *domos Ditis vacuas*, 534 *tristes sine sole domos*, Sen. *HF* 664 *Ditis invisi domus*, *Med.* 741 *opacam Ditis umbrosi domum*, *Pha.* 221, 1241 *aeterna domo*. Such phrases are modeled on the Greek "house of Hades," e.g. Hom. *Il.* 3.322 δόμον Ἄϊδος εἴσω, 22.52 εἰν Ἀΐδαο δόμοισιν, but where, as here, *domus* is not qualified by *Ditis*, it suggests the home of all the dead.

621 membra laetitia stupent. Such physical symptoms are an almost obligatory part of emotional reactions in Sen. Trag. (cf. 414 comm.). Not only is the language somewhat formulaic (cf. *Phoen.* 590 *membra quassantur metu*, *Med.* 926 *membra torpescunt gelu*), but the brevity of such phrases as the present one warrants Shelton's term "rhetorical shorthand" (30).

622 certa at sera. "Late but certain": for the inversion see 974f. comm. Such a phrase would normally describe *divine* action to right wrongs, cf. Sen. Rhet. *Contr.* 10 *praef.* 6 *sunt di immortales lenti quidem sed certi vindices generis humani* and other passages cited by Tarrant on *Ag.* 403a; the phrase therefore adds to our impression that Amphitryon regards Hercules as godlike.

623f. A's version *verumne cerno corpus an fallor videns / deceptus umbra*[95] is another example of drastic interpolation in that tradition. The clumsiness of the interpolation is evident: it loses the affective force of *teneo* and *fruor*, the participles *videns deceptus* are awkwardly juxtaposed, and

---

95. A variant *tua* for *videns* has slipped into the text in CS (cf. 96, also in an A interpolation).

deceptus is tautologous with *fallor*. The interpolator may have objected to the original reading on the grounds that an *umbra* could not be embraced, being insubstantial, but such an objection would clearly be overprecise in this context.

teneo. The *mot juste* in such a situation, as Gronovius pointed out, citing Plaut. *Rud.* 245f. *ut vix mihi / credo ego hoc, te tenere*, Ter. *Heaut.* 407f. *teneo te, / Antiphila, maxime animo exoptata meo*, Sen. *Phoen.* 501f. *teneo longo tempore / petita votis ora*, and Greek precedents such as Soph. *El.* 1226 ἔχω σὲ χερσίν, Eur. *El.* 578f. ὦ χρόνῳ φανεὶς / ἔχω σ' ἀέλπτως (both Electra to Orestes), *IT* 828f. ἔχω σ' Ὀρέστα (Iphigenia to Orestes). These parallels might suggest the conjecture *teneo te* for *teneone*, but elision of a personal pronoun is unparalleled in this metrical position. The contrast is actually between *editum* and *umbra*: "do I hold someone genuinely released from the underworld, or a mere shade?" *Tune es* is then an effective variation, asking the question more directly and personally.

624 tune es? The phrase sounds close to everyday speech. Compare the more elaborate phrase Ov. *Met.* 1.653f. (Inachus to Io) *tune es quaesita per omnes / nata mihi terras?*

624f. agnosco e.q.s. Reliance on tokens is a familiar element in dramatic recognition scenes, e.g. Soph. *El.* 1222f., Eur. *El.* 572f., Plaut. *Poen.* 1072ff.

625 alto nobilem trunco manum. The phrase *alto . . . trunco* is usually translated "with its great club," but Axelson 1967 88f. points out that *truncus* = "club" is unparalleled, and that *altus* is not a synonym for *vastus*; he believes that the phrase must mean "on your tall frame," and that *nobilem . . . manum* is therefore corrupt. But for *truncus* one may compare the similar use of *robur* and *stipes*; and *altus* is a natural description of the club, both because it is often held aloft (cf. *Oed.* 136 *manus . . . parat alta vulnus*, Hor. *Carm.* 3.26.1 *sublimi flagello*), whether in combat or at rest over Hercules' shoulder, and because its own length would then make it tower into the air. *Nobilem . . . manum* is something of a Senecan formula, cf. *Med.* 455, *Thy.* 685 (plural), both in the same metrical position.

626–28. For Megara's mourning garb cf. 202, 355f. Amphitryon's *squalor* and the *paedor* of the children are likewise due to mourning, as well as to their situation, which deprives them of all opportunity for *munditiae*. (For *squalor* of mourning cf. L-S s.v. II A3; for *paedor*, Cic.

Tusc. 3.26.62 *illa varia et detestabilia genera lugendi: paedores, muliebres lacerationes genarum* e.q.s.) In Eur. the situation is somewhat different, as Hercules finds his family dressed ready for death in grave-cerements (525ff.).

629f. For the extreme brevity of Amphitryon's explanation of the situation cf. *Ag.* 925–27, where Electra gives a highly compressed précis of events to Strophius. Tarrant (q.v. ad loc.) persuasively derives the style of these passages from the summaries of events with which tragic messengers tend to preface a detailed narrative (examples in Sen. are *Tro.* 1063f., *Pha.* 997). The fact that no further details are requested or given here is in keeping with the extremely condensed nature of this section of the Act (see introduction). In Eur. Hercules receives a much more detailed explanation of the situation (534–61).

631f. Hercules' complaint of the ingratitude of Thebes comes from the corresponding dialogue in Eur. 558–61. (Cf. also Amphitryon's criticism of Thebes at 217–29. Both passages in Eur. mention a specific benefit for which Thebes should be grateful, namely H.'s leadership against the Minyan enemy: Seneca omits reference to this obscure episode.)

631, 635 Herculeae, Alcidae. The proper names are of course significant: *Herculeae* implies the gratitude owed to the benefactor of mankind, and *Alcidae Lycus* juxtaposes hero with villain. Such significant references to the speaker's identity are not without parallel (cf. comm. on 509 *genitor Alcidae*), but the frequency with which Hercules makes them (cf. 957, 960, 991, 1155, 1163, 1168, 1218, 1295) is indicative of his vanity and self-centeredness.

632 vidit. That is, saw, without doing anything about the sight. Cf. *Pha.* 671ff. *magne regnator deum, / tam lentus audis scelera? tam lentus vides? / et quando saeva fulmen emittes manu* e.q.s., *Med.* 28ff. *spectat hoc nostri sator / Sol generis . . . / non redit in ortus ac remetitur diem?* But the verb has a more pregnant sense in the present passage, as it is not followed by any explicit indication of what action might have been taken.

633 defensus orbis. Compare 249 *orbe defenso caret.*

634 mactetur hostia. The MSS have *mactetur hostis*, which means that *hostis* appears in both 634 and 635: an insipid and pointless repetition. The *hostis* of 635 is part of a characteristic rhetorical point and must be allowed to stand, but that of 634 is colorless. Leo's conjecture *hostia* both removes the repetition and restores linguistic vigor. The somewhat brutal use of sacrificial imagery is characteristic of Hercules, cf. particularly 920–24, also 1036f. *tibi hunc dicatum, maximi coniunx Iovis, / gregem cecidi* and the bloodthirsty language of 636.[96] The rather awkward elision over punctuation may be paralleled by 1040 *stat ecce ad aras hostia, exspectat manum*; admittedly elision at the third-foot caesura is much rarer than at the fourth-foot caesura, but cf. *Ag.* 206 *captiva Pergama et diu victos Phrygas*.

634–36. In E this is part of Hercules' speech, but A attributes everything from *hanc ferat* to *inimicum feror* to Theseus, in which case *hanc ferat virtus notam* must be taken as an indignant question, as must 635. Few editors have followed A's arrangement, which is open to several objections: *virtus* would be awkward in the sense of *virtus tua*, 637 would be an odd response to Theseus' offer, and the bloodthirstiness of 636 suits Hercules better than Theseus. Two factors that may have contributed to A's error are the vocative *Theseu* in 637 and H.'s third-person reference to himself in 635. For the first factor as a probable cause of attribution error in A cf. 915, *Tro.* 533, *Ag.* 233; for the second, *Tro.* 979, *Pha.* 874.

notam. That is, the stigma of killing as unworthy an opponent as Lycus. Cf. the imitations in *HO* 816 (of the killing of Lichas) *facta inquinentur; fiat hic summus labor*, 1454f.

636 ad hauriendum sanguinem. The phrase is a brutal one, cf. Cic. *Sest.* 54 *me perculso ad meum sanguinem hauriendum ... advolaverunt*, Livy 26.13.13 *tanta sanguinis nostri hauriendi est sitis*, Ov. *Met.* 13.329ff., Sen. Rhet. *Suas.* 6.6 *Romanum sanguinem hausit Aegyptus*.

638 bella. For this word used of H.'s struggles v. 85 comm.

638f. differ ... differ. Examples of anadiplosis (use of the same word to begin and end a clause, sentence, etc.) in Sen. Trag. are collected by Canter 158. One of its uses, as here, is enumerative, the repeated word being attached to similar elements (*pater, coniunx*), cf. 1230, *Tro.* 465f. *talis incessu fuit / habituque talis*, *Med.* 984, *Ag.* 526, or, to take a Vergilian example, *socer arma Latinus habeto, / imperium sollemne socer* (*Aen.* 12.192f.). For a different use v. 907f. with comm.

---

96. Zwierlein 1966 200 n. 26 complains of the abruptness with which the sacrificial imagery is introduced, but much of this passage (i.e. 626–49) is compressed and abrupt.

639f. nuntiet e.q.s. For the idea of the newly dead bringing information to the underworld cf. V. *Aen.* 2.547ff. (Pyrrhus to Priam) *referes ergo haec et nuntius ibis / Pelidae genitori* e.q.s., Sen. *Tro.* 801ff., *Ag.* 1005ff. (Cassandra) *perferre prima nuntium Phrygibus meis / propero* e.q.s., *Apocol.* 13, Suet. *Tib.* 57.

640ᵇ–42ᵃ. Conceivably, but not necessarily, derived from Hercules' encouragement to his children and wife in Eur., 624f. ἀλλὰ θάρσος ἴσχετε / καὶ νάματ' ὄσσων μηκέτ' ἐξανίετε.

640f. flebilem ex oculis fuga ... vultum. The use of *vultus* for "expression of the eyes" is most unusual, and N. Heinsius was perhaps right to find it intolerable; he conjectured *luctum*. But it should be noted that *vultus* means "eyes" or "gaze" (a meaning not fully recognized in *OLD* s.v. 3a) several times in Sen. Trag., cf. 596, *Tro.* 966, *Phoen.* 43, *Thy.* 635, 950 (elsewhere cf. e.g. *Prov.* 2.8, Ov. *Met.* 5.30, 13.456). In these cases the expression of the eyes is occasionally indicated by an adjective, cf. 1022 *igneo vultu*, 953 and *Tro.* 1092 *vultus ... acres*. Of course *vultus* is often used of facial expression. For these reasons it seems conceivable that Sen. could have extended the meaning of the word to that required here.

641 regina. The use of the term is a polite assurance to Megara that she now has her rightful position: an instance of thoughtfulness and courtesy on Theseus' part. One may compare the addresses to Phaedra and Clytemnestra by their respective nurses, *Thesea coniunx, clara progenies Iovis* (*Pha.* 129) and *regina Danaum et inclitum Ledae genus* (*Ag.* 125); in each of these cases the purpose of the address is at least in part psychological, i.e. to remind the addressee of her true position, and of the fact that *noblesse oblige*.

642 si novi Herculem. A common type of phrase, which has the ring of everyday speech, cf. Balbus ap. Cic. *Att.* 9.7b.2 *si Caesarem bene novi*, Sen. *Ep.* 16.7, 18.3, 19.10 *si novi te*.

643 debitas poenas dabit. For the line-end cf. 729 *d.p. dare*, *Oed.* 976 *d.p. tulit*.

643f. dabit e.q.s. Ben Jonson could not resist imitating this rhetorical flourish, *Catiline* 3.3.174ff. "He shall die. / Shall, was too slowly said; he's dying. That / Is yet too slow; he's dead"; and Molière perhaps exploited its comic possibilities in *L'Avare* 4.7 *Je meurs, je suis mort, je suis enterré*. The Senecas had a weakness for this particular form of crescendo, cf. Sen. Rhet. *Contr.* 10.5.1 *caeditur: "parum est" inquit. uritur: "etiamnunc parum est." laniatur: "hoc" inquit "in irato Philippo satis est, sed nondum in irato Iove,"* Sen. *Ep.* 78.19 *inter haec tamen aliquis non gemuit. parum est: non rogavit. parum est: non respondit. parum est: risit, et quidem ex animo,* id. *Phoen.* 367ff. *hoc leve est quod sum nocens: / feci nocentes. hoc quoque etiamnunc leve est: / peperi nocentes.* Rhetorical points in Sen. Trag. are often based on self-correction by the speaker (*correctio,* v. H. Lausberg, *Handbuch der literarischen Rhetorik* [Munich 1960] § 785). Sometimes this involves picking up a word which has been used, as here, cf. 274f. *tenetque Thebas . . . Lycus.* / *sed non tenebit,* 907f.; at other times not, as at 1094ff., *Phoen.* 36f., *Ag.* 6 *video paternos, immo fraternos lares, Thy.* 411f.

644 lentum est "dabit." Examples of quoted words which stand outside the grammatical construction are rare in poetry, cf. Cat. 86.3 *totum illud "formosa" nego* with Fordyce ad loc.

645. "May God (who has the power) . . . " rather than "May the god who can" (Miller and others), which would be an odd prayer. Prayers frequently contain a reference to the god's ability to fulfill them (v. N–H on Hor. *Carm.* 1.28.28). Common formulas are δύνασαι γάρ, *namque potes;* for a third-person example cf. Callim. *Ap.* 29f. τὸν χορὸν ὡπόλλων, ὅ τι οἱ κατὰ θυμὸν ἀείδει, / τιμήσει· δύναται γάρ, ἐπεὶ Διὶ δεξιὸς ἧσται.

646 rebusque lassis. So EA, but many recc. alter *lassis* to *lapsis,* followed by Leo and Giardina; the same situation obtains at *Thy.* 615f. *nemo confidat nimium secundis, / nemo desperet meliora lassis,* 658 *hinc petere lassis rebus ac dubiis opem.* Other passages where *lassus* is the transmitted reading are *Cons. Polyb.* 16.6 *hunc principem lassis hominum rebus datum, Anth. Lat.* 405 Bücheler (attributed to Sen.) 1 *Crispe, meae vires lassarumque ancora rerum. Lassus* is strongly supported in these passages by the parallel use of *fessus* at *Thy.* 198f. *numquid secundis patitur in rebus modum, / fessis quietem,* cf. V. *Aen.* 3.145 *quam fessis finem rebus ferat,* 11.335 *rebus succurrite fessis.* In several other passages *res lassae* is very probably right, though not transmitted unanimously (the most usual variant being *lapsis*): V. *Georg.* 4.449 *venimus hinc lassis quaesitum oracula rebus,* Ov. *Tr.* 1.5.35f. *rebus succurrite lassis* (v. Luck ad loc.), 5.2.41 *unde petam lassis solacia rebus?, Pont.* 2.2.47, 2.3.93, Sen. *Ben.* 6.25.4 *quo . . . rebus lassis profligatisque succurrat.*

646f. magni . . . magnanime. For a somewhat similar instance of wordplay on simple and compound cf. Lucr. 1.895f. *verum semina multimodis immixta latere / multarum rerum in rebus communia debent.*

647 pande virtutum ordinem. Similar phrases eliciting a messenger speech are *Pha.* 999 *mortis effare ordinem, Tro.* 1065 *expone seriem caedis.* Such phrases are characteristic of Senecan noun-style (407–10 comm.), as Liebermann 27 illustrates by contrasting *Pha.* 999 with the corresponding question in Eur. *Hipp.* 1171 πῶς καὶ διώλετ'; εἰπέ. There are precedents at V. *Aen.* 3.179 *remque ordine pando*, 6.723 *ordine singula pandit* (cf. Ov. *Met.* 14.473 *referens tristes ex ordine casus*), but these use *ordo* adverbially.

pande. Note the variations *memorare* (650), *fare* (657), *ede* (760). Tarrant on *Ag.* 404a collects other instances of variation in such contexts, e.g. *Tro.* 1065ff., *Thy.* 633ff. *effare et istud pande . . . ede . . . indica . . . effare.*

virtutum. That is, *rerum virtute gestarum*, an unusual sense of the word which perhaps echoes V. *Aen.* 1.565f. *quis Troiae nesciat urbem / virtutesque virosque et tanti incendia belli?* Compare also the use of ἀρεταί in a concrete sense, e.g. Hdt. 1.176 μαχόμενοι ὀλίγοι πρὸς πολλοὺς ἀρετὰς ἀπεδείκνυντο, 9.40.

648f. The two questions correspond roughly to the two halves of Theseus' narrative, the first being concerned with the geography of the underworld, the second with Hercules' capture of the hound. Perhaps one sees here a touch of the orator's *divisio*. For the phrasing of 648 cf. 835 *ducit ad manes via qua remotos*, and for *maestos . . . manes* cf. 187 with comm.

650f. Tragic narratives are often prefaced by a statement that the speaker feels grief, horror, etc. at the events in question. For examples in epic cf. Hom. *Od.* 9.12f. σοὶ δ' ἐμὰ κήδεα θυμὸς ἐπετράπετο στονόεντα / εἴρεσθ', ὄφρ' ἔτι μᾶλλον ὀδυρόμενος στεναχίζω, V. *Aen.* 2.3ff. Such prefaces are frequent in Greek tragedy (v. Tarrant on *Ag.* 416ff.): in Sen. they become a standard feature and serve largely as a *praemunitio dinosis*, preparing the listener's mind for the narration of horrors (v. Smereka 1929), cf. *Tro.* 168ff., 1056ff., *Med.* 670, *Pha.* 991f., 995, *Oed.* 223f., 511, *Thy.* 634ff., *Ag.* 416ff. As a result of their emotions the speakers sometimes, as here, express reluctance to embark on their narratives, cf. e.g. *Ag.* 416ff. *acerba fatu poscis, infaustum iubes / miscere laeto nuntium. refugit loqui / mens aegra tantis atque inhorrescit malis.* The present passage is influenced somewhat in phrasing by V. *Aen.* 2.3 *infandum, regina, iubes renovare dolorem* (*cogis* ~ *iubes*) and 12 *quamquam animus meminisse horret luctuque refugit* (*menti* ~ *animus, horrenda* ~ *horret*), as is the passage in *Ag.*

Commentary: Act III

651f. vix adhuc e.q.s. Perhaps an echo of Ov. *Met.* 1.356f. (Deucalion after the flood) *haec quoque adhuc vitae non est fiducia nostrae / certa satis*. But *vitalis aura* is a Lucretian phrase (four uses); Vergil borrows it once, Sen. twice (cf. *Oed.* 650f.).

652f. torpet e.q.s. Similar phrasing at 1042f. *errat acies luminum / visusque maeror hebetat*; on formulaic language describing physical symptoms v. 414 comm., and for Vergilian influence (*Aen.* 2.605 *mortales hebetat visus*) see comm. on 1042^b–43^a.

653. Compare the similar words of Theseus at *Pha.* 837, again just after he has emerged from the underworld: *et vix cupitum sufferunt oculi diem*. (For such reactions cf. 292f. comm., but Theseus does not *fear* the light, not being a true denizen of the underworld.) The phrasing recalls Ov. *Fasti* 4.449f. *diurnum / lumen inadsueti vix patiuntur equi* [sc. *Ditis*].

654 alto in pectore. The phrase has an epic ring, cf. V. *Aen.* 6.599f. *sub alto / pectore*, 9.699f. *sub altum / pectus*.

655–57. The idea that hardships are enjoyable in retrospect was already proverbial in Homer's day and no doubt long before, cf. *Od.* 15.400f. μετὰ γάρ τε καὶ ἄλγεσιν τέρπεται ἀνήρ / ὅς τις δὴ μάλα πολλὰ πάθῃ καὶ πόλλ' ἐπαληθῇ. For later manifestations of it v. Otto s.v. *labor* (1) with the *Nachträge* pp. 40, 107, 239, adding Juv. 12.81f., 'Cato' *Collectio Monostichorum* 32 *aspera perpessu fiunt iucunda relatu*. Seneca's *meminisse* in particular comes from the Vergilian version of the idea, *forsan et haec olim meminisse iuvabit* (*Aen.* 1.203), which he quotes elsewhere at *Ep.* 78.15. There Sen. gives yet another version, *quod acerbum fuit ferre, tulisse iucundum est*, which is similar in its chiastic phrasing to the present passage.

The phrase *fructus laborum* recurs at 1253.

658–61. This apotropaic prayer is suggested by V. *Aen.* 6.264ff. *di quibus imperium est animarum, umbraeque silentes / et Chaos et Phlegethon, loca nocte tacentia late, / sit mihi fas audita loqui, sit numine vestro / pandere res alta terra et caligine mersas*, again at the beginning of an *inferorum descriptio*.

658 Fas omne mundi. An unusual phrase: invocations of *Fas* are rare, though examples occur at Livy 1.32.6, 8.5.8 *audite Ius Fasque*; *fas* with a dependent genitive is equally rare, though again instances may be found, cf. *TLL* 6.295.78ff., Sen. *Oed.* 1023 *per omne nostri nominis fas ac* *nefas.* The use of the word here may well have been suggested by the Vergilian passage cited above.

659 regno capaci. For *capax* of the underworld cf. *inc. inc. trag.* 250 R² *stagna capacis visere Averni,* Ov. *Met.* 4.439f. (in his *descriptio inferorum*) *mille capax aditus et apertas undique portas / urbs habet* [sc. *Ditis*] with Bömer ad loc.; similarly Sen. uses it of Charon's boat at 775 and *Oed.* 166, cf. also Hor. *Carm.* 3.1.16 *omne capax movet urna nomen.*

Seneca refers several times to the ability of the underworld to absorb the numbers of the dead, cf. 667, 673f. (This point may well derive from the similar emphasis in the Ovidian passage, which continues (440ff.) *utque fretum de tota flumina terra, / sic omnes animas locus accipit ille, nec ulli / exiguus populo est turbamve accedere sentit.*) This may be seen as part of the thematic emphasis in this play on the countless numbers of the dead, with the further implication of the universality of death; cf. 191 comm., 837ff., 868ff.

659f. teque quam e.q.s. In this prayer the relative clause has the function not only of mentioning a familiar detail concerning the deity (cf. 517f. comm.) but also of identifying her, as at Ar. *Thesm.* 315f. Ζεῦ μεγαλώνυμε, χρυσολύρα τε / Δῆλον ὅς ἔχεις ἱεράν. For invocation of a god by allusion rather than name cf. 205 comm.

I am not at all sure that the paradosis *tota . . . Aetna*⁹⁷ cannot stand, though it has often been suspected. *Totus* is common in indications of place in Sen. as elsewhere, e.g. Prop. 2.17.8 (Sisyphus) *difficile ut toto monte volutet onus,* Sen. *Ag.* 506 *toto . . . Ionio,* Pha. 1276 *Mopsopia . . . tota*; for the present phrase cf. ps.-V. *Aetna* 201 *fragor tota nunc rumpitur Aetna,* 329, and particularly Ov. *Met.* 14.188 (Polyphemus after Odysseus' escape) *totam gemebundus obambulat Aetnam*: the phrase is justified there and here by the massive size of the mountain (over 90 miles in circumference at its base). The objection to the paradosis is that Ceres actually searched all over the world, cf. Ov. *Met.* 5.462f., 489 *toto quaesitae virginis orbe,* 556 *quam postquam toto frustra quaesistis in orbe.* But Sen. chose to write *Aetna* rather than *orbe* because of the identifying function of this relative clause (so Pierrot): Etna is particularly well known in this context as the place where Ceres lit torches in order to continue her search at night, cf. Cic. *Verr.* 2.4.48.106, Ov. *Met.* 5.442, Claud. *Rapt. Pros.* 3.392ff. (The possibility that Sen. thinks of Etna, rather than Enna, as the place of the *rape* is much more doubtful; that tradition, though well attested, is late, v. Hall on Claud. *Rapt. Pros.* 1.122.)

Among conjectures, Heimsoeth's *amotam . . . Enna* (paleographically

---

97. Codd. *ethna*, as often, cf. *Med.* 410, *HO* 286, *TLL* 1.1160.77–82.

more plausible than Bentley's *raptam . . . Enna*) was accepted by Leo and Richter. Confusion of *Aetn-* (*ethn-*) and *Enn-* (*henn-*) is certainly common, cf. Claud. *Rapt. Pros.* 2.8, Hall on 1.122, and Stat. *Ach.* 1.825 where Gronovius corrected *Aetnaeas* to *Hennaeas*: for *quam* elided cf. *Thy.* 434, *Phoen.* 102, *Ag.* 131. But *amotam*, while tolerable, is not the most natural word in the context. To substitute *tota . . . Enna* for *tota . . . Aetna* with Avantius would turn a molehill into a mountain. Schmidt's *toto . . . orbe* (1865 18) is paleographically implausible. Readers who find the *tota* of the paradosis unacceptable may wish to consider replacing it with *nocte*, retaining *Aetna* (cf. *Tro.* 1175 *quaesita tota nocte*).

660 iure. The *iura* of the MSS is generally accepted, despite the fact that its meaning is quite uncertain. Various meanings are conceivable, e.g., "judgments," "powers," "laws," but none receives much support from the immediate context, and the abstract *iura* seems out of keeping with the physical *abdita et operta*. "Judgments" might be thought to accord with Theseus' description of trials and punishments in the underworld. But that is not his only topic, and he does not reach it for sixty lines; nothing *here* suggests "judgments" (contrast 728, where the context leaves no doubt that the word has this sense), and the emphasis on concealment in *abdita et operta* would be pointless.

In fact Theseus is asking permission to describe the underworld in general, not some special aspect of it. That is clear from the description into which he launches immediately, and it is confirmed by the Vergilian source of his request quoted above on 658–61. There can be little doubt, therefore, that Seneca wrote *iure abdita / et operta terris*, "things properly hidden and buried below the earth" (cf. Vergil's *res alta terra . . . mersas*). The simple correction, found already in Par. Lat. 8030 and 8035 (wrongly attributed to Par. Lat. 8034 in *TAPA* 111 [1981] 68), permits a convincing explanation of the corruption, i.e., accommodation of the noun to *abdita et operta*. Seneca's use of these participles as substantives governed by *eloqui* was perhaps suggested by Vergil's *audita loqui*.

661 impune eloqui. So A, but E has *impune loqui*; haplography of *e* by E seems the most probable cause of the divergence. *Eloqui* "speak out, declare" makes an effective contrast with *abdita et operta*. Admittedly Vergil has *loqui*, but there the contrast between secret and revelation is made elsewhere, i.e. in *pandere res . . . mersas*.

662–827. Theseus' report is divided into two sections: the description of the physical setting of the underworld, and the narrative of Hercules' capture of Cerberus (respectively, 662–759 and 762–827). This division may be seen as an outgrowth of the practice, common in epic and in the narratives of tragedy, of describing the location before recounting the action (Liebermann 65ff.). In Homer and in Greek tragedy, the place-descriptions are usually short (e.g. Hom. *Il.* 2.811ff., 11.711f., *Od.* 3.293ff., 22.126ff., Aesch. *PV* 846f., Soph. *Trach.* 752ff., Eur. *Hipp.* 1199f.), though longer examples are already found in Homer, e.g. *Od.* 9.116–41, 13.96–112, 15.403–14. Lengthy and elaborate examples are found in Ovid, e.g. *Met.* 2.1–18, 4.432–45, 11.592–616, and in Sen., cf. *Oed.* 530–47, *Thy.* 641–82. The present instance is remarkably long (longer in fact than the narrative for which it ostensibly sets the scene), because of the material available and the poetic precedents for such an *inferorum descriptio*: so long, in fact, that it contains subordinate examples of the ἔκφρασις τόπου pattern within it (v. 709ff. comm.), and the narrative proper has to begin with a new ἔκφρασις (762f.) to indicate where the exploit is located within the vast landscape which has been sketched in.

The strongest influence on Seneca's description of the underworld is *Aeneid* 6. This is particularly evident in the lines concerning the way down to the underworld, the personifications of human ills and the palace of Dis (v. comm. on 671f., 675 + 678ff., 690–96, 709ff.; cf. on 658–61), but there are also several more minor instances. The shorter catabasis of Juno in Ov. *Met.* 4 also contributes several details (v. comm. on 659 *regno capaci*, 686, 690–96 and 690, 717–20). Other topics are thoroughly traditional in treatments of the underworld, e.g. the punishments of the great sinners. Seneca adds several imaginative touches to the tradition, notably the substitution of Lethe for Styx, the evocation of the sterility of the underworld, and the description of Pluto. Even when following Vergil closely, as in listing the abstracts, he takes care to add new details of his own (v. comm. on 690–96 ad fin.). In the section on retribution for crimes committed on earth, Sen.'s emphasis on the punishment of tyrants is particularly striking and reflects the experience of his own generation.

Seneca does not attempt the daunting task of drawing a coherent picture of the whole underworld, but instead concentrates on certain areas of special interest. The series of questions with which Amphitryon punctuates Theseus' account not only helps to relieve the possible boredom of a long narrative (as in the messenger speeches at *Tro.* 1068ff., *Thy.* 641ff.), but also enables Sen. to move from one topic to another rather than giving a unified account. As the underworld cannot be visualized as a whole, so too Sen.'s descriptions are often impressionistic and evocative rather than specific: the appropriateness and effectiveness of this technique may be seen e.g. at 701–3 or 762–63.

662–67. A cave on the promontory of Taenarum (Cape Matapan, the southernmost point of Laconia) was believed to be one of the entrances to the underworld. Some authorities agree with Sen. in calling it the place of Hercules' descent (Eur. *Her.* 23, Apollod. 2.5.12), the only rival to my knowledge being a cave near Heraclea Pontica on the Black Sea (Xen. *An.* 6.2.2). Sen. also makes it the place where H. emerged from the underworld, but in this respect it has more rivals (v. comm. on 813).

662 attollit iugum. Cf. Liv. Andron. *trag.* 34 R² *Taenari celsos ocres.* For the topography see *RE* 4A.2034.

663. A vivid and atmospheric picture. Whatever Sen.'s sources, these woods may derive primarily from his imagination: deep woods make a suitable setting for such a sinister and awesome place. Compare particularly the *lucus niger* where Tiresias practices necromancy (*Oed.* 530ff.) and the *vetustum nemus* in which Atreus sacrifices Thyestes' children (*Thy.* 650ff.). Vergil similarly envisages woods around the entrances to the underworld at Cumae, *Aen.* 6.238, and at Amsanctus, 7.565f. *densis hunc frondibus atrum / urget utrumque latus nemoris.*

premit. The metaphor is a powerful one in the context, used of headlands again at *Phoen.* 22f. *vel qua alta maria vertice immenso premit / Inoa rupes, Pha.* 26f. *qua curvati litora ponti / Sunion urget.*

664, 666 ora, faucibus. A highly traditional metaphor in this context, cf. Pind. *P.* 4.43f. παρ χθόνιον / Ἀΐδα στόμα, Ταίναρον εἰς ἱερὰν, Eur. *Her.* 23f. Ταινάρου διὰ στόμα / βέβηκ' ἐς Ἅιδου, V. *Georg.* 4.467 *Taenarias ... fauces, alta atria Ditis, Aen.* 7.570 quoted below, Sen. *Pha.* 1201 *pallidi fauces Averni vosque, Taenarei specus,* and Marston's phrase about Death's "wide-mouthèd porch" (*Antonio and Mellida* 3.2.206). *Ora solvere* is used once by Lygdamus ([Tib. 3].5.14), and several times by Ovid (v. Bömer on *Met.* 1.181), in the sense of opening the mouth to speak.

Ditis invisi. Compare Hom. *Il.* 8.368 στυγεροῦ Ἀΐδαο; similarly in contexts of death Hor. *Carm.* 1.34.10f. *invisi horrida Taenari / sedes,* 2.14.23 *invisas cupressos,* V. *Aen.* 8.245 *regna ... pallida, dis invisa.* It would probably be overingenious to see a pun here on *invisus* "unseen" / Ἅιδης. A's *invicti* is no doubt an attempt to correct a meaningless *inviti, invitus* being a common corruption of *invisus* (*TLL* 7.2.192.8ff: so Gruter). For *domus* v. comm. on 620 *domum.*

Commentary: Act III

665f. More echoes of Vergilian entrances to the underworld: cf. *Aen.* 6.237 *spelunca alta fuit vastoque immanis hiatu*, and for *ingens vorago* cf. 7.569f. *ruptoque ingens Acheronte vorago / pestiferas aperit fauces*. Note the pleonasm of *alta, immenso, ingens, vastis*. Seneca likes to apply such adjectives to *specus* in particular: it is modified by *immensus* again at *Tro.* 178, by *ingens* at *HF* 94, *Tro.* 198, by *vastus* at *HF* 718, *Thy.* 9. All these phrases are of the underworld or entrances to it, cf. also Enn. *trag.* 155 R² *inferum vastos specus* and v. comm. on 718. Such impressionistic descriptions of caverns appear frequently in Vergil (but not usually with reference to the underworld).

667. The capaciousness of the way into the underworld is certainly traditional, cf. Hom. *Il.* 23.74, *Od.* 11.571 εὐρυπυλὲς Ἄϊδος δῶ, but it has a particular thematic importance in this play, v. comm. on 659 *capaci*.

668–72. This realistic picture of gradually increasing gloom is new in Seneca (Vergil dwells on the darkness of the journey, v. 671f. comm.); Sen. expands on it with characteristic ἐπιμονή.

670 dubius. Of light cf. *Pha.* 42 *dum lux dubia est, Tro.* 1142, *Oed.* 1. Pre-Senecan examples in *TLL* are Varro ap. Serv. *Aen.* 2.268 *de crepusculo, quod est dubia lux*, Ov. *Met.* 11.596 *dubiaeque crepuscula lucis*. Cf. also the somewhat more frequent use of *incertus*, e.g. Sall. *hist.* 4.40 *lumine incerto*, V. *Aen.* 6.270 (v. comm. 671f.) *per incertam lunam*.

affecti. The *afflicti* of the codd. could mean "broken, crushed, damaged, stricken," or "distressed, sad," but none of these meanings is appropriate in the context; and the application of the word to sunlight, or natural phenomena generally, would be very unusual. On the other hand the required sense of "weakened" could well be conveyed by *affecti* (the conjecture of Bentley), cf. e.g. Livy 5.18.4 *vires corporis affectae, sensus oculorum atque aurium hebetes, memoria labat* e.q.s.; *TLL* cites two examples of the word applied to natural phenomena, Cic. *Phil.* fr. 1.17 M *affecta iam prope aestate uvas a sole mitescere tempus est*, Sil. 15.502 *iamque hieme affecta mitescere coeperat annus*. It is not surprising that *afflictus* should have intruded, in view of its frequency in Sen. Trag. (twenty usages).

cadit. "Diminishes, grows weaker."

671f. A characteristic intermingling of Vergilian and Ovidian reminiscences. The introduction of a simile to describe the quality of the

Commentary: Act III

light at this point recalls V. *Aen.* 6.270ff. *quale per incertam lunam sub luce maligna / est iter in silvis, ubi caelum condidit umbra / Iuppiter, et rebus nox abstulit atra colorem*; but its content is different, evoking not pitch darkness but twilight, and echoes Ov. *Am.* 1.5.5f. *qualia sublucent fugiente crepuscula Phoebo, / aut ubi nox abiit, nec tamen orta dies.*

673 vacuis. Suggested by V. *Aen.* 6.269 (cf. previous comm.) *perque domos Ditis vacuas et inania regna.* Cf. also *Thy.* 1009 *chaos inane.*

674 mersum. For the word in such a context cf. *Pha.* 219f. *non umquam amplius / convexa tetigit supera qui mersus semel / adiit silentem nocte perpetua domum*, 1203, *HF* 317 *demersus* (with comm.), 422, *Tro.* 198. Acceptance of E's weak *versum* by Leo and Giardina is a result of excessive respect for that MS.

pergat. Codd. *pereat*; for the confusion cf. 408 *pereat* E *pergat* A. The correction was first suggested by Peiper in the 1867 Teubner, and later by Ageno as an improvement on Hoffa's *pergit* (1914 470, anticipated by the corrector of Par. Lat. 8034).

675, 678ff. The influence of *Aeneid* 6 is evident again, cf. 126f. *facilis descensus Averno: / . . . sed revocare gradum superasque evadere ad auras, / hoc opus, hic labor est.* Note *labor est*, and *gradum retro flectere* paraphrasing *revocare gradum. Retro flexit* again adds an Ovidian color to a Vergilian source, cf. *Met.* 3.187f. *oraque retro / flexit*, 10.51 *ne flectat retro sua lumina.*

676. Similes from seafaring are common in contexts of "being swept away out of control," cf. V. *Georg.* 1.201ff. *non aliter quam qui adverso vix flumine lembum / remigiis subigit, si bracchia forte remisit, / atque illum in praeceps prono rapit alveus amni*, Ov. *Her.* 20.41f., Sen. *Pha.* 181ff., *Thy.* 438f. Sometimes the brevity of the simile suggests that it is almost formulaic, as here or Ov. *Am.* 2.4.8 *auferor ut rapida concita puppis aqua.* The Senecan examples cited perhaps derive primarily from the simile in *Georg.*, as they share with it the picture of a struggle against natural forces which is finally unsuccessful (here reduced to *invitas*). Here note also the use of *rapit*, and *pronus* in 677 (*Pha.* 183 *prono . . . vado*).

677 pronus aer. *Pronus* as often has the sense of "moving downward," e.g. 125f. *prono . . . mundo. Urget* suggests that the wind is a strong one; Seneca's distinction *vehementior . . . spiritus ventus est, invicem spiritus leniter fluens aer* (*QNat.* 5.13.4) is not always observed in poetry, cf. Luc. 5.717f. *violentior aer / puppibus incubuit.*

[296]

avidum chaos. Compare *Tro.* 400 *tempus nos avidum devorat et chaos.* For the greed of death v. 291f. comm., and on *chaos* v. 610 comm.

679 umbrae tenaces. Some commentators take these *umbrae* in a personal sense and (because they have more power than usual) identify them with the *manes*, the grim and unforgiving spirits of the dead (cf. V. *Georg.* 4.489 *scirent si ignoscere manes*). Alternatively one might take *umbrae* as a synonym for the underworld, as at 977, *Tro.* 346; *tenaces* might seem to favor the personal sense, but note *Pha.* 625 *regni tenacis* (i.e. the underworld).

679–86. Vergil in *Aeneid* 6 consistently gives the impression that the underworld is bounded by a river and/or marsh, over which Charon ferries the shades, and which prevents their return. The names applied to these waters are usually Cocytus and Styx, though they are used primarily for color and not applied with precision (132, 295ff., 323, 439). Seneca here makes Lethe the boundary of the underworld (cf. *Oed.* 560), and at 777 the river on which Charon plies. (But he too is inconsistent, for at 715f. Acheron is the barrier preventing escape, and at 869f. it is Cocytus that the shades must cross.) Lethe is unusual in this role of boundary of the underworld, and Sen. perhaps uses it because it is also the boundary of identity (cf. *demitque curas*); having once crossed it and tasted of it, the shades forget their former selves (cf. 292 *oblitos sui*).

679 immensi sinus. *Sinus* here comes from *Aen.* 6.132 (again of the boundary of the underworld) *Cocytusque sinu labens circumvenit atro*. The genitive must be descriptive, "of immense sweep," i.e. "flowing in an immense curve"; Leo's view that it is governed by *intus* is improbable (Löfstedt *Syntactica* II 424 note). A has the variant *immenso sinu*: it is not unthinkable that two ablative phrases (the other being *placido . . . vado*) should modify one verb, as 665f. shows, but it seems probable that the ablative has been substituted by an interpolator for the slightly difficult genitive.

680. The golden line is appropriate to the unruffled flow of the river. *Placido quieta* is a further example of pairing of adjectives of similar meaning, particularly common in descriptions of waters, cf. 536 *mutis tacitum* with comm.

681 demitque curas. Compare V. *Aen.* 6.714f. *Lethaei ad fluminis undam / securos latices et longa oblivia potant*, Ov. *Pont.* 2.4.23 *securae pocula Lethes*; Plato *Rep.* 10.621a calls Lethe τὸν Ἀμέλητα ποταμόν.

Commentary: Act III

681–83. This winding and doubling back by the river, designed to prevent escape, is introduced because Lethe is here taking the place of Vergil's Styx, cf. *Aen.* 6.439 *noviens Styx interfusa coercet*. The concept of restraining rivers in the underworld is non-Homeric but appears in the Augustan poets, v. N-H on Hor. *Carm.* 2.14.9.

682 gravem. "Sluggish, slow-moving," a meaning sometimes found of people and animals (*TLL* 6.2284.9ff.), here unusually applied to a river. Adjectives meaning "sluggish" are often applied to certain rivers of the underworld, v. comm. on 554.

683 [Lethe] involvit amnem. The *amnis* is Lethe; for such "disjunctiveness" cf. e.g. V. *Aen.* 1.246 *it mare proruptum et pelago premit arva sonanti*, Manil. 1.539f. *quantum convexo mundus Olympo / obtineat spatium* (which means *q. mundus convexitate sua o. sp.*, as Housman notes), Prud. *Ham.* 793f. *scopulosaque semita longe / duceret . . . callem*. Further examples in *HF* are 712f., 1214 (v. ad locc.), 1326f.; on the subject see Housman on Manil. 1.539, 4.472 and Shackleton Bailey, *Propertiana* 33f.

involvit. A forceful usage, best rendered "entwines": the Latin word, like the English, would more normally apply to a situation where one loop crosses another (as at Cels. 7.31.1 *si [vena] curva est et velut in orbes quosdam implicatur pluresque inter se involvuntur*, cf. *TLL* 7.2.266.32ff.).

683–85. This is the third simile in Theseus' speech (cf. 671f., 677), whereas there are only two previously in the play (106, 478, the second very brief). Similes, particularly of the extended kind, are appropriate to the epic character of such a narrative; note the series in the messenger speech of *Pha.*, 1011ff., 1029ff., 1039ff., 1048f., 1072f., 1092ff., 1112.

The Maeander provides an opportunity for poets to show their paces; Seneca himself calls it *Maeander, poetarum omnium exercitatio et ludus* (*Ep.* 104.15). Naturally it appeals particularly to Ovid (*Met.* 2.246, 8.162ff., 9.451, *Her.* 9.55); in Sen. cf. *Phoen.* 605f. The present simile is based on the tour de force in *Met.* 8 (of the winding corridors of the labyrinth) *non secus ac liquidus Phrygiis Maeandrus in arvis / ludit et ambiguo lapsu refluitque fluitque / occurrensque sibi venturas aspicit undas / et nunc ad fontes nunc ad mare versus apertum / incertas exercet aquas*. Seneca's language here is similar to that at *Ag.* 140 *incerta dubitat unda cui cedat malo*; *dubitatio* ascribed to waters comes from Ovid, v. Introduction fn. 80.

683f. incerta vagus Maeander unda ludit. So A, but E *incertis . . . undis*. The singular is more stylish, cf. e.g. V. *Georg.* 4.479f. *tardaque*

Commentary: Act III

palus inamabilis unda / alligat, Sen. *HF* 378, 1323f., *Pha.* 6f. *amnis rapida currens / verberat unda.* The E tradition[98] occasionally alters the number of a noun out of a literal-minded idea of what the sense requires, as at 759, 1284 and *Med.* 430, and I suspect that has occurred here. On the other hand one cannot exclude the possibility of stylistic improvement by A.[99]

684 cedit sibi. "'Makes way for itself,' one bend appearing to have no other purpose than to leave space for another" (Kingery).

686. This *palus* of Cocytus derives from V. *Aen.* 6.323 *Cocyti stagna alta vides Stygiamque paludem,* and *foedus* probably from Vergilian descriptions of Cocytus and its environs, cf. *Georg.* 4.478ff. *quos circum limus niger et deformis harundo / Cocyti tardaque palus inamabilis unda / alligat, Aen.* 6.296f. *turbidus hic caeno vastaque voragine gurges / aestuat atque omnem Cocyto eructat harenam. Iners* on the other hand (cf. 869f. *inerti . . . Cocyto*) comes from *Styx nebulas exhalat iners* in Ovid's catabasis of Juno, *Met.* 4.434. *Iacet* means "lies motionless," cf. Ov. *Met.* 11.747f. *tunc iacet unda maris: ventos custodit et arcet / Aeolus egressu,* Sen. *QNat.* 6.20.7 *palustres et iacentes aquas.*

687f. The appearance of these ill-boding birds at large in the underworld is a new detail in Seneca, though Tityus is regularly punished by a vulture tearing at his liver (756 comm.). Here the *vultur* is not mentioned in that capacity, but for its more general associations as a devourer of corpses. Ovid couples it with the *strix* as a bird of evil (*Am.* 1.12.20), but its appearance was not per se a bad omen (e.g. Livy 1.7.1). On the other hand the *bubo* was regularly regarded as ominous of death, cf. Ov. *Met.* 5.549f. *volucris, venturi nuntia luctus, / ignavus bubo, dirum mortalibus omen* (a passage that influences the present lines: v. comm. below on *luctifer,* and n.b. *dirum . . . omen ~ omen . . . triste*), 10.452f., 15.791 and Pease on V. *Aen.* 4.462. The *strix* is the very epitome of the sinister, as the creature that witches can turn themselves

---

98. I use this phrase because much E interpolation undoubtedly took place before the date of the Etruscus itself: this is surely the case in 684, where the Etruscus faithfully copies both the correct *ludit* and the variant *errat.*

99. E actually wrote *incertus* before correcting himself, but the error is easily explained as a mechanical one due to the *-us* of *vagus,* and there is no need to conjecture *incertus vagis M. undis ludit* (cf. Leo 1876 432) or *incertus vaga M. unda ludit* (Viansino), particularly in view of *incertas . . . aquas* in the Ovidian source. *Ludit* is certainly right (as against *errat* which follows it in E), as *difficilior* and protected by the Ovidian passage (cf. also *Met.* 2.246 *quique recurvatis ludit Maeandros in undis*); *errat* is a variant which has slipped into the text, cf. *Med.* 766 *nemoris antiqui domus* A (*recte*), *nemoris antiqui domus decus* E, and v. Carlsson 1929 47.

into (v. K. F. Smith on Tib. 1.5.52); on its mythical nature v. S. Oliphant in *TAPA* 44 (1913) 133ff. Seneca couples *bubo* and *strix* again at *Med.* 733, as ingredients of Medea's magic potion.

Luctifer is not attested before Sen., and was suggested by Ovid's *venturi nuntia luctus*. On new compound adjectives in Sen. v. Appendix 4.

gemit. The cry of the *bubo* (βύας) was thought to be mournful, cf. V. *Aen.* 4.462f. *ferali carmine bubo / saepe queri et longas in fletum ducere voces,* Pliny *NH* 10.34 *nec cantu aliquo vocalis sed gemitu,* Apul. *Flor.* 13 *bubones gemulo [carmine].*

690–96. From the earliest times there appear lists of what we would regard as abstractions personified, cf. especially Hes. *Theog.* 211ff. (with West's Proleg. 33f.). By Sen.'s time lists of such figures, usually located in the underworld, are a familiar *locus* of poetry, cf. V. *Aen.* 6.274ff., Ov. *Met.* 4.484f., 502f., Petron. *Sat.* 124, Sen. *HF* 96ff., *Oed.* 589ff., 652, 1059ff., Stat. *Theb.* 7.47ff. Seneca is working closely from Vergil's list in *Aen.* 6, as seven of his eleven personifications come from there, the exceptions being Funus, Pavor, Pudor, and Dolor. But Funus is only an apparent exception, as it means "death" as often in the poets, and is therefore a substitute for Vergil's Letum (though not an exact equivalent, as *funus* usually connotes violent death).[100] The coupling of Pavor with Metus was suggested by Ovid's *et Pavor et Terror* (*Met.* 4.485; for the influence of that passage on *HF* v. comm. on 96–98 and 98), cf. also Homer's Δεῖμός τε Φόβος τε (*Il.* 11.37, cf. 4.440). Pudor personified appears at Ov. *Fasti* 5.29, but as a positive influence (cf. the altar to Αἰδώς at Athens, Paus. 1.17.1), whereas Sen. has in mind a punitive rather than preventive sense of shame, and therefore includes Pudor among the ills of mankind. Dolor is new in Sen., and also appears in two of the lists in *Oed.* In Vergil's list the personifications have a single adjective or none. Sen. adds more color by describing a characteristic activity of three of his figures, Fames, Pudor, and Senectus; compare the similar treatment in 97 *suumque lambens sanguinem Impietas ferox.*

690–92. The transmitted text of these lines requires considerable surgery. At the end of 691 the participle *iacens* must become *iacet* (thus

---

100. Madvig 1873 112 objected to *Funus* on the grounds that (a) it was out of place "inter animi illos affectus malaque vitae," and (b) the single asyndeton in a series of copulae in 693 suggested corruption. Suspicions of the word flourished for over half a century until quelled by Carlsson 1929 56f., who pointed out (a) that *Funus* replaces Vergil's *Letum*, and (b) that the syntactical usage is adequately paralleled by the opposite case of a single copula in a series of asyndeta at *Oed.* 652 *Letum Luesque, Mors Labor Tabes Dolor*. The most notable conjecture to result meanwhile had been Wilamowitz's *Metus Pavorque furvus* (teste Leo).

Commentary: Act III

paralleling *tegit* in 692: so Withof), as the sense of the verb indicates that *Fames* cannot be perched in the tree like *Sopor*; similarly in Vergil's list only the *Somnia* occupy the tree. In 690, Leo's *taxum imminentem qua tenet* removes the awkward ablative of place in the paradosis *taxo imminente quam tenet*. These corrections have been widely accepted, but the resulting text is open to two stylistic objections. First, the construction of 691 and 692 should be parallel to that of 690, but this means that all the important material of the sentence is subordinate to the less important material of 689. Second, the parallelism of 691 and 692 is jejune and unpleasing. It is tempting to adopt Withof's alteration of *Famesque maesta* to *Fames quoque istic*, which, though radical, is less improbable than appears at first sight; both *quoque* and *iste* are particularly subject to corruption in MSS, and a limited amount of mechanical corruption could have led to conjecture. But on balance I am inclined to regard the text with the corrections of Withof and Leo as tolerable, so long as 691f. are taken as main clauses.

690. Again a combination of motifs from the Vergilian and Ovidian *catabaseis*. The inspiration for this tree where *Sopor* perches comes from the end of Vergil's list of abstracts, *Aen.* 6.282ff. *in medio ramos annosaque bracchia pandit / ulmus opaca, ingens, quam sedem Somnia vulgo / vana tenere ferunt*. On the other hand its transformation into a *taxus* arises from Ov. *Met.* 4.432 *est via declivis funesta nubila taxo*, as that is apparently the first place in classical literature where the yew is associated with death and the underworld. That association, due no doubt to the tree's dark color and poisonous berries, becomes popular after Ovid, e.g. Luc. 6.645, Stat. *Silv.* 5.3.8.

imminentem. The tree which in Vergil is vast here becomes somewhat oppressive, even threatening—a detail characteristic of Sen.'s imagination, cf. *Oed.* 542f. *medio stat ingens arbor atque umbra gravi / silvas minores urget*, and comm. on 762f.

692 vultus tegit. For the gesture of shame cf. 1178 *uterque tacitus ora pudibunda obtegit* (with comm.), Ov. *AA* 2.583 (Mars and Venus trapped by Vulcan's net) *non vultus texisse suos . . . possunt*, *Met.* 10.411f.

694 aterque Luctus. For *ater* of similar emotions and personifications cf. V. *Aen.* 12.335 *atrae Formidinis ora*, 9.719 *atrumque Timorem*, Hor. *Carm.* 3.1.40 *atra Cura*, 3.14.13f. *atras . . . curas*, 4.11.35f., Petron. 89 v. 3 *atro . . . metu*. The adjective is particularly appropriate to *Luctus* as black is often the color of mourning clothes, cf. West on Hes. *Theog.* 406, Ov. *Met.* 6.288f. with Bömer ad loc.

Commentary: Act III

sequitur. Indicating the sequence in which these beings are viewed: in the forefront are Sopor, Fames, and Pudor, next are seen Metus, etc., and in the background is Senectus. There is no indication of movement on the part of the group as a whole (n.b. 690f. *tenet, iacet*).

696. Old Age personified (Γῆρας) is sometimes shown with a walking-stick in Greek vase paintings, such as that reproduced in *EAA* 3.840 ill. 1046 (839f. for bibliography). But a staff is characteristic of the old from at least as early as Aesch. *Ag.* 75 (cf. Sen. *Oed.* 657 *baculo senili*), and it is not necessary to postulate inspiration from such an illustration.

697ff. The absence of crops and vines, indicating the barrenness of the underworld, probably comes from Tib. 1.10.35f. *non seges est illic, non vinea culta, sed audax / Cerberus et Stygiae navita turpis aquae*, but the phrasing of 697 is also influenced by Ov. *Am.* 2.16.7 *terra ferax Cereris multoque feracior uvis*.

698–703. A series of negative clauses (often with initial *non, nullus,* etc.) followed by positive statement makes an effective descriptive technique, e.g. 550ff. and Tib. quoted above. Here the negative clauses evoke vividly the fertility missing from the underworld. Similar descriptions are V. *Georg.* 3.352ff. (of Scythia) *neque ullae / aut herbae campo apparent aut arbore frondes; / sed iacet aggeribus niveis informis et alto / terra gelu late* e.q.s., Ov. *Pont.* 1.3.51ff. *non ager hic pomum, non dulces educat uvas, / non salices ripa, robora monte virent / . . . quocumque aspicias, campi cultore carentes / vastaque, quae nemo vindicat, arva iacent.* Thus again descriptions of the frozen north influence Seneca's picture of the underworld. Cf. also *Anth. Lat.* 237 (description of Corsica, attributed to Seneca) 3f. *non poma autumnus, segetes non educat aestas, / canaque Palladio munere bruma caret*, Petron. 120.71ff. (region of Puteoli) *non haec autumno tellus viret aut alit herbas / caespite laetus ager, non* e.q.s. . . . / *sed chaos et nigro squalentia pumice saxa* e.q.s. On initial *non* in poetry v. A. Guillemin in *REL* 19 (1941) 101ff.

698 laeta. "Fertile, in good heart," a common usage of farmers (Cic. *de Orat.* 3.155) as well as poets, cf. *TLL* 7.2.883.80ff.

germinant. The first instance in *TLL* of intransitive *germinare* used of the place rather than plants, trees, etc., the only other instance being Mart. 10.94.3 (of a *hortus*).

699 fluctuat . . . seges. A stronger metaphor than "waving corn" in English, though by no means unparalleled: Livy uses it of a wavering battle-line (8.39.4), Gellius of a lion's waving mane (5.14.9), cf. also V. *Georg.* 2.437 *et iuvat undantem buxo spectare Cytorum*.

701. The use of an abstract noun as subject is not unusual in Sen. Trag. (cf. e.g. 617, 681f.) and may be seen as characteristic of his noun-style (407–10 comm.). Elsewhere it is found particularly in early drama (and in Cicero's letters), usually, however, with a transitive verb; cf. Acc. *trag.* 621f. R² *nam huius demum miseret, cuius nobilitas miserias / nobilitat*, Ter. *Ad.* 24f. *facite aequanimitas poetae ad scribendum augeat industriam*, and v. H. Haffter, *Unters. z. Altlat. Dichtersprache* ch. 4.

profundi vastitas. *Profundus* as an adjective of the underworld, Lucr. 3.978 *Acheronte profundo*, V. *Georg.* 1.243 *manesque profundi* and often in Sen. Trag.: as a *Kennwort* perhaps first here, then Stat. *Theb.* 1.615f. *profundo . . . Iovi*. *Vastitas* is extremely rare even in nondactylic poetry (and of course unusable in dactyls): it appears only here in Sen. Trag., and elsewhere only once in Accius. Seneca liked the collocation of the two words, cf. *de Otio* 5.6 (of extraterrestrial space) *utrumne profunda vastitas sit*, *Ep.* 99.10 *propone temporis profundi vastitatem*.

702 situ. Of lands cf. V. *Georg.* 1.72 *et segnem patiere situ durescere campum*, Ov. *Tr.* 3.10.70 *cessat iners rigido terra relicta situ*, Sen. *Pha.* 471 *orbis iacebit squalido turpis situ*, and of the underworld V. *Aen.* 6.462 *per loca senta situ*.

703. These phrases are in apposition to *tellus* in 702: "gloomy bourne of all things, the farthest region of the world." The *-que* is not a true connective but simply forms a correlative pair with *et*, cf. V. *Aen.* 8.731 *famamque et fata*, Ov. *Met.* 10.482 *inter mortisque metus et taedia vitae*, Sen. *Oed.* 264f., *TLL* 5.2.877.36ff.; Ovid provides a parallel instance in an appositional phrase at *Met.* 4.738f. *resoluta catenis / incedit virgo, pretiumque et causa doloris*. Seneca is here imitating line 4 of the passage by Pedo ap. Sen. Rhet. *Suas.* 1.15, *ad rerum metas extremaque litora mundi*; his second phrase also echoes Ov. *Tr.* 4.4.83 *haec . . . regio, magni paene ultima mundi*. Pedo and Ovid, however, are referring only to physical limits; what makes Sen.'s phrases particularly powerful is that both *finis* and *ultima* could have an additional temporal connotation, which is caught in Miller's rendering "sad end of things, the world's last estate."[101]

---

101. Gilbert Wakefield (on Lucr. 6.1267) opined that the verse "manifestissimus est νοθείας, et expellendus furca," and several editors of Sen. have deleted it. Presumably they were misled by taking *-que* as a true connective, with *finis* and *ultima* as further subjects of *torpet*, which would indeed be difficult. Seneca imitates Pedo, and Sen. Rhet. *Suas.* 1 generally, several times elsewhere (cf. comm. on 290, 540, 550–54, and Tarrant on *Ag.* 407ff.), and he echoes Ovid constantly; the line's authenticity is also supported by the fact that Lucan imitates its wording and appositional function in a similar context at 6.649f., and borrows the substantive use of *mundi ultima* at 4.147.

Commentary: Act III

705 marcore horrida. The transmitted reading *maerore horrida* has long been suspected, I believe rightly. It is one thing to transfer the adjective *maestus* from the shades themselves (648) to their abode (703, *HO* 1705 *maesta . . . regna*), and quite another to call the *scenery* of the underworld "disheveled with grief." The notion of *TLL* (8.42.84f.) that the phrase somehow has an active sense ("Orci aspectus maestum reddit intuentem") is plainly impossible. There can be little doubt that Richter's *marcore horrida* is the right correction. The unusual *marcor* would tend to be replaced by the more common *maeror*, particularly as *e/c* are easily confused in minuscule. *Marcor* is rare before Sen., but he uses it three times elsewhere, once of the effects of blight on crops (*QNat.* 3.27.4 *segetum sine fruge surgentium marcor*).[102]

706. Again Seneca rounds off with a summarizing line, epigrammatically shaped with paronomasia *morte-mortis* (cf. 5 comm.). Similar Senecan expressions with paronomasia are *Oed.* 180f. *o dira novi facies leti, / gravior leto*, *Thy.* 572 *peior est bello timor ipse belli*, cf. also *Tro.* 783 *o morte dira tristius leti genus*.

707 quid ille e.q.s. "What of him who . . ."; for the construction cf. 1194, *Pha.* 154, *Med.* 350, 355.

sceptro. Compare 65 comm., and the illustrations in Roscher, 1.1802, 1806, 1809.

708 populos leves. Compare Ov. *Met.* 10.14 *perque leves populos simulacraque functa sepulcro*. On *populos* v. comm. on 191; for *levis* cf. also Hor. *Carm.* 1.10.18f. *virgaque levem coerces / aurea turbam*, *TLL* 7.2.1204.49ff.

709ff. A smaller instance of the place-action sequence, enclosed within the larger place-description which constitutes this part of Theseus' report (cf. comm. on 662–827). We see here an instance of the formula whereby the ἔκφρασις τόπου begins *est locus* (*domus, turris,* etc.) and the return to human action is marked by a demonstrative pronoun or adverb (*huc*, etc., here *hanc* 720). This pattern is found already in

---

102. *Paedore horrida* was conjectured by Bentley, and (apparently independently) by F. Iacobs, *Animadvers. in Euripidis Tragoedias* (1790) 326 and by Wakefield loc. cit., with the precedents Lucr. 6.1268f. *membra videres / horrida paedore* and anon. ap. Cic. *Tusc.* 3.12 *barba paedore horrida*. But *paedore* is less attractive paleographically than *marcore*, and in addition the word is restricted to human contexts, *squalor* (here metrically impossible) having a more general application, e.g. Sen. *Tranq.* 2.13 *oculi longo locorum horrentium squalore releventur*.

[304]

Homer and remains common in epic, notably Vergil; it appears also in Greek tragedy, particularly in messengers' narratives (e.g. Aesch. *Pers.* 447ff. νῆσός τις ἐστὶ πρόσθε Σαλαμῖνος τόπων / . . . ἐνταῦθα . . .), and in Greek and Roman comedy: see Austin on V. *Aen.* 1.12 and 4.483. For other Senecan examples, all in messenger speeches, cf. *Tro.* 1068, *Pha.* 1057, *Oed.* 530, *Ag.* 558, *Thy.* 641, [*HO* 485].

These lines on the palace of Dis and its setting are influenced by Vergil's description in *Aen.* 6.549ff. of the castle in which Rhadamanthus holds court. That is encircled by Phlegethon, which *torquet . . . sonantia saxa* (551); just as here Acheron flows around the palace of Dis, and noisily rolls rocks along in its course. And the *porta adversa ingens* of Vergil's castle suggests both the *porta regni* of 720 and some of the wording of 717. Note also the similarity of *triplici circumdata muro* (549) to Seneca's *cingitur duplici vado*.

In 782 the palace of Dis appears on the far bank of Lethe, and there is no mention of its being encircled by Styx and Acheron. But the inconsistency is not obtrusive in view of the separation of the passages, and is excused by the vagueness of poetic geography, particularly concerning the underworld.

710. A line with powerful sound effects. Darkness covers the whole underworld (a constant theme, cf. 855–62 comm.), but here it is especially impenetrable.

711–16. Plato speaks of the rivers of the underworld as flowing from a great chasm, which the poets have called Tartarus (*Phaedo* 112a), but for springs in the underworld one may compare the Petelia inscription (Kern *Orph. Frag.* 32a). For other rivers separating from Styx cf. Hom. *Od.* 10.513f., where Cocytus is an ἀπορρώξ of Styx. Seneca need not have had a specific precedent for this common source of Styx and Acheron, for the post-Augustans like to draw such pictures of conjoined discord, cf. e.g. *Oed.* 321ff. *sed ecce pugnax ignis in partes duas / discedit, et se scindit unius sacri / discors favilla*, and the divided flame on the pyre of Oedipus' sons, for which v. 389 *totidem rogos* comm.

The sentence begins as if there were going to be two phrases in apposition to *latex*, i.e. *alter quieto similis, alter rapidus et ferox*, but the second is replaced by a full clause. The change is characteristic of Sen.'s tendency to avoid lengthy subordination and to prefer main clauses.

711 discors. "Discordant," referring to the opposite character of Styx and Acheron. Leo's odd view that it means no more than *duplex* (I 19) is found also in L-S. Leo took the same view of *Oed.* 323 *discors favilla*, where it is refuted by the phrase *pugnax ignis* only two lines earlier.

Commentary: Act III

712 quieto similis. If the reading is right, *quieto* must have a strongly participial sense, so that the phrase means "looking as though it were at rest" (or even "asleep," Kingery); *similis* apologizes for the personification as at *Thy*. 697f. *nutavit aula dubia quo pondus daret / et fluctuanti similis*. *Similis* is often found with a participle, particularly in Ovid, cf. Bömer on *Met*. 1.708 ad fin. But the phrase is surprising, as *quietus* is frequently used as an adjective, and may be applied without qualification to rivers, cf. 680 *quieta labitur Lethe*, Hor. *Carm*. 3.29.40f. *quietos amnes*, 1.31.7f. *Liris quieta . . . aqua*, Sen. *Apocol*. 7 v. 13 (Arar) *quietis . . . vadis*. There may therefore be room for conjecture.

hunc iurant dei. That the gods swear by Styx is established from the earliest times (Hom. *Il*. 15.37f., Hes. *Theog*. 793ff.); in Sen. cf. *Ag*. 755 (deleted by Tarrant), *Thy*. 667.

712f. alter [latex] . . . devehens fluvio Styga. All three nouns refer to the same thing, another example of "disjunctiveness," cf. 683 with comm. A similar example in which the water is said to carry along the river (rather than vice versa, as e.g. at *Thy*. 116f.) is *Pha*. 701 *rupesque et amnes, unda quos torrens rapit. Fluvio* perhaps has the sense "stream, current." It is a notably less common word than *amnis* and *flumen* in both poetry and prose (see the figures in *TLL* s.vv. *amnis* and *flumen*, and Axelson 126 with n. 19); Sen. uses *fluvius* only here in the tragedies.

713 sacram. Not infrequently used, like ἱερός, of springs and rivers, cf. *Phoen*. 126 *sacra . . . Dirce*, *Thy*. 116f. *sacer Alpheos*, N-H on Hor. *Carm*. 1.1.22; but particularly appropriate to Styx as the sanction of the gods' oaths.

714–16. This picture of Acheron is influenced by Vergil's description of Phlegethon (cf. comm. on 709ff.): Vergil's Acheron is different, being turbid and full of *caenum* and *harena* (*Aen*. 6.296f.). Seneca is more interested here in the contrast in character between the two streams, than in their mythical identity (though silence is not inappropriate to the awesome Styx); compare the freedom with which he treats the function of Lethe (cf. 679–86 comm.). Later writers also assimilate Acheron to Phlegethon in making it fiery, cf. Luc. 3.16, Sil. 11.473.

715f. invius renavigari. For the concept of the rivers of the underworld as preventing escape, v. comm. on 679–86 and 681–83. Acheron is not infrequently thought of as the river shades must cross on their way into the underworld (554 comm.), and thus in some sense as a boundary; the violent character Sen. here attributes to Acheron would make it an effective barrier.

The weighty compound *renavigari* was suggested in this context by Hor. *Carm.* 2.14.11 *unda . . . omnibus . . . enaviganda*. The dictionaries cite only this passage for *renavigo* in verse. For the infinitive dependent on an adjective, v. H-S 350f.; such explanatory infinitives are often passive, e.g. V. *Aen.* 6.49 *maiorque videri*, Hor. *Carm.* 2.4.11 *leviora tolli*, *Ars P.* 163 *cereus . . . flecti*, Luc. 3.347 *horrida cerni*.

716 duplici vado. "By this pair of rivers," i.e. Styx and Acheron.

717–20. "The house of Dis/Hades" is sometimes simply a metonymy for the world of death (see comm. on 620 *domum*), but here Sen. visualizes a specific building within the underworld, through whose gates the incoming spirits must pass. The picture is similar in general terms to that of Hes. *Theog.* 767ff. ἔνθα θεοῦ χθονίου πρόσθεν δόμοι ἠχήεντες κ.τ.λ. Ovid also envisages a *regia Ditis* (*Met.* 4.438: Sen. borrows the phrase), but he imagines the shades as inhabiting an *urbs Stygia*, and it is through the gates of this city, not of the palace, that they enter.

717 adversa. The front of the palace faces those newly arriving. Compare the *porta adversa ingens* of the Vergilian castle (709ff. comm.), and several other instances of *adversus* in *Aen.* 6 describing that which confronts those who make their way into the underworld (418, 631, 636).[103]

718 umbrante luco. The dark grove connotes awesome mystery, cf. 663 comm.

vasto specu. Seneca often uses *specus* in connection with the underworld or entrances to it (for adjectives such as *vastus* v. comm. 665f.). In some of these places, as here, the word refers to a particular enclosed space in the underworld, cf. 94, *Thy.* 9. The relationship between the palace and this entrance-cave is unclear: does the palace lie behind or within the cave, or is the cave part of the structure of the palace? The details here seem impressionistic rather than coherent.

720 campus. Such λειμῶνες or *campi* are a traditional feature of underworld descriptions: e.g. Vergil has both the *Lugentes Campi* of un-

---

103. All modern editors have rightly preferred E's *adversa* to A's *aversa*. The latter would have to mean either "facing away" or "remote, out-of-the-way," neither of which meanings would be appropriate in view of 718–20.

Commentary: Act III

happy lovers (*Aen.* 6.441) and the *campi . . . nitentes* of Elysium (ibid. 667). One may note particularly the λειμών on which Minos, Rhadamanthus, and Aeacus judge the dead (cf. 731f.) in Plato *Gorg.* 524a (called the πεδίον ἀληθείας in ps.-Plat. *Axioch.* 371c). See also *Hymn. Orph.* 18 (to Pluto) 1f. ὦ τὸν ὑποχθόνιον ναίων δόμον, ὀμβριμόθυμε, / Ταρτάριον λειμῶνα.

hanc circa. On postposition of prepositions v. comm. 148 *inter*.

721f. Earlier writers are unspecific about Pluto's functions with regard to the shades; Aeschylus is unusual in making him judge them (*Suppl.* 230f., where however ὡς λόγος probably indicates that the idea is not solely Aeschylean). Here the god "sorts out" (*digerit*) the souls, perhaps separating those who must stand trial (731ff.) from those who need not. Some later writers again make him a judge (Stat. *Theb.* 8.21ff., Sil. 13.601f.).

722. The line had been punctuated after *recentes* until Leo (I 190 n. 11) moved the full-stop to the end of the line to provide a subject for *digerit*, necessarily reading *dei* with E (A has *deo*). Modern editors have almost all followed his lead. But on an unprejudiced view it is evident that the phrases describing Pluto, beginning with *dira maiestas*, belong together. In particular the brevity of the phrase *frons torva* would be inappropriate at the beginning of a sentence but suitable for the second member of a list. As for the subject of the verb *digerit*, that is supplied without difficulty from *Ditis* (717) and *tyranni* (719). There are several parallels in this play for a change of subject without explicit identification of the new subject, cf. 33, 275, 312, 821. At the end of 722, then, we are left with a choice between A's *deo* and E's *dei*. The probable explanation of the divergence is simplification by E of the possessive dative; Leo's hypothesis that A has accommodated the case of the noun to that of *illi* (724) seems less likely. *Deo* is also supported by ps.-Sen. *HO* 1746 *tam placida frons est, tanta maiestas viro*, which imitates the present passage.

The use of an abstract noun as the subject of *digerit* would not in itself be an objection to Leo's punctuation (v. 701 comm.). There is a particularly similar instance at Phaedrus 2.5.23 *tum sic iocata est tanta maiestas ducis*. (Phaedrus is fond of this construction, cf. e.g. 1.13.12.)

animas recentes. Compare Ovid's phrase *umbrae . . . recentes, Met.* 4.434.

722–27. Commentators have often compared this description of Dis with that by Claudian, *Rapt. Pros.* 1.79ff., which is clearly influenced by these Senecan lines:

> ipse rudi fultus solio nigraque verendus
> maiestate sedet; squalent immania foedo
> sceptra situ, sublime caput maestissima nubes
> asperat et dirae riget inclementia formae;
> terrorem dolor augebat.

723 frons torva. *Torvus* is often used of the eyes or face. Vergil has the phrase in description of Polyphemus (*Aen.* 3.636), and Ovid of Tragoedia personified (*Am.* 3.1.12).

723–25. Jupiter, Dis, and Neptune are physically very similar in artistic representations, being distinguished primarily by their attributes (Roscher 1.1794.8ff.). Dis is sometimes called "the infernal Jove," though chiefly in reference to his status rather than appearance (47 *inferni Iovis* comm.).

723 specimen. The face of Dis "gives proof of who his brothers are, and of the greatness of his birth": a characteristically "pointed" notion. For *specimen* with such a genitive cf. V. *Aen.* 12.164 *Solis avi specimen.* Many editors have accepted the alteration by recc. to *speciem*, presumably because *speciem gerere* can be paralleled in the sense of "bearing a likeness to," cf. Lucr. 4.52, Cic. *Off.* 3.16 *similitudinem quandam gerebant speciemque sapientium*, Col. 3.17.2, 8.2.13. But the statement that Dis "bears a resemblance to his brothers and to his great family" (or "ancestors"?) lacks the pointed vigor of the transmitted reading. There is no reason to doubt *specimen gerere* in this context, cf. *Med.* 386 *furoris ore signa . . . gerens*, *Pha.* 829f. *regium in vultu decus / gerens*.

725f. magna pars e.q.s. For the characteristic rhetorical turn cf. *Ep.* 90.43 *nunc magna pars nostri metus tecta sunt*, 123.3 *magna pars libertatis est bene moratus venter*.

regni trucis. "The grimness of the realm," on the same principle as *ab urbe condita* = "from the foundation of the city" (cf. 1052 comm.).

726f. timet . . . timetur. On paronomasia of verb forms in Sen. cf. 116 comm.: similar examples include *Tro.* 1099f. *non flet e turba omnium / qui fletur*, *Med.* 218f. *petebant tunc meos thalamos proci, / qui nunc petuntur*.

Commentary: Act III

728 iam sera reddi iura. The slowness with which retribution overtakes the guilty is often remarked (622 comm.), though more usually in connection with punishment in this world than in the next.

I accept Ageno's simple correction *iam* for the transmitted *tam*. (For MSS confusion between these words cf. 614, *Oed.* 77, *HO* 1610, *Oct.* 872, 930). *Tam* puts too much emphasis on the lateness of the punishment, as though Amphitryon were incredulous at the idea: such incredulity would be out of keeping with the tone of 730. In view of the word-order, *iam* must go primarily with *sera*: for *iam serus* cf. ps.-V. *Culex* 32, Ov. *Tr.* 4.2.71, *TLL* 7.87.72f.

728f. oblitos sui sceleris. Through the passage of time, and the fact that the crime has long gone undetected: hardly through drinking from Lethe (681 comm.), as that would suggest some absurdity in the administration of infernal justice.

730 veri rector. Both Bentley and Withof found this phrase intolerable (Bentley conjecturing *veri exactor*), but in the context it yields a reasonably clear meaning, "one who oversees (or "guides") the discovery of truth." The phrase is certainly compressed and perhaps clumsy, but not impossible. The pairing of *rector* with *arbiter* was perhaps suggested to Sen. by a recollection of 205 *Olympi rector et mundi arbiter*.

731–34. Minos, Rhadamanthus, and Aeacus (father of Peleus, hence *Thetidis socer* 734) are traditionally the three judges of the dead.

Seneca's language in these lines echoes that of the Roman courts and their procedure. Thus *quaesitor* and *forum* are words with strongly Roman connotations. The phrase *alta sede* refers to a judge's tribunal: similarly at *Cons. Marc.* 19.4 Seneca mentions *tribunalia et reos* among the details of the mythological underworld. *Iudicia . . . sortitur* suggests Roman judicial procedure, though its precise interpretation is unclear (see ad loc.). Finally both *sedere* and *adire* are *voces propriae* in judicial contexts. For *sedere* of the judge cf. Prop. 4.11.19 *si quis posita sedet Aeacus urna* e.q.s., Tarrant on Sen. *Ag.* 730f. *Adire* is often used of appearing before magistrates, though more usually to lay an accusation, lodge an appeal, etc. than to stand trial (cf. *TLL* 1.617.50ff.). Such Roman coloring is seen also in Vergil's description of Minos at *Aen.* 6.432f. *quaesitor Minos urnam movet; ille silentum / consiliumque* [v.l. *conciliumque*] *vocat vitasque et crimina discit*. Seneca borrows *quaesitor* from Vergil both here and in a similar context at *Ag.* 24.

732 iudicia . . . sortitur. The casting of lots, or the judge's urn, is mentioned in several passages concerning *post mortem* judgment: apart from Prop. and Verg. cited above, cf. Sen. *Ag.* 23f. *omnes quos ob infandas manus / quaesitor urna Cnosius versat reos,* Stat. *Silv.* 2.1.219, 3.3.16, *Theb.* 4.530, 8.102, 11.571f., *Anth. Pal.* 7.384.5f. But the precise function of the lot is a matter of debate, cf. Shackleton Bailey, *Propertiana* 264, Tarrant on *Ag.* 24. In the present passage, *iudicia* might mean either "trials" or "verdicts, sentences." In the first case, the lot would decide the order of cases; this is the function of the urn in the Vergilian passage according to Servius, though his interpretation has been challenged (G. Williams, *Tradition and Originality* [Oxford 1968] 397f.). *Sera,* however, favors the second meaning, and in several other passages the lot seems to be associated (exactly how is unclear) with sentencing, so *Ag.* 23f. cited above, Stat. *Silv.* 3.3.15f. *si quis pulsatae conscius anguem / matris et inferna rigidum timet Aeacon urna, Theb.* 11.571f. *si modo Agenorei stat Gnosia iudicis urna, / qua reges punire datur,* Anth. Pal. 7.384.5f.

trepidis . . . reis. An Ovidian phrase, used four times by that author, but not in a context of underworld punishment. For other conventional poetic adjectives for *rei* v. N-H on Hor. *Carm.* 2.1.13.

735–47. Punishments in the underworld for sins committed in the upper world are mentioned as early as Homer, though there confined to a few notorious sinners (see comm. 750–59). By Plato's time the idea that transgressors in general would receive *post mortem* judgment and punishment was widespread (*Rep.* 330d–e, Paus. 10.28.4–5, Nilsson, *Greek Folk Religion* 117ff.), and Plato's myths of the afterlife in *Rep.* 614ff., *Phaedo* 113ff. and *Gorg.* 523ff. further strengthened it.

Seneca's treatment of the topic is remarkable for its concentration on the fate of rulers: contrast, for example, the wide variety of types punished and rewarded in Vergil's underworld. There are of course precedents: in Plato *Rep.* 615d and *Gorg.* 525d–e tyrants and despots are prominent among those to be punished. Nevertheless Sen.'s exclusive preoccupation with this class is clearly influenced by the political experience of his age (note too that the passage is imitated both by ps.-Sen. at *HO* 1559–63 and by Silius at 13.602–12); the praise of mild and bloodless rule (739ff.) anticipates Sen.'s advice to Nero in *Clem.* The brief homily at 745–47 which forms the climax of the passage, though formally addressed to all rulers (*quicumque, vestra*), could scarcely avoid being taken as directed especially at the reigning emperor.

735f. For the thought cf. *Thy.* 311 *saepe in magistrum scelera redierunt sua,* Shakespeare *Macbeth* 1.7.8ff.:

[*311*]

Commentary: Act III

>   that we but teach
> Bloody instructions, which, being taught, return
> To plague th' inventor. This even-handed justice
> Commends th' ingredients of our poison'd chalice
> To our own lips.[104]

737–39. This picture of tyrants being paid back in their own coin obviously gives Seneca a certain satisfaction: note the vigorous alliteration on *c* and *d* in 737. Similarly in *Apocol.* 14 Sen. has Aeacus condemn Claudius without hearing his defense—as Claudius was said to have treated defendants in life—quoting the saw αἴκε πάθοι τά τ' ἔρεξε, δίκη κ' ἰθεῖα γένοιτο. The focus on punishment of tyrants explains why Sen. insists on "an eye for an eye" in underworld justice, in contrast to his concern for *venia* and *clementia* in earthly administration of justice.

739 scindi. That is, with lashes, cf. Ov. *Ibis* 183 *hic tibi de Furiis scindet latus una flagello.*

739–42. The single idea "whoever rules mildly" is expressed in a variety of ways. Such variation and pleonasm is characteristic of Sen.'s style (cf. Carlsson 1925 71ff.). For 739^b cf. *Clem.* 1.13.4 *qui potentiam suam placide . . . exercet.*

740 dominus . . . vitae. That is, of life and death. The full phrase *dominus vitae necisque* occurs at Livy 2.35.2, 30.12.12, Curt. 4.1.22, Tac. *Hist.* 4. 62; cf. also Sen. *Thy.* 607f. *vos quibus rector maris atque terrae / ius dedit magnum necis atque vitae*, *Clem.* 1.1.2 *ego vitae necisque gentibus arbiter.*

741 imperium regit. Compare V. *Aen.* 1.340 *imperium Dido Tyria regit urbe profecta*, Ov. *Tr.* 2.166, *Pont.* 3.3.61f. *sic regat imperium terrasque coerceat omnis / Caesar*, Sen. *Pha.* 618 *te imperia regere, me decet iussa exsequi*. In the present passage *imperium* must have an abstract sense ("sway") and function as an internal object of *regit*; this is so also in *Pha.* and Vergil, but in the Ovidian passages *imperium* could conceivably mean "the empire."

---

104. Cunliffe 82 suggested that Shakespeare's lines were influenced by the present passage. But if there is Senecan influence, *Thy.* 311 seems the more likely source, being closer in language (for the teaching imagery cf. *magistrum*, and *doces* in 310) and context (crimes redounding on their authors in this world rather than the next). The immediate source of the idea is not Sen. but passages in the chronicles, cited by Muir and other editors: nevertheless the generality and epigrammatic quality with which Shakespeare endows it certainly has a Senecan ring.

Commentary: Act III

742 animaeque parcit. *Anima* as often is equivalent to *vita* (which Sen. used in 740), and the phrase is a variation on *vitae (capiti) parcere*, for which cf. *OLD* s.v. *parco* 3. The phrase is used in this sense at Hor. *Carm.* 3.9.12 *si parcent animae fata superstiti*; contrast Sen. *Tro.* 410f. *mors individua est, noxia corpori / nec parcens animae*, where *anima* means "soul" as opposed to "body." Zwierlein 1966 186ff. objects to *anima* meaning "life" in general, rather than an individual life as in the Horatian passage, but this seems an unnecessary scruple when *vita* in 740 has just this general sense.[105] Seneca no doubt avoided using the plural here because of its ambiguity.

longa permensus diu. Pleonasm is common enough in Sen. Trag., but it rarely involves adverbs; in fact this is the only pleonastic use of *diu* in the genuine tragedies, whereas it is often used loosely as a convenient line-end in ps.-Sen. *Oct*. The pleonasm underlines the long rule of the just king, in implied contrast to the brief tenure of the tyrant; for the contrast cf. e.g. *Tro.* 258f., *Clem.* 1.11.4 *quid enim est, cur reges consenuerint..., tyrannorum exsecrabilis et brevis potestas sit? Permensus* is an effective metaphor, suggesting that the just king has "full measure" of enjoyment from his long years as they pass. The word connotes length of years again at Mart. 9.29.1 *saecula Nestoreae permensa, Philaeni, senectae*.

743f. vivacis . . . felix. The MSS have *felicis . . . felix*. Word repetition without obvious rhetorical point is not unknown (43f. comm.), but corruption seems probable in view of the clumsiness of this instance. I am inclined to think *felix* genuine in 744 as it is (like *fortunatus*) applied to the inhabitants of Elysium, cf. 796f. *felices . . . umbras*, V. *Aen.* 6.669 *felices animae*, Luc. 6.784 *felicibus umbris*. Presumably, therefore, *felicis* in 743 arose through anticipation. Bentley's conjecture *vivacis* was part of a characteristically radical rewriting of 742^b–43^a as *summa permensus semel / vivacis aevi spatia*: taken by itself it admittedly adds a further degree of pleonasm to the clause, but that is hardly an objection in Sen. Trag.

---

105. The conjecture *animoque parcit* in τ T² recc., accepted by Giardina and Zwierlein, is not only unnecessary, but itself has difficulties of meaning. Gruter glossed it with *animo moderatur*, which suggests the meaning "controls his spirit," but it is most doubtful whether *parcit* could have that sense. The verb itself would point rather to the meaning "refrains from anger" (cf. such phrases as Hor. *Carm.* 3.14.11f. *male ominatis / parcite verbis*, Livy 8.7.21 *nullis verborum contumeliis parcere*, Sen. *Thy.* 221f. *ubi / sceleri pepercit?*), but *animus* in the sense of "anger" is usually plural.

743 vel caelum petit. The traditional belief that a few great souls had been rewarded by deification (the exemplar being Hercules himself) was not entirely out of keeping with the Stoic view that the pure soul rises to rejoin the heavenly fire, cf. E. V. Arnold, *Roman Stoicism* (London 1911) 263f., 268. Thus Cicero, for example, under Stoic influence, promises a place in heaven to just and good rulers (*Rep.* 6.13).

744f. The concept of a blessed existence in Elysium as a reward for goodness in this life is highly traditional, being found already in Pindar (*Ol.* 2.68ff.) and Plato (*Gorg.* 526c). The more usual form of reference is "the Elysian fields," Ἠλύσιον πεδίον Hom. *Od.* 4.563, *Elysii campi* Tib. 1.3.58, *campo . . . Elysio* Sen. *Tro.* 944; *nemoris* here comes from V. *Aen.* 6.638f. *amoena virecta / fortunatorum nemorum*. *Laetus* is frequently applied to the area, as *felix* to its inhabitants, cf. V. *Aen.* 6.638 *locos laetos*, 744 *laeta arva*, Hor. *Carm.* 1.10.17f.

745 iudex futurus. As great leaders on earth continue to hold sway below (Achilles in Hom. *Od.* 11.482ff., Agamemnon in Aesch. *Cho.* 354ff.), so it is appropriate that men distinguished for their justice during life should judge among the dead: cf. Plato *Apol.* 41a, where the judges are not only Minos, Rhadamanthus, and Aeacus but also Τριπτόλεμος καὶ ἄλλοι ὅσοι τῶν ἡμιθέων δίκαιοι ἐγένοντο ἐν τῷ ἑαυτῶν βίῳ; and Lucian *Ver. Hist.* 2.10, where Aristides ὁ δίκαιος and others sit on the bench with Rhadamanthus on the Isle of the Blest.

745–47 sanguine humano abstine e.q.s. Apostrophe addressed in this way to persons outside the dramatic framework is rare in the episodes (though less so in the odes, e.g. 178, 858, *Tro.* 407, 1018ff.), and though it could be explained as simply a more vivid form of *sanguine humano abstineat quicumque regnat*, its applicability to the reigning emperor could scarcely be missed (735–47 comm.). For the direct injunction imparting the moral to be drawn from underworld punishments, cf. V. *Aen.* 6.620 *discite iustitiam moniti et non temnere divos*. This advice is more general than Sen.'s, and is not addressed to a specific class.

747 vestra. *Quicumque regnas* in 746 suggests a class, and the plural *vestra* therefore corresponds to it in sense if not in grammatical number; for such adaptations cf. e.g. Plaut. *Men.* 82ff. *nam homini misero . . . maior lubido est . . .*; *nam se eximunt*, Livy 2.15.1 *missi . . . honoratissimus quisque*, K-S 634.

750–59. The punishment of the great sinners forms a standard element of an *inferorum descriptio* (Hom. *Od.* 11.576ff., V. *Aen.* 6.595ff.,

Commentary: Act III

Ov. *Met.* 4.457ff., 10.41ff.), and indeed is a favorite *locus* in Sen. Trag. (cf. *Med.* 744ff., *Pha.* 1229ff., *Ag.* 15ff., *Thy.* 4ff., ps.-Sen. *HO* 942ff., *Oct.* 621ff.). Seneca regularly includes Ixion, Sisyphus, Tantalus, and Tityus, as does ps.-Sen. (except that *Med.* and *HO* omit Tityos); for precedents v. Tarrant on *Ag.* 15ff. Here Sen. adds the Danaids, the Cadmeids, and Phineus, all of whom had Theban connections (Phineus being Cadmus' brother). The Danaids are not in fact uncommon in such lists: they occur in *Med.* (and *HO*), and earlier e.g. Lucr. 3.1008ff., Prop. 2.1.67f., Tib. 1.3.79f., Hor. *Carm.* 3.11.26f., ps.-V. *Culex* 245ff., Ov. locc. citt. and *Ibis* 173ff. But I find no parallel for the Cadmeids in the underworld, and only one (Prop. 3.5.41) for Phineus; it seems they are included because of their association with Thebes.

The list simply provides information in response to Amphitryon's question, and its six single-line entries are somewhat cataloguelike, with the verb standing enumeratively at the beginning (750, 756, 758f., cf. 141–46 comm.), or as a variation at the end (751, 757). (For this enumerative effect cf. e.g. *Oed.* 643ff. *petam* / . . . *traham,* / *traham* . . . / *vertam* . . . *obteram*.) This pattern is varied by the more elaborate treatment of Tantalus' punishment, however. In other plays the lists have a more dynamic relationship to the dramatic situation (e.g. at *Pha.* 1229ff. suggesting punishments for Theseus), and their emphasis is adjusted accordingly (M. E. Carbone in *Phoenix* 31 [1977] 53–55).

750. The *rota* provides an effective and useful line-ending in references to Ixion in both dactylics and iambics, and is often qualified by some such adjective as *celeris*, cf. Tib. 1.3.74 *versantur celeri noxia membra rota*, Ov. *Ibis* 176 *quique agitur rapidae vinctus ab orbe rotae*, 192, Sen. *Pha.* 1236f., *Ag.* 15f., *Thy.* 8 *aut membra celeri differens cursu rota*.

751. In most accounts of his punishment, Sisyphus rolls his stone uphill using hands and feet or hands and neck (v. Wilisch in Roscher 4.964.65ff.). The wording of some Roman accounts, however, suggests rather that he *carried* it: in addition to the present passage cf. Prop. 2.20.32 *tumque ego Sisyphio saxa labore geram*, Sen. *Pha.* 1229ff. *cervicibus / his, his repositum degravet fessas manus / saxum*, *Thy.* 6f. *Sisyphi numquid lapis / gestandus umeris . . . venit*, *Apocol.* 15.1 *irrita Sisyphio volvuntur pondera collo*, Mart. 10.5.15, ps.-Sen. *HO* 942f.; see also Schol. ad Lycophr. *Alex.* 176. (The different versions may go back to Homer's account in *Od.* 11, where 596 indicates pushing, but λᾶαν βαστάζοντα πελώριον 594 could be read to mean "lifting, carrying.") Here Sen. omits reference to the rock's frustrating elusiveness (e.g. *revolubilis* Ov. *Ibis* 189, *lubricus* Sen. *Med.* 747) and emphasizes rather its burdensome mass, for which cf. Homer's πελώριον, Prop. 4.11.23 *Sisyphe, mole vaces*, V. *Aen.* 6.616 *saxum ingens*.

Commentary: Act III

752-55. This version of Tantalus' punishment, according to which he is tantalized by unattainable water and fruit, appears in Hom. *Od.* 11.583ff., but in Greek literature it is generally ignored in favor of the punishment of the overhanging stone. Roman writers, however, usually follow Homer, though in many references (particularly of the shorter kind, e.g. Sen. *Med.* 745, *Pha.* 1232) the fruit is omitted, and indeed it appears in the present passage as something of an afterthought. For details v. K. F. Smith on Tib. 1.3.77f., Tarrant on *Ag.* 19ff.

senex. Applied allusively to Tantalus again at *Ag.* 22 and 769 (but to Sisyphus *Pha.* 1231), cf. *HO* 1075. The explanation of the term is presumably that Tantalus belongs to a relatively early generation of heroes and is frequently referred to as an ancestor of the Tantalids, cf. Eur. *Or.* 984ff. (Electra's words) ἵν' ἐν θρήνοισιν ἀναβοάσω / γέροντι πατρὶ Ταντάλῳ / ὅς ἔτεκεν ἔτεκε γενέτορας ἐμέθεν δόμων.

753 sectatur. Replaces the usual *captat* (Hor. *Sat.* 1.1.68, Ov. *Met.* 10. 42, *Am.* 2.2.43, *AA* 2.605, *Her.* 16.211, Sen. *Ag.* 770, *Thy.* 2), and appears only here in Sen. Trag.: the verb strengthens the harshly effective alliteration on *s* and *c* (*x*) in this clause.

mentum. Unusual in Roman accounts of Tantalus' punishment, but cf. *inc. inc. trag.* 111 R² *mento summam amnem attingens, enectus siti*; the ultimate source is Hom. *Od.* 11.583 [λίμνη] προσέπλαζε γενείῳ.

754. That is, "when it has convinced him (of its availability), though he has often been tricked before."

756. The wording recalls particularly Ov. *Ibis* 182 *visceraque adsiduae debita praebet avi*. The point that Tityus' liver regrows though consumed is sometimes conveyed by a single adjective, as in these examples or *Ag.* 18 *fecundum iecur*, Ov. *Ibis* 194 *inconsumpto viscere*, sometimes more fully as at V. *Aen.* 6.598f. *immortale iecur . . . fecundaque poenis / viscera*, Ov. *Pont.* 1.2.39f., Sen. *Thy.* 11 *nocte reparans quidquid amisit die*.

volucri. The two vultures attending Tityus at Hom. *Od.* 11.578f. become one at V. *Aen.* 6.597 and Hor. *Carm.* 3.4.78 and frequently, though not consistently, in later authors (v. Roscher 5.1037f.): e.g. singular here and *Pha.* 1233, *Ag.* 18, but plural *Thy.* 10.

757. The punishment of the Danaids, according to most authorities (see comm. on 750-59), consists of carrying water to a jar that leaks and can never be filled. At *Med.* 748 *urnis quas foratis inritus ludit labor* it

Commentary: Act III

seems that the pitchers in which they carry water are themselves leaky (unless *urnis . . . foratis* is simply a poetic plural); according to Costa (ad loc. and in *Mnemosyne* 26 [1973] 289–91) parallels for this variant are rare and late. Costa considers the present line to be ambiguous, but *plenas* surely indicates the standard version.

gerunt. E's reading is preferable in this context to A's *ferunt*, cf. Lucr. 3.1008f. *puellas / quod memorant laticem pertusum congerere in vas*, Ov. *Ibis* 177 *quaeque gerunt umeris perituras Belides undas*.

758. That is, they cannot rid themselves of the Bacchic frenzy; see the fragment of Accius' *Bacchae* in which Bacchus has maddened the women of Thebes (cf. Eur. *Bacch.* 35ff.): *deinde omni stirpe cum incluta Cadmeide / vagant matronae percitatae insania* (235f. R²). Seneca's line recalls also the frenzied wanderings of Dido, V. *Aen.* 4.68f. *uritur infelix Dido totaque vagatur / urbe furens*.

Cadmeides. On long Greek names at verse end v. comm. on 244, 246: Accius' *Cadmeide* is the only example from Republican tragedy.

759. Phineus was punished—either for an offence against the gods, or for blinding his children by an earlier marriage (cf. Roscher 3.2357ff.)—by blindness and by having his food fouled or stolen from his table by the Harpies. Most authorities locate this punishment on earth, but Propertius 3.5.41 places it in the underworld as does Sen. here. This variant is not inappropriate, for the punishment has a tantalizing quality reminiscent of other sinners' tortures (compare Phineus' inedible banquet with that of V. *Aen.* 6.604ff.), and the Harpies are sometimes associated with the underworld (V. *Aen.* 3.214f., 6.289; cf. Dieterich *Nekyia* 56).

761. For the question cf. Eur. 611f. Her. καὶ θηρά γ' εἰς φῶς τὸν τρίκρανον ἤγαγον. / Amph. μάχῃ κρατήσας ἢ θεᾶς δωρήμασιν; Here, however, *spolium* adds a suggestion of hubris, cf. 51f. *spolia iactantem patri / fraterna*. The following narrative leaves no doubt that though technically Pluto consented (805), the answer to Amphitryon's question is *spolium* rather than *munus*.

762–827. These lines provide the fullest extant treatment of Hercules' capture of Cerberus. Stesichorus' Κέρβερος is almost totally unknown to us, and the extant lines of Pindar's dithyramb which may have dealt with the subject (*POxy.* 1604 = fr. 70b Snell) are purely introductory. The most detailed account apart from Seneca's is that in

Apollodorus 2.5.12. It may well be justified to postulate a lost archaic epic on the subject, whose influence may be traced not only in Apollod. but also in the Pindaric fragment *POxy*. 2622 (conceivably part of the dithyramb referred to above), in Bacchylides *Dithyramb* 5, in the catabasis of Dionysus in Aristophanes' *Frogs* and in that of Aeneas in V. *Aen.* 6; cf. also ps.-Plat. *Axioch.* 371e, Diod. Sic. 4.25.1–26.1 (v. Norden *Aeneis VI* p. 5, H. Lloyd-Jones, *Maia* 19 [1967] 206ff.). This tradition made much of the fact that Hercules was initiated into the Eleusinian Mysteries before his descent, and consequently received cooperation from Pluto and Proserpina on his arrival in the underworld. Seneca's account omits several details found in this tradition, including H.'s initiation, his encounter in the underworld with Meleager, and his visit to Elysium. Some of these omissions could be seen as intended simply to shorten and concentrate the narrative, but H.'s relations with Pluto show a radically different concept of the hero. In Apollodorus, he asks Pluto for the hound, and abides by the god's condition that he subdue the creature without weapons, achieving his purpose by throttling it. Here he attacks it without asking leave of the rulers of the underworld, who are intimidated by his threatening presence (805f.). This is in keeping with Sen.'s general picture of him as a Harrower of Hell, and above all as one who relies to a hubristic degree on his own superhuman strength. The silence about Eleusis matches this picture; so does the silence about the help H. received from Hermes and Athena (e.g. Hom. *Od.* 11.625f., *Il.* 8.362ff.).

The very propriety of Hercules' behavior in the "Eleusinian" version implies an earlier version or versions in which he won Cerberus in a quite different manner, namely by *force majeure*. This supposition is strengthened by the consideration that fights with the god of death appear to be integral to the early Hercules myth, as is seen in his wounding of Hades (Hom. *Il.* 5.397) and in his struggle with Thanatos for the life of Alcestis. It is given substance by a Corinthian kotyle of the early sixth century B.C., which shows H. holding a stone threateningly while Pluto makes off behind his throne (Payne *Necrocorinthia* fig. 45c and p. 130). Possibly, then, Seneca's account is influenced, directly or indirectly, by a violent version of this kind.

The encounter with Charon (764–77) contains unmistakable echoes of the similar episode in V. *Aen.* 6 (see detailed comm.). Vergil had already drawn a contrast there between the violence of Hercules' catabasis and the peaceful nature of Aeneas', cf. 399f. *nullae hic insidiae tales (absiste moveri), / nec vim tela ferunt.* Seneca's purpose appears to be, while recalling Vergil, to make the contrast as evident as possible: characteristically H. resorts impatiently and unthinkingly to violence.

As for the actual subjugation of Cerberus, some element of violence is found even in most "Eleusinian" versions: thus H. fights the hound in Apollod. (cf. Eur. *Her.* 613), and vase paintings which show Proserpina's cooperation nevertheless sometimes have H. threatening Cerberus with his club.[106] Agreements over various details between Seneca's narrative and vase paintings or literary accounts suggest that Sen. has, characteristically, selected materials that appealed to him from a variety of sources (see comm. 797–802, 807f., 813–27). Also characteristic is his imitation of relevant passages from his great Roman predecessors: thus he borrows some elements from Vergil in his portrait of Cerberus (comm. on 783–85, 789, 792), and expands on Ovid in describing the hound's aversion to the daylight (comm. 813–27, also 808).

762f. The narrative of the exploit proper begins with a brief new ἔκφρασις τόπου (comm. on 662–827). Rocks are not an uncommon feature of infernal topography: cf. particularly that which stands by rivers in Hom. *Od.* 10.515, and v. Stanford on *Od.* 24.11 (adding Ar. *Frogs* 470f.). This one has no functional purpose but helps to create a grim, oppressive atmosphere. Such impressionistic use of detail is characteristic of Sen., and so is the detail itself—one of those threatening, overhanging masses so typical of Senecan landscape: cf. trees at 690, *Oed.* 542ff., *Thy.* 655; a palace *Thy.* 641ff.; a tower *Tro.* 1068ff.; a wall *Tro.* 1085ff.; a headland *Ag.* 562 (again with *imminet*).

763 stupente ubi unda segne torpescit fretum. So A; this is more stylish than E's *stupent ubi undae, segne t. f.*, and clearly right. Pleonasm in such Senecan descriptions regularly involves tautologous adjectives qualifying nouns in different cases, cf. 680 *placido quieta labitur Lethe vado*, 683f. *incerta vagus / Maeander unda ludit* and other passages cited on 536. E's error may be due either to loss of final *e* in *stupente* or to a literal-minded "correction" of the singular *unda*, for which cf. 683f. comm.

fretum. Unusual of a river, but paralleled at *Thy.* 73, 1017 (both of Phlegethon); *TLL* gives no instances before Sen. Compare *pelagus* of waters of the underworld at *HF* 554.

---

106. E.g. Boardman pl. Ib. The most peaceful version is that of Diodorus, who says that H. received Cerberus already tied up from Proserpina (4.25.1, cf. Timaeus ap. Plut. *Nic.* 1). Those vase paintings that show H. about to slip a chain onto a relatively docile Cerberus (see 807f. comm.) do not necessarily imply a complete absence of violence in the episode as a whole: Cerberus is necessarily pacific at this moment, otherwise he could not be chained.

Commentary: Act III

764–68. Closely modeled on Vergil's famous description in *Aen.* 6.298–304:

> portitor has horrendus aquas et flumina servat
> terribili squalore Charon, cui plurima mento
> canities inculta iacet, stant lumina flamma,
> sordidus ex umeris nodo dependet amictus.
> ipse ratem conto subigit velisque ministrat
> et ferruginea subvectat corpora cumba,
> iam senior, sed cruda deo viridisque senectus.

The tendency of Sen.'s reworking is toward a simple, direct, less elevated (and less evocative) style: thus *impexa pendet barba* replaces *cui plurima mento / canities inculta iacet*. He echoes the Vergilian lines elsewhere at *Oed.* 166–70 *quique capaci turbida cumba / flumina servat / durus senio navita crudo, / vix assiduo bracchia conto / lassata refert, / fessus turbam vectare novam*.

765 gestat. Des. Heraldus conjectured *vectat* (in book 1 of his *Adversaria* [Paris 1599] c. 12. p. 74), for which cf. V. *Aen.* 6.391 *corpora viva nefas Stygia vectare carina*, also ibid. 303 and Sen. *Oed.* 170, both quoted above. He has been followed by many modern editors including Leo, but Gronovius had already shown that *gestare* can be used of transporting by ship, cf. Curt. 4.7.24 *hunc . . . navigio aurato gestant sacerdotes*, Tac. *Hist.* 2.62 *ex urbe atque Italia inritamenta gulae gestabantur, strepentibus ab utroque mari itineribus*. Seneca likes *gestare* (though not usually in this sense); after Plautus (who has it thirteen times) the word is little used, but increases in popularity again with some of the post-Ovidians: Sen. has it eight times in the tragedies, thirteen in prose, Lucan has it eleven times, and *TLL* cites nine uses in Curtius.

senex. Charon was called γεραιός in the epic *Minyas*, our first literary reference to him, and so portrayed in Polygnotus' painting of the underworld (Paus. 10.28.2). Vergil calls him *senior*. The form *senex* (nom. and voc.) is rare, and *senior* common (4:20), in Vergil, but in Sen. the reverse is true (16:5); the reasons for this contrast may be lexical as well as metrical, cf. p. 470.

nodus. As in Vergil the point is that Charon's cloak is roughly knotted rather than secured by a *fibula*.

767 concavae lucent genae. *Genae* here = "eyes," and the phrase corresponds closely to a detail in the Vergilian source-passage, *stant lumina flamma*. In place of *lucent* (A), E has *squalent*, which has intruded from

765, perhaps because a copyist took *genae* as "cheeks" and could not understand *lucent*.[107] For *concavus* of sunken eyes cf. Cels. 2.6.1, Suet. *Cal.* 50.1.

769 onere vacuam. So E; A *onere vacuus*. The latter might be supported by the use of *vacuus* in 143 *vacuae reparant ubera matres*, and *plenus* in *Ag.* 857f. *linqueret cum iam nemus omne fulvo / plenus Alcides vacuum metallo*. But *onere vacuus* in the present phrase would represent a further extension in the use of the adjective, as Charon does not actually carry the burden in question. Seneca might have ventured on such a usage in a highly ornate passage, but hereabouts the style is relatively plain.

770 umbras. That is, those still awaiting passage.

770f. I doubt that *poscit viam* could mean "demands a passage, demands to be taken across", and in 772 Charon seems to be reacting to Hercules' movements rather than to such a demand (cf. V. *Aen.* 6.385ff. *navita quos iam inde ut Stygia prospexit ab unda / per tacitum nemus ire pedemque advertere ripae, / sic prior adgreditur dictis atque increpat ultro* e.q.s.). I take *viam*, therefore, to mean a path through the shades crowding the bank; in that case it is necessary to punctuate after *viam* (with Bentley) rather than after *turba* (the traditional punctuation).

771–75. Servius (on V. *Aen.* 6:392) says we read "in Orpheus" that when Charon saw Hercules he at once accepted him in terror into his boat. Seneca's Charon is made of sterner stuff, probably under the influence of Vergil's portrayal; his resistance enables Sen. to demonstrate H.'s violence.

771 dirus. Often used of the underworld and its dread inhabitants, v. 608 comm.

775–77. The immediate precedent for this detail is V. *Aen.* 6.413f., where upon Aeneas' embarkation *gemuit sub pondere cumba / sutilis et*

---

107. Housman conjectured *lurent* for *lucent* here (thus reviving a suggestion made by N. Heinsius 221) and at Ov. *Met.* 1.238f. *eadem violentia vultus, / idem oculi lucent, eadem feritatis imago est* (*TCPhS* 1890 140f. = 1972 162). But *lucent genae* is defended by the Vergilian precedent; it is also paralleled by a passage which is safe from *lurere*, Sen. *Pha.* 1041 [*oculi*] *relucent caerula insignes nota*, and may well be echoed at Stat. *Theb.* 1.104f. *sedet intus abactis / ferrea lux oculis*. With *lurent* (even if the verb were securely attested anywhere, which it is not) *genae* would be ambiguous, but would more naturally be taken of cheeks than eyes, and the result would not correspond to anything in Vergil's lines.

multam accepit rimosa paludem. One suspects that the detail was traditional to Hercules' catabasis and that Vergil transferred it to Aeneas (so Norden ad loc.); there may be another echo at Ap. Rhod. 1.531ff. (setting out of the *Argo*) μέσσῳ δ' Ἀγκαῖος μέγα τε σθένος Ἡρακλῆος / ἵζανον· ἄγχι δέ οἱ ῥόπαλον θέτο, καί οἱ ἔνερθεν / ποσσὶν ὑπεκλύσθη νηὸς τρόπις. Such motifs are found from the earliest times in connection with gods, e.g. Hom. *Il*. 5.838f. where a chariot-axle groans under the combined weight of Athena and Diomedes. Seneca's account is enlivened by the resolutions in *succubuit* and *latere titubanti*, which suggest the rocking of the boat (for the effect cf. 229 with comm.), and by alliteration in *titubanti bibit*.

775 cumba populorum capax. Cf. *Oed*. 166 *capaci . . . cumba*, also of Charon's boat. For emphasis on the numbers of the dead, and for *capax* in such contexts, v. 659 *regno capaci* comm. Charon's vessel is often designated by *cumba*: *TLL* 6.1588.11ff. has seventeen instances from V. *Georg*. to Corippus.

776 sedit. "Sank down, settled in the water." For *sedere* = "sink, settle," cf. Sen. *Oed*. 326, *QNat*. 6.20.3 *madefacta tellus . . . altius sedit*, *OLD* s.v. 12. There is no need for Gronovius' conjecture *sidit*.

777 Lethen. The river on which Charon plies is not usually called Lethe, but this identification is consistent with 679ff., where Lethe bounds the underworld (v. 679–86 comm.).

titubanti. A has *titubato*, which is paralleled at V. *Aen*. 5.331f. *vestigia presso / haud tenuit titubata solo*. But there the perfect has some point (Nisus cannot recover once his feet have begun to slip), whereas here the present *titubanti* (E) seems more appropriate (the boat takes in water as it rocks). For *titubare* of rocking on water cf. *Ag*. 685 *nido . . . titubante*, of the halcyon's floating nest.

778–81. That the shades of Hercules' *human* enemies scatter before him may be another traditional detail of his catabasis: at Apollod. 2.5.12 his appearance puts most of the shades to flight. The passage at Hom. *Od*. 11.605f., in which the souls flee from H.'s *wraith*, seems more likely to derive from such a traditional detail than to be its source. Vergil may well be reusing such a detail when he makes the shades of Greek warriors *ingenti trepidare metu* (cf. *trepidant* here) at the sight of Aeneas (*Aen*. 6.489–93).

Seneca's choice of Centaurs and Hydra is influenced by Vergil's list of monsters at the entrance to the underworld, *Aen*. 6.285ff. *multaque*

Commentary: Act III

praeterea variarum monstra ferarum, / Centauri in foribus stabulant . . . / . . . ac belua Lernae (cf. also another Hydra at 6.576). But Sen. puts them on the far bank of the river; similarly in Ar. *Frogs* Hercules warns Dionysus that θηρί' ὄψει μυρία / δεινότατα *after* riding on Charon's ferry (143f., cf. 278ff.).

778f. Hercules decimated the Centaurs when they attacked him and his host Pholus (Apollod. 2.5.4, Diod. Sic. 4.12.3ff.); he fought against the Lapiths at the invitation of their enemy Aegimius, king of the Dorians (Apollod. 2.7.7, Diod. Sic. 4.37.3). But the reference in 779 is very muddled: the Lapiths were not *monstra*; furthermore *multo in bella succensi mero* must allude to the famous battle between the Centaurs and the Lapiths, yet H. was not present on that occasion, and it was the Centaurs, not the Lapiths, who got drunk. These gross errors justify Ageno's tentative suggestion that 779 be excised. But deletion alone does not heal the passage, for 778 is incomplete in itself; one surmises therefore that 779 was added to fill a known lacuna, or else that it has displaced a genuine line. Presumably the interpolator had only the vaguest notion of the episode involving Aegimius, but thought that where there are Centaurs, Lapiths cannot be far off. His notion that the Lapiths were monsters could derive from a misunderstanding of V. *Aen.* 7.304f. *Mars perdere gentem / immanem Lapithum valuit*; or he may remember Hor. *Carm.* 2.12.5f. *saevos Lapithas et nimium mero / Hylaeum* but exchange the characteristics of Centaurs and Lapiths (in which case *Centauri truces* is also interpolated).

778 tum victa trepidant monstra. So E: A has *tunc vasta t. m. Victa* is obviously superior to *vasta*, and *tunc* is then ruled out by considerations of euphony.

780f. A lively picture: in the upper world the Hydra inhabited a swamp (Apollod. 2.5.2), and now its shade scuttles off to a similar habitat for safety. The underworld rivers are often said to be swampy (686 comm.); for *Stygiae paludis* cf. V. *Aen.* 6.323, 369, Ov. *Met.* 1.737, *Carm. Epig.* 1005.9.

781 fecunda . . . capita. For the adjective cf. 529 *serpentis resecet colla feracia* with comm.

Lernaeus labor. *Labor* is similarly used at 944f. *primus en noster labor . . . leo.* For *labor* used concretely of something on which toil has been expended, cf. also V. *Aen.* 7.248 *Iliadumque labor vestes*, *Georg.* 1.325 *sata laeta boumque labores.*

[323]

Commentary: Act III

782f. The reference to the palace of Dis suggests that Cerberus is conceived of as its watchdog. Cf. Hes. *Theog.* 767ff., Eur. *Her.* 1277 Ἄιδου πυλωρὸν κύνα, Tib. 1.3.71f. and the frequent use of *ianitor* for Cerberus, e.g. Hor. *Carm.* 3.11.15f., V. *Aen.* 8.296. This point naturally varies, as concepts of the underworld differ and as "the house of Dis" sometimes refers to the underworld as a whole rather than to a specific palace: thus in Vergil's account his cave is somewhat isolated (*Aen.* 6.417ff.), and in Apollodorus H. finds him at the gates of Acheron, which are distinct from the gates of Hades (2.5.12); even in this play Sen. elsewhere makes Cerberus guard the entrance to the underworld, rather than that of the palace (985). Of the vase paintings of Hercules and Cerberus, one type shows Hades' palace in the background, v. H. B. Walters in *JHS* 18 (1898) 297.

avari Ditis. See comm. on 291 *avida ... aetas*.

783–85. Cerberus' bark is sufficient to cow the shades, cf. 793f., V. *Aen.* 6.400f. *licet ingens ianitor antro / aeternum latrans exsanguis terreat umbras*; ibid. 417f. Vergil makes the point that it issues from three throats, *Cerberus hic ingens latratu regna trifauci / personat* (n.b. *regnum* here), as Sen. does again below at 796.

784 trina ... capita. Because forms from *trini* as well as the more common *terni* appear in several poets (Leo I 12 n. 10), there seems no reason to alter the transmitted *trina* to *terna* here (as Giardina does with many recc.) to conform with *terna colla* at 62 and *ora terna* at 796; for *trini* in Sen. cf. *Thy.* 675f. *latratu ... trino* (further details in Timpanaro 140).

785–87. Cerberus has a snaky chevelure like the Furies and Medusa. In art, snakes are shown growing from his body as early as the beginning of the sixth century B.C. (on the Corinthian kotyle mentioned above on 762–827), and later his tail sometimes ends in a single serpent's head (*EAA* 2 ill. 699, 700). In literature, references to the snakes on his neck include V. *Aen.* 6.419, Hor. *Carm.* 3.11.17f., Lygd. 4.87, Ov. *Met.* 10.21f.; references to the snake in his tail (787 *torta ... cauda* is abl. of place) are rarer, but cf. Apollod. 2.5.12 ad fin., who describes H. as bitten by it while fighting Cerberus, and Sil. 13.594. Note the threefold variation *colubrae-viperis-draco* articulating the tricolon.

785 caput. Withof 64f. objected to the word-repetition *capita-caput*, and thought *capita* corrupt. Repetition without rhetorical point is not in itself a strong objection (43f. comm.), but the singular *caput* for Cerberus' three heads is clumsy so soon after *terna . . . capita*. This is partly paralleled at 826, however, where *caput* singular follows equally soon upon *omni . . . cervice* ("with all his necks"). If correction is thought necessary, one might suggest e.g. *sordidum tabo latus* or *sordidas tabo genas*; *sordidus tabo* would be appropriate for Cerberus' mouths (cf. Hor. *Carm.* 3.11.19f. *saniesque manet / ore trilingui*), but nothing occurs to me along those lines.

789. Cerberus' snaky hackles rise as at V. *Aen.* 6.419 *vates horrere videns iam colla colubris*.

790 missum . . . sonum. *Mittere* is often used in the sense of *emittere* with objects such as *vocem* (cf. 795f. *fragor . . . missus*, TLL 8.1174.74ff.), but this usage is rare of nonvocal sounds.

792 antro. Another of the underworld's many caves (718 *vasto specu* comm.). This one has a precedent in Vergil's picture of Cerberus (cf. *Aen.* 6.400f. [quoted on 783–85], 418 *adverso recubans immanis in antro*, 8.299); earlier cf. Soph. *OC* 1572.

793 et uterque timuit. Sic codd. Hercules naturally feels a thrill of fear on facing terrible foes, cf. 45 *quae timuit et quae fudit* with comm. His apprehension in approaching Cerberus—though to chain him rather than to fight—is shown in several vase paintings (Boardman 8). There cannot therefore be any objection to the paradosis on these grounds. Admittedly it is somewhat awkward that Cerberus again becomes subject of the following clause without a noun or pronoun indicating this (so Bothe), but we have seen several instances in this play of unannounced subject change where context and sense make it evident, as here, what the new subject must be, cf. 33, 275, 312, 722. I therefore think conjecture unnecessary. Of the suggested alterations the best is Madvig's *leviterque timuit*. Bothe proposed *et utique timuit*, but *utique* is very rare in verse; I know of no certain instance of it in drama.

ecce. Sometimes used in narrative as here to mark a sudden and disruptive event, v. Köhler in *ALL* 5 p. 18, Austin on V. *Aen.* 2.203. For an example involving noise cf. Ov. *Fasti* 1.433f.

794f. totos . . . armos. "All his shoulders" Miller, perhaps rightly, for *toti* occasionally has the sense of *omnes* in the poets, including Sen. (cf. 1287, *Thy.* 1018, ps.-Sen. *HO* 383, H-S 203³, Bömer on Ov. *Met.* 1.253). But it is a moot point whether three necks would involve six shoulders, and *totos* may well have its more usual sense.

[325]

Commentary: Act III

796f. felices quoque exterret umbras. Thus Sen. follows Vergil in conceiving of Elysium as a region of the underworld, set apart but not totally separate. Other authorities think of it as a place, or group of islands, at the ends of the earth: for the various locations v. *RE* s.v. Elysion.

797–802. Apollod. 2.5.12 and Schol. B on Hom. *Il.* 5.395 agree with Sen. that Hercules used the lion-skin for a shield in this fight. But this is related to Pluto's stipulation that he must subdue Cerberus ἄνευ ἀσπίδος καὶ σιδήρου (Schol. B; cf. 762–827 comm.), whereas in Sen. it has no such significance. In the Scholiast's version, H. uses λιθίναις ἀκίσιν as offensive weapons: in Apollodorus he throttles him (cf. Ar. *Frogs* 468). For Sen.'s statement that H. used his club cf. Quint. Smyrn. 6.265; several vase paintings show H. threatening the hound with his club while leading him out of Hades (e.g. *RE* Suppl. 3.1080.64ff., Boardman pl. IIIb, Ib), which suggests the possibility that he has subdued him with that weapon.

797f. solvit a laeva . . . rictus. *A laeva* must mean "on his left" (*a laeva parte*), not "from his left hand" (*a laeva manu*), which would yield no sense. In art the lion-skin is usually shown as hanging symmetrically down Hercules' back, with its head covering the hero's; Seneca, however, conceives of it as normally worn over the left shoulder in the manner of a cloak (cf. 1150f. *cur latus laevum vacat / spolio leonis?*), following Ov. *Her.* 9.61f. *pestis Nemeaea . . . / . . . unde umerus tegmina laevus habet.* Evander wears a similar skin in the same fashion, *demissa ab laeva pantherae terga retorquens* (V. *Aen.* 8.460). Here H. unfastens the lion-skin and rearranges it so as to serve as a shield, presumably draping it over his left arm (cf. Pallas' use of the aegis on her left arm, 901^b–2 with comm. and Cadmus' use of a lion-skin as a shield at Ov. *Met.* 3.81f.). Withof 67 conjectured *at laeva* on the grounds that *laeva* should balance *dextera* in 800, but lack of balance is paralleled e.g. by Ov. *Met.* 11.167f. (Apollo) *instrictamque fidem gemmis et dentibus Indis / sustinet a laeva, tenuit manus altera plectrum.*

feros. So recc. The paradosis offers *ferox / tunc ipse*, which is unsatisfactory; it would presumably mean *post brevem timorem, ut canis, ita et ipse ferox rursus factus* (Ageno), but this is strained. Furthermore *rictus* would be bold without some qualification here; for *feros* cf. *Thy.* 77f. *feros / rictus leonum.* Confusion of *feros / ferox* is paralleled at 90, *Oed.* 90, 761, *Thy.* 96.

798. Ovid introduced *rictus* to high poetry, with twelve uses in *Met.* (Bömer on 1.741), though there are two instances of *rictum* (neuter) in

Commentary: Act III

Lucretius. Note also the Euripidean use of χάσμα, *Her.* 362f. (of H. wearing the lion-skin) ξανθὸν κρᾶτ' ἐπινωτίσας / δεινῷ χάσματι θηρός, *Rhes.* 209. The point of *rictus* and *caput* is of course that H. intends the head with its gaping jaws to frighten Cerberus. Seneca follows Ov. *Her.* 9.61f. (quoted above on 797f.) in identifying the skin as the Nemean Lion's (*Cleonaeum = Nemeaeum*). Apollod. 2.4.10 says that in early youth, after killing the lion of Cithaeron, H. wore its skin, but Stat. *Theb.* 1.485 adds that this was only until he killed the Nemean Lion.

799 tegmine ingenti tegit. At first sight one might take E's *tegit* as a trivialization and A's *clepit* as correct, particularly as this rare verb is paralleled in Sen. at *Med.* 155f. *levis est dolor qui capere consilium potest / et clepere sese.* But the connotations of the word must also be considered. *Clepere* regularly denotes theft, stealth, or improper concealment (cf. κλέπτειν), as the passages cited by *TLL* show, and Medea's use of it expresses her contempt for the course of action suggested by her nurse. Such a word is quite inappropriate for Hercules. Probably the A interpolator objected to the similarity of *tegmine* and *tegit*, and wrongly assumed from *Med.* 156 that *clepere sese* is interchangeable in meaning with *tegere sese*. For the *figura etymologica* of *tegmine tegit* cf. *Thy.* 1001 *meumque gemitu non meo pectus gemit*, and comm. on HF 1093 *virtusque viro*. Here it seems to be used for the sake of the complex alliterative pattern it creates with *ingenti*.

tegmine. The word is used of Hercules' lion-skin at Ov. *Her.* 9.62 (v. comm. 797f.) and below at 1151; of a similar lion-skin belonging to H.'s son Aventinus at V. *Aen.* 7.66, and of that belonging to Cadmus at Ov. *Met.* 3.52.

800f. *Rotat* in 801 must be transitive; I therefore place a semicolon at the end of 799, so that it may govern *robur* in 800 (ἀπὸ κοίνου with *gerens*). If we put a full-stop after 800 and a comma after 799 with Leo, Giardina et al., *rotat* must presumably govern *ictus*, which is impossibly awkward. My punctuation follows that of some early editors (e.g. Schroeder) and Bentley.

800 victrice . . . dextera. For the metrical flexibility of this phrase v. 399f. comm. The phrase is naturally used of Hercules, cf. Ov. *Her.* 9.75f. *victricem . . . manum* and two uses in Cicero's translation from Soph. *Trach.* at *Tusc.* 2.9 (*victrices manus, victrix manus*); but not exclusively, e.g. 399f. above (of Lycus), Prop. 3.22.22 (of the Romans), Ov. *Met.* 4.740 (of Perseus).

801f. Influenced by V. *Aen.* 5.457 *nunc dextra ingeminans ictus, nunc ille sinistra* (of Entellus boxing with Dares). A single *nunc* in place of a cor-

Commentary: Act III

relative pair is unusual, but cf. V. *Aen.* 5.830f. *una omnes fecere pedem pariterque sinistros, / nunc dextros solvere sinus*, Pers. 3.116. *Ingeminare* is first found in Vergil, who uses it twelve times; Sen. has it only here.

804 antroque toto cessit. "And emerged from the whole cave." The oddity of *toto* is explained by imitation of V. *Aen.* 6.422f. (Cerberus drugged by the Sibyl) *immania terga resolvit / fusus humi totoque ingens extenditur antro*. Seneca's point, like Vergil's, is that Cerberus' bulk is great enough to fill the cave; no doubt he could rely on his audience to recognize the Vergilian echo and so take the point.

805 uterque . . . dominus. That is, *dominus et domina*; analogous to Ovid's *ambo domini* with this sense, *Am.* 2.2.32. For *domini* = "master and mistress" cf. also *HF* 570 *umbrarum dominos*, Claud. *Rapt. Pros.* 2.314 (both of Pluto and Proserpina), *TLL* 5.1911.9ff.

solio. The throne is mentioned in the same context at V. *Aen.* 6.395f. *Tartareum ille manu custodem in vincla petivit / ipsius a solio regis traxitque trementem*. It also appears on the kotyle mentioned on 762–827. For the two deities shown enthroned together (though not in this episode) v. Roscher 1.1795f. with illustration.

806. Some accounts agree that Hercules was given permission to rescue Theseus, cf. Diod. Sic. 4.26.1 Θησέα μὲν ἀνήγαγεν . . . χαρισαμένης τῆς Κόρης, Hyg. *Fab.* 79. Others mention the detail that Theseus had to be torn from the rock, leaving part of his anatomy behind, which suggests a version in which his rescue owes more to H.'s strength than to the grace of the nether powers, cf. Schol. Ar. *Eq.* 1368, Gell. 10.16.13, Serv. ad V. *Aen.* 6.617. Seneca describes the rescue as economically as possible in order to concentrate on the fetching of Cerberus. The line has the same opening as that with which Theseus refers to his rescue at *Pha.* 845, *me quoque supernas pariter ad sedes tulit*.

807f. H.'s technique of soothing Cerberus while putting on the chain recalls the fine amphora by the Andocides Painter (P. E. Arias et al., *History of Greek Vase Painting* pl. 88, xxix) on which the hero pats one of the dog's muzzles with his right hand while holding a chain in his left, presumably intending to slip it onto the leash which is already in place. A few other vases similarly show Hercules or Hermes coaxing the dog (Arias 317, Boardman 8 with pl. IIa and IIb).

gravia. The point of the adjective is that Hercules endures to touch them although they are snake-covered and possibly fetid (785).

808 adamante texto. Seneca's immediate precedent for the adamantine chain was Ov. *Met.* 7.412f. (Hercules) *nexis adamante catenis / Cerberon abstraxit.*

810–12. Cerberus' "doggy" behavior is noteworthy in this episode: at 792ff. he realistically hesitates before starting to bark; here he drops his ears and wags his tail, as Odysseus' old hound does on recognizing his master, Hom. *Od.* 17.302. For such behavior by Cerberus on other occasions cf. Hes. *Theog.* 770f. ἐς μὲν ἰόντας / σαίνει ὁμῶς οὐρῇ τε καὶ οὔασιν ἀμφοτέροισιν, Soph. fr. 687 P (from the *Phaedra*) ἔσαινεν †οὐρὰν† ὦτα κυλλαίνων κάτω,[108] also Hor. *Carm.* 2.13.33ff. *illis carminibus stupens / demittit atras belua centiceps / aures,* 2.19.30ff.

It is difficult to be sure where one clause ends and the next begins: *componit* and *pulsat* may be linked either by *et* in 810 or by *-que* in 811.

810 componit. I take the verb to mean that he lays his ears back in such a way that they converge or even touch, but I have no parallel.

811 obsequens. This verb is avoided by the Augustan poets, but used twice by Ovid and occasionally thereafter (three times in Sen. Trag., once each in Luc. and Stat.).

812 anguifera. Earlier uses are of the Gorgon's head, Prop. 2.2.8, Ov. *Met.* 4.741 (on the snakes v. 785–87 comm.).

813–27. On the point that daylight terrifies creatures of the underworld, v. 292f. comm. That Cerberus balked at the light of day is probably an ancient tradition, to judge by the metope from the Temple of Zeus at Olympia, which shows the hound's head apparently just protruding from the mouth of hell, while Hercules attempts to drag him further (v. Ashmole and Yalouris, *Olympia* 28f.). (For dragging at some point in the journey cf. e.g. Boardman pl. Ic, V. *Aen.* 6.396 *traxitque trementem*). But Sen.'s immediate precedent was Ov. *Met.* 7.410ff. *Tirynthius heros / restantem contraque diem radiosque micantes / obliquantem oculos nexis adamante catenis / Cerberon abstraxit* (cf. 808 comm.). The whole of 813–27 may represent Sen.'s expansion on these lines of Ovid.

---

108. Probably from Theseus' narrative of his underworld experiences. Because of its similarity to the present passage, it has been thought to describe Cerberus' behavior after his capture (see Barrett's edition of Eur. *Hipp.*, p. 24), but in view of the parallel in Hesiod it may equally well concern someone's entry into the underworld.

813. On the association of Taenarum with Hercules' catabasis see 662-67 comm. Paus. 3.25.5 and Strabo 8.5.1 agree with Sen. that H. *emerged* there; rival locations include Hermione (Paus. 2.35.10, cf. Eur. *Her.* 615) or the nearby Troezen (Paus. 2.31.2, Apollod. 2.5.12 ad fin.), Mt Laphystius in Boeotia (Paus. 9.34.5), and the cave near Heraclea Pontica (Ov. *Met.* 7.407, Mela 1.103, Pliny *NH* 27.4). Earlier in the play H. seemed to emerge in Thebes itself, v. 520-22 with comm.

oras Taenari. "The verge, border of T."; i.e. they are not yet at the cave's mouth, but close enough to see the daylight. Zwierlein 1978 144 n. 10 proposes *ora Taenari* (cf. comm. on 664, 666), but despite Eur. *Her.* 23 Ταινάρου διὰ στόμα the unadorned metaphor seems bald here; contrast the fuller form at 664 *hic ora solvit Ditis invisi domus*. In any case there appears to be no need for conjecture. Zwierlein himself, in deference to Axelson's opinion, retains *oras* in the rare sense of "opening," for which there are parallels at V. *Georg.* 4.39, 188 (both of entrances to beehives), and perhaps at Enn. *Ann.* 80 Skutsch. But an audience would hardly detect this esoteric meaning when a more usual meaning offers satisfactory sense.

814 novos. *Bono*, the reading of the paradosis, cannot stand: it lacks point, and the construction of *lucis ignotae* ἀπὸ κοινοῦ with *nitor* and *bono* is strained. The best conservative corrections are those of Gronovius, who would write *ignoto bono* or *ignotum bonum*; for the sense cf. Stat. *Theb.* 8.33 (of Dis) *iucundaque offensus luce profatur*, and for *bonum* of light, Sen. *Ep.* 79.11 *adhuc non fruitur bono lucis*. Neither of Gronovius' conjectures gives a particularly Senecan phrase, however, whereas either *novos* (sc. *oculos*; so Ageno) or *novus* (Bücheler, reported in Leo's app. crit.) would yield the interweaving of two adjective-noun pairs which Seneca likes, and the equally characteristic juxtaposition of adjectives of similar sense (v. comm. on 216-48 ad fin. and on 536 *mutis tacitum*). I think *novos* more probable in view of the form of the corruption: *novus* would have been corrupted to *bonus*, whereas corruption of *novos* to *bonos* would prompt further alteration. For *novus* = "inexperienced" cf. *Tro.* 67f. *non rude vulgus lacrimisque novum / lugere iubes*, and for the word in this sense and in juxtaposition with a similar adjective *Thy.* 821f. *ipse insueto novus hospitio / Sol Auroram videt occiduus*.

Novos had earlier been proposed by Rutgers 494 in agreement with *animos*, a suggestion accepted by Zwierlein 1978 144 n. 10 *inter alios*.[109]

---

109. For the common confusion of *v/b* cf. *Pha.* 64 *bisontes/vi-*, *Ag.* 171 *vela/bella*, Zwierlein 1978 144 n. 10; if *novos* had been corrupted to *nobos*, "correction" to *bonos* would have followed naturally.

The pleonastic *re-* (of *resumit*) with *novos* is paralleled at Luc. 1.134 *reparare novas vires* and at ps.-Sen. *HO* 1418 *vires reparet . . . novas* (*novas* Axelson [1967 115] *nefas* E *suas* A). (But at Ov. *Met.* 1.11 *nova . . . reparabat cornua Phoebe* the force of *re-* is somewhat different, underlining the repeated nature of the action.) As for the sense-pause at the end of the fifth foot, Zwierlein compares particularly *Oed.* 943f. *novos / commenta partus*, cf. ps.-Sen. *Oct.* 420f. *novas / exstruxit urbes.* But *novos* with *oculos* seems to me more characteristic of Seneca's style, for the reasons indicated above.

815 resumit animos victus. This phrase and the play on *victus / victorem* (816) are influenced by V. *Aen.* 2.367f. *quondam etiam victis redit in praecordia virtus / victoresque cadunt Danai.* A's variant *vinctus* is therefore unlikely to be right here. *Sumere animos* is an Ovidian phrase, not found earlier (Bömer on *Met.* 3.544).

817 vexit. Equivalent to *traxit*, with no sense of "carrying" but a strong connotation of physical effort: an unusual use of the verb. Animals are sometimes said *vehere aliquem* by pulling a chariot, V. *Aen.* 5.105, Hor. *Carm.* 3.3.13ff. *te . . . Bacche . . . / vexere tigres indocili iugum / collo trahentes*, Ov. *Am.* 3.2.10, but that is less remarkable, as the animals are associated with the chariot. Cf. comm. on 604 *advexit*.

movit gradu. The phrase has a military ring: *gradus* is used in such contexts of a firm stance adopted for fighting. Cf. Livy 7.8.3 *primum gradu moverunt hostem, deinde pepulerunt*, 6.32.8 *hostes gradu demoti*, Sen. *Ag.* 515, 549, *TLL* 6.2145.16ff.

818 respexit. That is, looked to them for help, cf. Livy 4.46.8 *subsidia quae respicerent in re trepida*, Val. Fl. 7.624 (Hercules fighting the Hydra) *Palladios defessus respicit ignes*.

819 geminis uterque. A characteristically Senecan pleonasm, used elsewhere (with *utrimque*) of two seas, *Ag.* 563 *arx imminet praerupta quae spectat mare / utrimque geminum*, *Oed.* 267, *Thy.* 182.

821 clarum diem. A's *aethera* creates an unpleasing degree of tautology with 822, whereas E's *diem* varies the idea. I suspect that the A interpolator found *diem* flat and attempted to improve it: perhaps he objected also to its repetition in 824, but such repetition is not intolerable, v. 43f. comm. *Clara dies* is used in a similar context of emergence from the underworld at 586 (on the gender of *dies* see comm. there); for the phrase cf. also *Tro.* 756, *Med.* 5.

Commentary: Act III

822. For the phrase cf. *Med.* 30 *solita puri spatia . . . poli. Purus* is often used of a clear, cloudless sky, or of the heavenly bodies in such a sky; here it has the additional connotation of freedom from the contagion of the underworld. The form *spatia* is characteristic of Seneca's diction (eighteen occurrences), whereas it is uncommon in Vergil (five) and absent from Ovid; meter is partly responsible for this contrast, but Sen.'s liking for words with grandiose, expansive connotations also plays a part. Further examples of *spatia* used of the heavens are 593, 958, *Med.* 1026.

823. I accept Bothe's deletion of this line (also accepted by Leo and by Zwierlein 1976 182f. inter alios) for the following reasons: (a) *Oborta nox est* is so brief as to be ambiguous; was the *nox* the result of the sun's reaction to Cerberus (cf. 60f.) or vice versa? The next phrases make it clear that the latter was the case, but the awkwardness remains. Admittedly such phrases as *oborta nox est* are sometimes used without qualification of a psychosomatic "blackout," cf. Plaut. *Curc.* 309 *tenebrae oboriuntur, genua inedia succidunt*, Sen. Rhet. *Contr.* 7.1 *obortae sunt subito tenebrae, deriguit animus*; but here the preceding emphasis on light requires some clarification of the phrase and indeed some pointing of the paradox as at Ov. *Met.* 2.181 (Phaethon riding the Sun's chariot) *suntque oculis tenebrae per tantum lumen obortae*, which is the immediate source of the phrase. (b) *Lumina in terram dedit* is to a considerable degree duplicated in 825f. *omni petît / cervice terram*; the objection is not so much to word-repetition of *terra* (cf. 821 comm.) as to the similarity of action. (c) The whole sequence 823–26^a involves too much ἐπιμονή even for Sen., a fact that strengthens the case for excision of some part.

H. Weber in *Philologus* 66 (1907) 361f. retained the line but ingeniously conjectured *aborta vox est* for *oborta nox est* on the basis of Lucretius' list of physical symptoms of fear, 3.156ff. *videmus / . . . palloremque exsistere toto / corpore et infringi linguam vocemque aborire*; he should have cited also Sen. *Ag.* 859ff. *tractus ad caelum canis inferorum / . . . tacuit nec ullo / latravit ore*. But the point would again be too abrupt, and the alteration would not remove the other objections to the line. As to the origin of the line, Bothe suggested that Sen. himself drafted and then rejected it; the suggestion is supported by the similarity of 825^b–6^a to 823^b (reuse of a discarded idea), and by the line's reuse of an Ovidian paradox, but certainty is unobtainable.

825 aciemque retro flexit. Bothe criticized this phrase on the ground that having just closed his eyes, Cerberus could not avert his gaze. But C. is here trying out and *rejecting* various ways of avoiding the light. First he simply shuts his eyes; finding that unsatisfactory he presumably opens them again but turns his head back and down; finding that no improvement, he makes for a patch of shade, which he could scarcely have seen if his eyes were still closed. Bothe's conjecture *faciem* for *aciem* cannot be considered, as *facies* is very rarely used of the "face" of animals as opposed to humans. For the phrase as transmitted cf. 602 *aciem reflectat*, Ov. *Met.* 10.51 *ne flectat retro sua lumina* (of Orpheus).

825f. omni ... cervice ... caput.   See comm. 785 *caput*.

826f. sub Herculeas ... umbras.   This E reading is clearly preferable to A's *sub Herculea ... umbra*. The accusative is more accurate than an ablative, as Cerberus' action involved movement *toward* the shadow, and the plural is more likely to have been changed to a singular than vice versa.

827–29.   References to an entering Chorus are unusual in Sen. Trag., but this announcement of the approach of a choral *turba* whose arrival provides a reason for the end of the Act is paralleled at *Ag.* 586f. *sed ecce, turba tristis incomptae comas / Iliades adsunt.*[110] (The indication of the *content* of the ode in 829 is paralleled at *Oed.* 402 *populare Bacchi laudibus carmen sonet*.) The technique appears already in Eur. *Phoen.* 196f. ὄχλος γάρ, ὡς ταραγμὸς εἰσῆλθεν πόλιν, / χωρεῖ γυναικῶν; there are several examples in Greek New Comedy (usually involving an ὄχλος, cf. Men. *Aspis* 246ff., *Dysc.* 230ff. [with Handley ad loc.], *Epitr.* 169ff., *Peric.* 191ff.), and the technique was no doubt found in postclassical Greek tragedy. All the surviving Greek examples come at the end of the first episode or Act, whereas Sen.'s two examples differ in that they come later in the play.

The present passage has been taken as proving the absence of the Chorus from the scene during the preceding Act (Tarrant 1978 224f.). But it would be truer to say that a Senecan Chorus has no dramatic existence during the Acts, except when it is required, usually for strictly technical reasons, to participate in the action (cf. introduction to Ode II ad fin. and comm. 1032–34 ad fin.). The present passage simply provides a convenient means of breaking off Theseus' narrative.

This Chorus is somewhat reminiscent of Vergil's choruses at the Ara

---

110. In *Ag.* the *turba* is a secondary chorus of Trojan women accompanying Cassandra, but there is no need to infer from the parallel that we have here a secondary chorus of citizens specially favorable to Hercules. (For secondary choruses associated with a particular character see Tarrant 1978 225.) On the contrary, the negative attitudes expressed in the ode concerning the catabasis are entirely in keeping with those of Odes I and II; the celebration is no less natural here for people of good will, than hope for H.'s return was in Ode II.

Maxima, *hic iuvenum chorus, ille senum, qui carmine laudes / Herculeas et facta ferunt* (*Aen.* 8.287f.). But Vergil's singers are poplar-crowned; in Sen. the wearing of laurel in combination with praise-singing conveys a strong suggestion of a Roman triumph, cf. Livy 45.38.12 *militum quidem propria est causa, qui ipsi laureati triumphum nomine cient, suasque et imperatoris laudes canentes.*

Ode III (830–94)

Ode III takes its starting point from the third stasimon of Euripides' play (763–814), a song of rejoicing and praise for Hercules immediately preceding the catastrophe, but quickly diverges from it. The Euripidean Chorus maintains its joyful confidence throughout the stasimon, asserting that the hero's victory proves divine concern for justice (772ff., 813f.). But in Seneca the thought of Hercules' last labor leads the Chorus into a meditation on the world and condition of death, filled with powerful images and somber echoes of the Vergilian catabasis in *Aeneid* 6 (see comm. on 836, 838–47, 849–54, 854–57). All this quite undercuts the initial rejoicing, and although there is a brief resurgence of celebration in 875–94, marked by a change of meter, it is too little and too late to alter the atmosphere. Thus the ode is the strongest in a series of indications, from the prologue on, of the hollowness of Hercules' victory. Its concern with the world of death matches Theseus' *descriptio inferorum*, but the Chorus' attitudes are also consistent with those of the earlier odes: its abhorrence of the setting of the latest labor recalls that of Ode II, while the theme *quid iuvat durum properare fatum?* (867), with its implied criticism of H.'s undertaking (at least insofar as it represents symbolically the nature of all human striving), echoes the critique elaborated in Ode I.

A similar shift from optimism to pessimism may be seen at a similar dramatic point in Ode III of *Thy.* (546–622). Here too the Chorus' initial joy at the apparent reconciliation of the brothers gives way, via the notion of "sudden change" (560ff.) and the image of sea storm with its connotations of mutability (577ff.), to the thought of the chaotic instability of human affairs (596ff.). Both odes immediately precede the catastrophe or its revelation; in both cases the dramatic impact of the undercutting of initial optimism is evident.

The celebration of Hercules' achievement recalls the scene in *Aeneid* 8 in which the Arcadians at the site of future Rome offer sacrifice to H. (cf. 827–29 comm.): there too we have a narrative of one of his greatest exploits followed by a chorus singing his praises and by preparations for sacrifice; in both passages we find a *sacrificus* crowned with

Commentary: Ode III

poplar leaves, Evander in Vergil and H. himself in Seneca. There are also other Roman touches in the ode, though not obtrusive: the suggestion of a triumph at 828, the ritual details of touching the altar at 876, and covering the head at 893f. The picture of worldwide pacification in 882ff. has Roman overtones (see ad loc.), but it is also entirely appropriate to the theme of H.'s universal significance, seen throughout the play. (Elsewhere in the ode one finds a Roman note in 838f. but Grecisms in diction at 847 and 853.)

It is clear that the commands of 875–81 are not addressed to anyone onstage (note particularly 88of.), but rather indicate what activities would be appropriate on this occasion. Compare the commands in the marriage hymn of *Med.*, e.g. 61f. *Lucinam nivei femina corporis* / *intemptata iugo placet* (a sacrifice onstage is not envisaged), 108 *hinc illinc, iuvenes, mittite carmina*, 114 *solvat turba iocos*. Commands of this kind are reminiscent of those found in Hellenistic and Roman literary hymns, e.g. Callim. *Ap.* 8 οἱ δὲ νέοι μολπήν τε καὶ ἐς χορὸν ἐντύνεσθε, 17, 5.1 ὅσαι λωτροχόοι τᾶς Παλλάδος ἔξιτε πᾶσαι, 13ff., 45ff., 6.1ff., Cat. 61.76 *claustra pandite ianuae*, 117 *tollite, o pueri, faces*, 182ff., Hor. *Carm.* 1.21.1f. But in view of our relative ignorance of Hellenistic and Augustan stage conventions, we cannot necessarily conclude that commands of this type are incompatible with stage performance.[111]

The meter is Sapphic in 830–74 and glyconic in 875–94. The short glyconic line is appropriate for rejoicing and festive occasions, cf. Cat. 61, Sen. *Med.* 75ff.

830. When Hercules' birth was imminent, Jupiter had sworn that the prince of Perseus' house to be born that day would rule Mycenae. Thereupon Juno delayed the birth of Hercules and hastened that of Eurystheus, who had been only seven months in the womb; thus Eurystheus gained the throne. The story appears as early as Hom. *Il.* 19.95ff. Seneca's reference to the detail is not otiose, but explains why Eurystheus was in a position to give orders to H.

831ff. The Chorus need not specify whom Eurystheus commanded and whose were the labors, nor whom it is apostrophizing in 834, as the answer is obvious; compare the omission of Hercules as subject at 33, 275, 312, and for apostrophe without a vocative cf. 178, 547, 858, 1092, 1122. Euripides has several similar instances of apostrophe without vocative, v. Bond on *Her.* 434.

---

111. As early as Soph. *Trach.* 211–15 we find choral commands, in a context of religious celebration, which are not actually carried out onstage.

[*335*]

832. The implication is that Hercules has completed the tally of his tasks and so is free of servitude to Eurystheus. According to Diod. Sic. 4.9.5 it was stipulated that H. must perform twelve labors. (In Soph. *Trach.* 821ff., on the other hand, the stipulation is said to be for twelve *years*' servitude.) For the notion of "filling out a total" cf. 500 *dest una numero Danais: explebo nefas* with comm.

833. The line hints at the possibility of a hubristic concept of Hercules as "conqueror of all realms" (for *tertiae sortis* v. comm. on 599, 609), which becomes explicit in the maddened mind of H. himself at 955–57. *Spoliare* also points to the overbearing style of his capture of Cerberus (cf. Juno's description of the hero as *spolia iactantem patri / fraterna* 51f.), though it is not the Chorus' intention to suggest hubris on H.'s part.

834 ausus es. E's reading is superior to A's *ausus est*. Apostrophe is common in Senecan choral odes (186f. comm.), and especially appropriate here in a song of praise; cf. particularly V. *Aen.* 8.293ff. *tu nubigenas, invicte, bimembres, / . . . tu Cresia mactas / prodigia* e.q.s.

835. Similar wording to 648 *quam longa maestos ducat ad manes via.*

836 nigra metuenda silva. Elsewhere woods surround the opening that gives access to the underworld (663 comm.), but here they seem to shade the downward route itself; the idea perhaps came from Vergil's simile comparing the way down to a journey through dark woods, *Aen.* 6.270ff. *quale per incertam lunam sub luce maligna / est iter in silvis, ubi caelum condidit umbra / Iuppiter, et rebus nox abstulit atra colorem.*

Kapnukajas considered A's word-order *silva metuenda nigra* correct because it creates a chiasmus with 837 *magna comitante turba*: as evidence of Sen.'s liking for chiasmus he cited 551 *fluctibus aequora* × 553 *sidera navibus*. But the present ode provides an opposite instance, of parallelism rather than chiasmus, in 849f. *pars tarda graditur senecta, / tristis et longa satiata vita*. This is more closely similar to 836f., 850 in particular echoing 836. The balance of probability must therefore rest with E rather than A here.

837 magna comitante turba. An echo of the Vergilian phrase *magna comitante caterva*, *Aen.* 2.40, 370, 5.76 (cf. the variant *magna stipante caterva* 1.497, 4.136), though substitution of *turba* for *caterva* has an Ovidian precedent at *Met.* 6.594f. *concita per silvas turba comitante suarum / terribilis Procne* e.q.s. Seneca's reuse of the phrase is somewhat awkward since it is not evident who is the implied object of *comitante*: it may be *te*, the point being that on his way down Hercules was inevitably accompanied by the constant procession of newly dead souls; or it may be more general, "anyone who descends." I doubt the awkwardness is such as to justify conjecture. (Schmidt 1865 18f. proposed *magna volitante turba*, comparing *Oed.* 599 where *volitare* is used of the shades.)

838–47. A stately succession of images comparing the crowds of the dead to the throngs of the living. These magnificent lines will stand comparison with passages of similar content in later poetry (Herington 1966 434 with n. 31): with Dante's comparison of the sinners of the Eighth Circle to the crowds on the bridge at the Jubilee (*Inferno* 18.25ff.), and with Eliot's vision of the London crowd (*The Waste Land* I. The Burial of the Dead), which begins:

> Unreal City,
> Under the brown fog of a winter dawn,
> A crowd flowed over London Bridge, so many,
> I had not thought death had undone so many.

The effect of Seneca's lines lies partly in their formal qualities: the parallelism of the introductory words *quantus–quantus–quanta–tanta*, the solemn repetition of the Sapphic line, the lengthening of the third member of the tricolon. In content, the first two similes suggest a telling contrast between the brilliance and gaiety of such festivals on earth and the gloom of the underworld; the third simile with its Eleusinian content creates a more complex interplay between the themes of life and death (see comm. on 842–47). The impact of the similes also depends in part on the element of anachronism introduced in the first of them. It should also be remembered that both the Olympic Games and the Eleusinian Mysteries were still celebrated in Seneca's own day. By these means Sen. suggests that his theme of mortality is as relevant for his contemporaries as for the heroic age of Greece.

A *group* of similes to convey the numbers of the dead is traditional. Vergil has comparisons to leaves and birds at *Aen.* 6.309ff. (n.b. next to a list of the age categories of the dead, cf. 849–54 comm.); probably there were comparisons to leaves and waves in the catabasis-poem *POxy* 2622a lines 12–15 (see H. Lloyd-Jones in *Maia* 19 [1967] 215f.);[112] Seneca himself has leaves, flowers, waves and birds at *Oed.* 600ff. But in the present passage he appears to be original in the *content* of the similes which he applies to the dead.

---

112. Whether such a pair existed in the supposed epic *Catabasis of Hercules* must remain conjectural: v. G. Thaniel in *Phoenix* 25 (1971) 237–345.

838f. More suggestive of life in Hellenistic and Imperial times than in the heroic age. No doubt Sen. had heard accounts of the openings of many theaters and amphitheaters built before and during his lifetime in Italy and the provinces (see Bieber, *History of the Greek and Roman Theater* ch. 13, 14), as well as of the original openings of Rome's three theaters. He may be generalizing on the basis of several such events; if he is thinking of a particular occasion, we cannot be sure which.[113]

For comparisons drawn from the world of entertainment cf. Enn. *Ann.* 79ff. Skutsch (chariot racing); Lucr. 4.75ff., 6.109ff. (both of the theater), Ov. *Met.* 3.111ff. (theater), 11.25ff. (amphitheater), 12.102ff. (circus); ps.-V. *Aetna* 294ff. (theater); Luc. 9.808f. (theater), 4.285ff., 708ff. (gladiatorial shows). More generally cf. Sen. *Tro.* 1125 *theatri more*. Seneca sometimes uses imagery drawn from chariot racing (notably at *Tro.* 398 *velocis spatii meta novissima*), and there is an instance of gladiatorial language at *Ag.* 901 *habet, peractum est*.

839 avidus. This adjective has ironic overtones in the context: Death is as greedy for the crowds (291f. comm.) as they are for the spectacle.

840f. Not totally anachronistic, as the Olympic Games were founded by Hercules, but the lines clearly picture them as a well-established institution. There are several parallels for projection of the games in their developed form back into the heroic age: cf. particularly Sophocles' description (*El.* 681ff.) of Orestes as participating in the Pythian Games, though athletic contests were not added to the Delphic festival until the sixth century; also Ov. *Met.* 14.324f., *Her.* 18.166, Sen. *Ag.* 918f. (with Tarrant ad loc.), 938.

Eleum ... Tonantem. That is, *Iovem Olympium*. The Altis at Olympia was sacred to Zeus, and the games were held in his honor. For a similar reference to the games cf. *Ag.* 938 *Pisaei Iovis*. *Eleus* frequently = "Olympic," cf. particularly Prop. 3.2.20 *Iovis Elei caelum imitata domus*.

841 quinta ... aestas. By the usual inclusive reckoning, as e.g. at Pind. *Ol.* 11.57f. πενταετηρίδ' ... ἑορτὰν, Ov. *Met.* 14.325 *quinquennem ... pugnam*. *Quinta* is clearly chosen in part for assonance with *quantus, quanta*. The festival took place in high summer, at the time of the second or third full moon after the summer solstice.

---

113. Kapnukajas supposed that Seneca had in mind Claudius' rededication of the Theater of Pompey, at which games were given (Suet. *Claud.* 21.1); but we cannot be sure that Sen. was an eyewitness to that event, in view of his long exile. A reference to Nero's wooden amphitheater in the Campus Martius, built in A.D. 57, is ruled out by the date of *HF*.

842–47. Another Eleusinian element in the play is Megara's vow to celebrate the Mysteries if Hercules returns safely (300–302). These elements may have been suggested by H.'s association with Eleusis: he was said to have been initiated there before his catabasis, though Sen. does not include that detail in Theseus' narrative (762–827 comm.). The present simile also has a deeper thematic relevance. The Mysteries offered the hope of overcoming the power of death, but the context of the simile strongly suggests (though this is not, of course, the Chorus' intention) that that hope is as illusory as Orpheus' or Hercules' similar claims. Connotations of mortality are also present in the turning of the year and the approach of the *longa nox* (for that phrase can also mean "death," cf. 1076 with comm.) The poetic complexity and resonance of these lines is remarkable.

842–45 quanta ... turba ... Cererem frequentat. The Telesterion at Eleusis in the Periclean and Roman periods could accommodate about 3,000 worshippers (Mylonas, *Eleusis* 253 n. 137). The size of the procession from Athens to Eleusis may conceivably have been somewhat greater (but not 30,000: v. How and Wells on Hdt. 8.65). Whether Sen. had any accurate impression of the number of worshippers one cannot say.

842–44. The Greater Mysteries were celebrated in the month of Boedromion, i.e. September–early October.

I take the first clause to end with *crescere* and to mean "when the season returns for the night to grow long," i.e. at the autumnal equinox when night begins to exceed day in length (so Kingery), cf. Manil. 3.252f. *in Libra cum lucem vincere noctes / incipiunt*. Thus *longae* is a proleptic adjective which indicates the result of the verb *crescere*, cf. Eur. *Bacch.* 183 αὔξεσθαι μέγαν, anon. *Bell. Hisp.* 1 *maiores augebantur copiae*. The alternative is to take the clause as ending with *nocti* (*crescere* now being governed by *cupiens*) and meaning "when time is added again to the lengthened night," but this is inferior for two reasons: the proleptic use of *longae* is less acceptable in this version than the first; furthermore, the notion of Libra wanting sleep to increase (*crescere*) is somewhat inconsistent with the picture in 844 of Libra as balancing day and night equally. The A variant *cum longae redit hora noctis* must be excluded for reasons of sense, as "the season of long night" could only refer to winter.

843 somnos. Austin on *Aen.* 2.9 notes some of the connotations of the singular and plural of this word in Vergil. The plural often connotes "a means of enjoyment": so here and at *Pha.* 511f. *caespite aut nudo leves /*

duxisse somnos, though in both passages a properly plural sense (here "nights of sleep") cannot be excluded. The singular often means "the condition of sleep" in Sen. as in Vergil, e.g. *HF* 531, 1044, 1155.

844. The sun is in Libra at the autumnal equinox. For similar personifications of Libra cf. V. *Georg.* 1.208 *Libra die somnique pares ubi fecerit horas*, Manil. 3.659, Germ. *Arat.* 8 *quave Aries et Libra aequant divortia lucis*, Sen. *Pha.* 839.

845 secretam Cererem frequentat. The first two words paraphrase Horace's *Cereris . . . arcanae* (*Carm.* 3.2.26f.), with Ceres used by metonymy for her sanctuary, as Jupiter above for Olympia. For *secretam . . . frequentat* cf. V. *Aen.* 6.478 [*arva*] *quae bello clari secreta frequentant* (note the underworld context), also Ov. *Met.* 10.435f. *turba Cenchreis in illa / regis adest coniunx arcanaque sacra frequentat*, but an element of oxymoron is more evident in Sen.'s phrase than in these precedents.

846–50. These lines contain complex alliteration, particularly on *t* and *s*; notice also *c* and *i* in 846f., *-tur* in 848f. and *a* in 849f.

846f. Again it is uncertain how accurate a picture Sen. has of the Mysteries. I take these lines to refer to the famous journey from Athens to Eleusis, and the phrase *tectis . . . relictis* to mean "leaving behind their homes"; *noctem* alludes to the nocturnal τελεταί. Yet the couplet seems to imply a much shorter journey than the 15 miles covered by the procession. Individuals no doubt had to hurry from all over Athens to join the procession as it formed early in the morning, and that may be Sen.'s meaning in *citi . . . properant*, but once it had started the procession moved quite slowly.

The anomaly of a main clause (sc. *et citi . . . mystae*) made coordinate with a clause to which it is not parallel syntactically (sc. *quanta turba secretam Cererem frequentat*) is not infrequent: *Oed.* 332f. *quid istud est quod esse prolatum volunt / iterumque nolunt et truces iras tegunt? Med.* 821–23, *Pha.* 335–37.

847 mystae. A rare word in Latin literature, though it appears twice in Sen. Trag. (the other place being *Oed.* 431, cf. also *HO* 599). As so often, there is an Ovidian precedent (at *Fasti* 4.536).

848 campos . . . silentes. For the silence of the underworld v. comm. on 620 *silentem . . . domum*.

agitur. The passive verb suggests human helplessness, cf. 183f. *at gens hominum fertur rapidis / obvia fatis incerta sui* and 872 *tibi, Mors, paramur*.

Commentary: Ode III

849–54. The theme of the ages of the dead at once recalls Vergil's stately lines (*Georg.* 4.475–77 = *Aen.* 6.306–8)

> matres atque viri defunctaque corpora vita
> magnanimum heroum, pueri innuptaeque puellae,
> impositique rogis iuvenes ante ora parentum,

which in turn echo Homer (*Od.* 11.38–41)

> νύμφαι τ' ἠίθεοί τε πολύτλητοί τε γέροντες
> παρθενικαί τ' ἀταλαὶ νεοπενθέα θυμὸν ἔχουσαι,
> πολλοὶ δ' οὐτάμενοι χαλκήρεσιν ἐγχείῃσιν,
> ἄνδρες ἀρηίφατοι βεβροτωμένα τεύχε' ἔχοντες.

Seneca has the Vergilian passage in particular in mind: thus line 852 is an expansion of Vergil's phrase *innuptaeque puellae*. Seneca's weary elders may be suggested by Homer's πολύτλητοι γέροντες, though they may equally well come from his own imagination (see comm. on 850). In this lyric meditation on human frailty he omits the doughty warriors mentioned by the epic poets. His *currit* (851) may well be derived from Vergil's *ruebat* in *Aen.* 6.305 *huc omnis turba ad ripas effusa ruebat*, but he makes a new distinction between the movements of old and young. His chief addition is the pathetic instance of the infant, on which he capitalizes in the following lines (855f.).

850 longa satiata vita. A particularly Senecan thought, cf. *Brev. Vit.* 7.9 *quid enim est, quod iam ulla hora novae voluptatis possit adferre? omnia nota, omnia ad satietatem percepta sunt*, *Ep.* 24.26 *quosdam subit eadem faciendi videndique satietas et vitae non odium sed fastidium*, 30.12 (the man who meets a quiet death in old age should be grateful) *quod satiatus ad requiem homini necessariam, lasso gratam perductus est*.

851 melioris aevi. *Aetas* is somewhat more common in phrases of this kind, e.g. *bona aetas* at Cic. *Sen.* 14.48, Sen. *Ep.* 47.12, but *aevum* is paralleled at Ov. *Ibis* 441 *redire . . . aevi melioris in annos*.

853 comis nondum positis ephebi. A surprising phrase, as the term ephebe usually indicates one who has reached puberty, and it was at the onset of puberty, i.e. when a boy first became an ephebe, that the long hair of childhood was cut (cf. *RE* 7.2118.43ff., Hor. *Carm.* 4.10.2f.); it appears that here *ephebus* is used in a wider sense, to include preadolescent boys, as at Auson. *Parent.* 23.15f. *quam tener et primo nove flos decerperis aevo, / nondum purpureas cinctus, ephebe, genas!* *Ephebus* is by no means a synonym for *adulescens* or *iuvenis* in classical Latin, but is normally reserved for foreign youths, especially Greeks

[341]

Commentary: Ode III

(*TLL* s.v.). Seneca's use of it here, and of *mystae* in 847, gives a definitely Greek flavor to the vocabulary of this part of the ode.

854–57. Seneca's reference to infants among the dead was perhaps suggested by Vergil's mention of them in his description of the underworld, *Aen.* 6.426–29. The sentimental theme of children being frightened by their surroundings in the underworld seems likely to be Hellenistic in origin, cf. e.g. *Anth. Pal.* 7.365.5f. Seneca's picture of torches lighting the way for children is derived from the fact that Roman children's funerals took place at night and were torchlit, whereas adults' funerals normally took place in daylight. The picture may well come from Sen.'s imagination rather than a literary source, because in his prose works he mentions several times these nocturnal funerals, cf. *Tranq.* 11.7 *totiens in vicinia mea conclamatum est; totiens praeter limen immaturas exsequias fax cereusque praecessit*, *Brev. Vit.* 20.5, *Ep.* 122.10. It may be colored by memory of some such scene as the initiates carrying torches in the underworld at Ar. *Ran.* 340ff.

854. A reference to the fact that the word for "mother" is one of the first that a child learns (usually in baby talk, μάμμη, *mamma*).

855–62. Darkness is traditionally one of the terrors of the underworld, cf. Lucr. 3.1011 *Cerberus et Furiae iam vero et lucis egestas*; for its *oppressive* nature cf. *inc. inc. trag.* 75 R^2 *ubi rigida constat crassa caligo inferum*, Hor. *Carm.* 1.4.16 *iam te premet nox*, Sen. *Cons. Marc.* 19.4 *imminere mortuis tenebras*. In the *HF* Seneca alludes frequently to the gloom of the world of death, cf. 92, 280–82, 552f., 567, 608–11, 652f., 668–72, 689, 705, 709f., 813–27. These references strengthen the theme of 'light against darkness,' which is particularly evident at the end of the prologue, the beginning of Act III (see 592–95 comm.) and the onset of Hercules' madness (939ff.).

858–63. The Chorus suddenly addresses the dead directly, as if it has just appreciated fully their plight. For the apostrophe v. comm. on 186f. and 831ff. In content and structure the question is similar to the Chorus' question at *Tro.* 1047f. *quis status mentis miseris, ubi omnis / terra decrescet* e.q.s. The sense of oppressive darkness and claustrophobia conveyed is similar to that found in Sen.'s account of traveling through the Naples tunnel, *Ep.* 57.2 *nihil illo carcere longius, nihil illis facibus obscurius, quae nobis praestant non ut per tenebras videamus, sed ut ipsas. ceterum etiam si locus haberet lucem, pulvis auferret* (a comparison made by Gruter).

Commentary: Ode III

860–63. This succession of striking phrases combines to create the kind of apocalyptic vision, impressionistic rather than detailed, in which Sen.'s imagination excels, cf. e.g. 701ff. The use of polysyndeton is rhetorically effective (v. Canter 172), suggesting that there are infinite aspects of the underworld's grimness: one notes also the skillful variation of conjunctions.

861 stat chaos densum. The phrase evokes an overwhelmingly oppressive atmosphere. *Chaos* is often used by Sen. of the underworld, as here (610 comm.); at *Thy.* 1009 *inane chaos* it denotes an empty space, but here the description *densum* suggests conflation with another meaning of *chaos*, i.e. a formless conglomeration of matter, cf. Ov. *Met.* 1.7 *chaos — rudis indigestaque moles, / nec quicquam nisi pondus iners.* The phrase suggestively associates the formlessness of the world of death with chaos primeval. For initial *stat* emphasizing lack of motion v. 540 comm.

862 color noctis malus. *Color malus* is a phrase normally applied to persons, indicating poor health (Cels. 2.7.3, Scrib. 144, 186, Pliny *NH* 31.36): the present phrase therefore connotes not only darkness but also an unhealthy atmosphere.

862f. silentis otium mundi. The force of this phrase depends primarily on the word *otium*, which again is more normally used of people than of things. There are partial precedents at Ov. *Fasti* 1.68 *otia terra . . . habet*, 4.926 *otia mundus agit*, but there the *otium* pertains to the inhabitants of earth as much as earth herself, whereas here the context suggests a reference only to the physical setting of the underworld. In this context *otium* evokes an unhealthy torpidity, thus continuing the suggestion of the previous phrase.

863 vacuaeque nubes. In brief compass this phrase both evokes and negates the fertile cycle of nature, in which rain clouds play their part; a similar technique is used more expansively at 698ff. These clouds are as insubstantial as other things in the underworld, cf. 673 *vacuis . . . locis* and V. *Aen.* 6.269 *perque domos Ditis vacuas et inania regna*.

864–66. Note the simple diction of these lines, evident particularly in the use of the somewhat prosaic *illo* and *id*. Both diction and thought strongly recall Cat. 3.12 *illuc, unde negant redire quemquam*, a line Sen. quotes elsewhere (*Apocol.* 11). Seneca offsets this simplicity by the stylish "framing" of line 864 between adjective and noun, by the echoing effect of the repetitions *sera-sero* and *venit-venit* (in each case with metri-

Commentary: Ode III

cal variation) and by the interweaving of clauses in 865f. In *sera-sero* there is also a variation of meaning, from "late" to "too late." (The difference is made clear by the context, not by the forms, as both adjective and adverb can have either meaning.)

illo. Though it appeared some twenty-five times in Plautus and three times elsewhere in comedy, this adverbial form disappeared from poetry thereafter, perhaps because it was felt to be too prosaic; it reappears in Sen. Trag. (three uses), Lucan (one) and Statius (six).

865 id. Several poets, particularly in the first century A.D., show a reluctance to use the pronoun *is ea id*, perhaps because it was thought to be colorless or prosaic; however, there is some tolerance for the monosyllabic form *id*. Cf. Axelson 70ff., Austin on V. *Aen.* 1.413.

866 cum semel venit. For *semel* in subordinate clauses of the finality of death cf. Hor. *Carm.* 1.24.16ff., 4.7.21 *cum semel occideris*, Prop. 4.11.3 *cum semel infernas intrarunt funera leges*, Sen. *Pha.* 220f. *qui mersus semel / adiit silentem . . . domum.*

potuit. The gnomic perfect, as often, suggests that the statement is based on past experience, cf. Hor. *Sat.* 1.9.59f. *nil sine magno / vita labore dedit mortalibus*, Luc. 1.281 *semper nocuit differre paratis*: no one (in any generation) comes too late to death, from which he cannot return (as no one in any generation has been able to return).[114]

867. The line is perhaps echoed in A. E. Housman, *Last Poems*:

> Think no more, lad; laugh, be jolly:
> Why should men make haste to die?

For *properare fatum* cf. particularly Ov. *Met.* 10.31 *Eurydices, oro, properata retexite fata*, also V. *Aen.* 9.401, Prop. 2.28.25 *quod si forte tibi properarint fata quietem*, [Tib.] 4.1.205, Ov. *Tr.* 3.3.34 *vel praecepisset mors properata fugam.*

868–74. These ideas are found frequently in Sen.'s prose. For similar expressions of the universality of death cf. *QNat.* 2.59.6 *omnes reservamur ad mortem. totum hunc quem vides populum, totumque quem usquam cogitas esse, cito natura revocabit et condet, nec de re sed de die quaeritur: eodem citius tardius veniendum est*, *Cons. Marc.* 11.2 *hoc* (sc. *ad mortem*)

---

114. There seems no need for the conjecture *poterit* (Bentley, Bothe), which would in any case be at odds with the perfect *venit*.

omnis ista quae in foro litigat, in theatris <plaudit> [suppl. Madvig], *in templis precatur turba dispari gradu vadit.* For the notion that we begin to die from our time of birth (874) cf. *Cons. Marc.* 21.6 *ex illo* (sc. *die*) *quo primum lucem vidit, iter mortis ingressus est accessitque fato propior, et illi ipsi qui adiciebantur adulescentiae anni vitae detrahebantur.* The paradoxical direction of life's growth is conveyed with *crescere*, as in 870, at *Ep.* 24.19f. *non repente nos in mortem incidere, sed minutatim procedere; cotidie morimur. cotidie enim demitur aliqua pars vitae, et tunc quoque, cum crescimus, vita decrescit.* This process of 'dying day by day' is sometimes expressed by *carpere*, as in line 874: *Ep.* 26.4 *non enim subito impulsi et prostrati sumus: carpimur. singuli dies aliquid subtrahunt viribus,* 120.18 *ad mortem dies extremus pervenit, accedit omnis. carpit nos illa, non corripit.*

The present passage may have been influenced by Ov. *Met.* 10.32ff. (in Orpheus' address to the underworld divinities: these lines follow immediately on *properata . . . fata* cited in the previous note) *omnia debemur vobis, paulumque morati / serius aut citius sedem properamus ad unam. / tendimus huc omnes, haec est domus ultima, vosque / humani generis longissima regna tenetis.*

868 vaga. The epithet suggests that all mankind's busy traveling is pointless in comparison with the inexorable onward movement toward death; cf. *Anth. Pal.* 7.376 (Crinagoras) δείλαιοι, τί κεναῖσιν ἀλώμεθα θαρσήσαντες / ἐλπίσιν, ἀτηροῦ ληθόμενοι θανάτου;

869f. facietque inerti vela Cocyto. The phrase contains a hint of paradox, as on these lifeless waters there is unlikely to be enough breeze to fill a sail, cf. 550f. It is true that other writers speak of using sails in this context (V. *Aen.* 6.302 *velisque ministrat,* sc. Charon), but Seneca has dwelt in this play on the absence of movement in the infernal regions, and reintroduces the point here with *inerti*. For the sluggishness of infernal rivers v. comm. on 554; for the identity of the river which the shades must cross v. comm. on 679–86.

870^b–74. This passage appealed to many medieval and Renaissance readers: it appears, in full or in part, in several *florilegia* (Brux., Hier., Leid., Flor.), and is paraphrased in Thomas Hughes, *The Misfortunes of Arthur* 1.4:

> Thine (death) is all that East and West can see:
> For thee we live, our coming is not long:
> Spare us but whiles we may prepare our graves.
> Though thou wert slow, we hasten of ourselves.
> The hour that gave did also take our lives.

Commentary: Ode III

Edward Young, reusing the passage in his *Night Thoughts* (5.717ff.), adds a fine image: "While man is growing, life is in decrease; / . . . Our birth is nothing but our death begun; / As tapers waste, that instant they take fire."

870ᵇ–72. Arguing that the vocative *Mors* is too long postponed, Schmidt 1865 19 transposes 872ᵇ and 872ᵃ to the beginning of the apostrophe, followed by Zwierlein 1979 170f. who punctuates as follows:

$$870^a, 872^b \quad \text{vela Cocyto. tibi, Mors, paramur}$$
$$872^a, 870^b \quad \text{(parce venturis), tibi crescit omne}$$
$$871 \quad \text{et quod occasus videt et quod ortus.}$$

The explanation of the supposed error will be omission of 872^{b-a} through homoearchon (*tibi*) with 870ᵇ, followed by erroneous reinsertion; not a difficult hypothesis, cf. e.g. *Oed.* 583f., where 583ᵇ and 584ᵇ, both beginning *ipse*, are transposed by E. The alteration is perhaps justified, but one should note that in Senecan apostrophe the identity of the addressee must often be inferred, with a vocative either omitted completely (v. 831ff. comm.) or postponed as here, cf. e.g. 1057–60, *Tro.* 353–59, *Med.* 703f. See Addenda.

870 tibi crescit omne. Perhaps an echo of Hor. *Carm.* 2.8.17 *adde quod pubes tibi crescit omnis*, in a line of the same meter though very different in its subject. (N-H ad loc. suggest that *tibi crescit* may have been a phrase used of sacrificial victims, comparing the line *tibi nascitur omne pecus, tibi crescit haedus* cited by Caes. Bass. *gramm.* 6.256.) In the Senecan context, the verb conveys a touch of paradox: the active process of growth has as its goal the torpid inactivity that Sen. has described earlier.

871. "From the sunrise to the sunset" is a natural periphrasis for "throughout the whole world" (cf. comm. on 37f. ad fin.), but the phrasing here is perhaps indebted specifically to Ov. *Met.* 1.354 *terrarum quascumque vident occasus et ortus*.

872 parce venturis. Compare Ovid's phrase at *Tr.* 3.3.31 *quantum erat, o magni, morituro parcere, divi?*

873 sis licet segnis. Again conceivably an echo of an Horatian phrase in Sapphics, *Carm.* 3.27.13 *sis licet felix*, though again the subject matter is dissimilar.

Commentary: Ode III

874 carpit. So E: A has *carpsit*. In the two passages cited on 868–74 to illustrate the use of *carpere* here, the verb refers to a gradual wearing away of life, by attrition of strength or of the life span; I take it that here Sen. has in mind the latter. If a past tense were to be used here, an imperfect would be appropriate ("the hour which first gave life was already plucking away at it"), but a perfect would give the wrong impression, i.e. that the first hour of life was also the hour of death. The present must therefore be correct: "the hour which first gives [i.e. has given] life is already plucking away at it."

875. For the phrasing in reference to a religious celebration cf. Ov. *Met.* 12.150 *festa dies aderat* (followed as here by a reference to sacrifice), also Hor. *Carm.* 4.2.41f. *concines laetosque dies et urbis / publicum ludum* (for Augustus' return), Ov. *Fasti* 1.87 *salve, laeta dies.*

876 aras tangite. Touching the altar while making a sacrifice, prayer, etc. was a regular part of Roman ritual, cf. V. *Aen.* 4.219f. *talibus orantem dictis arasque tenentem / audiit omnipotens* with Pease ad loc., 12.201 *tango aras, medios ignes et numina testor*, Hor. *Carm.* 3.23.17, Ov. *Am.* 1.4.27 *tange manu mensam, tangunt quo more precantes.*

supplices. Not implying that the citizens of Thebes need to request protection or the like: the word here has a meaning connected with *supplicatio* = "thanksgiving," as at Hor. *Carm.* 3.14.6ff. (on Augustus' return from Spain) *prodeat . . . / et soror clari ducis et decorae / supplice vitta / virginum matres.*

878. For such phrasing in the context of a celebration cf. Ov. *Met.* 3.529 *mixtaeque viris matresque nurusque*, also V. *Aen.* 4.145f. *mixtique altaria circum / Cretesque Dryopesque fremunt pictique Agathyrsi*, Hor. *Carm.* 4.11.10f. *huc et illuc / cursitant mixtae pueris puellae*, Ov. *AA* 1.217 *laeti iuvenes mixtaeque puellae.*

880f. The wording and the theme of work being laid aside on a festival day recall Tib. 2.1.5ff. *luce sacra requiescat humus, requiescat arator, / et grave suspenso vomere cesset opus; / solvite vincla iugis.*

deposito iugo. A compressed phrase: more usually there would be mention of the animals that are unyoked, as at V. *Ecl.* 4.41 *tauris iuga solvet arator*, Hor. *Carm.* 3.6.41ff. *sol ubi . . . / iuga demeret / bubus*, Manil. 2.250 *Taurus depositis collo sopitus aratris.*

881 fertilis. Boeotia was known for its fertility, cf. *Phoen.* 129f. *Boeotios / colonus agros uberis tondes soli.* The adjective here is in keeping with the joyful atmosphere of the celebration; note also the thematic contrast with the infertility of the underworld.

incolae. The sense of the root *colo* = "cultivate" as well as "inhabit" (cf. *cultor, colonus*) is stronger here than is usual in *incola*; Heywood rightly translates "The Tillers of the fertile Soyle." Cf. Ov. *Tr.* 3.10.59f. *ruris opes parvae, pecus et stridentia plaustra / et quas divitias incola pauper habet.*

882–90. This description of the peace established by Hercules echoes the hyperbolic claims Romans make for the universality of their own empire and the *pax Romana*, claims in which *domare* (888) and *pacare* (890) are key words, cf. e.g. Cic. *Cat.* 2.11 *omnia sunt externa . . . terra marique pacata*, *Sest.* 67 *qui maximas nationes . . . domuisset, qui . . . imperium populi Romani orbis terrarum terminis definisset*, V. *Ecl.* 4.17 *pacatumque . . . reget orbem*, Livy 42.52.14 *Europa omni domita . . . aperuerint armis orbem terrarum*, Ov. *AA* 1.177f.; "from East to West" (883) often appears in such claims, e.g. Sall. *Cat.* 36.4 *ad occasum ab ortu solis omnia domita armis parerent*, Hor. *Carm.* 4.15.14ff. *imperi / porrecta maiestas ad ortus / solis ab Hesperio cubili*, v. Fraenkel *Horace* 451 n. 4. Line 890 in particular strikes a triumphal Roman note, cf. Livy 41.12.10 *pacatis provinciis Romam revertit.*

882 Herculea manu. The phrase has an Horatian precedent at *Carm.* 2.12.6f.

884. That is, in the south, specifically the tropics. For shadows disappearing as one reaches the tropics cf. Arist. *Meteor.* 362b. Syene in Upper Egypt was particularly famous as a place where the sun cast no shadow at noon on certain dates, cf. Strabo 17.1.48, Luc. 2.587, Pliny *NH* 2.75.183. But beyond this literal reference, the phrase *umbras corporibus negat* is wonderfully suggestive: a world where bodies cast no shadows is a *Gegenwelt*, a deathlike place (cf. e.g. Plut. *Mor.* 300c τῶν δ' ἀποθανόντων οἱ Πυθαγορικοὶ λέγουσι τὰς ψυχὰς μὴ ποιεῖν σκιάν) and the eeriness of the phrase is increased by the connotations of both *umbra* and *corpus*.

sol medium tenens. For the phrase cf. *Cons. Marc.* 22.6 *iter mortis ingressus sum et iam medium fere teneo*; I take it that in both passages *medium* functions as a noun, i.e. "midpoint (of the course)," rather than as an adjective with *iter* or *cursum* understood. Thus *sol medium tenens* is primarily an expanded version of *sol medius* = "the sun at midday" (Phaedr. 3.19.8, Val. Fl. 2.444, cf. Sen. *HF* 236 *medius dies* with my comm.). It is conceivable that there is some conflation with *medius* used of the midmost geoclimatic zone, i.e. that of the tropics, cf. e.g. Cic. *Rep.* 6.20 *cernis autem eandem terram quasi quibusdam redimitam et circumdatam cingulis, e quibus duos . . . obriguisse pruina vides, medium autem illum et maximum solis ardore torreri,* Luc. 2.586f. *calida medius mihi cognitus axis / Aegypto.*

886f. After listing east, west, and south, Sen. might have been expected to refer to the north, but in fact these lines provide a comprehensive summing-up, "every land throughout the world." (For listing of only three of the four compass points cf. 1139–41.) The means of expression is probably influenced by a similar passage in a very similar context at Ov. *Her.* 9 (Deianira to Hercules) 13f. *respice vindicibus pacatum viribus orbem, / qua latam Nereus caerulus ambit humum.*

887 Tethyos ambitu. An interesting juxtaposition of a poeticism with an essentially prosaic word. The use of *Tethys* by metonymy for the sea, Alexandrian in origin, was introduced into Latin poetry by Catullus (66.70, 88.5), but it was little used thereafter until taken up by Sen. and Lucan (five and nine uses, respectively). *Ambitus* is a word generally avoided by poets (*TLL* 1.1857.75ff.), but Sen. and Lucan use it guardedly (four and two uses, respectively); there is a poetic precedent, similar in sense to the present usage, at Hor. *Ars P.* 17 *aquae per amoenos ambitus agros.*

888 Alcidae . . . labor. For the periphrasis cf. Hor. *Carm.* 1.3.36 *perrupit Acheronta Herculeus labor.* Such phrases in Latin probably originated in imitation of Greek periphrases such as Hom. *Il.* 11.690 βίη Ἡρακλείη, 14.418 Ἕκτορος . . . μένος; v. Pease on V. *Aen.* 4.132, and for further Latin examples K-S 1.242f.

889 vada Tartari. Probably "the rivers of the Underworld," though at *Med.* 742 *Tartari ripis* Sen. may be thinking of Tartarus as a river, which could be the case here also.

893f. The traditional explanation of these lines is unsatisfactory. It assumes that the lines are addressed to an officiating priest, whose hair stands on end as a result of divine afflatus *in re divina*. For such a symptom of inspiration one might compare V. *Aen.* 6.48 (the Sibyl), Sen. *Oed.* 230 (the Pythia), Luc. 5.170f.; but although this is all very well for ecstatic prophetesses, no parallel is cited for so extravagant a symptom in a priest making sacrifice. Kapnukajas 68 is very probably right that the lines are addressed not to a priest but to Hercules him-

Commentary: Act IV

self. In this case we have another example of the dramatic technique whereby the Chorus at the end of an ode draws attention to the entrance of a character, and so effects a transition into the following Act; cf. the entry of Megara et al. at 202–4, with comm. *Stantes . . . comas* now refers simply to H.'s unkempt hair (cf. 468 *horrentes comae*, *Pha.* 833 *recta squalor incultus coma*), which will be somewhat disguised (n.b. *tege*) by the wreath. This explanation has the further advantage that the phrase *dilecta . . . populo* is more natural if addressed to H. (cf. V. *Ecl.* 7.61 *populus Alcidae gratissima*) than to a priest.

Seneca's wording properly reflects the Greek practice of wearing a wreath while sacrificing, as opposed to the usual Roman custom of covering the head with one's toga. Cf. Vergil's description of Evander's sacrifice at the Ara Maxima, where the Greek practice was observed in historical times: *Herculea bicolor cum populus umbra / velavitque comas foliisque innexa pependit* (*Aen.* 8.276f.). Vergil's *velavit* may well have suggested Seneca's *tege*. For the association of the poplar with Hercules, in addition to V. *Ecl.* 7.61 and *Aen.* 8.276f. cited above, cf. line 912 below, Ov. *Her.* 9.64 *aptior Herculeae populus alba comae*, N–H on Hor. *Carm.* 1.7.23.

Act IV (895–1053)

Basically, Act IV represents a translation into stage action of the Euripidean messenger speech describing Hercules' madness and the murder of his family (*Her.* 922–1015). Whether this adaptation is due to Seneca or to a predecessor we cannot know, but the latter is the more probable hypothesis (see Introduction). Nevertheless, it is highly unlikely a priori that Seneca would follow a single source at length without adding material of his own.

The chief divergencies from Euripides may be summarized as follows.

First, the private ritual of purification of the palace from bloodshed (Eur. 922–27) becomes a public rite of thanksgiving and is greatly expanded (Sen. 895–939). This expansion permits demonstration of Hercules' hubristic condescension toward the gods and disregard of religious requirements; it also allows the poignant juxtaposition between his prayer (926–39) and the onset of madness.

Second, in Hercules' madness a single impulse and hallucination, namely, an attack on Mycenae, is replaced by a series of shifting impulses and hallucinations, with great richness of psychological and thematic significance. Here the originator may well be Seneca himself in large measure (Introduction fn. 35).

Commentary: Act IV

The way in which the Euripidean material has been adapted shows an awareness of stage realities; there are in fact several stage directions written into the text, primarily in the murder-scene (987ff.), which leave little doubt about how the events are to be envisaged in terms of staging.[115] One of these occurs at 999ff., where Hercules breaks down the palace doors in pursuit of his children. Having smashed the doors and damaged the building he catches sight of one of his sons, and actually enters the palace at 1001f. to kill him. Amphitryon's description at 1002–7 must therefore be intended to inform the audience of events inside the palace, which Amphitryon himself can see through the ruined doorway.[116] Another clear stage direction is contained in Hercules' command *sequere* to Megara at 1018. This can only be intended to motivate an exit, in order to avoid having Megara and the third child being killed onstage; compare Orestes' command ἕπου to Clytemnestra at Aesch. *Cho.* 904 with a similar purpose, and the frequent use of *sequere* in Republican drama to motivate an exit (e.g. Plaut. *As.* 809, 941, *Aul.* 349, *Bac.* 108, *Capt.* 460, *Poen.* 1366). Amphitryon's description at 1022–26 must therefore have the same purpose as that at 1002–7, to inform the audience of what is happening offstage.[117] Clearly, then, Megara has fled from the palace (*e latebris*) at 1009, pursued by H.; hence they are onstage at 1018, which necessitates the command *sequere*. The indications concerning the first murder are less clear. It seems probable that the child's death is not to be visualized as taking place onstage, as the others do not. H. may exit at 990f. to make the shot, or he may shoot from the stage at a target unseen by the audience.[118] Finally it may be asked at what point he returns to the stage

---

115. The following analysis of how the murders are to be envisaged in stage terms is in general that accepted by most commentators and critics; cf. Zwierlein 1966 42 with further references.

116. Several ancient dramas contain descriptions of action which is happening simultaneously offstage, Aesch. *Suppl.* 713ff., Eur. *Phoen.* 101ff., Plaut. *Rud.* 166ff., Sen. *Phoen.* 394ff. For description of action taking place indoors there is a definite if brief precedent at Plaut. *Bac.* 834ff., where Chrysalus and Nicobulus look through the stage doors and comment on a banquet taking place within. (In Sen. *Thy.* 901ff. Atreus observes his brother dining within, but there we must envisage Thyestes' couch being wheeled onstage, cf. *Pha.* 384ff.) Sen. has an interesting adaptation of this technique at *Ag.* 867ff., where Cassandra describes the murder of Agamemnon indoors by her clairvoyant powers (see Tarrant ad loc. and 1978 253f., and cf. Eur. *Her.* 867–70 where Mania's ability to describe the hero becoming mad in the palace is presumably based on supernatural rather than ordinary vision).

117. Presumably again within the palace, cf. 1227f. *quis vos per omnem, liberi, sparsos domum / deflere digne poterit?*

118. In that case there is probably a close parallel in Soph. *Niobe*, in which Artemis seems to have shot from the roof of the stage palace at Niobe's daughters who were behind the scenes, v. W. S. Barrett in Carden, *The Papyrus Fragments of Sopho-*

[351]

Commentary: Act IV

after killing Megara. The fact that he does not respond immediately to Amphitryon's address to him ending in 1031, and that when he does speak in 1035ff. he appears not to have heard Amphitryon's words, suggests that he is just emerging from the palace at 1035. The content of 1035ff. would certainly suit a man just returning from a task well done; cf. *Oed.* 998 *bene habet, peractum est: iusta persolvi patri*, spoken as Oedipus comes out of the palace after blinding himself. Presumably, then, Amphitryon called into the shattered palace at 1028–31, but was not heard by H.[119]

The natural conclusion is this: not only is the murder-scene and the whole Act written within theatrical conventions, but it is deliberately designed to combine practicability for the stage with a maximum of emotional impact. It may be that this theatricality is due to a post-Euripidean source rather than to Seneca himself.

895 ultrice. So β (corrupted to *altrice* in δ), while E has *victrice*; for confusion of *ult-/vict-* in MSS v. 385 comm. Though the phrase *victrix dextra* is naturally used of Hercules (v. 800 comm.), the words *et poenae comes* in 897 suggest that here *ultrice* is the more apposite reading; furthermore *victor* in 898 would be somewhat otiose if preceded by *victrice* here.

895f. adverso ... terram cecidit ore. *Adverso ... ore* = "with face downward," *pronus*, though the ablative is instrumental rather than descriptive, thus giving a particularly violent image. The detail connotes ignominious defeat, cf. Hom. *Il.* 2.418 (Agamemnon's wish for the Trojans) πρηνέες ἐν κονίῃσιν ὀδὰξ λαζοίατο γαῖαν, Hor. *Carm.* 2.7.12 *turpe solum tetigere mento*, V. *Aen.* 11.484f., Ov. *Met.* 2.476f. (Juno attacking Callisto) *prensis a fronte capillis / stravit humi pronam*, Sen. *Oed.* 480 *ore deiecto petiere terram* (obeisance). Seneca's wording was probably influenced by Ov. *Her.* 12.63 *disiectamque comas adversaque in ora iacentem* (of Medea lying distraught on her bed). For *caedere* of smiting the earth in death cf. V. *Aen.* 10.403f. *curruque volutus / caedit semianimis Rutulorum calcibus arva*.

---

cles (Berlin 1974) 172f., 185. That scene provides a further parallel for a running description of what is happening within (fr. 8 lines 4–7, fr. 9.2 lines 3f.), though the speaker (Apollo) is not looking through the stage door.

In *HF* Act V all the bodies of Hercules' family are conventionally in the house (1227–28; actually on the *eccyclema*, see introduction to Act V); that would imply that the boy died in the house, but one cannot necessarily assume complete consistency between one Act and another.

119. For the technique of addressing someone within the stage building cf. Ter. *Ad.* 376ff. There the door is open, here it is broken down.

896f. Hercules is characteristically thorough in taking revenge (similarly in Eur. 568–73 he plans to kill *all* who have turned against him); later, in his madness, he will believe that he is destroying Lycus' family as well.

For the device of ending successive lines with the same word cf. the fine couplet *Thy.* 596f. *dolor ac voluptas / invicem cedunt; brevior voluptas,* and other examples collected by Canter 159. A possible source for the rhetorical point of the present passage (but without its sarcasm) is Ov. *Ibis* 628 *comites Rhesi tum necis, ante viae;* for the pointed use of *comes* in such contexts cf. Val. Max. 5.5.4 *comes fraternae necis non defuit,* Sen. *Ag.* 926 *comes paternae quaeritur natus neci, TLL* 3.1774.57ff.

897 iacuit. *Iacere* here and occasionally elsewhere denotes the *process* of collapsing, falling, etc. as much as the *condition* of lying prostrate, cf. Curt. 8.1.24 *[Philippum] debilitatum vulnere . . . iacuisse,* Phaedr. 1.24.9f. *[rana] dum vult validius / inflare sese, rupto iacuit corpore,* Tac. *Hist.* 1.42 *[Titus Vinius] ante aedem divi Iulii iacuit primo ictu in poplitem.* Compare the use of *stetit* = "stopped and stood still" at line 15 above.

899. Powerful tragic irony; the audience, knowing what is to come, understands *victimis* in its secondary sense of human "victims." This is not a difficult leap of thought, as *victima* is frequently used overtly in this sense in Sen. Trag. as in earlier Latin, v. comm. on 920–24. The effect of *Thy.* 545 *ego destinatas victimas superis dabo* is comparable to that of the present line, but not identical, as there Atreus is fully conscious of the ambiguity of *victima.* For similar effects cf. Eur. *Med.* 1053ff. χωρεῖτε, παῖδες, ἐς δόμους. ὅτῳ δὲ μὴ / θέμις παρεῖναι τοῖς ἐμοῖσι θύμασιν, / αὐτῷ μελήσει, and perhaps Aesch. *Ag.* 1056f.

900–906. Hercules emphasizes the warlike side of Minerva and Bacchus, which appeals to his own predilections: contrast the enervated Bacchus of 472ff. (However, in 906 Sen. is more interested in creating a paradoxical point than in revealing the attitude of the speaker).

900. The tradition of Minerva as Hercules' helper goes back as far as Hom. *Il.* 8.362f. οὐδέ τι τῶν μέμνηται, ὅ οἱ μάλα πολλάκις υἱὸν / τειρόμενον σώεσκον ὑπ' Εὐρυσθῆος ἀέθλων, cf. *Od.* 11.625f. It is particularly strong in artistic representations of the labors, cf. Brommer passim, *LIMC* s.v. Athena 511ff.

adiutrix. Seneca has a weakness for the rarer feminine agent-nouns in *-trix: adiutrix, dominatrix, domitrix, machinatrix, miratrix* occur once each in the tragedies. The last two were coined by Sen.; *dominatrix* and *domi-*

Commentary: Act IV

trix appear earlier, but rarely. *Adiutrix* is found in Republican drama, but then disappears from verse until used once by Ovid (*Met.* 7.195); Sen. borrows it from Ovid, as both use it in invocation of a goddess. Compare Sen.'s liking for the sound of adjectives in *-x*, for which see p. 470.

901 belligera Pallas. A variation on Ovid's *bellica Pallas, Met.* 5.46.

901^b–2. From the earliest times the aegis is regarded as an instrument of war, which may be used by Jupiter or Minerva either to hearten or to terrify mortal combatants (Hom. *Il.* 2.450ff., 5.738ff., 17.593ff.). Seneca envisages Minerva wearing the aegis spread over her left arm, as Hercules wears the lion-skin when attacking Cerberus at 797ff.; this use of the aegis by the goddess is illustrated in certain works of art, e.g. D-S 1.102 ill. 142, 143, *LIMC* s.v. Athena 59, 171, 387, though more usually it is depicted as worn over her shoulders, and in Latin literature it is often worn as a breastplate (V. *Aen.* 8.435ff., Ov. *Met.* 2.754, 6.79).

ciet . . . minas. Seneca has similar phrases at *Oed.* 351 *terrores cient*, *Phoen.* 389 *aera iam bellum cient*. His use of *ciere* in connection with the aegis may have been prompted by a reminiscence of V. *Aen.* 8.353f. [*Iuppiter*] *cum saepe nigrantem / aegida concuteret dextra nimbosque cieret*.

902 ore saxifico. The wording of this allusion to the Gorgon's head is derived from Ovid: *Ibis* 553 *saxificae videas infelix ora Medusae, Met.* 5.217 *saxificos vultus . . . Medusae*.

903 adsit. Gods are traditionally invited to attend a sacrifice, no doubt originally with the purpose of partaking of it, cf. Tib. 1.1.37 *adsitis, divi, nec vos e paupere mensa / dona . . . spernite* with K. F. Smith ad loc.

Lycurgi domitor. In the Homeric account (*Il.* 6.130ff.), it was Zeus who punished Lycurgus after he had attacked Bacchus and his attendants; later accounts, however, agree that Bacchus avenged himself, though they differ in details (Soph. *Ant.* 955ff., Apollod. 3.5.1, Hyg. *Fab.* 132, Serv. ad *Aen.* 3.14).

et rubri maris. This includes the more westerly portions of the Indian Ocean (including the Persian Gulf), as well as what is now called the Red Sea. It might be thought that Sen. refers in general terms to Bacchus' conquest of its coasts during his triumphant journey to India (for which cf. *Oed.* 114–20). More probably, however, he alludes to a specific, though ill-attested, episode during this journey, to which Horace also alludes at *Carm.* 2.19.17 *tu flectis amnes, tu mare barbarum* (n.b. immediately after mention of the *exitium Lycurgi* in line 16). This must have been a miraculous demonstration of Bacchus' power over the sea: N-H ad loc. present evidence suggesting a parting of the waters not unlike that attributed to Moses.

904. The thyrsus was originally nothing more warlike than a branch or a fennel-stalk tipped with leaves, but because of its magical power it could be used as a weapon, cf. Eur. *Bacch.* 25 κίσσινον βέλος, 762, 1099; hence in Alexandrian art and literature it became a full-fledged weapon, the θυρσόλογχος, with a metal spearpoint covered in leaves (v. D-S 5.295f., *RE* 6A. 751.65ff.). So in Latin literature the terms *hasta* and *cuspis* are frequently used of the thyrsus. For references to the point concealed by leaves cf. Cat. 64.256 *harum pars tecta quatiebant cuspide thyrsos*, Ov. *Met.* 3.667 *pampineis agitat velatam frondibus hastam.*

virenti. A's reading, whereas E has *virente*. Present participles with adjectival function normally have ablative singular in -*i*, but Sen. not infrequently substitutes the -*e* form for metrical convenience. Where meter would allow either form Sen. normally writes -*i*, but forms in -*e* are occasionally transmitted by EA unanimously: *Oed.* 1049 *tremente dextera* (contrast *Ag.* 890 *trementi . . . dextra*), *Ag.* 449 *iacente*, *Thy.* 780 *fluente*. Given those facts, it is difficult to know on what objective grounds one could make a decision when the MSS disagree: E writes -*e* and A -*i* here and at *Pha.* 1045, and the situation is reversed at *Tro.* 1079, *HO* 1005. In the present instance I choose *virenti* purely out of preference for its sound.

905 geminum . . . numen. A Senecan phrase for Apollo and Diana, cf. *Ag.* 399, *Med.* 700.

905f. A case of sand without lime, much rhetorical polishing masking emptiness of content. The paronomasia of 905 is not in itself unusual, cf. V. *Aen.* 1.325, Ov. *Fasti* 5.699 *Phoeben Phoebesque sororem*, Sen. *HF* 16, 482, *Tro.* 38 *Ithacus aut Ithaci comes*, *Phoen.* 647f., Canter 161. Somewhat more recherché is the figure of *regressio* (ἐπάνοδος) in 906, "a type of repetition which both repeats and differentiates what has been mentioned before" (Quint. 9.3.35, Canter 160), cf. *Med.* 695ff. (of Draco and the Bears) *descendat anguis, cuius immensos duae, / maior minorque, sentiunt nodos ferae / (maior Pelasgis apta, Sidoniis minor)*, *Pha.* 269f. Seneca's justification for the contrast of 906 would presumably be

Commentary: Act IV

that Diana is a full-time huntress whereas Apollo also has other interests, cf. Ov. *Am.* 3.2.51 *auguribus Phoebus, Phoebe venantibus adsit*, but it is clearly laughable to suggest that Apollo ἑκηβόλος is a less competent archer than his sister: Sen. could not resist the paradox of a sister more warlike than her brother. Such distinctions of talents are traditional for the other divine twins Castor and Pollux, and that may have suggested the idea here, cf. Prop. 3.14.18 *hic victor pugnis, ille futurus equis*, Ov. *Met.* 8.301f., Sen. *Med.* 88f. *cedet Castore cum suo / Pollux caestibus aptior* (n.b. the frequent use of *aptus* in such contrasts, cf. Ov. *Am.* 1.10.19 *nec Venus apta feris nec filius armis*, Sen. *Tro.* 816ff.), N-H on Hor. *Carm.* 1.12.26, *RE* 5.1093.29ff.

907f. frater . . . frater. Seneca quickly regains his rhetorical touch. One use of anadiplosis (638f. comm.) is to have the second occurrence of the repeated word qualify the first in some way, making a rhetorical point in the process: cf. *Med.* 922f. *placuit hoc poenae genus, / meritoque placuit*, 947f. *habeat incolumes pater, / dum et mater habeat*, *Thy.* 907. The present instance involves self-correction, which is the basis of many Senecan points, v. 643f. comm. ad fin. The catch-all phrase, reminiscent of those used in cult to prevent omission of any relevant deity (v. 600–603 comm.), also provides a convenient means of rounding off a prayer.

908 non ex noverca frater. This phrase recalls Juno's complaints in the prologue about Jupiter's bastards inhabiting heaven. Apart from the already-mentioned Bacchus and Phoebus, such brothers would include Orion, Perseus, and the Tyndarids (12ff.).

huc appellite. There are similar line-endings involving commands to anonymous attendants at *Oed.* 823 *ite propere accersite* and *Ag.* 787 *famuli attollite*.

909f. Hercules does things on the grand scale: there is characteristic hyperbole in the *quidquid* clauses. Horace uses a similar clause to indicate humorously the ambition of a man who is pleased *si proprio condidit horreo / quidquid de Libycis verritur areis*, *Carm.* 1.1.9f. On the other hand the poetic plural *greges* appears in Sen. in contexts where hyperbole seems unlikely, *Tro.* 296, 1108, *Med.* 96.

opimos. A technical term for animals fattened for sacrifice, cf. 922f. *victima . . . opima*, Varro *RR* 2.1.20 *boves altiles ad sacrificia publica saginati dicuntur opimi*, *TLL* 9.711.18ff.

quidquid Indi arvis secant. The transmitted text is *quidquid Indorum seges*: this makes sense only if one supplies some such verb as *reddit*, which is too large an ellipse.[120] Withof, who as often was the first to acknowledge the difficulty (78f.), conjectured *quidquid Indorum genus*, but this is open to two objections. First, *Indorum genus* would be simply a paraphrase for *Indi*, but so weak a use of *genus* is not paralleled in Sen. Trag.: at *Ag.* 523 *placetque mitti Doricum exitio genus* it has the connotation of "the whole race," which would not be appropriate here. Second, as Schmidt pointed out (1865 19), the wording of 910 seems to imply some *contrast* with the harvesting methods of the Indians: in particular one would normally expect variation of verbs in such multiple *quidquid* clauses, cf. 30ff. *quidquid horridum tellus creat / inimica, quidquid pontus aut aer tulit*, 333ff., *Med.* 212ff., *Pha.* 1161ff. *quidquid . . . Tethys . . . gestat, quidquid Oceanus . . . tegit*, *Thy.* 353ff. These two requirements are admirably met by Schmidt's conjecture, which I have printed.[121] For the wording cf. *Anth. Lat.* 444 (one of the epigrams doubtfully attributed to Sen.) 8 *quidquid Libyco secatur arvo*. The transmitted *Indorum seges* is best explained as part of a gloss that has ousted the true text. An alternative solution would be to accept Leo's suggestion that a line has been lost after *quidquid Indorum seges*: Leo supplements e.g. <*praestat colonis igne propioris dei*>. But the hypothesis of a lacuna means that the structure of the two clauses would be rather different, and that the first would be longer than the second; there is something to be said for closely parallel structure and an increasing dicolon, both of which are found in the two passages cited above and in Schmidt's conjecture.

It seems unlikely that Sen. has a particular spice in mind in 909 (cf. the vague *Indum gramen* Stat. *Theb.* 7.569): India was associated with several, notably *costum* (Ov. *Fasti* 1.341) and *tus* (ibid. 3.720). But in 910 (as at *Pha.* 67 *Arabs divite silva*) he clearly means cinnamon, in view of *Oed.* 117 *cinnami silvis Arabas beatos*. For the belief that cinnamon grew in Arabia cf. Diod. Sic. 2.49.3: in fact the bulk of it came from Indonesia, but via Arabian merchants, v. J. I. Miller, *The Spice Trade of the Roman Empire* (Oxford 1969) 153ff.

---

120. To understand *est*, or to insert it in the transmitted text after *Indorum* with Düring *Materialien* 4^b.483 and Ageno, would create inelegant Latin and doubtful sense: *quidquid Indorum est seges* would mean "whatever it is that the Indians happen to grow," which is not what Hercules intends.

121. The conjecture of Koetschau 134f. *quidquid Indo fert seges* makes a much less effective contrast, and the awkward metrical pattern it creates is normally avoided by Seneca (Strzelecki 22-25).

Commentary: Act IV

910 odoris. Often taken as a partitive genitive of *odor*, but the ablative plural of *odorus* would be more in keeping with Senecan style, which makes much use of noun-adjective pairs (v. p. 189): cf. Ov. *AA* 1.287 *arbore . . . odora*.

911 pinguis exundat vapor. This vigorous phrase matches the hyperbole of 909f. For *pinguis* used in such a context, cf. Ov. *Tr.* 5.5.11 *da mihi tura, puer, pingues facientia flammas*.

912f. Phrases such as *populea arbor* with adjectives derived from tree names are found both in high poetry, as at Enn. *trag.* 206 R² *abiegna trabes*, Ov. *Met.* 1.449 *aesculeae . . . frondis*, and in nonpoetic contexts, e.g. Cato *Agr.* 5.7 *frondem iligneam*, Col. 5.11.14 *arboris ficulneae*, cf. *TLL* 2.426.45ff. Though *arbor*, like *trabs*, is used of things made of wood such as ships' masts, its use by metonymy for a garland is remarkable; I know of no parallel closer than the use of *ramus* seen in 913 and frequently found in Vergil, e.g. *Aen.* 5.71 *cingite tempora ramis*. One might compare such a phrase as Ov. *Met.* 1.451 *tempora cingebat de qualibet arbore Phoebus*, which, however, does not involve metonymy.

913 gentili. As an adjective this word appears for the first time in Ovid, who uses it only once; it becomes slightly more common in Sen. Trag., Statius, and Silius.

914–17. These arrangements for the sacrifice are clearly designed to remove Theseus from the scene in preparation for the imminent mad-scene; probably Sen. borrowed the device from an earlier Hercules play, v. Introduction. On the question of when Theseus returns to the stage, v. 1032–34 comm.

915–17. Thebes was a city rich in sacred sites and historical monuments, as Pausanias' description makes clear (9.16ff.), and the detailed references to topography are therefore particularly appropriate, cf. e.g. Stat. *Theb.* 7.601ff.

silvestria trucis antra Zethi. The cave was no doubt that used as a home by the herdsman who rescued Zethus and Amphion as infants and reared them there, cf. Eur. *Antiope* in Page *Literary Papyri* p. 64 lines 26, 29f. δόμων στείχειν ἔσω / ἐς τήνδ' ἵν' ἡμεῖς καὶ πρὶν οἰκοῦμεν πέτραν, 37. It often happens that only one brother is mentioned, for the sake of convenience, in contexts where both might have been named (cf. 262f. comm.): thus their joint memorial is called Amphion's at Aesch. *Sept.* 528, Eur. *Suppl.* 663, but Zethus' at Eur. *Phoen.* 145. It may be that the cave is called Zethus' here because he took to the rough herdsman's life whereas his brother hankered after music and poetry (for the contrast between them v. Roscher 1.310.48ff.). That is certainly the explanation of the adjective *trucis* here, and Horace similarly calls Zethus *severus* (*Epist.* 1.18.42); cf. also Prop. 3.15.29f. *et durum Zethum et lacrimis Amphiona molem / experta est . . . mater*, and note that Sen. twice associates Zethus but not Amphion with the cruel punishment of Dirce (*Oed.* 610f., *Phoen.* 20).

Because the brothers had built the lower defensive walls of Thebes (v. 262f. comm.), they were regarded as cofounders of the city with Cadmus who had fortified the citadel, cf. e.g. Stat. *Theb.* 10.787f.

916 antra Zethi. Properly z as a double consonant would "make position," but Sen. ignores this again at *Oed.* 421 *retinentĕ zona*, 541, *Ag.* 433, *Thy.* 845, cf. Housman *CQ* 22 (1928) 7 = 1972 1143. Earlier this license tends to be used only when the word beginning in z would otherwise be inadmissible in verse, e.g. V. *Aen.* 3.270 *nemorosă Zacynthos*, but that is not the case in Sen.

nobilis Dircen aquae. The E reading (distorted in transmission to *Dircenaque*), clearly *lectio difficilior* and *potior* in comparison with A's *nobiles Dirces aquas*: the latter makes the phrase conform in construction with *antra Zethi* and *larem regis*, but E's version gives a stylish variation.

The stream that bore Dirce's name was considered particularly sacred, and sacrifices made to it might reasonably be regarded as made to Dirce herself, cf. Pind. *Isthm.* 6.74 Δίρκης ἁγνὸν ὕδωρ, Eur. *Bacch.* 520 πότνι' εὐπάρθενε Δίρκα, *IT* 401 ῥεύματα σεμνὰ Δίρκας, Sen. *Phoen.* 126 *sacra . . . Dirce*. At the so-called tomb of Dirce there was a minor cult, but this was very obscure (Plut. *Mor.* 578b).

917. The palace of Cadmus was identified in historical times with a ruined building on the Cadmeia (Paus. 9.12.3). In modern times, a Mycenaean palace, perhaps the selfsame building, has been excavated in that area (*RE* 5A. 1434f. with plan).

918 date tura flammis. *Dare* is not uncommonly used of offering incense, particularly in Ovid; there may be a ritual precedent in view of Serv. auct. ad V. *Aen.* 8.107 *dici solebat in sacris "da quod debes de manu dextra aris."* The combination of *dare tura* with *flammis* was probably suggested by Ovid, cf. *Met.* 6.164, 9.159 *tura dabant primis et verba precantia* *flammis* (n.b. before a "Hercules furens" scene), 13.636. Incense in the heroic age is an anachronism, though hardly an obtrusive one, frequently found in Ovid (v. Bömer on *Met.* 1.248 ff.).

918–24. Hercules' refusal to purify his hands before sacrifice reveals his hubristic assumption that he can ignore the normal standards governing behavior towards the gods: see Introduction with fn. 31. The focusing of attention here on his bloodstained hands is splendidly ominous: "blood will have blood."

919 cruenta caede. Seneca repeats this alliterative phrase at 1160. The two words appear together, in juxtaposition but not in agreement, once in Vergil, once in the *Culex*, and three times in Ovid.

920–24. Hercules' use of sacrificial language concerning human beings is indicative of his callousness, as at 634 *mactetur hostia*. Elsewhere in Sen. Trag. the word *victima* is consciously applied to human beings only by the murderous Pyrrhus and Medea (*Tro.* 306, *Med.* 970, cf. Atreus' ambiguity at *Thy.* 545), or to express the brutality of a murder such as that of Pelops (*Thy.* 146, cf. *Tro.* 140): compare the use of similar sacrificial imagery to convey condemnation at *Ag.* 166, 219, and above all the horror of Atreus' ritual butchering of his nephews, *Thy.* 682ff. Yet some qualification must be made in the case of the parallel passage *Pha.* 708f. (Hippolytus on the point of killing Phaedra) *iustior numquam focis / datus tuis est sanguis, arquitenens dea*, an expression not of habitual brutality but of extreme anger and detestation.

Thus the sentiment is somewhat distanced by the language in which it is couched. Nevertheless, Sen. surely expected his audience to see that this praise of tyrannicide might have a contemporary significance. Perhaps he also hoped that Roman emperors would take warning from it; compare the advice to rulers at 745–47, and v. comm. on 735–47 ad fin.

According to Tacitus' account of Sen.'s death, the philosopher, carried into a warm bath to hasten the end, sprinkled some of the water as a libation to Jove the Liberator (*Ann.* 15.64), and Thrasea Paetus, when forced to commit suicide, called his blood a similar libation (16.35).

920 cruorem. So A: E *cruore*. *Libare* in the sense required here is normally used transitively, the object being the liquid offered; the only certainly pre-Senecan example cited by *TLL* 7.2.1339.30ff. for an ablative of the thing offered is Pliny *NH* 14.88 *Romulum lacte non vino libasse*. (There is possibly a Vergilian inversion of the usual construction at *Aen.* 5.77 *mero libans carchesia Baccho*, where see R. D. Williams; at Tib.

1.10.21 the MSS divide exactly as here *seu quis libaverit uvam / uva*.) It may be that A has normalized an unusual construction, but I am more inclined to believe, because Sen. elsewhere employs the usual construction, that the simple error *cruore* for *cruorē* has arisen in E.

capitis invisi. The use of *caput* of a person in Latin, like the parallel Greek use of κάρα and κεφαλή (v. Barrett on Eur. *Hipp.* 651), is strongly emotional and may express either affection (1334 *o fidum caput*) and respect (*Pha.* 677, *Oed.* 291) or detestation: the latter is, not surprisingly, much the more common usage in Sen. Trag. (*Med.* 465, 1005, *Pha.* 1280, *Oed.* 521, 871, *Phoen.* 7, 233, *Ag.* 953, *Thy.* 188 *invisum caput* again, 244).

924 tuos. The transmitted word is *tuus*, accepted by Giardina, but this is awkward: in particular it is inappropriate here for Amphitryon to draw attention to the question of Hercules' paternity. The Renaissance conjecture *tuos* is simple, and the paradosis easily explained as assimilation of the adjective to the nearest noun. Defenders of the paradosis might argue that to refer *labores* to H. alone (*tuos*) conflicts with the point in 906 *fessis* that the whole family is exhausted. But since H.'s labors inevitably affect his family, the shift is not a difficult one: there is a similar shift, from the sufferings of Amphitryon to those of H., at 207–9 (v. ad loc.).

926ff. On this prayer for a new Golden Age, and the impossibility of its realization, see Introduction. Many details are traditional in descriptions of the Golden Age or similar utopias. The absence of war and its weapons (929–31) is compulsory, cf. Arat. *Phaen.* 107ff., V. *Aen.* 8.325ff., Tib. 1.3.47f., Ov. *Met.* 1.98ff., Calp. *Ecl.* 1.46ff., B. Gatz, *Weltalter, goldene Zeit und sinnverwandte Vorstellungen* (Hildesheim 1967) 299 B.1.4.b. Though normally the earth is spontaneously fertile (so e.g. Hes. *Erga* 117f., cf. Gatz 229 B.1.1–2), farming (930) is sometimes permitted in Golden Ages, cf. Arat. *Phaen.* 112f. ἀλλὰ βόες καὶ ἄροτρα καὶ αὐτή, πότνια λαῶν, / μυρία πάντα παρεῖχε Δίκη, Hyg. *Poet. Astr.* 2.25, *Einsied. Ecl.* 2.25ff. Temperate climate (931–34) marks the Golden Age (Ov. *Met.* 1.107f.), as it does Elysium, Olympus, and the Blessed Isles (respectively Hom. *Od.* 4.566, 6.43f., Hor. *Epod.* 16.53ff.), cf. Gatz 229 B.1.3. Absence of poisonous herbs (934f.) is a less common detail, which Sen. probably borrows from V. *Ecl.* 4.24f. *occidet et serpens et fallax herba veneni / occidet* (cf. *Georg.* 2.152–54). On the other hand the absence of tyrants (936f.) is a specifically Senecan detail, and in keeping with the detestation of them throughout the play (cf. 737ff. and 922ff. as well as the Lycus scene).

Commentary: Act IV

926f. Arrogance is evident in the snub to Amphitryon and in the hint that Hercules and Jupiter are equals. The phrase *Iove dignus* is Ovidian, used of H. in *Her.* 9.22 = *AA* 1.188, elsewhere to describe the quality of Jove's girls or of his anger; in conjunction with *concipere*, *Met.* 1.166 *dignas Iove concipit iras*.

927–29. That is, let the universe not collapse. Both Epicureans and Stoics thought that such a cataclysm would eventually occur, cf. Lucr. 1.1102ff., Sen. *QNat.* 3.27–30. Such images of cataclysm are also used by the poets in nonphilosophical contexts, cf. Ov. *Met.* 2.295ff. (speech of Earth in Phaethon episode) *fumat uterque polus: quos si vitiaverit ignis, / atria vestra ruent! . . . / si freta, si terrae pereunt, si regia caeli, / in chaos antiquum confundimur*, Sen. *Thy.* 830ff.

928 aequor. The certain correction of N. Heinsius 222 for the transmitted *aether*. The division "earth, sea, and sky" is a natural and familiar one (v. N-H on Hor. *Carm.* 1.12.15, Bömer on Ov. *Met.* 1.5), not least in contexts where the stability of the universe is in question: in addition to the last two passages cited in the previous comm. cf. V. *Aen.* 1.58f. *ni faciat, maria ac terras caelumque profundum / quippe ferant rapidi secum* (sc. *venti*). *Aether* is very occasionally used in contrast to *caelum* (Luc. 7.198 of regions of the heavens warring with each other), but it could hardly denote a major division of the universe as distinct from the *caelum*; nor would it be very meaningful to pray that the ill-defined *aether* stay in its proper place, whereas that clearly has point with reference to the seas.[122]

928f. astra inoffensos agant / aeterna cursus. Similar phrasing at 1332f. *astra transversos agunt / obliqua cursus* and *Pha.* 676f. *sidera obliquos agant / retorta cursus*.

929 alta pax gentes alat. *Alat* of course has special point, i.e. that peace fosters agriculture. For the wording and the personification of peace cf. particularly Tib. 1.10.45ff. *interea Pax arva colat. Pax candida primum / duxit araturos sub iuga curva boves: / Pax aluit vites* e.q.s. Peace is often personified as a giver of plenty, cf. Bacchyl. fr. 4.61f. τίκτει δέ τε θνατοῖσιν εἰρήνα μεγαλάνορα πλοῦτον, K. F. Smith on the Tibullan passage, Sen. *Med.* 65. There is probably some etymological play on *alta / alat*, cf. comm. on 1093 *virtusque viro*.

---

122. In support of the paradosis Pierrot cites Sen. *QNat.* 2.1.1 *omnis de universo quaestio in caelestia, sublimia, terrena dividitur*, but that is a scientist's division, not a poet's. Nor is it strictly parallel, for by *sublimia* Seneca means "the things between the *caelum* and the earth" (2.1.2); if that had been his meaning here, he would surely have written *aer* (cf. *QNat.* 2.4.1) not *aether*.

Commentary: Act IV

930f. The contrast between the instruments of agriculture and of war is a commonplace in contexts of peace, cf. Tib. ibid. 49f. *Pace bidens vomerque nitent, at tristia duri / militis in tenebris occupat arma situs* with K. F. Smith ad loc., Ov. *Fasti* 4.928f., *Einsied. Ecl.* 2.30f. (For the opposite *locus* of ploughshares beaten into swords cf. V. *Georg.* 1.508 with H. H. Huxley ad loc., *Aen.* 7.635f.).

931ᵇ-34. An increasing tricolon articulated by anaphora of the initial word, as e.g. in the similes at 838ff.

932 irato Iove. This might be taken as no more than a conventional poetic reference to the source of thunderbolts, but in the context of a prayer to Jupiter it surely has hubristic overtones: it hints that Jove's anger is as wayward and disruptive as storms at sea or flooding rivers. For Hercules' patronizing attitude cf. ps.-Sen. *HO* 29f. *iratis deis / non licuit esse.*

934 agros ... eversos trahat. *Agros* here denotes both the crops (for this metonymy cf. Stat. *Theb.* 11.42f. *ceu circumflantibus austris / alternus procumbit ager*) and the soil of the fields. A similarly wide meaning may be seen in *agros* at V. *Aen.* 2.305ff. *rapidus montano flumine torrens / sternit agros, sternit sata laeta boumque labores / praecipitesque trahit silvas.*

936. As at 585 (see comm.), *non* replaces *ne* when a particular part of a wish or command is emphasized: Hercules is not wishing that there should be no rulers, but that they should be nonviolent.

937–39. Powerful dramatic irony. This is inseparably combined here with character-revelation, for there is arrogance in Hercules' assumption, immediately disproved, that he can deal with any threat sent against him. There is also ambition underlying the urgency of *etiamnunc* and *properet*: H. feels that he has completed his labors, and is eager to take the promised reward of immortality. That this is in the forefront of his thoughts immediately becomes clear in the madness (955ff.).

939–52. Euripides with characteristic realism had dwelled on the physical symptoms that marked the onset of Hercules' madness, such as head-tossing and foaming at the mouth (*Her.* 868–70, 932–34; cf. *Or.* 35ff., 253, *IT* 282–84). Seneca could have followed suit, as he had done in Cassandra's trance at *Ag.* 710–19, but he was more interested here in the hallucinations themselves (see Introduction on "Hercules insane"). The content of these first hallucinations may well have been influenced by medical observations, for the Hippocratic περὶ διαίτης

[*363*]

Commentary: Act IV

(4.89) teaches that to see the heavenly bodies in disorder is prognostic of disease: in particular, to see a chase among the stars indicates imminent madness (4.89.7, cf. *HF* 947ff.). It is also noteworthy that medical authorities mention wild beasts among the hallucinations associated with epilepsy (Aretaeus *S.A.* 1.5) and certain forms of madness (Hipp. *Int.* 48).

Several parallels exist, however, between Hercules' madness and Cassandra's frenzy. Both begin with darkness dispelling daylight (cf. *Ag.* 7ff.), followed by a vision of evil and of the underworld. See further comm. on 960–64, 984–86, 1044^b–48^a, and 939.

939 sed quid hoc? A natural expression of surprise or shock (cf. 1042 *quid hoc est? Oed.* 353, v. Tarrant on *Ag.* 868 comparing ἔα · τί λεύσσω), and therefore useful to the dramatist to mark economically the onset of hallucination; cf. *Ag.* 868 *eheu quid hoc est?* at the beginning of Cassandra's clairvoyant vision.

939f. medium diem cinxere tenebrae. For *cingere* used in a similar context (storm clouds darkening the sky) cf. V. *Aen.* 5.13 *heu! quianam tanti cinxerunt aethera nimbi?* (The context at Manil. 3.397 [*dies*] *cingitur umbris* is less similar.)

941f. quis diem retro fugat e.q.s. Seneca probably intends the sun's turning back, albeit hallucinatory, as a reaction to a specific evil, i.e. the impending slaughter. It has that significance most notably in the Thyestes myth (*Thy.* 776–78, etc.) but is used also at *Med.* 31 *non redit in ortus et remetitur diem?* (reaction to Jason's infidelity). Reversal of the sun's course is also found in *adynata* (373f. comm.), however, and here it may be no more than an indication of disorder in the heavens.

942f. unde nox atrum caput ignota profert? Compare the use of this metaphor for heavenly bodies: constellations (e.g. Cic. *Arat.* 456f., Col. 10.156) and the sun (*HF* 594 with comm.). Here it has a sinister ring, particularly in combination with *ignota*, though the image is perhaps not as vivid as Lucr. 1.64f. [*religio*] *quae caput a caeli regionibus ostendebat, / horribili super aspectu mortalibus instans*.

944–52. The constellations are often described as adopting threatening postures, e.g. 12 *ferro minax hinc terret Orion deos*, and a distraught mind might well fear that they will burst into action, as Phaethon fears that he will actually be stung by Scorpio (Ov. *Met.* 2.195ff.).

There is rich poetic symbolism in this threatened rebellion of Leo, in addition to its psychological significance (v. 939–52 comm.). It suggests a disruption of the order for which H. prayed in 928f. *astra inoffensos agant / aeterna cursus*; and a corresponding chaos among the seasons, for the point of the references to autumn, winter, and spring is that Leo is the zodiacal constellation of summer (e.g. Hor. *Epist.* 1.10.16). Fire imagery is conventional for Leo, but Sen. heightens it (947–49 comm.) to strengthen the thematic association of fire with madness (v. 100–106 comm.).

In addition it seems probable that the Lion preparing for a murderous attack symbolizes Hercules himself about to commit murder (Trabert 15, cf. Mette 1966 485f.). A lion is a natural symbol for H. in view of its strength and ferocity; it is also a traditional symbol of anger (n.b. 946 *ira . . . fervet* and v. N-H on Hor. *Carm.* 1.16.15), which is one of the Senecan Hercules' leading characteristics. Furthermore H. wears the skin of this very lion, cf. 45f. *armatus venit / leone*. For identification of H. with a lion cf. Lycophr. 33 τριεσπέρου λέοντος.

944 primus en noster labor. The Nemean Lion is usually the first labor (Pind. *Isthm.* 6.48, Eur. *Her.* 359f., Sen. *Ag.* 829ff.). The identification of the constellation Leo with the Nemean Lion is first certainly attested in Nigidius (who says Juno was responsible for the catasterism, fr. 93 p.114 Swoboda), and becomes regular in Latin poetry, e.g. Germ. *Arat.* 547, Ov. *AA* 1.68 *cum sol Herculei terga Leonis adit.*

947 iam rapiet aliquod sidus. The unusual metrical pattern conveys a sense of urgency and alarm: for similar effects produced by initial dactyl plus trochee cf. 76 with comm., 100 *incipite famulae Ditis.*

947–49. Leo's vast open jaws and threatening mane are found in astronomical writers: for the first cf. e.g. Manil. 5.206 *vastos . . . hiatus* and v. Boll *Sphaera* 129, for the second Germ. *Arat.* 149 *horrentesque iubas et fulvum . . . Leonem*, *RE* 12.1977.64ff. (For mane tossing as characteristic of lions in general when aroused cf. *Oed.* 919f., *Pha.* 348f.) Leo is naturally called "fiery" in view of its zodiacal association with high summer (cf. 946 *fervet* and v. *RE* 12.1981.67ff.), but the detail that it *breathes* fire is unusual (though apparently imitated at Luc. 10.233f. *incensa Leonis / ora*) and clearly added by Sen. to heighten the thematic use of fire imagery. *Ignes efflare* is used at V. *Aen.* 7.786 of the Chimaera, at Ov. *Met.* 2.85 of the Sun's horses, cf. 7.104 of Colchian bulls.

948f. rutilat, iubam / cervice iactans. So A. E[1] first wrote the same, but then changed *rutilat* to *rutilam*: this is clearly wrong (*rutilam iubam* is unstylish), and the alteration is easily explained by unfamiliarity with *rutilare* leading to inability to understand the construction of *iubam*.

There are no grounds for suspecting *rutilat*, rare though the verb is: the intransitive use seen here is attested before Sen. at Accius *trag.* 675 R^2 (of Dawn) and at V. *Aen.* 8.529 (a portent of arms glittering in the sky), and Sen. has it again at *Oed.* 137 *aureo taurus rutilante cornu*. Admittedly the slight sense-pause before the sixth foot is unusual, but this scarcely warrants conjecture. (For the participial phrase cf. *Oed.* 919f., *Tro.* 467f.) The modern vulgate *rutila iubam cervice iactans* is not only unwarranted but weakens the text, because the mane tossing should belong to the threatening behavior of Leo which Hercules sees, not to the future action which he fears.

949f. quidquid autumnus e.q.s. That is, the zodiacal signs, of which there would actually be eight between Leo and Taurus. The form of the expression is chosen to suggest the confusion in the seasons which would result from Leo's attack.

gravis. "Unhealthy," cf. Caes. *BCiv.* 3.2.3 *gravis autumnus . . . exercitum valitudine temptaverat*, Hor. *Sat.* 2.6.19 *autumnusque gravis, Libitinae quaestus acerbae*, *TLL* 2.1603.63ff., N-H on Hor. *Carm.* 2.14.15. There may also be a hint of the sense *gravidus*, "heavy with fruit": for this sense of *gravis* cf. Quint. 8.3.8 *graves fructu vites*, Boeth. *Consol.* 4 poët. 6.28 *pomis gravis autumnus*.

950 frigidā spatio. The poets tend to avoid lengthening in such situations (i.e. when an open syllable containing a short vowel at the end of a word is followed by a word beginning with two consonants) with the exception of Vergil, who likes to lengthen *-que* in imitation of the Homeric treatment of τε. Lengthening is almost unknown (except in Catullus, and of course in Vergil) when the two consonants in question are a mute plus a liquid, and uncommon with other consonants, i.e. primarily *s* plus another (v. Fordyce on Cat. 4.9 and 17.24, Leo I 203 n. 4): Sen. has only one other certain example, *Pha.* 1026 *undiquē scopuli adstrepunt*. On the other hand, Augustan and later poets (except Propertius) are also reluctant to let a final short syllable stand open before a word which begins with *s* plus another consonant, tending to avoid such collocations of words altogether (Fordyce on Cat. 64.357). Seneca, however, permits such collocations relatively frequently in the middle of the third foot, where the scansion cannot be determined, e.g. *Med.* 13 *adeste sceleris*, 471 *expetita spolia*, 1026 *vade spatia*, *Pha.* 217 *verere sceptra*, 617, *Oed.* 670, 791.

951 uno impetu transiliet. An expressive metrical effect: the long word "overleaps" the third-foot caesura. Lines containing no word-

[*366*]

Commentary: Act IV

break in the third foot are unusual: in the 159 lines of Act IV there are only four (here, 973, 975, 985).

953f. The symptoms are much less extreme than in Eur., where Hercules' eyes roll and start from his head, 932–34 (cf. comm. on 939–52). For the phrasing of 953 cf. *Tro.* 1092 *vultus huc et huc acres tulit* (of Astyanax), and for that of both lines cf. *Phoen.* 473f. *quo vultus refers / acieque pavida fratris observas manum?* In these passages, as often, it is difficult to know whether *vultus* means "countenance" or "eyes, gaze" (for this meaning v. 640f. comm.). (*TLL* 1.359.62ff. is misleading on *vultus acer*: e.g. at Sen. *Ira* 3.4.1 *vultus* clearly means "face".)

955–57. On the heavens as the ultimate goal of the hubristic conqueror, see Introduction.

perdomita. This compound is much rarer than simple *domare* in Sen. Trag. (2:25) as in several poets, e.g. Ovid (3:40, v. Bömer on *Met.* 1.447). The intensive force of the prefix is clearly felt in both Senecan usages, here and at 444 *post monstra tot perdomita*.

tumida cesserunt freta. Such language is sometimes used, but clearly in a figurative sense, of Hercules' achievement in clearing the seas of monsters (cf. 30–32 comm.) or pirates, cf. Pind. *Isthm.* 4.57 ναυτίλιαισί τε πορθμὸν ἀμερώσαις, Eur. *Her.* 401f. θνατοῖς / γαλανείας τιθεὶς ἐρετμοῖς. Here, however, the claim is apparently meant literally. H. perhaps has in mind the occasion when Oceanus tested him by tossing his boat about on the voyage to Erythia, and was cowed by the threat of his archery (Pherecydes ap. Athen. 11.471d). At any rate, since the phrase suggests that the seas are permanently subdued, Sen. no doubt intends it as the exaggeration of a megalomaniac. World conquest encourages such hyperbole, cf. Hor. *Carm.* 4.5.19 *pacatum volitant per mare navitae*, with Quinn ad loc.

957 immune caelum est. Clearly double-edged: *immunis* often connotes freedom from something *undesirable*, and Sen. wants the audience to feel that connotation here.

959 astra promittit pater. The promise was made in the past (cf. 23 *astra promissa*), but the tense indicates its relevance and validity in the present ("the stars are my father's promise," Miller); cf. Xen. *An.* 2.1.4 ἀπαγγέλλετε Ἀριαίῳ ὅτι ἡμεῖς νικῶμεν βασιλέα ("that we are the victors"), Plaut. *Amph.* 1014 *sum defessus quaeritando: nusquam invenio Nau-*

Commentary: Act IV

cratem ("Naucrates is nowhere to be found"), Sen. *HF* 479 with comm., H-S 30f.

960–64. Hercules' sudden realization that there could be opposition (*quid si negaret?*) quickly hardens into a certainty (963 *una vetante*, 965 *dubitatur etiam*); for a similar pathological tendency on Juno's part to convert fears into certainties cf. 63–74 with comm.

The succession of short questions in these lines "gives a stylised impression of the *sermo praeruptus* which S. elsewhere (*Ira* 1.1.4, 3.4.2) calls characteristic of emotional states" (Tarrant on *Ag.* 724): similar passages include *Ag.* 722ff., *Med.* 934–39, 958–66, and much of *HF* 1138–85.

960 non capit terra Herculem. Compare Sen. Rhet. *Suas.* 1.5 *orbis illum suus non capit* (of Alexander), and in a context of ascent to heaven Varro *Men.* 298 *quem idcirco terra non cepit et caelum recepit.*

962 fores, 964 ianuam mundi. The image of the gates of heaven appears as early as Hom. *Il.* 5.749 αὐτόμαται δὲ πύλαι μύκον οὐρανοῦ, ἃς ἔχον Ὧραι (= 8.393), cf. Acc. *trag.* 531 R² *alto ab limine caeli*, V. *Georg.* 3.261 *porta tonat caeli*: it is particularly appropriate in contexts of human ascent to heaven, cf. *Anth. Pal.* 9.518.2 and Enn. *var.* 23f. *si fas endo plagas caelestum ascendere cuiquam est, / mi soli caeli maxima porta patet.* Seneca quotes the Ennian and Vergilian phrases, and refers to the Homeric antecedent, at *Ep.* 108.34 (to show his philosophical scorn of philologists who collect such parallels).

963 una vetante. For the allusive reference to Juno cf. V. *Aen.* 1.251 *navibus (infandum!) amissis unius ob iram.* A few lines earlier (960 *quid si negaret*) and a few lines later (966) H. sees his opponent as Jupiter, but the confusion and shifting of identity is characteristic of his madness (thus at 1018 he sees Megara as Juno, but at 1035ff. as Lycus' wife *sacrificed to* Juno). As a consequence it is quite uncertain whether the questions in 963 and 965 are addressed to Jupiter or Juno. Those who wish to bring order out of madness may write *uno vetante*, but I think the uncertainty is part of Seneca's portrayal of mental disturbance.

963ff. Hercules' truculent attitude recalls the megalomaniac Caligula's threats to Jupiter (Suet. *Cal.* 22.4).

reseras polum. The same phrase in the same position, but in a figurative sense, *Tro.* 354 (of Calchas) *arte qui reseras polum*: cf. also *Ag.* 756 *reserate . . . terga nigrantis poli* (i.e. the underworld).

964 traho. Not just "pull open" but "tear down, drag away." For the indicative instead of the more usual subjunctive in a deliberative question cf. Plaut. *Men.* 176 *iam fores ferio?*, Pers. 666 *Toxile, quid ago?*, Sen. *Phoen.* 450 *an dico et ex quo?*, H-S 308.

965 dubitatur etiam? "Are you still hesitating?" That seems the more likely meaning than "Am I still hesitating?" ("Do I yet doubt?" Heywood). The same phrase is transmitted at *Tro.* 246, where, however, the text has been suspected.

965–81. In its insanity Hercules' mind first plans a rebellion against Jupiter, and then swings around to fearing one. Such confused leaps of thought are found throughout Sen.'s portrayal of the madness: on that, and on the son's aggression against the father evident in H.'s planned rebellion, v. Introduction. There is also a thematic significance in these lines. As the original battle of the Giants against the Olympians was widely interpreted in art and literature as a struggle between barbarism and civilization, chaos and order (N-H on Hor. *Carm.* 2.12.7), so the rebellion envisaged by H. symbolizes a new assault by the forces of unreason (n.b. 968 *furentes*) and chaos against the orderly governance of the universe, in fact against that very cosmic order for which H. prayed so recently (927ff.). It is also poignantly relevant that H. himself helped to put down such a rebellion (84f. comm.). "To make, then break, this thought has come before, / the desperate exercise of failing power. / Samson in Gaza did no more." (Eliot, *Murder in the Cathedral*). The idea of employing the very forces which he opposed has a deep appropriateness to the Hercules myth, being embodied in his use of lion-skin and Hydra's poison.

Seneca may well have had in mind Hor. *Carm.* 3.4.42ff., a *locus classicus* on the Giants' rebellion, as that passage mentions the Titans, the feat of piling up mountains, several of the Giants, and Tityus (cf. 977f. comm.): it is noteworthy that Tityus and Typhoeus (also named in Hor. *Carm.* 3.4) appear in the parallel passage at *Thy.* 804–12. For the image of a new rebellion by the Giants cf., in addition to that passage, ps.-V. *Aetna* 203 *neve sepulta novi surgant in bella Gigantes.*

965–67. The motif of freeing prisoners from the underworld to help in the overthrow of the current regime is seen in Jupiter's own overthrow of Saturn, e.g. Hes. *Theog.* 501ff. (the Cyclopes), 624ff. (the Hundred-Handers), Apollod. 1.2.1. (That the defeated Saturn was imprisoned in the underworld is a long-established tradition, e.g. Hom. *Il.* 14.203f., Aesch. *PV* 219f., Ov. *Met.* 1.113.) Saturn is naturally associated with the Titans (967ff.) as their one-time leader and ruler.

966 impii. Sometimes taken as "unfilial" (i.e. in overthrowing Saturn: so Farnaby, Miller), but "unpaternal" makes much better sense. For *impius* of unnatural parents cf. Livy 1.53.8, Ov. *Met.* 7.396 (of Medea), Sen. *Med.* 779 (of Althaea) *piae sororis, impiae matris*.

968f. The idea of using rocks as missiles against the gods perhaps comes from descriptions of the Gigantomachy, cf. Apollod. 1.6.1 ἠκόντιζον δὲ εἰς οὐρανὸν πέτρας καὶ δρῦς ἡμμένας.

969 plena Centauris iuga. Centaurs are mountain dwellers already in Homer, cf. *Il.* 1.268 φηρσὶν ὀρεσκῴοισι. The primary point of *plena Centauris* is like that of *cum silvis*, i.e. to indicate the massive size of the crags that Hercules will use as missiles. It is also relevant, in view of what follows, that the Centaurs did not inhabit all mountains but specifically those of Thessaly. Is Hercules already thinking in 969 of *piling up* mountains, or does a random reference to Centaur-crowded peaks trigger that thought in his mind?

970–73. The idea of piling up mountains to scale heaven is clearly inspired by the feat of the Aloidae (often attributed to the Giants in Latin literature, v. *RE* Suppl. 3.735.15ff.). On the varying order in which the mountains are piled in narratives of that exploit v. Tarrant on *Ag.* 345 ff., Fantham on *Tro.* 828, adding Prop. 2.1.19f. (which follows the Homeric version); several accounts are elliptical, e.g. Hor. *Carm.* 3.4.52f., Sen. *Tro.* 830.

971. No doubt Chiron will see this sight from the heavens, to which he has been translated as a constellation (cf. *Thy.* 861); the line would have little point if taken otherwise.

972 tertio ... gradu. Compare *Tro.* 830 *tertius caelo gradus* of Pelion (also *gradus* in the same context *Ag.* 344).

974f. sani parum, magni tamen. The emphasis appears to fall on the wrong word: similarly at *Ag.* 403a *si propitios attamen lentos deos* we would say "if slow, yet favoring," at *HF* 622 *certa at sera Thebarum salus* "late but certain," at *Thy.* 206f. *facta domini cogitur populus sui / tam ferre quam laudare* "to praise as well as to endure." Schmidt 1865 12ff. regards such inversions as a peculiarity of Senecan style, and gives several instances from the prose works, e.g. *Ep.* 55.3 *nam quotiens aliquos amicitiae Asinii Galli, quotiens Seiani odium, deinde amor merserat (aeque enim offendisse illum quam amasse periculosum fuit)*, *Ben.* 1.13.3 (of Alexander) *tam hostium pernicies quam amicorum*.

Commentary: Act IV

975 compesce dementem impetum. Both *compescere* and *impetus* belong to the somewhat formulaic language which Sen. gives to those urging restraint of passion: for the first cf. *Med.* 174, *Pha.* 165 *compesce amoris impii flammas*; for the second, *Phoen.* 347 *mitte violentum impetum*, *Med.* 381, *Pha.* 255 *moderare . . . mentis effrenae impetus*, *Ag.* 126f., 203. The use of *impetus* in such contexts may be influenced by its occasional appearance in Stoic psychology as a technical term, equivalent to ὁρμή, e.g. Sen. *Ep.* 37.5 *non consilio adductus illo, sed impetu impactus est* (cf. J. M. Rist, *Stoic Philosophy* [Cambridge 1969] 225 and index s.v. "impulse").

977f. Tityus is known for his attempted rape of Latona, and his consequent punishment in the underworld, rather than for any part in the Giants' original rebellion. The reason for his inclusion here is very probably his appearance in Hor. *Carm.* 3.4.77, where he is associated with the rebellious Giants (a) as an example of *vis consili expers*, (b) in being imprisoned in the underworld, (c) as a son of Earth (cf. 965–81 comm. ad fin.). His wound is caused by the punishing vulture, cf. 756 with comm.

978 quam prope a caelo stetit. No doubt because of his gigantic size (cf. Hom. *Od.* 11.577 ὁ δ' ἐπ' ἐννέα κεῖτο πέλεθρα , V. *Aen.* 6.596f. *per tota novem cui iugera corpus / porrigitur*): however, *stetit* may also imply that he has taken his stand on some mountaintop. For the phrasing cf. *Tro.* 1177 *quam prope a Priamo steti*, also occupying the second half of the line.

979–81. Pallene is the site of the Giants' original rebellion (v. 979 comm.), and Tempe has relevant associations as it lies between Olympus and Ossa. Pindus, Cithaeron, and Oeta are added to make the struggle more impressive (such expansiveness is characteristic of Sen., cf. e.g. 1163ff.); the last two also bring it closer to Thebes.

979–80 labat Cithaeron, alta Pallene tremit, marcentque Tempe.
Probably these details denote a sympathetic reaction to the titanic battle, rather than physical damage caused directly by it, cf. e.g. Luc. 7.173f. (before Pharsalus) *multis concurrere visus Olympo / Pindus, et abruptis mergi convallibus Haemus*. The reaction may be influenced also by the presence on earth of evil creatures from the underworld: for a comparable instance of the pathetic fallacy cf. the reactions to Tantalus' ghost at *Thy.* 103–21, e.g. *domus . . . horruit* 104, *fontes liquor / introrsus actus linquat* 107f., *pallescit omnis arbor* 110.

At first sight *marcent* (A) is a surprising verb to apply to a gorge, but

Commentary: Act IV

for the ancients the beauty of Tempe lay in its fresh vegetation, cf. Cat. 64.285f. *viridantia Tempe, / Tempe quae silvae cingunt super impendentes*, Ov. *Met.* 1.568f., Luc. 8.1 *nemorosaque Tempe*, Pliny *NH* 4.31 *valle luco viridante*. Thus the verb would naturally be understood of the shriveling of trees and plants. With the A reading each proper noun has its own verb, and the double chiasmus permits the verbs to fall at the beginning or end of the line with enumerative effect, as e.g. at *Thy.* 755f. *erepta vivis exta pectoribus tremunt / spirantque venae corque adhuc pavidum salit* (cf. 750–59 comm. ad fin.). With the E reading *Macetumque Tempe* all this is lost. Furthermore, the poets rightly call Tempe "Thessalian," not "Macedonian," e.g. Hor. *Carm.* 1.7.4, Ov. *Met.* 7.222, Sen. *Tro.* 815, *Med.* 457; cf. also Mela 2.35 *per Thessalos Peneus excurrit*, Paus. 6.5.5. E's *Macetum* has all the air of a conjecture by someone who could not understand *marcent* or was faced with an already corrupt text.

979 alta Pallene. Pallene, the most westerly of the three promontories of Chalcidice, is sometimes substituted for Phlegra as the site where the Giants fought against the gods, cf. Diod. Sic. 4.15.1, Strabo 7 fr. 25, Luc. 7.150, *RE* Suppl. 3.661.57ff. In fact Pallene is relatively flat, but it is a not unnatural poetic assumption that Greek promontories are mountainous.[123]

981 Mimas. The generally accepted conjecture of Avantius[124] for codd. *minans*. The objection to the paradosis is that *saevit horrendum minans* gives too much personal detail to the anonymous *hic*, as well as destroying the formal balance established in the preceding clauses. Bentley retained *minans* and referred it to *Erinys*, putting a strong stop after *Oeten* and *Erinys*, but this scarcely improves matters: the two brief clauses *rapuit hic Pindi iuga, / hic rapuit Oeten* cry out for conclusion, and the change to the new topic of the Furies is better signaled by *flammifera Erinys* than by *saevit*. In favor of Mimas is the fact that he is named among the rebellious Giants in Hor. *Carm.* 3.4—a passage which Sen-

---

123. In place of the normal *Pallene* (A), E writes *Pellene*; properly this is the name of a town in Achaea, but the substitution is not uncommon in MSS, especially Greek (*RE* 19.355.15ff.). Leo's acceptance of *Pellene* (followed by most modern editors) results from his reverence for E, combined with a late-nineteenth-century enthusiasm for unusual forms. In general it seems unwise to print such anomalous forms without better evidence for their authenticity.

124. Corruption to *minans* suggests that the form in MSS before corruption may have been *Mimans*: cf. *Pha.* 68 *Garamans* E, *HO* 1604 *Poeans* ΣA, 1908 *Atlans* E, and analogous forms sometimes found in MSS of other writers, e.g. Statius. Whether Sen. himself intended such forms one cannot know (see fn. 123), despite the enthusiasm of modern editors for *Mimans* here.

[372]

Commentary: Act IV

eca has in mind hereabouts (965–81 comm. ad fin.)—and nowhere else in Latin poetry before Sen. For alternation of the indefinite *hic* with a specific noun cf. 154 *hic* comm.

982–84. The Furies are traditionally fiery and carry scourges, cf. 87f. with comm. (on fire imagery in *HF* v. 100–106 comm.). In particular the torches of the Furies are often prominent in the hallucinations of madness, or are used to cause it, cf. 100ff. This association occurs primarily in Roman literature. Ennius' *Alcmeo* contains such a hallucination, cf. 27f. R² = 24–27 J *fer mi auxilium, pestem abige a me, / flammiferam hanc vim quae me excruciat. / caeruleae incinctae igni incedunt, / circumstant cum ardentibus taedis,* and the Furies probably appeared onstage with torches in his *Eumenides* (Jocelyn p. 284). The maddening torches may well have figured in Augustan and later tragedy, as they do in other genres, V. *Aen.* 7.456f., Ov. *Met.* 4.481f., 508f.; another Senecan instance at *Med.* 962. Cf. the guilty Nero, Suet. *Nero* 34.4 *confessus exagitari se materna specie verberibusque Furiarum ac taedis ardentibus.* The brands thrust *in ora* here probably come from Ov. *Met.* 10.349ff. *sorores / quas facibus saevis oculos atque ora petentes / noxia corda vident,* cf. also Sen. *Med.* 965 *fige luminibus faces.*

It might be thought that the appearance of the Furies here confirms that they are fulfilling the orders Juno gave them in the prologue, with the detail that they carry brands from a burning pyre creating a specific reminiscence of line 103 (so Pratt 1963 206). But that detail is not unique to *HF* (see comm. 103), and visions of the Furies may be subjective as well as objective, e.g. Sen. *Med.* 958ff.

flammifera Erinys. Unidentifiable, as often where *Erinys* is used in Sen. Trag.—unless one sees a deliberate reminiscence of Act I here (see preceding comm.), in which case Megaera would be meant. *Flammifera* need not be suggested by the Ennian passage cited above, despite the similarity of context: Seneca's liking for the adjective probably derives from Ovid (593 *curru . . . flammifero* comm.).

984–86 saeva Tisiphone e.q.s. Again like Sen.'s Cassandra, Hercules sees into the underworld (cf. 939–52 comm., and *Ag.* 741ff., 759ff.). Cassandra's vision is that of clairvoyance, whereas H.'s is presumably a hallucination: compare Deianira's hallucination caused by guilt at ps.-Sen. *HO* 1008ff. The present passage would gain in point if the *porta* were actually the stage door (i.e. that broken down at 999f.), as in the following line the *proles* is an actual child. Tisiphone's task has been connected to the Giants' rebellion at 976ff., either as an attempt to stop their escape (Pierrot) or to prevent others escaping after them (Ageno);

[373]

Commentary: Act IV

but her appearance follows on from that of the Erinys, and seems to have no connection with the Giants.

Tisiphone's role as a replacement for Cerberus is *ad hoc*: Vergil speaks of her, and Ovid of all the Furies, as normally guarding Tartarus proper (*Aen.* 6.555f., *Met.* 4.456), though at *Aen.* 6.280 their *thalami* are by the gates of the underworld. (For a list of guardians of the gates other than Cerberus cf. *RE* 11.278f. Sometimes, as at 782f. above [v. comm.], Cerberus guards the entrance to the palace of Dis rather than the general entrance to the underworld.)

caput serpentibus vallata. For *vallare* used metaphorically of snakes cf. Lucr. 5.27 *Hydra venenatis ... vallata colubris*, and of something surrounding the head cf. Ov. *Her.* 4.159 *quod sit avus radiis frontem vallatus acutis* (of the Sun's crown of rays). In the latter passage the image is of a palisade of stakes, and a similar image is perhaps intended by Lucretius and Seneca. (On the other hand there is no such image at e.g. Prop. 3.16.29 or ps.-V. *Ciris* 79.)

987–1026. Comparison with Euripides shows the following similarities and differences in the deaths of the three sons and Megara:

		Eur.	Sen.
Son	(1)	Shot πρὸς ἧπαρ with arrow	Shot through neck with arrow
	(2)	Supplicates, killed with club	Supplicates, dashed against walls
	(3)	Shot with one arrow	Dies of fear
Meg.			Killed with club

The change in (1) is influenced by epic descriptions in Homer and Ovid (v. comm. 994f.); that in (2) is due to reminiscence of the Athamas scene in Ov. *Met.* 4 (see comm. on 1002–7); death by the club is then transferred to Megara; the change in (3) may well be Senecan invention, inspired by his love of the impressive and paradoxical (*perit ante vulnus* 1023).

Seneca's dependence on Eur., whether direct or indirect, is evident when one compares other accounts. Pherecydes has five sons dying by fire at Hercules' hand (*FGrH* 3 F14); Pindar says that eight sons died "bronze-equipped," i.e. in heroic battle and presumably not at Hercules' hand at all (*Isthm.* 4.63). Even in versions closer to Eur., Megara survives (*Megara* [Moschus 4], Nicolaus of Damascus *FGrH* 90 F13) or is not mentioned (Diod. Sic. 4.11.1, Philostr. *Imag.* 2.23.1–2);[125] when

---

125. Hyg. *Fab.* 32 says she was killed, but with only two children.

Commentary: Act IV

these accounts say how the children died, they mention only bow and arrows, not the club (*Megara*, Diod. Sic., Philostr.).

988 semen.   Rarely used simply of specific "offspring," though cf. V. *Georg.* 2.151f. *at rabidae tigres absunt et saeva leonum / semina*, Sen. *Tro.* 536 *generosa in ortus semina exsurgunt suos*. (In Ovid the word is used in this sense only of children in the womb, e.g. *Met.* 2.629, 10.470.)

989 leves.   Frequently used of arrows, cf. V. *Aen.* 5.68, 9.178 *iaculo celerem levibusque sagittis*, Germ. *Arat.* 690 *leve Telum* (translating Arat. 691 πτερόεντος Ὀϊστοῦ), Sen. *Ag.* 328f., *HF* 1127, *Apocol.* 12 poët. 8f. *levibusque sequi / Persida telis*.

990 sic.   That is, "against tyrants and the associates of tyrants" (Pierrot). Delrius explained "with such accuracy," but that would mean the shot has already been made, contrary to the indication of the present tenses in 993f. The chief point of the remark is no doubt its unconscious irony. Its brutal ring, when used of shooting down children, is not uncharacteristic even of the 'sane' Hercules.

mitti.   Contrast *emissa* 993. Simple *mittere* is regularly used in prose as well as verse of missiles (in Sen. Trag. six times, against two of *emittere*).

991 Herculea.   Speaker changes in these circumstances, i.e. before the caesura and without a strong sense-pause at the end of the previous line, are rare in Sen. Trag. (even sense-pauses in this position are unusual, v. 51f. comm.): other examples are *Tro.* 680, 926, 978, *Oed.* 337, *Thy.* 321, 638, 745, 1102. In the present instance the effect is to throw emphasis on *Herculea*, and expressive effects may be seen in some of the other instances, e.g. *Tro.* 679f. *iussa ocius / peragite!* (a brusque command by Ulysses), 925f. *vix lacrimas queo / retinere* (a pathetic sob by Helen), though not in all.

impegit.   A favorite word of Sen.'s in his prose writings, often used as here of the violent effects of passion. A close parallel is *Ira* 2.9.1 *quocumque visum est libido se impingit*; cf. also 1.3.5 *irasci dicit incitari, impingi*, 1.19.4 *quid [opus est] se in columnas impingere*, 3.24.4. In all, Sen. uses the verb twenty-seven times in prose (though only here in the tragedies): contrast three uses in Livy and four in Cicero. There is nothing to be said for the A variant *invergit*, which is less vigorous in sense and does not appear elsewhere in Senecan drama or prose.

[*375*]

992 cornibus. The context shows that the word refers to the tips of the bow, as at Ov. *Met.* 2.603f. *arma adsueta capit flexumque a cornibus arcum / tendit.* More usually *cornu(a)* of a bow means the whole weapon, e.g. V. *Ecl.* 10.59f. *libet Partho torquere Cydonia cornu / spicula.*

993 pharetramque solvit. Commentators compare Ov. *Met.* 5.379ff. *ille pharetram / solvit*, to which one may add *Am.* 1.1.21 *pharetra . . . soluta*, but the phrase is hardly recherché.

stridet. A familiar detail from epic, e.g. Hom. *Il.* 16.361 ὀϊστῶν . . . ῥοῖζον, V. *Aen.* 7.531 *stridente sagitta*, 9.632 *effugit horrendum stridens adducta sagitta.*

994f. medio spiculum collo fugit vulnere relicto. In Eur. the arrow strikes πρὸς ἧπαρ (979); Seneca's version is influenced by descriptions in epic, cf. Hom. *Od.* 22.16 (Odysseus shooting Antinous) ἀντικρὺ δ' ἁπαλοῖο δι' αὐχένος ἤλυθ' ἀκωκή, Ov. *Met.* 6.235f. (death of one of Niobe's sons) *summaque tremens cervice sagitta / haesit, et exstabat nudum de gutture ferrum.*[126] But Sen. is less gruesome than these writers, omitting the consequent outpouring of blood. He emphasizes the fatal accuracy of the shot (*medio . . . collo*) and its force (for *fugit* with this connotation cf. V. *Aen.* 10.339f. *traiecto missa lacerto / protinus hasta fugit*), and adds a characteristic touch of point in *vulnere relicto.*

995f. ceteram prolem eruam omnesque latebras. *Eruam* with the first object must mean roughly "drag out" (cf. Curt. 4.14.4 *imbelles ex latebris suis erutos*), with the second "tear open" (*Tro.* 663 *funditus busta eruam*). There is a similar zeugma at Claud. 24.304ff. *paludes / eruis et si quis defensus harundine . . . / . . . aper . . . dentes curvaverat*, though there *eruis* with *paludes* means roughly *perscrutaris*. (Use of *eruere* in that sense appears to be late, and not a possibility in the present passage.) For zeugma, particularly in the poets, v. H-S 831ff.

996–98 quid moror? e.q.s. The idea of attacking Mycenae derives from the Euripidean mad-scene, but Seneca makes very different use of it. In Eur., H.'s aggression is directed against Eurystheus from the very onset of his madness (936ff.): he collects siege equipment, 'marches' and 'arrives' at Mycenae (963), and thinks he is breaking through the Cyclopean walls (998ff.). In the Senecan version his fury is

---

126. Philostratus has Seneca's version rather than Euripides', *Imag.* 2.23.2 βέβληται δ' ὁ μὲν κατὰ τοῦ λαιμοῦ, καὶ δι' ἁπαλῆς γε τῆς φάρυγγος ἐκδεδράμηκεν ὁ οἰστός; perhaps, however, he took it from Homer, in view of ἁπαλῆς.

Commentary: Act IV

directed at Lycus' family, and the attack on Eurystheus is only briefly mentioned as a task for the future (cf. 1038 *Argos victimas alias dabit*); he does not mistake the palace for Mycenae, as several critics have supposed.

997f. Cyclopia . . . saxa. The adjective may be derived from the Euripidean mad-scene, cf. 944 τὰ Κυκλώπων βάθρα, 998 ἐπ' αὐτοῖς . . . Κυκλωπίοισιν, but such references to Mycenae's "Cyclopean" origin also occur several times elsewhere in Eur.'s plays. (*C. saxa* occurs at V. *Aen.* 1.201, but of Sicily not Mycenae.) At any rate, in Sen. the adjective acquires further connotations: walls built by Cyclopes can only be overthrown by similarly monstrous strength, particularly if it is to be done by hand (in contrast, Eur.'s Hercules relies on levers and crowbars for the task, 944, 946, 999).

999f. The Euripidean scene is not far in the background here, cf. 999 σκάπτει μοχλεύει θύρετρα, κἀκβαλὼν σταθμὰ κ.τ.λ. For the collapse of the roof cf. 905 συμπίπτει στέγη, 1007 πεσήματι στέγης. In Eur. it results from the earthquake promised by Lyssa at 864 (see Bond on 904f.); in Sen. there is no earthquake and Hercules is responsible for all the damage to the palace.

valva. The transmitted reading *aula*, "palace," entails several difficulties: *huc eat et illuc* is unclear (does it mean that the palace is to rock on its foundations, or that parts of the palace are to fall in various directions?); *obice* must presumably mean the door, but it is surprising in that sense without qualification; and *rumpatque postes* is an anticlimax. Baden's conjecture *valva*, generally accepted by modern editors, solves the last two difficulties: the *obex* is now properly the bar of the door, and mention of the door-posts is entirely apposite. The closeness of the Euripidean passage also favours *valva*, which corresponds to θύρετρα as *postes* does to σταθμά (for *obice* cf. 997 κλείει πύλας). "Let the door break its jambs" means that this will be the effect of its violent movement (*huc eat et illuc*), cf. V. *Aen.* 7.621f. *impulit ipsa manu portas et cardine verso / belli ferratos rumpit Saturnia postes.*[127] Singular *valva* is admittedly rare (for *valvae* of tragic stage doors cf. Acc. *trag.* 29, 470 R², Pacuv. *trag.* 214 R²)—the only instances cited are Petron. 96, Pompon. *fab. Atell.* 91 R², and Prop. 2.31.13f. where *valva* is understood—but one may compare the occasional use of πύλη in place of the more usual πύλαι for the stage doors of Greek tragedy (Soph. *Ajax* 11, *Ant.* 1186,

---

127. There seems no need of conjectures designed to avoid this expression, e.g. *ruptoque poste* (Schmidt 1865 20f.) or *ruantque postes* (Ageno 94f.).

Commentary: Act IV

El. 818, Eur. *Phaethon* 245 Diggle), and the more frequent use of *foris* for *fores* in Plautus (e.g. *Merc.* 699 *aperitur foris*). *Huc eat et illuc* may refer to the different directions in which the two leaves are to be pushed (cf. 287), or indicate that H. will swing the doors to and fro on their *cardines*.

An alternative is Withof's conjecture *clava* (83). This goes well with *huc eat et illuc* (Withof substituted *rotet* for *eat* from 801, which seems unnecessary) and *rumpatque postes*: paleographically it is as plausible as *valva* (haplography of *c* in *illuc clava*). There remains the objection to *obice* in the sense of "door," which would presumably be required.

deiecto. Assuming *valva* to be right, E's *deiecto* has a precise meaning: under H.'s violent battering on the door, the bar jumps from its place and falls to the ground, cf. Petron. 16 *sera sponte sua delapsa cecidit*, Ov. *Met.* 14.783 *Venus portae cecidisse repagula sensit*. The A reading *disiecto* yields satisfactory sense (cf. e.g. Livy 6.33.12 *inde effracta claustra portarum*), but the precision of E's reading speaks strongly for it.

1000 columen. So A, as against E *culmen*. Elsewhere in the tragedies Sen. uses *culmen* only when required by meter (four times), and *columen* when meter allows a choice: that supports *columen* here. So does the fact that *columen* is much the rarer form in literature from Ovid on, and would therefore tend to be altered to the more familiar form.

1001 perlucet. That is, light pours in through the shattered doorway and roof, cf. Plaut. *Rud.* 101f. *villam integundam intellego totam mihi, / nam nunc perlucet ea quam cribrum crebrius*, Juv. 11.13 *iam perlucente ruina*. A's *procumbat* is obviously inferior; perhaps the interpolator wrongly took 1143 *prostrata domo* to mean that the building is completely leveled (v. ad loc.).

1002–7. Though Eur. is the ultimate source, this sequence also has similarities to the madness of Athamas in Ov. *Met.* 4. In Eur. the second child makes a gesture of supplication and pleads with his father but is killed with the club (986ff.). The first two details are in Sen., but his description of the child's death is more immediately influenced by the way in which Ovid's Athamas kills one son, who is stretching out his arms (though in affection not supplication): *bracchia tendentem rapit et bis terque per auras / more rotat fundae, rigidoque infantia saxo / discutit ora ferox* (517ff.). There too the mother immediately flees (*fugit*) carrying another young son (*parvum*). (The story of Athamas in *Met.* 4.416–530 had considerable influence on *HF*.) There is also some similarity to Lichas' death at Hercules' hands at *Met.* 9.211ff.: Lichas makes the supplicating gesture and pleads, but *corripit Alcides, et terque quaterque rotatum / mittit in Euboicas . . . undas* (217f., cf. Sen.'s *rotatum misit*). Finally, one might suppose, in view of *cerebro tecta disperso madent* (*HF* 1007), that Sen. had been reminded of Lichas' death as Sophocles described it, *Trach.* 781 κόμης δὲ λευκὸν μυελὸν ἐκραίνει: but the gruesome detail is in fact not uncommon (Hom. *Il.* 3.300, *Od.* 9.458, Eur. fr. 388 N, *Cycl.* 402, Ter. *Ad.* 316f. *capite pronum in terra statuerem, / ut cerebro dispergat viam*, V. *Aen.* 5.413, 10.416).

1005 dextra precantem. A has *dextram precantem*, E *dextra precante* (the weaker of the two, as the omission of the object is uncharacteristic of Sen.). But it is one thing to say *manum precantem protendere* (V. *Aen.* 12.930f.) and another to use such a phrase when the hand is not that of the subject: the natural expression in that case would be *dextram precantis* (cf. e.g. Ov. *Met.* 3.721f. *dextramque precantis / abstulit*, *Her.* 4.175), but the readings of the MSS make it unlikely that that is what Sen. wrote. The correct version is undoubtedly *dextra precantem*, found in many recc.: admittedly there is some ambiguity about whose hand is meant (surely Hercules'), but careless writing seems more probable than the oddity of the A or E readings.

1006 bis ter. Not of course "six times" but an equivalent to the *bis terque* of the Ovidian source (1002–7 comm.), i.e. "several times": for such phrases v. Brink on Hor. *Ars P.* 358. Seneca uses the form *bis ter* again at *Thy.* 769, *bis terque* at *Thy.* 702 and *QNat.* 3.28.3.

ast. An archaic form that survives in poetry, but only before a word which begins with a vowel, that word usually being a pronoun or *ubi* (v. Leo I 214ff., Austin on V. *Aen.* 2.467). In Sen. Trag. it appears only once elsewhere, in the same position and again before *illi*, at *Thy.* 721f.

1007 sonuit. Usually the verb would be explained, e.g. by *muris illisum* (cf. 1100f. *nunc Herculeis percussa sonent / pectora palmis*): the stark use of the verb, further isolated by the abrupt metrical effect, emphasizes the brutal horror of the event.

1009 Megara. The Greek name is scanned with long final *a*, as at 203: Sen., like other Latin writers of iambics, avoids a tribrach constituted by a single word in the first foot (Strzelecki 69).

furenti similis. This may be derived from the Ovidian source, where Ino in flight is described as *male sana* and behaves like a Bacchante (*Met.* 4.521ff.): on the other hand such similes are highly conventional, cf. Hom. *Il.* 22.460 μαινάδι ἴση, Pacuv. *trag.* 422 R² *tamquam lymphata*, Sen. *Phoen.* 427 *furenti similis*.

1010. That is, Hercules now sees Megara as Juno. But though the audience may guess as much, their suspicion is not confirmed until 1018. The fact that H.'s words are not at first fully intelligible is part of Sen.'s portrayal of the madness.

1011 temet. Usually pronouns with -*met* are reflexive or emphatic, but no particular emphasis is evident here or at *Med.* 445, 546.

1012 latebram. So E, but A gives *latebras*. Has E altered an original plural to conform to the singular *fugam*, or has A normalized an original singular? Carlsson (1925 21) in his enthusiasm for A readings preferred *latebras*, citing *HO* 1408 *cur deinde latebras aut fugam vaecors petam?* He might have cited parallels for the agreement of *quam* with the first noun, e.g. Caes. *BGall.* 6.42.2 *ab ipso vallo portisque castrorum*, 7.35.5 *de suo iure et de legibus*, but parallels do not disguise the fact that *latebras* is particularly awkward here (at *HO* 1408 it is less awkward, and meter obliged the author to use the plural); I regard it, therefore, as a further instance of A's intolerance of anomalous forms. The singular is much less common than the plural: elsewhere in Sen. Trag. there are two instances of the singular (both *latebram*) against eight of the plural; in Vergil 1:11; in Ovid 2:12.

1014f. prece lenire tempta. The wording, though unremarkable, recalls Ov. *Pont.* 4.15.24f. *tempta lenire precando / numina*.

1015 parce ... precor. Alliteration on *p* is a common poetic device in prayers, particularly in this phrase, cf. e.g. Tib. 1.8.51, Hor. *Carm.* 4.1.2 *parce, precor, precor!* Ov. *Met.* 2.127 *parce, puer, stimulis* (with Bömer ad loc.), 361f. *parce, precor, mater ... / parce, precor*: in Sen. Trag. cf. *HF* 1249, *Med.* 595, *Oed.* 975, *Thy.* 995.

1016 Megaram. The proper name is used both for self-identification and with emotional implications ("your loving wife," etc.): for the latter aspect v. comm. on 509 *genitor Alcidae*.

1016f. vultus ... habitusque. Somewhat reminiscent, in such a context, of *Tro.* 464–66 (Andromache to Astyanax) *hos vultus meus / habebat Hector, talis incessu fuit / habituque talis*. In Eur. the Chorus notes the similarity of the children's gaze and bearing to their father's, but that is at a much earlier point in the play (130ff.).

Commentary: Act IV

1018f. This confusion of Megara with Juno is not found in Eur. It fits well with Sen.'s portrayal of Hercules as aggressively resentful toward his stepmother, cf. 604–6, 614f., 908, 963. The most violent shifts in H.'s hallucinations occur in regard to Juno: at 963 she is in heaven, preventing his entrance; here she is close enough, and powerless enough, to be caught and killed; at 1036ff. she is 'alive' and presumably distant again.

sequere. The command motivates an exit, in order to avoid having Megara's death occur onstage: see introduction to Act IV.

1019 iugo. Here the word neatly suggests both the yoke of marriage (e.g. Stat. *Silv.* 1.2.138 *thalami . . . iuga ferre secundi*) and that of humiliation, servitude, etc.

1020 parvulum. *Parvulus* has emotional overtones in its other appearances in Sen. Trag. (except at *Oed.* 463, where it is intensive); here presumably it expresses contempt. Sen. uses *parvulus* with unusual frequency both in verse and prose.

occidat. So E: A has *auferam*. It may be that the A interpolator, thinking (wrongly) that *occidat* must mean the child dies *coram populo*, substituted *auferam* to avoid a breach of the Horatian rule.

1021. Editors have followed A in assigning this line to Megara and 1022–31 to Amphitryon, but it should be noted that most E-branch MSS present 1021–31 as a single speech, which must be Amphitryon's.[128] I prefer this arrangement for two reasons. First, during the two previous murders Sen. avoids the tendency for Amphitryon to become an impersonal narrator by permitting him to react with horror *as the murders take place* (991, 1004): 1021 would serve the same function here if spoken by Amphitryon. (1025^b–31 is different, a deliberate response to the fact that the murders have happened rather than an instinctive reaction as they occur.) Second, A not infrequently tampers with speaker attributions (the clearest examples of deliberate alterations in this play are 634^b–36, 915–18, 1237 and 1239, 1263f., and

---

128. As in Σ, represented here by MN. (F^1 omits speaker-attributions from 895 on; F^2, which has inserted them, generally follows A, as here.) E's erroneous attribution to Hercules is easily understood on inspection of the MS. The scribe omitted space at the beginning of 1018 for a speaker-attribution, and the rubricator therefore inserted HER in the first attribution-space to offer itself, i.e. at the beginning of 1021; then, realizing the error, he squeezed HER in before 1018, but failed to correct the attribution before 1021.

Commentary: Act IV

1265f.) and has just tampered with the text at the end of 1020. Similarity of line 1021 to Megara's words at Eur. 975f. ὦ τεκών, τί δρᾷς; τέκνα / κτείνεις; is not a strong argument for attribution to Megara. Those words in Eur. occur at quite a different point in the mad-scene, *before* any of the murders.

1022 igneo vultu. The sane Hercules is sometimes said to have had fiery eyes, either habitually or at any rate in combat (Apollod. 2.4.9, Pind. fr. 52 u Snell line 13), but here the detail specifically indicates his madness; for blazing eyes as indicative of *furor*, whether anger or insanity, cf. e.g. Hom. *Od.* 4.662 ὄσσε δὲ οἱ πυρὶ λαμπετόωντι ἐΐκτην (Antinous in a rage), Plaut. *Capt.* 594 *ardent oculi* (an apparent madman), Cic. *Verr.* 4.148 *cum . . . oculis arderet* (a lunatic), Sen. *Ira* 1.1.4 *flagrant et micant oculi*, 2.35.5 *flammā lumina ardentia* (of *irati*). (These and similar parallels make it almost certain that *vultus* = "gaze" here, though for fire imagery used of the face cf. e.g. V. *Aen.* 12.101f.). On the association of fire imagery with *furor* and destruction in this play v. comm. on 100–106. In Eur., Hercules has a Gorgon-like glare as he kills the children (990).

1023 timor. Zwierlein 1980 194 n. 40 proposes to read *pavor*, which he regards as explaining both A's *puer* (viz. as a misreading influenced by *infans* in 1022) and E's *timor*.[129] But the repetition *pavefactus . . . pavor* would be most unskillful: because the clause beginning *spiritum* merely restates the first clause, there must be variation in vocabulary. Contrast rhetorically pointed repetition as at *Oed.* 792f. (Oed.) *sed pars magis metuenda fatorum manet.* / (Senex) *omnem paterna regna discutient metum.* Zwierlein likes the alliterative effect of *pavor*, but *timor* echoes *t* and *r* from earlier in the line. Admittedly A's *puer* is difficult to explain, but it is certainly influenced by *infans* above.

1025f. In Euripides Megara is shot with an arrow, but Sen. may be drawing on the death of the second son in Eur., 993f. ξύλον καθῆκε

---

129. *Pavor* appears already in recc. as an emendation of A's *puer*. Zwierlein explains E's *timor* with the comment that "derartige Synonymen-Vertauschungen begegnen noch öfter"; but although confusion of *tim-/met-* does often arise through metathesis, confusion with *pav-* is of course much less common: Zwierlein cites only *Thy.* 610 *expavescit* E *extimescit* A, where the words are certainly more similar *overall* than *pavor* and *timor*. A more natural assumption would be that *pavor* had already become *puer* in the archetype, and that E corrected the obvious error, as recc. emended it later in their turn; but one sees why Zwierlein wanted to avoid this hypothesis of a conservative A and a bold E.

παιδὸς εἰς ξανθὸν κάρα, / ἔρρηξε δ' ὀστᾶ (cf. *perfregit ossa*). There is no equivalent in the Greek to *corpori trunco* e.q.s. Similarly, Sen. has Agamemnon beheaded (*Ag.* 901ff.) without a precedent in Aeschylus. The image of a headless body is a particularly powerful one for the Romans, cf. V. *Aen.* 2.557f. *iacet ingens litore truncus, avulsumque umeris caput et sine nomine corpus*, Sen. *Tro.* 141 *Sigea premis litora truncus* (both of Priam), Luc. 2.171–73 (Sullan proscriptions), 8.607ff. (Pompey).

1026 nec usquam est. "It no longer exists" (having been obliterated), cf. Hor. *Sat.* 2.5.101f. *ergo nunc Dama sodalis / nusquam est?* Sen. *Tro.* 390ff. *nec amplius, / iuratos superis qui tetigit lacus, / usquam est*.

1026ff. Seneca's Amphitryon deliberately attempts to provoke Hercules into killing him, whereas H.'s attack on him in Eur. has no other prompting than that of madness (1001). Readiness to die in intolerable circumstances appears often in Sen. Trag., but is particularly characteristic of Amphitryon, cf. 509f., 1311f. Seneca's version also creates dramatic tension, similar to that in Act V over the imminent suicides of H. and Amphitryon.

1027 vivax senectus. The same phrase occurs in the same metrical position, again in self-address (Hecuba), at *Tro.* 42; the common source is Ov. *Met.* 13.518ff. (Hecuba again) *quo me servas, annosa senectus? / quid, di crudeles, nisi quo nova funera cernam, / vivacem differtis anum?*

1027f. habes mortem paratam. A familiar thought in the Stoicism of Sen.'s prose works: for an example with *paratus* cf. *Ep.* 30.16 *a quo enim non prope est* (sc. *mors*), *parata omnibus locis omnibusque momentis?* But utterance of it does not turn a dramatic character into a Stoic exemplar, unless one is willing to apply that label to Phaedra also (*Pha.* 878 *mori volenti desse mors numquam potest*). On this point cf. 1271f. comm.

1028–31. The transmitted text from the middle of 1028 to the beginning of 1030, *pectus in tela indue / vel stipitem istum caede monstrorum illitum / converte*, presents a difficulty: is Amphitryon addressing these words to himself or to Hercules? The immediately preceding phrases (1026^b–28^a) are clearly self-address; the immediately following phrases in 1030f. are equally clearly directed at H. But where does the change occur, and why is it not more clearly marked?

One solution would be to end self-address after *indue*, with *tela* taken in the general sense of "weapons," and *indue* meaning "thrust upon," for which there are good precedents, particularly Ov. *Am.* 2.10.31f.

[*383*]

induat adversis contraria pectora telis / miles (cf. *OLD* s.v. *induo* 5b).[130] I am more inclined to think that the balance offered by the paradosis between *tela* "arrows" and *stipitem* "club" is genuine, and that both clauses are therefore addressed to the same person. But it seems unlikely that they are self-address. First, the phrase *caede monstrorum illitum* would be pointless, and we should have to alter *monstrorum* to *nostrorum* with Schmidt 1865 23f.; admittedly not a major difficulty.[131] More serious is the fact that *pectus in tela indue* would have to mean "press your breast upon his arrows," an odd thought to say the least. Another serious objection lies in the fact that if Amphitryon begins to address H. at *falsum ac nomini turpem tuo*, there is no indication of the change of addressee in the Latin.

Probably, then, Amphitryon begins to address Hercules immediately after the words *mortem paratam* in 1028. It is noteworthy that Sen. nowhere else in verse or prose repeats *in* with *induere*, and Müller 10ff. persuasively suggested that the *in* of 1028^b conceals an original *en*. For *en* used to attract the attention of another to oneself cf. *Pha.* 54 *ades en comiti, diva virago*, and for closely similar situations in which the speaker uses *en* in inviting an attack upon himself/herself cf. *Med.* 966 *lania, perure, pectus en Furiis patet*, *HF* 1172f. *en nudus asto; vel meis armis licit / petas inermem*. This, then, gives the much-needed indication of the point at which Amphitryon begins to address H. Unfortunately Müller's conjecture in full, *pectus en telo indue*, is less persuasive: I do not know what it would mean if addressed to H. as Müller intended, nor did Müller explain. Instead I propose *pectori en tela indue*, "Here, plunge your arrows into my breast." For a parallel usage of *induere* cf. *Phoen.* 180 *nunc manum cerebro indue*, "Now plunge your hand into the brain" (for *induere* = "thrust into" cf. also Plaut. *Cas.* 113 *proin tu te in laqueum induas*, Cic. *Div.* 2.44 *cum autem [venti] se in nubem induerint*, Col. 8.11.4 *partes summae lingulas . . . habent, quae . . . foratis perticis induantur*); similar phrases with other verbs include *Oed.* 1036f. *pectori infigam meo / telum*, *Pha.* 1177 *pectori ferrum inseram*, *Ag.* 723 *flammas pectori infixas meo*. A parallel correction is necessary at 1312, from *ferro pectus . . .*

---

130. It will then be necessary to emend *vel* at the beginning of 1029. The best replacement would be *en*, used to attract Hercules' attention (on this use of *en* see further below); other possibilities would include *huc* or *iam*. The explanation of the corruption will lie in ambiguous compendia and/or an assumption that *indue* and *converte* are addressed to the same person.

131. Some have thought further emendation necessary to indicate the direction in which the *tela* are to be turned, but *convertere* can have the sense *convertere in se*, "attract, turn toward oneself," and although the object in this usage is normally other people's gaze or attention, there is a parallel for weapons at Sil. 9.392f.

induam to *ferrum pectori . . . induam.* No emendation will now be needed in 1029.[132]

Thus the whole of 1028^b–31 is addressed to Hercules. As H. will not return to the stage till 1035, Amphitryon must be calling into the palace, where H. fails to hear him (cf. introduction to Act IV).

1030f. falsum e.q.s. These striking words perhaps suggest a certain bitterness over the paternity question, which would be natural enough in Amphitryon's position as a surrogate father. They certainly reveal an understanding that one symptom that has emerged in Hercules' madness is a brutal megalomania which spurns human limitations and obligations altogether.

1032–34. Most MSS assign these lines to Theseus (surprisingly in the case of the A manuscripts, in view of their reading *genitor* for *senior*). But Theseus was sent away at 914–17 (v. comm. ad loc.), and it seems highly unlikely that Sen. brings him back at this point solely in order to speak these colorless lines, particularly as there is no other indication in the text that he has reappeared. It is true that he must return unheralded at some point before 1173, where the text shows him to be onstage; but such an unobtrusive entrance would come more appropriately at the beginning of Act V (unannounced entrances frequently occur as an Act begins) rather than in the midst of the mad-scene.

The only satisfactory solution is to give the present lines to the Chorus, an attribution found in M and perhaps in an ancestor of the Etruscus.[133] Indeed the timid tone of the lines suits the Chorus better than Theseus. As H. does not reappear onstage until 1035 (v. introduction to Act IV), this attribution is consistent with the Senecan practice of occasionally using the Chorus in dialogue when no alternative interlocutor is available, i.e. when there is only one speaking character onstage.[134]

---

132. One will not alter *monstrorum* to *nostrorum*: Amphitryon is attempting to fall in with H.'s heroic delusions (as in 1030f. and 1039–42), not to dispel them. *Converte* means simply "turn," the direction being easily supplied from the context.

133. Leo I 83f. drew attention to the scene-rubric in the Etruscus before 895, *Hercules. Amphytrion. Megera. Chorus.*, which might suggest that 1032–34 were properly attributed to the Chorus rather than Theseus in some ancestor of the Etruscus. However that may be, it seems unlikely that Σ somehow preserved the correct attribution independently of the Etruscus and handed it on to M; more probably M simply misread the abbreviation *the.* as *cho.*

134. It is sometimes said that choral interventions in dialogue (i.e. other than bridge-passages immediately subsequent to odes, on which see 202–4 comm.) occur *only* when no other interlocutor is present, but that formulation is too rigid. At *Oed.*

1032 te . . . ingeris. The reflexive use of this verb is popular with Sen., occurring seven times in the prose, though only here in the tragedies.

1033 profuge. This verb appears fourteen times in Sen. Trag., a remarkably high frequency in verse. It is completely avoided in most dactylic poetry and also absent from Cat. and used only once in Hor. (in *Epodes*); even Plaut. and Ter. have only five uses between them.

1034. The fear that Hercules will add crime to crime by killing his father possibly derives from Eur. 1075f. (Amphitryon) ἀλλ' εἴ με κανεῖ πατέρ' ὄντα, / πρὸς δὲ κακοῖς κακὰ μήσεται, but the play with "number" and "total" is characteristically Senecan, v. 500 comm.

1036–38. Tragic irony: he has sacrificed them to Juno in a truer sense than he knows. The meaning intended by Hercules is sarcastic (compare the tone of 614f.), for he assumes that Juno will be angered by the death of Lycus' family, as she certainly would be by the death of Eurystheus and his family (1038: the reference to Argos is pointed, as Juno was protectress of that city). *Te digna* suggests that the victims matched Juno in character, and/or that the merciless goddess delights in human victims. *Dicatum* and *vota* are also sarcastic, implying that H. made vows to Juno for safe return before setting out for the underworld.

The brutality of the references to human beings as sacrificial animals might be explained by H.'s insanity, if similar language had not been heard on the lips of the 'sane' Hercules at 634 and 920–24. His habitual tendency to devalue human life has caught up with him.

1037 cecidi. In Sen. Trag. the regular word for "kill" is *perimere*, and *caedere* = "kill" is used primarily of sacrificial animals (877, 899), or of people killed as *victimae* (here, *Tro.* 140, *Thy.* 1058: *Med.* 259 perhaps has specific overtones of "butchering" in view of the phrase *discissa membra*).

libens. Taken directly from religious language, as the word is frequently used in making *ex-voto* offerings; cf. the familiar formulas V.S.L.M. (*votum solvit libens merito*) or V.L.S. (*votum libens solvit*).

1004ff., 1040ff., although Jocasta is onstage, some explanation of her activities is necessitated by Oedipus' blindness, and is therefore given by the Chorus. In two passages in which the Chorus questions a messenger, I see no reason to deny that other characters are present, viz. Hecuba at *Tro.* 166f. (cf. 142–56) and Medea and Nutrix at *Med.* 879ff.

Commentary: Act IV

1038 Argos. Eurystheus is more usually associated with Mycenae (997, Eur. *Her.* 943, 963), but the two cities are frequently conflated (v. Tarrant 160f.); the name Argos is probably chosen here for its association with Juno (v. 1036–38 comm.).

1039–42. Amphitryon takes up the sacrificial metaphors, presumably intending to ensure his own death by encouraging H. to continue in his bloodthirsty frame of mind. The reference to the real situation in *nate* indicates to us that Amphitryon uses such language not only as a willing victim but also in bitter irony.

1039 litasti. The primary notion here is of completing the sacrifice successfully, perhaps with an implication that the previous victims were inadequate, cf. Gell. 4.6.6 *si primis hostiis litatum non erat, aliae post easdem ductae hostiae caedebantur*; probably there is an additional connotation of propitiation (but Miller's "atonement" does not seem appropriate here or at *Med.* 1020). The three uses of *litare* in Sen. Trag. all involve human victims (the third being *Ag.* 577, where see Tarrant).

1040 ad aras. The phrase could be purely metaphorical, but more probably Amphitryon should be imagined as actually stationing himself at the stage altar which has been mentioned several times, most recently at 911 (cf. comm. on 202–4 ad fin.).

1040f. exspectat manum cervice prona. Amphitryon envisages a powerful blow on the back of the neck, such as would fell a sacrificial animal (*Oed.* 135–39); there is similar phrasing in a similar context (Electra inviting Clytemnestra to kill her) at *Ag.* 974f. *seu more pecudum colla resecari placet, / intenta cervix vulnus exspectat tuum*.

1041 praebeo occurro insequor. For the strongly emotional effect of first-person verbs used in asyndeton cf. *Pha.* 566 *detestor omnes, horreo fugio exsecror, Med.* 507 *abdico eiuro abnuo, Tro.* 653 *potero perpetiar feram*. For similar effects with verbs in other persons and moods v. Canter 170.

1042 macta. This word with its sacral associations continues the imagery of the preceding lines. Sen. Trag. uses it several times in contexts of human sacrifice, cf. 634 *mactetur hostia*, 923, *Ag.* 219 (where see Tarrant), *Thy.* 713.

1042ᵇ–44ᵃ errat acies . . . manus trementes? That is, "do my eyes deceive me, or is what I see real?" There are alternative questions of

[*387*]

Commentary: Act IV

just this type at 618ff. (Amphitryon again) *utrumne visus vota decipiunt meos, / an ille domitor orbis . . . / tristi silentem nubilo liquit domum?* and at *Oed.* 203f. *adestne clarus sanguine et factis Creo / an aeger animus falsa pro veris videt?*—all three passages contain the suggestion that the speaker's mental state may be affecting his vision.

It has sometimes been thought that the words from *errat* to *hebetat* (1042^b–43^a) describe Hercules, marking the first symptoms of his collapse, but this involves acceptance of Wilamowitz's conjecture *marcor* for *maeror* (corrupted in E to *maemor*); *maeror* is supported by the fact that Boethius in the *Consol.*, a work full of echoes of Sen. Trag., twice uses the phrase *maeror hebetavit* (1 pr. 4.90 *sensus nostros m. h.*, pr. 6.40 *memoriam m. h.*).

1042^b–43^a errat acies luminum / visusque maeror hebetat. The similarity of these phrases to 652f. *torpet acies luminum / hebetesque visus vix diem insuetum ferunt* illustrates Sen.'s tendency to use formulas in description of physical symptoms (cf. 414 comm.). *Errat* may mean no more than "err" here (cf. Stat. *Theb.* 7.294f. *errore videndi falleris*), but probably it also contains some notion of physical "wandering", as e.g. at Petron. 128 poët. 2 *veluti cum somnia ludunt / errantes oculos. Hebetesque visus* at 653 and *visus . . . hebetat* here echo V. *Aen.* 2.604f. *[nubem] quae nunc obducta tuenti / mortales hebetat visus*: influence is certain as *hebes* occurs nowhere else in Sen. Trag., and *hebetare* only once elsewhere.

1044^b–48^a. Euripides' hero was felled by a rock thrown by Athena to prevent him killing his father, but Sen. substitutes a naturalistic collapse to end the mad-scene (cf. Eur. *IT* 307f.). The collapse of Cassandra in Sen. *Ag.* is closely parallel, both in language and in coming at the end of a series of visions: *iam pervagatus ipse se fregit furor / caditque flexo qualis ante aras genu / cervice taurus vulnus incertum gerens* (775ff.). Fainting spells are common not only in poetry (in Sen. cf. *HF* 1300ff. with comm., *Tro.* 949ff., *Pha.* 585ff.) but also in declamation with its poetic coloring, cf. Sen. Rhet. *Contr.* 1.1.16, 1.4.7 *cum oculorum caliginem, animi defectionem, membrorum omnium torporem descripsisset*, 7.1.6, 7.1.20.

The third-person description of Hercules' or Cassandra's collapse is not in itself undramatic, cf. Soph. *Phil.* 821ff.; but the presence of epic similes in both the Senecan passages gives them a notably formal quality. Sen. Trag. contains several examples of such formal descriptions, collected and discussed by Zwierlein 1966 56–63. The character of the long passages in particular is narrative more than dramatic, though their introduction is usually well motivated (Fitch 1974 257f.). In Greek tragedy detached descriptions are found only when a character enters,

Commentary: Act IV

and elsewhere descriptions are usually directed to the person concerned, as at Eur. *Hec.* 739f. τί μοι προσώπῳ νῶτον ἐγκλίνασα σὸν / δύρει, τὸ πραχθέν δ' οὐ λέγεις; or at any rate integrated more fully into the dramatic situation, as at Eur. *Tro.* 462f. Ἑκάβης γεραιᾶς φύλακες, οὐ δεδόρκατε / δέσποιναν ὡς ἄναυδος ἐκτάδην πίτνει. The contrast illustrates two related characteristics of Sen. Trag. vis-à-vis classical Greek tragedy, viz. increased formality and decreased interaction between characters.

1046–48. Seneca here uses the brief type of simile rather than the expansive type associated with epic (cf. Quint. 8.3.81, [Demetrius] *On Style* 89); the first type is usually marked, as here, by absence of a finite verb within the simile (v. Fitch in *TAPA* 106 [1976] 114). Double similes of the brief type are by no means uncommon in poetry, cf. e.g. V. *Aen.* 2.794 *par levibus ventis volucrique simillima somno*, 11.616, Hor. *Carm.* 2.16.23f. *ocior cervis et agente nimbos / ocior Euro*, Ov. *Met.* 11.771f. Seneca is in fact scaling down two Vergilian similes of the epic type. The first describes the fall of Troy, *Aen.* 2.626ff. *ac veluti summis antiquam in montibus <u>ornum</u> / cum ferro <u>accisam</u> crebrisque bipennibus instant / eruere agricolae certatim; illa usque minatur . . . / vulneribus donec paulatim evicta supremum / congemuit traxitque iugis avulsa ruinam.* The second is used of the collapse of the giant Bitias, *Aen.* 9.710ff. *talis in Euboico Baiarum litore quondam / saxea pila cadit, magnis quam molibus ante / constructam <u>ponto</u> iaciunt, sic illa ruinam / prona trahit penitusque vadis illisa recumbit* e.q.s. Seneca's version of the second simile is so abbreviated that its precise reference (to a mass of masonry dropped into the sea in the construction of a mole or pier) might be less than entirely clear without knowledge of the original, but he could no doubt rely on his audience to recognize the allusion.

1048f. leto dedit, misit ad mortem. Periphrases for "to kill" are found in poetry, particularly of the high style, from early tragedy on (notably in Ennius, v. Jocelyn p. 250). *Leto dare* is one of the more common (Jocelyn p. 409): it is used once each by Ennius and Pacuvius in tragedy, twice by Vergil, some seventeen times by Ovid, twice in Sen. Trag. The variant *neci dare* is also popular (three uses in Vergil, seven in Ovid, five in Sen. Trag.: my figures include compounds of *dare*). *Mittere* is not uncommon in such poetic periphrases (*TLL* 8.1184.52ff.), but *mittere ad mortem* is less strongly poetic (Cic. *Phil.* 9.10, *Tusc.* 1.97).

1050. Amphitryon's observation of Hercules' breathing may be derived from Eur. *Her.* 1059f. Amph. σῖγα, πνοὰς μάθω· φέρε πρὸς οὖς βαλῶ. / Cho. εὕδει; Amph. ναί, εὕδει, but that is not necessarily the case, cf. e.g. Eur. *Or.* 155 (Electra observing Orestes) ἔτι μὲν ἐμπνέει, βραχὺ δ' ἀναστένει.

reciprocos. *Reciprocus/-are* are most commonly used of tides, but of breathing cf. Livy 21.58 *vento mixtus imber . . . cum iam spiritum includeret nec reciprocare animam sineret*, Gell. 17.11.4 *in eam fistulam* (sc. the windpipe) *per quam spiritus reciprocatur*. There are three uses of *reciprocus/-are* in Republican tragedy, one in Plaut. and two in Sen. Trag. (cf. *Ag.* 449), but I know of no instances in nondramatic verse before Val. Fl. and Silius.

1051f. For sleep as helping to restore sanity cf. Eur. *Or.* 211 ὦ φίλον ὕπνου θέλγητρον, ἐπίκουρον νόσου, Cels. 3.18.12 *somnus et difficilis et praecipue necessarius est: sub hoc enim plerique sanescunt*. There may be deliberate wordplay on *gravi/levet*.

1052 vis victa morbi. "The curing of his powerful sickness": for the *ab urbe condita* construction cf. 442–45, 725 with comm., 985, H-S 393f.

1053. Hercules' weapons are not taken from him in Eur. In Sen. the fact that they have been removed, and H.'s demand for their return, has considerable importance in the shaping of the final Act, v. introduction to Act V.

famuli. On the anonymous slaves who are regularly on hand, in Latin as in Greek tragedy, to perform various tasks v. Tarrant on *Ag.* 787.

Ode IV (1054–1137)

To a greater extent than the other odes of the play, Ode IV is concerned throughout with commenting directly on what has just happened onstage and indeed on what is happening concurrently (1082ff.). Nevertheless it has links with the more general themes of the play: the idea that the whole universe should mourn, or re-echo Hercules' mourning (1054ff., 1103ff.), continues the theme of 'universal extension,' while the long celebration of the power of Sleep continues the thematic contrast, prominent since Ode I, between *quies* or *requies* on the one hand and frenetic activity on the other (see 1065ff. comm.).

The ode is naturally thought of as a mourning song. It is written in anapests, which are frequently associated with lament in Greek tragedy

Commentary: Ode IV

and in Sen. (*Tro.* 67ff., *Ag.* 664ff., *Apocol.* 12, cf. *HO* 173ff., 1863ff.). The element of ring-composition and repetition, to be seen in small compass in 1100–14 and on a larger scale in the double use of the 'universal extension' theme at 1054–62 and 1103–14, may be related to the repetitiousness frequently found in ancient laments (v. N-H on Hor. *Carm.* 2.1.38 *neniae* with further references); compare similar patterns in the first strophe of the *kommos* of *Tro.* (67f. *non rude vulgus lacrimisque novum / lugere iubes,* 80ff. *vulgus dominam vile sequemur:/ non indociles lugere sumus*). Only a small section at the end of the ode is actually concerned with mourning the dead (1122–37), however, and a much longer passage early in the ode (1063–97) is concerned not so much with mourning as with Hercules' present state and possible recovery. Thus the song is best seen as a choral commentary on the overall dramatic situation, which contains elements of lament.

Still less would it be possible to identify the ode with a particular genre of lament.[135] The motif of breast-beating is associated particularly with *kommoi*, and the section of the ode which contains it has affinities with the genuine *kommos* of *Tro.* (see above, and comm. on 1100–14), but the present song is not antiphonal. Praise for the achievements of the dead, such as that seen in 1126–29, is found in several genres such as the *laudatio funebris*, the ἐπικήδειον (v. M. Alexiou, *The Ritual Lament in Greek Tradition* [Cambridge 1971] 107f.) and the *nenia* (on which see S. Weinstock, *Divus Iulius* [Oxford 1971] 352ff.). In mourning for youths it is a natural *locus* to refer to the athletic and military glory which they might have won, as at 1122–25, and this cannot be associated with a particular genre; cf. Eur. *Tro.* 1209f. (Hecuba mourning Astyanax) οὐχ ἵπποισι νικήσαντά σε / οὐδ' ἥλικας τόξοισιν κ.τ.λ., V. *Aen.* 6.879ff. (on Marcellus) *non illi se quisquam impune tulisset / obvius armato, seu cum pedes iret in hostem / seu spumantis equi foderet calcaribus armos,* Sen. *Tro.* 766–82.

Although the ode uses many themes traditional to the lament, it is largely independent, so far as one can tell, of specific literary models. The only significant exception is the address to Sleep, modeled chiefly on a passage in Ovid. The sea simile at 1089ff. is also borrowed from Ovid, and as usual many turns of phrase are reminiscent of Vergil and Ovid; there is also some Horatian coloring, as in the other odes of *HF*. Influence from Euripides is not in evidence except perhaps at 1082ff.

The meter is anapestic monometers and dimeters; the colometry is discussed in Appendix 3.

---

135. Kapnukajas 87–89 rightly rejected the analysis of Mesk and Weinreich, who had classified the ode as a λόγος ἐπιτάφιος, and criticized it for not obeying the conventions of that genre.

1054–62. This appeal to the universe gives a sense of escape from the enclosed and horrific atmosphere of the preceding Act. In particular the invocation of the sun has the effect of bringing light into a world of darkness and evil: compare the similar contrasts at the beginning of Ode I and Act III.

The notion that the universe may react to human actions is not unusual in Sen. Trag., cf. e.g. 1332–34, *Oed.* 1ff., *Ag.* 908f., *Thy.* passim. At least four elements may be seen as contributing to the genesis of such passages: first, the Greek religious-mythological belief that the sun and other heavenly bodies, as well as the earth, are sentient and can react to human events (cf. 60f. comm.); second, the literary conceit of the pathetic fallacy; third, the traditional practice of divination, which assumes that the natural world reflects events in human life; and fourth, the Stoic doctrine of *sympatheia*, an interconnection of the universe which is both physical and moral in nature (Regenbogen 437f.). In this play the topic is particularly appropriate because of the universal extension of Hercules' exploits, as is clear from 1060–62.

1054bis magnusque parens aetheris alti. In brief compass this phrase combines the traditional concept of Zeus-Jupiter as a patriarchal sky-god, *pater aetherius* (Stat. *Silv.* 3.1.108), with a more philosophical concept of a creator-god, *ille ipse omnium conditor et rector* (Sen. *Prov.* 5.8). For a similar conflation v. 459 with comm. *Parens* is not infrequently used of a universal creative power, *OLD* s.v. 5; it appears in the similar opening of the penultimate ode of *Pha., o magna parens, Natura, deum* (959).

1056 vaga ponti mobilis unda. On Seneca's fondness for paired adjectives of similar meaning, particularly in descriptions of waters, v. 536 comm. *Vagus* is not often used of the sea or its waters, but there are two examples in Tibullus and two in Ovid (cf. Sen. *Pha.* 1162f. *vagis . . . undis*); for *mobilis* of the sea cf. Ov. *Her.* 2.128 *mobile . . . aequor*, Sen. *HF* 170, 540.

1057 tuque ante omnes. Similarly used at *Ag.* 400 to introduce the last in a series of invocations.

1057bis terras tractusque maris. A clear echo of V. *Ecl.* 4.51, *Georg.* 4.222 *terrasque tractusque maris caelumque profundum*, of which Sen. may have been reminded by the tripartite division of the world in 1054–56.

1059. *Ore decoro* in this context is probably influenced by Hor. *Sat.* 1.8.21f. *simul ac vaga luna decorum / protulit os.* For the attractive asso-

Commentary: Ode IV

nance of Sen.'s phrase cf. Hor. *Carm.* 1.10.3f. *decorae / more palaestrae*, also Sil. 16.486 *flaventiaque ora decori*, Stat. *Silv.* 2.6.43 *horrore decoro* (again *Theb.* 2.716); compare the similar but more emphatic pattern *unda profundi* in 1109 below. *Fugare* is a common metaphor in references to dawn, v. comm. on 136 *fugit*.

1060–62. For the point that Hercules' travels have extended as far as the Sun's cf. 37f. comm. ad fin. One doubts whether Sen. is alluding here to the celebrated story of Hercules traveling in the Sun's golden cup: it is unclear whether Stesichorus had H. sailing *with* the Sun in it (Athen. 11.781d), but Pherecydes clearly did not (ibid. 11.470c). *Pariter cum* need not imply accompaniment, cf. e.g. Cic. *Verr.* 2.5.173 *Siculi causam suam periisse . . . mecum pariter moleste ferent*, Sen. *Cons. Marc.* 20.5 *M. Cicero . . . Catilinae sicas devitavit, quibus pariter cum patria petitus est.*

1060^{bis}f. obitus . . . et ortus. *Obitus* is nowhere else coupled with *ortus* in Seneca's verse or prose, nor used in reference to sunset or (as here) "the West," though these usages are not uncommon in other writers; Sen.'s regular word is *occasus*. The poetic plural is also noteworthy, as *ortus/occasus* paired are regularly singular in Sen. Trag. (comm. on 24 *ortus*).

1062 tuas utrasque domos. From Ov. *Her.* 9.16 *implesti meritis solis utramque domum*, also in a Herculean context. In both passages *domus* no doubt means "abodes, haunts", in a general sense, rather than actual buildings, though there are occasional references to a palace of the Sun in the east (Stesich. 8 P, Mimnerm. 11 D, Ov. *Met.* 2.1ff., cf. the dwellings of Dawn at Hom. *Od.* 12.4) and to stables for his horses in the east (Eur. *Phaethon* 5 Diggle, Ov. *Met.* 2.120) or west (Eur. *Alc.* 593f., cf. pasture at Ov. *Met.* 4.214). For *uterque* used in the plural of two singular things, especially when regarded as a pair, v. OLD s.v. 3, H-S 200f.

1063f. Editors have generally printed A's version, *Solvite tantis animum monstris, / solvite superi*. But *solvite superi* is open to the objection that elsewhere in anapests Seneca avoids the sequence dactyl–anapest, whereas there are three examples in ps.-Sen., *HO* 186, 1883, *Oct.* 646; although Sen. likes to experiment metrically, one must note that other metrical sequences *within the individual anapestic metron* either occur frequently or are completely avoided. Suspicion is fueled by the fact that E has the unmetrical *solvite o superi* for *solvite superi*. The phrase at *HO* 186 *fingite superi* has been thought to imitate *solvite superi*, which would guarantee its authenticity. But although the author of *HO* frequently echoes *HF*, he may well have coined *fingite superi* independently, for he

[393]

uses vocative *superi* freely (whereas it appears nowhere else in the genuine tragedies): it occurs again at 1906 in the same position in an anapestic dimeter as in 186, and with imperatives at 1415 *favete superi* and 1758 *timete superi*. What I have printed is Leo's rearrangement (1876 440 n.) of E's text. This correction implies that the corruption was largely accidental; if one supposes deliberate interpolation in imitation of *HO* 186 (cf. fn. to 83 comm.), restoration of the original will be more difficult.[136]

1064bis rectam in melius flectite mentem. "Guide and turn his mind to a better state": for the somewhat tautologous participle cf. e.g. *Oed.* 416 *spargere effusos sine lege crines*. In such instances it is often difficult to decide whether the action denoted by the participle is virtually contemporaneous with that of the main verb, or whether the participle is proleptic; the latter is the case at 1128 [*telum*] *missum . . . librare*, but for more doubtful examples cf. e.g. V. *Aen.* 1.69 *submersasque obrue puppes*, 8.227 *fultosque emuniit obice postes*. On the usage v. Eden ad V. *Aen* 8.37. Alternatively *rectam* might be taken as a proleptic adjective (for *recta mens* cf. Enn. *Ann.* 199 Skutsch, Sen. *Vit. Beat.* 7.4, and for the adjective with *flectere* cf. e.g. *Pha.* 137 *ad recta flecti*, *Clem.* 2.7.5 *in rectum prava* [*ingenia*] *flectantur*), but the phrase *in melius* seems to conflict with the prolepsis.

1065ff. Addresses and prayers to Sleep include Hom. *Il.* 14.233ff. (by Hera), Eur. *Or.* 211ff. (by Orestes), Soph. *Phil.* 827ff. (a choral ode), *Hymn. Orph.* 85, Ov. *Met.* 11.623ff. (by Iris), Stat. *Silv.* 5.4 (by the poet himself), *Theb.* 10.126ff. (by Iris), Val. Fl. 8.70ff. (by Medea), Sil. 10.343ff. (by Juno). Quintilian even attests prose panegyrics of Sleep (3.7.28). Dramatically the situation is close to that of Soph. *Phil.*: the Chorus prays to Sleep for healing of the hero who lies on the ground. Verbally, however, Seneca's chief source was the Ovidian passage:

> Somne, quies rerum, placidissime, Somne, deorum,
> pax animi, quem cura fugit, qui corpora duris
> fessa ministeriis mulces reparasque labori,
> Somnia, quae veras aequant imitamine formas,
> Herculea Trachine iube sub imagine regis
> Alcyonen adeant e.q.s.   (*Met.* 11.623–28)

---

136. In the anapests of Greek tragedy, although a sequence of four or more short syllables is normally prohibited, this rule is relaxed in "threnodic" anapests, so that a dactyl–anapest sequence is occasionally found as at Eur. *IT* 215 Αὐλίδος ἐπέβασαν. *Solvite superi* might be taken as an imitation of this license in a mourning context, but elsewhere in Sen. there are none of the marked metrical differences between mourning and nonmourning anapests found in Greek tragedy.

Commentary: Ode IV

This not only supplied Sen. with two or three phrases (Ov. 624 *pax animi*—Sen. 1066 *requies animi*, Ov. 626—Sen. 1070, and v. comm. on Sen. 1072), but also suggested to him an expansive treatment of the familiar prayer-style listing of attributes in noun phrases, participial phrases, and relative clauses. The length of Sen.'s list, however, far surpasses Ovid's, and is more appropriate in a choral ode than it would be, for example, in an epic context.

Like most Senecan lists, this one has a tendency to expansion for its own sake and to independence from the immediate context. Nevertheless the emphasis on the power of Sleep, and the sustained parallel between Sleep and Death (1069 and 1075f., v. also comm. on 1072 and 1074) have a clear significance within the thematic structure of the play. The brothers Sleep and Death represent the principle of *quies*, the very opposite of Hercules' *animosa virtus* (v. Introduction).

Among passages of similar content in English literature one thinks particularly of *Macbeth* 2.2.33–37:

> the innocent sleep,
> Sleep that knits up the ravell'd sleave of care,
> The death of each day's life, sore labour's bath,
> Balm of hurt minds, great nature's second course,
> Chief nourisher in life's feast.

It is possible that both Ovid and Seneca had some influence on this passage (though theirs was not the only influence, as is noted by the commentators): Shakespeare's references to care and to labor are paralleled in Ovid's lines, and his allusion to death in Seneca's. If *1 Henry VI* 1.6.4 "Divinest creature, Astraea's daughter" is derived from the transmitted text of *HF* 1068 *matris genus Astraeae* (as seems possible, as children are not attributed to Astraea elsewhere in classical literature), that would confirm Shakespeare's knowledge of the Senecan passage.

1065 domitor Somne malorum. Compare *Ag.* 75 *curarum Somnus domitor*. Use of *domitor* in contexts of "taming" cares, emotions, etc. is rare, and not found before Sen. (*TLL* 5.1942.43ff.). Seneca's application of *domitor* to Sleep may well have been suggested by Homer's phrase ὕπνος πανδαμάτωρ (*Il.* 24.5, *Od.* 9.372f.), despite the difference between "tamer of troubles" and "tamer of all creatures."

1068 volucre o. The reading of the archetype was probably *volucer* (so EPCV; T's *volucre* is an individual adjustment to the gender of *genus*, perhaps assisted by ambiguous compendia). The isolated adjective is most unlike Sen.'s style, whereas Leo's correction gives the familiar

[395]

interwoven pattern seen e.g. in 1067 and 1069. For the wings of Sleep cf. Callim. *Del.* 234, Tib. 2.1.89f. *furvis circumdatus alis / Somnus*; already in Hesiod he travels over land and sea (*Theog.* 762f.), and in art he is often shown winged from at least the early fifth century B.C. (*EAA* s.v. Hypnos). In Vergil's phrase *volucrique simillima somno* (*Aen.* 2.794 = 6.702) *volucer* has a different sense, viz. "fleeting."

matris genus astriferae. The genealogical reference is in the accepted prayer style (examples in Norden *Agnostos Theos* 167). But there are several objections to the genealogy given by the transmitted reading *matris genus Astraeae*. First, the mother of Sleep is regularly Night (Hes. *Theog.* 211f., 758, Eur. *Cycl.* 601, Sil. 15.612, Hyg. *praef.* 1). Alternative versions are not thereby ruled out, but it would be surprising to find a son—or two, counting Death—foisted upon Astraea, as both Seneca and others call her a virgin (e.g. *Thy.* 857, Ov. *Met.* 1.149f.). Presumably this parentage would suggest an association between sleep and justice: some explain that law and order permit us to sleep without fear of danger; others that the just sleep sounder than the unjust (a thought which jars with that of 1074, though not contradicting it); others that sleep comes impartially to all, and so on. The plethora of weak explanations does not inspire confidence in the text.

Traina 1967 171f. points out that *matris* is somewhat otiose with the proper name *Astraeae* and therefore indicates an adjective at the end of the line, cf. *Med.* 845 *matris infaustae genus*, *HF* 1002 *natum scelesti patris*, *Tro.* 461 *magni certa progenies patris*. I suggest, then, that what Sen. wrote was *astriferae*; for this adjective in reference to night cf. Val. Fl. 6.752 *Nox simul astriferas profert optabilis umbras*, *Anth. Lat.* 583.1 *Nox abit astrifero velamine cincta micanti*. The adjective is first attested in Lucan, and it would therefore not be surprising to find it in Sen. (v. Appendix 4). The corruption envisaged would not be difficult in rustic capitals; nor indeed in minuscule, if the word were abbreviated *astrifae*.[137] Alternatively *Astraeae* may be an erroneous gloss which has displaced some

---

137. Traina's proposal to interpret the transmitted *astr(a)ee* as an adjective *astraeae* "starry," a Grecism from ἀστραῖος, will not persuade many, because the adjective is extremely rare even in Greek, and unparalleled in Latin. Bentley conjectured *Asteriae*, but Asteria has no better claim than Astraea to be mother of Sleep. Zwierlein proposes to read *asteriae* in the sense of "starry" (1980 182 n. 4), but this adjective appears only twice elsewhere in Latin, and there in a technical usage, as the name of a gem (*TLL* 2.949.36ff.). If it were correct here, it would allude to such phrases as Arat. *Phaen.* 695 ἀστερίη Νύξ or Callim. fr. 228.5 ἀστερία ἄμαξα, but Sen. is not normally allusive in that fashion; his loan-words from Greek, apart from proper names and adjectives derived from them, usually consist of easily recognized *nouns* such as *chelys, mystes, syrma*.

other adjective, e.g. *aligerae*, but in this case one could scarcely hope to recover the original.

For the high-poetic use of *genus* for a single child v. *TLL* 6.1890.69ff., Bömer on Ov. *Fasti* 6.433.

1069. Sleep is regularly Death's brother, cf. Hom. *Il.* 14.231, 16.672, Hes. *Theog.* 211f., 758f., V. *Aen.* 6.278. Hesiod draws a rather different contrast from Sen.'s, calling Sleep peaceful and kindly, Death pitiless and hateful (*Theog.* 762ff.). For death as *durus* v. 56 comm.

1070f. I take it that these two phrases are parallel in meaning: *veris miscens falsa* means that in regard to past, present or future, dreams sometimes contain fact, sometimes fiction; *futuri* e.q.s. means that specifically as prognostics they are variable, now accurate (*certus*), now unreliable (*pessimus*, cf. e.g. Cic. *Att.* 3.11.1 *non optimis ... auctoribus*). *Pessimus* has been interpreted differently, as meaning that the foreknowledge given by dreams is undesirable in comparison with blissful ignorance (for the thought cf. Aesch. *PV* 248, Hor. *Carm.* 3.29.29f., Sen. *Ep.* 5.9), but this interpretation would lose the parallel between the two phrases. Probably *veris miscens falsa* originates in *Somnia quae veras aequant imitamine formas* in the Ovidian passage (1065ff. comm.), though using *verus* in a different sense; it glances at Vergil's lines on true and false dreams (*veris umbris / falsa insomnia*, *Aen.* 6.894–96), and is shaped also by his phrase *obscuris vera involvens* (*Aen.* 6.100).

futuri. *Auctor* is occasionally found with a dative rather than the usual genitive (*TLL* 2.1201.22ff.), but not when *auctor* means "source of information"; the reading *futuris* in ET[1]P was no doubt caused by assimilation to *veris* (cf. assimilation of *sui* to *fatis* at 184 by E).

1072 pax o rerum. The paradosis has *pater o rerum*, a grandiose title for Sleep, though *pater* itself is a common title of divinities (v. Carter *Epitheta Deorum*, index s.v.: of Sleep Val. Fl. 8.70 *Somne pater*). One must discard the specious traditional explanation that Sleep is so called because it nurtures and refreshes living creatures (so e.g. Trevet and Delrius); the fact is that Sleep is not the *source* of things, which alone would justify the use of *pater rerum* in this sense.[138] Elsewhere *pater*

---

138. Cf. Boeth. *Consol.* 3 poët. 6.1f. *omne hominum genus in terris simili surgit ab ortu; / unus enim rerum pater est*, also Luc. 2.7 *parens rerum*. Similarly at V. *Georg.* 4.383 the appellation *patrem rerum* for Ocean probably alludes to the doctrine of water as the prime substance.

Commentary: Ode IV

rerum is used of a supreme god, Jove (ps.-Sen. *HO* 1587) or Jehovah (e.g. Auson. 3.2.6 p. 18 Peiper). One might defend its use here on the grounds that Hypnos is sometimes addressed in terms that would befit Zeus, cf. Hom. *Il.* 14.233 Ὕπνε, ἄναξ πάντων τε θεῶν πάντων τ' ἀνθρώπων (elaborated *Hymn. Orph.* 85.1ff.), Ap. Rhod. 4.145 θεῶν ὕπατον. But there is a difference: those appellations, appropriately to their contexts, emphasize the *power* of Sleep, whereas *pater rerum* here would imply fatherly control, a less appropriate idea in the context.

Rerum recalls *quies rerum* at the opening of the Ovidian source-passage, and this suggests that Sen. wrote *pax o rerum* (Traina 1967 179; compare Luc. 4.190 *o rerum mixtique salus Concordia mundi*); this has the additional advantage that it matches *portus vitae* better than does the transmitted reading. The cause of corruption will have been misreading of *pax* as a compendium for *pater*, perhaps assisted by the fact that *pater rerum* is a common Christian appellation for God (Traina 1968 289). The earlier conjecture of Wilamowitz *pax errorum* is no less plausible paleographically, but lacks the Ovidian recommendation.

portus vitae. "Harbor" is a common metaphor (v. Kamerbeek on Soph. *Ajax* 683), particularly frequently used of death, e.g. Soph. *Ant.* 1284, *Anth. Pal.* 7.452, "Longinus" 9.7, Cic. *Tusc.* 1.118, 5.117, Sen. *Ag.* 592, *Cons. Pol.* 9.7, *Cons. Marc.* 20.2, *Ep.* 70.3. Its transference here to sleep is appropriate in view of the connections Sen. draws in this passage between sleep and death (1069 and 1075f.). A precedent for its application to sleep occurs at Critias 6.20 D ὕπνον . . . τῶν καμάτων λιμένα.

1074. Again borrowed, appropriately, from a commonplace concerning death. For death's impartiality cf. e.g. *Tro.* 434 *certe aequa mors est*, *QNat.* 2.59.4 *mors omnes aeque vocat*; for those of high and low estate mentioned in this context cf. Pind. *Nem.* 7.19f. ἀφνεὸς πενιχρός τε θανάτου πέρας / ἅμα νέονται, Kaibel *Epigr. Gr.* 459.7, Hor. *Carm.* 1.4.13f. *pallida Mors aequo pulsat pede pauperum tabernas / regumque turres*, 2.3.21ff., 2.14.11f. *sive reges / sive inopes erimus coloni*, 2.18.32ff., 3.1.10ff. Seneca may be taking the topic specifically from Horace in view of its frequency there and the use of *rex*, but kings are naturally often mentioned in such contexts, e.g. Lucr. 3.1025f. *multi reges rerumque potentes / occiderunt*, v. N-H on Hor. *Carm.* 1.4.14.

1075f. The similarity of the condition of death to that of sleep tends to be mentioned by those who would minimize the fearful nature of death (Plat. *Apol.* 40d, Lucr. 3.919ff., Cic. *Tusc.* 1.92), but the notion of sleep as actually a *praeparatio mortis* is more unusual and striking. Partially comparable are passages that call sleep a practice (μελέτη) for death: Philo in a fragment *On Sleep* p. II 667 M, *Anth. Pal.* 11.25.2, *Hymn. Orph.* 85.7. Similarly [Plut.] *Mor.* 107e calls it a προμύησις for death.

Discere is a characteristically Senecan touch, for he often speaks of learning to understand death and face it bravely; see the passages cited on 426 *nescit mori*, especially *Ep.* 26.9 *egregia res est mortem condiscere*, also 30.4, *Prov.* 6.8, *Brev. Vit.* 7.3 *tota vita discendum est mori*. Normally the lesson is to be mastered by philosophical contemplation of death (*Ep.* 28.8ff., 30.18, 70.17), but here—again an unusual point—the preparation is psychological rather than philosophical, being based on our daily experience of sleep.

noctem. This conjecture of I. Douza the younger (ad Cat. 5.6) is necessary because the whole cast of the passage requires continuation of the parallel between sleep and death; the flat *mortem* of the codd. is probably an intrusive gloss. For the long night of death in the poets cf. Hor. *Carm.* 4.9.27ff. *sed omnes illacrimabiles / urgentur ignotique longa / nocte*, Prop. 2.15.24 *nox tibi longa venit, nec reditura dies*, *Anth. Pal.* 12.50.7f. (Asclepiades) μετά τοι χρόνον οὐκέτι πουλύν, / ὀχέτλιε, τὴν μακρὰν νύκτ' ἀναπαυσόμεθα, and the passages cited on 610 ad fin.

1077. As both E and A read *fove*, the natural assumption is that E is correct in placing the line before 1078 with its parallel imperative *preme*; A puts the line before 1075. Withof 93 objected that the line would be more appropriate, with *foves* (the reading of many recc.) and in the position assigned to it by A, as a description of one of the *permanent* functions of sleep, for which there would be a precedent in the Ovidian passage, *Met.* 11.624f. *qui corpora duris / fessa ministeriis mulces reparasque dolori*.[139] But *fessum* as a description of Hercules' condition is adequately defended by 1044f.; the adjective can refer to physical and emotional infirmity as well as ordinary weariness, cf. Tac. *Hist.* 2.94 *fessi morbis*, *Ann.* 2.29 *metu et aegritudine fessus*. Assuming E to be right, A's text is explained by initial omission of 175–76 through homoearchon with 177, followed by erroneous reinsertion. If we adopt the A order with *foves*, the explanation of the paradosis will be loss of *s* on *foves* in the archetype, followed by conjectural rearrangement of the lines in E or, more probably, by accidental displacement of 177 result-

---

139. Zwierlein 1980 181f., who accepts the A order, adopts Scaliger's *fovens* rather than *foves*, wishing to attach 1077 closely to 1074 for imaginative stylistic reasons; but then the singular *fessum* comes most awkwardly after *regi famuloque*, to which it must refer if *fovens* is read.

Commentary: Ode IV

ing from homoearchon with 175: a more elaborate, though by no means incredible, hypothesis.

placidus. Not only "calm" but also "calming"; for this occasional extension of meaning cf. V. *Aen.* 1.521 *maximus Ilioneus placido sic pectore coepit* (Serv. auct. ad loc. "ergo *placido* ad placandum apto"), Livy 28.25.4 *ad quorum primum adventum exasperati animi; mox ipsis placido sermone permulcentibus notos . . . leniti sunt*, Ov. *AA* 3.545 (of poets) *ingenium placida mollitur ab arte.* The adjective appears in the Ovidian source (623 *Somne . . . placidissime . . . deorum*), where however this connotation is less evident.

1078 devinctum. For this verb used of sleep cf. Lucr. 4.453f. *devinxit membra sopore / somnus*, 1027 *somno devincti*, Cat. 64.122, ps.-V. *Ciris* 206, *Carm. Epigr.* 481.3 *hic iacet aeterno devinctus membra sopore.* The metaphor is taken up in *alliget* in the next line. Thus the weak *devictum* of ETP is clearly wrong: it would be particularly inappropriate in the neighborhood of *indomitos*. The confusion is of course an easy one (cf. e.g. 52).

1078ᵇ–79. There are close similarities of phrasing at Ov. *Met.* 1.548 *torpor gravis occupat artus* (Daphne transformed into a tree), also V. *Aen.* 3.511 *fessos sopor irrigat artus*, Germ. *Arat.* 294 *nautis tremor alligat artus*, Sen. *Oed.* 181f. *piger ignavos / alliget artus languor*, Luc. 4.290 *frigidus artus alligat . . . torpor*, Val. Fl. 1.48 *sopor alligat artus*; on the tendency to use formulas in such contexts in poetry v. 414 comm.

1081 mens . . . pristina. The phrase here and at *Ag.* 288 *surgit residuus pristinae mentis pudor* is probably derived from Ov. *Met.* 3.203 *mens tantum pristina mansit*, as *pristinus* occurs only in these places in the two authors' poetry. In the present instance one might speak of the adjective as transferred from *cursum*, contrast Hyg. *Poet. Astr.* 2.23 p. 65.18 *quo . . . ad pristinum statum mentis perveniret.*

1082–88. At Eur. 1068ff., Hercules' stirring in his sleep creates dramatic tension, based on fear lest he awake, and there is a similar effect at *Or.* 165ff. The dramatic point of Sen.'s lines seems to be not so much to create tension as to point out that H. is still suffering from madness or its aftereffects.

Detailed observation of a sleeper's movements, with inference about the nature of the dreams which cause them, may well owe something to the vivid passage in Lucr. 4.987–1036. Lucretius, however, is concerned simply with daytime activities being pursued in dreams, whereas Sen. implies that it is the *furor* and guilt of the preceding

Commentary: Ode IV

bloodshed that causes broken sleep: in this respect a closely comparable passage, very probably inspired by *HF*, is Luc. 7.766f. (Julius Caesar's troops after Pharsalus) *invigilat cunctis saevum scelus, armaque tota / mente agitant, capuloque manus absente movetur.*

1082 fusus humi. Perhaps from V. *Aen.* 6.423 *fusus humi* of Cerberus, in a passage much in Sen.'s mind (v. particularly 804 comm.), though the phrase occurs again at Ov. *Met.* 8.530.

1082^{bis}f. corde volutat somnia. *Corde volutat* is a borrowing from Vergil, cf. *Aen.* 1.50 *flammato corde volutans*, 4.533 *secumque ita corde volutat*, 6.185 *tristi cum corde volutat* (earlier Lucil. 1017 Marx *in corde volutas*); the verb appears nowhere else in Sen. Trag. *Somnia volutare* appears to be a Senecan coinage, *volutare* normally being used of a *conscious* turning over of ideas in the mind.

1085f. The notion of the club as a pillow is probably borrowed from Ov. *Met.* 9.236 *imposita clavae cervice recumbis*, though that refers to reclining on the pyre, not to a regular habit; for the influence of that passage on *HF* see comm. on 1152 and 1216. An anonymous tragic fragment (*TrGF* adesp. F416) speaks rather of the hero grasping the club in his right hand while sleeping.

clavae ... mandare caput. An unusual phrase; somewhat similar uses of *mandare* are the periphrases for sleep (Lucr. 4.848 *fessum corpus mandare quieti*, ps.-V. *Culex* 160 *somno mandaverat artus*) and burial (V. *Aen.* 9.213f. *me ... / mandet humo*).

1088–93. The sea imagery of the simile extends into the language of the surrounding phrases in the form of metaphor, viz. *aestus, fluctus*. The same process is found, again with sea imagery, at *Ag.* 138ff. *fluctibus variis agor, / ut, cum hinc profundum ventus, hinc aestus rapit, / incerta dubitat unda cui cedat malo. / proinde omisi regimen e manibus meis,* and *Med.* 939ff. *anceps aestus incertam rapit; / ut, saeva rapidi bella cum venti gerunt, / utrimque fluctus maria discordes agunt / dubiumque fervet pelagus, haut aliter meum / cor fluctuatur*; cf. also *HF* 171f.

Imagery drawn from the sea is abundant in Seneca (Pratt 1963 passim), but also common in earlier writers: precedents for similes about waves and wind include Hom. *Il.* 4.422ff., Cat. 64.269ff., Prop. 3.15.31ff., but Sen.'s immediate model here is undoubtedly Ov. *Fasti* 2. 775ff. *ut solet a magno fluctus languescere flatu, / sed tamen a vento, qui fuit, unda tumet, / sic, quamvis aberat placitae praesentia formae, / quem dederat praesens forma, manebat amor.* (There is therefore no need to suggest,

Commentary: Ode IV

with Cattin 82, influence from Eur. *Her.* 1091f. ὡς δ' ἐν κλύδωνι καὶ φρενῶν ταράγματι / πέπτωκα δεινῷ, though nautical imagery is certainly prominent in Eur.'s play.) Seneca was sufficiently struck by the simile to use it also in prose, *Tranq.* 2.1, *Brev. Vit.* 2.3, and the phenomenon to which it refers is discussed by Gell. 2.30.

The present simile lacks a formal application to the context, such as is given in the Ovidian model by the passage beginning *sic*. There are several examples in Latin poetry of "epic" similes which are elliptical in just this way, cf. V. *Aen.* 2.626ff., 4.402ff., 6.707ff. (any or all of these passages may be incomplete, but they seem nevertheless to have served as precedents for later writers); Stat. *Theb.* 4.363ff., 5.599ff., 7.436ff.; Sil. 4.302ff.; Claud. *Rapt. Pros.* 2.209ff.[140]

1092–1121. The Chorus continues to speak of Hercules in the third person, but with intermittent apostrophe (*pelle*, 1097 *te*, 1110 *tua*) which is in the manner of Senecan choral odes (186f. comm.) and here indicates sympathy with the sleeping hero. Some early commentators took *pelle* as addressed to Somnus, but that would seem to require an indication of the addressee both with *pelle* and at 1097 where H. is certainly addressed; the parallelism of the phrases *expulit aestus* (1089) and *pelle . . . fluctus* (1092f.) suggests that both have the same subject, viz. Hercules.

1093 virtusque viro. A Vergilian *figura etymologica*, with *vir* in the sense of "hero," *is quem virtus decet*, cf. *Aen.* 1.566, 4.3 *viri virtus*, 8.500 *virtusque virum* (for the connection between the two words cf. Cic. *Tusc.* 2.43). Etymological play is not common in Sen. Trag., but other examples include 799 *tegmine . . . tegit*, 929 *alta pax . . . alat*, *Phoen.* 307 *indomitum domas*, *Thy.* 692 *carmen . . . canit*, 1001 *gemitu . . . gemit*; cf. Canter 162, and on the figure in general H-S 790ff.

1094–99. Use of self-correction (*vel sit potius*) to create a rhetorical point is characteristic of Sen. (643f. comm.). The basic notion of the passage, that continuation of madness may be less painful than understanding reality, occurs in comparable tragic contexts at Soph. *Ajax* 271ff., Eur. *Bacch.* 1259ff., but to wish on these grounds that the madness should actually continue is typical of Senecan paradox and exaggeration, and appealed to another rhetorical writer, [Quint.] *Decl.* 256

---

140. In view of these parallels it is unnecessary to alter *sed ut* to *velut* with Withof and Bothe, or to postulate a lacuna after *tumet* with Leo. Vahlen defended the paradosis on the grounds that the simile turns into a metaphor before *tumet* is reached, thus giving a main clause which is otherwise lacking (*Opuscula Academica*, 1907–8, 1.302f.); but this interpretation is plainly impossible.

(on a father who killed two sons in madness) *abstulisti mihi ignorantiam malorum . . . unde tantum boni, ut reddere possis illam valetudinem, illum furorem?* For the more general commonplace that ignorance of evils is a boon cf. Soph. *Ajax* 552ff., Eur. fr. 205 N τὸ μὴ εἰδέναι γὰρ ἡδονὴν ἔχει τινὰ / νοσοῦντα, κέρδος δ' ἐν κακοῖς ἀγνωσία, Publ. Syr. 877 *nam sapere nil doloris expers est malum,* [Plut.] *Mor.* 115e μετ' ἀγνοίας γὰρ τῶν οἰκείων κακῶν ἀλυπότατος ὁ βίος.

1095 vesano concita motu. Ovidian phrasing, cf. *Met.* 3.711 *insano concita cursu,* 6.158 *divino concita motu. Vesanus,* which occurs only here in Sen. Trag., provides variation on *insanus* (1092) and euphony with *mens.*

1097f. solus . . . insontem. In view of the phrase *nescire nefas* below, the issue here is presumably not Hercules' technical responsibility for what he has done (that question arises at 1237f., v. comm.), but the sense of guilt he is bound to feel once he realizes the truth.

1098[bis] puris . . . manibus. "Clean hands" is a natural metonymy for "innocence" (Hor. *Epod.* 17.49, *Sat.* 1.4.68, Sen. *QNat.* 3 *praef.* 14, Suet. *Tit.* 9), but with special significance here in view of the thematic importance of Hercules' bloodstained hands, v. 122 comm.

1100–14. This passage has several similarities with the *kommos* of *Tro.*, to be explained by the traditional themes of lament rather than by specific reminiscence of *Tro.* in *HF* or vice versa. In addition to the point mentioned in the introduction to this ode, one may note parallels with *Tro.* 106–15: references to breast beating and *gemitus* with emphasis on their magnitude; the idea of the natural world hearing and re-echoing these sounds.

1101 percussa . . . pectora palmis. Alliteration on *p* was felt as appropriate to such contexts: for similar wording cf. e.g. V. *Aen.* 1.481, Ov. *Met.* 3.481 with Bömer, 5.473 *percussit pectora palmis,* Sen. *Apocol.* 12 poët. 27, *Tro.* 64; for variations v. Bömer on Ov. *Met.* 6.248, Pease on V. *Aen.* 4.673.

1101bis. The device of exaggerating a single instance into a regular practice comes from declamation, and frequently involves *solere,* cf. e.g. Sen. Rhet. *Contr.* 9.1.5 *cogita qualium misereri soleas* (referring specifically to Cimon son of Miltiades), 7.5.15 *facit . . . quod solet: pro amatore sanguini suo non parcit* (referring to a single earlier occasion). The tragedies offer plentiful instances, e.g. *HF* 1343, *Tro.* 360 *dant fata Danais quo*

Commentary: Ode IV

solent pretio viam (Iphigenia), *Pha.* 780f. *Naides . . . / formosos solitae claudere fontibus* (Hylas: on generalizing plurals v. *HF* 1284 comm.), 1164f. *o dure Theseu semper, o numquam ad tuos / tuto reverse* (alluding to his return from Crete); see further Leo I 149ff. Frequently (though not here) the device is related to Sen.'s general tendency to use "precedent" as the basis of a rhetorical point, cf. 386–96 comm.

1102 ultrice. The transmitted *victrice* is entirely out of place: interpretations that see the word as ironic (Kapnukajas) or as contrasting previous glorious victories and the present hollow one (Pierrot) are oversubtle. Correction to *ultrice* (N. Heinsius 222, Bentley) is easy and justified by the frequent confusion of *ult-/vict-* in codd., cf. 385 comm. (M appears to have *uitrice* (sic), not *ultrice* as Leo I 102 read.)

1103, 1105. The fact that *vastus* appears twice in three lines need not cast doubt on its authenticity in either place (43f. comm.), particularly as Sen. likes the adjective: it occurs forty-three times in the tragedies, which gives a relative frequency slightly greater than in Vergil and approximately four times greater than that in Ovid. The word has already been used of Cerberus' chains at 815.

1104 atri . . . poli. For such periphrases for the underworld cf. 607 *deterior polus* with comm., and for *ater* of the underworld v. 59 comm. I know of no earlier instance of the adjective used as a *Kennwort* for the underworld, but there are several later examples, e.g. Sil. 7.229f. *ab atris / . . . sedibus*, Stat. *Silv.* 2.1.227.

1105–7. Cerberus is back in the underworld, but still wearing his chains, and still terror-stricken (1107). How did he return? When last mentioned he was onstage with Hercules (594–604 comm.). Probably Sen. has seized an opportunity to make a striking point, without worrying about the practical details. It might be objected that H. should have presented Cerberus to Eurystheus before releasing him, but in 592ff. he clearly regards his task as complete, and Juno as his real taskmaster (contrast Eur. 1386f., where H. makes plans to convey Cerberus to Argos). (According to Apollod. 2.5.12, H. showed Cerberus to Eurystheus and then returned him to the underworld; Hesych. s.v. ἐλεύθερον ὕδωρ [cf. Eustath. 1747.10ff.] says the hound escaped and gained his freedom in Argos.)

1107 imo latitans . . . antro. The content and shape of the phrase are influenced by Ov. *Met.* 1.583, where the grief-stricken Inachus is *imo . . . reconditus antro*. Seneca's *imo . . . antro* might mean several things (and Ovid's phrase is equally ambiguous): (a) "in his (regular) cave deep below," (b) "in the nethermost cave (of the underworld)," (c) "in the depths of his cave." But (c) is probably ruled out by the tradition that the great dog filled the whole cave (804 with comm.); (b) implies that in terror he has found a more remote hiding place than his usual cave (for a similar notion cf. 780), but this would seem to require more elaboration in the Latin. So (a) is probably right; the required sense of *imus* is seen e.g. at *Tro.* 146 *liber manes vadit ad imos.*

1108–14. The motif of the earth or heavens re-echoing human cries, etc., is found in high poetry from the earliest times; Sen. here expands it to include the underworld, in keeping with the theme of universality associated with Hercules. Earlier examples of the motif include Hes. *Theog.* 835, Aesch. *Pers.* 389ff., Soph. *Trach.* 787 ἀμφὶ δ' ἐκτύπουν πέτραι (to the cries of H.), Eur. *Suppl.* 710 ὥσθ' ὑπηχῆσαι χθόνα, Pacuv. *trag.* 223 R², Acc. *praet.* 2 R² *clamore et gemitu templum resonit caelitum,* V. *Aen.* 4.668 *resonat magnis plangoribus aether,* 5.228, Ov. *AA* 3.375 *resonat clamoribus aether.*

1109 latique patens. The line is so typically Senecan, both in its juxtaposition of adjectives of similar meaning in description of waters (536 comm.) and in its interweaving of two adjective-noun pairs (216–48 comm.), that there is no need to consider the Renaissance conjecture *lateque patens,* despite the frequency in Latin of the phrase *late patere* (*OLD* s.v. *patere* 7).

unda profundi. The sound-repetition suggests the constant succession of waves, as at *Aetna* 320 *velut unda profundo;* similar effects are used more forcefully at Acc. *trag.* 570 R² *unda sub undis labunda sonit,* Cat. 11.4 *tunditur unda,* Tib. 2.4.10 *tunderet unda.* In Greek cf. Hom. *Od.* 1.162 κῦμα κυλίνδει, Alcaeus 326.2 L-P κῦμα κυλίνδεται.

1110f. et (qui melius tua tela tamen senserat) aer. The allusion is to Hercules' shooting of the Stymphalian Birds. Leo I 102f., following Schmidt, deleted these words on the grounds that the *tria regna* of 1114 have already been enumerated by the end of 1109, so that *aer* only duplicates the *aether* of 1104, but Birt adumbrated the correct defense in *RhM* 34 (1879) 545f.: *resonet* is to be distinguished from the *audiat* of 1104, and opens a new period which is closed appropriately by *sonent* (1114). In fact the sentence beginning *audiat aether* might have enumerated the three realms, but it became diverted, so to speak, by the personalities of the underworld, especially Cerberus; Sen. therefore started a fresh enumeration under the new topic *resonet.*

[405]

Aer is the transmitted reading in 1111 and provides verbal variation on *aether* of 1104; on both counts the variant *aether* (CS) is inferior. The realm in question (cf. 1114 *tria regna* and 599 comm.) is Jupiter's; therefore *aer* must be used in its general sense in which it is not distinct from the *caelum* (cf. Manil. 1.13f. *iuvat ire per ipsum / aera et immenso spatiantem vivere caelo*, Pliny *NH* 2.102 *hoc caelum appellavere maiores, quod alio nomine aera*, *TLL* 1.1048.1ff.). This consideration must exclude the E reading *medius* (A *melius*), because that adjective, whatever its precise meaning,[141] would make it impossible for *aer* to have the required sense. For confusion of *medius/melius* in codd. cf. *HF* 72, *Pha.* 766.

There are two possible interpretations of *melius*: *melius quam liberi tui* (Farnaby, Pierrot, Ageno) or *melius quam clamorem tuum* (Baden 1798). The first seems more appropriate to the dramatic context, and it better explains the pluperfect tense, as the skies had felt H.'s arrows before the children did. Its difficulty lies in *tamen*, which could not have an adversative force, but would simply mark the parenthesis, a function that normally belongs to *autem* (*OLD* s.v. *autem* 4a, *TLL* 2.1592.58ff.); most grammars do not recognize this function for *tamen*, although H-S 473 acknowledge an occasional example in Cicero. (One might conjecture *olim* for *tamen*, but this is not plausible paleographically, nor is *olim* used elsewhere in Sen. Trag. in the sense of "once.") On the second interpretation the point is somewhat strained, but that is not necessarily an objection in Sen. Trag. This interpretation gives a normal adversative sense to *tamen* (viz. *sentiat aer clamorem tuum, quamquam melius senserat tela tua*), and this use of *qui tamen* is well established, e.g. Cic. *Sest.* 53.114 *alter, qui tamen se continuerat, tulerat nihil, senserat tantum de re publica aliud atque homines exspectabant*, Sen. *Tranq.* 1.10, 4.5, L-S s.v. *tamen* IIG, *OLD* s.v. 6. Unless the use of *tamen* involved in the first interpretation can be better supported, or the word can be convincingly emended, I am inclined to prefer the second interpretation. For the postponement of *tamen* involved in either case cf. *Phoen.* 542f. *ut recedas, magna pars sceleris tamen / vestri peracta est*, *Tro.* 737.

1114 planctu. Particularly appropriate to mourning songs by virtue of its meaning; thus six of the ten uses in Sen. Trag. are concentrated in or around the *kommos* of *Tro.*, cf. also Scaevus Memor *trag.* 1 R² *scin-*

---

141. The natural interpretation would be *medius inter caelum et terram* (Manil. 1.154, Sen. *QNat.* 2.4.1), but (in addition to the fatal objection noted above) the position of this clause in the list would suggest, absurdly, *medius inter inferos et mare*. In itself *medius aer* might mean *media pars aeris* (Sen. *QNat.* 2.10.4), i.e. *medius inter summum et imum aera*, but (again as a further objection) this would seem altogether too precise and scientific.

dimus atras veteri planctu / Cissei genas. The word is post-Augustan, and the uses in Sen. Trag. seem to be the earliest surviving in verse.

1115–21. Somewhat at odds with 1085ff. where the Chorus knows that the weapons have been removed. The point is developed without great concern for its consistency with the dramatic context.

1115. The idea of the quiver with its arrows as *collo decus* is influenced by Hor. *Carm.* 1.21.11f. *insignemque pharetra / fraternaque umerum lyra*, whereas the wording comes from V. *Aen.* 10.135 *[gemma] aut collo decus aut capiti* (particularly in view of the unusual dative, cf. 257 comm.). For arms as *decora* cf. more generally e.g. Hor. *Carm. Saec.* 61 *augur et fulgente decorus arcu*, V. *Aen.* 11.194 *galeas ensesque decoros*, Ov. *Met.* 2.773 *deam . . . formaque armisque decoram.*

1116 fortis harundo. Singular for plural, while *pharetrae* is plural for singular. *Fortis* describes the arrows themselves, but also suggests that they share their owner's *fortitudo*, cf. Prop. 3.12.2 *Augusti fortia signa*.

1117 graves. With arrows, cf. Hor. *Carm.* 1.22.3f. *venenatis gravida sagittis, / Fusce, pharetra*, Sen. *Ag.* 328f. *graves levibus telis / pone pharetras*. On the other hand, quivers are sometimes called *leves* as part of the equipment of light-armed warriors (V. *Aen.* 10.169, Stat. *Theb.* 6.931; for *levis* of arrows v. 989f. comm.); hence the A variant *leves* here, but *graves* is clearly more appropriate to a context of giving blows.

1119 potens. Because it is commonly used of people and rarely of things (except of medicinal or magical herbs), this adjective provides a touch of personification here. It is used of arms at Vell. 2.108.2 *cum propter potentiora arma refugisset*, but clearly in a transferred sense.

1120 duris . . . nodis. The knots in the club do the damage, cf. V. *Aen.* 7.506f. *hic torre armatus obusto, / stipitis hic gravidi nodis.* Ovid calls Hercules' club *trinodis*, *Fasti* 1.575.

oneret. For the metaphor of "loading" someone with blows, wounds, etc. cf. Plaut. *Amph.* 328 *onerandus est pugnis probe*, *Aul.* 412 *onustos fustibus*, Phaedr. 3.2.3f. *alii fustes congerunt, / alii onerant saxis [pantheram]*, Front. *Strat.* 2.13.5 *vulneribus oneratus*, Tac. *Ann.* 2.15.2 *onusta vulneribus terga.* Gronovius, citing only the first of these parallels, wondered whether the metaphor was not too redolent of comedy, and several critics have condemned the reading on those grounds, but the other parallels given above suggest that the usage comes from everyday

Commentary: Ode IV

speech rather than specifically from comedy; for Sen.'s use of wording not normally associated with high poetry cf. pp. 185–86, index s.v. "vocabulary," and Tarrant's index s.v. "colloquialism." Conjecture (such as the *laceret* of Cornelissen 175 and Leo)[142] therefore seems unnecessary.

1122ff. As often, the identity of the new addressee is left to be understood from the context and content of the address, cf. e.g. 178, 547, 834, 858, 1092, *Tro.* 353, *Pha.* 774. *Estis* is to be supplied with *ulti, docti* and *ausi*: "You have not taken vengeance . . . , you have not been trained . . . , but you have already dared." *Vos* is inserted for reasons of sense, as is normal in ellipse of first- and second-person forms of *esse*, e.g. V. *Aen.* 3.45 *nam Polydorus ego*, *Ecl.* 5.21 *vos coryli testes*; the phrase *patriae laudis comites* is in apposition to *vos*, "sharing in your father's glory." Ellipse of *esse* in the first and second persons is rare in Sen. Trag., but paralleled at *Oed.* 709 *non tu tantis causa periclis*.

1122–23. The point that the children will not gain a reputation of their own to match their father's is similar to *Tro.* 768ff. *genetricis o spes vana, cui demens ego / laudes parentis bellicas . . . / . . . precabar, vota destituit deus,* less similar to Eur. *Her.* 1369f. ἀγὼ παρεσκεύαζον ἐκμοχθῶν βίᾳ / εὔκλειαν ὑμῖν, πατρὸς ἀπόλαυσιν καλήν, where the reference is rather to reflected glory.

1124 Argiva . . . palaestra. Another touch of local color, like *mystae* and *ephebi* in the last ode, though *palaestra* is less unusual in Latin than either of those words. The adjective means "Greek," implying that the boys would have been brought up in the proper Hellenic manner. Less probably, *TLL* 2.533.75 takes it to mean "of Argos" (cf. 1180f. *Argivae . . . urbis*); that would presumably imply plans on Hercules' part to move his family back to Argos, plans that are mentioned in Eur. (13ff.) but not elsewhere in Sen.

1125[bis] **fortesque manu.** The contrast with *fortes caestu* suggests a reference to fighting without gloves, viz. in the pancration or wrestling; for the contrast cf. *Ben.* 5.3.1 *pancratio aut caestu decernere*, *Ep.* 88.19 *vincere luctatione vel caestu*. Alternatively the phrase may refer to more general strength of hand, such as would be seen also in throwing the discus or javelin.

---

142. Garrod 214 proposed *inaret*, but *TLL* has no parallel earlier than Ambrose for the required metaphorical sense of the verb. Gronovius tentatively suggested *urat* (cf. Hor. *Sat.* 2.7.58, *Epist.* 1.15.47 of flogging), but *duris urat* makes an awkward sound-pattern.

1126–30. Hunting was regarded as good training for youths in handling weapons of war, cf. Xen. *Cyn.* 1.18–2.1. Boys would begin at an early age with hares and deer (the boys' hunts seen in Roman mosaics probably had some basis in reality, v. K. Dunbabin *Mosaics of Roman North Africa* [Oxford 1978] 85–87) and later graduate to fiercer animals; hence Hercules' boys were able to hunt deer and lion cubs, but nothing more dangerous as yet. (In contrast Astyanax was not yet old enough to have begun hunting, *Tro.* 775–77.) Leo I 104 illustrates this training with several passages, among them V. *Aen.* 9.590f. (Ascanius, cf. 4.156–59 and 7.477f.), Ov. *Fasti* 5.173 (Hyas) *dum nova lanugo est, pavidos formidine cervos / terret, et est illi praeda benigna lupus. / at postquam virtus annis adolevit, in apros / audet et hirsutas comminus ire feras,* Mart. *spect.* 23.1f.

1127–30. These lines are unmistakably echoed in the *nenia* of *Apocol.* 12: see Introduction on "Date."

1127 telum . . . leve. A common periphrasis for "arrow" (v. 989 comm.), but perhaps the adjective also suggests here that such weapons were manageable for the children.

Scythicis . . . gorytis. The noun is another Grecism, from γωρυτός; it appears in Latin only twice before the present passage, at V. *Aen.* 10.169 and Ov. *Tr.* 5.7.15. In literature it generally means "quiver," though ancient grammarians also recognized another meaning "bow-case" (Serv. ad V. *Aen.* 10.169). The E reading with its poetic plural is more stylish than A's genitive singular; A perhaps objected to the brachylogy "shot from a quiver," but that is hardly exceptionable in poetic diction. *Scythicis* alludes to the well-known penchant of that people for archery (indeed γωρυτός may be a loan-word from Scythian, v. Frisk *Gr. Etym. Wörterbuch* s.v.). It may have been suggested here by the fact that Ovid ascribes use of the *gorytus* to the tribesmen around Tomis, but in the present context it is purely conventional, as e.g. at Ov. *Met.* 10.588f. (Atalanta) *Scythica non setius ire sagitta / Aonio visa est iuveni.*

1128. Similar language to 118f. *ut certo exeant / emissa nervo tela, librabo manu* (on *mittere / emittere* v. 990 comm.). But here the participle *missum* is proleptic, cf. e.g. V. *Georg.* 4.547 *placatam Eurydicen vitula venerabere caesa,* *Aen.* 3.236f. *tectosque per herbam / disponunt enses;* v. 1064 comm., K-S 1.239f. *Certus* frequently appears in references to archery, etc.: in addition to *HF* 118f. cf. e.g. Cat. 68.113f. *certa Stymphalia monstra sagitta*

Commentary: Ode IV

/ *perculit,* Prop. 1.7.15, Ov. *Am.* 3.10.26 *figentem certa terga ferina manu, TLL* 3.924.18ff.

1129 tutos. In a pregnant sense, i.e. "normally safe," "relying on": Bentley's conjecture *fretos* simplifies the sense but overwhelms the delicate alliteration of *fuga figere.* For *tutus fuga* cf. Lucr. 5.863 *tutatast . . . fuga cervos,* Cic. *Nat. D.* 2.129 [*bestiae*] *aliae fuga se . . . tutantur,* Ov. *AA* 1.216, *Rem. Am.* 224 *tutus adhuc Parthus ab hoste fuga est.*

1130 nondumque ferae . . . iubatae. That is, of a lion cub that has not yet grown its mane (contrast the adult *iubatus . . . leo* of *Thy.* 732); the point of the phrase is illustrated by the elder Pliny's remark that the high spirit of lions becomes evident *tum cum colla armosque vestiunt iubae* (*NH* 8.42). Hunting of lion cubs is mentioned by Jul. Poll. *Onomast.* 5.84. For *nondum* used in indications of youth cf. 142 *nondum rupta fronte iuvencus* with comm., 852f. *virgines nondum thalamis iugatae / et comis nondum positis ephebi.* The separation of *nondum* from the word which it modifies seems awkward but is paralleled at 1219 *nondum tumultu pectus attonito carens.* It was perhaps this separation that led some early commentators to misinterpret the line as meaning *sed nondum ausi leonem iubatum aggredi,* with *-que* in its adversative sense; this may be dismissed, since after the positive statements of *iam tamen ausi* e.q.s. it would be an awkward anticlimax to return to a negative statement like those of 1122–26.

ferae terga. Perhaps influenced by epic phrasing, cf. Ov. *Met.* 4.719 *terga ferae, terga ferarum* at V. *Aen.* 7.20, Ov. *Met.* 14.66, Stat. *Ach.* 1.115, 415, and Ovid's *terga ferina* (1128 comm.).

1131–37. T. S. Eliot remarked on the beauty of these lines, both in the original and in Jasper Heywood's translation:

> Go hurtless souls, whom mischief hath oppressed
> —Even in first porch of life but lately had—
> And father's fury. Go unhappy kind,
> O little children, by the way full sad
> > Of journey known.
> Go see the angry kings.

1131 Stygios . . . portus. An interesting combination of the metaphorical use of *portus* for "death" (v. 1072 comm.) with a literal reference to crossing the waters of the underworld.

1133 in primo limine[143] **vitae.** Possibly borrowed from V. *Aen.* 6.427ff. *infantumque animae flentes in limine primo / quos dulcis vitae exsortes et ab ubere raptos / abstulit atra dies* e.q.s.; but ancient interpreters took *in limine primo* there to mean the entrance to Limbo, though some modern editors would punctuate after *flentes* and take *limine* with *vitae* (see Austin ad loc.). A more certain precedent is Lucr. 3.681 *cum gignimur et vitae cum limen inimus.*

1134 scelus. "A criminal act," not necessarily implying deliberate guilt; cf. the usage at 1004, and v. comm. on 1237f.

1135f. Leo I 104f. thought these two lines should be transposed to the beginning of the address to the children, i.e. immediately after 1121, but his reasons are unconvincing.[144] First, he believed that *estis* could not be supplied in 1122–30 because he had found no parallel for such ellipse in Sen. Trag. (cf. I 192); concluding that in the transmitted text the whole of 1122–30 must be subordinate to *ite* in 1131, he objected both to the length of the subordination and to the clash between the masculine participles *ulti, docti* and *ausi* and the feminine *umbrae*. These problems would be solved, he thought, by making 1135–36 the beginning of the apostrophe, with 1122–30 dependent on them. But Leo had overlooked ellipse of *es* at *Oed.* 709 *non tu tantis causa periclis*; and even without this parallel one would be justified in assuming ellipse of *estis* in our passage in view of *vos* in 1122, which functions like that of V. *Ecl.* 5.21 *vos coryli testes* (see on 1122ff.; it is indicative of the error of Leo's transposition that *vos* becomes awkward and redundant). Second, Leo argued that "in fine carminis nimius est chorus in compellandis pueris, quos quater ire iubet, primum umbras, dein pueros vocat." But Sen. would not have thought the four imperatives excessive, for he uses *sume* thrice at *Tro.* 806–8 and *audite* four times at *Thy.* 1069–71; for other examples of multiple anaphora v. Canter 155. The vocative phrases with *pueri* following *umbrae* might be criticized if their purpose were to identify the persons addressed, but in fact they are intended to arouse pathos (cf. Heywood's "O little chil-

---

143. *Limite*, which Moricca and Giardina print as if it were the transmitted reading, has no authority but appears in the closely related fourteenth-century MSS Laurentianus plut. 24 sin. 4 and Neapolitanus Bibl. Nat. IV.d.47.

144. Leo's prime motive in altering the passage was to eliminate the examples of *syllaba debilis* which occur in the final syllables of both *furor* and *laboris* in E's colometry; but the reformed colometry (for which see Appendix 3) brings both words to line-end, and so removes the problem. To Leo's credit he did not argue, as Withof 101 had done before him, that the apostrophe to the children starting after 1121 should be marked *ab initio* by a vocative: see on 1122ff.

Commentary: Act V

dren"). A positive objection to Leo's proposal is that the thought of 1137 grows directly out of 1136 (Pluto and Proserpina are angry because of Hercules' visit: the father's glorious exploit will bring trouble on the innocent sons), and this wry and very Senecan ending would be much weakened by separation of the two lines.

1135. Similar language to *Med.* 845 *ite ite nati, matris infaustae genus*. *Infaustus* suits the portentous atmosphere of Sen. Trag., where it appears fifteen times; contrast four uses in Vergil and two in Ovid.

1137. See comm. on 1135f. ad fin. The line will be a reminiscence of *Pha.* 946f. *non cernat ultra lucidum Hippolytus diem, / adeatque manes iuvenis iratos patri*, if my relative dating of the tragedies is correct. Almost certainly the *irati reges* are Pluto and Proserpina: for *reges = rex et regina* cf. Caes. *BCiv.* 3.109.1, Livy 1.39.2, 37.3.9, and compare *domini = dominus et domina* at 570 (v. 805 comm.). Some have taken them to be the tyrants dispatched to the underworld by Hercules (i.e. the *reges* of 1123), but presumably they cannot now represent a threat (cf. 737ff.). The close of the ode is absolutely characteristic of Seneca: for the new ironic twist in a tragic context cf. *Oed.* 201, *Tro.* 860; more generally one may compare the endings of *Ag., Med.,* and *Thy.*

Act V (1138–1344)

In Act V one may notice two important differences from Euripides' dramatic handling. The first lies in the increased importance of Amphitryon; it is he who takes the leading part in arguing against Hercules' impulse to kill himself, whereas in Euripides that part is played by Theseus. The change is appropriate, in that throughout Seneca's play Amphitryon represents qualities that are the opposite of Herculean aggression and violence.

A second change concerns the new issue of the return of Hercules' *arma*, which were removed at the end of Act IV. At one level the *arma* provide a physical, tangible focus for the argument of the second half of the Act, that is, from the moment Hercules determines on suicide (1218) and begins to demand their return (1229ff.). But they also function as a symbol of his heroic-aggressive *persona*, so much so that the very loss of them in his sleep constitutes a defeat to his mind (1153–56). For a brief and moving moment he realizes that his Herculean *persona* is responsible for his inability to weep for his children (1226ff.). Consequently his immediate decision to destroy the weapons implies not only atonement for the murders but also a rejection of that

Commentary: Act V

rigid *persona*, to which the weapons are an essential adjunct. For that reason it has some of the poignancy of Prospero's

> I'll break my staff,
> Bury it certain fathoms in the earth,
> And deeper than did ever plummet sound
> I'll drown my book.

But by an irrational shift of thought similar to those in the madness, the return of the arms quickly changes its significance and becomes a means by which he can kill himself (1242ff.). This intention of using the weapons in retributive violence shows that he has once again donned the heroic straitjacket, which he wears till the end of the play.

The Act may be classified typologically with the Passion-Restraint scenes characteristic of Senecan tragedy. (Such scenes normally occur in Act II, but there are parallels outside Act II at *Med.* 380ff., 891ff.)[145] The person urging restraint is usually a servant, but Amphitryon has that role again (significantly) at *HF* 309ff., and Agamemnon at *Tro.* 203ff. There are particular similarities between the present scene and *Pha.* 85–273, in the appeals of the restraint-figure (see comm. on 1250f. and 1309) and in the abrupt final change of heart by the passion-figure.

The stage situation envisaged is consistent with Act IV, in that the bodies are within the house (1143f., 1227). Yet Hercules' address to them at 1230ff. implies closeness, and at 1194ff. he can see the fatal arrow close at hand. The obvious explanation is that at the end of Ode IV the bodies are wheeled out on the *eccyclema*, as they are at Eur. *Her.* 1029ff., thus becoming visible onstage while remaining 'indoors' by convention.[146] The visibility of the indoor scene is explained in Euripides by the opening of the doors (1029f.), and in Seneca by the phrase *prostrata domo* (1143). As a result of this arrangement, Euripides' Hercules, like Seneca's, can address his dead family close at hand (1367ff.). Other instances of persons being wheeled out in Seneca are *Pha.* 384ff. (n.b. *patescunt regiae fastigia*) and *Thy.* 901ff. (n.b. *fores / templi relaxa*). But the fact that Seneca observes the conventions of stage drama in such passages need not mean that he wrote primarily for stage performance.

---

145. The Act II pattern was recognized by Herington 1966 453f. (see introduction to Act II), who also noted *Med.* 380ff.; Act V of *HF* and *Med.* 891ff. are added by Liebermann 59 n. 181.

146. Zwierlein 1966 43 interprets the contrast between 1227 (children in the house) and 1230ff. (children close at hand) as an indication of Seneca's inconsistency in envisaging the stage situation. But it would be remarkable if such an inconsistency should occur within the space of four lines in a single address to the children; and it seems perverse to choose this explanation when the alternative, viz. use of the *eccyclema*, has a Euripidean precedent.

Commentary: Act V

1138ff. The broken, choppy style of much of this speech reflects Hercules' emotional turmoil (on *sermo praeruptus* v. 960–64 comm.), and the spate of questions down to 1163, with a second series beginning in 1173, conveys his bewilderment.

1138–41. What might seem to be merely otiose amplification of the question "where am I?" in fact has particular relevance to the speaker, Hercules the world-traveler: it is *because* H. has been to the ends of the earth that he now feels he might be anywhere at all.

1138. This fine line is used evocatively by Eliot as the motto of his poem "Marina."
   Association of *locus* and *regio* goes back to earlier Latin, e.g. Plaut. *Rud.* 227 *haec loca atque hae regiones,* Lucr. 4.786 *regione locoque*: in questions cf. V. *Aen.* 1.459f., 6.670 *quae regio Anchisen, quis habet locus?* with Austin ad loc., Sen. *Tro.* 498 *quis te locus, quae regio seducta invia* e.q.s.

1139 cardine. *Cardo* is frequently used of the northern or southern pole, v. *TLL* 3.443.84ff.; here the usage is particularly appropriate as the northern pole is the turning-point for the Bears, cf. Cic. *Nat. D.* 2.105 *hunc circum Arctoe duae feruntur,* Vitr. 9.5.4 *Septentriones circum axis cardinem versantes.*

1140 glacialis Ursae. The same phrase at *Pha.* 288; cf. 6 comm.

numquid. This use of *numquid* as an interrogative particle, virtually equivalent in meaning to *num,* is somewhat colloquial, and therefore more appropriate to some forms of poetry, notably drama, than to others. Thus it is common in Republican comedy, and Sen. Trag. has twelve uses of it as against six of *num* (in his prose *numquid* is three times more frequent than *num*); Horace has five uses of it, but all in *Sat.*; Ovid has seven uses, but six of them are outside *Met.* and *Fasti*; it is avoided by Lucr., Cat., Prop., Tib. and Verg.

1140f. Hesperii maris extrema tellus. The furthest point of land on the western Mediterranean, viz. Gibraltar, the meeting place of the *mare internum* and Ocean. The phrase *tellus maris* seems awkward, but scarcely warrants conjecture.

1142 quas trahimus auras. The reference to breathing possibly derives from the corresponding speech in Eur. (cf. 1144^b–46 comm.), 1089 ἔμπνους μέν εἰμι, 1092f. πνοὰς θερμὰς πνέω / μετάρσι', οὐ βέβαια, πνευμόνων ἄπο: compare 1050 comm. *Aura* is governed by a variety of verbs in periphrases for breathing, e.g. *auras carpere, ducere,* *haurire, suscipere, auris vesci*. The only pre-Senecan example of *trahere* cited by *TLL* is Ov. *Met.* 2.229f. (Phaethon) *ferventesque auras . . . / ore trahit*; there the verb may suggest difficulty in breathing, but no such connotation is evident in the other Senecan examples, *Oed.* 599 and *Phoen.* 220.

1143. *Certe* implies doubt about something *else,* and I take it to be the state of the palace, i.e. "I have certainly returned, but why do I see," etc. Alternatively the doubt may be more general ("but I don't know what else has happened"), in which case H. notices the palace only *after* saying *certe redimus*; then a full-stop or dash would convey the sense better.

prostrata domo. Schmidt 1865 24f. thought this excessive as a description of the damage to the palace, and therefore wrote *prostrata ad domum* to agree with *corpora*. His conjecture has won considerable acceptance, but it is inconsistent with the clear indications both in Act IV and in 1227f. that the bodies are *inside* the house; although Sen. sometimes perpetrates such inconsistencies, there is no justification for foisting this one upon him. In the mad-scene H. did not just break down the door (as Zwierlein 1966 43 n. 9 oddly thinks), but left the house a roofless ruin (1000f. *culmen impulsum labet. / perlucet omnis regia*); so it would be strange here if he did *not* notice the destruction as well as the bodies lying in it. *Prostrata* may mean "ruined" rather than literally "leveled with the ground," cf. e.g. Livy 22.5.8 [*motus terrae*] *qui multarum urbium . . . magnas partes prostravit*, Mart. 5.42.2 *prosternet patrios impia flamma Lares*. The ablative *prostrata domo* may be causal (he can see the bodies *because* the house is ruined) or local, and it would probably be wrong to exclude either of these senses.

1144ᵇ–46. Probably derived from Eur. 1101f. where the hero wonders, on seeing the corpses, whether he has returned to Hades—though the question in Sen. is rather different.

1144ᵇ–45ᵃ. The use of *simulacra* here of images or pictures held in the mind has a somewhat Lucretian ring, cf. e.g. 4.758f. (in sleep) *simulacra lacessunt / haec eadem nostros animos quae cum vigilamus*, 881f.; the word is particularly appropriate in the present context as it can also mean "ghost," e.g. Lucr. 1.123, V. *Aen.* 2.772 *infelix simulacrum atque ipsius umbra Creusae*, Ov. *Met.* 4.435.

1146 oberrat oculis . . . meis. The transitive use of *oberrare* seen in A's variant *oculos . . . meos* is not found elsewhere before Apuleius, and then in the different sense of "wander over."

Commentary: Act V

1147ᵇ–48. The language is somewhat formulaic, particularly in drama: for presentiments of evil cf. Ter. *Heaut.* 236 *sed nescioquid profecto mi animu' praesagit mali*, Plaut. *Bac.* 679 *animus iam istoc dicto plus praesagitur mali*, V. *Aen.* 10.843 *praesaga mali mens*, Sen. *Phoen.* 278f. *magna praesagit mala / paternus animus*, *Thy.* 958 *mens ante sui praesaga mali* (for other instances of such presentiments v. Jocelyn 192 nn. 1, 2); more generally, Pacuv. *trag.* 294 R² *sed nescioquidnam est: animi horrescit, gliscit gaudium*, Sen. *Med.* 917f. *nescioquid ferox / decrevit animus intus*, *Thy.* 267ff. *nescioquid animus maius et solito amplius / . . . tumet / . . . haud quid sit scio, / sed grande quiddam est.*

The effect of the repetition of *nescioquod* is perhaps one of pathos and doubt, cf. *Thy.* 829f. *trepidant, trepidant pectora magno / percussa metu*. Short scansion of *o* in *nescioquis, nescioqui* is found already in Plautus and had become standard by Sen.'s time (on short final -*o* generally v. 109 comm.). Metrically, Sen., like Plautus, treats such forms as a single word (Strzelecki 22f., 71, 83).

1149 ubi es, parens. So E, but A has *est*. For similar instances with a vocative taken as a nominative cf. 109 *Iuno, cur nondum furis (furit* A), 259 *ferax deorum terra, quem dominum tremis? (tremit* A). On the other hand a second-person form is sometimes intrusive in such circumstances, as at 1038 *Argos victimas alias dabit (dabis* A).

1149f. illa natorum grege animosa coniunx. Influenced by Latona's words at Ov. *Met.* 6.206 *en ego vestra parens, vobis animosa creatis* (echoed again at *Tro.* 588 *animosa mater*), though Latona's pride is hubristic, Megara's creditable.

1150f. On the lion-skin as normally draped over H.'s left shoulder, and on *tegimen* used of the skin, v. comm. on 797f. and 799 *tegmine* (both details from Ovid).

1151 spolio leonis. Another Ovidian phrase for Hercules' lion-skin, *Met.* 9.113 (also 3.81 of Cadmus' lion-skin), *Fasti* 2.725, 5.393, *Her.* 9.113; echoed elsewhere at Manil. 2.32, Sen. *Pha.* 318.

quonam. Like *quinam/quisnam* (introduction to Act II), the interrogatives *quonam* and *ubinam* seem at home in the vigorous diction of drama. *Ubinam* is common in comedy, though *quonam* appears only twice in Republican drama. Thereafter they appear sporadically and infrequently in prose, and even more infrequently in verse (one use of *quonam* in Vergil, one of *ubinam* in Catullus). Probably they have colloquial overtones, though it is noteworthy that Sen., who has *quonam* four times and *ubinam* twice in the tragedies, uses neither word in prose.

1152. Like Hercules' use of his club as a pillow (1085f.), this detail probably comes from Ovid's description of him reclining on his pyre, *Met.* 9.235f. *congeriem silvae Nemeaeo vellere summam / sternis.* The detail is not merely decorative, but implies that he would normally expect to find the cloak spread under him. *Mollis* of course conveys a point, viz. that the shaggy pelt spread on the ground would not seem like soft bedding to ordinary mortals (cf. the contrast at Ov. *Her.* 9.111f. *hirsuti . . . leonis / aspera texerunt vellera molle latus,* of Omphale wearing H.'s lion-skin).

1156 libet . . . libet. Here the force of the anadiplosis is simply emphatic, as e.g. at *Tro.* 94 *placet hic habitus, placet*; for other uses of the figure see comm. on 638f. and 907f.

1157–59. *Exsurge, virtus* (A's *victor* has intruded from 1156) must mean "rouse yourself, my courage," indicating that Hercules intends to fight his 'conqueror'. The clauses beginning *quem* and *cuius* may be relative clauses referring to *victorem*, but I take them as questions in view of the spate of questions in this speech up to 1163. Gronovius interpreted *exsurge, virtus* as "rise up, great hero," addressed to Hercules' 'conqueror,' but it is very doubtful that *virtus* could carry this sense.[147]

1158 fetu. "Begetting, conception," an unusual sense, but cf. Pliny *NH* 22.36 *si quadripes fetum non admittat, urtica naturam fricandam monstrant.* A's variant *incestu* for *in fetu* is entertainingly inappropriate.

1160–61ª. Similar phrasing is found at *Ag.* 925 *pater peremptus scelere materno iacet, Tro.* 238 *iacuit peremptus Hector,* 312 *saevo peremptus ense quod Priamus iacet, Oed.* 1040 *iacet perempta.* The alliteration here is almost worthy of Ennius. For *cruenta caede* v. 919 comm.

1161 quis Lycus regnum obtinet? Apart from its immediate dramatic irony, the question has rich thematic significance in view of the parallels established earlier between Lycus' behavior and that of Hercules.

1162. Leo I vii brusquely rejected this line as "post v. 1161 non tolerabilem"; presumably he found it flat after the conceit of 1161ᵇ, but (as

---

147. The affective use of abstracts for concretes is reserved for abuse (*exitium, scelus* etc.) or endearments, the latter usually with a possessive (Cic. *Att.* 1.8.3 *Tulliola, deliciae nostrae,* Plaut. *Bac.* 1176 *mea pietas,* H-S 746). The use of an abstract in a *collective* sense is rather different (H-S 747; for *virtus* so used cf. Petron. 89 poët. 8f. *huc* [in the Wooden Horse] *decenni proelio / irata virtus abditur,* Stat. *Ach.* 1.14 *Itala virtus*), as is the use of abstracts indicating social status, etc. (e.g. *servitium* for *servus, coniugium* for *coniunx*: H-S 748).

much of this speech demonstrates) Senecan rhetoric tends not to use one question when two will do.[148]

1163–66. A poetic adaptation of the traditional cry for help addressed to the populace (Lat. *quiritatio*), for which cf. e.g. Eur. *Or.* 1621f. ὦ γαῖα Δαναῶν ἱππίου τ' Ἄργους κτίται, / οὐκ εἶ' ἐνόπλῳ ποδὶ βοηδρομήσετε; Plaut. *Rud.* 615 *pro Cyrenses populares, vostram ego imploro fidem*, Hor. *Ars P.* 459f. *licet "succurrite" longum / clamet "io cives,"* Ov. *Fasti* 6.517 *dique virique loci, miserae succurrite matri* (note *succurrere* in the last two examples as here), Sen. *Pha.* 725 *adeste Athenae*, and v. Brink on Hor. *Ars P.* 460, W. Schulze *Kleine Schriften* 160ff. The appeal to neighboring peoples as well as Thebans reflects Hercules' belief that there has been a coup d'état in Thebes, as that would necessitate powerful allies; but it owes more to his habit of thinking in broad terms than to immediately practical considerations. For *Ismeni loca* in reference to Thebes v. comm. on 334 *quidquid Ismenos rigat*.

1164 Actaea. This adjective is generally much rarer than *Atticus*, and all citations of it in *TLL* are from verse. Ovid has it some eight times, but before him it occurs only once in Latin and occasionally in Hellenistic verse (Bömer on *Met.* 2.554).

1164ᵇ–65. Pelops is normally associated with Argos, but "beaten by twin seas" might suggest the Isthmus (cf. Ov. *Her.* 12.104 *quique maris gemini distinet Isthmos aquas*, Sen. *Oed.* 266f. *pater Neptune, qui . . . / utrimque nostro geminus alludis solo*, Anth. Lat. 440.5 *mari gemino semper pulsata Corinthos*, Tarrant on *Ag.* 563). Similarly at *Med.* 891f. *effer citatum sede Pelopea gradum, / Medea* the context might suggest a reference to Corinth despite *Pelopea*. On the other hand at *Thy.* 181 Atreus, wishing that his fleets were harrying the *geminum mare*, is indubitably in Argos.

Perhaps in all these places Sen. has in mind the northeastern Pelo-

---

148. Zwierlein, *Gnomon* 38(1966) 685 objects that in Sen. Trag. we find *scelus, facinus, nefas* as direct objects of *audere* (cf. *audere* with direct objects such as *aliquid, omnia, magnum, plura*, etc. in criminal contexts), and that the explanatory infinitive is paralleled only in ps.-Sen. *HO* 767f. *audent fata . . . nefas / admittere*. But although this establishes Seneca's usual practice, it scarcely excludes the possibility that he might on occasion use an infinitive; for *moliri* in this position cf. *Phoen.* 303 *scio quo ferantur, quanta moliri parent*, *Oed.* 28 *iam iam aliquid in nos fata moliri parant*, *Ag.* 230. There is no metrical objection to the line-end *ausus est*. For metrical purposes Seneca treats *est* as part of the preceding word (Strzelecki 82f.). Hence in the present line and in *Med.* 692 *caelo petam venena. iam iam tempus est* (cf. also *HO* 939) he does not contravene his usual rule that, after word-break in the middle of the fifth foot, word-break may not occur elsewhere than at the end of the fifth foot (Strzelecki 16f.).

Commentary: Act V

ponnese, i.e. roughly Argolis-Corinthia, washed by the Myrtoan Sea (Argolic and Saronic Gulfs) on the east and the Corinthian Gulf on the west; or the references to Pelops may indicate that he means the whole of the Peloponnese. It is even conceivable that with a poet's vagueness about geography he thinks of Argos as lying on or very near the Isthmus, in which case he may have had a precedent in the tragic fragment which he quotes at *Ep.* 80.7, *en impero Argis, regna mihi liquit Pelops, / qua ponto ab Helles atque ab Ionio mari / urgetur Isthmos*. Finally, it has been suggested that the *HF* and *Med*. passages refer to Corinth as inherited by Pelops from Tantalus (Costa on *Med*. 891f.), but the story that Tantalus reigned in Corinth is poorly attested (Serv. ad V. *Aen*. 6.603, *Myth. Vat*. 2.102, 3.6.21) and there is no need to see an allusion to it at *Med*. 745.

1165 Pelopis ... Dardanii. Pelops is sometimes called "Phrygian," an allusion to his birth and youth in Tantalus' kingdom in Asia Minor (Bacchyl. 7.53, Hdt. 7.8, Strabo 12.8.2, Prop. 1.2.19, Sen. *Thy*. 662f.). Seneca calls him "Dardanian" by association between Troy and Phrygia, as "Phrygian" is often used loosely for "Trojan." Aeschylus in his *Niobe* associates the family specifically with Mt Ida (frr. 158, 159, 162, 163 N), but Sen. is probably using *Dardanius* in a much more general sense.

1167 ruat ira in omnes. For "objectification" of passion in Sen. Trag. v. 27–29 comm. Anger is characteristically directed against all and sundry without discrimination, in Sen.'s view; in his essay on the subject he describes Anger as *omnium odio laborantem, sui maxime, si aliter nocere non possit, terras maria caelum ruere cupientem* (*Ira* 2.35.5). Hercules later shows precisely this willingness to cause universal destruction, at 1285ff. and especially 1293f., and so does Medea at *Med*. 426ff. *sola est quies / mecum ruina cuncta si video obruta; / mecum omnia abeant. trahere, cum pereas, licet.*

1169f. seu tu ... sive. *Tu* is sometimes added to one part of a disjunction without any clearly emphatic force; to the first e.g. Hor. *Carm. Saec.* 15f. *sive tu Lucina probas vocari, / seu Genitalis*, to the second e.g. *HF* 1247f., Ov. *Fasti* 2.677 *et seu vomeribus seu tu pulsabere rastris*, v. H-S 501 ad fin.

currus. By metonymy for "horses," as often, but clearly implying that Diomedes *had* chariots, as at *Ag.* 845f. *tinxitque crudos / ultimus rictus sanguis aurigae*. Cf. Eur. *Alc*. 66f. Εὐρυσθέως πέμψαντος ἵππειον μέτα / ὄχημα, 483 Θρηκὸς τέτρωρον ἅρμα Διομήδους μέτα; if Dale ad loc. is

[419]

Commentary: Act V

right that ὄχημα and ἅρμα here refer to horses alone, Seneca or a predecessor was perhaps misled by that usage. Certainly at Eur. *Her.* 380ff. the horses appear to have been unbroken until H. bridled and teamed them.

1171 Libyaeve dominos. Probably a reference to Antaeus and Busiris, who tend to be associated together (v. p.195fn.), with *Libya* in its general sense of "Africa." Diod. Sic. 4.18 mentions other anonymous tyrants Hercules suppressed in the same region as Antaeus, but one doubts whether they are sufficiently prominent for Sen. to be thinking of them here.

1173ff. The dramatic technique of this passage and of 1192–1200 is noteworthy: over a space of several lines the speaker alternates between direct address and commentary "aside" on the behavior of the persons addressed. This represents an extension of the sequence "aside"—address as seen e.g. at *Med.* 549ff. or at the end of some entrance monologues, e.g. at *Med.* 186ff., *Thy.* 505ff. Other examples of the technique in Sen. Trag. include *Tro.* 607–31 and 949–54; for an instance outside drama cf. Hor. *Epod.* 7.13ff. *furorne caecus an rapit vis acrior / an culpa? responsum date! / tacent et albus ora pallor inficit / mentesque perculsae stupent.*

1173–79. Similarly Eur.'s Amphitryon weeps and covers his face, avoiding his son's eyes, 1111f. πάτερ, τί κλαίεις καὶ συναμπίσχει κόρας, / τοῦ φιλτάτου σου τηλόθεν παιδὸς βεβώς; Theseus is not present at that point, but he weeps later (1238).

1174 ora . . . condunt. An echo of the Ovidian phrase *vultus condere*, though only one of Ovid's four uses of the phrase designates an emotional gesture (*Met.* 2.330).

1175 differte fletus. The parallel with 638f. *differ amplexus, parens, / coniunxque differ* is a close and significant one: Hercules characteristically puts a higher priority on violent retribution than on natural expression of love or grief.[149]

dederit neci. On the periphrases *neci, leto dare* for "to kill" v. 1048f. comm.

---

149. There is no justification for doubts about the reading such as those entertained by several critics from N. Heinsius to Schmidt 1868 869: they arose from excessive respect for E (which has the obviously corrupt *defer tellus*) combined with the strange view that because Hercules mentions the weeping at 1179 he cannot see or anticipate it earlier (Withof 105ff.).

Commentary: Act V

1177 at tu. "But *you* at least," i.e. if my father will not. Rather different is the use of *at tu* to *introduce* an appeal, for which cf. [Tib.] 3.12.7 *at tu, sancta, fove*, *TLL* 2.995.54ff.

Theseu . . . Theseu. The effect is not quite the same as in immediate repetition of a proper name in the vocative, e.g. Hom. *Il.* 5.31 Ἆρες Ἆρες, Theoc. 11.72f. ὦ Κύκλωψ Κύκλωψ, V. *Ecl.* 2.69 *a Corydon Corydon*, Hor. *Carm.* 2.14.1 *Postume Postume*; here the first vocative identifies the addressee as Theseus rather than Amphitryon, while the second gives added emotional force as Hercules redoubles his appeal. The verse accent changes from *Théseu* to *Theséu*, cf. 50 *vidi ipsa vidi* with comm.

sed tua . . . fide. *Sed* will mean that *at tu ede, Theseu* has met with no response: so Miller, "But do thou tell, Theseus! Nay, Theseus, tell me. . . ." Reference to *fides* is frequently made in appeals to gods, fellow citizens, friends, etc. for help or protection (Plaut. *Amph.* 373 *tuam fidem opsecro*, Cic. *Verr.* 5.129 *fidem et misericordiam vestram requirebat*, *Q.Rosc.* 23 *pro deum hominumque fidem!*), but here in addition there is a special allusion to Theseus' characteristic loyalty, for which cf. 1334 *o fidum caput* with comm. *Fides* in appeals is normally in the accusative, governed either by a verb or *per/pro*: the ablative here perhaps points to the special significance of the word.

1178f. In addition to the Euripidean precedent cited on 1173–79, cf. for actions and phrasing Ov. *Fasti* 2.819f. (the ravished Lucretia) *illa diu reticet, pudibundaque celat amictu / ora, fluunt lacrimae more perennis aquae*. The phrase *ora pudibunda* is specifically Ovidian, always used by him in contexts of covering the face, as here, but always of females (*Met.* 3.393f., 6.604f., 10.421f.).

1178, 1180 pudibunda, pudendum. Hercules not unnaturally interprets their gesture as one of shame, cf. 692 with comm. But its meaning is presumably more complex here, including grief (cf. Hom. *Od.* 4.114f., Eur. *Suppl.* 110f., Ov. *Met.* 2.329f.) and reluctance to meet H.'s eyes and questions.

1181 dominator. This rare noun is a favorite of Sen.'s, for he uses it six times (all in verse); elsewhere it appears only thrice before the end of the first century, at Cic. *Nat.D.* 2.4, ps.-V. *Eleg. Maec.* 87, Sil. 14.79. Seneca is fond of the more recondite agent-nouns in *-tor*, as of their female equivalents in *-trix* (900 comm.): two of those which appear in the tragedies are ἅπαξ λεγόμενα, *mactator* and *sortitor*; four more are not

Commentary: Act V

previously attested, *deceptor, donator, peremptor,* and *stuprator*; two others are not previously used in verse, *aestimator* and *machinator*.

1182 pereuntis. The time reference of present participles is sometimes prior to that of the verb on which they are dependent, rather than strictly contemporaneous (e.g. V. *Aen.* 1.305ff. *at pius Aeneas, per noctem plurima volvens, / ut primum lux alma data est, exire . . . / . . . constituit,* v. K-S 757, H-S 386f.), and *pereuntis* has been compared with such instances; but normally in these cases the subject of the participle is the same as that of the finite verb, which helps to blur the distinction between past and present. Here it seems better to regard the participle as essentially atemporal, and the whole phrase as meaning *agmen Lyci, infestum propter mortem domini*. To understand "sent by Lycus as he died" is impossible in view of lines 895–97.

1183. Personal pronouns tend to move close to the beginning of their clause in appeals, frequently coming between πρός/*per* and their objects, cf. Soph. *Trach.* 436, Eur. *Hipp.* 605 ναί, πρός σε τῆς σῆς δεξιᾶς, Ter. *Andr.* 538 *per te deos oro,* Tib. 1.5.7f., Sen. *Ag.* 929 *per te parentis memoriam obtestor mei,* K-S 1.584f., 2.593.

facinorum. Seneca is sparing in his use of this metrical pattern, in which a single word covers a resolved third-foot arsis and the whole of the fourth foot, because of the conflict between ictus and word-accent in the third-foot arsis (Strzelecki 58f., cf. 408 comm.).

1184f. tuique nominis . . . numen secundum. That is, second only to the *numen* of Jove. In Sen. there is none of the rejection of Jove's paternity seen in Eur. 1265 πατέρα γὰρ ἀντὶ Ζηνὸς ἡγοῦμαί σ' ἐγώ: Hercules consistently *calls* Amphitryon "father," but without intending any denial of his divine parentage (1246–48 comm.). The extravagant reference to an individual human being as a *numen* has occasional precedents in Ovid (who also uses *numen* frequently of members of the imperial family), cf. Ov. *Her.* 13.159 *per reditus corpusque tuum, mea numina, iuro,* 3.105, *Am.* 2.18.17, *Fasti* 2.842. Here it is softened by the fact that the *numen* is that of the holy name "father" rather than purely of Amphitryon as an individual. The word is used in part for the play on *nomen* (compare the pun *nomen-omen,* Otto 1235 with *Nachträge*; on such wordplay in Sen. Trag. see introduction to Ode II).

1185 quis fudit domum? *Domus* here means "family, household" as at 1250, as *fundere* in the sense of *prosternere* regularly has people or animals as its object (*TLL* 6.1569.71ff.: ibid. 1570.20f. both the present passage and Val. Fl. 4.167 are wrongly classified).

1186 cui praeda iacui.   A Lucretian phrase, cf. 5.875 *haec* (sc. *genera animalium*) *aliis praedae lucroque iacebant.*

1186ff.   Antilabe here suggests Amphitryon's extreme reluctance to speak, whereas at 1263f. it suits the vehemence of the argument. The present passage and 1295ff. illustrate Sen.'s tendency to use on occasion very broken dialogue in which speeches of half, full, and one and a half lines are intermingled, cf. also 426–29.

sic abeant.   That is, things should be left as they are, Hercules should take no further action. For the colloquial-sounding phrase cf. 27 *non sic abibunt odia* with comm. Euripides' Amphitryon similarly advises his son to enquire no further (1125 τοσοῦτον ἴσθι τῶν κακῶν, τὰ δ' ἄλλ' ἔα), but before he has discovered the death of his family.

1187.   The exchange perfectly characterizes the two men, Hercules obsessed with retribution and the need to maintain his heroic image, Amphitryon perceiving the complexities of life and action. *Saepe vindicta obfuit* of course coincides with Sen.'s own view, illustrated several times in the *de Ira,* cf. 2.22.4–23.1, 3.27.1 *ultio . . . multis se iniuriis obicit, dum una dolet,* 28.3. For *ut ego, egone ut,* etc. in indignant questions in drama see introduction to Act II.

1191 quota.   "How small," as regularly with *pars* in Sen., cf. 383 comm.

1192–94.   The fact that Hercules' *manus* reveal the truth is telling in view of their thematic significance throughout the play (122 comm.). Compare particularly the blood on his hands *before* the mad-scene: there too it was revelatory, though for the audience rather than for the hero himself.

1193 manus refugit.   *Manus* is probably accusative plural, *pace* Delrius and others who take it as nominative singular citing 1318f. *dextra contactus pios / scelerata refugit*; in the present passage the avoidance would have to be *involuntary* (at 1318f. it is intentional), and though Sen. might have liked such a notion, he would have conveyed it with more force.

Commentary: Act V

hic errat. That is, it is somewhere hereabouts. The uncertainty implicit in *errat* is actually that of H. concerning the location of the *scelus*: a rare usage, but cf. *Thy.* 473 *rogat? timendum est. errat hic aliquis dolus.*

1195f. *Tincta Lernaea est nece* is Leo's convincing correction. The MSS have *tincta Lernaea nece* (E *t. Lernae n.*) which TPCS take, by their punctuation, to qualify *harundo* (E is ambiguous, punctuating both after *leto* and after *nece*). Many editors accept this and punctuate as follows:

> unde hic cruor? quid illa puerili madens
> harundo leto, tincta Lernaea nece?
> iam tela video nostra. non quaero manum.

But this reduces *tincta Lernaea nece* to an afterthought or fact of minor importance, rather than the crucial new discovery which leads to the conclusion *iam tela video nostra*. Bothe and others therefore prefer to take the phrase as qualifying *tela*:

> unde hic cruor? quid illa puerili madens
> harundo leto? tincta Lernaea nece
> iam tela video nostra. non quaero manum.

But the sentence from *tincta* to *nostra* would properly have the ridiculous meaning "*Now* I see that my arrows are dipped in the Hydra's poison," as if he had not noticed this fact previously. The context shows that it must be causal, explaining why he recognizes the arrows, but the awkward subordination lacks Senecan vigor and point. Those qualities are restored by Leo's insertion of *est*.[150]

Iam tela video nostra means not "Now I see that the arrows are *mine*," but "*Now* I see my arrows," whereas previously I could not (1153 *ubi tela? ubi arcus?*). The second interpretation suits the Latin word order much better than the first, and is rhetorically superior. This constitutes a further objection to Bothe's text, because *tincta Lernaea nece* suggests that it is a matter of *recognition* (as of course it is), whereas *iam tela* e.q.s. suggests rhetorically that it is a matter of *timing*: the two phrases would therefore be in conflict with each other if linked grammatically.

1195. *Leto* means "gore": *caedes* is frequently used in this sense (e.g. 483, 919), but *TLL* gives no other instance of *letum* so used (7.2.1191.40). *Nece* alludes to the poison that flowed from the dying

---

150. For omission of *est* cf. e.g. *HO* 49 (A), 1763 (E). E's *Lernae* conceivably suggests that at an earlier stage *Lernaea ē* had become *Lernaeae* (which was then misread as the genitive of *Lerna*), as at *Phoen.* 499 *hasta ē* became *hastae*.

Hydra, an analogous use to *leto* (for *nex* = "gore" cf. Ov. *AA* 2.714 [*manus*] *imbutae Phrygia nece*). But the context also suggests a secondary meaning, *id quod necat*: compare the occasional use of *mors* for the *source* of death, e.g. Sen. Rhet. *Contr.* 7.3.8 (poison), Luc. 9.706f. *inde petuntur / huc Libycae mortes* (sc. asps). "Fatal blood" might catch the ambiguity of the usage, if not its force.

1197f. A characteristic rhetorical heightening (though perhaps influenced by reminiscence of *Odyssey* 21); earlier accounts envisage no difficulty for lesser heroes, notably Philoctetes, in using the bow.

1198 sinuare nervum.[151] *Sinuare* appears only here in Sen. Trag., and the phrase clearly echoes Ov. *Met.* 8.30 *sinuaverat arcus*, 380f. *sagittam / imposuit nervo sinuatoque expulit arcu*. *Sinuare* seems less appropriate to the angle formed by the bowstring than to the curve of the bow.

vix recedentem mihi. *Re-* indicates the drawing *back* of the bowstring before shooting (Quint. 10.3.6 *bracchia reducimus et expulsuri tela nervos retro tendimus*). The ponderous metrical effect of *recedentem* suggests the difficulty of the task, cf. 504 *nec orbe si remolito queat* e.q.s. with comm.

1199 ad vos revertor, genitor. Though the address is plural (i.e. to Amphitryon and Theseus) only one person is mentioned in the vocative: this pattern occurs chiefly in informal contexts, notably in comedy, but is also found occasionally in high poetry, e.g. V. *Aen.* 1.140, 9.525 *vos, o Calliope, precor, aspirate canenti*, cf. H-S 433. Editors have traditionally punctuated with a semicolon before *genitor* rather than after it, presumably to avoid the conflict of number between *vos* and *genitor*; but *tacuere* shows that the whole of 1199 is addressed to both men, so there seems no reason not to attach *genitor* to the first clause of the apostrophe, as is done by ETPCS.

The words *ad vos revertor*, though scarcely recherché, probably echo Ov. *Tr.* 4.10.91 *ad vos studiosa revertor / pectora*, similarly in apostrophe of an audience previously addressed.

1200f. Juno's responsibility is mentioned several times in the final episode of Eur.'s play (1127, 1191, 1253, 1302ff., 1311f., 1393), but not as here with the purpose of asserting Hercules' innocence of intention;

---

151. Housman 1077 explains the E reading *nervos* as corrupted from an original *nervom*: for forms in *-vo-* for *-vu-* v. Housman 178f., M. Leumann, *Lateinische Laut- und Formenlehre* (Munich 1977) 49.

[425]

Commentary: Act V

in fact the distinction between guilt and innocence of intention is not made in Eur.'s play (see below comm. on 1237f.)

1200 istic. Pronominal and adjectival forms of *istic istaec istuc* (as opposed to the adverbs *istic istinc istuc*) are extremely rare in Latin poetry outside Republican comedy and tragedy; before the fourth century A.D. *TLL* s.v. *iste* notes only one instance in the archaic poem *Carm. Epigr.* 331.5, a handful in Lucilius, two in Cat. 67 and the present instance. One may therefore see this as a further instance of "dramatic" diction.

1201. Compare [Cato] *Monostich.* (Duff *Minor Lat. Poets* 624.25) *haut homo culpandus, quando est in crimine casus.* On the argument v. 1237f. comm. For the line-ending, and for *crimen* and *culpa* as virtual synonyms, cf. *Med.* 935 *crimine et culpa carent, Thy.* 321 *crimine et culpa vacent.*

1202ff. Similar prayers are voiced at comparable moments of revelation by other Senecan characters: Medea at *Med.* 531ff., Hippolytus at *Pha.* 671ff., Thyestes at *Thy.* 1077ff. In all cases the speakers pray to Jupiter to destroy them with his thunderbolts, though they are in varying degrees innocent of the wrong that evokes the prayer. Each passage also contains some reference to the physical turmoil in the heavens (*mundus*—usually mistranslated by the Loeb editor) which will accompany Jove's hurling of his thunderbolts. These prayers therefore contribute to the characteristic tendency of Sen. Trag. to present human crimes as leading, potentially and sometimes actually, to disruption of the very fabric of the universe (cf. 1054–62 comm.).

1202. Very similar language appears in two of the prayers referred to above, *Med.* 531 *nunc summe toto Iuppiter caelo tona, Thy.* 1080 *omni parte violentum intona.* The phrases *parte ab omni, omni parte* refer to the segments of the sky from which thunder was thought to appear. Thus at V. *Aen.* 8.427f. [*fulmina*] *toto genitor quae plurima caelo / deicit in terras* Servius' comment on *toto . . . caelo* is "ab omni parte caeli: nam dicunt physici de sedecim partibus caeli iaci fulmina." These divisions are known to Pliny the Elder, who says they have an Etruscan origin (*NH* 2.143), and they are listed by Mart. Cap. 1.45ff.; they appear to be represented also on the bronze liver found at Piacenza (M. Pallottino, *The Etruscans* [London 1975] 144ff.).

1203 oblite nostri. That is, "though you have forgotten *me* (in not protecting me from Juno), at least avenge your grandsons." That is preferable to "forget me (i.e. do not spare me) and avenge . . . ," which would seem to require *oblitus* rather than *oblite*. The first interpretation has the advantage also of giving a clear meaning to *saltem*, though under the second a meaning could probably be discerned (e.g. "since you can do nothing for *me*, at least . . ."). This phrase (on the first interpretation) together with *sera manu* represents Hercules' only criticism of his divine father after the mad-scene: in Eur. the criticism is more prominent and more bitter in tone (1247, 1263, 1265).

sera manu. Observations are frequently made on the slowness of divine punishment, cf. Curt. 3.13.17 *dii seri saepe ultores,* Juv. 13.100 *lenta ira deorum est,* Otto s.v. *deus* (11) and my comm. on 622. Schmidt 1865 25 proposed *saeva manu* (cf. *Pha.* 673, *Oed.* 1029 in similar contexts), protesting that Jupiter could not be accused of slowness so soon after the event; but probably H. implies that vengeance should have been instantaneous, cf. *Pha.* 671f. (directly after Phaedra's confession) *magne regnator deum, / tam lentus audis scelera? tam lentus vides?*

The phrase *sera . . . manu* is used by Ovid at *Pont.* 3.4.62, but not in a similar context.

1204 saltem. There is always a note of pathos when this word is used in Vergil (so Austin ad *Aen.* 4.327); the same is true of its three appearances in Sen. Trag. (cf. *Med.* 1015, *Ag.* 492), and it is usually the case in Ovid also. Prayers and appeals are the usual context for the word's appearance in all three authors.

stelliger. A somewhat surprising form, for two reasons. First, *stellifer* is found at *Pha.* 785, and in no other compound does Sen. use both *-fer* and *-ger* forms. (At *Pha.* 909 A's *armigerae* probably represents an intrusion of the more usual form, as does the *armigeri* of β at *Med.* 980.) Second, Sen. elsewhere uses *-ger* only when it has a special appropriateness as against *-fer*: in *belliger* (*bellum gerere*), and when the first half of the compound is something held in the hand (*securiger, thyrsiger*) or part of an animal's body (*aliger, corniger, laniger, saetiger*). But although Sen. is more careful than some other writers (e.g. Cicero uses *auriger,* Ovid *piniger,* Statius *flammiger*), his use of such forms as *sceptrifer* and *squamifer* shows that he does not make a rigid distinction, and I am therefore not inclined to write *stellifer* here.

1205 et hic et ille . . . polus. The two extremes stand for the whole of the heavens, just as East and West can stand for the whole world (37f. comm.); the expression is Ovidian, cf. *Met.* 2.295 *fumat uterque polus, Fasti* 2.489f. *Iuppiter adnuerat, nutu tremefactus uterque / est polus,* the latter echoed also at Sen. *Ag.* 402f. *cuius nutu simul extremi / tremuere poli.*

[427]

Commentary: Act V

1206ff. For the rehearsal of various possible methods of punishment cf. *Pha.* 1223ff., *Oed.* 930ff. The punishments proposed often have a special relevance to the speaker: Hercules thinks of Prometheus' torment because he himself freed Prometheus from it (cf. also 1216f. comm.), Theseus thinks of punishments he has imposed or witnessed, Oedipus thinks of Cithaeron and punishments suffered by Thebans. The topic is closely related to 'choosing a way of death' which is seen at 1284–94. (The point at which death becomes H.'s central concern is clearly marked at 1218.) In Eur. the hero considers ways of death immediately after the full revelation of what he has done, 1148ff.; one of those lines (1148 οὐκ εἶμι πέτρας λισσάδος πρὸς ἅλματα) may conceivably have suggested the crags of Sen. 1206–10, and another (1151 ἢ σάρκα †τὴν ἐμὴν† ἐμπρήσας πυρὶ) the pyre of Sen. 1216f.

1206 rupes . . . Caspiae. Compare *Thy.* 374f. *Caspia . . . iuga*: not solely an instance of poetic association, as geographers too call part of the Taurus "Caspian" (Mela 1.109, Pliny *NH* 5.99).

trahant. Not an easy usage to explain, but roughly equivalent to *distrahant*: his body will be "pulled apart" when spread-eagled on jagged rocks and torn by the vulture. One might think of translating "ravage, plunder," cf. Sall. *Hist.* 4.69.17 *quibus non humana ulla neque divina obstant, quin socios amicos . . . trahant excindant*, but *trahere* in this usage properly refers to goods (cf. *rapere trahere*) rather than the persons themselves. "Drag off" (for punishment, cf. *OLD* s.v. 1b) is unlikely in view of *ligatum*. Ageno 114 proposes *terant*, which would suit *rupes* but not *ales*; one would then have to suppose aposiopesis of the verb of *ales*, but that would seem pointless because *cur Promethei vacant scopuli* does not introduce a new idea but simply elaborates 1206.

1207. *Ales avida* recurs at *Ag.* 18 of the bird that afflicted Tityus; cf. *avida . . . avis* of a Harpy at *HF* 759. *Promethei* is the adjective rather than the genitive of the proper name, in view of Sen.'s avoidance of iambic fifth feet and his liking for noun-adjective phrases.

1208 vacat cur. Leo's certain correction: it presupposes, persuasively enough, that E's *vagetur* faithfully preserves the original corruption despite its meaninglessness, whereas the A interpolator has substituted the bland *paretur* (further corrupted to *parent* in δ, no doubt by misreading of a compendium). For *cur* postponed in the second of two questions cf. 1173f., *Pha.* 174 *cur monstra cessant? aula cur fratris vacat?*, 856, *Oed.* 1024.

[428]

1208f. feras volucresque pascens. Primarily the phrase indicates that the area is a savage wilderness; *pascere* is used in the sense of τρέφειν. There is a strong secondary implication that the beasts and birds will devour human flesh given the chance, however, and this is conveyed not least by *pascens*: cf. *Tro.* 566f. *numquid immanis ferae / morsu peremptus pascis Idaeas aves?*, *Thy.* 10, 1033f. *utrumne saevis pabulum alitibus iacent, / . . . an pascunt feras?* The same double meaning can be seen in *alere* at *Phoen.* 255ff. *feris / avibusque saevis quas Cithaeron noxius / cruore saepe regio tinctas alit.*

1210–15. H. wants each of his arms to be fastened to one of the Symplegades, so that they will be stretched apart when the rocks diverge, and his body will be crushed when they converge.

1210 Pontum Scythen. An Ovidian phrase, cf. *Tr.* 3.4.46 *Scythicus cetera Pontus habet*, 4.1.45, echoed again at *Med.* 212.

1211 Symplegas. The first instance in Latin of the singular form; in Greek the singular is transmitted at Eur. *IT* 241 and *Andr.* 794, though critics tend to be skeptical of the authenticity of those forms.

1212 revocata vice. "As the regular change recurs," viz. the change from diverging to converging. The form of the phrase was possibly suggested by Ovid's uses of *vice/vicibus* plus participle, *Fasti* 4.353 *vicibus factis*, *Tr.* 4.1.99 *vice mutata*, but the choice of verb was clearly influenced by the movement of the rocks themselves, which are "recalled" after moving apart. I have considered conjecturing *revocata invicem*, "recalled alternately with being separated" (for the ellipse cf. 377 *vicibus alternis fugax*), but I doubt whether correction is necessary.

1213. *Saxa* is the subject of both *coibunt* and *expriment*. It sometimes happens that a word common to two phrases or clauses stands at the beginning of the second with *-que* attached to it, cf. Tib. 1.6.81f. *hanc animo gaudente vident iuvenumque catervae / commemorant merito tot mala ferre senem*, Sen. *Med.* 570f. *domūs / decusque regni*, Orelli on Hor. *Carm.* 1.30.6, Housman *CQ* 10 (1916) 150 = 1972 938. More usually the word in question is a verb, e.g. Hor. *Carm.* 2.19.31f.

1214 rupibus. Virtually identical with the *saxa* of 1213; for "disjunctiveness" in general cf. 683f. comm., and in this context cf. Val. Fl. 4.658 *Cyaneae iuga praecipites inlisa remittunt.*

Commentary: Act V

1215 montium. *Variatio* on *saxa* and *rupes* above, creating a fine sound-pattern with *iaceam mora*; as a reference to the Symplegades (so also at *Med.* 342), borrowed from Ov. *Met.* 7.62f. *mediis concurrere in undis / dicuntur montes.*

mora. There are several examples in Sen. and earlier of *mora* used of a person (cf. V. *Aen.* 10.428 *pugnae nodumque moramque* of Abas, Livy 23.9, Sen. *Ag.* 211 *Danais Hector et bello mora* with Tarrant ad loc.), but in none of them does *mora* have so strongly physical a sense as here.

1216f. As at 1285–87, Sen. shows H. contemplating the sort of death which he will in fact eventually choose. The pyre is also foreshadowed in the reference to Oeta at 133.

1216. *Agger* of a pyre (cf. *Phoen.* 110) comes from Ov. *Met.* 9.234ff. (of Hercules on Oeta) *dumque avidis comprenditur ignibus agger, / congeriem silvae Nemeaeo vellere summam / sternis.* The phrase *congeriem silvae* in the same passage suggests both *congerite silvas* at *HF* 506 and *nemore congesto* here, and Ovid's next detail, that H. rested his head on his club, is echoed at 1085f.

1218. The idea of death emerges here, to remain prominent in Hercules' mind almost to the end of the Act. As often in Sen. Trag. one can observe the process of thought by which the idea is formed: the pyre of 1216f. is first proposed as a *punishment*, but the prospect of *death* which it offers then captures H.'s attention.

sic sic. For anaphora of this kind in the first foot v. 99 comm.: here it marks the vehement acceptance of an idea that has just occurred to the speaker, as at *Oed.* 668 *iam iam tenemus callidi socios doli.*

1219–21. Amphitryon sees Hercules' speech as evidence of the lingering effects of insanity, but in fact it is typical of H.'s tendency to exact summary punishment. For Seneca's perception that *ira* and *furor* turn against the self cf. 98 *in se semper armatus Furor*, *Ira* 2.35.5 *[Iram] omnium odio laborantem, sui maxime*, 3.1.5 *in se ipsa morsus suos vertit.*

1219. Compare *Thy.* 260 *fateor. tumultus pectora attonitus quatit. Nondum* goes with *carens*; the hyperbaton is paralleled at 1130 *nondumque ferae terga iubatae*, but its unfamiliarity caused A to write *caret* for *carens*.

[430]

1221–23. The vocatives express longing, and perhaps imply an appeal such as *recipite me*: compare the similar effect of *Pha.* 718 *o silvae, o ferae!* Alternatively one might punctuate with a dash after *turbae*, indicating that H. was about to say something like *recipite me* or *abdite me* but broke off when struck by the thought of an even more remote hiding-place. (I do not know why Leo II 376 and Giardina compare the construction at *Oed.* 691ff.) A's insertion of *et* before *si quod exilium* in 1223 produces syntactical chaos.

1221 dira Furiarum loca. The adjective *dirus* is sometimes used of the Furies themselves, no doubt in allusion to the name *Dirae*, cf. V. *Aen.* 7.324 *dirarum ab sede dearum*, 7.454, 12.914, Sen. *Thy.* 78, 250 *dira Furiarum cohors*, and for its use of the underworld generally v. 608 comm.

1222 carcer. Seneca likes this metaphor for the underworld, using it on eight occasions including *HF* 57; there are Ovidian precedents at *Met.* 4.453, *Ibis* 80, and it matches traditional descriptions of Tartarus as enclosed by walls, e.g. Hes. *Theog.* 732f., V. *Aen.* 6.548ff.

1222f. sonti plaga decreta turbae. That is, Tartarus. Seneca usually calls its inmates the *nocentes*, as at 93; *sons* probably echoes Vergil's description, 6.570f. *continuo sontes ultrix accincta flagello / Tisiphone quatit insultans*.

1223–26. Sen. Trag. has several comparable passages containing an appeal to Earth to hide the person concerned, usually after the discovery of guilt incurred unintentionally, cf. *Pha.* 1225–42, *Oed.* 868–70, *Thy.* 1006–19, *Tro.* 519–21 (an appeal to Earth to protect Astyanax). Such appeals are highly traditional from Homer on, in a context of shame or guilt; often the earth is asked to open to *prevent* some shameful occurrence. Cf. e.g. Hom. *Il.* 4.182 τότε μοι χάνοι εὐρεῖα χθών, Aesch. *Ag.* 1538f. ἰὼ γᾶ, γᾶ, εἴθ' ἔμ' ἐδέξω / πρὶν τόνδ' ἐπιδεῖν κ.τ.λ., Eur. *Suppl.* 829 κατά με πέδον γᾶς ἕλοι, V. *Aen.* 4.24ff. *sed mihi vel tellus optem prius ima dehiscat / . . . / ante, pudor, quam te violo* (with Pease ad loc.), Ov. *Her.* 6.144 *hiscere nempe tibi terra roganda fuit*.

1223f. The idea of a secret hiding-place in the depths of the underworld is characteristically Senecan and regularly expressed in this fashion, cf. 92f. *in alta conditam caligine, / ultra nocentum exilia, discordem deam*, *Phoen.* 144f. *Tartaro condi iuvat, / et si quid ultra Tartarum est*, *Thy.* 1013 *si quid infra Tartara est*. More generally one may compare, from

Commentary: Act V

the passages cited above, *Oed.* 869 *in Tartara ima*, *Tro.* 520f. *Stygis / sinu profundo*. For *exilium* in such contexts v. 93 comm.[152]

1225 hoc. E preserves this form of the adverb here and at *Ag.* 143, *Thy.* 710, 1014; in all cases A normalizes to *huc*, except that at *Ag.* 143 C has *hoc*. That *hoc* in the present passage is the adverb, not the ablative of the pronoun, is confirmed by *Thy.* 1013f. where *si quid infra Tartara est* is taken up by *hoc . . . demitte*; for *huc/hoc* with *abdere* cf. Petron. 89 poët. 8f. *huc decenni proelio / irata virtus abditur*. The fortunes of *hoc* in verse are similar to those of the comparable form *illo* (v. 864 comm.), with which it is coupled at *Thy.* 710f. *flectit hoc rictus suos, / illo reflectit*: it appears frequently in Republican drama and occasionally in the satires of Lucilius and Varro, but then virtually disappears from verse until Sen. Trag. (one certain use at V. *Aen.* 8.423).

1226 mansurus. That is, "not to return again"; cf. *non rediturus* of Orpheus *Med.* 633, *non exiturum* of Theseus *Pha.* 1242. In each case the point is that the person concerned *has* previously returned from the underworld.

1226ᵇ–29ᵃ. A significant contrast with Eur.'s Hercules, who does weep (1354ff.). Seneca makes him incapable of tears and presents this not as heroic endurance but as a disability caused by his unnatural way of life: compare his impatience with embraces and with the tears of others (638, 1175). (For the significant inversion of a Euripidean detail cf. Introduction fn. 31.) What is particularly telling is that H. perceives, at least momentarily, his disability and its cause.

The language of *Ep.* 99.15 is reminiscent of this passage: *quid? nunc ego duritiam suadeo et in funere ipso rigere vultum volo?*

1227f. quis vos . . . deflere digne poterit? Compare 258 *quis satis Thebas fleat? Ag.* 667ff., 670ff. *non . . . / . . . tristis aedon / . . . / lugere tuam poterit digne / conquesta domum*, ps.-Sen. *Oct.* 914f. *quis mea digne deflere potest / mala?* But in those passages the main point is the greatness of the tragedy; here it is rather the speaker's inability to mourn properly.

---

152. Zwierlein 1980 180 proposes to replace *latet* with *patet* on the basis of the hyperbolic imitation at *HO* 742f. *quaere si quid ulterius patet / terris freto sideribus Oceano inferis*. (MSS confusion of *latere/patere* is not uncommon.) But in *HO* the idea of "an available place" (for refuge) is conveyed chiefly by the verb *patet*; in the present passage it is conveyed by the noun *exilium*, and *latet* adds a further idea, of seclusion, which is strongly supported by 1224 *ignotum*, 1225 *abde*, and later 1335 *latebram quaere longinquam abditam*.

Commentary: Act V

1229ᵇ–36. On the new significance of the *arma* in Seneca, and their relationship to Hercules' suicidal impulse, see introduction to Act V. There is a partial precedent for this passage at Eur. 1377ff., where H. wonders—again immediately after an address to his dead family—whether he should keep the arms which were involved in their murders. (But the overall context is different, for Eur.'s hero has decided to live on, whereas Sen.'s plans to destroy himself along with the weapons.)

For the motif of destroying harmful weapons cf. *Anth. Pal.* 5.179, Tib. 2.6.15f. with Smith ad loc. (both on the bow and arrows of Eros-Amor).

1229 arcum. The transmitted reading *ensem* is inappropriate. Although a sword is occasionally found among Hercules' accoutrements in literature (Hes. *Theog.* 316, Bacchyl. 12.50ff., Apollod. 2.4.11, Diod. Sic. 4.14.3) and more frequently in art (see e.g. M. Robertson in *CQ* N.S. 19 [1969] 212f.), that is normally in the context of the earliest labors, viz. the Nemean Lion and the Hydra. Certainly there would be no point in planning to destroy the sword here, as it did not contribute to the murders as did the other weapons. A further objection is the lack of correspondence with 1231ff. which mentions arrows, *bow*, and club. The natural correction is therefore to *arcum* (Bentley, Withof 121, and Jortin 406 all seem to have reached this conclusion independently). The motive for the interpolation is not easily divined—perhaps no more than a desire for variety—but its source appears to have been ps.-Sen. *HO* 869 *Herculeus ensis*. The fullest discussion is in Ageno 115ff.

1231–34. The natural assumption is that each of these four clauses is addressed to a different victim, viz. to the three sons individually and to Megara (not necessarily in that order); certainly *tibi . . . tibi* in 1231 seems likely to be enumerative, cf. 584f. *tu . . . tu* with comm. Yet, as is often the case, one cannot be certain that Sen. had a firm grasp of such details—for example, one might have expected a vocative to distinguish Megara from the boys—and it is not inconceivable that he thinks of more sons (n.b. *liberi* 1227) than the three of Act IV.

1231 tela. Arrows, as at 119, 990, 1110, 1127, 1234.

1235ᵇ–36. The idea of blaming hands as well as weapons was perhaps suggested by Ov. *Met.* 2.615f. (Apollo, after shooting Coronis in error) *nec non arcumque manumque / odit cumque manu temeraria tela, sagittas.* But the notion of *burning* the offending hands surely derives from

[433]

Commentary: Act V

the action of Mucius Scaevola, mentioned several times by Sen. in the *philosophica* (*Prov.* 3.4f., *Clem.* 1.3.5, *Ben.* 4.27.2, 7.15.2, *Ep.* 24.5, 66.51ff., 98.12).

infaustas meis . . . telis. An arresting expression, but perfectly clear: the hands "brought ill-fortune" upon the weapons by guiding them in the murders and so destroying their renown; the hands were the agency of Juno's will, the weapons only the passive instrument. Some have taken *meis . . . telis* as an ablative of accompaniment (so e.g. Miller), but that would require *cum*; as an ablative without a preposition the phrase would have to be instrumental, which seems highly unlikely here.

1236 novercales manus. A powerful compression: they have treated the children as a proverbial stepmother might, and have done the work of his own stepmother Juno. The Senecas appear to provide the first three extant uses of *novercalis*: the elder has *novercalibus oculis* at *Contr.* 4. *exc.* 6, and the younger writes *novercales manus* again at *Ag.* 118.

1237–39. Both here and in 1263–66 E identifies H.'s interlocutor as Amphitryon, whereas A calls him Theseus. A is proved to be wrong in the second of these interchanges by Theseus' words at 1272–74; Amphitryon's third-person references to himself at 1263f. may have led to the alteration by A. This, coupled with A's general tendency to tamper with attributions (1021 comm.), makes it likely that E is also right in the present exchange. Against this it might be argued that the call to Herculean endurance in 1239 should belong to Theseus (cf. 1274–77 and Eur. 1248ff., 1410ff.), but on the other hand 1237 looks like Amphitryon resuming his argument of 1200f. The vocative *Theseu* in 1242 does not affect the issue (though it may have influenced A) because H. turns rapidly from one addressee to another (n.b. *referte* 1244, *pater* 1245, cf. 1173ff.).

1237f. Amphitryon takes up the argument he used briefly at 1201. Similarly in *Oed.* and *Phoen.* Jocasta argues that unconscious wrongdoing creates no guilt, whereas Oedipus implicitly rejects the argument: *Oed.* 1019 *fati ista culpa est: nemo fit fato nocens* (but contrast 1024ff.), *Phoen.* 451ff. *error invitos quoque / fecit nocentes, omne Fortunae fuit / peccantis in nos crimen,* 538f. *scelere . . . nullo nocens, / erroris a se dura supplicia exigens,* 554f. (cf. also ps.-Sen. *HO* 884ff., 898ff., 983). It is noteworthy that the distinction between guilt and innocence of intention is not made in Eur. *Her.* or Soph. *OT,* but appears prominently in the later *OC* (266ff., etc.).

Commentary: Act V

The use of *scelus*/*error* [153] to make the distinction is Ovidian (for earlier approximations to it v. *TLL* 5.2.817.63ff.), *Met.* 3.141f. *at bene si quaeras, Fortunae crimen in illo, / non scelus invenies; quod enim scelus error habebat?*, *Tr.* 3.11.34, 4.10.89f. *scite, precor, causam . . . / errorem iussae, non scelus, esse fugae*. In prose Sen. generally uses *error* in a more Stoic sense, with reference to the initial mistake of judgment which leads to wrongdoing. He has little use for legalistic distinctions of guilt and innocence, because no human soul is innocent in the fullest sense (*Ira* 2.28).

1237 usquam (E). More stylish than A's *umquam*, which appears to be a normalization (further corrupted in CS to *numquam*). *Usquam* is not infrequently so used, e.g. *Ep.* 93.9 [*Natura*] *quemadmodum omnia, quae usquam erant, cluserit*, i.e. "how she has brought to an end all things that ever existed," *QNat.* 6.29.3.

nomen . . . addidit. For *addere* used in a context where the name is erroneous cf. *Pha.* 197 [*libido*] *titulum furori numinis falsi addidit*. Earlier instances of *nomen addere* include Afran. *tog.* 57 R² *novercae nomen huc adde impium*, Ov. *Met.* 5.525, 9.357 (apart from the technical sense of adding a *cognomen* to existing names, *TLL* 1.585.82ff.). There is no need for Avantius' much-repeated conjecture *indidit*.

1239–45. The connection of thought between the two speeches is clear enough, though not explicit. Amphitryon attempts to recall his son to "heroic" behavior; but he, unable to achieve Herculean endurance as recommended, seizes upon the only other approach suggested by the Herculean *persona*—violent retribution, destruction of the evil.

1239 Hercule. For the significant use of the proper name cf. Eur. 1250 ὁ πολλὰ δὴ τλὰς Ἡρακλῆς λέγει τάδε; and 1414 ὁ κλεινὸς Ἡρακλῆς ποῦ κεῖνος ὤν; (both spoken by Theseus); however the usage is familiar in Sen. (v. comm. on 631, 635, 1016), and this instance of it need not have been borrowed direct from Eur.

molem mali. This alliterative phrase occurs several times before Sen.: Lucr. 3.1056; Cic. *Cat.* 3.17, *Tusc.* 3.29 (in tragic trimeters); Livy 5.37.1; Ov. *Met.* 11.494; for similar alliterative patterns v. *TLL* 8.1379.44.

---

153. For *saepe error* in 1238 Moricca reads *saepe furor* (*furor* from E); but a trochaic–pyrrhic sequence of words, violating word accent, is avoided by Sen. at the beginning of the line (Strzelecki 72).

Commentary: Act V

1240. Similar phrasing to *Pha.* 250 *non omnis animo cessit ingenuo pudor*.

1242–95. Originally Hercules demanded his arms with the intention of destroying them (1229ff.), but now he clearly intends to use them for suicide. The dilemma that consequently faces the others, whether to return arms to their owner when he is mentally unbalanced, was a familiar moral issue: it is discussed somewhat simplistically at Plato *Rep.* 331c 5ff. and Cic. *Off.* 3.25.95 (in these cases the owner is actually insane), and "supplying arms to an angry man" (or "madman") became a proverbial act of folly, cf. Publ. Syr. 184 *eripere telum non dare irato decet*, Sen. *Ira* 1.19.8 *male irato ferrum committitur*. Here the situation is made more complex by the danger that a refusal will further enrage H.: hence Amphitryon and Theseus avoid responding to the demand directly.

1242f. mihi / . . . mihi. Although certain disyllabic words appear frequently at line-end, e.g. *meus, domus, locus, potest, mare, nefas*, Sen. generally avoids repeating the same word, or the same root with a different ending, in successive line-ends, unless this has an expressive purpose. I have noticed only seven examples of nonexpressive repetition (here, *Pha.* 1053f., *Ag.* 111f., 152f., 404af., 661f., *Thy.* 81f.: at *HF* 446f. *Iovem* is a *Stichwort*). That suggests a more deliberate avoidance than e.g. by Eur. (v. Collard on *Suppl.* 17). Even so careful a writer as Vergil has occasional instances, which are not necessarily to be seen as a sign of incomplete revision (v. Eden on *Aen.* 8.396f.).

arma arma. Such repetition in a call for weapons is a very ancient custom, cf. e.g. Aesch. fr. 140 N ὅπλων ὅπλων δεῖ, *inc. inc. trag.* 138 R^2 *tela famuli tela propere ferte*, V. *Aen.* 2.668 *arma viri ferte arma*, Ov. *Met.* 11.377f. *arma, / arma capessamus*, v. N-H on Hor. *Carm.* 1.35.15.

propere. Much more common in drama than in other verse. Seneca has it six times in the tragedies and once in tragic rhesis at *Apocol.* 7, and there are some fifty uses of it or *properiter* in Republican drama (thirty-eight in Plaut., six in Ter., six in the comic and tragic fragments). In contrast, no nondramatic poet before Sen. employs it more than once, except for Vergil who uses it thrice.

1243–45. Such rehearsal of antithetical alternatives is characteristic of declamation, cf. e.g. Sen. Rhet. *Contr.* 1.7.8 *si non tenuero causam, fame moriar; si tenuero, hoc tantum consequar, ne fame moriar*, 1.8.15 *Diocles Carystius dixit*: ἂν ἐπιτύχῃς, μίαν προσθήσεις ἀριστείαν· ἂν ἀποτύχῃς, τρεῖς ἀριστείας ἀπολέσεις. In this Act of *HF* alone cf. 1247f.,

1269f., 1278, and in the other tragedies e.g. *Tro.* 510ff., *Phoen.* 76, 455ff., *Med.* 194, *Pha.* 1184f.

1245 recede. That is, to avoid suffering the same fate as the rest of my family.

mortis inveniam viam. A sad echo of characteristic Herculean confidence, cf. 276f. *inveniet viam / aut faciet*. For the phrase cf. *Phoen.* 5f. *melius inveniam viam, / quam quaero, solus*, where the *via* is similarly that leading to death; and more generally V. *Aen.* 2.645 *ipse manu mortem inveniam.*

1246–48. Amphitryon is not suggesting that H. might deny the paternity of Jupiter, which is never questioned in the play except by Lycus. The issue is simply what name H. *calls* him by (n.b. *nominis, vocas*): *altor* would mean that he regards him simply as a foster-father, whereas *parens* would imply a closer relationship akin to that of adoption. But there is no question of H. actually regarding Amphitryon as his biological father. (Consequently *generis* in 1246 means "family," not "birth" [Miller]). *Altorem* is the certain Renaissance correction for the transmitted *auctorem*, which does not yield a meaningful contrast with *parentem*.

sacra. For this unusually abstract sense of the noun, "sacred ties," cf. Ov. *Her.* 16.3 *hospitii temeratis . . . sacris*, *OLD* s.v. *sacrum* 5.

1248 seu tu parentem. For *tu* used in one half of a disjunction cf. 1169f. comm.: here it may also have some affective force, indicating Amphitryon's preference for the second of the two alternatives.

1249 parce . . . precor. On this prayer formula v. 1015 comm.

1250f. For the wording cf. particularly the nurse's appeal to Phaedra at *Pha.* 267 *solamen annis unicum fessis, era*; earlier she appealed by her grey hairs (246f.), as Amphitryon above. *Annis fessis* diverges slightly from such precedents as Lucr. 3.458 *aevo fessa*, Ov. *Met.* 7.163 *fessusque senilibus annis*, by making *fessus* agree with the noun indicating age, cf. later e.g. Luc. 2.128 *fessa senectus*, Tac. *Ann.* 14.33 *fessa aetas*.

unicum lapsae domus firmamen.[154] Such phrases with an abstract noun, modified by *unicus*, describing a person are a speciality of Sen.

---

[154] "Quomodo firmamen, si domus iam lapsa?" asked N. Heinsius 224, but the objection is overliteral; cf. e.g. Ov. *Tr.* 1.6.5 *te mea supposita veluti trabe fulta ruina est,*

Trag. The nouns are usually neuter, so *solamen* thrice, *auxilium*, *levamen* once each, but there is one feminine instance with *spes*. Two examples, which are particularly close in that they share a dependent *domus*, are *Med.* 945f. *unicum afflictae domus / solamen*, and *Tro.* 462 *spes una Phrygibus, unica afflictae domus*. Earlier instances include Cic. *Rep.* 3.8 *cum ipse sis quasi unicum exemplum antiquae probitatis*, Livy 3.26.8 *spes unica imperii populi Romani, L. Quinctius*.

Firmamen first appears in Ovid, who likes to coin nouns in *-men*; in fact it is found only at *Met.* 10.491 and here in classical Latin. The usual form is *firmamentum*, applied to individuals at Afran. *com.* 241 R², Sen. *Cons. Helv.* 20.4.

1251 lumen. This metaphor may have been inspired by Eur. 531 ὦ φίλτατ' ἀνδρῶν, ὦ φάος μολὼν πατρί, also spoken by Amphitryon to his son though at a different stage in the play; but as the usage "light" = "salvation" is not uncommon (see below), the point cannot be proved, though it is noteworthy that the usage does not occur elsewhere in Sen. Trag.

D. Heinsius' conjecture *columen*[155] has been noted by most editors and accepted by some, but to my knowledge no justification of it has been given, and none exists. Heinsius may have disliked the change of metaphor from *firmamen* to *lumen*, but such variation is by no means unparalleled in phrases of this kind, cf. e.g. Cic. *Cat.* 4.11 *lucem orbis terrarum atque arcem omnium gentium*, Sen. *Phoen.* 1f. *regimen ... levamen*, *Tro.* 124 *columen patriae, mora fatorum*, 961, ps.-Sen. *Oct.* 168 *modo sidus orbis, columen augustae domus*. Admittedly *lumen* when applied to a person usually has the connotation "leading light, luminary" (*TLL* 7.2.1851.15ff.) rather than "salvation" as in the present passage, but there is at least one parallel for the latter, at Livy 1.39.3 *scire licet hunc lumen quondam rebus nostris dubiis futurum praesidiumque regiae adflictae*. These connotations are, after all, determined by context rather than by the word itself: thus *lux* can suggest either "salvation" (e.g. Enn. *trag.* 57 R², Plaut. *Stich.* 618) or "glory" (e.g. Sil. 13.707).

---

where it would be equally futile to object that a ruin cannot be shored up. For *lapsae domus* in a phrase of this sort cf. *Tro.* 766 *o decus lapsae domus*. There is no need to write *quassae domus* with Heinsius, or to follow Bothe in accepting the Renaissance reading *lassae domus*, which no doubt arose through error (cf. 646 comm.); *lassae* would come awkwardly after *fessis*.

155. It is not always noted that N. Heinsius 224, wanting the metaphor of *quassae domus firmamen* to be continued more consistently, wrote *columen afflictae*, whereas his father had been content with *columen afflicto*.

1252ᵇ–57. These are standing complaints of Amphitryon's, cf. 207ff. The present lines in particular are reminiscent of Ov. *Her.* 9.33ff., where Deianira speaks of Hercules' absences and lists the various dangers that make her afraid for him; this passage (itself an elaboration of Soph. *Trach.* 27ff.) is echoed by Sen. again at *Pha.* 91. Cf. also Megara's complaint of how rarely she sees her husband in the *Megara* ([Moschus] 4) 41ff.

1253 fructus laborum. An echo, probably unintentional, of 655f. *fructu . . . laborum.*

dubium mare. Specific nautical dangers encountered by H. include a storm en route to Erythia (Pherecydes ap. Athen. 11.471d) and another that blew him to Cos (Hom. *Il.* 14.250ff., 15.18ff.), and the shipwreck alluded to at 319–24 above. This and similar phrases (*Med.* 942, *Thy.* 292, *Ag.* 407a) may well derive from Ov. *Pont.* 4.10.10 *iactatus dubio per duo lustra mari.*

1255 manibus aut aris. Though the allusions to Eryx and Busiris are clear enough, the nouns make an ill-balanced pair. One wishes that Sen. had written *gregibus aut aris* with Bentley (for *greges* in allusion to Diomedes cf. ps.-Sen. *HO* 1898), but that is paleographically improbable, and no other convincing correction suggests itself. The paradosis is given some support by the wording of 481ff. *ipsius opus est caestibus fractus suis / Eryx et Eryci iunctus Antaeus Libys, / et qui hospitali caede manantes foci / bibere iustum sanguinem Busiridis.*

1257 fructum. Repeated from 1253, with emphatic effect.

1258–62. Once again, as at 920ff., Hercules rejects a crucial appeal from Amphitryon. With characteristic self-centeredness he dwells on his own situation, and cannot conceive that his father's need for him might provide a reason for living on. Contrast Sen.'s own decision in a comparable situation (v. Introduction fn. 54), and note his comment *ille qui non uxorem, non amicum tanti putat ut diutius in vita commoretur, qui perseverabit mori, delicatus est* (*Ep.* 104.3).

Chapman adapts the passage in *Byron's Tragedy* 5.4.69–72:

> Why should I keep my soul in this dark light,
> Whose black beams lighted me to lose myself?
> When I have lost my arms, my fame, my mind,
> Friends, brother, hopes, fortunes, and even my fury.

Commentary: Act V

1258f. Possibly derived from Eur. 1301f. τί δῆτά με ζῆν δεῖ; τί κέρδος ἕξομεν / βίοτον ἀχρεῖον ἀνόσιον κεκτημένοι; The phrasing is similar to Evander's words at V. Aen. 11.177f. *quod vitam moror invisam Pallante perempto / dextera causa tua est*; both this parallel and the balance of Sen.'s sentence suggest that *morer* is transitive.

1259ᵇ–61ᵃ. It has been suggested that this enumeration, by someone contemplating suicide, of the disadvantages of his life has a Stoic ring, cf. Cic. *Fin.* 3.60 *in quo enim plura sunt quae secundum naturam sunt, huius officium est in vita manere: in quo autem aut sunt plura contraria aut fore videntur, huius officium est e vita excedere*, Sen. *Ep.* 70.5 *cogitat semper, qualis vita, non quanta sit. si multa occurrunt molesta et tranquillitatem turbantia, emittit se*. But it is equally natural for non-Stoics to count over their losses in desperate straits, cf. e.g. Ov. *Her.* 7.5f. (Dido) *sed merita et famam corpusque animamque pudicam / cum male perdiderim*, Shakespeare, *Macbeth* 5.3.24ff. "And that which should accompany old age, / As honor, love, obedience, troops of friends, / I must not look to have." Furthermore, to apply the term *bona* to such things is blatantly non-Stoic, because Stoics are adamant that the only *bonum* is virtue.

1260. For the line filled with nouns in asyndeton cf. 32 comm.

mentem. Some translators say "reason," but H. is not now insane; the meaning is closer to "self-possession, composure, mental control," for which cf. Cic. *Phil.* 3.24 *adlato nuntio . . . mente concidit*, Hor. *Carm.* 1.13.5f. *tunc nec mens mihi nec color / certa sede manet*, Ov. *Met.* 14.519 *mox ubi mens rediit et contempsere sequentem*, OLD s.v. 10.

manus. That is, as reliable instruments for the doing of glorious deeds. For the thematic importance of the *manus* v. 122 comm.

1261 etiam furorem. This paradoxical point was developed more fully in the last ode, cf. 1094–99 with comm. For the "capping" of the list by a paradox cf. particularly *Phoen.* 313ff. *hic Oedipus Aegaea transnabit freta / iubente te . . . / iubente te praebebit alitibus iecur, / iubente te vel vivet.*

1263 perimes parentem. For the play on similar-sounding words v. introduction to Ode II.

1264. Possibly influenced by V. Aen. 2.538f. *qui nati <u>coram</u> me <u>cernere</u> letum / fecisti et patrios foedasti funere vultus*, particularly as *coram oc-*

[440]

Commentary: Act V

curs only here in Sen. Trag. For postposition of prepositions v. 148 comm.

docui. For the pointed use of *docere* cf. 242 [*Hydram*] *docuit mori*, *Pha.* 593f. *qui timide rogat, / docet negare.* Here a single occasion is exaggerated into a whole course of "instruction," as at *Ag.* 932, *Thy.* 310 *in patre facient quidquid in patruo doces.* Such passages, like those involving "learning" (398 comm.), illustrate Sen.'s exploitation of "precedent" as a basis of rhetorical points, cf. 386–96 comm.

1265 memoranda . . . facta. The same phrase at 442; for *memorandus* with connotations of *praeclarus* v. *TLL* 8.693.62ff.

1266f. Hercules' response to Amphitryon reveals his characteristic harshness; it also shows once again his inflexibility in assimilating the present situation to that of the labors, despite the essential differences between them. In the *de Ira* Seneca frequently commends the exercise of *venia*, on the grounds that to refuse it is to deny what one needs oneself, along with every other member of the human race (1.14.2, 2.10.2, 4, 2.34.2ff., 3.26.3, cf. *Ag.* 267). Hercules' present situation perfectly illustrates the argument. Like H., Sen. criticizes the inconsistency of those who seek *venia* for themselves after denying it to others (2.34.4 *quam saepe veniam qui negavit petit! quam saepe eius pedibus advolutus est, quem a suis reppulit!* cf. *Clem.* 1.6.2), but his point is quite different from H.'s, that they should have shown *venia* earlier, in order to qualify for it themselves. (At *Clem.* 2.7 Sen. draws a sharp distinction between *venia* and *clementia*, condemning the former and approving the latter; but that is later than either *Ira* or *HF*, and in any case such philosophical rigor should not be looked for in the present literary context.)

1268 hoc unum meum est. *Hoc unum* takes up 1266 *unius . . . criminis* (rhetorically H.'s answer is well turned), and refers to the same thing, namely, the murder of his family. *Meum est* in this context echoes two key phrases of the play, 938f. *si quod parat / monstrum, meum sit* and 1200 *tacuere: nostrum est.*

1270 fatum. The A reading is clearly superior to E's *factum*. H. is arguing that there are honorable reasons for Amphitryon to help him commit suicide, the other two being *pietas* and a desire to free his *virtus* from taint. *Triste fatum* suggests both H.'s innocence of intention (cf. *fortuna* in 1272) and his anguish over what has happened, and so implies that he is worthy of Amphitryon's pity, which would be a motive

Commentary: Act V

in keeping with the other two. *Factum* is less clear in its implications: it seems to suggest a motive of punishment or vengeance that is less appropriate in the context. For *factum* displacing *fatum* in MSS cf. *HF* 184 (*factis* S¹, corr. m.2 mg.), *TLL* 6.355.19ff.

violatum decus virtutis. E's *violatum* has a strong claim against A's *violatae*, and is preferred by Leo and later editors. Logically speaking, the appeal for Amphitryon's help is not based on Hercules' glorious *virtus* but on the *damage* to it, which needs to be made good: the *ab urbe condita* construction is needed, and *violatum decus* provides it. But one cannot ignore the fact that the word group *violatae decus virtutis* is more characteristic of Sen.'s style, nor the possibility that E has accommodated the participle to the gender of *decus*. Can A's phrase give the required sense? In the context it will have to mean "the glory of my *virtus*, which has been tainted (but can be cleansed by my suicide)"; *decus* will have a proleptic sense, indicating a glory that is at present obscured but will reappear. But the phrase comes close to a nonsensical implication that it is his tainted *virtus* which is glorious. On balance I prefer E's version.

1271f. vincatur . . . Fortuna. The struggle to conquer Fortune, in the sense of remaining impervious to her wiles and attacks, is a constant theme of Sen.'s prose works. But a stoic-sounding phrase does not make a Stoic character—unless one is willing to admit Medea too into that category (cf. *Med.* 159, 176, 520 *fortuna semper omnis infra me stetit*): cf. comm. on 1027f. *habes / mortem paratam*.

1272f. Theseus shows characteristic tact and thoughtfulness in his intervention, cf. 640–44 with comm. on 641 *regina*. For the adjective *patriae* in place of *patris* v. comm. on 255 *paterni*. The phrase *preces efficaces* occurs twice in Livy (1.9.16, 9.20.20); *efficax* appears only here in Sen. Trag., and is rare in poetry generally (unusable in dactylic verse).

1274–77. For Theseus' weeping cf. 1173–79 with comm. Euripides' Theseus similarly argues (1248ff., 1410ff.), that Hercules' identity and achievements require that he show heroic endurance now. In Sen., Amphitryon has already introduced the argument briefly at 1239.

1277 irasci. His emotional reactions have already been identified as *ira* at 1167 and 1220.

1278. For such rehearsing of alternatives v. 1243–45 comm.: an especially similar example is *Phoen.* 76 *si moreris, antecedo; si vivis, sequor*. On

Commentary: Act V

the use of present tenses (*vivo, morior*) with reference to the future in a protasis v. comm. on 1284 *arma nisi dantur* (p. 446).

1279 purgare terras propero. Both the ill-considered haste and the impossible wish for a world cleansed of evil are characteristic of Hercules: for the first cf. 636f., 937f.; for the second, the prayer at 927ff. He is completely immersed again in the Herculean *persona*, though its manifestations are far from what Theseus had hoped for.

1279ᵇ–81ᵃ. That is, the *image* of such a monster (himself) floats before him: there are several instances of *oberrare* with dat. used of something present in the imagination, cf. 1146, Curt. 8.6.26 *tanti periculi . . . imago oculis oberrat*, Stat. *Theb.* 8.436f. *dilecta genis morientis oberrant / Taygeta*, Pliny *Pan.* 61.7, *Ep.* 9.13.25; similarly *errare* Ov. *Tr.* 3.4.57, Sen. *Thy.* 281f. *tota iam ante oculos meos / imago caedis errat*.

Once again Hercules is reducing the situation to the formula of the labors; but here the equation has a deeper significance than intended, for he has indeed taken on some qualities of his monstrous foes. (For various earlier hints of this, v. comm. on 46, 944–52, 965–81. The author of *HO* characteristically turns suggestion into bald statement, 55f. *Hercules monstri loco / iam coepit esse.*)

iamdudum. A psychological interpretation is tempting, viz. that Hercules here "expresses a long-standing repulsion with himself. It is as though throughout his labors, not merely now, he has felt himself to be a monster" (A. Rose 1978 124). But it seems more probable that *iamdudum* is rhetorical exaggeration (for which cf. 614f. *iam diu pateris manus / cessare nostras, Iuno, Tro.* 308f., *Thy.* 1022), here indicating the reason for H.'s haste (*propero*).

1281–84. The combination of hesitation with (self-)encouragement to take some fearful action is frequently encountered in Sen. Trag., often with similar phrasing, cf. *Tro.* 1000ff. *Pyrrhe quid cessas? age* e.q.s., *Phoen.* 44ff., 91ff. *dextra quid cessas iners* e.q.s.; *Med.* 41ff., 895ff. *quid anime cessas* e.q.s., 988ff.; *Pha.* 592ff.; *Ag.* 49ff., 108ff., 192ff., 228ff.; *Thy.* 241f., 283f., 324f.; [*HO* 307ff., 842ff.]. For a similar phrase from prose cf. *Prov.* 2.10 (Cato's soliloquy before suicide) *aggredere, anime, diu meditatum opus.*

1282 labore bis seno. "The twelvefold labors," not "the twelfth labor" (cf. Miller). The same phrase at *Ag.* 812f., where the meaning is clear: *tuus ille bis seno meruit labore / adlegi caelo magnus Alcides* (v. Tarrant ad loc.). These appear to be the earliest instances of a singular distribu-

[443]

tive used in place of a plural cardinal or distributive number in such phrases, v. B. Löfstedt, *Eranos* 56 (1958) 196.

1283f. Hercules' hesitation may be purely momentary, caused by suicide having become a more immediate reality in 1281f. (similar reactions to the prospect of immediate action at *Med.* 895ff., 988ff., *Thy.* 283f.). In that case we infer from the vehemence of what follows that he has fiercely quelled the hesitation and determined to prevent its recurrence. Alternatively *cessas* may indicate a recognition that the delay since 1242ff. has really been due to his own lack of insistence. (Passages in which the hesitation is more than momentary, among those cited on 1281–84, include *Phoen.* 44ff., 91ff.; *Med.* 41ff.; *Ag.* 192ff.; cf. also *Thy.* 176ff. *ignave, iners, enervis* e.q.s.) In that case the vehemence of 1285ff. shows that he is determined to put an end to such trifling.

ignave. The younger Gronovius' conjecture *ignava*, continuing the address to the *dextra*, has been accepted by most modern editors and may be right. In support of it one may cite *Med.* 895ff., where the MSS have *quid, anime, cessas? . . . amas adhuc, furiosa* but Bentley's correction to *furiose* is shown to be necessary by 904 *violentus hauri*. But a contrary example is provided by Clytemnestra's words at *Ag.* 192f. *accingere, anime . . . pigra, quem exspectas diem?*, and the sense of the present passage does not strongly require the change. Indeed, the second interpretation of *cessas* given above, if correct, would probably exclude *ignava*, as the question would follow on not just from 1281f. where the *dextra* is addressed, but from H.'s behavior ever since 1242.

fortis in pueros modo. Compare *Tro.* 755 *fortis in pueri necem*, and for the scornful use of *fortis* also *Phoen.* 45 *fortis in partem tui*, "brave only against a part of yourself."

1284 pavidasque matres.[156] The single actual instance (Megara) is generalized, a natural and effective rhetorical device, cf. *Phoen.* 479 *post ista fratrum exempla* (Eteocles), *Med.* 278f. *quidquid etiam nunc novas / docet maritus coniuges* (Creusa),[157] 1007f. *i nunc, superbe, virginum thalamos pete, / relinque matres* (Creusa, Medea). (Cf. the use of *solere* to exaggerate a single instance into a regular habit, v. 1101[bis] comm.) In Eur. *Her.* cf. 455 ὁμοῦ γέροντες καὶ νέοι καὶ μητέρες (Amphitryon, the boys,

---

156. E's weak variant *pavidamque matrem* is proved wrong by hiatus within the trimeter, which Sen. avoids. For E's tendency to make an overliteral "correction" to the number of a noun v. 683f. comm.

157. I suspect the *HO* author is clumsily imitating the device at 555 *amare discat coniuges* (*coniugem* E).

[444]

Megara—a close parallel to the present passage), 1309f. τοὺς εὐεργέτας / Ἑλλάδος (H. himself); other instances from Greek tragedy in Leo I 150 n. 3.

1284ᵇ-94. "Ercles' vein" indeed, and a magnificent example of it. What separates such a passage from the empty rantings of a Laertes (*Hamlet* 5.1.250ff.) is our sense that Hercules could indeed do these things; or at least that it is not inappropriate for a man of such mighty achievements to *imagine* that he could do them. Such threats befit a Hercules, a Medea (Sen. *Med.* 32ff., 424ff.) or a Tamburlaine (e.g. Pt. 2, 5.3.48ff.), but not a Laertes. The notion of pulling down buildings upon himself and others is somehow in keeping with the essence of the Herculean hero and the ambivalence of his strength, as is shown by the similar feats of Samson and of Cleomedes of Astypalaea, the "last of the heroes" (Kirk 207; for Cleomedes v. Paus. 6.9.6). A more specific appropriateness to H. is seen in the way in which the first threat, in 1285-87ᵃ, foreshadows in hyperbolic terms his eventual mode of death (cf. 132f. with comm. and 1216f.). And the last threat, to pull down the heavens, is suggested by H.'s knowledge that he had the strength to *support* them on an earlier occasion: as Juno said in a slightly different sense, *posse caelum viribus vinci suis / didicit ferendo* (69f.).

Although the passage is rhetorically magnificent and mythologically appropriate, it is also, of course, evidence of the most extreme *ira* and *furor*. On the willingness of the *iratus* to cause universal destruction in satisfaction of his anger, v. 1167 comm. Particularly revealing is the impiety that runs through these lines: this is evident in the threat to the *Bacchi lucos*, especially in view of Bacchus' importance in Thebes; talk of razing temples with their gods is comparable with Lycus' *templa supplicibus suis / iniecta flagrent* (506f.); and the threat to bring the heavens down can only be compared with the ravings of the mad-scene (964ff.).

1284ᵇ-87. *Aut* in 1287, omitted by the paradosis, is supplied by several recc. including the manuscript of the tragedies used by Trevet. Haplography of *t* or an illegible compendium for *aut* may have contributed to causing the omission. Instead of inserting this *aut*, some critics have preferred to alter 1284ᵇ *arma nisi dantur* (E: A *dentur*) *mihi* into a command, so that the *aut* of 1285 means "otherwise, or else" (*OLD* s.v. 7); Bentley wrote *arma reddantur mihi* using E, Cornelissen 175f. *arma cito dentur mihi* using A. But this use of *aut* is infrequent in poetry, and I have found no instance of it in Sen. Trag. (though *vel* is so used *Oed.* 518). Furthermore, H.'s threats in 1285-87ᵃ and in 1287ᵇff. are al-

ternatives, as each would result in his death, and asyndeton between them is therefore improbable.[158] The second objection applies also to Axelson's proposal (1967 50f.) to retain *arma nisi dantur mihi* but write *altum omne Pindi Thracis excidam nemus* in 1285. In addition there is no parallel in Sen. Trag. or ps.-Sen. for *omnis* immediately preceded by an adjective qualifying the same noun: the usual word order is *omne clarum facinus, omne vipereum genus* (*HF* 247, *Oed.* 587).[159]

1284 arma nisi dantur. The protasis of a condition sometimes has a present indicative though referring to future time; in such cases the reference is often to the *immediate* future, though by no means always so, cf. Ernout-Thomas, *Syntaxe Latine*, 2d ed. 375f. In verse cf. e.g. V. *Aen.* 3.606 *si pereo, hominum manibus periisse iuvabit*, Ov. *Met.* 15.594f. *quem vos nisi pellitis urbe, / rex erit*. Instances in Sen. Trag. in which the apodosis has a future indicative include *Tro.* 307, *Med.* 299, *Pha.* 596, *Thy.* 541; all of these except *Pha.* 596 are like the present passage in containing a threat.

1285 Pindi Thracis. Properly Thessalian, but Sen. puts it in Thrace again at *Oed.* 434f., and similarly calls Thessalian Ossa "Thracian" at *Thy.* 812. Poets' geography is particularly vague about northern regions: Statius seems to put Ossa and Othrys in Thrace at *Theb.* 2.82, 4.655, and Valerius Flaccus conversely moves Haemus from Thrace to Thessaly at 1.24; see also comm. on 533–46 ad fin.

excidam. *Excindam* (i.e. *exscindam*) in P and C is probably an error that arose independently in those two MSS, as ETS agree on *excidam*. *Exscindam* would mean "smash, destroy," less appropriate in the context than "cut down," sc. for burning.

1286–87ᵃ. It seems likely that *Bacchi lucos* refers to forests where the Bacchae roam in his worship, rather than to specific sacred groves: similarly the *Bacchi nemus* on Tmolus at Ov. *Fasti* 2.313 may well be the

---

158. There is no change of construction such as accounts for the single *vel* at Lucr. 5.383, *pace* Munro ad loc. who regards the paradosis as authentic here.

159. Axelson 1967 48ff. objects to insertion of *aut* in 1287 on two grounds: first, that elision over a definite pause is not permitted by Sen. at this point in the line, and second, that only *et* and a limited number of monosyllables, not including *aut*, are allowed in this position when there is elision (statistics in Zwierlein 1983 215). But the first point is not entirely persuasive as "pause" is so vague a term: there seems to be a definite pause in some examples with *et*, e.g. *HF* 101. And the second point carries little weight because the conjectural *at* in 622, which is clearly essential, is equally unparalleled in elision in this position. (Other monosyllables are allowed in elision over a pause in thesis elsewhere in the line, e.g. *Tro.* 656 *at*, *Thy.* 894 *ut*.)

vineyards mentioned in the same line. Probably *lucos* is the object of *cremabo* rather than *excidam*, as that moderates the boldness of *iuga* = "mountain forests" (paralleled, so far as I know, only later, at Mart. 7.27.6). So it refers to Cithaeron (cf. 134f. with comm.), the holy mountain of Bacchus (*Oed.* 483); if governed by *excidam* it would mean the Thracian forests roamed by the Bacchae (cf. e.g. Ov. *Met.* 6.587ff., Sen. *Oed.* 432ff.).

1287f. tota cum domibus suis dominisque tecta. The traditional, and I think correct, interpretation is that *domibus* means "households." Axelson 1967 50 n. argues that *tecta* here means "city," a usage associated particularly with Sen. and Lucan, cf. Sen. *Thy.* 404, 1010f. *non tota ab imo tecta convellens solo / vertis Mycenas, Phoen.* 322, *Ag.* 613, Luc. 2.479f. *at te Corfini validis circumdata muris / tecta tenent, pugnax Domiti,* 3.73, 368, 5.270 (earlier cf. Ov. *Met.* 4.86). Therefore, in his view, *domibus* can and does have its normal meaning of "houses." But it is difficult to accept that this transferred sense of *tecta* is so distinct from its usual sense that it could have the dependent phrase *cum domibus suis* = "with its dwellings." Furthermore, the parallel *cum deis templa* suggests that the *cum* phrase should indicate the *inhabitants* of the *tecta*.

Others have found it difficult to believe that *tecta cum domibus suis* could mean "buildings with the households living in them." I think it conceivable, but I have no parallel for *tecta* and *domus* juxtaposed in these senses. Certainly the required sense of *domus* is well established, and *domibus dominisque* makes a neat alliterative pair, cf. Cat. 68.68, 156, Mart. 11.93.3f. *o magnum facinus crimenque deorum, / non arsit pariter quod domus et dominus,* Juv. 3.72 *magnarum domuum dominique futuri, TLL* 5.1. 1912.49ff., 1955.82ff. If emendation is thought necessary, Peiper's *laribus* for *domibus* is attractive as it parallels *cum deis* below: *domibus* will be explained as an erroneous gloss which has crept into the text. Damsté's *regna* for *tecta* also merits consideration.[160]

cum ... dominis ... tecta, cum deis templa. Particularly similar instances of the pointed use of *cum* are ps.-V. *Aetna* 610f. *ardebant ... mitia cultu / iugera cum dominis,* Ov. *Met.* 1.286f. *cumque satis arbusta simul*

---

160. Munro 76 proposed to take *tota* with *iuga*, omitting the conjectural *aut*, and then to write *cumve opibus suis*. But one very rarely finds *-ve* corresponding to *aut* in a formal disjunction, viz. when the existence of alternatives is indicated *ab initio* as in 1285: there are no examples in Sen. Trag., and elsewhere I know only of Stat. *Theb.* 4.608f. *non ille aut sanguinis haustus, / cetera ceu plebes, aliumve accedit ad imbrem.* Of course *-ve* not infrequently appears in poetry as a variation on *aut* when alternatives are simply being tacked on, as at 1324f., *Med.* 411f. *non procellosum mare, / Pontusve ... aut vis ignium.*

[447]

pecudesque virosque, / tectaque cumque suis rapiunt penetralia sacris. More generally cf. e.g. Ov. *Met.* 2.215f. *cumque suis totas populis incendia gentes / in cinerem vertunt; silvae cum montibus ardent,* 3.92, 561, Sen. *HF* 258, 968, *Phoen.* 108, *Ag.* 550, *Thy.* 1009 *ad chaos inane regna cum rege abripis.*

Cum deis templa recalls the Senecan paradox of temples falling upon their own gods, for which v. 506f. comm. Properly, of course, *deis* refers to the gods' statues (cf. K. F. Smith on Tib. 2.5.22, *TLL* 5.1.859.7ff.), but in the context it clearly suggests an identification of the gods with their statues, which carries impious overtones.

1291 immissa incident. The assonance strengthens the expressive force of the elision, cf. 1312 *impresso induam.*

1293f. The *onus* is the vault of heaven, once supported by H. (for *onus* in that context cf. 425 *nullo premetur onere, qui caelum tulit,* Petron. 139 poët. 3 [Hercules] *onus caeli tulit*); that experience contributes to his notion that he can destroy it (cf. 68ff.). It "separates off the gods" in the sense that they are above it; the phrase suggests that it is one of the *rerum termini,* the natural boundaries of the universe (290 comm.). Thus the periphrasis emphasizes first the weight that would fall on H., and second the consequent destruction of universal order, both physical and hierarchical.

The probable meaning of *media parte . . . mundi* is "in the central part of the heavens": so the whole periphrasis from *onus* to *superos* is equivalent to *medium caelum.* H. might attack it directly by piling up mountains (cf. 970ff.), or indirectly by undermining its foundations, e.g. where Atlas supports it. Less probably *media* might mean "between the gods and subcelestial creatures," with *mundi* in the sense of "universe."

Several interpreters have followed Gronovius in taking the *onus* to be the earth (cf. Ov. *Fasti* 6.270, 276), but it is difficult to see how H. could bring that down upon his own head.

1295 reddo arma. Seneca can leave Amphitryon's motives to be inferred from the context: clearly he sees that withholding the arms only enrages Hercules. The terseness perhaps indicates Amphitryon's reluctance, cf. e.g. 1186ff. and Creon's brief answers to Oedipus' longer questions at *Oed.* 509ff., also Thyestes' grudging *eatur* and *accipio* (*Thy.* 488, 542).

The A reading *redde* cannot be separated from A's speaker-attributions in 1295–1300[a], which are rightly rejected as inferior to E's by modern editors. Lessing and others make Amphitryon say *redde arma* to a servant, but such an address would have to be differentiated by a plural, a vocative or an *aliquis* (*HF* 506, 1053, *Oed.* 862); an address to Theseus (Thomann) would also require some identification.

digna genitore Herculis.   For the notion cf. 509f. with comm. on *genitor Alcidae*.

1296. Rhetorically the line is effective, emphasizing Hercules' guilt (hence Amphitryon's reply) and suggesting the appropriateness of his using this *spiculum* against himself. Theatrically there is a minor difficulty: one assumes that this arrow has just come from offstage with the other *arma*, but H. shot only one boy with an arrow (992ff.), and that arrow was lying onstage at 1194ff. The problem could be solved in production if someone picked up the arrow at 1295 and added it to the *arma*, but the inconsistency in the writing is undeniable, if unobtrusive.

1297 immisit.   So E: *emisit* A. Characteristically A has interpolated a more obvious and less forceful word. *Immisit* will presumably mean "shot it at the boy by means of your hands" (*TLL* 7.1.471.34ff.), not "put it into your hands" as *TLL* weakly takes it (ibid. 469.77).

1298ᵇ–99.   Such descriptions of physical symptoms of emotion are often found in Sen. Trag., v. 414 comm. What follows makes it likely that Amphitryon addresses this to Hercules, drawing attention to his distressed condition (v. 1301ᵇ–13 comm.), though *ecce* is not impossible in self-address (cf. *Med.* 992).

cor palpitat.   In verse the usual verbs are *salire* or *micare* (*TLL* 4.931.51ff., 8.929.36ff.). *Palpitare* is more prosaic (of the *cor* Cic. *Nat. D.* 2.9.24, Sen. *Ira* 3.14.3), at least until Ovid introduces it into verse at *Met.* 6.560 (of a severed tongue); Sen. follows suit only here.

cor . . . pectus . . . ferit.   *Pectus* is Gronovius' alteration of the transmitted *corpus* (apparently made by inadvertence rather than conjecture, as he wrongly attributes *pectus* to E). These two words are often confused in codd. (*TLL* 4.999.63ff.), and here there is the additional possibility that *cor* brought *corpus* to the scribe's mind. *Pectus* is obviously the right word, cf. Hom. *Il.* 13.282 ἐν δέ τέ οἱ κραδίη . . . στέρνοισι κατάσσει, Aesch. *PV* 881 κραδία . . . φρένα λακτίζει, *Ag.* 996f., Plaut. *Aul.* 627, *Cas.* 414 *cor . . . pectus tundit*, Ov. *AA* 3.722 *pulsantur trepidi corde micante sinus*, Luc. 7.128f. The case is different at *Phoen.* 159f. *effringe corpus corque tot scelerum capax / evelle*, where many editors alter *corpus* to *pectus* with N. Heinsius: there the context might be thought to support *corpus*, as Oedipus is speaking of his whole body as guilty and deserving punishment. But I see no reason why the two passages should stand or fall together.

1300ᵇ–1313. There are several problems concerning the dramatic developments in these lines, fortunately capable of solution. First, 1301ᵇ *pande, quid fieri iubes?* forms part of Amphitryon's speech in the paradosis, but we must transfer it to Hercules with Rutgers 494 and modern editors: the words make little sense if spoken by Amphitryon, but they are perfect as a first sign of wavering on H.'s part, and *nihil rogamus* is then a perfect response (see below on these phrases). But that raises another difficulty: what new argument of Amphitryon's has prompted this crucial hesitation of Hercules? None, if *scelus* in 1300ᵇ means H.'s suicide. A further difficulty lies in lines 1302–10, where Amphitryon indicates that he is on the very point of death (*hanc animam levem . . . in ore primo habeo*), and will not survive H.'s suicide but die simultaneously with him. How will his death come about, and why does he convey the idea with such indirection in 1302–7? If we take into consideration 1298ᵇ–99 *ecce quam miserum metu / cor palpitat pectusque sollicitum ferit* and 1317f. *artus alleva afflictos solo, / Theseu, parentis*, the interpretation becomes clear. Amphitryon has reached a state of physical collapse by 1300,[161] and he is warning, there and in 1302ff., that the shock of his son's death will be too much for him. The *scelus* which H. is about to commit in 1300 is therefore not suicide, but causing Amphitryon's death. We must imagine *ecce iam facies scelus / sciens volensque* (1300ᵇ–1301ᵃ) as accompanied by some stage-business (perhaps Amphitryon falls to his knees, perhaps to the ground) which will explain both it and the otherwise obscure statements of 1302ff. This interpretation of *scelus* is confirmed by 1313 *hic hic iacebit Herculis sani scelus*, which is so similar to 1300ᵇ–1301ᵃ that the *scelus* must be the same, viz. responsibility for Amphitryon's death. Furthermore the parallel between *ecce* in 1298 and 1300 suggests that they should have a parallel function, and on this interpretation they have, i.e. to draw Hercules' attention to Amphitryon's physical condition.

Some commentators have interpreted Amphitryon's talk of imminent death in 1302–10 as a threat to commit suicide simultaneously with H. Again it will be necessary, in my view, to imagine some stage-business in 1300, to account both for H.'s wavering in 1301 and for the allusiveness of 1302–7. Presumably Amphitryon seizes a weapon and

---

161. For collapse from emotional stress as a feature of Sen.'s dramaturgy v. 1044ᵇ–48ᵃ comm., and cf. particularly *Tro.* 949ff. with a reference to closeness to death (952) comparable to that at 1308–10.

directs it at himself. The *scelus* will, as on the other interpretation, be responsibility for Amphitryon's death. But this interpretation loses the parallel between the *ecce* statements of 1298f. and 1300f., and the special point of *artus alleva afflictos solo* (1317): in addition, the words *hanc animam levem / fessamque senio nec minus fessam malis / in ore primo teneo* refer more naturally to a state of collapse, caused by age and exhaustion, than to imminent suicide (for *in ore primo teneo* of an aged person's soul cf. *Ep.* 104.3 *spiritus . . . in ipso ore retinendus est*, 30.14 *senilis anima in primis labris esset*). Of course Amphitryon does threaten suicide in 1311f., but that is a new development caused by anger at H.'s hesitation and by determination to force his hand.

1300ᵇ–1301ᵃ. For the warning against adding intentional wrongdoing to unintentional cf. *Phoen.* 451ff. *error invitos adhuc / fecit nocentes . . . / . . . hoc primum nefas / inter scientes geritur*.

1301 volensque sciensque. The standard formula is *sciens prudensque* or vice versa, cf. Otto s.v. *scire* (2) with the *Nachträge*, adding *Leges XII Tab.* 8.10, Cael. ap. Cic. *Att.* 10.9A.5. Seneca uses that at *Cons. Marc.* 17.6, but varies it (apparently the first to do so) here and at *Ira* 2.28.5 *volentes scientesque*, *Ep.* 114.21 *scientes volentesque*.

pande, quid fieri iubes? Logically absurd, as it is evident what Amphitryon wants. But this is a battle of wills, not a logical argument. Hercules has lost the initiative, but he will not yield ground too quickly. Compare Oedipus at a similar moment of tactical retreat at Soph. *OT* 655 οἶσθ' οὖν ἃ χρῄζεις . . . φράζε δὴ τί φῄς.

The paradosis makes the question part of Amphitryon's speech (see comm. on 1300ᵇ–13). In this case the sense will be "Are we both to die or not" (which would suit either explanation of Amphitryon's imminent death)—though one would have expected a question with *utrum*. *Nihil rogamus* will then mean "I do not *request* either course, I simply fall in with your decision" (cf. *Phoen.* 74 *non deprecor, non hortor*, spoken by Antigone, who will similarly live or die with Oedipus). But this is strained, and attribution of the question to Hercules allows a more natural interpretation.

1302 nihil rogamus. Sensing that he has the advantage, Amphitryon refuses to humble himself by further pleading, but makes H. accept full responsibility. The response reflects Amphitryon's bitterness at having had to plead so long unsuccessfully, cf. *Ben.* 2.5.1f. *nihil aeque amarum quam diu pendere; aequiore quidam animo ferunt praecidi spem suam quam trahi . . . inde illae voces, quas ingenuus dolor exprimit, "fac, si quid facis," et "nihil tanti est; malo iam mihi neges."*

noster in tuto est dolor. Not an easy phrase, but it cannot mean "cessat dolor" (Gronovius), and Kingery's interpretation, "sorrow is assured for me in any case," is contradicted by everything that follows, especially in 1305. The reference must be to Amphitryon's certainty that he will not suffer grief over H.'s death, because he will die simultaneously with him; for *tutus* used in reference to the immunity from suffering guaranteed by death or its imminent prospect, cf. *Tro.* 574 *tuta est, perire quae potest debet cupit*, 655f. *hic suam poenam potest / sentire, at illum fata iam in tuto locant* (*hic* being Astyanax, *illum* the dead Hector). The best interpretation is therefore "My grief is safely protected from any increase" (so Pierrot). The alternative, "My prospective grief at your death is safely forestalled," is conceivable but less probable. For prepositional phrases such as *in tuto* v. comm. on 1307.

1304 nec tu. "Not even you," cf. *OLD* s.v. *neque* 2b, Sen. *Phoen.* 201 *iam nec tu potes*.

1306 sic . . . ut. "With this proviso, that . . .": for this restrictive use of *sic* followed by *ut* cf. *OLD* s.v. *sic* 8b, Quint. 10.1.31 *historia quoque alere oratorem . . . potest. verum et ipsa sic est legenda ut sciamus plerasque eius virtutes oratori esse vitandas*.

causam. That is, the question of guilt or innocence, which is the issue at hand: Hercules believes death will establish his innocence (1278); Amphitryon argues that it will make him guilty of parricide, without even the excuse of madness.

1307 in arto . . . et ancipiti. Seneca appears to be the first to use *in ancipiti*, "in a critical situation," here and at *Tranq.* 10.6 (*TLL* 2.25.54f.). *In arto* is generally taken to mean virtually the same as *in ancipiti* ("at hazard" Miller, cf. *OLD* s.v. *artum* 2). But the metaphorical use of *in arto/-um* normally denotes restricted scope, circumscribed opportunities (Hor. Ars P. 134, Ov. *Met.* 9.683, Sen. *Tranq.* 9.3, *Cons. Marc.* 16.1 *quis autem dixit naturam maligne cum mulierum ingeniis egisse et virtutes illarum in artum retraxisse?*). So the primary sense of the phrase here is probably that H. has restricted room for maneuver, his choices are strictly limited (*aut vivis aut occidis*). At Livy 26.17.5, another alleged example of *in arto* = "in danger" (*OLD* ibid., *TLL* 2.723.83ff.), the reference is surely to the physical restrictions of the *fauces*.

Seneca is fond of such prepositional phrases: often they simply indicate physical location (*in aperto, convexo, extremo* [*HF* 695], *propinquo*, etc.), but frequently they connote doubt, difficulty, or danger, cf. *in abdito* "in secret" (*Ira* 1.1.5), *in alto* "in mystery" (*Oed.* 330, *Ben.* 7.1.5), *in*

Commentary: Act V

ambiguo (*Oed.* 208), *in dubio* (*Ag.* 59, *Cons. Pol.* 5.3), *in incerto* (*Pha.* 630, *Thy.* 422, *Brev. Vit.* 9.1, *QNat.* 5.18.4), *in lubrico* (*Cons. Marc.* 9.2, *Ep.* 71.28, 75.10, 84.12), *in praecipiti* (*Ag.* 58, *Ep.* 23.6), *in praerupto* (*Ep.* 84.12). The opposite indication, of safety, etc., is less common, but note *in plano, in sereno, in tuto* (*HF* 1302 al.).

1308 occīdis. This verb is common in early poetry but used very sparingly from Lucretius on, presumably because of prosaic connotations (*TLL* 9.2.344.64ff.). Seneca shares the general caution, using it only four times in the tragedies. (Meter identifies *occĭdere* at *Pha.* 1117, *pace TLL* ibid. 68). Clearly it is chosen here for the sake of a pun on *occĭdis*, which would be a more normal alternative to *vivis*.

levem. That is, ready to fly forth, cf. *Tro.* 952 (of Hecuba, similarly in a state of collapse) *quam tenuis anima vinculo pendet levi!*, *Ep.* 30.14 *senilis anima in primis labris esset nec magna vi distraheretur a corpore.*

1309. For *fessus senio* and similar phrases v. 1250f. comm.; *fessam malis* gives a further parallel to the appeal of Phaedra's old nurse, cf. *Pha.* 247 *fessumque curis pectus.*

1310 (animam) in ore primo teneo. For this vivid phrase indicating that one is on the point of death cf. Herondas 3.3f., *Anth. Pal.* 5.197.5 βαιὸν ἔχω τό γε λειφθέν . . . ἐπὶ χείλεσι πνεῦμα. In Latin it is associated particularly with Sen., who intensifies it by addition of *primus*, cf. *Ep.* 30.14 cited above, *QNat.* 3 *praef.* 16 *in primis labris animam habere*, *Ep.* 104.3 *spiritus . . . revocandus et in ipso ore retinendus est*. *Teneo* must be given its full force: he restrains the soul which would otherwise fly forth.

1311 non feram . . . moram. For such phrases, more usually with *pati*, v. 588 comm.

1312. The MSS have *letale ferro pectus impresso* (E: *impressum* A) *induam*. Now *letale* cannot qualify *pectus*, for it does not mean "close to death," nor does it yield any meaning if taken proleptically.[162] But it is a perfectly appropriate adjective for *ferrum*, and *letale ferrum* is therefore

---

162. Peiper in the Teubner of 1867 wrote *letale ferro vulnus impresso induam* (*letale vulnus* occurs twice in Vergil), but *vulnus* is a strange object for *induam*, particularly in the absence of an indirect object; to write *l. f. vulnus impressum induam* (cf. particularly *Ep.* 24.8 *impressit deinde mortiferum corpori vulnus*, *Anth. Lat.* 396 [attributed to Sen.] 3f. *victori vulnus iniquo / mortiferum impressit*) would palliate the difficulty but not, I think, remove it.

likely to be the correct beginning of the line. Given that, the most natural correction of the line as a whole is to *letale ferrum pectori impressum induam* (found in some recc. and in early editions, e.g. Ascensius) or *l. f. pectori impresso induam* (not previously proposed).[163] For *induere* in the sense of "thrust into" cf. *Phoen.* 180 *nunc manum cerebro indue* and *HF* 1028 *pectori en tela indue* (corrected from *pectus in tela indue*) with comm. ad loc.; for similar phrases with other verbs cf. *Oed.* 1036f. *pectori infigam meo / telum*, *Pha.* 1177 *pectori ferrum inseram*, *Ag.* 723 *flammas pectori infixas meo*. What of the choice between *impressum* and *impresso*? *Impressum induam* would give a pleonastic participle of the *submersasque obrue puppes* type, which, though paralleled (1064f. comm.), is not particularly common in Sen. Trag. But Sen. does like lines composed of two noun-modifier pairs and a verb: although he prefers the interwoven pattern (v. comm. 216–48 ad fin.), lines without interweaving are also deliberately created, cf. e.g. 29 *aeterna bella pace sublata geret*, 666, 670 *fulgorque dubius solis affecti cadit*, 691f., *Thy.* 692 *letale carmen ore violento canit*. For the idea of the breast thrust onto the sword cf. e.g. *Oed.* 964 [*oculi*] *vulneri occurrunt suo*, 341 *iuvenca ferro semet imposito induit*.[164]

letale ferrum. *Letale* is not simply decorative, but rather suggests the effect of the weapon on this occasion, cf. e.g. V. *Aen.* 4.73 *haeret lateri letalis harundo*, Ov. *Met.* 11.515, 13.391f. [*Aiax*] *in pectus . . . , / qua patuit ferro, letalem condidit ensem*. The *ferrum* is presumably Amphitryon's own sword: other civilians too have swords when needed (*Oed.* 935, *Pha.* 706). Some commentators have supposed the *letale ferrum* to be one of H.'s poisoned arrows, but the text gives no indication of the elaborate stage-business that would be involved in purloining one of them.

---

163. One may exclude *l. f. in pectus impressum induam* as Sen. does not elsewhere repeat *in* with *imprimere* or *induere*, and rarely allows monosyllables other than *et* in elision at the beginning of the third foot (1284ᵇ–87 comm.).

164. Withof's conjecture (127) *senile* for *letale*, with the rest of the line reading *ferro pectus impresso induam*, is supported with enthusiasm by Zwierlein, *Gnomon* 38 (1966) 683 and 41 (1969) 765. Its effect would be one of pathos, as at ps.-Sen. *HO* 1857f. *agedum senile pectus, o miserae manus, / pulsate*, which might be thought an echo of it. Zwierlein points out that *senile* would take up 1308f. *animam levem / fessamque senio*, cf. the repetition in *Med.* 258ff. *senio trementem debili atque aevo gravem / patrem peremptum queritur et caesi senis / discissa membra*. But that might actually be thought an argument against it, in view of the evident change of mood in the middle of 1310. After the pathos of *hanc animam levem* e.q.s., Amphitryon becomes disgusted with Hercules' hesitation, and summons his energies to force the issue; decisiveness is now more evident than pathos. The chief objection to *senile* is paleographical: Zwierlein diligently parallels corruption of *s* to *l*, *t* to *n* (!) and *i* to *a*, but fails to explain why all three should have occurred together.

Commentary: Act V

1314. For repeated *parce* with *iam* cf. V. *Aen*. 3.41f. *iam parce sepulto, / parce pias scelerare manus*, *Anth. Lat.* 236 (to Corsica, attributed to Sen.) 7 *parce relegatis: hoc est, iam parce solutis*. *Geminatio* is a feature of prayers and *parce* is a ritual word (N-H on Hor. *Carm.* 2.19.7), so repetition of *parce* is not uncommon in prayers and hence in appeals; for the tendency to alliteration on *p* in prayers v. 1015 comm. For the phrase *iam parce* cf. also Sen. *HF* 1015, *Phoen.* 40, *Med.* 1004; ps.-Sen. *HO* 982; in several instances, as here, *iam* strengthens the appeal but has little temporal reference.

1315f. Characteristically, Hercules reduces the morally demanding situation to the simplistic formula of the labors (cf. 1267ff., 1279ff.). The comparison may derive ultimately from Eur. 1410f., at a similar point in the action, but note that there H. rejects the parallel implied by Theseus: Thes. οὕτω πόνων σῶν οὐκέτι μνήμην ἔχεις; / Her. ἅπαντ' ἐλάσσω κεῖνα τῶνδ' ἔτλην κακά. Again characteristically, the Senecan Hercules thinks here of his self-image, and in his next speech of his own immediate future; his concern for Amphitryon in 1317ff. is purely momentary.

1315 succumbe, virtus. A similar phrase is used by Ovid at *Met.* 5.177 *verum ubi virtutem turbae succumbere vidit*, but of a purely involuntary yielding to larger numbers.

imperium patris. Perhaps echoed in the letter in which Sen. describes his own rejection of suicide out of consideration for his father: *itaque imperavi mihi ut viverem* (*Ep.* 78.2). But the different source of the *imperium* points to the difference in quality between the two men's decisions (v. Introduction fn. 54).

1316 eat ad. "Be added to," a rare variation on *accedat ad*: *OLD* s.v. *eo* 21c cites only two parallels, Ov. *Medic.* 66 and Luc. 10.343, whereas *TLL* 5.2.650.33f. knows of none.

labores . . . Herculeos. The phrase occurs elswhere in poetry at Hor. *Carm.* 1.3.36 (in a rather different sense), Prop. 3.18.4, Ov. *Fasti* 5.696.

1317 vivamus. The unusual sense-pause has an expressive effect. It conveys resignation again at *Tro.* 475f. *quod captis sat est, / vivamus*. For a different but equally fine effect with *vivere* cf. *Med.* 19f. *mihi peius aliquid, quod precer sponso, malum est: / vivat*. Other instances where emotional and/or rhetorical expressiveness is heightened by a sense-pause

Commentary: Act V

early in the line include (e.g.) *HF* 51f. (v. ad loc.), *Tro.* 888f. *hoc derat unum Phrygibus eversis malum,* / *gaudere, Med.* 25f., 881f.

artus alleva. Ovidian, cf. *Met.* 6.249 *allevet artus,* 7.343; *allevare* does not appear in verse before Ovid.

1318ᵇ–21ᵃ. Hercules shows a momentary concern, at least, for his father; but he characteristically allows his obsession with guilt to prevent warm human contact (cf. 638–39). Equally characteristically, Amphitryon does the opposite, expressing his love for his son through physical contact, cf. 624 *teneo,* 628 *amplexus,* 1257 *fructum tui tactumque et aspectum peto.* The passage derives from Eur. 1233f., where Theseus rather than Amphitryon is the interlocutor: H. φεῦγ', ὦ ταλαίπωρ', ἀνόσιον μίασμ' ἐμόν. / Thes. οὐδεὶς ἀλάστωρ τοῖς φίλοις ἐκ τῶν φίλων. But the archaic concern about transmitting pollution in the technical sense has disappeared in Sen.; and the idea that love outweighs such scruples is effectively conveyed by action, rather than explicitly stated.

1318f. contactus pios . . . refugit. More Ovidian phrasing, cf. *Met.* 7.239f. *refugitque viriles* / *contactus.*

1321–41. "Where can I turn?" is a natural dilemma of tragic characters, who often point out the objections to places that might be suggested (1331f., 1341), cf. Eur. *Med.* 502ff. νῦν ποῖ τράπωμαι; πότερα πρὸς πατρὸς δόμους, / οὓς σοὶ προδοῦσα καὶ πάτραν ἀφικόμην; / ἢ πρὸς ταλαίνας Πελιάδας; καλῶς γ' ἂν οὖν / δέξαιντό μ' οἴκοις ὧν πατέρα κατέκτανον, *Her.* 1281ff., 1285ff. ἀλλ' Ἄργος ἔλθω; πῶς, ἐπεὶ φεύγω πάτραν; / φέρ' ἀλλ' ἐς ἄλλην δή τιν' ὁρμήσω πόλιν; / κἄπειθ' ὑποβλεπώμεθ' ὡς ἐγνωσμένοι κ.τ.λ., Enn. *trag.* 231f. R² (Medea) with Jocelyn ad loc. (217f. J), Acc. *trag.* 231f. R² (Thyestes), Cat. 64.177ff., Sen. *Med.* 451ff.; compare also Plato *Apol.* 37d, Cic. *de Orat.* 3.214 (Caius Gracchus) *quo me miser conferam? quo vertam? in Capitoliumne? at fratris sanguine madet,* e.q.s., *Mur.* 88, ps.-Sall. *Inv.* 1.

The development of this commonplace into the notion that the whole universe rejects Hercules (1331ff.), while entirely Senecan and in keeping with the play's themes (see comm. on 1329ᵇ–41), may well have been suggested by a parallel development in Eur., 1295ff. φωνὴν γὰρ ἥσει χθὼν ἀπεννέπουσά με / μὴ θιγγάνειν γῆς καὶ θάλασσα μὴ περᾶν / πηγαί τε ποταμῶν. In that case, Eur.'s mention of sea and rivers probably triggered Sen.'s use of the *locus* "no river or sea can purify me" in 1323–29. Certainly there is a notable shift of theme from 'exile' to 'purification' (1323) and then back to 'exile' (1329).

1323–29. "Living water" from streams, rivers, or the sea was used in purification (v. Frazer on Ov. *Fasti* 2.45); hence the literary conceit of the crime so heinous that neither the greatest rivers nor the whole Ocean can cleanse it, cf. Aesch. *Cho.* 72ff., Soph. *OT* 1227f. οἶμαι γὰρ οὔτ' ἂν Ἴστρον οὔτε Φᾶσιν ἂν / νίψαι καθαρμῷ τήνδε τὴν στέγην, *Anth. Pal.* 14.71.3f., Lucr. 6.1075ff. (a witty transference of the *locus* to the indelibility of purple dye) *dirimi qui non queat usquam, / non si Neptuni fluctu renovare operam des, / non mare si totum velit eluere omnibus undis*, Cat. 88.5f. *suscipit, o Gelli, quantum [sceleris] non ultima Tethys / nec genitor Nympharum abluit Oceanus*, Sen. *Pha.* 715ff. *quis eluet me Tanais aut quae barbaris / Maeotis undis Pontico incumbens mari? / non ipse toto magnus Oceano pater / tantum expiarit sceleris.*

Of the two Senecan passages, that in *Pha.* is primary, as the Amazon theme of that play explains the choice of Tanais and Maeotis (cf. *Pha.* 401 *Tanaitis aut Maeotis* and my comm. on *HF* 533–46). The present passage expands on that in *Pha.*, adding several rivers. These additions contribute little conceptually, but when rhetoric has such energy and poise, much may be forgiven it. The catalogue of exotic places is characteristically Roman (cf. Canter 8off., Walter 136 n. 272), but not inappropriate to Hercules the world-traveler.

In postclassical literature the most famous example of the *locus* is Shakespeare, *Macbeth* 2.2.57–60:

> Will all great Neptune's ocean wash this blood
> Clean from my hand? No: this my hand will rather
> The multitudinous seas incarnadine,
> Making the green one red.

If this has a classical source (not necessarily the case), a likely candidate would be that in *Pha.*, particularly if Shakespeare knew it in Studley's translation: "not Neptune, graundsire grave, / With all his Ocean foulding floud can purge and wash away / This dunghill foule of stane." But the impossibility of cleansing *hands* of their bloodguilt comes closer to *HF* than to the other classical passages.

1323 Persica. Seneca's student Nero also misplaces the Tigris in Persia, fr. 1.1f. Morel *quique pererratam subductus Persida Tigris / deserit*. For the poetic looseness of the term cf. e.g. *Apocol.* 12 poët. 8–12 where "Parthian," "Persian," and "Mede" are interchangeable, and *Pha.* 325 where Persia is coupled with Lydia in reference to Omphale. Diod. Sic. 2.11.2 and Curt. Ruf. 5.1.14 say incorrectly that the Tigris flows through Media.

[457]

1324. Both rivers were well known for their swift currents: for the Tigris cf. Strabo 11.14.8 ὀξύτητα, Dio Cass. 68.28.4 ὀξύτητος, Varro *LL* 5.20.100 *vehementissum*, Hor. *Carm.* 4.14.46 *rapidus*, Curt. Ruf. 4.9.16 *violentus*; for the Rhine, Strabo 4.3.3 ὀξύς, Caes. *BGall.* 4.10.3 *citatus*, 4.17.2 *rapiditatem*, Tac. *Ann.* 2.6 *violentiam cursus servans*, *Anth. Lat.* 425.1 *rapidum*. Epithets for rivers are sometimes transferred from neighboring peoples (for the Rhine cf. Ov. *Fasti* 1.286 *tradiderat famulas iam tibi Rhenus aquas*, Luc. 2.52 *indomitum Rheni caput*), and *ferox* may have some such color here (Miller renders "warlike Rhine"), as is certainly the case at Sil. 4.61 *Rhodanumve ferocem*; however, Luc. 4.138 uses *ferox* of another river with no such connotation.

1325. The gold of Tagus is a commonplace in Roman poetry, cf. Cat. 29.19 *amnis aurifer Tagus*, Ov. *Am.* 1.15.34, ps.-V. *Cat.* 9.52 *aurea . . . flumina*, Sen. *Thy.* 354f. *[quidquid] aut unda Tagus aurea / claro devehit alveo*; for further examples v. Otto s.v. *Tagus* with *Nachträge*, *RE* 7.1564.13ff., 4A.2025.54ff. Both here and in *Thy.* Sen. provides something more elaborate than the usual passing reference. In such a context *gaza* is not simply a synonym for *aurum* but carries connotations of exotic foreign treasure (more usually Eastern, see Austin on V. *Aen.* 2.763), cf. *Med.* 483–85.

1326ᵇ–27. Maeotis, like Tanais, is borrowed from *Pha.*, see comm. on 1323–29. The *mare* is the Maeotis itself, cf. 683 comm. Seneca's liking for heavy trisyllabic words in the penultimate position in the line leads him into unusual diction in both *arctoum* and *transfundat*. *Arctous* is first attested in Sen. Trag. (four times), and *transfundere* occurs here for the first time in verse, so far as I know, though there are several earlier uses in prose.

1328 Tethys. On this high-poetic metonymy for "ocean" v. 887 comm. Note that one of the few pre-Senecan uses of it occurs in the same *locus*, at Cat. 88.5.

1329 altum. "Deep" both physically (i.e. indelible) and metaphorically ("grave, heinous," *OLD* s.v. 15c).

1329ᵇ–41. A final appearance of the play's constant theme concerning the universal significance and fame of Hercules' exploits (cf. comm. on 30–32, 37f. ad fin., 250, 1054–62, 1108–14, 1284ᵇ–94), with a most effective reversal of its usual meaning. "The expansive terrain has now, with pathetic irony, become the guarantor of the hero's contamination. . . . The very lands and stars that knew his fame now, by that knowledge, prevent him from hiding himself and his guilt" (Owen 307).

These lines are echoed in the words of the grief-stricken Thésée at Racine, *Phèdre* 5.7.14–18:

> Confus, persécuté d'un mortel souvenir,
> De l'Univers entier je voudrais me bannir.
> Tout semble s'élever contre mon injustice.
> L'éclat de mon nom même augmente mon supplice.
> Moins connu des mortels je me cacherais mieux.

1330 recedes, petes. Contrast 1327f. *me, meas,* 1331 *perdidi.* Such changes of person tend to occur in emotional self-address: compare Sostratos' speech in Men. *Dis Exap.* which shifts from third person (19) to first (20) to second (23) to first (25), also Sen. *HF* 109ff. *furis . . . me . . . apparo,* Med. 126 *meis,* 128 *tuae,* 131 *nefandae virginis,* Thy. 177 *reor,* 179 *agis.*

ortum an occasum. He is known at both ends of the earth, cf. 37f. comm. ad fin. On the singular forms see comm. on 24 *ortus.*

1332–34. On such physical reactions on the part of the universe to events on earth, v. 1054–62 comm. Here Sen. leaves some ambiguity about whether the reaction actually occurs or is in the eye of the beholder; the latter was the case in Hercules' madness (939ff.) and in Cassandra's vision (*Ag.* 726ff.).

1332f. astra transversos agunt / obliqua cursus. Similar phrasing to *Pha.* 676f. *sidera obliquos agent / retorta cursus,* one of those passages in which people *pray* for such a universal reaction to crime (v. comm. on 1202ff.); and to *HF* 928f. *astra inoffensos agant / aeterna cursus,* where H. prays that such universal disorder will *not* occur.

1333ᵇ–34ᵃ. The sight of Cerberus terrified the Sun, cf. 6of. *viso labantem Cerbero vidi diem / pavidumque Solem* with comm. ad loc. and on 594–604.

1334 meliore vultu. The slightly prosaic-sounding phrase *vultus bonus* does not occur in verse before Ovid, and then only in one section of *Met.* (5.501, 7.862, 8.677). In Sen. Trag. cf. *Thy.* 936 *redeant vultus ad laeta boni,* also *Med.* 751 *pessimos induta vultus* (of the moon).

o fidum caput. Loyalty is one of Theseus' leading characteristics. Ovid treats the *fides* shown by Theseus to Pirithous as exemplary, cf. *Tr.* 1.3.66 *o mihi Thesea pectora iuncta fide!* and 1.5.19, 1.9.31, *Pont.* 2.3.43, 2.6.26, 4.10.74f., 78: later instances in Otto s.v. *Theseus*. This gives a special edge to Phaedra's sarcasm at Sen. *Pha.* 92 *praestatque nuptae quam solet Theseus fidem.*

This is the only instance in Sen. Trag. where *caput* is used affectionately of another person, whereas κάρα is more commonly so used in Greek tragedy: for other emotional uses v. 920 *capitis invisi* comm. For *fidus* with *caput* so used cf. Prop. 2.1.36 *fidele* (also Ov. *Ibis* 85 *male fido*, Val. Max. 6.8.3 *perfidum*). The fact that *fidus* is more common than *fidelis* in Sen. Trag. (18:6), whereas the opposite is the case in his prose (4:20), is due in part, at least, to metrical convenience.

1336f. A reference to Theseus' having loyally accompanied Pirithous to the underworld despite his impious designs (with *arbiter* in the sense of "witness"), and to his having succored Oedipus in Athens (with *arbiter* meaning "one having jurisdiction over"). Probably *semper* is not based solely on those episodes (though they would be an ample basis for such a generalization in Senecan rhetoric, cf. 1101bis comm.), but rather indicates that Hercules perceives, from Theseus' presence and concern, that his attitude is comparable on this occasion. At any rate that interpretation is suggested by other hyperbolic uses of *semper* in Sen. Trag., where the reference is both to the past and to the present, cf. *Tro.* 164 *o longa Danais semper in portu mora* (viz. at Aulis and now at Troy), *Pha.* 128, 1164f. *o dure Theseu semper, o numquam ad tuos / tuto reverse* (Theseus' return from Crete and now from the underworld), 1167. *Amas* is an interesting usage, erotic in reference to Pirithous but nonerotic vis-à-vis Oedipus and Hercules.

Though the primary reference is to these three cases, the wording carries overtones of a mild and humane attitude towards wrongdoing, such as Sen. advocates in the *de Ira*, cf. 1.14.2f. *non est autem prudentis errantes odisse; alioqui ipse sibi odio erit . . . quanto humanius mitem et patrium animum praestare peccantibus et illos non persequi, sed revocare!* and compare his commendation of *venia* (1266f. comm.) and later of *clementia* (*Clem.* passim). Of course H. himself is quite incapable of such an attitude (1267).

1338 vicem. "A return, recompense," i.e. a practical paying back, cf. Ov. *AA* 1.370 *non poteras ipse referre vicem*, *Am.* 1.6.23 *redde vicem meritis*, Sen. *Med.* 482 (Medea to Jason) *redde . . . vicem* (where Miller and Costa mistranslate).

Commentary: Act V

1338ᵇ–41ᵃ. There is a mirror image of this prayer at *Pha.* 1217ff., where Theseus prays Hercules to return him to the underworld: n.b. 1218f. *ereptos mihi* / <u>*restitute*</u> *manes.* Note also 1211f. *sidera et manes et undas scelere complevi meo:* / . . . *regna* <u>*me norunt*</u> *tria.* The similarities between *HF* 1223ff. (v. ad loc.) and *Pha.* 1225ff. are less specific, being largely accounted for by the commonplace *dehisce, Tellus*.

redde me. For the rhetorical use of this phrase with similar implications, "return me to what *appears* worse," cf. Sen. Rhet. *Contr.* 3.4 *redde me hosti,* Sen. *Ben.* 2.11.1 *redde me Caesari,* 7.10.6.

1339 reductum. For the pleonastic participle cf. 1064bis comm.

1339f. meque subiectum tuis restitue vinclis. "And restore me, as your substitute, to your chains," i.e. let me take the place of punishment which you have vacated in the underworld. For *restituere* used of "restoring" a substitute rather than the original cf. Sen. *Ep.* 91.14 (on the burning of Lyons) *veri simile est certaturos omnes ut maiora celsioraque quam amisere restituant,* Suet. *Tib.* 48.1 *munificentiam . . . exhibuit . . . quibusdam dominis insularum, quae in monte Caelio deflagrarant, pretio restituto*: here the usage is clarified by the addition of *subiectum*. Admittedly *subicere* = "to substitute" does not occur elsewhere in Sen., but other authors use it so (Cic. *Or.* 27.92, anon. *B.Alex.* 26.2, Quint. 3.6.28, 6.3.74). A less probable but conceivable alternative is that *subiectum* might mean "placed in, loaded with," cf. [Tib.] 3.7.117 *libera Romanae subiecit colla catenae* and the phrase *sub vinculis habere* at *Tranq.* 9.2; but that would make the use of *restitue* more difficult.

I see no strong justification for conjecture. Bentley and (independently) Leo wished to replace *restitue* with *substitue*. The phrase would then mean "substitute me for yourself as one placed in your chains." There is perhaps something to be said for *subiectum-substitue* as parallel to *reductum-redde*. But apart from one's reservations about the required meaning of *subiectum*, word-order suggests that *tuis . . . vinclis* should be governed at least ἀπὸ κοινοῦ by the first word of 1340, which is the case with *restitue* but becomes impossible with *substitue* ("substitute me for your chains"!).

For the notion of filling Theseus' vacant place in the underworld cf. *Pha.* 1153 *constat inferno numerus tyranno* (sc. by Hippolytus' death): cf. also *HF* 500 *dest una numero Danais: explebo nefas,* with comm. ad loc.

1341 novit. That is, "and so it will not receive me," cf. 1331.

Commentary: Act V

1341ᵇ–44. Seneca follows Eur.'s "Athenian" version of H.'s purification, 1323f. ἕπου δ' ἅμ' ἡμῖν πρὸς πόλισμα Παλλάδος. / ἐκεῖ χέρας σὰς ἁγνίσας μιάσματος κ.τ.λ. Other versions are extant: Apollod. 2.4.12 says that he was purified by King Thespius in Boeotia, ps.-Sen. *HO* 907f. that he cleansed himself in the waters of the Cinyps in Libya, Hyg. *Fab.* 32 and Serv. auct. ad V. *Aen.* 8.300 that he sought advice from Apollo as to how he should purify himself, but was not favored with a reply.

1342f. Mars had a daughter Alcippe, whom Halirrothius, son of Neptune, raped or attempted to rape in Athens. Mars killed him, and on Neptune's complaint he was then tried by the gods on the Areopagus, the first murder trial to be held there. The general understanding is that he won acquittal (stated specifically by Din. 1.87, Apollod. 3.14.2 and Schol. Hom. *Il.* 18.483); purification, important in Sen. for the parallel with Hercules, is not mentioned in any other source, though the need for it is indicated at Eur. *IT* 945f. ἔστιν γὰρ ὁσία ψῆφος, ἣν Ἄρει ποτὲ / Ζεὺς εἶσατ' ἔκ του δὴ χερῶν μιάσματος. Other references to the episode are listed at *RE* 7.2.2268.64ff.

Gradiuus. This title of Mars is much less common than *Mars/Mavors* in poetry; on its uncertain origin v. Bömer on Ov. *Fasti* 2.861.

1344. The single instance (Mars) is generalized, in rhetorical style, into a regular custom, cf. 1101f. comm. *Superos* need refer only to Mars, but probably it also hints at Hercules' eventual deification, often anticipated in the play (21ff., 423, 437, 462). (It therefore glances at the standard version of H.'s fate, rather than the future envisaged in Eur. 1331ff., viz. to die in Athens and receive heroic honors there.) Nevertheless the hint, even in the last line of the play, is only a hint. Hercules is so obsessed with his bloodguilt that he can scarcely conceive of any future for himself. Deification was in the forefront of his ambition before the mad-scene, but now it can only be a very distant prospect.

APPENDIX 1

Further Details of T (Par. Lat. 8031)

For reasons explained in the Introduction, I list here certain details eliminated from my apparatus criticus. Even this list is selective: I do not record corrections for which I am confident that the first hand is responsible, nor cases in which another hand merely expands an abbreviation or otherwise clarifies an original reading. Marginal and interlinear variants entered by secondary hands have also been omitted.

7 sublime: d *supr.* l *add.* T^2 ∥ 9 tyria T^{pc} (a *in ras. ex* e) ∥ 11 athlantides ∥ 31 aut aer: aut aut aer T^{ac}, *postea corr.* ∥ 38 ting⁻t T^1 tingit T^{2pc} | ethiopas ∥ 54 hereboque ∥ 58 superbifica: b *in ras. 2 litt.* T^2 ∥ 66 astria veniet lenta T^{ac}, *sed prima* i *postea era. et ord. verborum corr.* ∥ 75 ira: ita T^1, *corr. m.2* ∥ 97 lambens: labens T^1, *corr. m.2* ∥ 98 erorque T^1, *corr. m.2* ∥ 101 primum T^{ac} pinum T^{pc} ∥ 104 petite: capite ∥ 110 sorores: e *in ras.* T^2 ∥ 203 megera *ut* P CS (*et sic semper*) ∥ 222 prolusit T^1 prelusit T^2 (re *in ras.*) ∥ 224 maximus *om.* T^1, *add.* $T^2mg.$ ∥ 231 hesperie: ⁻ *supra* i T^1, *postea era.* ∥ 232 ˍharcesii T^1 chartesii T^2 (c *in ras.*) ∥ 239 post hoc ∥ 251 prosperm (*sic:* prospm) ∥ 252 vocictur T^1, *corr. m.2* ∥ 260 arvis: vi T^2 *in ras.* ∥ 263 canoro: canora T^{ac}, *postea corr.* ∥ 281 clausum: cla T^2 *in ras.* | iterque: interque T^{ac}, *postea corr.* ∥ 290 terinos (*sic:* t'īos) ∥ 297 amplectaˍr T^1 amplectar T^{2pc} ∥ 307 deffende ∥ 316 *post* est *una litt. primum expunct., postea era.* ∥ 324 pupe ∥ 328 transit T^2 *in ras.* (n *ex* s) ∥ 334 *ante* phocis ras. 3 litt. (fˍ) ∥ 342 omnis est in ferro salus T^1, *corr. m.2* ∥ 344 tuetur T^2 (u *in ras. 2 vel 3 litt.*) ∥ 355 tristi nestis T^1 *ut vid.* tristis vestis T^2 ∥ 357 *ras. aliquot litt. ante* adheret ∥ 364 paret: e *in ras.* T^2 ∥ 366 scalebit ∥ 377 alternis: alterius T^1, *corr. m.2* ∥ 380 quid ultra? (est *om.*) ∥ 388 coniungis, *altera* n (*sic:* ⁻) *postea era.* ∥ 415 aut T^1 haud T^2 ∥ 417 circumsonaret: civū sonaret T^1 *ut vid., corr. m.2* ∥ 423 tetigit: g *in ras. ex* d T^2 ∥ 427 quod T^2 *in ras.* ∥ 444 phlegram T^2 *in ras.* ∥ 468 horrentes comae: s *et* come *in ras.* T^2 ∥ 477 eurytis ∥ 478 virginum: unginum ∥ 489 lesere T^2 (*altera* e *in ras.*) ∥ 491 magistro: magistrum T^1, *corr. m.2* ∥ 498 egypti T^1 egysti T^2 ∥ 501 pertinax T^2 (tin *in ras.*) ∥ 513 veta T^2 (t *in ras., ex* r *ut vid.*) ∥ *ante* 516 *notam Amphitryonis om.* T^1, *inser.* T^2 ∥ 526 euristeus ∥ 529 resecet T^1 reseret T^2 ∥ 545 peltam T^2 (lta *in ras.*) ∥ 552 tindaride T^2 (e *ex* i, *et* t *post hanc* i *era.*) ∥ 553 *post* timidis *ras. 4 litt.* (ˍeˍ) | navibus T^2 *in ras., et postea ras. aliquot litt.*

Appendix 1

‖ 559 colus T^1 colos T^2 ‖ 561 Pylon: *praeter* p *in ras.* T^2 (n *ex* ō) ‖ 563 ter gemina T^1 (=P), *corr. m.2* ‖ 586 obtulerit: obtuleris T^1, *corr. m.2* ‖ 587 Spartani: ni (ī) *in ras.* T^2 ‖ 599 qui: que T^1, *corr. m.2* ‖ 605 atque: t *in ras. m.2* ‖ 611 quiddam: ddam T^2 *in ras.* ‖ 627 unde T^2 *in ras.* ‖ 637 qua vis: quamvis T^1, *corr. m.2* ‖ 645 deus: de_us T^1, *corr. m.2* ‖ 652 luminum: umi *corr.* T^2 ‖ 656 quae (*sic:* q̄) T^1 quod T^2 ‖ 660 *post* quesivit *ras. 2 litt.* (e_) ‖ 676 innitas ‖ 683 involvit T^2 *in ras.* ‖ 686 inhertis cocyti iacet feda T^1, *ord. corr.* T^2 ‖ 691 tabido T^1 rabido T^2 ‖ 695 cuncta T^1, *corr. m.2* ‖ 711 uno: imo ‖ 715 volvunt T^1, *corr. m.2* ‖ 716 renavigari T^1 remigari T^2 ‖ 719 lumina T^1, *corr. m.2* ‖ 721 digerit T^1 dirigit T^2 ‖ 728 sera T^1 fera T^2 ‖ 738 plebeia: plebia T^1 (=P), *corr. m.2* ‖ 741 mitis: militis T^1, *corr. m.2* | regit T^2 *in ras.* ‖ 750 volucri: volucer T^1, *corr. m.2* ‖ 755 in ore: more T^1, *corr. m.2* ‖ 756 ticius ‖ 759 phynceas T^1, *corr. m.2* ‖ 769 pupim ‖ 777 lethen: n *in ras.* T^2, *ex* u *ut vid.* ‖ 781 post hoc T^1, *corr. m.2* ‖ 784 vasta T^{ac}, *postea corr.* ‖ 789 vibrato: v *in ras.* T^2 ‖ 797 laeva: lena T^1, *corr. m.2* ‖ 802 ictus: r (*ut vid.*) era. *ante* i ‖ 805 uterque T^1 utrumque T^2 *ut vid.* ‖ 819 geminis T^1 geminisque T^2 ‖ 830 euristheus ‖ 855 solis: solum T^1, *corr. m.2* ‖ 870 velo T^{ac}, *postea corr.* | cocyto T^1 cochito T^2 ‖ 886 alluitur: alluiur T^1 abluiur T^2 ‖ 902 sacrifico T^1 *ut vid.* saxifico T^2 ‖ 903 assit T^1 assis T^2 | ligurgi ‖ 939 monstrum T^2 (rum *in ras.*) ‖ 940 cinxere T^1 tinxere T^2 ‖ 942 unde T^2 *in ras.* ‖ 951 transiliet: tra T^2 *in ras.* ‖ 960 terra: terre T^1, *corr. m.2* ‖ 966 impii: imperii T^1, *corr. m.2* ‖ 977 ticius ‖ 981 etheu T^1 ethan T^2 ‖ 983 sudes: u *in ras.* T^2, *ex* e *ut vid.* ‖ 984 thesiphone ‖ 1002 scelesti: celesti T^1, *corr. m.2* ‖ 1011 undecumque: de T^2 *in ras.* ‖ 1012 pergis: pargis T^1, *corr. m.2* ‖ 1032 ingeris: iugeris T^1, *corr. m.2* ‖ 1037 cecidi: cicidi T^1, *corr. m.2* ‖ 1039 sacrum: saccum T^1, *corr. m.2* ‖ 1080 prius: r T^2 *in ras.* ‖ 1088 vano: narro T^1, *corr. m.2* ‖ 1102 lacertos: certos T^2 *in ras.* ‖ 1114 tria T^2 *in ras.* ‖ 1117 fero: sero T^1, *corr. m.2* ‖ 1120 pectora: pectoris T^1, *corr. m.2* ‖ 1163 Ismeni: ismehi T^1, *corr. m.2* ‖ 1164 acthea ‖ 1172 en: an T^1, *corr. m.2* ‖ 1193 hic: hoc T^1, *corr. m.2* ‖ 1199 reverto T^1, *corr. m.2* ‖ 1200 tacuere T^1 iacuere T^2 ‖ 1212 distendat: distentat T^1, *corr. m.2* ‖ 1216 quim ‖ 1224 erebo: *prima* e *et* o *in ras.* T^2 (o *ex* ro) ‖ 1225 ultimum: ulterim T^1 *ut vid., corr. m.2* ‖ 1232 rumpemus: r *in ras.* T^2 (*ex* p *ut vid.*) | at T^{ac} ac T^{pc} ‖ 1235 quoque T^2 *in ras.* ‖ 1244 referte: efer T^2 *in ras.* ‖ 1257 fructum T^1 fructumque T^2 | et *om.* T^1, *add.* T^2 ‖ 1265 intens ‖ 1267 qui: que ‖ 1296 en: e *in ras.* T^2 ‖ 1307 famamque: que *om.* T^1, *add. m.2* ‖ 1331 notus: nothus T^1, *corr. m.2*

APPENDIX 2

Addenda and Corrigenda to Giardina's Apparatus Criticus

Singular errors of the A manuscripts, eliminated from my apparatus criticus and from Zwierlein's, are usually recorded in the apparatus of Giardina's edition. The chief purpose of this appendix is to supplement Giardina by listing the more notable errors of this kind (usually in P) omitted by him. I have not included mere spelling variations or instances of self-correction by the first hand, nor the frequent detachment of a prefix (especially *in-*) from its word (though this last phenomenon is noted in my apparatus criticus when it occurs in two or more MSS). In addition to the large number of singular errors that stand uncorrected in P, there are many that have been corrected, usually in such a way that one cannot identify the corrector: I have generally not recorded these.

I have also taken the opportunity to list a few corrections to Giardina concerning matters not covered in my own apparatus criticus. In these cases even minutiae are noted where Giardina's report is erroneous.

6 glacialis: *altera* i E^2 *in ras. ex* e ‖ 9 vector: v P^2 *in ras. 2 litt.* ‖ 81 gigante *FM* -anti *N* ‖ 91 *suo loco MN, ante* 90 *F* ‖ 108 prius: pirus *P* ‖ 113 reversus: u E^{pc} *in ras.* ‖ 117 inferis: inferus *P* ‖ 176 tempore *P* ‖ 232 carcesii E^1 carthesii E^{2pc} ‖ 258 fleatur *P* ‖ 273 fertque: que *om. P* ‖ 322 diserta *P* ‖ 336 ysmos exulis *P* ‖ 352 invida *P* ‖ 366 tectis: rectis *Sd* ‖ 378 euiboica *P* eubogica *S* ‖ 387 sclera P^1, *corr. m.2* ‖ 426 cogi: cgi *P* ‖ 432 et: qui *P* ‖ 435 pirtutis *P (errore rubricantis)* ‖ 452 sed: qui *P* ‖ 454 Phoebus *om. P* ‖ 465 cuivis *P* ‖ *ante* 479ª Amphitryonis *notam habent SV* ‖ 506 suis: tuis *P* ‖ 514 trabibus accrescit: turbidus accersit *P* ‖ 533 multi vagas *P* ‖ 539 itonsis *P* ‖ 549 vidististi *P* ‖ 556 inumera *P* ‖ 564 tenui: teneri *P, postea corr.* ‖ 606 omibus *P* ‖ 624 desceptus *P* ‖ 663 silvis: silus C^{pc} *(altera* s *in ras.)* ‖ 668 prima P^1, *corr. m.2* ‖ 670 afflictu adit P^{ac} afflictum cadit P^{pc} ‖ 686 concyti P^{pc} (y *ex* i) chochiti *C* ‖ 698 non: ion P^1 *(errore rubricantis), corr. m.2* ‖ 707 loca: loco *P, postea corr.* ‖ 738 terga plebeia: plebia terga *P* ‖

Appendix 2

756 ticius *P* tycius *CS* ‖ 760 nunc: c E^2 *in ras., et ras. unius lit. post* c ‖ 762 iminet *P* ‖ 820 irritam *P, postea corr.* ‖ 822 puta *P* ‖ 830 eristeus *P* ‖ 850 saciata *CS* ‖ 859 sensit: sentit *P, postea corr.* ‖ 884 et: e *P* | tenens: teneris *P* ‖ 925 detur: dent *P* ‖ 935 nulla *P (recte)* ‖ 951 peter *S ut vid.* ‖ 953 quo: quod *P* ‖ 976 quid: qui *P* ‖ 977 gerens: gemis *P, postea corr.* ‖ 978 prope: ppe *P* | a celo C^{1pc} (*ex* ac celo) ‖ 981 *nonne* horrendum *S? (sic:* -nd') ‖ 989 excutiat: -tiet *P, postea corr.* ‖ 993 pharetramque *P* (= *T*) far- *CS* ‖ 1003 miseranda: mif- *vel* imf- *P* ‖ 1005 rapuit: rapiunt P^1, *corr. m.2* ‖ 1037 cicidi *P* (= T^1) ‖ 1042 luminum *P (recte)* ‖ 1074 par: ̱par (*sc.* parar *vel* perar*) P* ‖ 1102 lacertos: lactos *P* ‖ 1132 in: inde (*vel* vide) *P* ‖ 1151 meum: in eum *P* ‖ 1160 confecti: confe_i *P* (*an* conferri?) ‖ 1163 reverso: verso P^1, re *add. supr. m.2* ‖ 1165 pulsata: pinsata *P ut vid.* ‖ 1180 Argivae: arguto C^{pc} *in textu,* argive *sup.* ‖ 1198 vix recendem *P* ‖ 1224 alterius *P* ‖ 1237 quis: q *om. P errore rubricantis* ‖ 1242 propere: prope *P* ‖ 1262 sanandus *P Leid* ‖ 1283 in pueros: impueros *C* ‖ 1307 famamque tuam P^1, tuam *exp. m.2* ‖ 1335 longingram *P*

APPENDIX 3

The Colometry of the Anapestic Odes

The transmitted colometry of Seneca's anapestic odes is rendered suspect by the fact that it creates eleven cases of hiatus or *syllaba debilis* in the middle of a dimeter. The conservative solution has been to eliminate these anomalies either by conjecture or by altering the colometry so as to bring each anomaly to the end of a line, whether dimeter or monometer. However, G. Richter in his *Kritische Untersuchungen zu Senecas Tragödien* (progr. Jena 1899) 32–47 made the crucial observation that if Seneca's original colometry has been disturbed, as it certainly has, it is extremely unlikely that these disturbances were confined to places where they could later be detected by hiatus or *s. debilis*; in other words, we must assume disruptions in many more than the eleven places unmasked by these anomalies. This assumption is strengthened by the fact that the colometry continued to be tampered with after the division of the transmission, that is, in E and A separately, as is shown by their not infrequent disagreements over colometry. Richter further observed that in the majority of anapestic lines Seneca aims at a correspondence of metrical unit with the unit of sense and syntax; and that where the presence of hiatus or *s. debilis* enables us to detect and correct erroneous colometry, the correction usually restores such correspondence. He therefore suggested rightly that correspondence of this kind provides a criterion by which the original colometry can be restored.

Though Richter's criterion has not been used with confidence by critics and editors since (with the notable exception of Zwierlein in his discussions of text problems), my investigations of the metrical patterns of the dimeters confirm its complete reliability. If we study those passages where the transmitted colometry does preserve correspondence, we find certain definite metrical differences between the first and second metron of the dimeter. The sequence dactyl–spondee is a favorite pattern in the second metron, occurring in just over one-half of all cases, but much less common in the first metron, where its frequency is

Appendix 3

only 15 percent. Conversely, a double spondee is relatively frequent in the first metron, accounting for just over one-quarter of all cases, but is avoided because of its heaviness in the second metron, where it occurs at only 4 percent, almost always after the sequence spondee–anapest in the first metron. If we then study dimeters which, in the transmitted colometry, violate correspondence, we find that these patterns are reversed, with dactyl–spondee becoming much more common in the first metron than the second, and vice versa with double spondee—a clear indication of error; and when correspondence is restored in these passages, metrical normality is also restored. (Restoration of correspondence creates a far larger number of monometers than exists in the transmitted colometry; this led Richter to suggest persuasively that the motive of the copyist who altered the original colometry was to save space by eliminating monometers where possible.) In those few cases where sense and syntax do not provide clear guidance, meter alone may be used as a criterion for colometry.

Finally, the criterion of correspondence might suggest that sense-units covering *three* metra should be written as trimeters, e.g. *Tro.* 71f. *secuitque fretum pinus matri sacra Cybebae.* But in my opinion the weight of evidence from metrical patterns is against the existence of trimeters. Those trimeters which E and A offer sporadically (but almost never jointly) appear to have arisen through scribal inadvertence or economy.

My colometry of the two anapestic odes in *HF*, viz. 125–203 and 1054–1137, is based on these criteria and conclusions; I hope to treat the subject more fully in a forthcoming study.

APPENDIX 4

Compound Adjectives and Adjectives in -x

There are nine compound adjectives that appear for the first time in Sen. Trag.: *castificus, incestificus, letificus, nidificus, superbificus* (*HF* 58); *luctifer* (*HF* 687), *monstrifer, squamifer*; *multivagus* (*HF* 533). This frequency of new compounds is about the same as in Lucan, Statius, and Valerius Flaccus (cf. F. Seitz, *De Adiectivis Poetarum Latinorum Compositis*, Diss. Bonn 1878: in Vergil and Ovid it is more difficult to be sure what proportion of compounds is actually new). On the subject of compound adjectives see the references collected by R. D. Williams on V. *Aen.* 5.452, adding Leumann *Kleine Schriften* 150ff.

Compound adjectives in *-ficus* are particularly associated with drama, though not absent from other genres. Jocelyn 250 lists the examples used in Republican tragedy and comedy. Cicero's translations from Greek tragedy in *Tusc.* 2 contain *vastificus* and *luctificus*. Sen. Trag. has fourteen such adjectives[1] in a total of twenty-three usages. By contrast, the corresponding figures for Vergil are four and eight. Ovid uses such adjectives rather more often than Vergil, but with nothing like the same frequency as Seneca. In *superbificus* and some other adjectives of this type, such as *castificus* (*Pha.* 169), *ingratificus, regificus*, the *-ficus* suffix adds little in terms of meaning.

Compounds in *-fer* are associated with high poetry, both iambic and dactylic. Their frequency in Sen. Trag. (an average of one every 202 lines)[2] is similar to that in several dactylic writers: Lucretius (one in 239

---

1. They are: *castificus* (1) *incestificus* (1) *laetificus* (1) *letificus* (1) *luctificus* (5) *magnificus* (2) *maleficus* (1) *nidificus* (1) *sacrificus* (4) *saxificus* (1) *superbificus* (1) *tabificus* (1) *terrificus* (2) *vulnificus* (1).

2. The following are used, once each unless noted: *aestifer, anguifer, armifer* (3), *aurifer, bacifer, caelifer, flammifer* (3), *florifer, frondifer, frugifer, gemmifer, horrifer, ignifer, imbrifer* (2), *lucifer, luctifer, monstrifer, mortifer* (6), *pestifer* (4), *pinifer, pomifer, rorifer, sceptrifer, signifer* (2), *squamifer, stellifer, velifer*.

[469]

Appendix 4

lines), Ovid in *Met.* and *Fasti* (one in 202 lines), Lucan (one in 168 lines), Valerius Flaccus (one in 180 lines). Cicero is unusually freehanded (an overall average for the poetica of one in 55 lines), Vergil unusually sparing (one in 497 lines). Outside the high style such adjectives are notably less common: Horace uses only one, *pomifer*; in Ovid their frequency outside *Met.* and *Fasti* is less than half that in those poems; in comedy they are rare, but relatively more frequent in Republican tragedy.³ The *-fer* element, like *-ficus*, is in some cases void of meaning: thus *aurifer HF* 240 = *aureus*, *squamifer Med.* 685 = *squameus*, *flammifer Thy.* 855 = *flammeus*. In such cases style, meter, and the influence of early poetry may play a part.

The most popular compounds in *-vagus* before Sen. are *montivagus* (Lucr., Cic.), *noctivagus* (Lucr., Verg.) and *solivagus* (Cic.). Many compounds in *multi-* have Greek precedents in πολυ-, thus *multivagus* = πολυπλανής, πολυπλάνητος.

Seneca has a definite liking for adjectives in *-x*; twenty-five of them are used more frequently, proportionally speaking, in the tragedies than in either Vergil or Ovid.⁴ Of these only three (*contumax, pertinax, pervicax*) were inaccessible for metrical reasons in dactylic poetry. Three of the adjectives Sen. found useful as iambic line-ends (*minax* and *capax* are each used six times in this way, and *ferox* fifteen times), but that does not explain the whole phenomenon. The explanation must lie at least partly in the strong sound-effects provided by such words; contrast for example the smoother sound of adjectives in *-osus*, of which Vergil uses many more than Seneca.

---

3. The figures for Cicero, Lucretius, Vergil, Ovid, and Valerius are based on the lists of adjectives in *-fer* given by Arens in *Mnemosyne* ser. 4.3 (1950) 242f. For comedy and Republican tragedy see Jocelyn 200; however, his statement about the relative frequency of *-fer* adjectives in later poetry is erroneous.

4. These are: *atrox, audax, capax, contumax, dicax, fallax, felix, ferax, ferox, minax, pernox, pertinax, pervicax, praecox, procax, pugnax, rapax, redux, sagax, supplex, trux, velox, verax, victrix, vivax.*

BIBLIOGRAPHY

This Bibliography is limited almost exclusively to works cited in abbreviated form in my Introduction or Commentary. When a work is cited only once, bibliographical information is usually given in that citation rather than in the Bibliography. Fuller bibliographies are provided by Coffey (for 1922–55), Mette 1964 (for 1945–64), Hiltbrunner (for 1965–75), and Seidensticker and Armstrong (for 1978–c.1983).

Editions in the first section are of the whole corpus, except where otherwise noted. They are listed in chronological order.

Editions Consulted

Ascensius, Iodocus Badius. Paris 1514. With commentaries of Ascensius, Marmita, and Caietanus.

Avantius, Hieronymus. Venice 1517.

Delrius, Martinus Antonius. *In Lucii Annaei Senecae . . . Adversaria.* Antwerp 1576.

———. *Syntagma Tragoediae Latinae.* 3 vols. Antwerp 1593–94 (Paris 1607, 1619–20).

Raphelengius, Franciscus, and Justus Lipsius. 2 vols. Leiden 1588–89 (1601).

Commelinus, H., with notes of J. Gruter. Heidelberg 1600.

Gruter, J. (see preceding entry).

Scaliger, J. J., and Danielis Heinsius. Leiden 1611.

Farnaby, Thomas. Leiden 1623.

Gronovius, Jacobus. Amsterdam 1682. With the important notes of the elder Gronovius.

Schroeder, J. J. 2 vols. Delft 1728. A useful edition with the notes of Gronovius *père* (from the 1682 edition) and a selection from those of D. and N. Heinsius, Delrius, Farnaby, and others.

Baden, Torkill. *Hercules Furens. Specimen Novae Recensionis Tragoediarum Senecae.* Kilonii 1798.

———. Copenhagen 1819 (Leipzig 1821).

Bibliography

Editio Lemairiana. 3 vols. (vol. 1, containing *HF* etc., ed. J. Pierrot). Paris 1829–32.
Pierrot, J. (see preceding entry).
Bothe, F. H. Vol. 3 of *Poetae Scaenici Latini.* 2d ed. Leipzig 1834 (1st ed. Leipzig 1819).
Peiper, Rudolf, and Gustav Richter. Leipzig (Teubner) 1867. An eccentric edition.
Leo, Friedrich. 2 vols. Berlin 1878–79 (reprinted Berlin 1963).
Richter, Gustav (with Rudolf Peiper). Leipzig (Teubner) 1902 (1921, 1937).
Kingery, H. M. *Three Tragedies of Seneca.* New York 1908 (reprinted 1966). *HF, Tro., Med.*
Miller, F. J. 2 vols. London and Cambridge, Mass. (Loeb) 1917 (1927, etc.). With English translation.
Herrmann, Léon. 2 vols. Paris (Budé) 1924–26 (1961). With French translation.
Ageno, F. *L'Ercole Furioso.* Padua 1925. Italian translation, critical notes.
Moricca, Umberto. 3 vols. 2d ed. Turin (Paravia) 1947 (1st ed. 1917–23).
Thomann, T. 2 vols. Zurich 1961–69. With German translation.
Viansino, Giovanni. 3 vols. Turin (Paravia) 1965 (vol. 1, 2d ed. 1968).
Giardina, Gian Carlo. 2 vols. Bologna 1966.
Costa, C. D. N. *Medea.* Oxford 1973.
Tarrant, R. J. *Agamemnon.* Cambridge 1976.
Caviglia, Franco. *Il Furore di Ercole.* Rome 1979. With Italian translation and commentary.
Fantham, Elaine. *Troades.* Princeton 1982.
Tarrant, R. J. *Thyestes.* Atlanta 1985.
Zwierlein, Otto. Oxford 1986.

Other Works

Ahl, Frederick M. *Lucan: An Introduction.* Ithaca 1976.
Anderson, A. R. "Heracles and His Successors." *HSCP* 39 (1928) 7–58.
Anliker, K. *Prologe und Akteinteilung in Senecas Tragödien.* Bern 1960.
Axelson, Bertil. *Unpoetische Wörter.* Lund 1945 ("Axelson").
―――. *Korruptelenkult: Studien zur Textkritik der unechten Seneca-Tragödie "Hercules Oetaeus."* Lund 1967.
Baldwin, T. W. *William Shakspere's Small Latine & Lesse Greeke.* 2 vols. Urbana 1944.
(Bentley, Richard.) Hedicke, Edmund. "Seneca Bentleianus." In *Studia Bentleiana.* Freienwalde 1899. (Publication of Bentley's marginal jottings.)
Bishop, J. D. "Seneca's *Hercules Furens*: Tragedy from *modus vitae.*" *C&M* 27 (1969) 216–24.
Boardman, J. "Herakles, Peisistratos and Eleusis." *JHS* 95 (1975) 1–12.
Bond, Godfrey W., ed. *Euripides: Heracles.* Oxford 1981.
Bonner, S. F. *Roman Declamation.* Liverpool 1949.

Braden, Gordon. "The Rhetoric and Psychology of Power in the Dramas of Seneca." *Arion* 9 (1970) 5–41.
_____. *Renaissance Tragedy and the Senecan Tradition.* New Haven and London 1985.
Brommer, F. *Herakles. Die zwölf Taten des Helden in antiker Kunst und Literatur.* Münster and Cologne 1953.
Busa, R., and A. Zampolli. *Concordantiae Senecae.* 2 vols. Hildesheim and New York 1975.
Canter, Howard Vernon. *Rhetorical Elements in the Tragedies of Seneca.* Univ. of Illinois Studies in Language and Literature X.1. 1925.
Carlsson, Gunnar. *Die Überlieferung der Seneca-Tragödien.* Lunds Universitets Årsskrift N. F. 21.5. 1925.
_____. "Zu Senecas Tragödien: Lesungen und Deutungen." *Kungl. Human. Vetenskapssamfundet i Lund.* Årsberättelse 1928–29, pp. 39–72. Lund 1929.
_____. "Seneca's Tragedies: Notes and Interpretations." *C&M* 10 (1948) 39–59.
Cattin, Aurèle. *Les thèmes lyriques dans les tragédies de Sénèque.* Neuchatel 1963.
Charlier, J. *Ovide et Sénèque.* Diss. Brussels 1954.
Coffey, Michael. "Seneca, Tragedies . . . 1922–1955." *Lustrum* 2 (1957) 113–86.
Cohon, B. J. *Seneca's Tragedies in Florilegia and Elizabethan Drama.* Diss. Columbia University 1960.
Cornelissen, I. I. "Ad Senecae tragoedias." *Mnemosyne* N. S. 5 (1877) 175–87.
Cropp, Martin J. *A Stylistic and Analytical Commentary on Euripides' Herakles 1–814, with an Introduction to the Play as a Whole.* Diss. Toronto 1975.
Cunliffe, J. *The Influence of Seneca on Elizabethan Tragedy.* London 1893.
Damsté, P. H. "Ad Senecae Herculem Furentem." *Mnemosyne* N. S. 46 (1918) 428–34.
Dingel, Joachim. *Seneca und die Dichtung.* Heidelberg 1974.
Düring, T.: see Hoffa.
Edert, O. *Über Senecas Herakles und den Herakles auf dem Oeta.* Diss. Kiel 1909.
Eliot, T. S. "Shakespeare and the Stoicism of Seneca" (1927) and "Seneca in Elizabethan Translation." In *Selected Essays*, 3d ed., pp. 126–40; 65–105. London 1951 (1953 etc.).
Fitch, John G. *Character in Senecan Tragedy.* Diss. Cornell University 1974.
_____. "*Pectus o nimium ferum*: Act V of Seneca's *Hercules Furens*." *Hermes* 107 (1979) 240–48.
_____. "Sense-pauses and Relative Dating in Seneca, Sophocles, and Shakespeare." *AJP* 102 (1981) 289–307.
_____. "Notes on Seneca's *Hercules Furens*." *TAPA* 111 (1981) 65–70.
_____. "Seneca's *Troades* in a New Edition: A Review Article." *Classical Views* 29 (1985) 435–53.
Frenzel, Friedrich. *Die Prologe der Tragödien Senecas.* Diss. Leipzig 1914.
Friedrich, Wolf-Hartmut. *Untersuchungen zu Senecas dramatischer Technik.* Diss. Freiburg. Leipzig 1933.
_____. "Euripides' Herakles und die römische Tragödie." *Hermes* 69 (1934) 303–10.

———. "Die Raserei des Hercules." In *Vorbild und Neugestaltung*, pp. 88–111. Göttingen 1967.
Galinsky, G. Karl. *The Herakles Theme*. Oxford 1972.
Garrod, H. W. "Seneca Tragoedus Again." *CQ* 5 (1911) 209–19.
Griffin, M. T. *Seneca: A Philosopher in Politics*. Oxford 1975.
Haar Romeny, H. M. B. Ter. *De Auctore Tragoediarum quae sub Senecae Nomine Feruntur, Vergilii Imitatore*. Diss. Leiden 1877.
Hahlbrock, Peter. "Beobachtungen zum jambischen Trimeter in den Tragödien des L. Annaeus Seneca." *WS* N. F. 2 (1968) 171–92.
Hancock, J. L. *Studies in Stichomythia*. Chicago 1917.
Harder, Franz. "Bemerkungen zu den Tragödien des Seneca." In *Festschrift für J. Vahlen*, pp. 443–63. Berlin 1900.
Haywood, R. M. "Was Seneca's Hercules Modelled on an Earlier Latin Play?" *CJ* 38 (1942) 98–101.
Heinsius, Nicolaus. *Adversariorum Libri IV*. Haarlem 1742.
Henry, D., and B. Walker. "The Futility of Action. A Study of Seneca's *Hercules Furens*." *CPh* 60 (1965) 11–22.
Herington, C. J. "A Thirteenth-century Manuscript of the *Octavia praetexta* in Exeter." *RhM* 101 (1958) 353–77.
———. "The Exeter Manuscript of the *Octavia*: A Correction." *RhM* 103 (1960) 96.
———. "Senecan Tragedy." *Arion* 5 (1966) 422–71.
———. "The Younger Seneca." In *The Cambridge History of Classical Literature*. Ed. E. J. Kenney (2.511–32). Cambridge 1982.
Heywood, Jasper. Translation of *HF* in Thomas Newton, ed., *Seneca His Tenne Tragedies Translated into English*. London 1581 (reprinted London 1927).
Hiltbrunner, Otto. "Seneca als Tragödiendichter in der Forschung von 1965 bis 1975." *ANRW* 2.32.2 (1985) 961–1051.
Hoche, Max. *Die Metra des Tragikers Seneca*. Halle 1862.
Hoffa, Wilhelm. "Textkritische Untersuchungen zu Senecas Tragödien." *Hermes* 49 (1914) 464–75.
Hoffa, Wilhelm, and T. Düring. Materialien für eine Neueausgabe von Senecas Tragödien (1914). Niedersächsische Staats- und Universitätsbibliothek Göttingen, MS 4° Philol. 142ⁿ.
Housman, A. E. *Classical Papers*. Ed. J. Diggle and F. R. Goodyear. 3 vols. Cambridge 1972.
Jortin, J. "Philological Remarks on Seneca Tragicus." In *Tracts II*, pp. 404–24. London 1790.
Kapnukajas, Christos K. *Die Nachahmungstechnik Senecas in den Chorleidern des Hercules Furens und der Medea*. Diss. Leipzig 1930.
Karsten, H. T. *Spicilegium Criticum*. Lyons 1881.
Kirk, G. S. *The Nature of Greek Myths*. Harmondsworth 1974.
Koetschau, Paul. "Zu Senecas Tragödien." *Philologus* 61 (1902) 133–59.
Kroll, Wilhelm. *Gott und Hölle. Der Mythos vom Descensus-Kampfe*. Leipzig 1932.
Lawall, Gilbert. "Virtus and Pietas in Seneca's *Hercules Furens*." *Ramus* 12 (1983) 6–26.

Bibliography

Leo, Friedrich. "De recensendis Senecae tragoediis." *Hermes* 10 (1876) 423–46.
———. *Der Monolog im Drama*. Berlin 1908.
Lessing, G. E. "Von den lateinischen Trauerspielen, welche unter dem Namen des Seneca bekannt sind." In *Theatralischen Bibliothek*. 1754.
Liebermann, Wolf-Lüder. *Studien zu Senecas Tragödien*. Meisenheim 1974.
MacGregor, A. P. "The MS Tradition of Seneca's Tragedies: *Ante renatas in Italia litteras*." *TAPA* 102 (1971) 327–56.
———. "Parisinus 8031: *Codex optimus* for the A-MSS of Seneca's Tragedies." *Philologus* 122 (1978) 88–110.
———. "The Manuscripts of Seneca's Tragedies: A Survey." *ANRW* 2.32.2 (1985) 1134–1241.
Madvig, I. N. "Seneca Tragicus." In *Adversaria Critica* (2.109–27). Hauniae 1873.
Marcosignori, A. M. "Il concetti di virtus tragica nel teatro di Seneca." *Aevum* 34 (1960) 217–33.
Mette, H. J. "Die römische Tragödie . . . 1945–1964." *Lustrum* 9 (1964) 5–211.
———. "Die Funktion des Löwengleichnisses in Senecas *Hercules Furens*." *WS* 79 (1966) 477–89.
Motto, Anna L., and John R. Clark. "*Maxima virtus* in Seneca's *Hercules Furens*." *CPh* 76 (1981) 101–17.
Müller, Michael. *In Senecae Tragoedias Quaestiones Criticae*. Diss. Berlin 1898.
Munro, H. A. J. "Seneca's Tragedies." *JPh* 6 (1876) 70–79.
Mylonas, G. *Eleusis and the Eleusinian Mysteries*. Princeton 1961.
Oldfather, W. A. (with A. S. Pease and H. V. Canter). *Index Verborum quae in Senecae Tragoediis . . . Reperiuntur*. *Univ. of Illinois Studies in Language and Literature* IV.2. 1918 (reprinted Hildesheim 1964).
Opelt, I. "Une description du globe céleste dans l'*Hercule furieux* de Sénèque." *StudClas* 15 (1973) 109–14.
Owen, W. H. "Commonplace and Dramatic Symbol in Seneca's Tragedies." *TAPA* 99 (1968) 291–313.
Paratore, Ettore. "Il prologo dello *Hercules furens* di Seneca e l'*Eracle* di Euripide." *ALGP* 2 (1965) 277–308. Printed separately, Rome 1966 (*Quaderni della RCCM* 9).
Peiper, Rudolf. *Observatorum in Senecae Tragoediis Libellus*. Breslau 1863.
Philp, R. H. "The Manuscript Tradition of Seneca's Tragedies." *CQ* 18 (1968) 150–79.
Pratt, N. T. *Dramatic Suspense in Seneca and His Greek Precursors*. Diss. Princeton University 1939.
———. "Major Systems of Figurative Language in Senecan Melodrama." *TAPA* 94 (1963) 199–234.
Regenbogen, Otto. "Schmerz und Tod in den Tragödien des Seneca." *Vorträge Bibl. Warburg* 7 (1927–28) 167–218. = *Kleine Schriften*, pp. 411–64. Munich 1961.
Richter, Gustav. *De Corruptis Quibusdam Senecae Tragoediarum Locis*. Jena 1894.
Rose, Amy. *Studies in Seneca's Hercules Furens*. Diss. Univ. of Colorado 1978.
———. "Seneca's *HF*: A Politico-Didactic Reading." *CJ* 75 (1979) 135–42.

———. "Seneca and Suicide: The End of the *Hercules Furens*." *CO* 60 (1983) 109–11.
Rose, H. J. *Handbook of Greek Mythology*. 6th ed. London 1958.
Runchina, Giovanni. "Tecnica drammatica e retorica nelle tragedie di Seneca." *Annali della Facoltà di Lettere, Filosofia e Magistero della Università di Cagliari* 28 (1960) 165–324.
Rutgers, J. *Variarum Lectionum Libri IV*. Lyons 1618.
Schmidt, Bernhard. *De Emendandarum Senecae Tragoediarum Rationibus Prosodiacis et Metricis*. Diss. Berlin 1860.
———. *Observationes Criticae in L. Annaei Senecae Tragoedias*. Jena 1865.
Schulze, W. *Untersuchungen zur Eigenart der Tragödien Senecas*. Diss. Halle 1937.
Seidensticker, Bernd. *Die Gesprächsverdichtung in den Tragödien Senecas*. Heidelberg 1969.
Seidensticker, Bernd, and David Armstrong, "Seneca tragicus 1878–1978 (with Addenda 1979ff.)." *ANRW* 2.32.2 (1985) 916–68.
Shelton, Jo-Ann. *Seneca's Hercules Furens: Theme, Structure and Style*. Göttingen 1978.
Smereka, J. "De Senecae tragoediis dinosis colore fucatis." *Eos* 32 (1929) 615–50.
———. "De Senecae tragici vocabulorum copiae certa quadam lege." In *Munera Philologica L. Cwiklinski Oblata*, pp. 253–61. Posnan 1936.
Soellner, R. "The Madness of Herakles and the Elizabethans." *CompLit* 10 (1958) 309–24.
Soubiran, J. "Recherches sur la clausule du sénaire (trimètre) latin. Les mots longs finaux." *REL* 42 (1964) 429–69.
Spika, J. *De Imitatione Horatiana in Senecae Canticis Choris*. Vienna 1890.
Strzelecki, L. *De Senecae Trimetro Iambico*. Krakow 1938.
Tarrant, R. J. "Senecan Drama and Its Antecedents." *HSCP* 82 (1978) 213–63.
Timpanaro, Sebastiano. "Uno nuovo commento all' *Hercules Furens* di Seneca nel quadro della critica recente." *A&R* 26 (1981) 113–41.
Tobin, R. W. "Tragedy and Catastrophe in Seneca's Theater." *CJ* 62 (1966) 64–70.
Trabert, K. *Studien zur Darstellung des Pathologischen in den Tragödien des Seneca*. Diss. Erlangen 1953.
Traina, A. "Le litanie del sonno nello *Hercules Furens* di Seneca." *RFIC* 95 (1967) 169–79.
———. "Ancora sulle litanie del sonno." *RFIC* 96 (1968) 288–89.
Trevetus, Nicolaus. *Expositio Herculis Furentis*. Ed. V. Ussani, Jr. Rome 1959.
Wagenvoort, H. "Ad Senecae Herculem furentem." *Mnemosyne* 60 (1933) 170–78.
Waith, Eugene M. *The Herculean Hero*. New York and London 1962.
Walter, Stefan. *Interpretationen zum römischen in Senecas Tragödien*. Zurich 1975.
Wellmann-Bretzigheimer, G. "Senecas *Hercules Furens*." *WS* N. F. 12 (1978) 111–50.
Wilamowitz-Moellendorf, U. von, ed. *Euripides Herakles*. 2d. ed. 3 vols. Berlin 1895 (reprinted 1959).
Wilkinson, L. P. *Golden Latin Artistry*. Cambridge 1963.

Bibliography

Withof, I. H. *Praemetium Crucium Criticarum Praecipue ex Seneca Tragico.* Lyons 1749.

Zintzen, Clemens. "*Alte virtus animosa cadit.* Gedanken zur Darstellung des Tragischen in Senecas *Hercules Furens.*" In E. Lefèvre, ed., *Senecas Tragödien,* pp. 149–209. Darmstadt 1972.

Zwierlein, Otto. *Die Rezitationsdramen Senecas.* Meisenheim am Glan 1966.

──────. "Kritisches und Exegetisches zu den Tragödien Senecas." *Philologus* 113 (1969) 254–67.

──────. "Versinterpolation und Korruptelen in den Tragödien Senecas." *WJA* N. F. 2 (1976) 181–217.

──────. "Weiteres zum Seneca tragicus (II)." *WJA* N. F. 4 (1978) 143–60.

──────. "Weiteres zum Seneca tragicus (III)." *WJA* N. F. 5 (1979) 163–87.

──────. "Weiteres zum Seneca tragicus (IV)." *WJA* N. F. 6 (1980) 181–95.

──────. *Prolegomena zu einer kritischen Ausgabe der Tragödien Senecas.* Wiesbaden 1983.

──────. *Senecas Hercules im Lichte kaiserzeitlicher und spätantiker Dichtung.* Wiesbaden 1984.

ADDENDA

The following points arise from Professor Zwierlein's text of Seneca's tragedies, which appeared while this edition was in proof. References are to lines of *HF*.

20. Axelson's conjecture *matribus sparsa impiis* for E's *nuribus sparsa impiis* is highly persuasive; it represents exactly the pointed kind of usage which tends to puzzle scribes.

146–51. Z.'s relocation of these lines between 136 and 137 may well be right. It gives a better focus in 139–58 on *human* activities (herding, sailing, fishing), in keeping with the preamble (137f.). The fact that it comes closer to the Euripidean order of topics (comm. p. 159), by keeping the nightingale before the shepherd, strengthens the case. Having fallen out, the passage will have been replaced after 145 because its initial verb *pendet* matched *ludit* and *errat*, and because its subject-matter seemed to match that of 141–45.

390. Z. accepts Ascensius' conjecture *superbo* for *superba*, but although it is stylistically attractive (cabAB), Pierrot p.178 had shown it to be inappropriate to the context: Megara is concerned with the *punishment* of pride, not its defiant continuation, and this is confirmed by 391 with its emphasis on sadness and tears. Supporters of *superbo* cite Stat. *Theb.* 4.576 *Tantalis et tumido percenset funera luctu*, but that picture of Niobe in the underworld still counting her children with defiant pride is inspired by *Oed.* 613–15 rather than *HF*.

867. Z. accepts Axelson's punctuation: *quid iuvat, durum, properare, fatum?* This provides a referent for the *tibi* in 870, and consequently Z. now prints 870–72 in the transmitted order. But one is suspicious of interpretations which rely heavily on modern punctuation, and Sen. Trag. nowhere else has *fatum* in the vocative.

Addenda

However, Axelson's understanding of 867 could be retained by taking *fatum* as the object of *iuvat* (viz. "Why does cruel fate delight to make haste?"), and this is initially appealing as unifying the thought of 867–74: death need not hasten because our own lives move toward death quickly and inevitably. But in fact the thought is more complex, and very like that of Ode I (177–91): though our lives move quickly toward death, we wilfully hasten the process further (*fertur obvia* 183f., *quaerimus* 185, *properare* 867), as Hercules has deliberately sought out the world of death (186ff.).

1317. For *afflictos* Z. prints *afflicti*, which appears in some recc. and appealed to Bentley; *solo* will presumably be ablative of separation. Admittedly *afflictus* is often used of persons in a metaphorical sense, "emotionally stricken", as at 1251. But there is no reason why it should not have a more physical sense here, "stricken to the ground" (*solo* dative) with the physical *artus*; cf. e.g. Ov. *Met.* 14.205f. *vidi bina meorum / ter quater affligi sociorum corpora terrae*, Luc. 2.30f. *hae pectora duro / afflixere solo*, ps.-Sen. *Oct.* 685f. *affligat humo violenta manus / similes nimium vultus domini*, Flor. 2.22.5 *infantes suos afflictos humi.*

INDEXES

References in roman are to the Commentary by line number; references in italics are to pages.

1. INDEX OF LATIN WORDS

Actaeus poetic, 1164
addere (nomen), 1237
adiutrix, 900
advehere, *51–52*
aer, 677, 1110f.
agedum in drama, *186*
ager, 934
aliquando unpoetic, *185*
alternus, 362
ambitus unpoetic, 887
amovere with abstract objects, 397
arbor, 912f.
arctous, 1326ᵇ–27
artum (in arto), 1307
ascendere, 21f.
aspergere, 20, 134f.
ast, 1006
ater, 59, 694
ātrox, 32
audere, 79, 1162fn.

bellum of Hercules' struggles, 85
bis ter(que), 1006

caedere = "kill," 1037
caeruleus, 132
caeles, 89
caelestis, genitive plural forms of, 516
caelifer, 528
capax of the underworld, 659
caput for a person, 920, 1334
carcer for the underworld, 1222
chaos of the underworld, 610, 861
circumsonare, 416f.
clarescere, 123f.

clepere, 799
colorem ducere, 347f.
color malus, 862
columen/culmen (spelling), 1000
constare (metaphorical), 461f.
contrahere of gathering troops, 126–28
cornu of tip of bow, 992
croceus, 124
culmen/columen (spelling), 1000
cum (pointed use), 1287f.

decipere, 155
densus, 228f.
devincire of sleep, 1078
dies, 8f.; gender, 586
dirus, 608, 1221
dives = "precious," 532
dominator, 1181
domitor, 1065; *d. orbis*, 619
domus, 239, 1185, 1287f.
dubius of light, 670
ductor, 299–301

efficax, 1272f.
egone ut in drama, *186*
en, *384*
Eous (scansion), 25
ephebus, 853
ergo, 354
error and *scelus*, 1237f.
escendere, 21
esse, ellipse of, 224, 233, 1122ff.
evehere, 132
exagitare, 528
excoquere (metaphorical), 105

Index of Latin Words

exitium used of an individual, 358
exserere, 10–11

facies of a fearful form, 600
facinus (meter), 408, 1183
Fas, 658
Favonius, 550
ferre = "have children" (of father), 494
fides in appeals, 1177
fidus, 1334
flammifer, 593
fluctuare (metaphorical), 699
fluvius, 52, 713
fore ut unpoetic, 185
fundere = *prosternere*, 1185

gentilis (adjective), 913
germinare intransitive, 698
gestare, 765
gorytus, 1127
gradus, 291f., 817

hic in lists, 154, 164–72
hoc (adverb), 1225
hoc agere, 104

i (*i nunc*), 89
iacere, 686, 897; with *peremptus*, 1160f.
iam: in appeals, 1314; repeated, 125ff.
igitur, 354
illo (adverb), 864
impetus, 975
impingere, 991
impius, 966
incola, 881
induere, 1028–31
ingeminare, 801f.
ingerere reflexive, 1032
inremeabilis, 548
inter, 148
intrare = "come among," 533f.
intueri in drama, 62
invisus, 664
involvere = "entwine," 683
ire ad = *accedere ad*, 1316
is unpoetic, 865
istic (pronoun), 1200
iuridicus = "judge," 581

lassus (*res lassae*), 646
latebra (singular), 1012
laxare, 121
lentus in *sermo amatorius*, 298
letum, 1195
libare with ablative, 920
loca of underworld, 576
locus and *regio*, 1138

lues, 358
lumen (metaphorical), 1251
[*lurere*], 767

magnanimus, 310
manare, 391
manes (*imi*), 55
marcor, 705
medius, 884
Megara (scansion), 203, 1009
memor in *sermo amatorius*, 298
memoria (meter), 408
mergere of sinking into underworld, 674
-*met* non-emphatic, 1011
mittere = *emittere*, 790, 990
mixtus in contexts of celebration, 878
modulatus, modulor, 263
moles mali, 1239
mora in periphrases, 573; of a person, 1215; with *ferre, pati*, 588
mortale genus, 448
movere, 469f.
mystes, 847

nec . . . aut, 16
neci dare et sim., 1048f.
nefas of objects, 603
nemo in drama, 186
nescioqui, -quis, 1147[b]–48
nex, 1195
nimis = "extremely," 579; in hyperbaton, 313f.
non in negative descriptions, 698–703; in prohibitions, 585
novercalis, 1236
novitas, 337–41, 348
nox aeterna of underworld, 610
numen of a human being, 1184f.
numquid, 1140
nunc, correlative, 801f.
nurus, 129

O in address, 309
oberrare, 1146, 1279[b]–81[a]
obicere, obex (scansion), 434f.
obitus, 1060[bis]f.
obsequi, 811
obtinere unpoetic, 185
occīdere, 1308
Oedipodes, 496
onerare of blows etc., 1120
opima, 48; *opimus*, 909
ortus (forms), 24

paelex, 4f.
palpitare, 1298[b]–99
parce in prayers, 1314

Index of Latin Words

pars quota, 383
particeps (dependent cases), 369ff.
parum est, *137fn.*, *138*
parumper in drama, *186*
parvulus, 1020
pater of divinities, 1072
pati = "to endure living," 353; *p. moram*, 588
perdomare and *domare*, 955
peremptus, *51*
pertimescere, 565
pestifer, 562
pestilens, 32
Phosphorus, 128
pictus, 467
placidus = "calm/calming," 1077
planctus, 1114
poena = "suffering," 604
polus for underworld, 606f.
populi of dead, 191
potens of gods, 300; of things, 1119
praeceps, 547
pristinus, 1081
profugere, 1033
profundus of underworld, 701
propere in drama, 1242
Prŏserpina, 549
puella, *126*

-que: at beginning of questions, 430; used correlatively with *et*, 703
querulus, *queri*, *querella*, 148, 298
quisnam and *quinam* in drama, *185–86*
quonam in drama, 1151

recidere, 269
reciprocus, *reciprocare*, 1050
rector, 205, 517, 730
redire in contexts of mortality, 136
regio and *locus*, 1138
remoliri, 504
reparare = "refill," 143
revocabilis, 559
rictus in poetry, 798
rutilare, 948f.

saltem in appeals, 1204
sator, 357
scelus and *error*, 1237f.
sciens prudensque vel sim., 1301
semel of finality of death, 866
semen of offspring, 988
senex and *senior* in verse, 765
senium in drama, 204
sic abire, 27
sinuare, 1198
sociare of marriage, 370

sollicitus = "causing anxiety," 461f.
somnus (number), 843
spatium, 822
specus, 665f., 718
stare of stance, 285, 458; as line-opening, 540
stipes = "club," *51*
stuprum, 488
supplex, 876
surdus, 576
suus, 481
Symplegas, 1211
syrma, 475

tecta, 1287f.
tegmen, 799
telum = "arrow," 1231
temnere, 89f.
templum, 3
tendere, perfect stem of, 538
tenere in emotional greetings, 623f.
tergum of water, 535
terrere = "threaten," 502
terribilis, 32
terror, 617
Tethys = "sea," 887, 1328
Titan = "sun," 124
totus of place, 659f.; plural = *omnes*, 794f.
trabs, 103
trahere, 1206; *t. auras*, 1142
transfundere in verse, 1326^b–27
tremulus, 158
trini in verse, 784
tristis of underworld, 566, 611
truncus = "club"?, 625
tu in prayers, 299–301; in disjunctions, 1169f.
tutus, 1302

ubinam in drama, 1151
umbrae of underworld, 679
unde + acc., 296f.
unicus with abstract noun, 1250f.
usquam for *umquam*, 1237
utrum(ne) . . . an in verse, 618f.

vacuus, 143
vagari of stars, 11
vagus of the sea, 1056
vallare, *374*
valva singular, 999f.
vastitas in verse, 701
vastus common in S., 1103, 1105
vector = *qui vehit*, 9
vehere = *trahere*, 817
victima of humans, 899
victor − *victus* play, 278

[483]

General Index

victrix dextra, 399, 800
videre in pregnant sense, 632
viduus, 3
virtus and deification, 39; in concrete senses, 647, 1157
vis of gods' power, 516

vitalis with *aura*, 651f.
vitiare, 104
volens sciensque, 1301
volutare, 1082[bis]
vultus = "eyes, gaze," 640f., 953f.; *v. bonus*, 1334

2. GENERAL INDEX

The rubric "influence of (a certain writer) on S[eneca]" covers everything from certainty to mere possibility, the degree of probability being indicated in the particular discussion.

abstractions personified, 96–98, 690–96
Act: technique of closing, 252, 827–29; technique of opening, 202–4, 893f.
adjectives: compound, 427, 469–70; diminutive, 1020; with explanatory infinitive, 715f.; in place of gen. of noun, 201; of similar meaning in proximity, 536; from tree-names, 912f.; in -*x*, 470
adynata, 223–24
aegis, 901[b]–2
Ageno, F., 105, 674, 728, 778f., 797f., 814, 357*fn*., 377*fn*., 1206, 1229
Albinovanus Pedo, influence on S., 548, 550–54, 703
Alexander the Great, 18–19
alliteration, 221, 278, 572–74, 254, 737–39, 753, 775–77, 799, 846–50, 919, 1015, 1100, 1160–61[a], 1239
allusiveness, 6–18, 205, 386–89, 460; in invocations, 205, 300, 659f.
Amazons, 545; location of, 246, 533–46
Amphion, 262f., 915–17
Amphitryon: characterization of, 24–25, 205–308, 439ff., 509f., 1026ff., 1030f., 1039–42, 1187, 1295, 1302, 1318[b]–21[a]; role of in play, 22–23, 36, 274–75, 351–52, 1021, 412–13
anachronism, 58f., *162*, 838–47, 840f., 918 (*see also* Roman coloring); mythological, 477f.
anadiplosis, 638f., 907f., 1156. See also repetition of words
anapests, 144, 1063f., 467–68
anger, characteristics of, 25, 31, 77, 403–5, 1167, 1219–21; of Hercules, 25, 41; of Juno, 33, 28[b]–29
antilabe, 426–29, 1186ff.
Apollo, *119*, 15, 235–36, 905f.
apostrophe, 745–47; in choral odes, 177, 186f., 831ff., 834, 870[b]–72, 1092–1121, 1122ff.

appeals, language of, 1177, 1183, 1250f.; to Earth, 1223–26
Ariadne and her crown, 18
'aside.' *See* dramatic technique
asyndeton: in lists, 32, 289; with verbs, 1041
Axelson, B., *185–86*, 625, 813, 814, *446fn*., 1284[b]–87, 1287f., *478–79*

Bacchus, 16, 66, 457f., *240–41*, *354–55*
Baden, T., 52–54, 430, 999f., *406*
Bears (constellations), *120*, *164–66*
Bentley, R., *137fn*., 94, 103, 478, *272fn*., 659f., 670, *304fn*., 730, 743f., 770f., 800f., *344fn*., 981, *396fn*., 1102, 1129, 1229, 1255, 1283f., 1284[b]–87, 1339f., *479*
Boeotia, *214–15*
Bothe, F. H., 793, 823, 825, *344fn*., *402fn*., 1195f., *438fn*.
boundaries, natural, *19–20*, 49, 290, 1293f.
Bücheler, F., *128fn*., *260fn*., 814

Caesar, Julius, *19–20*, *23–24*
Carlsson, G., *55fn*., 21f., 72, 272, *299fn*., *300fn*., 739–42, 1012
Castor and Pollux, 14, 553, 905f.
cataclysm, 365–67, 927–29
catalogues, 6–18, 1065ff.
Catullus, influence on S., 864–66
Cerberus, 62, 595–604, *324–25*, *328–29*, 825, 1105–7. *See also* Hercules: Labors, catabasis
characterization, by appearance, 204, 329–31, 474
Charon, *320–22*
chiasmus, 457f., 836, 979–80
choral odes, relationship to Acts, *161*, *163*, 202–4, 207–13, 255–56, 334
Chorus: consistency of attitudes, *333fn*.,

[484]

General Index

Chorus (*continued*)
334; dramatic use of, *255–56*, 827–29, 1032–34
Cicero, influence on S., 14, 224f., 240, 309
clausular effects, 5, 59, 158, 278, 328, 367
conditions, syntax of, 365–67, 1284
constructio ad sensum, 747, 846f.
conventional language with special reference, 194bis, 1138–41, 1206ff.
Costa, C. D. N., 104, 234, *196*, 620, 757, 1164^b–65
Creon, 255; sons of, 255
Cycnus, *243–44*

Danaids, *315–17*
darkness-light contrast, *29fn.*, *161*, 592–95, 939–52, 1054–62
dead: ages of, *341–42*; characteristics of, 292f.
death: descriptions of, 56, 291f., *398–99*; as guarantee of freedom, 426; personified, 291, 555; preparation for, 107f. *See also* Underworld
declamation, *116fn.*, 1044^b–48^a, 1101bis, 1243–45
descriptions *160*, 764–68; impressionistic style of, 762f., 860–63; of physical and emotional reactions, 414, 621, 1042^b–43^a (*see also* characterization); of places, 662–827; technique of, 698–703, 762f., 1044^b–48^a
Dis, 563, *270–71*, 709ff., *307–9*
Discordia, *148–49*
disjunctiveness, 683
dramatic irony, 27, 592–617, 605, 613–15, 899, 1036–38
dramatic technique, *36fn.*, 45–50, 115–17, 202–4, *183*, 515, 274–76, 592–617, 624f., 827–29, 334–35, 939–52 ad fin., 939, 1173ff. *See also* Act; entrances; exits; monologue
ecphrasis, 662–827, 709ff., 762f.
Eleusinia, *209–10*, *337*, *339–40*
Eliot, T. S., 9, 422ff., *337*, 965–81, 1131–37, 1138
elision, 606f., 634, *446fn.*, 1291
ellipse: of addressee, 1122ff.; of forms of *esse*, 224, 233, 1122ff.; of subject, 33f., 722; of subject-accusative of infinitive, 91, 117f.; of verb, 159, 406f.
emotions: as cause of hallucinations, 618–24, 1042^b–44^a; obsessive, 381; personification and reification of, 27–29, 75, 380–83; sudden shifts of, 295ff.
entrances, technique of, 329–31, 332–57, 520–22, 592–617, 827–29
Epicurean elements, *161*, 175

epigrammatic lines, 5, 541, 706
Eryx, *243–44*
Etna, 80–82, 106, 659f.
Euripides and his influence on S., *115*, *127*, 356, 500, 831ff.; *Heracles,* 17, 22–26, *29fn.*, *31fn.*, 32, 44–47, 50, *134fn.*, 59, 72, *183*f., *182–86*, 218f., 232, *196*, 249ff., 255f., *202*, 269, *219*, 434f., 439ff., 444f., 477f., *247–50*, 252, 255, 258, *261–62*, 274–75, 595–604, 618–24, 285, 640^b–42^a, 664+666, 761, *334*, *350–51*, 896f., 367, 987–1026, *376–78*, *380–83*, 1034, *388–89*, 1082–88, *412–15*, *419–20*, *422–23*, 1200ff., 1206ff., *432–33*, 1239, 1251, *1258*f., 1274–77, 1284, *455–56*, *462*; *Phaethon, 158–60*, 139f., 146–49, 152–54, 159
excerpt collections, *59–61*
exits, motives for, 515, 914–17

Fantham, E., *53fn.*, 227, 298, 970–73
figura etymologica, 1093
fishing, *172–73*
formulas, 414, 621, 625, 652, 975, 1042^b–43^a, 1078^b–79, 1147^b–48, 1160–61^a, 1201, 1202, 1223f., 1250f., 1281–84, 1332f.
Fortune, 524–32, 1271f.
Friedrich, W.-H., 44, 46, 48, *205–308*
funerals: of children, 854–57; torches of, 101, 103
Furies, *146–47*, *151–52*, *373–74*

Galinsky, G. K., *15fn.*, *16fn.*, *21fn.*, *32fn.*
generalizing of single instance, 1101bis, 1284
genitive plural: in *-um* and *-ium*, 516; in *-um* for *-ium*, 93
geography, poetic vagueness concerning, 1164^b–65, 1285, 1323
Giants, *144–45*, *369–72*
Giardina, G. C., *58–59*, 674, *465*
glosses, intrusive, 460, 577, 1075f.
Golden Age, 27, 926ff.
"golden" line. *See* iambic trimeter
Greek names, 203, 244+246
Greek nouns, 847, 853, 1124, 1127
Gronovius, J., 157, 161^bf., 233, 237f., 248, *225fn.*, 498f., 499, *284*, 765, 776, 814, 1120, *408fn.*, 1157–59, 1293f., 1298^b–99, 1302
Gronovius, J. F., 268, 1283f.
Gruter, J., 430, 664+666, *313fn.*, 858–63

heaven, gates of, 962; human attacks on, *19-20*
Heinsius, D., 76–82, 1251

[*485*]

General Index

Heinsius, N., *124fn.*, 103, 137f., 238, 268, *214fn.*, 466, 485, *248fn.*, 640f., *321fn.*, 928, 1102, *437fn.*, *438fn.*

Hercules:

——Attributes: club, 1085f., 1120; hands, 122, 1192–94; lionskin, 797f., 1152; sword, 1229; weapons, *412–13*

——Characterization of by S.: *21–44*, *253–55*, 592–617, 631+635, 636, 762–827, *350*, 896f., 909f., 918–24, 920–24, 926f., 937–39, 990, 1036–38, 1175, 1187, *432–33*, 1258–62, 1266f., *443–45*, 1315f., 1318[b]–21[a]

——Labors, *16–17*, 216–48, 239; Apples of Hesperides, *195–96*, 530–32; catabasis, *47–57*, 59, *252–53*, 662–67, 762–827, *321–34*; Cyreneian Hind, *191*; Erymanthian Boar, 228f.; Geryon, *193–94*, *212*, 480–88; Girdle of Hippolyte, 245f., 533–46, *261–62*; Horses of Diomedes, *191–92*, *419–20*; Hydra, 241f.; Nemean Lion, 83, 224f. (*see also* Leo); Stymphalian Birds, *197*

——Other episodes: Atlas' burden, bearing of, 70–74, 72; birth, 830; conception, *130*; Eleusinia, initiation in, 300–302, *318*; Gigantomachy, part in, 84; harrier of women, 478; Iole episode, 477f.; madness, *21fn.*, 28–33, 939–52, 963, 965–81, 996–98, 1018f., 1044[b]–48[a]; nautical dangers encountered, 1253; Omphale, *238–40*; promised immortality, 23; purification after murders, 1341[b]–44; Pylos, fight at, 560–65; seas, conquest of, 955; snakes, strangled in cradle, *189–91*, 456; Straits of Gibraltar, opening of, *194–95*; Syrtes, shipwreck in, *212–13*; Thespius, daughters of, 478; Vale of Tempe, opening of, *206*; voyage in cup of Sun, 1060–62

——Status: ambivalence of heroism, *15–20*, *39*; chastiser of tyrants, 271f., 480–88; divine honors, *18, 22–23, 39*; exemplar of *sapiens*, *43*; fame and significance, 30–32, 37f., 250, 1054–62, 1108–14, 1284[b]–94, 1329[b]–41; model for emperors, *18–19, 39–40*; for θεῖος ἀνήρ, *18–20, 39*; savior of dead, *17–18, 34–35*, 566; superhuman status, *22*, 277f.; universal scope of conquests, *22*, 30–32, 37f., 833, 955–57

Hercules (constellation), 23
Herington, C. J., *9*, *61fn.*, *183fn.*, *413fn.*
Heywood, J., 881, 965, 1131–37
Hoffa, W., 207–13, 308, 380, 427f., 674
Homer, influence on S., 1065f., 1197
Horace, influence on S., 93, *160–61*, 139f., 141–46, 166–68, 169–71, 179, 340f., 360f., 533f., 541, 549, 554, 555, 573, 715f., 742, 845, 870, 873, 882, 888, 965–81, 977f., 981, 1059, 1074, 1115

Housman, A. E., *126*, 155, 456, 553, *321fn.*, 867, 916, *425fn.*
hunting, 1126–30, 1130
hyperbaton, 63, 313f., 1130, 1219
hyperbole, 52–54, 244, 303–5, 380, 504, 909f., 955–57, 1336f.

iambic trimeter, 20; consisting of asyndetic list, 32; "framing," 59, 95, *189*; "golden" line, *189*, 594, 680; ictus, 50, 422ff., 1183; line-endings, 92f., 244+246, 504, 908, 1242f.; resolutions, 76, 100–105, 229, 263, 775–77, 947; sense-pauses, positioning of, 51f., 276f., 373, 380, 1317; "silver" line, 59, *189*, 367; speaker changes, position in line, 991; third foot, 950, 951; third and fourth, 1183; fourth and fifth, 504; fifth, 20, 408, 1162fn. *See also* meter

identity, 112; meaningful reference to, 509, 631–35

imagery, 105, 1088–93; animal, 478 ad fin.; appropriate, 137f.; of body, 942f.; cycle of year, 180; financial, 461f.; fire, 100–106, 105, 106; flight, 136; 'harbor,' *398*; 'loading' with blows, etc., 1120; military, 126–28, 126, 136; public life, 189–91; sacrificial, 104, 634, 870, 920–24, 1036–38, 1039, 1040f., 1042; sea, 170, 171, 1088–93; seafaring, 676; theatrical, 838f. *See also* darkness-light contrast; simile

imitation of S., 72, 84f., *185fn.*, 241f., 251–53, 313f., 328, 341–45, 569–89, 634–36, 643f., 703, 722–27, 867, 870[b]–74, 947–49, *395*, 1082–88, 1258–62, 1323–29, 1329[b]–41

imperatives, effect of, 100–105, 279ff.
inconsistency, *45*, *252*, 618–25, 1115–21, 1296
indefinite clauses and phrases, 30–32, 611, *356–57*, 1223f.
influence of S., 463f., 1138. *See also* imitation of S.
interpolation: in A, 12, 36f., 76, 104, 112, 116, 161[b]f., 212, 219, 362, 597, 623f., 799, 821, 1001, 1020, 1208; in archetype, 83, 336, 778f., 1229; in E tradition, 683f., 948f.
interweaving. *See* noun-adjective phrases
inversion of emphasis, 974f.

Jocelyn, H. D., 37f., 86ff., 129–31, *185*, 469, *470fn.*
Juno, *116–17*; role in play, *21, 32–33*

General Index

Jupiter, 460; concept of, 459, 1054bis; "J. of underworld," 47; of Olympia, 840; titles of, 517, 597f.
juxtaposition, 51f., 228f., 536, 631+635, 887

Kapnukajas, C. K., *158fn., 262fn.*, 836, *338fn.*, 893f.
Kingery, H. M., 121f., 143, 684, 712, 842–44, 1302

lament, *390–91*
"learning," in rhetorical points, 69f., 398, 1264
Leo (constellation), *364–66*
Leo, F., 55, *58fn.*, *116fn.*, 19ff., 49, 83, 130f., 207–13, 224, *203fn.*, 287, 321, 336, 489–92, 573, 612, 634, 674, 679, 690–92, 711, 722, 784, *357, 372fn., 385fn.*, 1063f., 1068, *402fn.*, 1101bis, 1110f., 1126–30, 1135f., 1162, 1195f., 1208, 1221–23, 1270
Liebermann, W.-L., 63, 329, 380–83, 403–5, 407–10, 647, *293, 413fn.*
line-endings. *See* iambic trimeter
love-elegy, influence on S., 165, 298, 545
Lucretius, influence on S., 144f., 651f., 1144^b–45^a, 1186
Lycus, *45–46, 184–85*, 269, 515, *274*; characterization of by S., 28, 269, 329–31, *216–18*

MacGregor, A. P., *53fn.*, 56
manuscripts, *53–61. See also* glosses; interpolation; speaker-attributions; transposition of lines
Mars, tried for murder, 1342f.
Megara: appearance of, 202, 355f.; characterization of by S., *183–84*, 205–308, 279ff., 308
metaphor. *See* imagery
meter, expressive use of, 76, 100–105, 144, 229, 263, 504, 775–77, 947, 951, 1198. *See also* anapests; elision; iambic trimeter
Miller, F. J., 3, 96, 143, 155, 188–91, 205, 220, 352f., 469f., 472f., 478, 645, 703, 794f., 959, 966, 1039, 1177, 1235^b–36, 1246–48, 1282, 1307, 1324, 1338
monologue, *115–17*, 604ff.; entrance-monologue, 332–57, 592–617
mourning garb, 202, 355f., 626–28

narrative, *275*; technique of, 647, 650f., 662–827, 683–85, 709ff., 793
nightingale, *170–71*
Niobe, *227–28*
noun-adjective phrases, 454; interweaving of, 14, 216–48, 248, 1068

nouns: abstract, 617, 701 (as subjects), 1157–59fn., 1250f. (for concretes); importance in S.'s style, 396, 407–10, 573, 647, 701; in *-tor*, 1181; in *-trix*, 900. *See also* Greek nouns; vocabulary
novi homines, 337–41
number: poetic expression of, 1282; rhetorical use of, 487, 500. *See also* singular

Oeta, 133
omission, significant, 33ff. *See also* ellipse
Orion, 12
Orpheus, *253, 268–71, 273*
Ovid, influence on S., *116–18*, 6–7, 9, *132–35*, 49, *144*, 86ff., 96–98, *159–60*, 126–28, *168–69*, 157, 172f., 221, *192–93*, 298, 316, 349, 381, *227–28*, 413, 454, *463f.*, 469–71, 498f., *247, 257–59*, 563, 569–89, *270–74, 277–78*, 606f., 651f., 653, 662–827, *295–96, 298–303, 307–8*, 732, 756, *326–27, 329*, 815, 823, 837, 847, *344–47*, 886f., *352–54*, 918, 982–84, 993, *373–79*, 1014f., 1027, *393–95, 397–98, 400–402*, 1095, 1107, *416–17*, 1164, *420–22*, 425, 1205, *429–31*, 1235^b–36, 1237f., *438–39, 455–56*, 1334

paradox, 166–68, 567f., 869f., 870, 1094–99, 1261
parallelism, *252–54*, 590f., 838–47
paratactic style, 188–91, *354*, 433–37, 560–65, 569–89
paronomasia, 116, 273, 278, 457f., 482, 706, 726f., 905f.
participles: perfect, 1064bis (tautologous), 1128 (proleptic); present, 93, 904 (forms), 1182 (use)
Passion-Restraint scenes, *183–84, 279ff., 412*
passions. *See* emotions
Peiper, R., *142fn., 181fn., 194fn.*, 336, *218fn., 224fn.*, 674, 1287f., *453fn.*
Pelops, *418–19*
perfect tense: forms, 244; gnomic, 866
periphrases, 37f., 92–94, 124ff., 871, 888, 1142, 1293f.; for "to kill," 431, 1048f. *See also* Underworld, phrases for
personifications, 27–29, 75ff., 96–98, 193f., 403–5, 690–96, 696, 929, *394–98*
Phineus, 750–59, 759
Pierrot, J., *136fn.*, 138, 203, 273, *217fn.*, 659f., *362fn.*, 990, 1302, *478*
Pleiades, *122–23*, 129–31
pleonasm, 536, 739–42, 742, 763, 819
"poetic" words. *See* vocabulary
postponement of words, 63, 148, 454
prayers, technique of, 205, 277f., 283ff.,

[487]

General Index

prayers (*continued*)
  299–301, 517f., 592–95, 600–603, 645, 659f., 1015, *395*, 1314
precedent, in rhetorical points, 386–96, 398, 1101bis, 1264
prepositional phrases, 9, 1307
present tense: with future sense, 306, 1284; indicating present significance, 479, 959
proper names: rhetorical use of, 631+635, 1016, 1239; significant omission of, 33ff.
Propertius, influence on S., 15, 559, 759
proverbial elements, 21, 253, 313f., 316, 340f., 375, 377f., 437, 524–32, 655–57
punishment as harmful, *25–26*, 1187

quies, as theme of play, *23–24, 35, 41, 390, 395*

Regenbogen, O., *9*, 1054–62
repetition of words: in comparisons, 381; conveying 'addition,' 482; emphatic, 50, 99, 1156; enumerative, 125ff., 254–57, 584f., 638f.; "framing," 1156; immediate, 50; of monosyllables, 99, 1218; multiple, 1135f.; with pathetic effect, 1147^b–48; in prayers, 299–301, 1314; of proper name, 1177; with rhetorical point, 251, 441–45, 905ff.; without rhetorical point, 43f., 1103–5, 1242f.; in self-correction, etc., 274f., 907f.
resolutions. *See* iambic trimeter; meter
rhetorical devices, 43f., 63, 79–85, 116, 251, 274f., 359–71, 386–96, 406f., 457f., 480–88, 643f., 648f., 845, 860–63, 905f., 995f. *See also anadiplosis*; apostrophe; chiasmus; declamation; generalizing of single instance; hyperbole; juxtaposition; paronomasia; personifications; precedent; repetition of words
Richter, G., *127fn.*, 353, *270fn.*, 705, 467–68
Roman coloring, 250, 337–41, 731–34, 827–29, *335*, 882–90. *See also* anachronism; triumph
Rose, A., *21fn.*, *158fn.*, 1279^b–81

sacrifice, 299f., 893f.; as motive for exit, 515, 914–17. *See also* imagery, sacrificial
salutatio, *174–75*
scansion: of final -*o*, 109, 1147^b–48; of open final syllable, 916, 950
Schmidt, B., 161^bf., 577, 659f., 837, 870^b–72, 357, 974f., *377fn.*, 384, 1110f., 1143, 1203
Seidensticker, B., 422ff., 433–37
self-address, *154–55*, 1330
self-correction, 274f., 643f.

Seneca Rhetor, influence on S., 290, 540, 548, 550–54, 643f., 703
Seneca's tragedies: dating of, absolute, *50–53*; dating of, relative, *53, 154–55, 181, 412, 457*; endings of, *37–38*; text of, *53–61*; world-picture of, *41*
sense-pauses, positioning of. *See* iambic trimeter
sententiae, 59–60, 433–37
sermo amatorius, 165, 298, 545
sermo praeruptus, 960–64
Shelton, J.-A., *21fn.*, 621
"silver" line. *See* iambic trimeter
simile, 676, 683–85, 337–38, 1044^b–48^a, 1046–48, 1088–93. *See also* imagery
simple life, theme of, 196–201
singular: of collective nouns, 616; and plural in first-person forms, *127*; of poetic nouns, 683f.; used by Chorus, 196
Sisyphus, 751
Sleep (personified), *394–98*
snakes, supernatural, 216, 218f., 240
sound-effects, 581, 710, 841, 1059, 1109, 1215, 1291, *470*. *See also* alliteration
speaker-attributions, errors in, 205–308, 634–36, 1021, 1032–34, 1237–39, 1295
stage setting, 202–4, 356, 506, 984–86, 1040
staging, 86ff., 202–4, 503, *351–52*, 1040, *413*, 1143, 1300^b–13; difficulties of, 47, 595–604, 1105–7, 1296
stars: description, 11, 126; setting, *125–27*
stichomythia, 352f., 422ff., 463f. *See also antilabe*
Stoic elements, 329–31, 426, *459*, 464, 743, 975, 1027f., 1054–62, 1259^b–61^a, 1271f.
Stoicism, *30–31, 40–44*
Strzelecki, L., 20, 229, 244, 408, *357fn.*, 1009, 1147^b–48, *418fn.*, 1183, *435fn.*
subject of sentence, unannounced change in, 33ff., 722, 793
suicide, *36, 42–43*
Sun, 37f., 60f., 595–604, 607, 941f.; attributes of, 132, 593, 594, 1062; expressions for, *124*; sunrises, poetic, 124ff.
symbolism, 944–52
sympathy, universal, 250, *390*, 1054–62, 1108–14

Taenarum, 587, *294*, 813
Tantalus, *316*
Tarrant, R. J., *49–50, 53fn., 54fn.*, 5, 15, 21, 27–29, 47, *137fn.*, 170, 149, 196–201, 206, 240, 257, 300–302, 329–31, 332–57, 334, 351, *225fn.*, 429, 517, *252fn., 255fn.*, 524–32, 552, 622, 629f.,

Tarrant, R. J. (*continued*)
647, 650f., *303fn.*, 712, 732, 750–59, 752–55, 827–29, 840f., *351fn.*, 939, 960–64, 970–73, 1038, 1039, 1042, 1053, 1120, 1164^b–65, 1215, 1282

Taurus (constellation), *120–22*

Tempe, 284, 979–80

Thebes, *358–59*; disasters of, 386–96, 495; foundation of, 262f.

"theme and variation," *254*, 583–87

Theseus, characterization of, 641, 1272f., 1334; presence on stage, *46–47*, 914–17, 1032–34; in underworld, 806

"thinking aloud," *115–16*, 19ff., 33ff., 63–74, 76–82, 108f., 604ff., 1218

three-speaker rule, *272–75*

Tibullus, influence on S., 697ff., 880f.

time (dramatic), *117*, 114f., 123f., *161*, 161^{b}f.

Timpanaro, S., *21fn.*, 183f., 784

Titans, *144–45*

Tityus, 756, 965–81, 977f., 978

transposition of lines, 49, 1077, 1135f.

tripartite division of the world, 30–32; between gods, 53, 599

triumph (Roman), language of, 58f., 195, *334*

tyrants: characteristics of, 341–45, 351, 353, 511–13; punishment of, 271f., 480–88, 735–47; threats of, 419–21, 429, 502

Underworld: barrenness of, 597f.; birds of, 687f., 756; capaciousness of, *33*, 659, 667; characters of, 59, 96–98, 690–96; darkness of, as source of terror, 611, 855–62; description of, 576, 662–827, 709ff., 717–20, 718, 720, 762f., 876, 863; door of, 47; emergence from, 520–22; gloom of, 566; gods of, 578; judges of, 271, *310–11*, 745; judgments and punishments, 735–47, *314–17*; messages sent to, 639f.; opening of, 47–57; phrases for, 185, 606f., 610, 620, 1104f.; power of, *33–35*; silence of, 620; water of, *263–64*, *297–98*, *305–6*, *322–23*

universe, sympathy of. See sympathy

"unpoetic" words. See vocabulary

variatio, 70–74, 647, 739–42, 785–87; in structure, 216–48; in verb tenses, 272, 473f.

venia, need for, *25–26*, 1266f.

verbs: in deliberative question, 964; of eating and drinking, 234; paronomasia of, 116; simple for compound, 409f., 790; tense changes, 272, 776; used enumeratively, 141–46, 750–59. *See also* ellipse; participles; perfect tense; present tense

Vergil, influence on S., *116–17*, 1f., 21, 28^b–29, 36f., 55, 71f., *146–47*, 101, 105, *160*, 125–27, *168–71*, 169, 216–22, 227, 237f., 257, 266, 299–300, 310, 323, 365f., 376, 416f., 438, 475, 500, *262*, *264–65*, *267–68*, 583–87, 587, *289–93*, *295–302*, 709ff., 714–16, 731–34, 744f., *318*, *320–28*, 815, *334–37*, 849–54, 854–57, *350*, 901^{b}f., 926ff., 1042^b–43^a, 1046–48, 1057bis, 1082bis, 1093, 1115, 1133, 1258f., 1264

virtus, 22–25, 28, 39, *162*, 337–41, 437

vocabulary: everyday, 27, *185*, 396, 624, 642, 864–66, 1120, 1140; new in S., 417, 715f., 1114, *469*; "poetic" and "unpoetic," *185*, 310, 345, 348, 415, 417, 701, 864–66, 865, 887, 913, 1006, 1317; similarities to Republican drama, 62, 89f., 204, *185–86*, 206, 618f., *344*, 1050, 1140, 1151, 1200, 1225, 1242f.

Wain, 131. *See also* Bears

welcome, *topoi* of, *208*

Wilamowitz-Moellendorf, U. von, *31fn.*, 185, 207–13, 251, 427f., *300fn.*, 1042^b–44^a, 1072

Withof, I. H., *137fn.*, *194fn.*, 251, 577, 690–92, 730, 785, 797f., *357*, *378*, 1077, *402fn.*, 1229, *454fn.*

word-order, 385, 836. *See also* hyperbaton; noun–adjective phrases; postponement of words

wordplay, *254*, 567f., 581, 586, 646f., 1093, 1184f., 1263, 1308. *See also figura etymologica*; paronomasia

words, long, 244 + 246, 416f. *See also* Greek names; Greek nouns; vocabulary

Zethus, 262f.; *and* Amphion, 915–17

Zwierlein, O., *21fn.*, *53fn.*, *54fn.*, 57–59, *60fn.*, 8f., 72, *155fn.*, 130f., 205, 362, 586, *273fn.*, *274fn.*, *286fn.*, 742, 813, 814, 823, 870^b–72, *351fn.*, 1023, 1044^b–48^a, *396fn.*, *399fn.*, *413fn.*, 1143, *418fn.*, *432fn.*, *446fn.*, *454fn.*, 467, 478–79

Library of Congress Cataloging-in-Publication Data

Fitch, John G.
   Seneca's Hercules furens.

   (Cornell studies in classical philology; v. 45)
   Bibliography: p.
   Includes indexes.
   1. Seneca, Lucius Annaeus, ca. 4 B.C.–65 A.D. Hercules furens. 2. Hercules (Roman mythology) in literature. 3. Hercules (Roman mythology)—Drama. I. Seneca, Lucius Annaeus, ca. 4 B.C.–65 A.D. Hercules furens. II. Title. III. Series.
PA6664.H43F58 1987   872'.01   86-11582
ISBN 0-8014-1876-3 (alk. paper)